W9-CYD-290

AN OUTLINE HISTORY OF CHINA

(Revised Edition)

Bai Shouyi

Contributors

Yang Zhao, Fang Linggui, Gong Shuduo, Zhu Zhongyu, Wang Guilin, Guo Dajun, Lu Zhenxiang

FOREIGN LANGUAGES PRESS BEIJING

First Edition 2008

ISBN 978-7-119-05296-0

Published by

Foreign Languages Press

24 Baiwanzhuang Road, Beijing 100037, China

http: //www.flp.com.cn

Distributed by

China International Book Trading Corporation

35 Chegongzhuang Xilu, Beijing 100044, China

Printed in the People's Republic of China

Preface

This book combines, in one volume, the English editions of *An Outline History of China*, published in 1982, and *An Outline History of China 1919-1949*, published in 1993.

In the autumn of 1997, the *History of China* in Chinese containing 22 sections bound in 12 volumes, of which I was chief editor, was completed. Mr. Wu Canfei, an editor at the Foreign Languages Press (FLP) in Beijing, suggested that the two English edition books, which had been published and distributed for many years, be bound into one volume titled *An Outline History of China* (revised edition), and be officially published by FLP after it had revised the translation. Prior to this, they had translated the Chinese editions of the two books into English, Japanese, Spanish, German, French and other languages. This was something I had wanted to do for many years. When I drew up the plan for compiling *An Outline History of China*, I considered writing about the period from 1919 to 1949 in the book, but failed to do so due to factual difficulties. The idea was realized in late 1987, and the second volume of the book came into being. It covers Chinese history from 1919 to 1949, and is now Chapter 11 in this revised edition of *An Outline History of China*. Though *An Outline History of China*, which now includes the second volume, cannot be regarded as a complete Chinese history, readers can gain an overall understanding of Chinese history more conveniently through this single-volume edition.

This combined book retains the original edition's style, content and features. However, there have been some necessary revisions and corrections made to specific historical facts, figures and regions, and some linguistic corrections. Here I would like to express my gratitude to Mr. Wu Canfei for his patient work.

We are still endeavoring to apply correct historical theories in our study of the course and characteristics of the development of Chinese history. To what degree we have managed to achieve this will be decided by our readers.

An Outline History of China and its follow-up have been popular among a broad range of readers since they were first published. Chinese editions have sold nearly one million copies, and foreign-language editions have sold out. The history departments of many colleges and universities use them as textbooks, showing the social demand and readers' appreciation of the work. We would like to express our deep gratitude for this. There are some issues in Chinese history of interest to everyone that, owing to a shortage of materials or research, we have been unable to address. We hope to do so in the future.

Bai Shouyi
December 1998, Beijing

CONTENTS

Chapter I
Introduction

1. A Land of 9,600,000 Square Kilometres

The People's Republic of China is situated in Eurasia, on the western shores of the Pacific Ocean. Its borders reach from the central line of the main navigation channel of the Heilongjiang (Heilungkiang) River near Mohe in the north to the Zengmu Reef in the Nansha Archipelago in the south, and from the Pamirs in the west to the confluence of the Heilongjiang and the Wusuli (Ussuri) River in the east. The total area is about 9.6 million square kilometres, making China one of the largest countries in land size in the world. With a continental land boundary of more than 20,000 kilometres, China adjoins Korea in the east, Mongolia in the north, Russia in the northeast, Kazakhstan, Kirghizstan and Tajikistan in the northwest, Afghanistan, Pakistan, India, Nepal, Sikkim and Bhutan in the west and southwest, and Myanmar, Laos and Viet Nam in the south. The continental coastline is more than 18,000 kilometres long, and looks across the seas towards South Korea, Japan, the Philippines, Malaysia, Indonesia and Brunei.

The primary administrative divisions in China today are the four municipalities directly under the central government, the twenty-three provinces, the five autonomous regions and two special administrative regions (Table I). The capital of China is Beijing.

TABLE I

The Four Municipalities Directly Under the Central Government

Beijing	Shanghai	Tianjin	Chongqing

The Twenty-three Provinces

North Hebei Shanxi
Northeast Liaoning Jilin Heilongjiang
Northwest Shaanxi Gansu Qinghai
East Shandong Jiangsu Zhejiang Anhui Jiangxi
Southeast Fujian Taiwan
Southwest Sichuan Guizhou Yunnan
Central South Henan Hubei Hunan
South Guangdong Hainan

The Five Autonomous Regions

The Inner Mongolia Autonomous Region (north)
The Ningxia Hui Autonomous Region (north)
The Xinjiang Uygur Autonomous Region (northwest)
The Guangxi Zhuang Autonomous Region (south)
The Tibet Autonomous Region (southwest)

The Two Special Administrative Regions

Hong Kong Special Administrative Region
Macao Special Administrative Region

Underneath the provinces and autonomous regions are cities, autonomous prefectures, counties, autonomous counties and other divisions. The municipalities directly under the central government are subdivided into urban districts and suburban counties. Under the autonomous prefectures are counties, autonomous counties and cities, and under the counties and autonomous counties are townships, ethnic group townships and towns.

China has many mountain ranges, most of the major ones being located in the western regions. Running west-east are the Altay, Tianshan, Kunlun, Qilian, Karakorum, Gangdise, Himalaya, Yinshan, Qinling and Nanling mountains. Running north-south is the Hengduan Range, which is formed from the Daxue, Nushan and Gaoligong mountains lying side by side from east to west. In the eastern part of the country are mountain ranges running from the northeast to the southwest: to the west are the Greater Hinggan Range, the Taihang Mountains, and the Wushan, Wuling, Dalou and Xuefeng ranges; to the east are the Changbai Mountains and the Liaodong, Shandong and Minzhe highlands. These mountain ranges and highlands determine the basic features of China's topography.

The Chinese terrain varies conspicuously in elevation and consists of three tiers descending from west to east. The Qinghai-Tibet Plateau, the highest and largest plateau on earth, is commonly known as "the roof of the world." To the north it is bounded by the northern branch of the Kunlun and Qilian mountain ranges and to the south and west by the Karakorum, Himalaya and Hengduan mountain ranges. Its average elevation is more than 4,000 metres above sea level. Mount Qomolangma in the Himalaya Mountains, located on the border between China and Nepal, is the world's highest peak, with an elevation of 8,848.13 metres. The Qaidam (Tsaidam) Basin northeast of the Qinghai-Tibet Plateau is somewhat lower even though it has an elevation of almost 3,000 metres. This area forms the highest tier in China's topography. The northern and eastern faces of the Qinghai-Tibet Plateau descend to plateaus and basins mostly between 1,000 and 2,000 metres above sea level. They include the Yunnan-Guizhou Plateau; the loess plateau which takes in central and eastern Gansu, eastern and southern Ningxia, northern Shaanxi, the whole province of Shanxi and western Henan; the Inner Mongolia Plateau; the Sichuan Basin; the Tarim Basin and the Junggar Basin in Xinjiang. These plateaus and basins form the second tier. East of the Greater Hinggan Range and the Xuefeng Range are hilly country with an elevation of less than 1,000 metres and plains of less than 200 metres. The three main plains of China, the Northeast Plain, the North China Plain and the Lower and Middle Changjiang (Yangtze River) Plain are all in this area. The coastal plains have an elevation of less than 50 metres above sea level. These hills and plains form the third tier in the Chinese terrain.

Most Chinese rivers flow from west to east and empty into the Pacific Ocean. The major rivers all flow east along most of their courses, such as the Changjiang (Yangtze River), Huanghe (Yellow River), Heilongjiang, Zhujiang (Pearl River). Songhuajiang (Sungari River), Liaohe, Haihe and Huaihe. (*Jiang* and *he* are both Chinese words for medium-sized and large rivers.) Some of the south-flowing rivers, such as the Yarlung Zangbu Jiang (the Yalutsangpo or Brahmaputra) River and Nujiang (the Salwèen River), pass through India, Bangladesh and Myanmar to empty into the Indian Ocean; others, such as the Lancangjiang, the Mekong River and Yuanjiang, flow through Myanmar, Laos, Thailand, Kampuchea and Viet Nam into the Pacific Ocean. The Ertixhe (the Kara-Irtysh River) flows north from Xinjiang into the U.S.S.R. There are also inland rivers with no ocean outlet, such as the Tarimhe, Qaidamhe and Shulehe; these are mostly confined to Northwest and West China.

The longest river in China is the Changjiang at 6,300 kilometres, which passes through Qinghai, Sichuan, Tibet, Yunnan, Hubei, Hunan, Jiangxi, Anhui, Jiangsu and Shanghai, with tributaries flowing through several other provinces including Guizhou, Shaanxi, Gansu and Henan. Next is the Huanghe, which passes through Qinghai, Sichuan, Gansu, Ningxia, Inner Mongolia, Shanxi, Shaanxi, Henan and Shandong. The part of the Heilongjiang which lies within Chinese territory and forms the border between China and Russia has a drainage basin which covers the greater part of the northeastern provinces. The Tarim which has few tributaries has a relatively small drainage basin. The Zhujiang, originating in the Nanpanjiang in the upper reaches of the Xijiang (Sikiang or West River), passes through Yunnan, Guizhou, Guangxi and Guangdong. The Songhuajiang in the northeast has a relatively large drainage basin, and the drainage basins of the Yarlung Zangbu Jiang (within China) and the Haihe are both more than 200,000 square kilometres.

TABLE II

The Longest Rivers in China

Name	Length	Drainage basin
Changjiang (Yangtze River)	6,300 km	1,800,000 km^2
Huanghe (Yellow River)	5,464 km	750,000 km^2
Heilongjiang (Heilungkiang or Amur River)	2,965 km*	
Tarimhe (Tarim River)	2,179 km	198,000 km^2
Zhujiang (Pearl River)	2,129 km	425,700 km^2
Songhuajiang (Soungari River)	1,840 km	545,600 km^2

Lakes of all sizes are scattered throughout China but are more concentrated on the Lower and Middle Changjiang Plain and the Qinghai-Tibet Plateau. The largest fresh water lakes are the Poyang in Jiangxi, the Dongting in Hunan, the Hongze in western Jiangsu and Taihu in southern Jiangsu. The most important of the salt lakes are the Qinghai Lake (Koko Nor) in Qinghai and the Lop Nur (Lob Nor) in Xinjiang; the latter has changed greatly over the last two thousand years and is now dried up. Lake Xingkai (Hsingkai) is a fresh water lake which straddles the Sino-Russian border.

---

* Length within China and along the Sino-Soviet border.

TABLE III

The Largest Lakes in China

Name	Type	Area
Qinghai Lake (Koko Nor)	Salt	4,635 km^2
Poyang Lake	Fresh	3,960 km^2
Dongting Lake (Tungting Lake)	Fresh	3,940 km^2
Hongze Lake (Hungtse Lake)	fresh	3,180
Taihu	fresh	2,425 km^2
Lop Nur (Lob Nor or Lop Nor)	salt	
Lake Xingkai* (Lake Hsingkai or Hanka)	fresh	4,380 km^2

In addition to the natural rivers and lakes, there are also many canals in China. The most famous is the Grand Canal between Beijing and Hangzhou (Hangchou), 1,801 kilometres in length, which passes through the city of Tianjin and four provinces (Hebei, Shandong, Jiangsu and Zhejiang) and links up with five major rivers: the Haihe, Huanghe, Huaihe, Changjiang and Qiantangjiang (Chientang River).

The continent of China faces east and south towards the seas. In the east, the most northerly sea is known as Bohai (Po Hai): the Liaodong peninsula and the Shandong peninsula confront each other forming a natural gateway known as the Bohai straits. Southeast of Bohai is the Huanghai (Yellow Sea), south of the mouth of the Changjiang is Donghai (East China Sea), and south of the Taiwan Straits is Nanhai (South China Sea). The Bohai is a gulf while the other three are all marginal seas of the Pacific. More than 5,000 islands are scattered across the seas, with half of them located in Dong-

* Belongs in part to China, in part to the U.S.S.R.

hai, forming a total area of about 80,000 square kilometres. The largest island is Taiwan (35,700 square km), followed by Hainan Island (over 34,000 square km) and Chongming Island (1,083 square km). Also well known are the Miaodao Archipelago at the entrance to the Bohai, the Zhoushan (Choushan or Chusan) Archipelago beyond the mouth of the Qiantangjiang, and the Penghu Islands (Pescadores) in the Taiwan Straits. The most southerly islands are the coral reefs or atolls known as the Dongsha (Tungsha), Xisha (Sisha), Zhongsha (Chungsha) and Nansha archipelagos. These Nanhai archipelagos are composed of varying numbers of islets, sandbars and reefs totalling more than 170; the Nansha Archipelago consists of close to 100, and the Xisha comes next with about 30.

Many seaports are strung out along China's lengthy and winding coastline. The river estuary ports of Tianjin, Shanghai and Guangzhou-Huangpu (Canton-Whampoa) are important centres for foreign trade and economic exchange within China. The port of Tianjin stands on the western shores of Bohai Bay at the lower reaches of the Haihe; the port of Shanghai stands at the confluence of the Changjiang, Huangpujiang (Whangpoo River) and Wusongjiang (Woosung River); the ports of Guangzhou-Huangpu stand at the Zhujiang delta which is the confluence of the lower reaches of the Dongjiang, Beijiang and Xijiang (the East, North and West rivers). The bay ports of Dalian (Dairen) on the Liaodong peninsula, Qingdao (Tsingtao) on the Shandong peninsula, Jilong (Keelung) in Taiwan and Zhanjiang (Chankiang) on the Leizhou (Leichow) peninsula all have good natural harbours and are key to sea and land communications.

Due to the monsoon climate created by the difference in temperature between continent and ocean, plus the vastness of the land and the complexity of the terrain, there are considerable variations in air temperature and rainfall in different parts of China, and a wide variety of climates. In summer, the temperature throughout China is generally rather high. The average temperature in July is above 20°C in Heilongjiang, 15°C in Lhasa and 28°C in Hangzhou. The average temperature in winter is about minus 30°C in the most northerly part of Heilongjiang but above 10°C in places like Guangdong, Guangxi and Fujian, while in Hainan it can go as high as 15°C or more. While the north is a frozen land, coconut groves flourish in the south.

The vastness of the land, the complexity of the terrain and the variation in climate, together with the related regional differences in natural characteristics, combine to make China's natural resources extremely rich and multifarious. The fertile plains produce cereal crops such as wheat, rice, maize, millet, sorghum (gaoliang) and soybean, and cash crops such as cotton, hemp, sugar and oil-bearing plants. The vast mountain areas produce, in addition to foodstuffs, tea, tea oil, tung oil, silk, wax and medicinal materials. Inner Mongolia, Xinjiang, Qinghai and Tibet have large areas of prairie land providing rich pastures for raising cattle, sheep, horses and camels, including many excellent breeds. The forests are mostly concentrated in the northeast and southwest, and are also to be found in Fujian and the eastern part of Taiwan. The forests are complex with many different types of plants: there are more than 2,800 species of trees alone, of which almost 1,000 provide timber of considerable economic value. The fauna that live wild in every region throughout China include about 1,150 bird species, more than 400 species of mammals, and over 420 species of reptiles and amphibians, many of them rare. China is very rich in water resources. According to preliminary estimates, the total volume of flow of Chinese rivers is 2,700,000 million cubic metres, with a potential of 680 million kilowatts of hydro-electric power. All the major rivers are open to navigation, with a total of about 160,000 kilometres of navigable waters. Rich reserves of oil, coal and iron are found in various regions of the country. Non-ferrous minerals such as copper, aluminium, tungsten, antimony, molybdenum, tin, manganese, lead, zinc and mercury, along with oil shale, phosphorus, sulphur, magnesite, salt, gypsum are also widely distributed.

2. Fifty-Six Ethnic Groups and a Population of More Than 1,000,000,000

The People's Republic of China is a unitary multi-ethnic state, comprising the Han people and over fifty ethnic minorities. The Han people are the most numerous, with a population of about 1.042 billion, and live all over the country; their highest concentrations are in the Huanghe, Changjiang and Zhujiang river basins and on the Songhuajiang-Liaohe Plain in the northeast, occupying forty to fifty per cent of the total area of China. According to 1990 statistics, the ethnic minorities have a total population of 117.535 million, accounting for ten percent of the total 1.1601 billion population of China. They inhabit fifty to sixty per cent of the country's total area.

TABLE IV

China's Ethnic Minorities

(Based on 1990 Statistics)

Name	Region	Population
Northeast		
Manchu	Mainly in Liaoning, Jilin, Heilongjiang and Hebei	8,921,180
Korean	Mainly in Jilin, Heilongjiang, Liaoning	1,970,597
Daur Ewenki Oroqen Hezhen	Mainly in Heilongjiang	
North		
Mongolian	Mainly in Inner Mongolia, also in Liaoning, Jilin, Heilongjiang, Qinghai, Gansu, Hebei, Henan, Xinjiang, and Ningxia	4,806,849

TABLE IV (cont.)

Name	Region	Population
Northwest		
Uygur Kazak Kirgiz Xibe Tajik Ozbek Tartar Russian	In or mainly in Xinjiang	7,214,431
Hui	Widely distributed, but mostly in Ningxia and Gansu; also in Shandong, Yunnan, Qinghai, Hebei, Henan, etc.	8,692,978
Dongxiang Yugur Bonan	Mainly in Gansu	
Tu Salar	Mainly in Qinghai	
Southwest		4,593,330
Tibetan	Tibet, Gansu, Qinghai, Sichuan, Yunnan, etc.	
Lhoba Moinba	In Tibet, but mostly in Moinyü and Lhoyü regions now occupied by India	
Yi	Mainly in Sichuan and Yunnan; some in Guizhou and Guangxi	6,572,173
Miao	More than half in Guizhou, the rest in Hunan, Yunnan, etc.	7,398,035
Bouyei	Guizhou	3,545,059

TABLE IV (cont.)

Name	Region	Population
Dong	Guizhou, Hunan and Guangxi	2,545,059
Bai	Mostly in Yunnan; small numbers in Sichuan and Guizhou	1,594,827
Hani		1,253,952
Dai		
Lisu		
Lahu		
Va		
Jingpo		
Blang	In or mainly in Yunnan	
Achang		
Pumi		
Nu		
Jino		
Benglong		
Drung		
Naxi	Mostly in Yunnan, also in Sichuan and Tibet	
Shui	Mostly in Guizhou, a small number in Guangxi	
Gelo		
Qiang	Sichuan	
South and Central-south		
Zhuang	Mostly in Guangxi, small numbers in Yunnan, Hunan, Guangdong, etc.	15,489,630
Yao	In Guangxi and also in Hunan, Yunnan, Guangdong, Guizhou, Jiangxi, etc.	2,134,013
Tujia	Hunan and Hubei	
Li	Guangdong	
Gaoshan	Taiwan	

Name	Region	Population
She	In Fujian and Zhejiang, also in Guangdong, Anhui, etc.	
Mulam Maonan Jing	Guangxi	

Apart from the fifty-five ethnic minorities listed in the above table, there are still some groups whose ethnic status remains unclear.

The language and script of the Han ethnic group are the most widely used in China, and are commonly known as the Chinese language and script. Each of the other ethnic groups, with the exception of the Hui which uses Chinese, has its own language. The language of the She is very close to Chinese. Increasing numbers of people among the ethnic minorities are using Chinese in addition to their own languages. Many of them have no script of their own and use either the Chinese script or the script of a related ethnic group.

The Chinese (Han) language belongs to the Sino-Tibetan family. It is often said to be monosyllabic because the smallest meaningful units of speech generally consist of one syllable each. However, very many words of the modern language are polysyllabic compounds of two or more of the one-syllable basic units. Chinese is also described as a tonal language, which means that a syllable generally is pronounced with a characteristic tone (even, rising, falling-rising or falling). On the whole, Chinese lacks the inflections (suffixes, prefixes etc.) that are characteristic of many other languages. These are partly replaced by grammatical "particles", and the parts of speech in a sentence are chiefly determined by the word order.

Over the vast area throughout which the Chinese language is spoken, there are many different dialects, some of which are mutually unintelligible. In the last few decades a standard language has gradually been formed, based on the language of the north, with the Beijing pronunciation as the norm and a grammar modelled on modern vernacular writing. This language is called *putonghua* and is gradually being popularized. It will eventually become the form of spoken and written Chinese in universal use.

The Han script consists of pictographs and ideographs commonly known as Chinese characters, some of which go back more than three thousand years. The earliest characters consisted of a single pictographic or ideographic element: the characters 日 and 月 were, as they still are, pictographs for the sun and the moon, while 丄(上) and 丅(下) conveyed the meaning of "upper" and "lower" in terms of the relative position of the vertical stroke to the horizontal. The structure of such characters was relatively primitive and simple. A second step was taken when two or more simple characters were combined to form a more complex character to express a new meaning. For example, the characters 日 and 月 were combined to form 明, meaning "bright", and the character 人 (man) with the character 戈 (spear) forms the character 戍, meaning "defend". Still later a third type of character was developed, consisting of one element which stood for the meaning and another for the pronunciation, e.g.:

芳 fāng: fragrance
房 fáng: house
访 fǎng: visit
放 fàng: set down
钫 fāng: francium
妨 fáng: hinder
舫 fǎng: pleasure boat

The character 方 fāng, which means direction, only indicates the pronunciation and does not contribute anything to the meaning; the other element indicates the meaning. Over a long period of time, Chinese characters have undergone very great changes in appearance, and many new characters have been invented, but the principles for the formation of new characters have persisted. In the development of Chinese culture, the Chinese or Han script has played a very great role in facilitating communication between different regions in China and strengthening the unity of the country. But because each character has its own separate form, the Chinese script is much more difficult to learn, write and print than an alphabetic script. For this reason, the Chinese government has set up a committee for the reform of the Chinese script to study and carry out gradual reforms.

Twenty-eight of the languages of China's ethnic minorities belong to the Sino-Tibetan family, including Tibetan, Yi, Zhuang, Bouyei, Dai, Miao and Yao. Another eighteen belong to the Altaic family, including Uygur, Kazak, Mongolian, Manchu and Korean. Va, Blang and Benglong belong to the Austroasiatic family, Gaoshan to the Austronesian family, and Tajik and Russian to the Indo-European family. Some people claim that the Jing language belongs to the Austroasiatic family, but this has not been fully established.

Some national minorities, such as the Mongolians, Tibetans, Uygurs, Kazaks, Koreans, Xibes and Dais, have their own alphabetic scripts. The Tibetan script has a history of more than 1,300 years. The Uygurs and Mongolians have used different alphabetic scripts over periods of more than a thousand years and seven or eight hundred years respectively. The Yi language has a syllabic script which also has a history of over a thousand years. The Naxi script consists of two elements, ideographs and a syllabary, and the ideographs go back more than a thousand years. Ethnic minorities which had no script or incomplete scripts have created or improved their scripts in recent years. Ten of them have devised their phonetic alphabets, and nine of these are being tried out.

Both in economic and cultural life many of the ethnic groups have much in common with each other, yet each has its distinctive characteristics.

Han people have had a very long history of agricultural production, and their handicrafts also reached a fairly high level at an early stage. Their inventions, such as printing, the compass, gunpowder and the manufacture of porcelain, tea, silk and paper, have long been famous throughout the world. Han culture is extremely rich in ancient books and records, literature and history. Many great thinkers, scientists, inventors, statesmen, military strategists, writers and artists have appeared in the course of Chinese history, and great revolutionary movements have taken place. The Han people have made a very great contribution to the development of Chinese society.

Of the twenty-one ethnic minorities that live in North China, twelve are mainly engaged in agriculture, including the Manchus, Koreans, Huis and Uygurs. Among them the Tus, Xibes and Yugurs turned from stock-breeding or fishing and hunting to agriculture only during the last few centuries. The achievements of the Koreans in rice paddy cultivation and improvement are well known. The Uygurs are skilled in establishing green oases on basin peripheries and at constructing karez (an irrigation system of wells connected by underground channels), demonstrating their mastery of agricultural production. The Xinjiang Uygur Autonomous Region was one of the first areas in China where cotton was planted. The Kazak, Kirgiz and Tajik minorities are mainly engaged in stock-breeding. The Kazak regions are famous for their livestock. Agricultural crops flourish in the Ili Basin, which is known as "the granary of northern Xinjiang". The Mongolians on the northern plateau are mainly engaged in stock-breeding, while those on the Hetao Plain at the Yellow River Bend are mainly engaged in agriculture. The Mongolians raise famous breeds of horses, oxen, sheep and camels. The Hezhens are mainly hunters and fishers, and the Oroqens are mainly hunters, but both also practise some agriculture. The Ozbeks and Tartars are for the most part engaged in commerce, but a few also practise agriculture.

Of the thirty-four ethnic minorities in the south, the majority are chiefly engaged in agriculture, some in combination with stock-breeding, hunting and fishing, or forestry. The Tibetans practise both stock-breeding and agriculture, the former on the extensive, high grasslands and the latter in the river valleys. The large and long-haired yak is unique to the Tibetan highlands. The Jings are the only minority which chiefly subsists on fishing, with some agriculture as well.

Most of the ethnic minorities have a rich cultural tradition embracing song, dance, oral literature and art. The colourful dances of the Uygurs, Kazaks, Mongolians and Koreans are particularly well known. The Uygurs, Mongolians, Huis, Manchus, Tibetans, Bais and Dais all possess substantial bodies of literature and art as well as historical and technological works and religious classics.

Modern industry began in China around the middle of the nineteenth century. After the founding of the People's Republic in 1949, an all-round development of the national economy got underway, and all kinds of industries were established. At the same time education and cultural activities were improved and popularized. The economic and cultural life of each ethnic group took on a new look. Ethnic minorities which had lingered in a backward condition for a long period achieved a rapid development both economically and culturally, and exhibited striking changes.

In Chinese history no one ethnic group has developed in isolation from the others. Each has contributed to the creation of Chinese history and each shares the destiny of the nation as a whole. In the protracted struggle against feudalism, colonialism and imperialism, each group has battled side by side with the others. In every aspect, economic, political and cultural, each group absorbs nourishment from its fraternal groups for its own enrichment, and each language is under the constant influence of its fraternal tongues. Even the formation and development of each ethnic group is a constant process of association, separation and fusion, a constant process of emigration and immigration between different groups. After the founding of the People's Republic, a policy of equality and unity between its ethnic groups was put into effect, autonomous areas for minorities living in compact communities were established, the languages and customs of the minorities were respected, and the state helped each of them to develop its economy and culture. Unprecedented unity has been achieved.

3. 1,700,000 Years and 3,600 Years

Human life existed in many parts of China in remote antiquity, leaving behind traces of primitive society. The earliest man discovered in China is Yuanmou Man, who lived roughly 1,700,000 years ago. The famous Peking Man lived approximately 400,000 to 500,000 years ago. The gradual formation of a matriarchal commune took place approximately 40,000 or 50,000 years ago, and the patriarchal commune appeared more than 5,000 years ago.

Because of low productivity, exploitation did not appear in primitive society; it was a society of communal production and consumption, and the productive relations were based on the public ownership of the means of production. Primitive society was followed by slave society, in which the relations of production were based on the slave-owners possessing both the means of production and the productive workers, the slaves. It was in slave society that exploitation, classes and the state appeared for the first time. We still lack concrete evidence to determine when slave society came into being in China. According to traditional ideas, the first dynasty in Chinese history was the Xia, which ruled for more than four hundred years. Its activities were centred around the juncture of modern Shanxi, Shaanxi and Henan. It is generally thought that this dynasty lasted roughly from the 21st century to the 16th century B.C. and saw the beginning of slave society in China. Archaeologists are still trying to find out the truth about the Xia, knowledge of which exists only from traditional legend.

The first dynasty which can be traced from archaeological discoveries and from records corroborated by these discoveries was the Shang, having begun some 3,600 years ago when, according to our present knowledge, recorded history started in China. By the Shang, which lasted roughly from the 16th century to the 11th century B.C., China had entered the stage of slave society. The Western Zhou Dynasty, which succeeded the Shang in the 11th century B.C., was also based on the slave system. The centre of Shang activity was initially around Shangqiu in the southeast of modern Henan, but after repeated moves the rulers finally settled around Anyang in modern Henan. The Zhou capital, Hao, was on the western outskirts of modern Xi'an in Shaanxi. The centre of Zhou activity was the region around the lower reaches of two rivers, the Jinghe and Weihe. In addition, the Zhou had an eastern capital at Luoyi, on the west bank of the Luoshui (present-day Luohe) near modern Luoyang in Henan, which formed another centre of activity around the lower reaches of the Yihe and Luoshui. The Jing-Wei plain and the Yi-Luo plain were both well suited for agriculture, with fertile soil, a mild climate and relatively adequate rainfall. Other natural resources were also fairly abundant there. These two regions subsequently experienced several periods of prosperity and decline, but they enjoyed an important political position up until the end of the 9th century. Considerable bodies of cultural relics, legends and records have also been preserved in other regions within China.

The period from 770 to 221 B.C. is known in traditional history as the early Eastern Zhou, Spring and Autumn, and Warring States periods. It was a time when slave society was gradually disintegrating and feudal society taking shape, a period of transition from slave to feudal society. The relations of production in feudal society were the landlords' ownership of the means of production and their partial ownership of the productive workers. In addition, there was an individual economy where peasants and artisans owned tools and other means of production on the basis of their own labour. But these individual labourers were the objects of landlord control and exploitation. The landlords and peasants were the two antagonistic classes in feudal society, although the different ranks into which the society was divided generally obscured the class division.

In the Spring and Autumn and Warring States periods, the feudal hierarchy of land ownership gradually replaced the land ownership by the slave-owning aristocracy; the labour of individual peasants replaced collective slave labour in agriculture, the dependence of the labour force on the land replaced an unstable relationship between the labour force and the land, and the individual peasant family combining ploughing and weaving gradually became the dominant form of labour organization. As for the political system, the system of enfeoffment initiated in the early years of Western Zhou underwent changes, giving rise to a prefectural system of local administration: local government officials were appointed by the court to serve limited terms in a succession of different places, as opposed to the system of hereditary posts. With the appearance and development of the prefectural system, contacts between the various regions increased, the political organization of each locality was strengthened and history progressed further along the path to unification of the country. In 221 B.C., Qin Shi Huang (First Emperor of the Qin) established the first imperial dynasty, marking the beginning of feudal predominance throughout the country.

The period from 221 B.C. to A.D. 196 was a time when feudalism reached maturity under the three imperial dynasties of Qin, Western Han and Eastern Han. The hierarchical feudal order matured both economically and politically. The emperor possessed supreme political power, and at the same time was the supreme landowner. Under the emperor were landowners with different kinds of hereditary status and privileges including the imperial relatives on the male and female lines and persons who had rendered meritorious services to the throne. These landed aristocrats with hereditary titles occupied the dominant position in the landlord class. In addition there were the landowners from powerful families and the mercantile landowners thriving on usury. Both possessed considerable strength in property and social influence, but they did not belong to the higher ranks in social status, and some even ranked very low. The hereditary aristocrats subjected to exploitation peasants who were registered by household and bestowed to them by the feudal state. This was the main type of peasant at the time. The registered peasants had a private economic sphere and a certain degree of personal freedom. Although they were exploited, they were better off than the slaves. But they too varied in socio-economic status. Their household registration status could not be altered after they were attached to hereditary aristocrats by state decision. The land rent they paid to the landed aristocracy also served as their state tax, the two being combined in one. The relations of production stated above were established in the period of unity under the Qin and grew continuously under the Western and Eastern Han. Slavery did not vanish in the Qin and Han period but persisted in government and private handicraft industries, and existed in households throughout the feudal era. However, these remnants of the slave system were insignificant in social production.

As for the political system, Qin Shi Huang started a unitary prefectural system of administration, but no historical records survive which describe how it was carried out. Under the Western and Eastern Han the system coexisted with the fiefs. Underneath the prefectures and fiefs were counties and underneath the counties were administrative organizations at the gressroots. These were the different levels in the political structure, each with some relative independence. Beginning in the 3rd century, the prefectural system gradually superseded the fiefs and changed continually. But generally speaking, power became more and more concentrated in the hands of the court and restricted at the local levels.

The capital of the Qin Dynasty was Xianyang, and the capital of Western Han was Chang'an; the Eastern Han moved its capital east to

Luoyang after Chang'an had been devastated by war. The Jing-Wei plain, the Yi-Luo plain and the lower reaches of the Huanghe were the most fertile regions in these periods. The sphere of activity of the Qin and Han was much wider than those of previous dynasties and included the Huanghe, Changjiang and Zhujiang river basins. There were more extensive records of the history of the ethnic minorities than before. The Han people, the major ethnic group in China, was formed in the Qin and Han periods through the fusion of related tribes and ethnic groups. The name of the Han people is that of a great dynasty.

Chinese feudalism experienced its earlier period of ascendancy from 196 to 907, which covered a period of disunity—the Three Kingdoms, the Western and Eastern Jin, and the Northern and Southern Dynasties—as well as the dynasties of Sui and Tang. The period witnessed protracted struggles as well as large-scale displacement and migration among the ethnic groups. As a result the territory shared by various groups expanded both northward and southward. The Han group replenished itself, and the ethnic minorities raised their production level and standard of living. A new phase in national fusion appeared, and feudalism developed among groups sharing the same territory. This is an important feature of the earlier period of ascendancy of Chinese feudalism.

The hereditary landed aristocracy of the previous era crumbled under the onslaught of peasant uprisings, and was replaced with the newly arisen landlords of privileged families. Like the landed aristocracy, the privileged families enjoyed political status and hereditary rights. But they built themselves up by relying on their traditional position in the feudal officialdom and not as a result of imperial fiat. Their land ownership had a more private character than had been the case with the landed aristocrats. The privileged landowners mainly controlled peasants who had attached themselves to these manorial lords for protection against exorbitant taxes and levies. These manorial peasants were omitted from the household registers of the state and the land rent they paid was no longer part of the state tax. Their position in society was lower than the state-registered peasants, but they were relieved of state taxes which included a heavy burden of labour service. This change in the relations of production was favourable to the growth of the productive forces of society. It was another sign of the ascendancy of Chinese feudalism.

The Wei (one of the Three Kingdoms), the Western Jin, and the Later Wei (one of the Northern Dynasties) all set up their capitals at Luoyang. The Sui and Tang had their capitals at Chang'an and maintained an eastern capital at Luoyang. The Wu (another of the Three Kingdoms), Eastern Jin and the four Southern Dynasties of Song, Qi, Liang and Chen all had their capitals at Nanjing (Nanking). The northerners who began to move south in the Wei and Jin dynasties lent fresh impetus to agricultural production in the southeast by increasing the labour force and spreading productive skills. The lasting prominence of Nanjing as a political centre was inseparable from the prosperity of the southeast. The economic growth in the middle and lower reaches of the Changjiang, emulating that in the fertile areas of the Huanghe river basin, was another feature of the ascendancy of Chinese feudalism.

The years from 907 to 1368 were the later period of ascendancy of Chinese feudalism. It began with the Five Dynasties and Ten Kingdoms, followed by the Liao, Western Xia and Jin dynasties on one side and the Northern and Southern Song dynasties on another, and finally reunification under the Yuan Dynasty. Extensive border regions from the northeast to the northwest and again in the southwest entered the stage of feudal society in most important respects at this time. This was a significant feature of Chinese feudalism in the later period of its ascendancy. The economic growth in the southeast surpassed that in the north, and the middle and lower reaches of the Changjiang became the most prosperous parts of the country.

The privileged stratum of landowners of the previous historical period crumbled under the onslaught of peasant uprisings. It was replaced, under the Northern and Southern Song, by bureaucrat landlords who enjoyed certain political status and privileges. With few hereditary privileges, these bureaucrat landlords obtained most of their land through purchase or seizure. The law put no limit on the amount of land they might hold. They were obliged by regulations to pay taxes to the state, and in their turn collected rent from the peasants. The distinction between taxes and rent became clearer. Apart from the bureaucrat landlords there were also the plutocrat landlords and mercantile landlords. Some of the peasants owned small amounts of land, but the majority were tenant-farmers who worked on the lands of the various kinds of landlords. They had a better social position in society and more personal freedom than the manorial peasants in the previous period. Listed in the state household registers, they had to contribute a poll tax and some labour services to the feudal state in addition to payment of rent to the landlords. But generally they were not registered with a certain landlord on the order of the feudal state. This was a major difference between them and the state-registered peasants of the Western and Eastern Han. The imprint of feudal bondage on both landlords and peasants tended to fade away, and the agrarian relations of exploitation in terms of property rights became more distinct. This marked the feudal relations of production in the Northern and Southern Song dynasties.

The strength of the Southern Song landlord class was largely preserved after national unification under the Yuan Dynasty, and a most typical feudal economic order prevailed in the regions under its domination. The Yuan Dynasty saw the emergence of a huge stratum of Mongolian aristocratic landowners, many commoner households bearing feudal duties, and a greater number of slaves. This kind of relations of production was, however, confined to the north and was merely a partial phenomenon of retrogression. The feudalization of extensive border regions was a new phenomenon in the development of production in Yuan society.

The states of Liang, Jin (936-946), Han and Zhou in the period of the Five Dynasties established their capitals at Kaifeng, which also served as the capital for the Northern Song and as a secondary capital for Jin (1115-1234). Modern Beijing was the capital for three dynasties: the Liao, which called it Nanjing; the Jin (1115-1234), which called it Zhongdu; and the Yuan, which called it Dadu. Since ancient times this site has been of strategic, political and economic importance. After the Yuan, the Ming and Qing dynasties retained it as their capital and today it is the capital of the People's Republic. The development of Beijing is a joint creation of the Han, Qidan, Nüzhen, Mongolian and other ethnic groups. Although the Song capital of Kaifeng and the

Yuan capital of Beijing were rather distant from the fertile regions of the Southeast, they both used the Grand Canal linking north and south to facilitate the transport of foodstuffs from the south to the north and to bring in the wealth of the southeast.

The period from 1368 to 1840, which includes the Ming Dynasty and a large part of the Qing, saw the decline of Chinese feudalism. The majority of peasants under the Ming were still tenant-farmers. From the legal point of view, the feudal dependence of the tenant-farmer on the landlord was somewhat weakened. Peasants could choose their own landlords and could reject the landlords' excessive demands for labour service. Hired labourers selling their labour power for material recompense also made their appearance. The tax law of the Qing converted the poll tax and the land tax into a single tax, so that those with land were taxed and those without were not, giving the tax the character of a pure property tax. These conditions showed that feudal bonds had eased considerably. But this did not arise from the kindness of the rulers, but from the necessities of socio-economic development and the fierce struggles of the labouring people. Nevertheless, this was only one aspect of the social phenomena of that time. The other aspect was the rapacious plunder and oppression carried out by the landlord class, especially its ruling group, by using the power in their hands. The unscrupulous use of eunuchs at the Ming court and the strengthening of military rule during the Qing period were attempts to preserve a highly feudalized government. These two aspects may appear to be in disagreement with each other, but they are simply different manifestations of the moribund condition of feudal society. The second manifestation by no means showed the vitality of the feudal landlord class, but revealed its weakness. The two apparently contradictory phenomena were both signs of decline.

The bureaucrat landlords of the previous historical period and their successors, together with the Mongolian aristocratic landlords, crumbled as before under heavy attacks from peasant uprisings. Taking their position were the newly arisen scholar-official landlords. Apart from officials it included fairly large numbers of intellectuals who had passed the Ming and Qing civil service examinations. The wealthier members of this class not only owned much land but also took up trade, operated pawnshops and issued high-interest loans. This was a reflection of the development of commodity production and a money economy, which nevertheless could not be developed normally because those people were dependent on feudal power.

The Ming court directly occupied large areas of land in the form of imperial estates. This, like its appointment of palace eunuchs to collect taxes on commerce and mining and to look for and store up tremendous amounts of gold and silver, revealed the greed of the rulers of a falling dynasty. The estates of the imperial clan and the nobles and bureaucrats, along with the grain allowance of the imperial clan, amounted to fantastic sums, growing into a malignant tumour on the social economy and national finance. Although the Qing court also had imperial estates, they were aware of the possible harmful effects and kept the area much smaller than under the Ming. However, for a fairly long period, the Manchu homeland of the Qing court in the northeast was a forbidden area, which largely hindered local economic development.

"Sprouts of capitalism" could be found as early as the beginning of the Ming Dynasty. They appeared in greater quantity after mid-Ming and showed a further development in early Qing. But these "sprouts" could never grow to full maturity or break through the declining feudal system because of their insufficient strength.

In external relations, the Sui, Tang, Song and Yuan were all in a position to take the initiative, but under the Ming and Qing external relations took a distinct turn for the worse. In early Ming there were landings by "Japanese invaders" (*wokou*), pirates operating off the Chinese and Korean coasts from the 14th to the 16th century, but the Ming court did little against them. From the mid-Ming on, coastal harassment by the "Japanese invaders" brought great destruction to the south. During the Ming and Qing period, capitalism had already arisen in the West, but Chinese feudalism hobbled along its own course, and the autocratic rulers knew nothing of world developments. By the beginning of the 16th century, the Portuguese, Spanish, Dutch and others had come east to carry out colonial activities and had invaded Chinese territory. They were subsequently followed by Tsarist Russia, England and the United States, whose ambitions in regard to

China grew constantly. The eunuch admiral Zheng He's voyages to Southeast Asia and the Indian Ocean in early the Ming and China's resistance to Tsarist Russian invasion in the early Qing were major events in external affairs, but the overall situation worsened continually, and it was not by chance that the Opium War was followed by a series of national disasters.

The history of semi-feudal and semi-colonial China lasted from 1840 to 1949. At the same time, this was an era of resistance to imperialism and feudalism by all of China's ethnic groups. The first stage, up to the May Fourth Movement of 1919, was the period of the old democratic revolution. The second stage, from 1919 on, was the period of the new-democratic revolution.

The period of the old democratic revolution lasted almost eighty years, taking in the final years of the Qing Dynasty and the first years of the Republic. In this period, due to the invasion of foreign imperialism and its brutal rule over China, China's social economy underwent major changes, becoming more complex than that in feudal society. In addition to the feudal landlord economy and the individual economy of the peasants and handicraftsmen, which continued to exist, the newly arisen capitalist economy became a major sector in the social economy. The capitalist economy comprised three parts: imperialist capital, bureaucrat-comprador capital and national capital. While imperialism gained control over China's economic lifelines, the feudal landlord class occupied a dominant position in the economy, and the two were in mutual collaboration. Bureaucrat-comprador capital was an appendage to the imperialist economy and was also closely connected with feudal exploitation. The national capitalist economy was extremely weak. It did not form an independent economic system or occupy an important position in socio-economic life, and it also had ties with imperialism and feudalism. Foreign imperialist aggression brought ruin to the self-sufficient natural economy in the countryside; commodity production developed, but agricultural production and the peasants' economic life was drawn deeper and deeper into the vortex of the world capitalist market. These were the main features of China's semi-colonial, semi-feudal social economy.

Along with the violent changes in the social economy, changes also developed in class relations. Following its penetration into China, the foreign bourgeoisie became a dominant power in Chinese social life, controlling the country's economy, politics, military affairs and culture. It not only propped up the feudal landlord class as the mainstay of their rule over China, but also created a comprador class to serve the needs of their aggression. Within the feudal landlord class, the newly arisen warlord-bureaucrat landlords, with the support of the international bourgeoisie, replaced the scholar-official landowners as the dominant force. The warlord-bureaucrat landlords were an appendage to the international bourgeoisie and were generally the earliest bureaucrat-capitalists of a strong comprador character. They held the real power in the regime of the landlord class and became the decisive force. This was an important manifestation of the compradorization of the landlord regime. The peasant class mostly comprised owner-peasants, tenant-peasants and farm labourers, and accounted for about 70 or 80 per cent of the national population. Under the oppression and exploitation of feudalism and imperialism, the peasants became increasingly impoverished and bankrupt, so that the owner-peasants became ever fewer and the tenant-peasants ever more numerous. The national bourgeoisie and the proletariat were the two new classes arising in this period. The national bourgeoisie, as determined by their economic position, was a class with a dual character: on the one hand it exhibited an anti-imperialist, anti-feudal revolutionary character in certain periods and to a certain extent, but on the other hand it tended towards compromise with the enemies of revolution. The proletariat was the greatest, most progressive and most revolutionary class. In the period of the old democratic revolution, however, it did not constitute an independent political force, but took part in revolution as a follower of the petty bourgeoisie and the bourgeoisie.

The socio-economic conditions and class relations in semi-colonial, semi-feudal China determined that the basic task of the Chinese revolution was to overthrow the rule of imperialism and feudalism. In the period of the old democratic revolution, the people of all ethnic groups in China carried out a bitter, unremitting struggle against the internal and external enemies and for the winning of national independence and freedom and happiness for the people. However, they did not find the road to liberation and did not gain the final victory. After the May Fourth Movement of 1919, the proletariat grew in strength, Marxism-Leninism spread to China, the Chinese Communist Party was established and the Chinese revolution took on an entirely new appearance. Under the leadership of the Chinese Communist Party, the people of each ethnic group in China gained the final victory in China's democratic revolution. In 1949, the People's Republic of China was established and China entered a new age of socialism.

Chapter II
Traces of Remote Antiquity

1. From Yuanmou Man to Peking Man; the Making of Tools and the Use of Fire

The first primitive man so far known to have existed in China is Yuanmou Man, who lived about 1.70 million years ago. In 1965, two fossil front teeth of primitive ape men were discovered in Yuanmou County, Yunnan Province. Later, stone artifacts, pieces of animal bone showing signs of human work and ash from campfires were also dug up. The primitive ape man who had inhabited the site came to be known as Yuanmou Man.

In 1963 and 1964, a fossil skullcap, the upper and lower jawbones, and three teeth of the ape man were discovered together with stone artifacts and animal fossils in Lantian County, Shaanxi Province. The "Lantian Man" inhabited this site 500,000 to 600,000 years ago. [1] Other traces of the ape man have also been found in Hebei, Shanxi, Henan, Hubei, and Guizhou. But the best-known of all is "Peking Man".

Peking Man, whose remains were discovered at Zhoukoudian to the southwest of Beijing (Peking), lived some 400,000 to 500,000 years ago. In excavations before and since liberation in 1949, a wealth of fossils and other evidence of this culture have been uncovered. In 1966, a relatively complete fossil skullcap was discovered at the site. To date, fossil bones deriving from more than forty individuals of both sexes and various ages, and more than 100,000 pieces of stone worked

---

[1] Paleogeomagnetic examination reveals that the skullcap and the lower jawbone date from different periods. The former is a million years old, while the latter dates back 500,000 years.

by man, fossils of more than a hundred kinds of animals, and traces of campfires have been discovered there.

Though still retaining some of the features of the ape, Peking Man's physical structure already possessed the basic characteristics of man. He was relatively short, the male averaging 1.558 metres, the female 1.435. His face was shorter than that of modern man, his mouth protruded, and he had no chin, while his forehead was low, flat, and receding. His skull was about twice as thick as modern man's, with the cap smaller at the top and widening towards the base. Cranial capacity averaged 1,075 cc., approximately 80 per cent of contemporary man's, more than twice that of the modern anthropoid ape (415 cc.), and much greater than Lantian Man's 780 cc. The brain structure was incomparably more advanced than that of present-day anthropoid apes. Peking Man had two inter-locking heavy brow bones above the eye sockets which screened his eyes, his nose was flat, his cheekbones were prominent, his teeth strong and their grinding surfaces relatively complex.

Peking Man's lower limbs already had the basic form of those of modern man. In size, shape, proportion, and muscular attachment, his thighbones were similar to those of present-day man, though they still possessed some primitive features. The bone walls were thicker and the medullary cavities inside the bones smaller, while the transverse diameter of the middle section of the femur was slightly greater than the diameter measured front to back—more like that of the ape than of contemporary man, whose femoral cross-section is the reverse. But Peking Man could already walk and even run erect, though he was somewhat stooped.

Through labour over long periods, Peking Man's hands had become dexterous, as they had had to adapt to complex movements. The humerus and collar bone of the upper arm resembled those of modern man, though the humerus was still somewhat primitive, with a relatively small medullary cavity and a thicker wall. Research on the inner surface of the cranium shows that the left cerebral hemisphere was bigger than the right, testifying to the fact that Peking Man normally used the right hand in labour. This point is verified by reference to the stone tools he used.

It is clear that the uneven development of the various parts of Peking Man's physique was due to the nature of the labour in which he was engaged. Hand labour led to the functional differentiation between the upper and lower limbs, with the upper limbs developing faster than the lower. The development of the brain occurred gradually as a result of hand labour and differentiation of the limbs, and thus the primitive character of Peking Man's head is rather more pronounced. The role of labour in the physical development process proves the truth enunciated by Engels: "Labour created man."[1]

Peking Man was already able to make and use tools: tools of wood and bone, but especially of stone. He already had several ways of making stone tools. He used one piece of stone to strike or hammer another stone to pieces, or broke a stone held in his hand by pounding it against a bigger stone, thus knocking off large numbers of usable sharp flakes which could be fashioned into various kinds of tools. Most of the tools were made of stone flakes worked on one edge. Only a few were made of unworked stone flakes. The stone tools can be roughly classified as choppers, scrapers, or knife-shaped tools, according to their different forms and uses. Some were suitable for cutting and fashioning wooden hunting clubs, others for cutting animal skins or meat. The tools made and used by Peking Man prove that he was essentially different from the animals and had already come a long way on the road of human development.

A great deal of ash, some of it in piles and some in layers, has been discovered in the caves once inhabited by Peking Man. The ash contains pieces of burnt animal bones and stones of various colours, hackberry seeds, and charred Chinese redbud wood, showing that animal meat was often roasted, and that Peking Man was already able to preserve, use, and control fire.

The use of fire allowed Peking Man to cook his food, and thus shorten the digestive process and promote the absorption of more nutrients, thereby spurring physical evolution and enhancing health. At the same time, fire could be used to ward off cold and defend against attacks by fierce animals. It could serve as an effective aid in hunting as well.

In his mutual relations, Peking Man had already formed links which do not and cannot exist in the animal realm, namely, the links

---

[1] *Dialectics of Nature*, Foreign Languages Publishing House, Moscow, 1966, p. 170.

involved in the cooperative creation and use of tools, and the creation of speech through the common labour process. The size of the part of the brain where the speech centre is located shows that he could already speak. Speech originated in joint labour, and in turn promoted the evolution of man's body; it had an especially great influence on the development of man's brain.

Peking Man's main productive activities were hunting and gathering. The great quantities of smashed and burnt deer bones discovered in the caves where he lived indicate that deer were his principal game. Probably his most effective hunting weapons were the firebrand and the wooden club. Although no clubs have been preserved, the discovery of many choppers and big convex tools suitable for scraping wood, provides indirect evidence of their existence.

Peking Man led an extremely difficult life in primitive collectives. He used his crude tools, his limited labour experience, and his simple cooperative labour to confront every kind of natural hazard, to stave off repeated attacks by wild beasts, and to procure his essential food. His lifespan was generally not long; of the more than forty individuals whose remains have been discovered, approximately one-third died before the age of fourteen years.

2. Dingcun (Tingtsun) Man and Upper Cave Man; the Improvement of Tools and the Emergence of Ornaments

About 100,000 years ago, China's ancient culture entered the "Neanderthaloid" stage.[1] Human fossils from this period are relatively widely distributed in China, but the most significant among them are

[1] The evolution of man may be roughly divided into the Pithecanthropine ("Apeman"), Neanderthaloid, and "Modern" stages. Some scholars hold that beginning with the time man began to create tools, his morphological development may be divided into three stages, namely, the "Australopithecus" stage, a Homo erectus stage, and the Homo sapiens stage which includes contemporary man.

those of "Maba Man", discovered in Qujiang County in South China's Guangdong Province; "Changyang Man", found in Changyang County in Central China's Hubei Province; and "Dingcun Man", uncovered in Xiangfen County in North China's Shanxi Province. Their physical appearance was already different from that of Peking Man. Maba Man's skull bones were thinner than those of Peking Man, and his forehead was higher. Changyang Man's upper jawbone did not protrude so much as Peking Man's. And both the roots and the crowns of Dingcun Man's teeth were more advanced than those of Peking Man, closer to those of modern man.

Dingcun Man lived in the Fenhe River basin to the west of the Taihang Mountains. His chief tools were still stone implements, but they were more advanced than those of Peking Man, both in terms of flaking and fashioning technique. In making the flakes, Dingcun Man commonly used a flinging technique, forcefully hurling a large piece of stone against another stone. Dingcun Man's stone implements were also more clearly differentiated as to type than were those of Peking Man, with tools like the prismatic knife-edge and stone balls appearing for the first time.

About 40,000 years ago, China's ancient culture entered the stage of "modern man". Starting then, the hunting and fishing economy underwent a remarkable advance and the matriarchal commune gradually took shape. Traces of the peoples of that period have been found at many places across China's wide territory. Typical examples are Liujiang Man and Qilinshan Man found in Liujiang and Laibin counties respectively in Guangxi, South China; Hetao Man found along both banks of the Sjara-osso-gol River in Uxin Banner, Inner Mongolia and in Lingwu County in Ningxia; the Shiyu Culture which existed 28,000 years ago in what is now Shuoxian in North China's Shanxi Province; and the Upper Cave Man who lived about 18,000 years ago in caves near the top of Dragon Bone Hill at Zhoukoudian, where Peking Man was discovered.

Upper Cave Man's physical make-up and outward appearance were hardly different from those of present-day man. As a result of working with the hands and walking erect, the load on the skeletal muscles had been diminishing. Thus the walls of the bones of the limbs had become thinner, and the medullary cavity larger. As for the head, the cranial capacity had expanded and the structure of the brain was reaching a higher level of complexity and perfection. Peking Man's cranial capacity had averaged 1,075 cc., but Liujiang Man's and Upper Cave Man's was between 1,300 and 1,500 cc., similar to that of present man. As the brain gradually grew, the forehead became progressively higher, the cranium progressively thinner, and the point of maximum breadth of the skull shifted from above the ears to the region where the parietal bones link up. The brow-ridges had become thinner and flatter, and the teeth smaller and less complex. The mouth had receded so that the lower jaw and nasal bridge were more prominent as in modern man. The cranium of Liujiang Man and Upper Cave Man possessed the basic characteristics of that of modern man. From the point of view of race, their heads bore the primeval features of the Mongoloid peoples, and they represent an important stage in the formation of Mongoloid physical characteristics.

Upper Cave Man's labour experience and skill surpassed that of his predecessors. Though his stone implements were still basically made by striking stones against each other and by rough fashioning, he had already acquired the new skills of polishing, scraping, drilling, carving and colouring. Among the tools he left behind were two bone implements, a polished dear antler and a lower jawbone. The polished antler bears carved designs consisting of both straight and curved lines. The best reflection of Upper Cave Man's improved tool-making techniques is a bone needle. With a length of 82 mm and a diameter varying from 3.1 to 3.3 mm, the needle is round and sharp, and the eye small. To fashion such a needle, an animal bone had to be cut and scraped, the eye had to be gouged out, and then the whole thing had to be polished. By these complex techniques Upper Cave Man created a needle which could be used to sew animal skins into clothing.

Among the ornaments belonging to Upper Cave Man that have been discovered are drilled stone beads, pebbles, the eye-socket bones of black carp, perforated animal teeth and clam shells, and carved tubes made of bird bones. The making of these ornaments involved selection of materials, chipping, drilling, abrading and colouring. Some of the ornaments were dyed red with hematite.

Upper Cave Man's main economic activities were hunting and fishing. Hare, red deer, sika, wild boar, antelope, badger and fox were his chief game. He also caught ostrich and other birds. He caught various fish, including black carp a metre in length, and he collected fresh-water clams. He gathered fruit and roots as supplementary food.

Upper Cave Man, or even his predecessors, probably already knew how to make fire. Making fire instead of just preserving it marked another big step forward in man's effort to control nature. Engels considered the discovery of the fire-making technique to be even more important than the discovery of the steam engine. He pointed out that "the generation of fire by friction for the first time gave man command over one of the forces of nature, and thus separated him for ever from the animal kingdom."[1] The invention of the fire-making technique paved the way for many subsequent inventions, such as the making of pottery and metal tools.

The shells of salt-water clams found in the upper cave were not local, but could only be obtained at the seaside quite a distance away. Whether obtained by exchange or collected directly, they show that man had expanded the scope of his activities and contacts, and was in a better position to do battle with nature.

The upper cave is approximately 12 metres long and about 8 metres wide, with an area of more than 90 square metres, and could accommodate a dozen or so inhabitants. The cave was divided naturally into "upper" and "lower" chambers. The upper chamber, near the cave mouth, was the common living quarters, while the lower, located deep inside, served as a burial ground. A vast region around the cave served as the base for hunting, fishing, and gathering activities.

A young female, another of middle age, and an elderly male were interred in the lower chamber of the cave. Hematite powder was scattered around the dead, and stone implements and ornaments were interred with them. The arrangements for the dead give an idea of the activities of the living in the upper chamber. The burial of men and women, old and young together, with production tools and ornaments around them, reflects the closeness of a blood relationship and the

[1] *Anti-Dühring*, Foreign Languages Press, Beijing, 1976, p. 145.

production relations of communal labour and consumption. The fact that there is no great differentiation in burial objects suggests equality of the clan members. The hematite powder and accompanying burial objects show that Upper Cave Man adhered to certain burial customs and that his thinking had developed to a new level at which he had begun to formulate primitive religious beliefs with a superstitious tinge and ideas that went beyond actual existence.

3. The Yangshao Culture and Its Matriarchal Communes

Some 6,000 to 7,000 years ago, clans and tribes, big and small, were scattered across China, leaving behind rich cultural remains. A microlithic culture extended from the Northeast through Inner Mongolia and Ningxia to Xinjiang and Tibet.[1] There was the Yangshao culture[2] on the middle reaches of the Huanghe (Yellow River), and the Majiayao culture[3] on its upper reaches. Other primitive cultures were distributed elsewhere.

The features of the matriarchal commune are displayed relatively distinctly by the Yangshao culture. Mainly discovered in central Shaanxi, western Henan and southern Shanxi, it stretched as far as the upper and middle reaches of the Hanshui River in the south and the Hetao (Yellow River Bend) region in the north, the upper reaches of the Weihe River in Gansu in the west, and Shandong in the east. The remains of many settlements have been found in these places, and in some cases they were clustered relatively close together.

The inhabitants of the Huanghe River region were engaged

---

[1] The name "microlith" derives from the small size of the stone implements. The term "culture" is used here in its archaeological sense, referring to an entire body of archaeological remains with common characteristics from a single period and a single region. Such a culture is commonly identified by the name of the spot of the first discovery or the name of a characteristic site or relic.

[2] The name comes from Yangshao Village, Mianchi County, Henan Province, where the culture was first discovered.

[3] First discovered in Majiayao, Lintao County, Gansu Province.

mainly in a primitive agriculture, supplemented by animal husbandry. They used pointed wooden sticks for digging the earth, and their stone implements were no longer the roughly fashioned ones made by striking stones, but comparatively refined ones made primarily by abrading techniques. They had stone axes for cutting away the ground cover, stone and bone spades for loosening and levelling the soil, and various kinds of stone knives for harvesting grain. The main agricultural crop was grain,[1] but they also planted vegetables. Some simple tools for processing crops had already been invented. Grain was placed on a millstone and ground with a hand-held stone pin or disc until it was husked or powdered.

Once man took up agriculture, he was able to produce the food he needed, and thus could settle down. Of course, the methods of cultivation used in primitive agriculture were still in an early stage, and production was always subject to the whims of nature. The yields were low or even came to nothing. In such circumstances a part of or even an entire clan settlement had to move.

Hunting and fishing was second only to agriculture in man's productive activities, occupying a relatively important position in the economic life of the time. The principal weapons included bows and arrows, stone-tipped spears, fishing lances, fish-hooks, and nets with stone weights attached. Household animal husbandry developed as another sideline. From the pens and animal skeletons found at the Banpo site at Xi'an, we can see that the main livestock were pigs and dogs. Cattle, sheep, horses and chickens may also have been domesticated. But gathering was still an indispensable part of production. Many hazelnuts, pinenuts, chestnuts, hackberry seeds, snail and clam shells were discovered in the homes and cellars at the Banpo site.

The rise in the quantity and quality of production and household implements is an indication of the advance of handicraft industry. The

---

[1] Between 1973 and 1978, archaeologists unearthed large quantities of carbonated rice remains and bone and wood spade-shaped implements used in rice planting at the site of Hemudu Village in Yuyao County, Zhejiang Province. These remains go back approximately 7,000 years. To date, they are the first signs of the domestic cultivation of rice in China.

Bust of a reconstruction of Peking Man

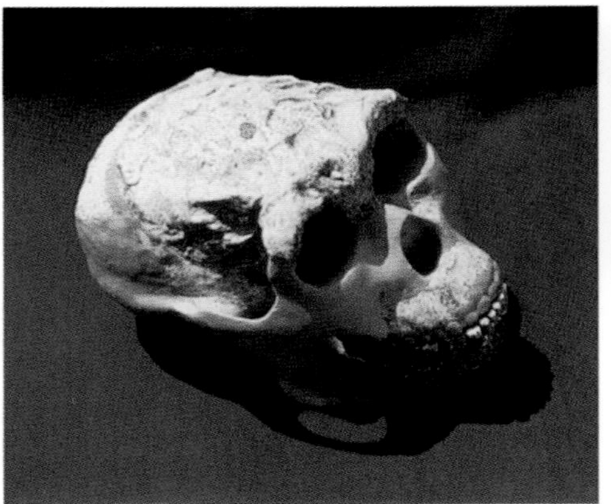

The reconstructed cranium of Lantian Man

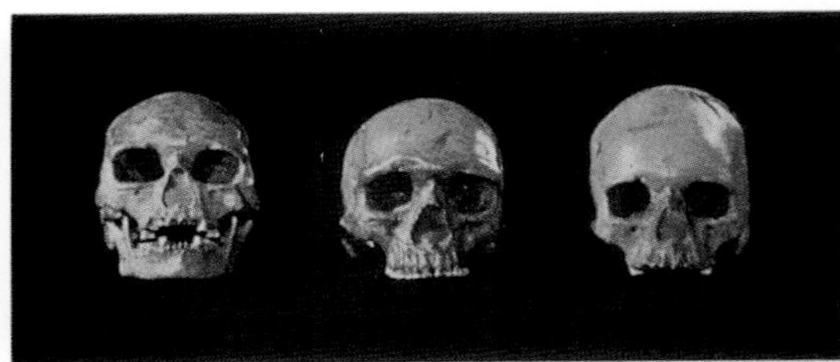

The fossilized cranium of Upper Cave Man (unearthed in Upper Cave, Zhoukoudian, Beijing)

The earliest known Chinese dragon on the left, made from clamshells, and a tiger on the right (unearthed in Xipo, Puyang County, Henan Province)

Vessel in the shape of a naked human figure (unearthed in Liuwan, Ledu County, Qinghai Province)

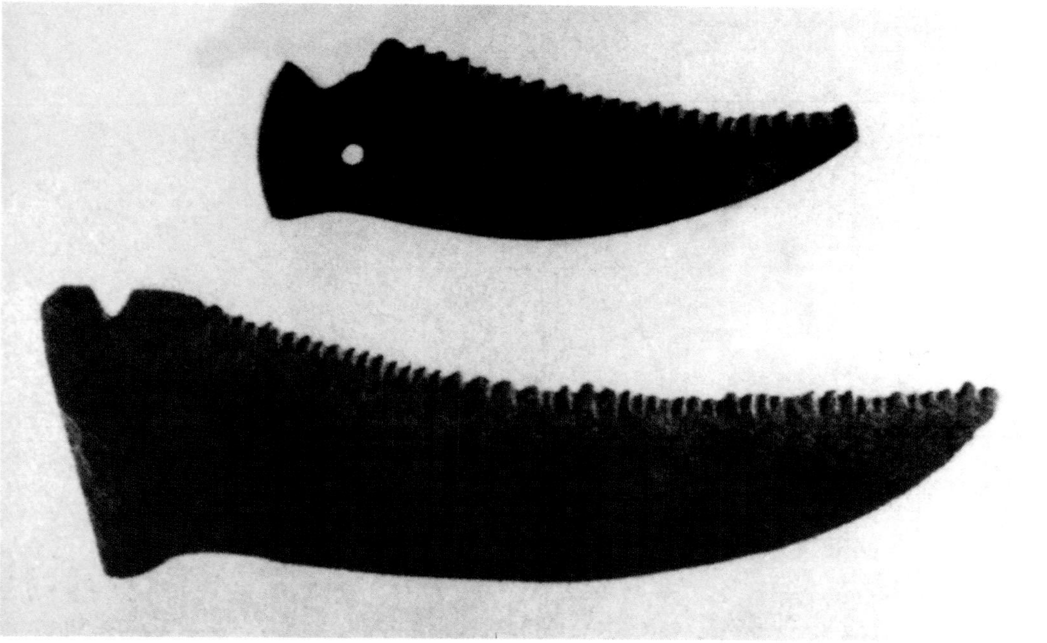

Stone sickles with saw-tooth edges (unearthed in Peiligang, Xinzheng County, Henan Province)

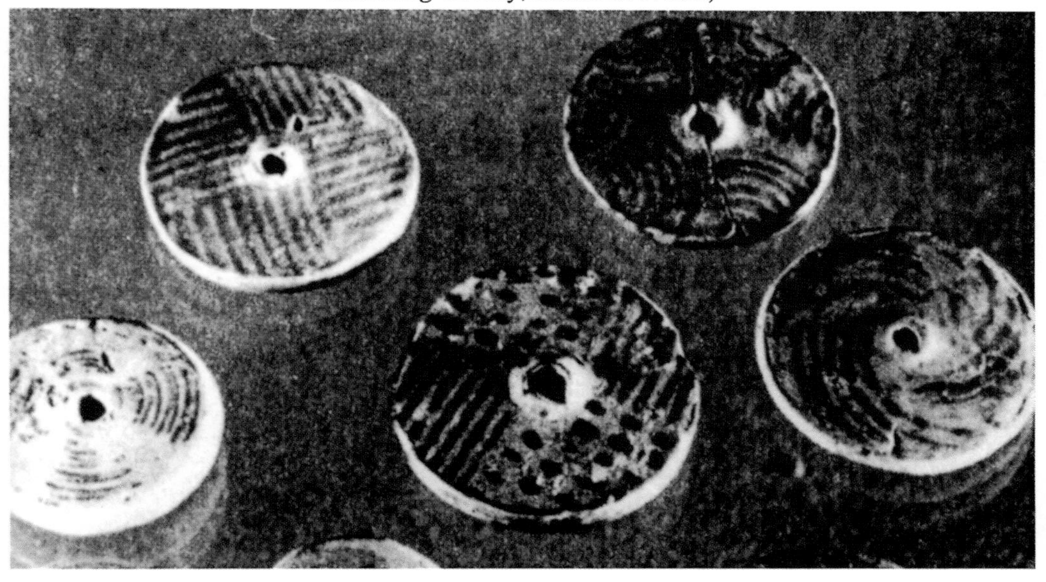

Painted spinning wheels (unearthed in Jingshan County, Hubei Province and Xichuan County, Henan Province)

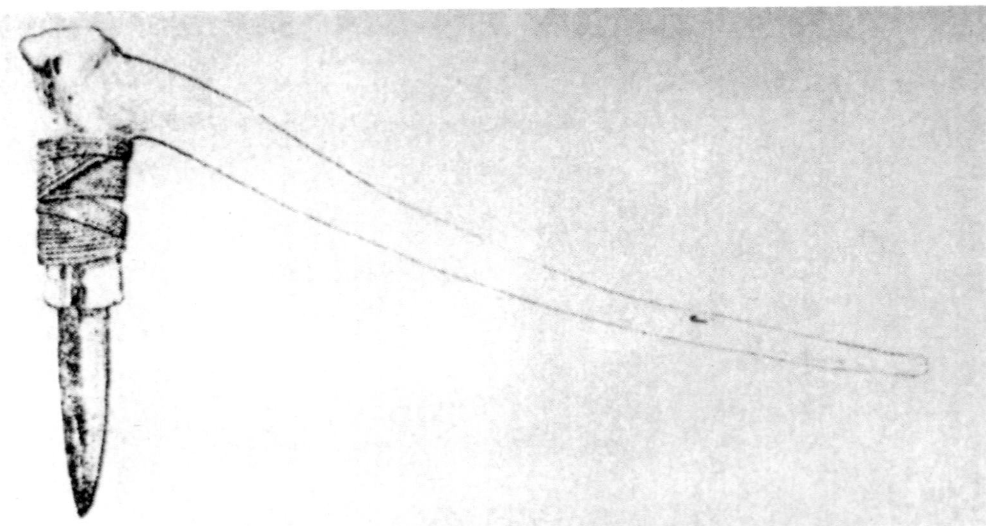

A stone pickaxe (restored) from the Yangshao Culture

Reconstruction of a round house at the Banpo site from the Yangshao Culture

Inscriptions on bone and tortoise shell

Left: Zai Feng Inscription

Lower: Dagu inscription

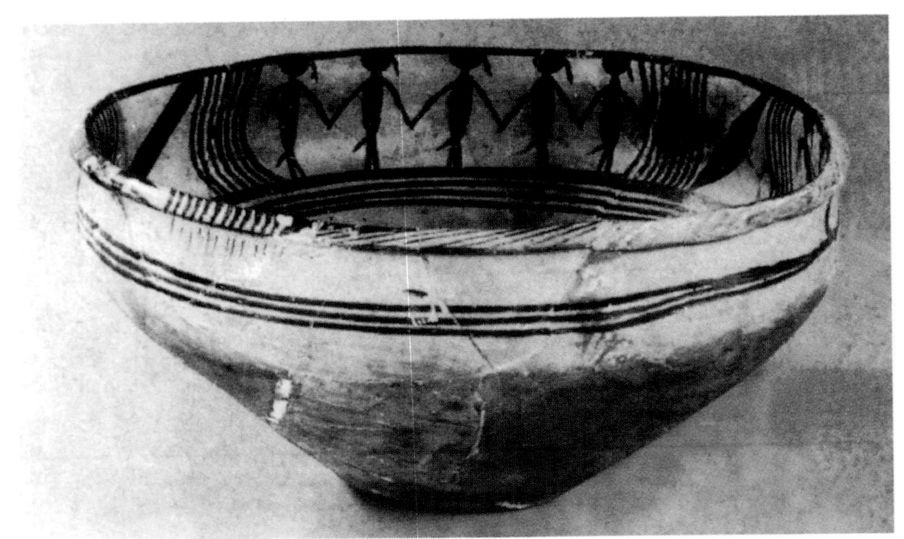

Pottery basin with dancing designs (unearthed in Datong, Qinghai Province)

A pottery wine container from the Longshan Culture (unearthed in Dafanzhuang, Linyi City, Shandong Province)

Designs on copperware from the Shang Dynasty

Rubbing taking from the Shiqiang Plate

A rectangular *si mu wu ding* ritual cauldron from the Shang Dynasty (unearthed in Wuguan Village, Anyang County, Henan Province)

The Shiqiang Plate from the middle period of the Western Zhou Dynasty (unearthed in Zhuangbai, Fufeng County, Shaanxi Province)

creation of large numbers of ground and polished tools provided man with new tools and spurred the overall development of social production. That cutting, paring, grinding and drilling techniques were being used can be seen from the axes, adzes, spades, chisels, knives, needles and hairpins. The reflex-barbed fishing spear, the fish-hook and the perforated bone needle had already appeared, indicating the relatively high level of the bone-working techniques of primitive handicraft industry.

Weaving and sewing had also made relatively rapid progress. Fibre could be stripped from wild hemp and twisted into thread with the use of pottery or stone spinning wheels, and then be woven into cloth. Animal skins were also used to make clothing. The ingenious bone needles or bone and antler awls could be used to sew cloth and leather into various kinds of clothing.

Pottery manufacture was a new, distinctive handicraft at the time. One of the characteristics of the Yangshao and Majiayao cultures was that they had various kinds of painted pottery. Remains of pottery kilns have been found at the sites of numerous clan settlements. The pottery paste was prepared from relatively fine loess soil to the proper degree of viscosity. After mixing, it was rolled into cords and then either folded to make a rough blank or coiled into an embryonic shape. Small pieces were molded directly into finished form. The next step was decoration of the blank and the addition of handles, ears, noses, etc. by adhesion or inlay. After the blanks were half dry, the inner and outer walls were again scraped and polished. Hematite and manganese oxide were applied with brush-like tools to paint pictures on finer household utensils. Sometimes, before applying the paint, a white or light red ground was applied to make the whole image more colourful. As the kilns were not completely sealed, the iron oxides in the clay would oxidize fully, hence the bulk of the pottery is red or brown.

Part of the pottery articles were production tools while most were household utensils: basic cooking utensils such as stoves, steamers, footed vessels and cauldrons for steaming or boiling various kinds of foods; drinking and eating vessels like cups, basins, plates, bowls and tumblers; and jars and pots for storing things in. There was an amphora-shaped bottle for drawing water which utilized the principle of equilibrium: placed on the surface of the water, it would automatically tilt, allowing the water to flow in.

Pottery was one of the most important inventions of the matriarchal commune period. It indicates that man's wisdom was not limited to the working of natural objects, but could create entirely new things. Pottery could be used to cook food, thereby allowing the human body to absorb more fully the nutritious substances of foodstuffs, and it could be used to store liquids, which was beneficial to agricultural irrigation. This contributed to making the sedentary life style more stable. And the principles of pottery-making could also be applied in making ceramic spinning wheels, pellets for hunting, and sinkers for fishing nets. Fire could also be used to bake the earth walls and foundations of primitive buildings. All of this had very great significance for the advance of human production and livelihood.

Painted pottery was not only practical, but was also a fine handicraft art. The painted designs, patterns, birds and animals on the pottery reflect the agricultural labour and hunting and fishing activities of the time with much liveliness and imagination. There are also many marks carved into the surfaces of the pottery which may have been used as symbols for the utensils themselves. Some scholars believe that they are a kind of primitive script. The birds, fish, deer and frogs depicted on the pottery may have been the clan totems.[1]

The settlements of that era had a fixed layout in keeping with clan structure. The Banpo site is a typical clan settlement. It covers an area of about 50,000 square metres and includes three components: a residential section, a pottery-kiln quarter, and a common burial ground. Cellars of various shapes within the village were the clan's common storehouses. The homes in the residential section are themselves arranged according to a pattern. There was one very large square building, a place for public activities, while other medium- and small-sized buildings served as the clan members' dwellings. A ditch, approxi-

---

[1] Totems served as both the names and emblems of the clans. In general, names of animals, plants or inanimate objects were adopted. The function of the totem was to preserve the common pedigree of all clan members bearing its name, thereby serving to distinguish between clans.

mately five or six metres deep and wide, was dug around the residential section, and the clan's common burial ground was to the north of the ditch, the kiln quarter to the east. This layout demonstrates that the clan members lived in equality, labouring and consuming in common, and the fact that they were buried together when they died shows that they all belonged to a single clan.

Women enjoyed a high status in the clan. They played an important role in production and other activities. The custom of burying the females in the centre prevailed in some places: dozens of joint matriarchal clan graves have been discovered at Yuanjunmiao, Huaxian County, and Hengzhen Village, Huayin County, in Shaanxi Province. The bodies of the deceased, found in common pits, were all moved there to be buried together; the number of bodies in each pit was uneven, and there were men and women, old and young. The removal and joint burial process was quite complex. When a person died, the corpse was probably first dealt with in an interim fashion, but when a woman of fairly high status in the matriarchal clan died, her body was immediately placed in one of these grave pits in a supine position. Then the remains of the predeceased of the same clan were brought, laid out together, and buried in the same grave. This burial custom, with the women at the centre, is one reflection of the important position women occupied in the clans. But what is more, at the Banpo site and at the Jiangzhai site in Lintong County in Shaanxi, the buried objects accompanying the females generally outnumbered those of the males. This is further demonstration that the women's social status was high.

Collective labour and the public character of ownership of the means of production determined that the distribution of goods within the matriarchal commune was perforce one of common consumption by all members. The cellars for storing things at the Banpo and Jiangzhai sites are distributed closely together around the dwellings. In some spots there are more than ten clustered together in one place, forming a cellar complex. This may have been a form of collective storage. From the graves we can see that after death the majority of clan members were buried in a common burial ground according to a basically similar burial style, and that the great majority of burial objects were ornaments and pottery used in daily life. The maximum number of burial objects in any one of the seventy-one graves containing such objects at Banpo was ten, the minimum one, and the average 4.3.

Although by that time, people's livelihood had improved somewhat, it was still very difficult. According to the result of a survey of human bones at the Yuanjunmiao site, the people of the time were afflicted with bone-compression spurs because of the excessively heavy burdens they had to bear. And because their food was coarse and they had to expend a lot of energy in chewing, their lower jaws were still more sturdy than those of modern man and their teeth show serious wear and tear. The remains in the various grave groups reveal that the life expectancy of the majority was only around thirty or forty years, and that there was a high rate of infant mortality. Because the level of the productive forces was still very low, and the means of livelihood very limited, it was only possible for them to maintain such an arduous, poor life for members of the clan by living, producing and consuming in common.

4. The Patriarchal Clan Society of the Longshan Culture

Approximately 5,000 years ago, the tribes of the Huanghe River and Changjiang (Yangtze River) valleys gradually entered the era of the patriarchal clan commune. In general, the Longshan, Qijia, Qujialing, Qingliangang, Liangzhu and Dawenkou tribal cultural remains belong to this period.[1]

The Longshanoid tribes were widely distributed, from the seacoast in the east to the middle reaches of the Weishui River in the west, from the Bohai Gulf coastline of the Liaodong Peninshula in the north

---

[1] These cultures take their names from their places of first discovery: Longshan Township, Zhangqiu County, Shandong; Qijia Green, Guanghe County, Gansu; Qujialing, Jingshan County, Hubei; Qingliangang, Huaian County, Jiangsu; Liangzhu, Hangzhou City, Zhejiang; and Dawenkou, Taian County, Shandong.

to the northern parts of Hubei, Anhui and Jiangsu in the south. The principal area was Henan, Shandong and Hebei, the southern part of Shanxi, and the Weishui River basin in Shaanxi. Taken as a whole, it was greater in extent than the Yangshao culture, and the regional differences were more pronounced. Tribes belonging to the Qijia culture lived on the upper reaches of the Huanghe River in the eastern part of Gansu and the northeastern part of Qinghai. The stone implements and pottery from the late New Stone Age sites found in Tibet have an affinity to those of Qijia; the jade bi (a piece of jade for ceremonial purposes) and jade beads of the New Stone Age cultural remains of the Wusuli River basin in the Northeast are also similar to those of the Huanghe River basin. The Qujialing culture was distributed mainly in the Hanshui River basin in Hubei, while the Qingliangang culture was scattered along the lower reaches of the Changjiang River, principally within what is now Jiangsu Province. The Liangzhu culture extended along the lower reaches of the Qiantang River and the area around Lake Taihu. The Dawenkou culture was scattered mainly throughout Shandong and the northern parts of Jiangsu and Anhui.

Production reached new levels of development, especially in agriculture and animal husbandry, during the Longshanoid period. The rise in handicraft levels was marked by the introduction of the potter's wheel and by the beginning of the metallurgical manufacture of copper. Two new agricultural tools appeared at this time: the wooden fork and the stone or clamshell sickle. It was discovered that by using a stone or clamshell sickle with handle attached, a change could be made from picking the ears of grain to harvesting it with the stems connected. This raised labour efficiency and made it possible to bring in fodder for the livestock. The development of Longshanoid agriculture is also reflected in the increase in the numbers of reaping tools. At some sites in Hebei, Henan and Shaanxi, reaping tools in the form of stone knives have been found in numbers roughly equal to those of tools for clearing and planting, as represented by the stone axe and stone spade. In some places the reaping tools even outnumber the clearing and planting tools by two to four times. There was also an improvement in the stone knives, which became broader, longer and sharper. By way of contrast, among the agricultural implements of the

Yangshao culture, clearing and planting tools normally outnumbered reaping tools by a couple of times. The increase and improvement in the Longshanoid culture's reaping tools indicate the better harvests in that period.

The tribes of the Qujialing, Qingliangang and Liangzhu cultures living on the middle and lower reaches of the Changjiang opened up the grass-covered marshy regions, turned them into paddy fields, and planted rice.

The numbers and variety of domesticated animals also increased in this period. Herds of pigs and dogs were raised everywhere, and there were cattle and goats as well as horses and chickens. The bones of livestock excavated from twenty-six firepits of the Longshanoid culture at Miaodigou, Shanxian County, Henan, are more plentiful than those from 168 Yangshao firepits; among them, pig bones are especially numerous. Bones from twenty-one pigs were excavated from a single firepit in Jiangou, Handan County, Hebei. More than one-third of a total of 133 graves excavated at Dawenkou yielded pig bones which had been interred with the corpses, the richest tomb in this respect yielding fourteen pig skulls. Of the domesticated animals, pigs have the advantage of reproducing quickly and of tolerating coarse food. The growth of pig raising provided a source of meat for man and made him less reliant on hunting.

Livestock raising had already become a new means of livelihood and it gradually took on increasing importance in economic life. While participating in agricultural labour, the males also devoted themselves to animal husbandry and thus the acquisition of means of livelihood became a primarily male affair. The products from such pursuits accrued more to the males, while the women were confined to labouring chiefly within the household. It was these herds that became the major private property of the patriarchal family.

The hunting-fishing-gathering economy served as a supplementary means of livelihood and underwent development to varying degrees. Of the hunting implements discovered, the stone, bone and shell arrowheads are highly polished, but in specific areas we still find a few struck flint ones. People of the Liangzhu culture of Shuitianfan at Hangzhou and Qianshanyang in Wuxing, Zhejiang, were already using fishing boats to go out into open waters to fish on a relatively large scale.

At the time under discussion, the potter's wheel had already been created. The clay was fashioned into containers by using the force of the rapidly spinning wheel. Pottery made this way was regular in shape and of even thickness, but a more important result was the sharp rise in productivity. The structure of the pottery kilns had also been perfected and people had mastered the technique of sealing them. High temperatures and sealing caused the reduction of the ferrites in the fired blanks, giving rise to a grey-coloured pottery. The wheel-thrown pottery of the Shandong Longshanoid clans was particularly well-developed. Because the blanks were polished, the kilns were tightly sealed, and the smoke was intentionally allowed to colour it, the fired pottery was pitch-black, with a glossy surface. Black pottery could even be made which was thin as eggshell. And kaolin clay was used to fire a small number of tripod pitchers with a very white surface.

The metallurgical industry was one of the outstanding production accomplishments of the patriarchal clan period. Copper tablets have been discovered at the Dacheng Mountain site near Tangshan in Hebei and such things have also been discovered in some quantity in several dwelling sites and graves of the Qijia culture which came a bit later than that of Longshan. Copper products—knives, awls, chisels and rings—and fragments of copper utensils have been found at Huangniangniangtai in Wuwei County in Gansu. Copper daggers, awls and rings have also been found at Qinweijia and Dahezhuang in Linxia County, Gansu. All these items were made of very pure copper; there were small amounts of impurities, but no tin or lead was added in the working process. Such copper was relatively soft and could be directly hammered into various kinds of tools and ornaments. Copper is malleable and can be shaped at will and even recast, and is thus much superior to stone. The discovery of copper marks a break with the several tens of thousands of years of stone tool technology of primitive Chinese society; it was a creative new technology which brought about a fresh rise in the productive forces. Making copper implements involved a series of steps—mining, smelting, hammering, pattern making and casting—which required much more complex production techniques than did the making of either stone implements or pottery. People came to specialize in this profession, furthering the division of handicraft labour. As those who turned out the copper utensils came to know the properties of metals, they also opened the road for subsequent metal manufacture.

At the time of the patriarchal clan communes, people still lived under a primitive communal system with collective ownership and sharing, and the clans were still held together by blood ties. In the layout of the clan settlements, the dwellings and the cellars are still tightly interknit and there are common graveyards close to the dwelling areas. The common burial grounds of the clans are especially ordered and best reflect the characteristics of the clan system. The clan gravesite of the Longshanoid culture at Miaodigou is situated on the western edge of the site. Within an area of something over 1,100 square metres, 145 graves are laid out, aligned north-south, the heads of the dead pointing invariably to the south. The public burial ground of the Qijia culture at Qinweijia has more than a hundred graves in six north-south rows and the heads of the dead all face northwest. Somewhat over twenty metres to the east is a smaller burial area with three east-west rows and twenty-nine graves, the heads of the deceased all facing west. These arrangements suggest that the different clans adhered strictly to their own traditional customs for burying the dead and that the members of the clans did not easily leave their own clans under normal circumstances.

An important symbol of the patriarchal clan commune was the appearance in marriage relations of a more firm and enduring system of monogamy, with succession fixed through the male line. By that time they had adopted the formula of joint burial after death. There are quite a few joint graves of adult men and women at the Dawenkou cultural site and they are also found at the Longshanoid Hengzhencun site in Huayin County, Shaanxi. In the joint graves of the Qijia culture at Qinweijia, the males are invariably on the right-hand side, stretched out, their faces upward, while the females are always on the left, reclining on their sides facing the males, legs flexed. This burial style seems to show that the males were in the dominant position and the females in a position of submission and dependence.

In the separate conjugal families, the diverse household chores had been transformed from the previous service to the commune to a kind of service to the individual—this marks them off completely from the matriarchal households. It has been discovered that in the graves of the Dawenkou culture at Dawenkou, Liulin and Dadunzi of Pixian in Jiangsu, all those whose heads are ornamented have spinning wheels, while those without ornaments have more production tools. In the graves of Majiayao culture discovered at Liuwan in Ledu County in Qinghai, the majority of the burial objects with the males are ground stone axes, adzes, knives and chisels, while the majority of those with the females are pottery or stone spinning wheels, and bone awls and needles. These things all give expression to the division of labour between males and females, the women being excluded from social production and hence losing their previous social status. What is more, pottery and stone sculptures symbolizing male ancestor worship have been found at the Longshanoid sites at Keshengzhuang in Xi'an and Quanhucun, Huaxian County in Shaanxi, and the Qijia culture site at Zhangjiazui, Linxia County in Gansu. This too is an important sign of the formation of the patriarchal clan.

The patriarchal clan commune represented a transitional social stage between primitive communal and slave society. Private ownership, polarization between rich and poor, class division, and the possession of slaves all made their appearance in the patriarchal clan commune period. As we have noted, the most important item of private property at the time was the livestock herd. It was the fashion for tribes in various places to use pig palate bones as a yardstick for measuring wealth. The private wealth which people accumulated while alive went into their graves as burial objects after their death. About one-third of 133 Dawenkou culture graves have pig skulls in them, the maximum number being fourteen. In a few graves belonging to the Dawenkou culture at Gangshangcun, Tengxian County, and Yaoguanzhuang, Weifang City in Shandong, there were also unequal numbers of pig palate bones. Fourteen such bones were found in a grave belonging to the Longshanoid culture at Qinglongquan, Yuanxian County in Hubei, thirty-six pieces were placed in a grave belonging to the Qijia culture at Dahezhuang and sixty-eight pieces were discovered in a grave at Qinweijia. Pig bones in varying numbers have also been found in graves in other places. This shows both that the pigs were owned personally by the grave occupant while alive and that the accumulation of personal property had already reached substantial proportions.

The beginning of private ownership was accompanied by polarization between rich and poor. Some wealthy people used grain to brew alcohol. A set of wine containers such as tripod pitchers, kettles and long-stemmed cups discovered in a Dawenkou grave testifies to this situation. There is a clearer reflection of this division between rich and poor and of the inequality in property in the Dawenkou burial grounds. The burials of the wealthy were very extravagant and the pits very big—more than four metres long and three metres wide. The pits were lined with wood, wooden floors were laid to form outer coffins, and some of the coffin bases were daubed with red pigment. The wealthy had fifty or sixty burial objects—the richest more than 160—including elegant painted, jet-black and pure white pottery, delicate production tools, and various kinds of ornaments made of polished stone and bone. Some graves also had ivory combs and containers with perforated patterns carved in them. In contrast to the lavish burials of the wealthy, of the 133 graves already excavated at Dawenkou, eighty employ only common production tools and household utensils as burial objects, and eight have no burial objects at all. In graves of the same age and style excavated at Liuwan, differences in size and great disparities in number of grave objects also appear. The differences in the number of grave objects and their presence or absence, are a record of the wealth possessed by the grave occupants during their lifetimes, a reflection of the division into poor and wealthy, and evidence that some people expropriated the fruits of others' labour and made them their own.

In the patriarchal clans, relations of bondage were taking root. At the Huangniangniangtai site, one joint adult grave was discovered, containing one male and two females. The male lay face upward in the middle with a female on either side; both females lay on their sides facing the male with limbs bent, the lower limbs behind them and their two hands in front of their faces. In graves belonging to the Qijia culture at Liuwan, some males lay in coffins, face upwards with their limbs straight, while young females lay on their sides outside the coffins, their limbs bent and facing towards the males. The women in these graves, whether their relations with the males were conjugal or not, were obviously in a subordinate position and seem to have been in the status of slaves.

Oracle bones have been discovered in many of the Longshan and Qijia culture sites. They are the result of a method of divination which used fire to scorch the upper surface of pig, oxen or sheep scapulae to produce cracking patterns which were then used to determine good or bad fortune. The development of this kind of activity later led to the emergence of sorcerers who specialized in divination, becoming daily more divorced from physical labour. Their activities probably were not limited to making entreaties to nature, but may also gradually have assumed the character of class oppression.

Chapter III
Myth and Legend

1. The Legends of Ancient Tribes

Tradition has it that in remote antiquity there were two famous tribes in the Huanghe River valley. One was Ji and had Huang Di (the Yellow Emperor) as its chief. The other, Jiang, was headed by Yan Di. Being closely related, they formed a tribal alliance. They lived at first in the Weihe (Wei River) area and later moved eastwards along the Huanghe River to areas belonging to today's Shanxi, Henan and Hebei provinces. In old Chinese books there are many legends and stories about Huang Di. He is described as a god, resourceful in inventions as well as war, and is credited with the invention of many things, such as carts and boats, clothes, houses, writing, and silkworm breeding and silk weaving.

Yao and Shun are two leaders who have been much praised in historical tradition and are supposed to be descendants of Huang Di. In Yao's time disastrous floods occurred and he called together some tribal chiefs to discuss what should be done. Some suggested that a man called Gun be sent to deal with the flooding and Yao followed their advice. Later Shun succeeded to Yao's position and also summoned some of the tribal chiefs to discuss how their tasks should be assigned to different people. Shun agreed with the recommendation and only functioned as the chairman of the meeting. Stories like this give us an idea of the primitive democracy at meetings of tribal alliances.

Tribes originally occupying East China were called Yi. They were first active in southern Shandong and later expanded north to northern Shandong and southern Hebei, west to easten Henan, south to central Anhui, and east to the sea coast. They were famous for their workmanship in bows and arrows and the written character Yi (夷) was originally a picture of a man (人) carrying a bow (弓). Taihao, Shaohao and Chiyou were renowned leaders among the Yi people. Chiyou once engaged in a long and fierce battle against Huang Di on the outskirts of Zhuolu, which according to tradition was in present Hebei. Chiyou was very resourceful and could summon wind and rain. But Huang Di outdid him by sending goddesses to disperse the wind and rain and finally Chiyou was defeated. After he died, Chiyou ascended to Heaven, and became a constellation known as "the Banner of Chiyou". Both Huang Di and Chiyou were worshipped later as gods of war.

Another chief of the Yi people, according to legend, was the celebrated archer Yi. In his days, there were ten suns in the sky, which burned all the crops, so that the people had nothing to eat. There were also many evil demons harming mankind. The archer Yi shot down nine suns, leaving only one in the sky, and killed all the demons. Because of his great exploits he became revered as a god.

Along the Changjiang River valley down south, in modern Hubei, Hunan and Jiangxi provinces the Miao and other tribes once lived. Among the leaders of these tribes, Fuxi and Nüwa were the best known. Fuxi was said to be the first man who used ropes to make nets for hunting and fishing. In the days of Nüwa, the four pillars supporting heaven collapsed and the earth cracked. So flames spread wildly, torrential waters flooded all the land, while fierce birds and beasts preyed on men. Nüwa smelted rocks to make five-coloured stones with which she patched up heaven. To replace the broken pillars she cut off the four legs of a huge turtle and used them to prop up the fallen sky. With water and land restored to order and the fierce animals killed, the people could once again live in peace and happiness. Nüwa in return was regarded as a goddess for her great achievements.

The tribes mentioned earlier, namely, the Huang Di, Yan Di and Yi tribes, can be regarded as three tribal groups. Though it is difficult to separate legend and reality, we know for certain that they once did exist and had an influence on later historical development.

2. Tribal Chiefs, Gods and Their Sons

According to myth and tradition, chiefs made important contributions to their tribes, especially in flood control, farming and animal husbandry. They were regarded as gods, the sons of gods or both.

There was once a tribe called Jintian living in areas belonging to modern Shanxi. Both its chief, Mei, and his son Taitai, were skilful in water control work. Taitai dredged the Fenshui (Fen River) and constructed the storage lake of Daze so the people in the Taiyuan area could live a stable life. And Taitai became the god of Fenshui, enjoying sacrifices offered by the four states established by his descendants. Xiu and Xi, chiefs of the Shaohao tribe in Shandong, were likewise known for being good at flood control. Their work was carried on by their sons and grandsons while they themselves became water gods. Gonggong in northern Henan was another tribe known for its success in water control work. The people of the tribe invented the method of building dikes to prevent floods. Due to overdependence on the dikes, however, they suffered severe losses when their dikes eventually failed them. Nevertheless their chief, Houtu, was respected as a god of the soil. Later, when helping Yu the Great with water control work, the Gonggong tribe adopted his method too with very good results. The above stories illustrate the fact that water conservation was of great importance in the lives of people in primitive societies. When the chiefs brought relief to the sufferings of the people, they were deified. However, their achievements were limited by a tribal nature, and it was only Yao's and Shu's contemporary, Yu the Great, who made contributions in water works construction that affected a larger number of tribal groups.

Yu was conceived by some mysterious force. According to one legend, Yu's mother was called Xiuji, and bore her son after swallowing the *Yiyi* plant (Job's-tears). According to another legend, Yu emerged into the world from the body of the above-mentioned Gun, who had been dead for three years, when his body, which had not decayed, was cut open. Both accounts agree in making the birth of Yu the Great a miracle.

Yu was entrusted by Shun with the task of conquering floods in cooperation with fraternal tribes. Having learned from previous failures, Yu studied the characteristics of flowing water, the direction of its flow and the topography, and adopted the method of dredging the waterways. Canals were dug to direct flood water into proper water courses. Furthermore, he led people in digging irrigation canals which were beneficial to farm production. Thanks to all these efforts, people could settle down peacefully on the plains without the constant threat of floods.

Yu was so devoted to his work that he did not visit his home for thirteen years, although he travelled nearby three times. He worked tirelessly, regardless of wind and rain, until his hands and feet were severely calloused. In order to open some water courses, he summoned a divine winged dragon. Once, while cutting through a mountain, he even turned himself into a bear so as to complete a task beyond man's ability. His celebrated contributions won him the respect of the people who honoured him as "Yu the Great" and god of the soil. Stories about Yu's exploits in water conservation spread far and wide beyond the boundaries of individual tribes.

Shennong was one of those tribes that were good at farming and it had a gifted man as its chief. Not only did he invent tools for turning over the soil and teach his men how to farm, but he also discovered many medicinal herbs by personal experimentation. Zhu, chief of the Lieshan tribe, became god of agriculture because of his miraculous talent in growing grain crops and vegetables.

Above all, Qi, chief of the Zhou tribe, was famous for his achievements in farming and was often compared to Yu the Great in fame. Qi was a son of god and a god himself. Once when walking in the wilderness, his mother, Jiang Yuan, stepped onto a huge footprint of a giant and her body was jolted. She had become pregnant and later bore a son. At first she dared not keep the child so she abandoned him in small lanes, in the woods, and on frozen waterways. But to her great surprise, the child always remained protected and did not die. So she took it back and named it "Qi", meaning "abandoned". The child proved to be very handy in farm work when he was still very small. The beans, millet, hemp, wheat, melons and fruit he cultivated all grew well, and the crops he helped others grow were so heavy they bent. He was also good at discovering better varieties of plants and ways of processing grain. The food he made was so good it even pleased the Lord on High. Later he became god of agriculture under the name of Houji, Lord of Agriculture.

Houji lived at the same time as Yu the Great and helped in the water control work together with Xie, Gaoyao, Boyi and Dafei. Gaoyao and Boyi were both from the Yi people in the east. Boyi invented the sinking of wells. Xie's mother, Jiandi, was once standing on a high platform when she saw a swallow fly by. She swallowed an egg it had laid and later gave birth to Xie. Dafei, about whose birth a similar story is told, was an expert in animal husbandry and the animals under his care were very obedient. Shun married a woman from his clan to Dafei and said to him that his descendants would surely be promising. As it happened, descendants of Yu, Xie and Houji founded the Xia, Shang and Zhou dynasties respectively, while Dafei became the ancestor of the founder of the Qin Dynasty.

That the tribal chiefs were said to be sons of gods actually reflects the fact that in a society of matriarchal clans people knew only who their mothers were but not their fathers. Another reason for men becoming gods was that they had distinguished themselves by performing the most important social function in a primitive society with a low productivity, namely, the organization of work in water conservation, farming and animal husbandry. Despite repeated changes made according to each story-teller's imagination, these myths to some extent reflect the historical reality of primitive society.

As historical conditions changed, so did the role played by the tribal chief. He became less a public servant than a kind of power above society. History entered a new stage as classless primitive society changed into civilized society with its class distinctions.

3. The Hereditary Monarchy of the Xia Dynasty

The Xia Dynasty is traditionally supposed to have begun with the reign of Yu the Great and ended with the fall of Jie, lasting for more than 400 years, from approximately the 21st century B.C. or a little earlier to the 16th century B.C. There were altogether seventeen kings in fourteen generations. According to an ancient version of history, however, it was not Yu, but his son Qi, who founded the dynasty.

The Xia people lived on loess plains formed by alluvial deposits suitable for primitive farming. Their territory extended from western Henan and southern Shanxi eastwards along the Yellow River to the point where the borders of modern Henan, Hebei, and Shandong provinces meet and extended south to Hunan and north to Hebei next to the territory of other tribes living there. Since flooding had already been brought under control and people could settle down, we may suppose that animal husbandry and agriculture underwent further development.

Development of animal husbandry and agriculture required more knowledge of astronomy and a better calendar to mark seasonal changes. After carefully observing the movements of the sun, the moon and the stars, Yao is said to have worked out a calendar dividing a year into spring, summer, autumn and winter to coincide with the seasons of stockbreeding and farming. What was used in Yao's time was a lunar calendar with the months determined by the phases of the moon. Since a year of twelve lunar months is shorter than the solar year, an intercalary month was inserted in certain years. At the time of Yao and Shun the solar year was thought to have 366 days which, of course, was not quite correct. It is not known whether the calendar of the Xia Dynasty represented an improvement upon that of Yao but the so-called Xia calendar was much praised by people of later generations.

Bronze vessels came into use at the time of the Xia. There was little opportunity to use bronze directly in farming but it could have been useful in the making of farm tools. Some tribes are said to have presented bronze to the Xia as tribute, Yu is supposed to have cast bronze tripods, and the Xia used bronze to make weapons.

The Xia was an alliance formed by over a dozen closely related tribes of which the Xiahou tribe was the leading one. Included in the alliance were also some more distantly related tribes and some of the Yi tribes in the east. According to historical tradition, the leadership of the alliance originally alternated between the Yi and the Xia. Due to Yu's great achievements in water control and his victories over the Sanmiao tribes, his personal prestige increased so much that the chief of the clan wielded ever greater authority over the other clan members. As Yu was getting old, the renowned chief Gaoyao of the Eastern Yi was elected to succeed him. But Gaoyao unexpectedly died before Yu, so Boyi of the Eastern Yi tribes was chosen to replace him. After Yu's death, the Xia tribes, relying on their great strength and Yu's prestige, promoted Yu's son Qi to the position of king. They asked Qi to grant them audiences and mediate in disputes, and praised him to the sky. As a result the principle of electing leaders was violated and a new hereditary system came into being. In ancient times this was considered to be the beginning of a system whereby the ruler "takes all under Heaven as his family possession". The founding of the Xia Dynasty is regarded as a major turning point in history.

One tribe named Youhu criticized Qi for having violated the old system. But Youhu was defeated by Xia in a battle at Gan in modern Huxian in Shaanxi. The defeated survivors were made into "mushu", which may be a term for prisoners of war who became slaves collectively owned by the victorious tribe.

After attaining kingship, Qi turned out to be fond of drinking, hunting, singing and dancing. Qi's successor, Taikang, cared nothing for state affairs but rather spent months on end hunting on the northern bank of the Luo River. This behaviour aroused strong resentment among the people. Houyi, known as a good archer from the Youqiong clan of the Eastern Yi, took the opportunity to attack Xia and made himself king. But the throne was again seized by Houyi's trusted follower Hanzhuo who bribed Houyi's family servants to kill him.

Taikang, the overthrown ruler, had fled and died in exile, leaving as his heir his younger brother Zhongkang. Zhongkang's son Xiang was attacked and killed by Hanzhuo while taking refuge with the Zhenguan and Zhenxun clans. But Xiang's wife, already pregnant, climbed through a hole in the wall and escaped to her mother's family of the Youreng tribe where she later bore her son Shaokang. When the son grew up, he was put in charge of stockbreeding in the clan, but being pursued again by Hanzhuo, he escaped to the Youyu clan which was descended from Shun. There he was made responsible for food preparation and the tribal chief Yusi married two daughters to him. Shaokang gathered together some other closely related tribes, defeated

Hanzhuo, and restored the Xia Dynasty.

In order to counter the good marksmanship of the Yi people, Shaokang's son Shu invented coats of mail which played an important role in the defeat of Hanzhuo. After he came to the throne, Shu went on a punitive expedition against the Eastern Yi and drove them back to the sea coast. Because of his great exploits, Shu was regarded by the Xia people as the only worthy heir of Yu, and they made magnificent sacrifices to him after his death. The Yi tribes were one by one brought under Xia's control, and Yi chiefs even accepted noble titles and became officials of the Xia court offering tribute. After many long years of struggle, Xia's ruling position was eventually recognized by the other tribes, and the new hereditary monarchy had in effect replaced the traditional system of election.

The establishment of hereditary monarchy eliminated the function of the tribe as an organization representing the will of its members and taking care of its own affairs. What was emerging instead was a state apparatus in which one class ruled over another. The Xia Dynasty by then had not only erected city walls with moats, but also established its own army, penal code and prisons. The tribes conquered by Xia or forced to recognize its position were made to pay tribute which usually consisted of local products. But some defeated tribes were forced to offer their sons and daughters as tribute.

Towards the end of the Xia Dynasty, social conflict grew sharper. Tradition has it that in the 16th century B.C., the last ruler of Xia, Jie, abused his power and increased oppression. He exhausted the resources of the people to build palaces and pavilions for himself. The people were also forced to go to war frequently to exact children, as well as jade and silk, from neighbouring tribes. Filled with hatred for Jie, the people could no longer put up with his despotic rule and fled in large numbers. Even his court officials cursed him and wished his death, although that might mean that they themselves would perish. Jie, however, still thinking of restoring and strengthening his control over other tribes, gathered all the tribal chiefs together for a punitive expedition against the Youmin clan. But this made the existing conflicts more acute and alienated the tribes further. Shang Tang took this opportunity to revolt and overthrew the Xia Dynasty.

Chapter IV
The Slave State of the Shang and Zhou Dynasties

1. The Earliest Written History

The Shang and Zhou dynasties were the earliest to have a written history. The Shang (c. 16th-11th century B.C.) lasted over 600 years, with 31 kings belonging to 17 generations. The early Zhou Dynasty is known as Western Zhou because the capital was located in the west. This period (c. mid-11th century to 771 B.C.) lasted more than 290 years, with 12 kings belonging to 11 generations.

It was during these 900 years that historical records became consciously and systematically written instead of being spontaneous and fragmentary. This was made possible by the emergence of two essential conditions, a written script and a calendar, during the Shang Dynasty.

The Shang nobles were superstitious and believed that everything in the world was controlled by gods. They often sought the divine will through oracles and used a method of divination by which a spot on a tortoise shell or an animal bone was heated until it cracked and the oracle was then interpreted on the basis of the pattern of the cracks. This method has been called scapulimancy, since the scapulae or shoulder blades of cattle were often used. In many cases the question and the answer and sometimes the subsequent events were written on the bone or shell and these records are known as oracle-bone inscriptions.

Oracle-bone inscriptions were first discovered in Xiaotun Village, in the northwest of Anyang County in Henan. People began to collect and identify them in 1899, and there have since been more discoveries. According to preliminary research, these inscriptions contain about 4,500 characters, of which some, 1,700 have been deciphered. The written characters were already formed in four different ways; there were pictographs, ideographs, associative compounds and phonetic compounds. A method of "borrowing" was used, that is, a synonym or homonym was adopted to express a different thing. For example, the character *lai* 来, which gave the image of wheat, was borrowed for a homophonous word meaning "to come"; *feng* 凤, meaning phoenix, was borrowed to write the word *feng* meaning wind (now written 风). Compared with later Han characters, the oracle-bone script was more detailed in making distinctions between animals of different species and sexes. For instance, the character *yu* 驭, meaning "to drive a chariot", would take the radical *ma* 马 (horse) or *xiang* 象 (elephant), depending on which animal was used. Again, the character *mu* 牧 (herding) would take the radical 牛 *niu* (cattle) or 羊 *yang* (sheep), depending on whether the herd was cattle or sheep. The characters 马 *ma* (horse), 羊 *yang* (sheep), 豕 *shi* (pig), 犬 *quan* (dog) and 鹿 *lu* (deer) might have additional marks to indicate whether the animal was male or female. The characters 牝 *pin* and 牡 *mu*, which at first meant male and female cattle, were later applied to the males and females of all animals. Some of the oracle-bone characters did not have a fixed form, such as that for the character 龟 *gui* (tortoise). The character sometimes depicted the figure of a turtle from the front and sometimes from the side, with or without a tail. In general, however, the oracle-bone script is the foundation of later Han characters. Judging from the forms of the oracle-bone characters and the grammar of the inscriptions, they must have gone through a rather long period of development, but the origin of this script remains to be ascertained.

The number of characters on any given piece of oracle bone could range from a handful to over a hundred. The actual content of the oracles was related to various activities of the ruling house, indicating the circumstances at the time. As divinations of good or evil, the oracle-bone inscriptions are the earliest historical records known to us and are invaluable in a study of the Shang Dynasty.

From these inscriptions we know that the Shang used a lunar calendar which was combined with the solar year through the addition of an intercalary month, once every few years, to make up the difference between a year of twelve lunar months and a solar year. The number of days in a month was fixed at 30 for a long month and 29 for a short one. The intercalary month was at first added at the end of the year as a 13th month, but later inserted in the middle of the year. Years and months were recorded by numerals in oracle-bone inscriptions. Ten characters known as "heavenly stems" and twelve others known as "earthly branches" were used to name the days in a cycle of sixty days. The stems are *jia* 甲, *yi* 乙, *bing* 丙, *ding* 丁, *wu* 戊, *ji* 己, *geng* 庚, *xin* 辛, *ren* 壬, *gui* 癸, and the branches are *zi* 子, *chou* 丑, *yin* 寅, *mao* 卯, *chen* 辰, *si* 巳, *wu* 午, *wei* 未, *shen* 申, *you* 酉, *xu* 戌, *hai* 亥. Calendar-making has since gone through many changes and the calculations have become increasingly exact, but the lunar calendar bound to the solar year, and the 60-day cycles continued in use for over 3,000 years.

The use of a calendar was of great significance to the development of historical records. Most of the oracle-bone inscriptions only recorded the day and not the year or month. Some recorded all three, but with the day preceding the recorded event, followed by the month and then the year. A record of the year alone, however, did not indicate which king's reign it referred to. Such information has to be sought by other means. In other words, while records of some form did exist, they were incomplete. Only through a study of both written sources and archaeological finds are we able to obtain more comprehensive information on the Shang Dynasty.

The engravings on Shang bronzes are an important form of documentation. A vessel may have one or a few characters, while some late Shang bronzes are inscribed with as many as 45 characters. These inscriptions are generally called *jin wen* (writings on bronzes) or *zhong ding wen* (writings on bells and tripods). Up till now, not very many of such inscriptions have been found, but they are a primary source of historical material for the Shang period.

Oracle-bone inscriptions of the Zhou Dynasty have been discovered in recent years. The characters are so small that they can only be read with a magnifier. The content of these inscriptions are still under study, but there is a clear increase in writing on bronze vessels from the Zhou period, not only in the number of pieces but in the length of the inscriptions. For example, *ling yi*, an inscription dating from the early Zhou, has 187 characters; *Mao gong ding* of the late Zhou has 499 characters. A large number of the bronze inscriptions from the Zhou Dynasty had 100-300 characters each, and show a wider vocabulary than the oracle-bone inscriptions.

Most of the Zhou Dynasty bronze inscriptions are written in praise of great achievements or to celebrate grants and rewards. Detailed descriptions are often given on military expeditions, the capture of war prisoners, and grants of servants and slaves, land, chariots, horses, banners, dresses, ceremonial vessels, and gold and shell articles. Some famous inscriptions contain data about the scale of warfare and number of servants bestowed; others record the circumstances concerning grants of land and enfeoffment.

The Zhou inscriptions frequently end with the words: "For eternal preservation by our descendants." This is clearly an expression of hope for the handing down of the inscribed bronzes from generation to generation, and of the fact that the inscriptions were written in a way to suit such a purpose. In other words, they were deliberately written as historical records and, in this sense, represent an advance over the oracle-bone texts. Some of the bronzes do not record the time, but there are more bronzes than oracle bones which give years and dates. Unlike the oracle bones, the bronzes indicate the time by using the month-day-year or year-month-day sequence, the latter subsequently becoming the common practice in Chinese historical records.

There were also some Shang and Zhou historical records written on bamboo slips or silk. The main part of what has been preserved is contained in the *Book of History* (*Shang Shu*) and the *Book of Odes* (*Shijing*). The *Book of History* is a collection of political documents from the Shang, the Western Zhou and the Spring and Autumn periods. The *Book of Odes* dates from the Western Zhou and the Spring and Autumn periods. These two works had a far-reaching influence on the philosophy, political ideas and literature of later times. From the point of view of historical value, the *Book of History* has about twenty papers on Shang and Zhou history that are comparatively reliable and more or less contemporaneous with the historical events they covered. These include accounts of historical figures, speeches and events. The way in which the material is presented shows a further step forward in making conscious historical records as compared to the bronze inscriptions. The *Book of Odes* contains 74 "Lesser Odes", 31 "Greater Odes" and 31 "Sacrificial Odes of Zhou". Most of these odes deal with events, and some with offerings to gods, and they were written mainly during the Zhou Dynasty. The book also includes 160 "Lessons from the States", 4 "Praise-odes of Lu" and 5 "Sacrificial Odes of Shang", most of which were works of later times. The odes throw light on the historical conditions and are highly valuable for an understanding of history.

It can be seen that the various sources for Shang and early Zhou history, whether the oracle-bone inscriptions, bronze inscriptions or the *Book of History* and *Book of Odes*, all developed independently of each other and do not give a complete year by year record of these periods. The situation started to change towards the end of the Western Zhou. From 841 B.C., the Zhou royal house began to keep annals, and some vassal states did the same about this time. Henceforth China had historical records for each year. Thus the year 841 B.C. marked the beginning of conscious, systematic records.

Although historical records of the Shang and Western Zhou are still rather inadequate to help us understand the history of this period, they nevertheless free us from dependence on legends.

2. The Slave-owning Shang Dynasty

According to legend the Shang Dynasty traced its origin to an ancient tribe on the lower reaches of the Huanghe River. As stated in the previous chapter, the founder of the Shang Dynasty, Xie, had assisted Yu in harnessing rivers. The legendary accounts tell us that Xie was also an official in charge of education during the reign of Shun. This may be attributable to the fact that the Shang tribe had a relatively high cultural level.

The Shang moved its centre of activities five times under the three kings from Xie to Xiang Tu, and three times after Xiang Tu, during the eleven generations from Chang Ruo to Tang. These moves occurred mainly along the Huanghe River in present-day Shandong and Henan provinces.

Shang rule became powerful under Xiang Tu, its influence extending eastward to Mount Tai and north to the coast of Bohai Sea. It grew still stronger under Tang, who was also called Tai Yi.

State organization already existed under Tang. He had two men, Yi Yin and Zhong Hui, as his ministers, both known as capable officials. At that time Jie, the ruler of the Xia Dynasty, was opposed by the people. From Bo, a place south of present-day Caoxian in Shandong, Tang launched attacks against Xia rule. He first conquered a dozen nearby tribes and small states and then started an expedition against the Xia king, Jie. He issued a proclamation denouncing Jie for his misrule and the harm he had done to the people's productive pursuits. He said that the house of Xia had committed such crimes that the Lord on High had commanded him to destroy it, and since he feared the Lord on High, he dared not disobey. Tang also told people that they would be richly rewarded if they followed him and succeeded in their god-given task. If they did not follow him, he would enslave them or kill them and they should not expect to be able to save themselves. Tang's words show that the soldiers were free men and not slaves but that Tang himself behaved in the manner of a slave-owner. Jie was defeated in a battle fought at Mingtiao (present-day Fengqiu in Henan) and fled to Nanchao (present-day Chaoxian in Anhui), where he died. The Xia Dynasty was overthrown, and the Shang Dynasty established, with present-day Shangqiu city in Henan Province as the centre of its activities.

The state power of the Shang Dynasty was exercised by the king and the slave-owning nobility. The king was assisted by ministers and vice-ministers. Other officials with religious functions were the shamans, the recorders and the diviners. Actually the ministers were also religious officials. Others took charge of military affairs, production, etc. The numerous official posts were mostly hereditary for members of noble families.

The dynasty had a large and powerful army. Oracle-bone inscriptions state that "the king has set up three army units, right, centre and left." The core of the army consisted of members of the nobility, while the soldiers were mainly commoners. A number of slaves were pressed into service as foot-soldiers or for the performance of miscellaneous duties. Sometimes a clan constituted a unit of the army. The oracles record orders for "three clans", "five clans" or "a clan with many sons" to go to battle. The army was armed with bronze weapons, the commonly used ones being axes, battle-axes, lances, spears, swords, javelins, and bronze battle-axes with iron edges. It was also equipped with bronze helmets and leather shields. In the late Shang, chariots became the principal combat force. Each chariot was drawn by two horses and carried three soldiers clad in armour—one driving, one holding a lance or spear, and the third carrying a bow and arrows; alongside the chariots marched foot-soldiers. The number of soldiers in war usually varied from three to five thousand, and could reach thirty thousand.

Prisons were set up and punishments were instituted for more than ten different crimes.

The Shang kings claimed that their first ancestor was the son of the Lord on High on whose command the dynasty had been founded. Thus a central element in Shang religion was the identification of the earliest royal ancestor with the supreme god. The Shang kings were born to become masters of the people and became gods after death. While they lived they ruled over the living, and after they died they ruled over the dead. In remote antiquity, the tribal heads who had worked for the good of the people and made contributions to their common cause were venerated as gods. The Shang still regarded their chiefs as gods, but these were gods who stood above the people and ruled them as kings and so were no longer the servants of the people.

The Shang possessed a complete set of instruments of violence and weapons of spiritual control as well as a well-developed written language. It was already a slave-owning state of considerable scale but retained a great many customs of primitive society. Special sacrifices were offered to a person's deceased mother and the heavenly stems were used for the titles of deceased grandmothers. This shows the great respect the Shang people paid to matriarchal authority.

After the death of Tang, as his eldest son Tai Ding had died young, he was succeeded by Tai Ding's younger brother Wai Bing who was in turn succeeded by another brother, Zhong Ren. A few years later, Tai Ding's son Tai Jia became the fourth king of Shang. He refused to take the advice of Yi Yin, the prime minister, who then dethroned him, but restored him when he changed for the better a few years later. Another story says that Tai Jia was at first put under house arrest by Yi Yin. He escaped, killed Yi Yin and seized the throne. This restoration marked the beginning of a period of stability under six kings from Tai Jia to Tai Wu.

After Zhong Ding succeeded Tai Wu, struggles for the throne occurred many times, and the internal contentions among the nobility intensified. Misery spread wide among the people, and the dynasty declined. Small states that had submitted to the Shang now renounced their allegiance. Conditions improved somewhat under the rule of King Zu Yi, the fourth successor of Zhong Ding. Oracle-bone inscriptions show that sacrifices were offered to three kings together—Tai Yi, Tai Jia and Zu Yi, the last posthumously given the title of Zhong Zong. To honour them, 300 head of cattle and sheep were used in the sacrifices. However, struggles for the throne continued throughout the period from Zhong Ding to Yang Jia.

During the reign of King Pan Geng, the Shang removed its capital to Yin (modern Anyang in Henan), laying a new foundation for Shang rule which from then on was also called the Yin Dynasty (or Yin-Shang). One of the next kings, Wu Ding, is supposed to have spent his early years among the common people and was therefore familiar with their difficulties in making a living. After becoming king he appointed Gan Pan and Fu Yue as ministers and made great efforts to consolidate his rule.

Wu Ding also launched many military expeditions against the surrounding tribes and states. These campaigns centred on present Shanxi, northern Shaanxi and Inner Mongolia. The Tu Fang tribe and another nomadic tribe north of the Hetao (the Yellow River Bend) had joined forces to attack the Shang. For each campaign Wu Ding conscripted three to five thousand men. The more powerful nomadic tribe Gui Fang, which lived in present Shaanxi, Inner Mongolia and further north, resisted the forces of Wu Ding for three years before they were conquered. In the northwest there was also the Qiang Fang tribe against which Wu Ding once employed 13,000 men. In the south he also attacked the Jing Chu people and extended his influence to the Changjiang basin. His reign lasted 59 years and he received the posthumous title of Gao Zong.

Wu Ding was succeeded by Zu Geng and then by Zu Jia. The rulers after Zu Jia were mostly pleasure-seeking and paid little attention to state affairs while social contradictions deepened. The last two kings were Di Yi and Di Xin. Di Yi launched many expeditions against the Yi (Eastern Yi) tribes between the Changjiang and Huai rivers and was victorious. He moved the capital to Zhaoge, present-day Qixian in Henan. Di Xin or Zhou is known in history as an infamous tyrant. He devised many cruel laws and means of torture, oppressing and exploiting the slaves and common people. Building luxurious palaces and gardens, he led a life of debauchery with companions from the nobility. By tradition, the old nobles held power in Shang. But by the end of the dynasty, particularly under King Zhou, the centralized autocracy had the effect of setting aside the "elders" and only favouring those congenial to the king. This aggravated the contradictions among the nobility and caused internal dissension. Zhou also spent nearly a year personally leading a war against the Yi. Although he won a victory after one year's bitter fighting, he exhausted much of the resources of his realm and increased the burdens of the people. The intensification of class contradictions brought about great confusion. Taking advantage of the opportunity, King Wu of the Zhou Dynasty launched an attack and overthrow the Shang Dynasty.

3. The Social Economy of the Shang Dynasty

Animal husbandry had a long history already in Shang times. In the late Shang period, the number of cattle and sheep used in a single sacrifice might be 300-400, sometimes up to a thousand. The oracle-bone inscriptions many times mention hunting, e.g., in one hunting trip 384 deer were captured, and hunting was common for quite a long period. The inscriptions also record the kind and sexes of the animals, showing the developed state of animal husbandry.

Agriculture was the principal part of production with many kinds of crops. In the ruins of the Shang capital at Zhengzhou in Henan, remains of rice have been found. In the oracle-bone inscriptions we find the names of the main cereals and some other plants, e.g., *he* 禾, meaning growing grain; *shu* 黍, sticky millet; *su* 粟, rice or millet in husk; *mai* 麦, wheat; *ji* 稷, millet; *mi* 米, rice; *sang* 桑, mulberry; and *ma* 麻, hemp. In the ruins of Yin at Anyang cellars have been discovered for storing grain. Some of the walls and floors of these cellars had been plastered with a mixture of mud and straw. The character *ling* 廪 in the oracle-bone inscriptions, which means granary, applied to such cellars.

Different kinds of wine were brewed—sweet wine was made of rice and fragrant wine was made of black millet. The many wine vessels found in the Yin ruins show that drinking wine was common among the nobility. Wine making and drinking were a result of the advances in agriculture.

Iron had been discovered and was already in use. Iron-blade bronze battle-axes of the Shang have been unearthed recently but not iron farm implements. Tools were mainly made of wood or stone, such as wooden spades to dig earth, stone hoes for weeding grass and stone sickles for harvesting. Hundreds of sickles have been found near the royal palace among the Yin ruins, mostly showing signs of having been used. The handicraft tools included the axe, adze, knife, saw, chisel, drill, awl, needle, shovel, etc.—all made of bronze.

Bronze metallurgy was the most highly developed among the handicrafts. Remains of bronze foundries under the direct control of the royal house have been discovered at Zhengzhou, Anyang and other places. The raw material consisted of malachite (copper oxide ore), tin and lead, and charcoal was used for fuel. Pottery moulds were first made, into which molten bronze was poured. The mould was removed after the liquid had cooled off and solidified. The bronze was then decorated by carving to make it more attractive. The famous large rectangular cauldron *si mu wu ding* can be taken as a representative of the advanced bronze metallurgy of the late Shang. The height is 133 cm to the top of the handles, the opening 110 × 78 cm, and the weight 875 kgs. The furnace used for smelting bronze was made of red pottery with a thick inside wall and could stand high temperature without breaking. Usually it could only take 12.5 kgs of molten bronze. To make the above-mentioned large cauldron, 70-80 furnaces were required. A couple of hundred skilled craftsmen performing different tasks were needed, not including those making the mould and handling transport. Chemical analysis has shown the tripod to contain 84.77 per cent of copper, 11.64 per cent of tin and 2.79 per cent of lead. Separate moulds were made for the ears, the body and the legs, each requiring from two to eight pieces.

Besides the common gray, black and red pottery, there were white and hard pottery and primitive porcelain made of porcelain clay fired in a kiln. These were heated to a high temperature, so that they became hard and did not easily absorb water. The white pottery has a clear pure colour with fine texture and beautiful decorations. The surface has a thin, blue or yellowish green glaze, the body is greyish white, the structure is solid, and the vessels emit a metallic sound when struck. Experimental analysis has shown that the temperature of firing was about 1,200 ± 30°C. The vessels were still quite rough, but may be said to be primitive porcelain.

The Shang people already had linen and silk textiles. On the bronzes, traces of silk fabrics have been found—rough silk with plain design and damask with lozenge design.

Cowrie shells and a small number of copper shells have been unearthed from Shang ruins. The oracle-bone inscriptions record the acquisition and bestowal of shells. The shell was at first used as an ornament. It began to be used as money with the growth of exchange. Documents of the early period of the Zhou Dynasty mention traders driving ox-carts carrying goods to distant places. At Zhengzhou and Anyang, hard pottery with impressed design, sea shells, clam shells, whale and tortoise scapulae (used for divination) have been found to have come from far away.

The development of production was closely connected with the advance of scientific knowledge. Astronomy was needed to determine the seasons for farming and animal husbandry. And mathematics and mechanics helped water conservency planning and design and construction in the cities. The oracle-bone inscriptions have records of solar and lunar eclipses and of some constellations and newly discovered stars. The Shang calendar shows the important results of astronomy and mathematics of that time. Numerals from one to ten thousand with a decimal system were used.

Tradition says that Xie, the founder of the Shang royal lineage, worked together with Yu in harnessing the rivers and that Ming, Tang's ancestor eight generations before, was drowned while doing the same work. In its early period the Shang people had inhabited the lower reaches of the Huanghe River and had much to do with water control. There must have been many records concerning this, but now they are no longer available.

The Shang capital cities were built according to a plan that determined the arrangement of palaces, temples and various workshops. The characteristic of Chinese architecture based on wooden structures had already taken shape. The foundations of the palaces and temples of Yin ruins were generally of pounded earth, one of them as large as 46.7 by 10.7 metres. The remains of the stone or bronze bases of the rows of columns allow us to see the complicated structure of the palaces with heavy gates and compound rooms. These building foundations, with a north-south or east-west direction, formed groups of mutually compatible structures. Their style and technique exercised a far-reaching influence on the architecture of later ages, and the knowledge of applied mechanics was already fairly advanced.

In the relations of production, the Shang Dynasty had entered slave society. The slaves were engaged in farming, domestication of animals and primitive handicrafts, or did household work for slave-owners. The oracle-bone inscriptions record using war prisoners for farming and animal husbandry. There is not much historical material on the actual conditions under the slave system. In the oracle-bone inscriptions the character 众 *zhong*, (meaning many people), resembles a picture of three men under the sun and has commonly been interpreted as slaves labouring in the fields. In a large tomb at Wuguan Village at Anyang, which had been twice plundered, 79 skeletons were found, buried with the man the tomb was made for. The other

Genealogical Table of the Shang Dynasty

I. Up to Tang

Xie — Zhao Ming — Xiang Tu — Chang Ruo — Cao Yu — Ming — Wang Hai
Wang Heng

Shang Jia Wei — Bao Yi — Bao Bing — Bao Ding — Shi Ren — Shi Gui — Tang (Tai Yi)

II. The Shang Dynasty

(8) Xiao Jia
|
(6) Wo Ding (9) Yong Ji
| |
(1) Tang — (2) Tai Ding — (5) Tai Jia — (7) Tai Geng — (10) Tai Wu — (11) Zhong Ding
| |
(3) Wai Bing (12) Wai Ren
| |
(4) Zhong Ren (13) He Dan Jia

(19) Yang Jia
|
(20) Pan Geng
|
(21) Xiao Xin
|
(14) Zu Yi (Zhong Zong) — (15) Zu Xin — (17) Zu Ding — (22) Xiao Yi — (23) Wu Ding (Gao Zong)
| |
(16) Wo Jia (18) Nan Geng

(24) Zu Geng (26) Ling Xin
| |
(25) Zu Jia — (27) Kang Ding — (28) Wu Yi — (29) Wen Ding — (30) Di Yi — (31) Di Xin (Zhou)

tombs of the Yin ruins also contain the remains of people buried alive with the dead or killed as sacrifices. It is generally explained that these people were slaves. That is more or less guesswork and does not clarify the position of slaves in social production. Not until the Zhou Dynasty did more factual data on the slave system appear.

4. The Rise of the Zhou and the Establishment of the Slave-owning Zhou Dynasty

The people of Zhou were an ancient tribe on the loess plateau in the middle reaches of the Weishui (the Wei River). The ruling clan's family name was Ji. Their earliest ancestor, Qi, was worshipped as the god of agriculture.

Qi lived in Tai, which is said to be present Wugong County in Shaanxi. His great-grandson Gongliu started a settlement in Bin, the area around Binxian and Xunyi counties in Shaanxi. He studied the topography, found the water sources and organized production, developing agriculture and the domestication of animals. Ten generations from Gongliu to Gugong Tanfu lived in Bin. Threatened by the Rong and Di* tribes from the northwest, Gugong Tanfu led his people to Zhouyuan (the Zhou plain) at the foot of Mount Qi (now Qishan County in Shaanxi). People in his time gave up cave-dwelling and built houses and city walls and began to live in cities called *yi*, which were administered by officials. Making use of the rich soil of Zhouyuan, the people developed farm production and laid the foundation for the rise of the Zhou. About this time Zhou began to have contacts with the Shang.

Gugong Tanfu was later honoured as Great King. He was succeeded by Ji Li, or King Ji, during whose reign the Zhou state grew strong. In the wars against the Rong Di tribes the captured prisoners

---

* "Rong" or "Xi Rong" was the ancient name applied to ethnic groups in Northwest China, while "Di" or "Bei Di" was the name used for ethnic groups in North China. The groups in both Northwest and North China were also generally referred to under the name of "Rong Di".

were made slaves. The relations between the Zhou and the Shang became closer; Ji Li married the Shang woman Tai Ren and was received in court by the Shang king who granted him some land and gave him horses, jade and other valuables. He was also appointed an official in charge of livestock. However, later he was killed by King Wen Ding of the Shang.

Ji Li was succeeded by his son Chang, who later became the celebrated King Wen of the Zhou. Seeing that the Shang king, Zhou, had earned the hatred of the nobility by his efforts to win over and recruit the slaves of certain tribes and states, Chang proposed an agreement among the slave-owners. It authorized searches for escaped slaves, who should be returned to their respective owners and must not be hidden by anyone. This agreement won the support of the nobility and raised King Wen's prestige among the tribes and states.

He carried out a series of campaigns against hostile tribes and states and subdued them. Then he attacked Chong (now Huxian in Shaanxi), a powerful state on the Zhou's eastern border. Chong was friendly to the Shang and was treated as an enemy by the Zhou. With the help of his allies King Wen subdued Chong, capturing many of its people. He then moved his capital to Fengyi (on the west bank of the Feng River in Shaanxi), ready for eastward expansion. The many rivers and rich soil in this area favoured agriculture. In King Wen's last years, his power extended to the southwestern part of present Shanxi and the western part of present Henan, posing a threat to Zhaoge, the Shang capital.

Ji Fa, King Wen's son, succeeded as King Wu. He moved the capital to Hao (southwest of present-day Xi'an in Shaanxi). In the ninth year of his reign when the contradictions in Shang society sharpened, he attacked Shang which had been exhausted in its wars against the Eastern Yi tribes. When his forces reached Mengjin (now Mengxian, Henan), 800 enfeoffed lords spontaneously joined him, but he did not continue his drive until two years later. Then he advanced eastward with 300 war chariots, a shock brigade of 3,000 men and 45,000 armoured soldiers. The forces of the tribes of the southwest also joined in when he started the campaign against King Zhou of the Shang. At Muye to the southwest of the Shang capital of Zhaoge, he and his men took an oath denouncing King Zhou for failing to offer sacrifices to ancestors and distrusting his kinsmen and for shielding people who had committed crimes and slaves who had escaped from their masters. The Zhou and Shang armies fought a battle at Muye. As the Shang soldiers turned against their ruler, King Wu quickly captured Zhaoge, where the Shang king burnt himself of death.

Having vanquished the Shang, King Wu established the Zhou Dynasty. Among his chief ministers were Dan, the Duke of Zhou; Shi, the Duke of Zhao; and the Venerable Duke Jiang (Lü Shang, also known as Taigong Wang or Jiang Taigong). He enfeoffed Wu Geng, the son of King Zhou of the Shang, at Yin and appointed his own brothers Guan Shu, Cai Shu and Huo Shu to watch over Wu Geng. King Wu died two years later and was succeeded by his young son Song as King Cheng with his uncle, the Duke of Zhou, as regent. Guan Shu and Cai Shu and other nobles were dissatisfied and Wu Geng took this opportunity to rebel against Zhou rule in collaboration with these nobles and some tribes and small states in the east. The Duke of Zhou led his forces in an eastern expedition, crushed the rebellion in three years, and extended the influence of the Zhou Dynasty to the lower reaches of the Huanghe and Huaihe rivers.

The Zhou capital city, Hao, was far removed from the east where the Duke of Zhou was carrying on his military campaign. Luoyi, now Luoyang city in Henan, was then chosen as the eastern capital and as a strategic centre from which the east could be controlled politically and militarily. Here many people who remained loyal to the Shang were forced to move and troops were stationed to watch them. The new dynasty was stabilized only after the eastern expedition of the Duke of Zhou and the building of the eastern capital.

The Zhou regime was a dictatorship by the slave-owning nobility. It was based on a coalition of the royal clan and other noble clans, with or without the same surname as the royal family, under the supreme authority of the king. In each of the fiefs, power was based on a similar coalition of the ruling family and other noble clans, with or without the same surname, under the supreme authority of the fiefholder.

Under Zhou rule there were many fiefdoms, some ruled by clans with the same surname as the royal house and some ruled by clans with other surnames. Of the latter there were those who were related by marriage to the Zhou rulers, leading clans surviving from the Shang period, and also fiefdoms transformed from old tribes. Some had been set up before and were then recognized by the Zhou ruling house; others were established after the reclamation of land and construction of city walls and ancestral temples. The Zhou enfeoffment policy had a positive significance in the development of production. The principal fiefdoms were Jin, Wei and Yan to the north of the Huanghe River, and Xu, Cai, Chen, Song, Cao, Lu and Qi to the south of the river. The state of Wu in the far southeast gradually became important, and so did Qin and Zheng which were established later.

This enfeoffment policy benefited vassals who were related to the royal house in one way or another. It also preserved the power of the noble class which, though unrelated to the new dynasty, did not challenge its authority. In this way the Zhou Dynasty won the general support of the nobility.

At the height of its power, the Zhou domain extended south across the Changjiang River, northeast to present-day Liaoning, west to Gansu, and east to Shandong. In the northeast the Su Shen tribe inhabiting the vast area from the Songhuajiang to the Heilongjiang rivers presented King Wu with an arrow that had a head made of stone and a shaft made of wood. King Wu inscribed some words on the shaft and gave it to the state of Chen which kept it in its treasury down to the Spring and Autumn period. After the successful eastern expedition of the Duke of Zhou, this tribe again sent an emissary to offer congratulations.

The Zhou Dynasty established a patriarchal clan system. Within the clan there was a distinction between major and minor lineages. The king made the eldest son born of his wife heir to the throne—this was the major lineage. The other sons born of his wife and of his concubines became the heads of minor lineages. The vassal lords with the royal surname belonged to minor lineages in relation to the king, but in their own states they established the same kind of lineage system with a major lineage and many minor ones. A *dafu* (great officer) belonged to a minor lineage in relation to the vassal lord, but within his own fief he also maintained a system under which the first son of his wife was his legitimate heir representing the major lineage. Thus by combining blood relationship with an enfeoffment policy, the nobles bearing the same surname were united. At the same time, the royal house intermarried with the ruling families of the fiefdoms and became related to those with different surnames. The king of Zhou of a younger generation called the vassal lords with the same surname paternal uncles and those with different surnames maternal uncles. Such a clan relationship, coupled with intermarriages, strengthened the ties between the royal house and the vassal lords.

Of the various officials under the king the *taishi* or *taibao* (prime minister) was the most powerful. There were a minister of civil administration and land affairs (*situ*), a minister of military affairs (*sima*), a minister of construction (*sikong*), a minister of justice (*sikou*), and officials in charge of agriculture. Most of the official posts were held by nobles by hereditary right; the fiefs were, of course, also hereditary. The political organization in each fiefdom was similar to that at the royal court.

The king and the vassal lords each had his own armed forces. As in the Shang Dynasty, the main fighting force was composed of soldiers riding in chariots.

To maintain the rule of the dynasty, rites and laws were formulated. Punishments were used to control the slaves and common people while the function of ritual was to maintain the hierarchy within the nobility. Mainly an expression of different political status, the ranks also indicated seniority and the relative position of men and women.

The power of the king was bestowed by Heaven or the Lord on High. Like the Shang, the Zhou Dynasty identified its ancestral god with the supreme god. The Zhou admitted that the Shang kings were the elder sons of the Lord on High, but since they had failed to live up to his expectations, the Lord on High shifted his favour from the east to the west. As the Zhou Dynasty embodied the divine will, it was given supreme power over the human world. But the mandate of Heaven was not permanent; it depended on whether the conduct of posterity met with the approval of Heaven. Here again the ancestral

Genealogical Table of the Zhou Dynasty

I. Before King Wu

Qi (Houji) — Bu Zhu — Ju — Gong Liu — Qing Jie — Huang Pu —

— Cha Fu — Hui Yu — Gong Fei — Gao Yu — Ya Yu — Gongshu Zulei —

— Gugong Tanfu (Tai Wang) — Ji Li (Gong Ji, Wang Ji) — Chang (Xi Bo, King Wen)

II. The Zhou Dynasty

(1) King Wu (Fa) — (2) King Cheng (Song) — (3) King Kang (Zhao) — (4) King Zhao (Xia) —

— (5) King Mu (Man) — (6) King Gong (Yi Hu) — (7) King Yi (Jian) — (9) King Yi (Xie) —

(8) King Xiao (Pifang)

— (10) King Li (Hu) — *Gonghe* Period — (11) King Xuan (Jing) — (12) King You (Gongnie) god became separated from the supreme god, because the former was not the only son of the latter. It seems that the supreme god of the Shang was autocratic, while that of the Zhou, though autocratic, was also rational. The Shang god belonged to the Shang alone, while the Zhou god did not, but stood above dynasties and tribes. In this respect the Zhou religion was more developed than the Shang religion, and this also reflected the political ideas of the Zhou Dynasty in its early period.

5. Economic Development Under Zhou Slavery

The slave system was well developed under Zhou rule. The king, vassals and high officials owned slaves of different status and under different names and forced them to create great wealth for them. The slave-owners held power and were also dominant economically. The common people living in the capital cities were called *guo ren*, also interpreted as "freemen". The peasants in rural communes were called *ye ren* or "people in the fields".

After the Zhou conquest a large number of the Shang people and their slaves became slaves of the new rulers. Ancient records state that King Wu attacked 99 states, taking prisoner large numbers of people who possibly became slaves. The kings of Zhou conducted expeditions to the east and the south and frequently fought against the Gui Fang tribe in the north. In one battle 13,081 men and many chariots, horses, cattle and sheep were captured. Convicts were another source of slaves. The common people who revolted against the nobles were considered to have "committed crimes" and criminals were often converted into slaves and forced to perform all sorts of labour. But they were not necessarily slaves for life, and were generally released after serving their sentences.

Bronze inscriptions record the grants by the Zhou kings and nobles of tens, hundreds or thousands of slave families. One of the characteristics of the slave system in ancient China was the organization of the slaves on a family basis, although this was not the case with all slaves. In these inscriptions gifts of slaves are often mentioned along with gifts of all kinds of utensils, money, cattle, horses and land. This shows that slaves were treated in the same way as utensils or animals. They could be bought and sold. According to one inscription, five slaves were worth a horse and a bundle of silk.

There were fewer cases of slaughtering slaves and prisoners of war under Zhou rule than under the Shang, but it was still rather common to bury people alive to accompany the dead, though in smaller numbers. This shows that, under the Zhou slave system, production could obviously absorb a greater labour force than under the Shang. In the bronze inscriptions there are many examples of slaves being forced to perform productive labour—mostly farming and in some cases handicraft work.

The royal house was nombinally the owner of all land in the country. The royal domain around the capital was directly owned while the nobles and officials each had his own fief. These fiefs were hereditary and, to a large extent, could be handled freely by their owners. The land system was one of ownership by the slave-holding nobility.

A poem from the Zhou Dynasty describes thousands of people working in the fields. The grain of the slave-owner piled high on the farms. The poem says that a thousand granaries and ten thousand baskets should be prepared to handled the grain. This is probably a description of a bumper harvest with the slaves working collectively on the land.

Within the rural commune, farmland was periodically distributed on the basis of fertility. An able-bodied peasant could use 100 mu of the best land and 50 mu of fallow; or 100 mu of middle-grade land and 100 mu of fallow; or 100 mu of poor land and 200 mu of fallow. The peasant worked a piece of land distributed to him and let another piece lie fallow. Land was redistributed after several years. Between the fields were irrigation canals along which roads were built. Although there is no definitive proof, this may have been the farming system that was later referred to as the "well fields" (*jingtian* 井田). Eight households are supposed to have cultivated one plot of land each with a common field in the middle. According to one interpretation, the crops from the central field were given to a lord. The character *jing* 井, "well", resembles such a group of nine fields.

The peasant clans lived together in the rural communes. The settlements were called *yi* or *she* and were surrounded by open fields. They had their own houses, gardens or orchards. Between them there was equality, but the neighbourhood leaders controlled who was joining or leaving these communities. Women were brought together for "making ropes at night". The peasants were given land by the commune to produce grain, vegetables, fruits, domestic animals, fuel and clothing to support themselves.

Tools for farm production used during the Zhou period were not much different from those of the Shang Dynasty. But production was improved as the slaves and the peasants of the communes had accumulated much experience over a long period. The main method of farming was called *ou geng*, or "two men working together". This was probably designed to make deeper ploughing possible. The system of fallow was a progressive development and gradually replaced the slash and burn method. The technique of simple drainage and irrigation was also improved as were weeding, seed breeding and pest control. People grew rice, sorghum, sticky millet, wheat, beans, millet, mulberry, hemp, melons and fruits. There was a greater variety than in the Shang period, covering nearly all the principal crops we have today.

Handicrafts continued to develop. After conquering Shang, the Zhou kings sent the "six clans of Yin people" and "seven clans of Yin people" to the states of Lu and Wei, and among these there were ropemakers, makers of two different kinds of vessels and potters as well as makers of flags, horse harnesses, files and axes, fences and mallets. These captured handicraftsmen played an important role in the development of Zhou handicrafts.

Bronze casting continued to be an important handicraft, especially the building of chariots which were not only a means of conveyance for the nobility but, more importantly, a kind of military equipment. As more fiefs were estblished, the construction of buildings also developed.

Zhou handicrafts and trade were mainly controlled by the nobles or officials and served the nobility. The status of the workers and their leaders was inherited. At this time slaves, cattle and horses, arms and jewellery were exchanged through barter, and in the capital there were markets under state control. Cowries were still used as money, with strings of shells as the units of calculation. Metals were also used as means of exchange. Among the common people barter mostly involved daily necessities.

6. The Zhou Dynasty from Prosperity to Decline

After the death of King Wu, the Duke of Zhou was in charge of state affairs for seven years until King Cheng came of age. The four decades under King Cheng and his son King Kang were marked by political stability and economic prosperity.

Under the next rulers, King Zhao and King Mu, the strength of the dynasty was at its height and wars were fought against the peoples of the surrounding areas. These conflicts intensified with the Zhou side enjoying the initiative. King Mu, powerful and ambitious, is said to have toured the regions far out in the west.

After King Mu and throughout the reigns of King Gong, King Yi, King Xiao, King Yi and King Li, the prestige of the dynasty gradually declined and contradictions between the royal house and the people began to surface. King Li exploited the capital residents or freemen more mercilessly than ever and that roused general opposition. His ministers advised him to stop his oppression, but he refused to listen. Instead, he suppressed all public discussion. His tyranny continued for three years; then the capital residents could no longer tolerate it and rose in armed revolt. They attacked the royal palace and forced the king to flee. Then they surrounded the residence of the Duke of Zhao where they had heard that Prince Jing, heir to the throne, was hiding. The Duke made his own son take the place of the prince, thus saving the heir who later became King Xuan.

After King Li had fled, the Duke of Zhou and the Duke of Zhao, descendants of the two mentioned earlier, took charge of the government; this period was called the *gonghe*. One account says that the man in power was Duke He of the state of Gong, hence the name *gonghe*. The first year of *gonghe* was 841 B.C. From that year on, we have accurate dates of recorded Chinese history.

King Li died in Zhi (now Huoxian in Shanxi) 14 years after his flight. The Dukes of Zhou and Zhao had Prince Jing enthroned as King Xuan. In the first years of his rule severe droughts occurred, but they did not develop into a serious situation. Later King Xuan carried out wars against some neighbouring tribes and states and won some victories, but was defeated in wars against the Jiang Rong tribe[1] and agaisnt the Tiao Rong and the Ben Rong tribes.[2] For a time during King Xuan's reign there were signs of prosperity. But the contradictions between the Zhou state and the neighbouring peoples and the social contradictions in the Zhou-controlled areas were not resolved. Moreover, continuous wars consumed much of the dynasty's manpower and material resources.

King You, who succeeded King Xuan, was a stupid, self-indulgent and cruel ruler. The existing contradictions grew worse. As the *Book of Odes* pointed out: "Some people leisurely stay at home, some work untiringly for the country, some lie in bed doing nothing, some always have to go to war, some drink and make merry, some are fearful of meeting disaster, some talk nonsense or gossip, some have to do all kinds of work." The struggles between big and small slave-owners became sharper with the small slave-owners complaining: "People have land, you take it away; people own slaves, you seize them!" Uninterrupted famine and severe earthquakes compelled people to leave their homes and wander about. Those who were politically sharp used the earthquakes as a pretext to warn that "high cliffs may turn into deep valleys, while valleys may become hills and mountains." The Zhou Dynasty faced a crisis.

During King You's reign the neighbouring people made continuous attacks. He dismissed Queen Shen and the crown prince Yi Jia and

---

[1] The Jiang Rong tribe first inhabited Gua Zhou (west of present-day Dunhuang County in Gansu Province) and later moved eastward.

[2] The Tiao Rong and Ben Rong tribes lived in the area around present-day Mingtiaogang north of the Zhongtiao Mountains near Yuncheng County in Shanxi Province.

made his favourite concubine Bao Si queen and her son heir to the throne. Marquis Shen, father of Queen Shen, attacked the king in collaboration with the Quan Rong tribe[1] and Lü, Zeng and other states. As the vassals refused to send him reinforcements, King You was killed at the foot of Mount Li. The capital was sacked and its treasures plundered. Under the threat of the Quan Rong and their allies, the Zhou ruler had lost control of the old capital by 771 B.C. In the following year King You's successor, King Ping, moved the capital to Luoyi with the support of some of the nobles and vassals. From this year the dynasty is known as Eastern Zhou. The dynasty's power and prestige had declined sharply, and history entered a new stage.

---

[1] The Quan Rong tribe led a nomadic life in the Jing and Wei river valleys, or present-day Binxian and Qishan counties in Shaanxi Province, during the Shang and Zhou dynasties.

Chapter V
The Early Eastern Zhou, Spring and Autumn, and Warring States Periods: Transition from Slavery to Feudalism

1. The Early Eastern Zhou and the Spring and Autumn Period: Contention for Supremacy Among the Major States

In 770 B.C., King Ping moved the centre of political power eastward to Luoyi (present-day Luoyang), and the Eastern Zhou Dynasty came into being. In 256 B.C. the Eastern Zhou came to an end after 514 years of existence under 25 successive kings. The period from 722 B.C., 49 years after the Zhou capital was moved east, to 481 B.C. is known to historians as the Spring and Autumn Period and the subsequent period, to 221 B.C., is known as the Warring States Period.[1]

The eastward move by the Zhou was an important political event. This was followed by annexation among the vassal states. During the Spring and Autumn Period, big states conquered 30 or more small states, some as many as 40 or 50 small states. It is said that there were 1,800 states under the Western Zhou, but the number dwindled to 100 by the Spring and Autumn Period as the result of conquest and an-

[1] The term "Spring and Autumn Period" refers to the period covered by the book *The Spring and Autumn Annals*, namely from 722 to 481 B.C. There are three definitions, however, for the Warring States Period. Some hold that it began in 475 B.C., others say 476 B.C., and still others cite 403 B.C. The third definition is used in the present book. The 76 years (480 B.C. to 404 B.C.) lying between the two periods are regarded as part of the Spring and Autumn Period.

nexation. Of the 100 only about a dozen were politically significant. During the Warring States Period, only 7 states, plus a few smaller ones, remained before they were finally absorbed by the Qin. The early years of the Eastern Zhou, the Spring and Autumn Period, and the Warring States Period were all marked by great upheaval.

After moving his capital to the east, King Ping reestablished the power of the dynasty with the help of such states as Jin, Zheng, Wei and Qin. He relied particularly on Jin and Zheng for support. The capital of Zheng was located at modern Huaxian, Shaanxi Province; it was then moved to modern Xinzheng, Henan Province, at the time when the Eastern Zhou moved its capital. Duke Zhuang of Zheng was active politically during the first two decades of the Spring and Autumn Period. Jin, located in the southern section of modern Shaanxi Province, was a state of fertile land where Han communities were interspersed with Rong and Di tribes. It gained considerable strength during the first few years of the Eastern Zhou Dynasty. Qin, a newcomer among the states, grew in power amidst struggles against the Rong; it extended its jurisdiction to the eastern section of modern Gansu Province and the central section of modern Shaanxi Province. Among the strong powers of this time were Jin, Qin, Qi (in today's Shandong Province) and Chu (in the Changjiang and Huanghe river basins and the southern section of modern Henan Province). Because of its continuing expansion to the north, Chu became a formidable threat to the northern states and an object of their defence. In 679 B.C., Duke Huan of Qi stopped the civil war in Song; then he called a meeting that was attended by the various states and thus established the supremacy of his state. The state was set for the contention of power, of which the previous 90 years had been only a preparatory stage.

Duke Huan designated a statesman named Guan Zhong to carry out reforms, the purpose of which was to build up a rich state with strong armed forces. He succeeded in uniting some of the vassal lords by invoking the slogan of "loyalty to the King of Zhou" and by putting up strong resistance against Chu, Rong, and Di that had been a menace to the allied states. As the Bei Rong (Northern Rong) was harassing the state of Yan and as the Di was attacking the state of Xing after having conquered the state of Wei, Qi supported Yan in defeating the Bei Rong and helped Wei to reestablish itself, besides moving Xing to a safer region. In 656 B.C., Duke Huan led an alliance of Qi, Lu, Song, Zheng, Chen, Wei, Xu, and Cao to attack Cai and Chu. The allied army fought its way to Zhaoling (modern Yancheng, Henan Province) and forced Chu to pay tribute to the king of Zhou. Qi's supremacy had now reached its apex. It is said that the great alliance headed by the duke met on nine occasions. At the well-known conference held at Kuiqiu (to the east of modern Lankao, Henan Province) in 651 B.C., a treaty to be observed by all the participants was signed. In 643 B.C., Duke Huan died, and his death was followed by intense contention for succession. Before long, hegemony passed to the state of Jin.

Duke Wen of Jin was the second overlord of this period. He became the sovereign of his state when he was over 60, after nineteen years of exile during which he learned to understand contemporary society better than any other sovereign of his time. Hu Yan, Zhao Cui and others who had accompanied him during the exile were all outstanding political figures. Duke Wen ascended the throne in 636 B.C. and, the very next year, raised the slogan of "loyalty to the King of Zhou". He brought back to the capital King Xiang of Zhou who had left the capital because of fratricidal fighting within the court itself. He also succeeded in putting down rebellions. In 632 B.C., the state of Chu led an alliance with Chen, Cai, Zheng and Xu in an attack against Song on account of the latter's pro-Jin policies. In response, Jin led the forces of Song, Qi and Qin and met the invaders at Chengpu (today's Linpu township to the southwest of Juancheng County, Shandong Province) and decisively defeated them. For the first time, Chu suffered a serious setback in its expansion towards the north. The successful encounter enabled Duke Wen to enjoy a fame more widespread than that of Duke Huan of Qi. For next 80 years and more, the contention between Jin and Chu for supremacy was the dominant feature of Chinese history and each side had victories and losses. In 597 B.C. Chu defeated Jin's forces at Bi (near modern Zhengzhou, Henan Province), and the victory made Duke Zhuang of Chu an overlord of the states.

Duke Mu of Qin, aided by able statesmen, was also ambitious. He assisted two princes of Jin to return to their homeland as rulers, and Duke Wen of Jin was one of the two. In 627 BC., Duke Mu took the advantage of Duke Wen's death to launch a surprise attack on Zheng. He was defeated by Jin, and all his three generals were captured. From then on as Qin could not expand much to the east, it concentrated its efforts on the west. As a result, Duke Mu became famous as an overlord in the western regions.

Wars among big states in the Huanghe River valley brought nothing but disasters to the small states which, as the bones of contention, could not cope with the situation. In the meantime, the intermittent wars intensified the fighting within the ruling classes in each state, and the resulting rise and fall of different political forces left it powerless to cope with a big state's aggression. Not surprisingly, many states were longing for a change. In 579 B.C. and again in 546 B.C., the state of Song, which had suffered enormously from the warfare among the big states, called a peace conference. It succeeded in attaining its goal during the second conference. It was agreed that the eight small states of Song, Lu, Zheng, Wei, Cao, Xu, Chen and Cai would pay tribute to both Jin and Chu, and that the two big states of Qi and Qin would enter into an alliance relationship with Jin and Chu respectively. Thus Jin and Chu had an equal share of the supremacy. The agreement temporarily put an end to the contention for hegemony among the states in the Huanghe River valley.

After the peace conference, China entered the late Spring and Autumn Period, which was marked by two important events: the intensification of struggle between the leading noble families and the houses of the sovereigns within each state and expansion to the Huanghe River area by two new states, Wu and Yue, that rose to prominence in the lower reaches of the Changjiang River.

Like the overlords among rulers of the states, the leading noble families held real power within each state. After the death of Duke Wen, some nobles in Jin gradually attained prominence during wars against foreign states. By the late Spring and Autumn Period, political power in each state had passed from the sovereign to the nobles. Having no control over generals and soldiers, the sovereign led a life of luxury and self-indulgence and paid little attention to the lot of the common people. The nobles, on the other hand, were stronger than the ruler because they were supported by able advisers and armed forces. They also attached some importance to the winning of the masses. As a result, contradictions continued to sharpen between the sovereign and the nobles and among the nobles themselves. In the state of Jin, six noble families, Zhi, Zhao, Wei, Han, Fan and Zhonghang emerged and ruled the state among them. Later the Fan and Zhonghang families collapsed as a political force, and only four families remained active. In 453 B.C., Zhao, Wei and Han divided Zhi among them. The ground was then set for the three remaining families to divide the state of Jin whenever they liked.

Like Jin, the noble families in Qi grew in power after the death of Duke Huan. Among them were Guo, Gao, Luan, Bao, Cui, Qing, Yan and Tian, the last one eventually overwhelming all the others by intrigues and brutal force. In 489 B.C., the Tians went as far as killing the sovereign of Qi. They did the same thing again in 481 B.C. They held the political power in Qi beginning in 480 B.C. From then on, they could replace the sovereign of Qi anytime they wished.

Smaller states had their noble families, too. In Lu, for example, there were the families of Jisun, Mengsun, and Shusun, all of whom had originally belonged to the ruling house. In 562 B.C., they divided the land and labourers of the ruling duke, virtually partitioning Lu into three separate states. The duke could only live on the tributes paid by the noble families.

The capital of Wu was located in today's Suzhou, Jiangsu Province. The ruling family of Wu had the same surname as the king of Zhou's, but the state later became a dependency of Chu. In 584 B.C., having learned archery and the use of war horses and chariots from the people of Jin, Wu strengthened its armed forces and began to communicate with the northern states. The relationship between Wu and Chu also underwent a change. The prince of Wu, He Lü, appointed Wu Zixu to be his military adviser and Sun Wu commander of the army. In 506 B.C., Wu launched five separate attacks against Chu and won them all. It captured Chu's capital Yingdu (now Jiangling County, Hubei Province). King Zhao of Chu fled, and the whole state was on the verge of being exterminated. Qin then sent troops to help Chu; meanwhile, infighting broke out among the Wu aristocrats. Yue took advantage of the situation to attack Wu, and the latter was compelled to withdraw from Chu.

Yue, whose capital was located at modern Shaoxing County, Zhejiang Province, grew quickly in power with the help of Chu. Led by Prince Gou Jian, it defeated Wu in a decisive battle, in which Prince He Lü suffered an injury which led to his death. He was succeeded by his son Fu Chai, who sought revenge. In 494 B.C., Wu defeated Yue and reduced the latter to a dependency. Debasing himself as a Wu subject, Prince Gou Jian prepared to restore his state. In 482 B.C., when Prince Fu Chai was in the north to confer with other princes, Yue attacked and captured Wu's capital. In 473 B.C., it ended Wu's existence altogether.

After victory over Yue, Prince Fu Chai of Wu had met with other princes at Huangchi (modern Fengqiu County, Henan Province) in his attempt to seize hegemony from the prince of Jin. After Yue defeated Wu, Prince Gou Jian also went to the north to confer with other princes for the same purpose. Both journeys indicated that the relationship between the north and the south had been greatly strengthened by then. The attempt of Wu and Yue to seize hegemony nevertheless marked the last days of the Spring and Autumn Period when the struggle for supremacy was no longer as significant as before.

2. The Seven Powers of the Warring States Period

In 403 B.C., Jin was divided into three independent states, Han, Zhao and Wei. In 386 B.C., the Tian family openly seized state power in Qi. These four states plus Qin, Chu and Yan are referred to by historians as the seven powers of the Warring States Period. Geographically Chu was located in the south, Zhao in the north, Yan in the northeast, Qin in the west, Qi in the east, and Han and Wei in the centre. By this time, none of the states used the slogan of "loyalty to the King of Zhou" any more as Zhou had become a much smaller state. Instead of confrontation between Chu and the northern states of the

Spring and Autumn Period, the seven powers of the Warring States Period contended with one another. Fierce fighting went on among the seven as each tried to annex its neighbours until Qin succeeded in conquering all the rival powers.

Greater social changes took place during the Warring States Period than in the preceding period. Far-sighted statesmen perceived these changes and took the initiative to expedite them politically. This brought up the issue of political reforms. During the earlier stage of this period there were men like Li Kui in Wei, Wu Qi in Chu, and later Shang Yang in Qin, whose reforms had a great impact on history.

In the early Warring States Period, Wei was a powerful and prosperous state. Marquis Wen of Wei, as a monarch of high aspirations, searched for talented men and found Li Kui whom he put in charge of reforms. Li Kui, in his turn, appointed people according to their abilities instead of their social status, and gave high positions to those who had rendered meritorious services to the state. Having studied the budget of farmers, he realized their financial difficulties and proposed measures to raise production. He introduced a system of stabilizing grain prices whereby the government bought grain at a reasonable price during a good harvest and sold it at a reasonable price during a bad harvest. In this way, grain prices would not rise or fall drastically, and both producer and consumer would benefit and lead a more secure life. Measures of this kind played a significant role in maintaining social stability, strengthening the government, and building a rich and powerful Wei.

Wu Qi, a famous statesman and strategist, had won victories on the battlefield for both Lu and Wei. He had also distinguished himself as an administrator in Wei. Yet the aristocrats in both states rejected and persecuted him, and he had to leave Wei for Chu in 382 B.C. In Chu King Dao made him his chief minister. As chief minister, Wu Qi introduced new laws, invalidated sinecure, and abolished the privileges of the king's distant relatives. Money thus saved was used for the strengthening of the armed forces. He also stipulated that the enfeoffed land of the nobles must be returned to the state after three generations. These reform measures certainly benefited the state, but they aroused the resentment of the nobles. As soon as King Dao died in 381 B.C., the nobles sought him out and wanted to kill him. He died taking refuge behind the king's corpse, and some of the arrows aimed at him pierced the king's body as well. When the crown prince ascended the throne and became King Su of Chu, he ordered the execution of all the nobles who desecrated the late king's body while killing Wu Qi, and more than seventy families were eliminated as a result. The execution dealt a heavy blow to the conservative forces of Chu and provided new impetus to the development of the state.

In 359 B.C., Shang Yang launched his reform in Qin, a reform that historians regard as the most significant event in the Warring States Period. The reform also indicated that the middle stage of the Warring States Period had arrived.

Shang Yang was a native of Wei, and his surname was Gongsun. Shang was the title of his fief, and Yang his personal name. Having won the confidence of Duke Xiao of Qin, he began to introduce reforms. He made clear what the laws were, rewarding those who had distinguished themselves in farming or on the battlefield. The purpose was to strengthen monarchal rule. He abolished the land-owning system of the past, promoted production by individual peasants, and carried out a policy of "elevating agriculture and downgrading commerce". Land now could be sold or bought. Measures were adopted for a full utilization of labour power for agricultural development. For isntance, families with two or more male adults living in the same house were required to pay twice the amount of taxes compared to families with only one male adult. Those who harvested more grain or produced more silk would be exempted from corvée, while merchants and those too lazy to work would be condemned to slavery together with their wives and children. Shang Yang abolished the traditional privileges of the nobles and introduced a new system in which there were 20 ranks of honour, which were granted to those who deserved them. Social hierarchy was clearily defined, and a person with rank would be entitled to an appropriate amount of land, houses, retainers, concubines, and clothing. A member of nobility who had not distinguished himself on the battlefield would see his name deleted from the royal roster. On the other hand, he who had distinguished himself on the battlefield would be rewarded with honour, which was denied to those without military credit, no matter how wealthy they were. To establish a political system of autocratic monarchy, Shang Yang grouped all villages and towns of the state into 30 to 40 counties governed by magistrates and their deputies, who were appointed and removed by the sovereign himself. He also divided households into groups of five or ten, responsible for one another's behaviour. Those who failed to report a criminal act would be cut in two at the waist; those who reported would be rewarded as if they had killed an enemy; those who harboured a criminal would be severely punished as if they had surrendered to an enemy. Shang Yang also standardized and made uniform weights and measures.

These reforms were opposed by many people. When the crown prince Si broke the law, Shang Yang said that since the resistance to law enforcement came from above, the crown prince must be punished. However, since the culprit was the heir apparent and could not be punished, he punished the prince's two tutors instead. Those who opposed his reform were also punished. From then on, his reform became very effective. However, like Wu Qi, he aroused resentment as well. After the death of Duke Xiao, those who had opposed the reform wrongly accused him of having started a rebellion. Subsequently he and his whole family were put to death.

The reform of Shang Yang lasted more than twenty years and greatly strengthened Qin. Qin became a power held in awe by all other states. The reform also paved the way for the Qin rulers to realize their imperial ambition.

In the third year of Shang Yang's reform, Prince Wei ascended the throne in Qi. He rewarded the officials who had reclaimed wasteland and made people wealthy; he punished those who had failed to promote production, driven people to poverty, accepted bribes, or lied to the sovereign. He appointed Zou Ji to be the prime minister and put the strategist Sun Bin in charge of military reform. The purpose was to strengthen the state of Qi both politically and militarily.

As Qin and Qi became powerful, Wei, which had held a superior position during the early Warring States Period, now became a victim of attacks by both Qin and Qi and grew weak daily. However, Wei launched an attack on Zhao in the year 354 B.C. The next year Qi sent out troops to rescue Zhao at the latter's request. Qi's army, adopting Sun Bin's strategy, launched a sudden attack on Daliang (modern Kaifeng City, Henan Province), Wei's capital. The Wei forces were compelled to withdraw so as to defend their capital. The Qi army intercepted and routed Wei forces at Kuiling (to the west of modern Changyuan County, Henan Province). The strategy has come to be known in Chinese military history as "besieging Wei in order to rescue Zhao", or rescuing the besieged by attacking the base of the besiegers. In 342 B.C. Wei attacked Han; once again, Qi dispatched troops to help the victim. This time, Sun Bin lured the enemy to as far as Maling (to the southwest of modern Daming County, Hebei Province) where the Qi army dealt him a severe blow. Wei's crown prince, Shen, was captured; Wei's general, Pang Juan, committed suicide. During the time when Shang Yang was carrying out his reforms, Qin made repeated attacks on Wei. In 352 B.C., Qin captured Anyi (modern Xiaxian County, Shanxi Province) of Wei. In 340 B.C., the Qin army, led by Shang Yang himself, attacked again and this time captured Wei's top commander, Prince Qiong. From then on, the Qin army repeatedly marched eastward, and Wei was forced to cede Yinjin (modern Huayin County, Shaanxi Province) to Qin. The occupation of Yinjin provided the Qin army with a strategic passageway for advancing eastward. Wei was forced to cede its land west of the Huanghe, enabling Qin to use the river as natural barrier.

The war between Wei on one side and Qi and Qin on the other weakened Wei considerably and gave Qin footholds in its march eastward. Qin also defeated Yiqurong[1] to its west and exterminated Shu[2] in the south, and grew more powerful as a result. The six other states, threatened by Qin, were susceptible to the idea that they should form an alliance for defence. As the allies had contradictions among themselves, the alliance was anything but solid. Qin took advantage of this situation and tried to separate them from one another. It persuaded

---

[1] "Yiqurong" was a ethnic group in ancient China, residing in an area around today's Qingyang and Jingchuan counties in Gansu Province.

[2] "Shu" was also a ethnic group in ancient China, residing in the central and western section of modern Sichuan Province. It was also the name of the state.

each of them to form an alliance with it instead. Qi and Chu had a treaty of alliance between them, but Qin succeeded in making the treaty ineffective and repeatedly attacked Chu, which lost both men and territory in the process. In 299 B.C., Prince Huai of Chu went to Qin with which he was hoping to form an alliance, but he was held as a captive at Qin's capital Xianyang, where he later died. From then on, Chu became weaker and weaker.

As Qin and Chu fought against each other, changes also took place in Zhao, Qi and Yan. In 307 B.C., Prince Wuling of Zhao carried out military reforms by organizing a powerful cavalry and clothing the cavalry men in the style of nomadic peoples, making it easier for them to ride and to shoot their arrows. Qi, taking advantage of the internal turmoil of Yan, attacked and captured its capital in 314 B.C. The invader killed Prince Kuai and stationed troops on Yan's soil. In 284 B.C., Prince Zhao of Yan dispatched general Yue Yi to attack Qi and, in five years, took more than seventy cities, leaving only two cities still in Qi's control. Prince Zhao died in 279 B.C., and his successor, being suspicious of Yue Yi, replaced him with Qi Jie as commander. Qi's general Tian Dan took advantage of Yue Yi's absence by launching an offensive and succeeded in routing Yan's army. He killed Qi Jie and recovered the lost territories. The war between Qi and Yan, lasting 35 years, exhausted the strength of both, weakening the eastern states in their confrontation with Qin in the west. As the war between Qi and Yan lingered on, Qin launched an all-out offensive against Chu and succeeded in taking over half of the latter's territory. Finally, in 278 B.C., Qin's army marched into Chu's capital, Ying. By then the later stage of the Warring States Period had arrived, a stage in which Qin tried to unify the country by its own strength.

During the late stage of the Warring States Period, Qin first concentrated on attacking Han, Zhao and Wei. In 260 B.C., Qin and Zhao fought at Changping (modern Gaoping County, Shanxi Province). Before the battle, Qin succeeded in sowing discord in the enemy's ranks, making Zhao replace the experienced general Lian Po with the armchair strategist Zhao Kuo. Then General Bao Qi of Qin lured the Zhao forces into a trap where they were surrounded on all sides and their route of retreat cut off. When the battle was over, Zhao lost more than 400,000 men, including Zhao Kuo who was killed in action.

Apart from military offensives, Qin also adopted a policy of befriending distant states while attacking those nearby. It bought support in the enemy's ranks with cash and resorted to assassination as well. In 246 B.C., Prince Ying Zheng ascended the throne, and the new ruler was later known as the First Emperor of the Qin Dynasty. In 230 B.C., Qin conquered Han and, in nine years, conquered Zhao, Wei, Chu, Yan and Qi as well. Since the nobles in Qi had taken more gold from Qin than those in any other state, Qi surrendered to Qin without a fight in 221 B.C.

3. The Transition from Slavery to Feudalism

Great changes had taken place in productive forces during the early period of the Eastern Zhou Dynasty and the Spring and Autumn Period. When consequent changes took place in production relations, the time had arrived for the slave society to be transformed into a feudal society.

The development of social productive forces in the period that covered the early Eastern Zhou, Spring and Autumn and Warring States periods was marked by the increasing popularity of iron tools. Iron had been discovered and used as early as the Shang Dynasty. By the late period of the Western Zhou Dynasty, iron tools were in common use. In the Spring and Autumn and Warring States periods, people knew quite a bit about exploring and mining iron. It was recorded then that wherever reddish-brown objects were seen in the mountains, there might be iron deposits underneath. The record also said that there were 3,609 mountains yielding iron. The iron-smelting site in Linzi County, Shandong Province, covered an area of over 100,000 square metres. At the iron mining site of Tonglu Mountains, in Daye County, Hubei Province, the mine tunnel supports since discovered were quite advanced and complete. Facilities and installations for transportation, ventilation, and water drainage have also been found. Normally, the ore first went through a selection process in the pit before it was brought up by winches. As part of the iron-smelting equipment, the bellows were made of leather, connected to the furnace by a tube at one end and a handle made of porcelain at the other end. The turning of the handle forced air into the furnace, causing the charcoal to burn and the heat of the furnace to go up. In the late Spring and Autumn Period, craftsmen in the state of Wu already knew how to cast iron into sharp swords. In 513 B.C., with iron collected as tax, the state of Jin made a tripod on which the entire criminal code was cast. All this demonstrated that iron instruments had become quite popular among the common people after a considerable period of development.

Iron weapons dating back to the Warring States Period include armours, sticks, swords, broad swords, awls, halberds and daggers. A study of the steel swords and halberds unearthed at the secondary capital of Yan, located in modern Yixian County, Hebei Province shows that the final product came about through carbonization and repeated heating and hammering, followed by a sudden immersion in water. The steel thus obtained was martensitic, noted for its hardness and strength. At this time, people also discovered that a magnet attracted iron and that a magnetic needle always ran in a north-south direction. They invented the early form of a compass, known as *Sinan*.

In the middle Spring and Autumn Period, farm tools made of iron were in use in Qi. The iron farm tools in common use during the Warring States Period included plough, pick, hoe, spade and sickle and the common iron-made tools for handicraft work were axe, chopper, saw, awl, chisel and hammer. For women, the iron-made tools were needle, knife, awl, etc. People in Yan used iron moulds to mass-produce farming tools, handicraft tools, and spare parts for wagons.

The use of iron tools made it possible to employ draught animals for agricultural production. Oxen ploughing the fields became a common sight in the Spring and Autumn Period. Horses were also employed for ploughing during the Warring States Period. All this helped intensive farming and did much to increase agricultural productivity.

Closely related to the development of agricultural productivity in the Warring States Period was the construction of water conservancy projects. In 486 B.C., King Fu Chai of Wu, in an attempt to seek supremacy in the north, constructed the Han Canal from Jiangdu to

Huai'an, both in modern Jiangsu Province, so that the Huaihe River was linked with the Changjiang River. Later, he constructed a deeper canal connecting the Yishui River in the north with the Jishui River in the west, joining the drainage of the Huaihe and the Huanghe. This was a gigantic project constructed primarily for water transportation. Ximen Bao of Wei in the Warring States Period irrigated farmland in Ye (modern Linzhang County, Hebei Province) with water from the Zhanghe River, turning large tracts of saline-alkaline soil into fertile fields, demonstrating the important role that water conservancy projects could play in improving agriculture. Li Bing of Qin built in modern Guanxian County, Sichuan Province, the Dujiang Weir, cutting Minjiang River into an inner and an outer tributary. The project prevented flood and facilitated water transportation, and provided irrigation which turned the Chengdu Plain into a vast expanse of rich farmland. The state of Qin also employed Zheng Guo, an expert in water conservancy from the state of Han, to build a 150-kilometre-long canal connecting the Jingshui with the Beiluoshui rivers. The use of silt-laden water from these two rivers for irrigation transformed over 40,000 hectares of saline land into fertile fields. At this time, well sweeps were in use to bring water from low to high areas.

Farmers in the Warring States Period could already tell the differences among various types of soil and knew how to transform one type of soil into another. They classified soil into 9 categories and selected the suitable crops. They used a variety of manure, ranging from animal droppings to wood ashes and green manure. They mixed crop seeds with animal bones and called the mixture "fertilized seeds". In crop management, they paid attention to the right distance between plants, straight rows, selection of healthy young plants and root protection. They knew the importance of weeding and the elimination of locusts and snout moths. Books on agriculture were in existence. The ancient book *Lu's Almanac* and some other works all contained chapters on agriculture.

During the Warring States Period, progress was made in salt making, lacquerware manufacturing and the casting of bronzes. Sea salt in Qi and Yan, lake salt in Anyi of Wei, and well salt in Ba and Shu were well-known. Beginning with the middle of the Warring

States Period, musical instruments, weapons, outer coffins, and many utensils for daily household use were coated with lacquer. In the casting of bronzes, such new techniques as etching, inlaying of gold and silver, enchasing and gilding were all used.

The increase of social productivity in agriculture during the early Eastern Zhou, the Spring and Autumn, and the Warring States periods gradually changed the nature of the productive forces. Apart from the newly invented farming tools, slaves who had been engaged in collective farming were now replaced as labourers by peasants each working on his own. Independent peasants also replaced those who formerly worked in communal villages.

The inadequate manpower resulting from slowdown or the escape of slaves worried the slave-owners during the late stage of slave society. A poem from Qi in the middle of the Spring and Autumn Period says: "Stop ploughing the fields, for wild grass is shooting up." Touring the state of Chen, an envoy from the Eastern Zhou complained that the crops there had all been covered up by weeds. Clearly, land lay waste in some areas owing to the shortage of manpower. Under these circumstances, slave-owners were compelled to give up the practice of using slave labour, as they realized that it was more advantageous to exploit individual peasants.

The old practice of distributing land according to its fertility gradually lost its appeal. Now peasants could make their own arrangement regarding land rotation, since it was no longer necessary to rotate land on a community basis. A special relationship was thus established between a peasant and the land he tilled permanently. This in turn gave birth to the concept of the family as a productive unit. We now know that Jin was the first state to use administrative power to promote such a practice in 645 B.C.

The individual peasant had two distinct features. First, he was tied to land, unlike the relationship between slaves and land or between a village commune and land. Secondly, an individual family, where the husband tilled and the wife wove became known as a "household", or a productive unit. All this further increased the peasants' dependence on land.

The change in social productive forces inevitably led to changes in production relations. The production relations of the slave system could no longer suit the new productive forces and had to be replaced by the production relations of the feudal system. The representative of the new productive forces must be one who had a certain degree of freedom and was engaged in private economy, not simply a tool that could speak. When exploiters took individual peasants as their main target of exploitation, they could no longer own the producer as completely as they did the slave. Now the ownership was only partial. Under these conditions, the exploiters became landlords. The beginning of confrontation between peasants and landlords marked the appearance of the feudal relations of production.

Beginning with the middle of the Spring and Autumn Period and particularly during the Warring States Period, some princes and dukes changed from slave-owners to landlords. Most of the landlords acquired land through grants as a reward for their military deeds. Some of the individual peasants might also grow into landlords. In places where land could be traded, merchants might also become landlords.

Feudal landownership was a system where land was owned by landlords. Different landlords occupied different political and social positions. Such ranks were merely a reflection of different grades of landownership. After its inception in the Spring and Autumn and Warring States periods, feudal landownership in China always represented a hierarchy.

In all of the reforms carried out by Shang Yang in the state of Qin, including the encouragement of married sons to live in separate households, the rewarding of those who had done well in farming and weaving, the registration and organization of households, and the suppression of commerce, he tried to transform a household into a production unit where men tilled and women wove, thus tying the labour force to the land. His other measures of reform, such as the granting of the twenty ranks of honour according to military deeds, the distribution of land and houses according to merit, and the downgrading of nobles who had failed to distinguish themselves in war, were all aimed at the replacement of the slave-owning class by the new landlord class. The reform, enforced through administrative power, accelerated the development of the new productive forces and the corresponding feudal landownership based on a system of ranks.

The change in production relationship was no easy matter and was bound to be accompanied by complicated struggle. Class struggle, including the struggle among the exploiting classes, was inevitable. The reforms of Wu Qi and Shang Yang posed, from the very beginning, a confrontation with the nobility of the old order. The fact that they were killed for their reforms indicated the harshness of the struggle. The running away of slaves, the roaming about of "thieves and robbers" and the "fleeing of citizens" in general were actually different forms of class struggle that went on all the time. History recorded the "fleeing of male and female slaves" and the "fleeing of masses"; all this indicated that ordinary citizens or slaves ran away because they could no longer bear the heavy burden of military and labour services imposed upon them by the ruling classes.

In 641 B.C., rulers of Liang (to the south of modern Hancheng County, Shaanxi Province) forced people to build they city walls. When they ordered the weary labourers to dig a moat, they caused a "mass fleeing of citizens". Qin seized the occasion to attack Liang and succeeded in conquering it. A hundred and twenty-two years later, when Chu built its capital at Yingcheng in 519 B.C., the above incident was still regarded as a lesson to be avoided, indicating its far-reaching impact. "Thieves and robbers" were a serious threat to the ruling classes of various states. They could be found on the highways of Chu, or in the capital city of Jin. According to legends, there was a leader of a mass uprising named Zhi, referred to by rulers of various states as Thief Zhi. He had a strong force of several thousand people under his command and dealt telling blows to the ruling classes. Struggles of this kind might be small in scale and did not have many slaves as participators, but whoever participated fought bravely against the slave-owning class, weakened the rule of the slave system, and paved the way for the rise of feudalism.

Industry and commerce during the early Eastern Zhou, the Spring and Autumn, and the Warring States periods, unlike agriculture, did not play a dominant role in the social economy as a whole. As far as the record goes, the traders and the industrialists all had considerable influence. Two stories about merchants during the Spring and Autumn Period deserve special mention. In 627 B.C., while journeying to Zhou on a business trip, Xuan Gao, a merchant of Zheng, encountered Qin's army on its way to attack Zheng by surprise. He gave four pieces of tanned leather and twelve oxen to the Qin army in the name of the sovereign of Zheng. The Qin army mistakenly thought that news of their projected attack must have leaked out, and it decided to withdraw. During the battle at Bi between Jin and Chu in 597 B.C., an official of Jin, Xun Ying, was captured. Merchants of Zheng planned to smuggle him out of Chu in a cart loaded with merchandise. Before the plan was carried out, Chu released him. The Zheng merchants in these two stories might not be ordinary businessmen but people with political status. Zi Gong, a disciple of Confucius, was not a professional merchant, and all his commercial activities were closely related to politics. Lü Buwei was not only a successful merchant of the late Warring States Period, but also a political manipulator. He masterminded and financed the return to Qin of Prince Yi Ren, who had been held in Zhao as a hostage. After Zi Chu ascended the throne as Prince Zhuangxiang, Lü Buwei became his prime minister.

Agricultural and side-line products were the main trade items during the Warring States Period. They included grain, silk, bast fibre, textile, ko-hemp cloth, special local products of various regions, and luxuries used by the ruling class. Bai Gui, a merchant of Wei, amassed a huge fortune by purchasing grain and selling silk and lacquerware in years of good harvest and by selling grain and buying textile and cotton goods in years of bad harvest. Iron-smelting and salt-making were both profitable trades. Guo Zong and the Zhuo family of Zhao, Cheng Zheng of Qi, the Kong family of Liang, and the Bing family of Cao all made fortunes by smelting iron. Yi Dun of Lu and Diao Jian of Qi became rich by making salt or trading in fish. All of them employed slaves for production. Slavery persisted for a long time in the iron-smelting and salt-manufacturing industries.

4. Confucius, Mo Zi, Other Thinkers and the *Elegies of Chu*

During the early Eastern Zhou, the Spring and Autumn, and the

Warring states periods, persistent social upheavals gradually broke up the monopoly of culture and literature by members of the nobility, a monopoly that began as early as the Western Zhou. Private schools became a trendy development. During the late Spring and Autumn Period, Confucius started the trend by providing private teaching. Then, in the Warring States Period, many schools of thought came into existence and began to contend with one another. *Ci,* a new form of literature reflecting the trend of the time, appeared in the middle of the Warring States Period.

Confucius, whose personal name was Qiu and courtesy name Zhongni, was born in 551 B.C., in Zhou Yi, modern Qufu County, Shandong Province, then a part of the state of Lu. He died in 479 B.C. His ancestors used to be slave-owners in Song, but his great grandfather fled to Lu due to failure in his political career. By his father's time, the noble family had declined financially. During his youth, Confucius was for a time a low-ranking official managing warehouses; then he tended sheep and oxen. For the most part of his life, however, he was a private teacher. It is said that he had more than 3,000 students, 70 of whom were considered to be excellent. He often took some of his students with him while touring the various states. The rulers of these states all received him courteously and consulted him. Nevertheless, Confucius never had the opportunity to put his theory of government into practice. Not until his fifties did he become an official in charge of criminal punishment and the maintenance of social order in the state of Lu. He was then able to participate in state administration, but held the post for only three months. He devoted his later years to the collation and editing of literary works. He was said to have edited the *Book of History* and the *Book of Odes*. He added explanatory notes to the *Book of Changes*, a work on divination. He compiled the *Spring and Autumn Annals*. The *Book of Rites* and the *Book of Music* were examined and revised by him, too. Except for the *Book of Music* which has been lost, the other five books, in later years, became known as the Confucian classics which followers of Confucianism must read and abide by. The *spring and Autumn Annals* was the earliest and more or less complete chronicle, which had great impact on later historical works. After Confucius' death, his disciples compiled his statements to form a book entitled *The Analects*.

His lectures and tours indicated clearly that, like many others who did not enjoy the political status of the nobles, Confucius intended to take part in politics. These people were a rising force in a time of turmoil. Most of them were commoners, but some may have been nobles in origin who had lost their status. Confucius said that those who did well in studies could become officials. Thus the purpose of his teaching was to help his students acquire the necessary skill to get into politics. He often praised his students by saying that this one would do well in politics and that one could become a prime minister.

The content of Confucius' private teaching was antagonistic to that taught by the official schools of the nobles. He held that men were alike in nature, a teaching that was contrary to the basic concept of a slave society where social status was preordained. Speaking about politics, Confucius proposed that good and capable people should be appointed to official posts, a proposal that was contrary to the practice of hereditary rule. All this reflects the progressive aspect of his thinking.

As for the rites that supposedly governed the behaviour of the nobles beginning with the Western Zhou Dynasty, Confucius believed that they should not be merely a formality but should instead be combined with benevolence. Rites without benevolence would be totally meaningless.

Confucius, nevertheless, was only a reformist. He did not carry his ideas to their logical conclusion. Though he initiated private teaching, what he taught was nevertheless the same as the nobles used to learn. He did not believe that the noble status was preordained, but he defended the hierarchy of the nobility. He advocated the elevation of good and capable people, but he never raised objection to the official hereditary system, even advising good and capable men to be satisfied with their poverty and lowly position. He emphasized the importance of benevolence and regarded it as the highest ideal of morality. Yet, according to him, benevolence meant different grades of love—more love for those who were close and less for those who were distant, more for the highly placed and less for the lowly. Only the socially elevated could be loving, he said, while those below were merely objects of love. On the one hand, he stressed that rites should be combined with benevolence. On the other, he held that benevolence should be practised within the strict boundary of rites. Attempting to solve problems involving rites and benevolence, Confucius failed to use the new ideas to replace the old formality; instead, he adhered to the old formality as a means of reshaping old ideas. While his activities contained some progressive elements, such as his aspiration to be a statesman, basically, he defended the interests of the slave-owning nobles without being able to break through the shackles of the old order. Confucius viewed the upheavals of the Spring and Autumn Period as an abnormal situation in which society was not guided by right principles; he longed for the return of the Western Zhou times when society was guided by such principles. Rationally he knew that the Western Zhou times would never return; emotionally, however, he could not bring himself to face the fact. Many described him as a man who "does what he knows is impossible".

As the first private teacher who brought education to a large number of people, Confucius was properly regarded as having made great contributions in the cultural history of China. We must be reminded, however, that being politically conservative, he worked against the tide of history.

The school of thought founded by Confucius was known as Confucianism. A later school of thought which had equal influence was the school of Mohism founded by Mo Zi.

Mo Zi, whose personal name was Di, was a native of either Lu or Song. He was active during the period of 468-376 B.C. More in line with the interest of the common people, some of his important theories were in direct conflict with those of Confucius. His ideas could be found in a book entitled *Mo Zi*.

Mo Zi advocated universal love, the love for all without discrimination. One must treat another person, his family and his country in the same way as one treated oneself, one's own family, and one's own country. Thus Mo Zi's love was totally different from the concept of benevolence taught by Confucius. Mo Zi had no use for rites and music; his teaching of frugality on funerals and other occasions was in sharp contrast with the kind of life the nobles had and the kind of advice Confucius gave.

In politics, Mo Zi believed that people with ability should be elevated; he was opposed to inherited wealth or nobility. He said that a man with ability should become a government official even though he might be a lowly peasant or an ordinary worker. This idea of his was different from that of Confucius who did not clearly oppose the hereditary system in the officialdom.

According to Mo Zi, heaven and the demons rewarded the good and punished the evil. King Jie of Xia, King Zhou of Shang, and King You and King Li of Zhou, being tyrannical rulers, were punished for their opposition to the will of heaven, while Great Yu of Xia, King Tang of Shang, and King Wen and King Wu of Zhou, being saintly leaders, were rewarded for their compliance with the wishes of heaven. He believed that reward and punishment were meted out by heaven and the demons in accordance with the way people behaved. Poverty and wealth and people's status were neither preordained nor immutable. He invoked the will of heaven to persuade rulers to display kindness, so that "the starving may have food, those suffering from cold may have clothes, and the toilers may have some rest". Though all this was merely a wish, his opposition to fatalism was nevertheless progressive.

Ideologically speaking, both Confucius and Mo Zi were idealists. But there are noteworthy elements of materialism in Mo Zi's theory of knowledge. Some of his criteria of authentic knowledge had to do with proof by facts and objective result. Mohists of later days inherited this fine tradition and developed the materialistic view of the theory of knowledge. They made their contributions in the realm of natural sciences.

Mohism was an organized school of philosophers. After the death of Mo Zi, Ju Zi emerged as the leader of the school, which not only enforced its own discipline but also put its beliefs into practice.

During the Warring States Period, apart from Confucianism and Mohism, there were also Taoism and Legalism. In addition, there was the school of Logicians that studied the distinction between name and reality—a school that emphasized the importance of logic and debate. The *yin-yang* school, on the other hand, tried to explain natural and social phenomena by an analysis of *yin* and *yang*—the negative and the positive forces in the universe. The author of the book *Lao Zi* and Zhuang Zi of the Taoist school, Mencius and Xun Zi of the Confucian school, and Han Fei of the Legalist school were the best known scholars.

Lao Zi, whose surname was Li and personal name Er, was also known as Lao Dan. Roughly a contemporary of Confucius, he hailed from the state of Chu. The book *Lao Zi*, which has been attributed to him, was actually a work of the Warring States Period. It may not fully express his ideas.

The book repudiated the theory of a god, a heaven, or a supreme authority that had been popular since the Shang Dynasty. It replaced the theory with the Way, an absolute, overriding spirit transcending time and space and encompassing the whole universe. They Way had existed long before the physical universe came into being; it was in fact the source of everything in the universe. This represented the standpoint of objective idealism.

In the area of political thought, the book *Lao Zi* refuted the Confucian theory of benevolence and the Mohist concept of elevating good, virtuous people. It was in favour of letting nature take its own course and of non-interference in people's life. People would be better off without knowledge or desire. An ideal society was one small in population and territory, where there were no advanced implements and tools, no boats or vehicles, and no wars. People recorded events by making knots with ropes, and they never visited people of a neighbour state for the duration of their lives even though "they could hear the crowing of cocks and the barking of dogs on the other side of the border". The idea expressed above reflected the pessimism among rulers of the village communes in decline.

The book *Lao Zi* contained some naive ideas of dialectics. It unveiled the unity of opposites in the objective world such as disaster and fortune, soft and hard, strong and weak, more and less, above and below, early and late, true and false, honour and shame, clever and stupid, etc. Lao Zi realized the contradictions in things and the transformation of the opposites. In his view, however, the changes in things did not develop in a forward fashion; instead, it went on in an endless cycle. Besides, the transformation of the opposites was absolute and unconditional. He attempted to resolve contradictions in a subjective way, and this attempt gave birth to the idea of "acting without striving" in politics.

Zhuang Zi (c. 369 B.C.-286 B.C.), whose personal name was Zhou, hailed from the state of Song. Among the over 30 chapters in the book *Zhuang Zi*, some were his own writing.

Like the author of *Lao Zi*, Zhuang Zi regarded the Way as the substance of the universe. By claiming that he had identified himself with the Way, he changed the objective idealism in *Lao Zi* into a subjective idealism.

From Zhuang Zi's point of view, only the Way was absolute, while everything else was relative. He equated the subject with the object, life with death, longevity with short life, right with wrong, and disaster with fortune. He dismissed all difference between opposites and advanced a theory of relativism or nihilism. He denied the validity of the concepts of right and wrong debated between Confucians and Mohists, and regarded all cultural progress as meaningless. He once said that there would be peace and order if the learned men gave up their knowledge, and all fighting would stop with the abolition of weights and measures. His ideal society was one in which people lived in harmony with animals and birds.

Zhuang Zi's denial of the differences between right and wrong, life and death, oneself and others, illusion and reality, his antagonism to progress and his longing for a return to the prehistoric times, reflected a deep sense of pessimism, similar to that expressed in *Lao Zi*. The pessimistic view of both struck a sympathetic chord among the classes in decline throughout Chinese history. By refusing to recognize reality, however, the author of *Lao Zi* and Zhuang Zi also took a negative view of the "early kings", including Great Yu, King Tang of Shang, and King Wen and King Wu of Zhou, revered and extolled by Confucians and Mohists. In so doing they helped people, albeit unconsciously, to emancipate their minds.

Mencius, active during 372-289 B.C., was a native of Zou (modern Zouxian County in Shandong Province). His personal name was Ke and courtesy name Ziyu. His life experience was similar to that of Confucius. He too was a private teacher and took his students with him while touring the various states. While travelling, he was at one time accompanied by several hundred disciples and scores of chariots. He was also received with courtesy by rulers of various states, but none accepted his political ideas. His teachings were contained in a book entitled *Mencius*.

Mencius condemned tyranny, describing it as a system that "directs beasts to eat people". He was concerned with the sharpening of social contradictions, especially the fleeing of labour from productive pursuits. He inherited the Confucian concept of benevolence and developed it further by emphasizing its importance as a governmental policy. He believed that every person should have his own immovable property. A family of eight should have 100 *mu* of land in order to grow enough food to eat. It should raise domestic animals for meat, and plant mulberry trees and cultivate silk worms for clothing. In addition, there should be schools to teach people to be dutiful towards their parents and respectful towards all elders. If all this was done, people would be "friendly towards one another, helping one another in difficulties or in poor health." In that case, they would have no desire to move to other places all their lives. All this, in Mencius' opinion, would be beneficial to the building of a strong state. The purpose of having immovable property for everyone, as proposed by Mencius, was to combine tilling with weaving to create a small-scale agricultural economy where labour would be permanently tied to land. This meant the feudalization of the socio-economy that had apparently taken place during the time of Mencius. He wanted to promote it by administrative method.

The basis for Mencius' theory of a government by benevolence was that man was born with goodness. Man possessed the inherent quality of benevolence, righteousness, propriety and wisdom, which some people were able to preserve, while others could not. In Mencius' view, every sovereign was able to rule by a policy of benevolence, and every citizen was able to accept it. Both the rulers and the ruled were able to be good. In other words, the moral standards for two different classes were preordained. He made this point even clearer when he said that "those who labour with their minds govern others; those who labour with their hands are governed by others."

The constant wars of annexation were strongly opposed by Mencius. He maintained that those who loved to wage wars should be severely punished. As he realized that the trend during the period of the Warring States was towards unification, he stated, "only those who hate killing will be able to unify the country". He meant that one could unify the country only through benevolence, not by violence.

Mencius advocated the democratic principle that the people were more important than kings. A king enjoying popular support deserved to be called a king; a king who had lost popular support would be a lonely tyrant, who deserved to be put to death by anyone. A king who had done harm to the state should be replaced.

Representing the landlord class, Mencius was an idealist in thought, and the measures he preached were those of reconciliation. Nevertheless, he was progressive in the sense that he hated despotic rule and attached great importance to people's economic life and their importance to the government.

Xun Zi, also known as Xun Kuang or Xun Qing, hailed from the state of Zhao. He was active during 298-238 B.C. He travelled to the state of Qi twice as a visiting teacher and served on two occasions in Chu as magistrate of Lanling (located to the southwest of Zaozhuang City, modern Shandong Province). While touring Qin, he met with King Zhao whose political system he admired. In his old age, he retired to Chu, where he concentrated on writing. He extant *Xun Zi* contains his works.

Han Fei, a student of Xun Zi, was a native of the state of Han. He died in 233 B.C., but the year of birth is not known. Seeing the decline of his native state, he repeatedly presented ideas of reform to the king of Han. But none was accepted. When his written works were brought to Qin, the king of Qin admired it greatly. Han Fei went to Qin, only to be murdered by Li Si and other Qin officials. His written works were preserved in a book entitled *Han Fei Zi*.

Xun Zi and Han Fei lived in the late Warring States Period, shortly before the state of Qin unified China. By this time, the feudal landlord class had already established its position of supremacy, and the political trend was clearly the development of an autocratic monarchy and the unification of China. This trend showed itself in academic and political thought in the predominance of the school of Legalism and in comprehensive criticism of previous schools. Both Xun Zi and Han Fei had evaluated and criticized the various schools of thought before their time. "Criticism of the Twelve Schools" in *Xun Zi*, and "Prominent Schools of Learning" and "Five Evils" in *Han Fei Zi* are well-written examples of this kind.

Xun Zi's concept of nature was a step forward compared to the naive materialism or atheism initiated during the Spring and Autumn Period. He viewed the stars, days and months, the four seasons, wind and rain, cold and heat, *yin* and *yang* as phenomena of change in nature. They were governed by their own rules, without will or aim. Nature could not dispense with winter no matter how much human beings were afraid of cold, and land would not shrink no matter how much people wanted to hurry from one place to another. The laws that governed the motion of nature did not come about because of the existence of a wise king named Yao; they would not disappear because of the rise of a tyrant named Jie. Xun Zi noted that people were afraid of the falling of meteors or the strange sound caused by wind blowing against trees, but these phenomena indicated nothing but some rare changes in the *yin-yang* equilibrium that governed the normal function of the universe. They were not something to be afraid of. He believed that if people would work harder in agriculture and practise frugality, nature could not make them poor; if people would wear enough clothes, eat properly, and do physical exercise, nature could not make them ill. On the other hand, if people gave up agricultural production and were given to extravagance nature could in no way bring them prosperity. If they did not have enough food or clothes and did not do much physical exercise, nature could not do much about their health. Man, in his view, had the capacity of adapting himself to his environment and of making good use of natural laws so as to make everything in the universe serve his own ends. The idea of Xun Zi represented the upward movement of a feudal society dominated by landlords; it was different from that of Confucius, Mencius, Zhuang Zi, Mo Zi and the author of *Lao Zi*.

Xun Zi also spoke of benevolence, but he emphasized the importance of rites. He believed that learning should begin with the study of the *Book of Odes*, the *Book of History*, and other classics; it should end with a study of rites, which marked the apex of the learning process. He carried forward Confucius; view on rites, though with some reservation. On the one hand, he realized that the purpose of emphasizing the importance of rites was to maintain the class difference between the rich and the poor, the noble and the humble. On the other hand, he often mentioned law and rites in the same breath and considered them almost synonymous. In particular, he emphasized the importance of law, saying that no country could be governed without it. He explained the origin of rites with the supposition that man was born with evil. Beginning with his birth, man desired material things and sought among themselves for the satisfaction of such a desire, and the fight, in turn, caused social disorder. The need to maintain social order gave rise to rites. Xun Zi's view on rites showed his preference, sometimes, for Legalist ideas. His disciple Han Fei carried the argument further and became an important Legalist.

According to Xun Zi's theory of innate evil, the good qualities man had were acquired through learning after birth. He held that studying hard would enable one to change from being foolish to being wise and that those who studied most diligently might even become "sages". Though Xun Zi's theory was in direct conflict with that of Mencius who maintained that people were born with goodness, both philosophers talked about man's nature in the abstract without taking into consideration the factor of class influence. Both were idealists. Nevertheless, Xun Zi explained his theory from the viewpoint of material desire, emphasized learning after one's birth, and paid particular attention to the influence of environment on man. As a philosopher, he tended towards materialism. He was a progressive in his time. According to him, a major reason for the chaos during the Warring States Period was "too many schools of thought expressing too many different ideologies". To ensure social stability, there should be no more than one school of thought, from which even sages should not differ. By this point of view, he was in favour of thought control under an autocratic feudal government.

Han Fei held that history was evolutionary, each era being more progressive than the preceding one. He classified history into three stages, the early ancient times, the middle ancient times, and the late ancient times. In the early ancient times, wild animals outnumbered human beings. To protect humans from attack by wild animals, one sage invented a tree house that was very much like a bird's nest, so humans had a place to live in. To prevent diseases caused by food, another sage invented fire by drilling wood, so they could cook their food and eat better. In the middle ancient times, there was a big flood, which Gun and Yu succeeded in controlling, eventually. In the late ancient times, King Jie of Xia and King Zhou of Shang imposed such despotic rule upon humans that King Tang of Shang and King Wu of Zhou led uprisings to depose them. If, at the time of the Xia Dynasty, someone still lived in trees and made fire by drilling wood, he would be laughed at by Gun and Yu. If, at the time of the Shang Dynasty, someone still regarded flood control as the most pressing priority, he would be laughed at by King Tang of Shang and King Wu of Zhou. If, at the present time, someone still eulogized Yao, Shun, Gun, Yu, Tang, and Wu as perfect sages, he would and should be laughed at by all of today's sages. Han Fei concluded that today's sages should neither long for the past nor copy obsolete rules. They should, instead, take a long, hard look at today's social conditions and adopt appropriate measures.

Having studied political history and learned its lessons, Han Fei made a political proposal for the purpose of strengthening feudal rule, a proposal that combined the use of law, tactics, and power. "Law", enacted by the monarch, consisted of written regulations whereby the people were subjected to his rule. "Tactics" were the means by which the monarch governed his citizens. Han Fei maintained that law and tactics were equally important. Ruling with laws minus tactics could not prevent officials from building up their own power at the expense of the monarch's authority. On the other hand, ruling with tactics minus law would weaken the stability of the government. In addition to law and tactics, power was necessary. By power was meant the monarch's supreme authority, which alone could make law and tactics effective. All the three—law, tactics, and power—were the indispensable tools for the monarchy. Han Fei proposed that all power be concentrated in the hands of the monarch who would then use a combination of the three to govern the people effectively.

Han Fei's opposition to conservatism was clear-cut and his advocacy of reform positive. Representing the interests of the feudal landlord class, he was laying the ideological foundation for the advent of feudal autocracy.

New successes in art and literature were achieved during the later part of the middle Warring States Period. A typical example was the *Elegies of Chu*, a collection of poetic verses and songs written in the local dialect and tone of Chu. It possessed strong regional characteristics and a unique style. Qu Yuan, whose personal name was Ping, became famous as the author of these works. A native of Chu, he was born around 340 B.C. and died in 278 B.C. In his works, he told impressive stories of Chu's mountains and rivers, products, local customs, and songs and dances. He narrated many fairy tales and popular legends. More significantly, his works portrayed vividly the actual situation in Chu during the drastic changes in the late Warring States Period. They reflected his sincere love for his country and people.

Chu was still powerful and prosperous when Qu Yuan was young. With an aristocratic family background, he intended to pursue a political career. He won the trust of the Prince of Chu and was appointed the Left Minister. As an senior official, he was able to participate in the making of decisions involving the state's internal and foreign affairs. He advocated the choosing of virtuous and capable men as officials and the enactment of good laws to strengthen the state. In foreign affairs, he was in favour of a military alliance with the state of Qi against the state of Qin. However, the prince soon distrusted him and banished him from the capital. Meanwhile, corruption and incompetence, combined with repeated defeat by Qin, gradually weakened Chu. Refusing to be as corrupt as other members of Chu's nobility, he was hoping that he could regain the prince's trust and receive an appointment again. But he hoped in vain. He was so worried that he wanted to give up everything. Yet there was the suffering of the people a patriot must face. Where should Chu stand, now that the unification of China had become a distinctive trend? Torn by all these contradictions, he could not help feeling irritated and frustrated. When he poured out his sorrows and anger in the form of poems, the splendid works of the *Elegies of Chu* were born. When Chu's capital Ying was captured by Qin and when his state was on the verge of extinction, he committed suicide by drowning himself in a river.

Unlike poets before his time who were anonymous, Qu Yuan was the first poet to leave his name in the history of Chinese literature. His works exerted tremendous influence on the development of Chinese literature.

Chapter VI
The Qin and Han Dynasties: the Growth of Feudal Society

1. The Qin, China's First Feudal Dynasty

Feudal society reached maturity in the Qin and Han dynasties. The Qin Dynasty, the first feudal empire in China, unified the country on a scale unknown in China since the Shang and Zhou dynasties and established a form of government which had a lasting influence on Chinese feudalism. Among the accomplishments of the Qin Dynasty was the construction of the Great Wall. In power only 15 years (c. 221-207 B.C.) through the reigns of two emperors, the Qin Dynasty gave way to four years of Chu-Han conflict before the Han Dynasty was established which lasted over 400 years.

Historians divide the Han Dynasty into Western Han (c. 202 B.C.-A.D. 5) which continued through 11 emperors and an empress regent belonging to ten generations and Eastern Han (c. 25-220) which was ruled by 14 emperors through eight generations. There was a short interval of 18 years between the Western and Eastern Han when Wang Mang, then Liu Xuan ruled. Starting in 196, as the Three Kingdoms—Wei, Shu and Wu—began to evolve, the Han Dynasty existed in name only.

The Qin in 221 B.C. conquered its six rival states (Han, Zhao, Wei, Chu, Yan and Qi) at the end of the Warring States Period, a period in which all seven states contributed to a trend of regional unification. In fact, the Qin was able to prevail not only through war but, more significantly, through this existing unity and its own developed productive forces and political organization. The Qin then further expanded along the lands of the middle and lower Huanghe and

Changjiang rivers, as well as the Zhujiang River.

Given the scope of the Qin domain, King Ying Zheng of Qin decided to give himself a more distinguished title, the First Emperor (Shi Huang Di), and decreed that his successors be titled the Second Emperor, the Third Emperor, and so on. He hoped that the Qin empire would be passed on in this way forever through his descendants. He also devised some exclusive terminology for the emperor's use only in issuing edicts and in addressing himself.

The First Emperor (Qin Shi Huang, as he is generally known) set up a complete autocratic system of state administration extending from the central court to the local levels. In the imperial court, the *cheng xiang* (prime minister) assisted the emperor in governing the country, the *tai wei* (marshal) took charge of military affairs, and the *yu shi* (censor) supervised officials of all ranks. The whole empire was divided into 36 prefectures (later increased to more than 40), each of which comprised a number of counties. These prefectures and counties had officials who were counterparts of the prime minister, marshal and censor at the central level. Under the counties, township officials administered education, justice and taxation, and public security. And under the townships, households, consisting of individual families in which men farmed and women wove at home, were organized in groups of five or ten.

This administrative set-up was like a pyramid. Perched on top, the imperial court extended its control right down to the grass-roots units of the household groups which supplied labour, grains and draftees. The First Emperor understood the basic importance of the individual families to the feudal empire. "Men are satisfied with farming their land and women are engaged at home" was a phrase he coined to describe the foundation of Qin rule.

The prefecture-county system instituted by the First Emperor had gradually evolved in the Spring and Autumn and Warring States periods. This system was different from the feudal fiefdoms in the Western Zhou Dynasty in that, in the first place, the throne and offices held by the nobles in the fiefdoms were hereditary while officials under the prefecture-county system were appointed and dismissed by the imperial court; secondly, the prefectures and counties had to accept orders from the central government which was not necessarily so with the hereditary fiefdoms. Devised to meet the requirements of feudal autocracy, the Qin system was to have a lasting influence on government in China's feudal society. However, records give no details on the extent to which the prefecture-county system was actually carried out during the reign of the First Emperor. For instance, the state of Wei, born in the beginning of the Western Zhou period, disappeared as a state as late as 12 years after the introduction of the Qin government system. This indicates that the First Emperor's new system could not have prevailed in the whole country within a short time.

To rule more effectively, the First Emperor ordered that the written language and weights and measures be standardized. The first step was aimed at simplifying communication in official documents, and the second at making easier the collection of grain, silk and other materials as tax in kind and tribute, and metrological calculations for construction projects. These standards all proved helpful for cultural, production and trade development.

The First Emperor also ordered large-scale road and canal building. Two broad highways with pines planted on both sides, called "imperial chariot roads", were constructed with Xianyang, the capital, as centre, one stretching eastwards through present-day Hebei and Shandong provinces to the sea-coast, and the other southwards to modern Jiangsu and Zhejiang provinces. Roads were also built between Hunan, Jiangxi, Guangdong and Guangxi, and in the remote provinces of Yunnan and Guizhou. The First Emperor ordered his general, Meng Tian, to build another road leading from Xianyang through Yunyang (north of today's Chunhua County in Shaanxi Province) and Shangjun (in north Shaanxi) to Jiuyuan (northwest of present-day Baotou in the Inner Mongolia Autonomous Region). Besides roads, the First Emperor also built the Lingqu Canal, dug in the northeast part of modern Guangxi Zhuang Autonomous Region to connect the Lijiang and Xiangjiang rivers and serve as a passage between the Changjiang and Zhujiang river systems. Although inspired by the military and political needs of the First Emperor, the opening up of land and water routes developed a transport network which furthered communications throughout the country.

The first Emperor took various measures to suppress or forestall anti-Qin activities. He collected and destroyed weapons from the vanquished states. Fortifications that might be of military use, and even some city walls, were demolished. He had 120,000 rich families from all over the country moved to the imperial capital, weakening the old local powers and strengthening the court's command over them. Primarily as a show of strength, he often toured the empire, mostly to the territories of the former states of Qi and Chu.

At a court banquet in 213 B.C., some scholars spoke in favour of the fief system. Li Si, the Prime Minister, held that any dissension over the emperor's decrees could hurt the authority of the sovereign. So he proposed that all historical records in the imperial archives except those written by Qin historians be burned; that the *Book of Odes*, the *Book of History* and works by scholars of different schools be handed in to the local authorities for burning; that anyone discussing these two particular books be executed; that those using ancient examples to satirize contemporary politics be put to death and their families killed; and that those who had not burned the listed books within 30 days of the decree be sentenced to four years' imprisonment. The First Emperor accepted all these proposals to exercise autocratic control over thinking and culture. But critics of the imperial regime were not silenced. In the second year of the burning of books, the First Emperor heard of people criticizing him. Regarding this as slander, he ordered an investigation and finally had more than 460 implicated scholars buried alive.

During the Warring States Period, a powerful nomadic people called the Xiongnu (the Huns) lived north of the states of Qin, Zhao and Yan. To keep out these nomads who often clashed with them, the three states built wall fortifications along their northern frontiers. The First Emperor had these defence works linked together to form the Great Wall extending from Lintao (present-day Minxian County, Gansu Province) in the west to the Liaodong Peninsula in the east. Although this engineering feat did not check the southward invasions of the Xiongnu, it stands as a monument to the knowledge and creative powers of the labouring people in ancient China.

Li Si, the First Emperor's trusted Prime Minister, came from Shangcai (in present-day Henan Province) of the state of Chu. As a Legalist, he was responsible for many of the policies under the feudal dynasty of Qin.

2. Peasant Uprisings in the Late Qin Dynasty

The First Emperor played a progressive role in establishing the unified Qin Dynasty, promoting the growth of social productive forces and developing production. On the other hand, he became increasingly tyrannical. Peasants were forced to fight expeditionary wars, guard frontiers, transport provisions for the army and build the Great Wall. The emperor ordered a string of palaces to be built. For the construction of the Epang (Efang) Palace alone, some 700,000 peasants were conscripted, and the same number laboured to build the First Emperor's mausoleum. Many peasants died working on these projects. Moreover, they never knew when they might be punished at any moment on any pretext under the harsh laws of the Qin Dynasty.

Though progressive in nature compared with slave society, feudal society is a prison for labouring people, especially when a despotic ruler is on the throne. Even though the First Emperor of the Qin was aware of the importance of the individual families to his feudal empire, he enslaved the common people. In his later years, people began to organize against the Qin Dynasty. They were like kindling, ready to be ignited to destory the imperial regime.

In 210 B.C., the First Emperor died in Shaqiu (northeast of modern Pingxiang County, Hebei Province) while on an inspection tour. The eunuch Zhao Gao and Prime Minister Li Si conspired to forge an imperial decree ordering their opponents, the Crown Prince Fu Su, and General Meng Tian, to commit suicide, and declaring as successor the emperor's second son, Hu Hai, who was then placed on the throne as the Second Emperor. Zhao Gao encouraged the new emperor to indulge in debauchery and to deal harshly with those he disliked or suspected. All this sharpened the class contradictions in society and the contradictions within the ranks of the ruling class. Not to mention the labouring people, many members of the imperial house, many ministers and even some of the First Emperor's sons and daughters were

A stone fresco of the tilling of land by oxen-drawn plough (unearthed in Mizhi County, Shaanxi Province)

A fishing, hunting and harvesting scene carved on brick (unearthed in Yangzishan, Chengdu City, Sichuan Province)

A market scene on brick (unearthed in Guanghan County, Sichuan Province)

Confucius (551- 479 AD)

A chime of bells from the Warring States Period (unearthed in Leigudun, Suixian County, Hubei Province)

The present-day Dujiang Dam in Guanxian County, Sichuan Province

A cortege of terracotta warriors at Qin Shihuang's mausoleum (unearthed in Lintong County, Shaanxi Province)

A Western Han Dynasty gauzy jacket, which is as fine as cicada's wings and weighs only 49 grams (unearthed from a tomb at Mawangdui, Changsha, Hunan Province)

A lacquered container with images of the Twenty-eight Constellations (unearthed in Leigudun, Suixian County, Hubei Province)

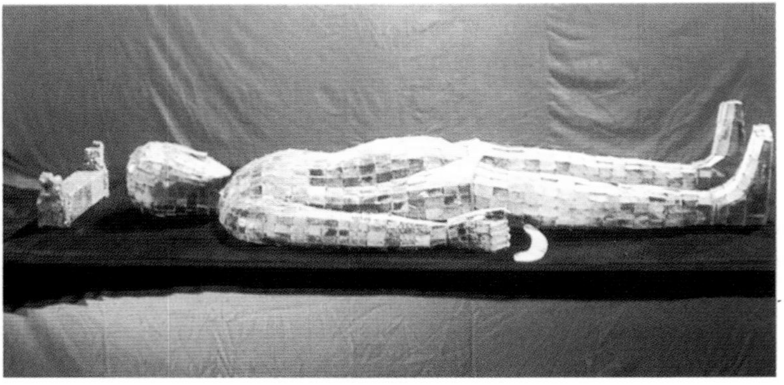

A Western Han jade suit sewn with gold thread (unearthed from Liu Sheng's tomb in Mancheng, Hebei Province)

Lao Zi (said to have lived at the end of the Spring and Autumn Period)

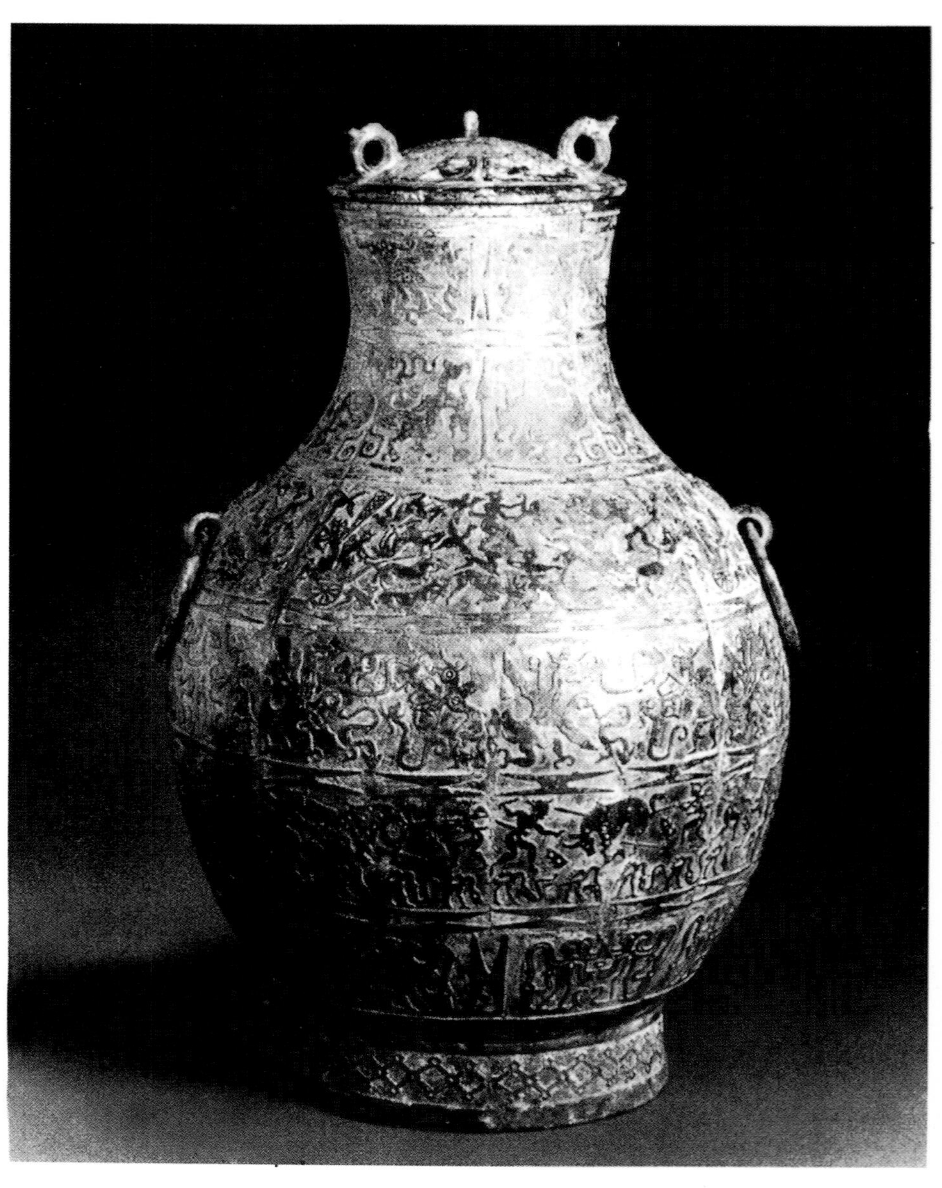

A wine container from the early Warring States Period, engraved with hunting designs

An astronomical painting on silk from the Han Dynasty (unearthed from a tomb at Mawangdui, Changsha, Hunan Province)

Designs on a bronze wine container unearthed in Baihuatan, Chengdu City, Sichuan Province

A tiger-shaped tally from the State of Qin
(unearthed in the suburbs of Xi'an, Shaanxi Province)

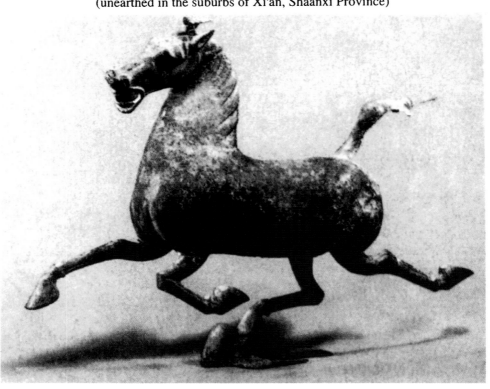

Bronze horse—god of the wind
(unearthed in Leitai, Wuwei, Gansu Province)

killed. In 209 B.C., when the Second Emperor had been barely 10 months on the throne, Chen Sheng and Wu Guang hoisted the anti-Qin standard at the head of an insurgent peasant army.

Chen Sheng, whose other name was Chen She, was a native of Yangcheng (southeast of modern Dengfeng County, Henan Province) while Wu Guang, also known as Wu Shu, came from Yangxia (modern Taikang County, also in Henan). Chen and Wu were among the 900 conscripted peasants assembled in Daze Township (part of today's Suxian County in Anhui Province). While heading for Yuyang (in modern Miyun County, Beijing), they were delayed by heavy rain that made the roads impassable, which meant they could not arrive on time. The law required those failing to report on time to be executed. At this point, Chen Sheng and Wu Guang considered their options. According to the Han Dynasty historian, Sima Qian, in his *Records of the Historian*, Wu argued: "Since we will have to die anyway, why not rise in revolt?" And Chen said, "the common people have suffered more than enough. So we have only to raise the standard of rebellion for them to answer like an echo." They then thought up a plan to lay the foundation for an uprising.

Not long afterwards, one of the conscripts found in the belly of a fish he had bought a piece of silk with the vermilion characters, "Chen Sheng will be the king". This amazed the other conscripts. Late that night, somebody saw a sort of will-o'-the-wisp in a temple in the nearby woods and then heard, amid a howl like a fox, a voice saying, "The great State of Chu has been restored. Chen Sheng has become its king." The voice was so loud that it woke the peasant conscripts. When they saw Chen Sheng the next morning, they quietly exchanged remarks about him. And so he became the centre of attention.

One day, Wu Guang intentionally quarrelled with the officer in charge of the conscripts when the officer was drunk. The infuriated man beat Wu and threatened him by drawing his sword. Wu seized his weapon and killed him. Meanwhile, Chen Sheng killed two other officers. Then, again according to the historian Sima Qian, Chen and Wu said to the other conscripts, "We were delayed by rain and will be executed according to law. Even though we are able to survive this time, we would most likely die when we are put on guard duty later on.

We will die like men and for a worthy cause, if we have to. We can be great men, too. For no kings, dukes, generals and ministers are such by birth." The soldiers responded by vowing to fight together for the overthrow of the Qin Dynasty and made Chen their general and Wu their field commander.

The anti-Qin war led by Chen Sheng and Wu Guang was the first large-scale peasant rebellion ever recorded in Chinese history. The idea advanced by Chen, that royalty, officers and ministers were not so by birth, was a revolutionary political thought negating the idea of hereditary aristocracy that had been in existence since the Shang and Zhou dynasties.

Having first occupied Daze, Qi (south of present-day Suxian in Anhui) and several other neighbouring towns, the insurgent army took Chenxian County (modern Huaiyang County in Henan). Now it had 600-700 war chariots, more than 1,000 mounted soldiers and several tens of thousands of foot soldiers. The insurgents set up the state of Zhang Chu and made Chen Sheng king. Peasants all over the country responded, rising and killing local officials. Chen's army quickly grew.

Basing himself in Chenxian County, Chen Sheng divided his forces for attacks on government-held areas. One route, commanded by Wu Guang, launched an attack on the strategically important Xingyang (in modern Henan). Another route, under Wu Cheng, Zhang Er and Chen Yu, crossed the Huanghe River and advanced on Hebei Province. A third route, directed by Zhou Wen, pushed towards the imperial capital of Xianyang. Many smaller detachments of peasant insurgents occupied lesser towns.

Zhou Wen's troops swiftly expanded their ranks along the way until they numbered several hundred thousand armed men with 1,000 war chariots. Crossing the Hangu Pass (southwest of modern Lingbao County, Henan Province), they came to the Xishui River (east of modern Lintong County, Shaanxi Province) in the vicinity of Xianyang. But they failed to withstand the counter-attacks by the imperial army under General Zhang Han. Badly defeated, Zhou Wen fled to Mianchi (west of the modern county of the same name in Henan) with Zhang in hot pursuit. Finally, he committed suicide, and his troops scattered. Zhang followed up his victory by marching eastwards to Xingyang. By then Wu Guang had been killed by a subordinate named Tian Zang. Zhang defeated Tian's detachment, occupied Xingyang and approached Chenxian. Chen Sheng retreated to Chengfu (northwest of present-day Mengcheng County in Anhui), where he was murdered by a carriage driver. This was in the beginning of 208 B.C., only six months after the outbreak of his uprising.

Though the rebellious army suffered setbacks in Zhou Wen's defeat and Chen Sheng's murder, the movement went on to bring down the Qin regime in less than two years after Chen's death.

After Chen, two men—Xiang Yu and Liu Bang—emerged as leaders of the two strongest peasant forces. With the defeat of the Qin, they would become rivals themselves for power. Liu, a native of Peixian County (in modern Jiangsu Province), came from a peasant family (or the family of a small landlord, according to other historical records). Responding to the call of Chen Sheng and Wu Guang, he gathered a number of peasant rebels around himself and occupied his native county with the help of Xiao He and Cao Can, local petty officials. Unlike Xiang Yu, who slaughtered people in the cities he captured and killed surrendering enemy soldiers and commanders, Liu Bang respected the welfare of the people and treated well those Qin military commanders who surrendered. Xiang Yu was a noble of the former state of Chu and his uncle, Xiang Liang, was the son of a Chu general named Xiang Yan. Uncle and nephew staged an uprising in Guiji (modern Suzhou in Jiangsu Province) and then led 8,000 men northwards across the Changjiang River. Learning of the death of Chen Sheng, they put the grandson of King Huai of the former state of Chu on the throne and addressed him as "King Huai of Chu". They allied themselves with some other insurgent forces, including those under Liu Bang, and quickly gained in influence and prestige.

Growing arrogant and off guard in his northward march against the Qin empire, Xiang Liang was defeated and killed in Dingtao (in modern Shandong Province) after the Qin general Zhang Han hit his army in a surprise attack. Soon afterwards, Zhang surrounded the peasant force in Julu (modern Pingxiang County in Hebei). Song Yi and Xiang Yu were ordered by King Huai to lead their troops to the rescue of the encircled rebels. However, Song refused to advance after arriving at Anyang (in modern Henan Province), whereupon Xiang Yu had him executed. Then Xiang led his unit across the Zhanghe River where—to make clear that no one could turn back unless victorious—he had all the boats and cooking vessels destroyed and ordered his soldiers to carry enough rations for only three days. With this mandate, the rebel soldiers drove forward with resounding battle cries against Zhang Han's army. After nine engagements, in which the peasant army pitted one against ten, the imperial army was routed and Zhang Han surrendered with his 200,000 remaining forces. This marked the virtual annihilation of the military strength of the Qin Dynasty.

When Song Yi was advancing north, Liu Bang was marching west, also on the order of King Huai of Chu. He fought his way forward almost unopposed. In a year's time his troops took the Wuguan Pass (west of modern Shaanxian, Henan), gateway to the heartland of the Qin regime, threatening the capital city of Xianyang. It was during this period that the Qin Prime Minister, Li Si, died at the hands of his eunuch colleague Zhao Gao, who also murdered the Second Emperor and placed the emperor's nephew, Zi Ying, on the throne. Before long, Zi Ying, who assumed the title "King of Qin" instead of the Third Emperor, had the chief eunuch killed. Then Liu Bang laid siege to the imperial capital, forcing Zi Ying to surrender at Bashang (east of modern Xi'an in Shaanxi). This finished the Qin regime in the winter of 207 B.C. and marked for the first time in Chinese history the overthrow of a feudal dynasty by peasant insurgents.

3. Establishment and Consolidation of the Western Han Dynasty

Following the downfall of the Qin Dynasty, the struggle for power began among the leaders of the victorious rebel armies. Although Liu Bang prevailed in 202 B.C. to become the first emperor of the Han Dynasty, the struggle to establish and consolidate the feudal dynasty of Han went on about 66 years (207-141 B.C.), beginning with Liu Bang's entry into Xianyang and going through the reigns of Emperor Hui Di, Empress Lü, Emperor Wen Di and Emperor Jing Di. A characteristic of these early days of the Western Han Dynasty was that the emperor and most of his subordinate rulers were of humble origin, a marked change—which proved Chen Sheng's view that royalty was not a matter of birthright—in China's political life from the time of the Shang and Zhou dynasties. After he entered Xianyang, Liu Bang declined with thanks all gifts presented by the people as a token of respect to his army and further won acclaim by assembling the local people to announce the repeal of the harsh laws of the Qin government. He wanted them to observe only this law: "Let those who kill be executed, and those who inflict injuries on or rob others be punished." This announcement was of great political significance in that it reflected the popular demand of the time for personal safety and the right to survival.

Liu Bang's first confrontation with Xiang Yu following the overthrow of the Qin Dynasty came when Xiang Yu reached the Hangu Pass. Earlier, King Huai of Chu had promised the territory west of the pass to the first man who entered it. Having had the good fortune to be that man, Liu Bang made himself supreme in the region and ordered his men to guard against intrusions by other forces. When Xiang Yu reached there with an army of 400,000—claimed to be a million strong—and found his way barred, he was furious and prepared to attack Liu Bang. Because Liu Bang had only 100,000 men, he was forced to sue for peace. This helped to stabilize the situation for the time being.

A few days later, Xiang Yu marched into Xianyang where he slaughtered people and burned houses. The fires raged for three months. He called himself the "Hegemonic King of Western Chu" and made Pengcheng (now Xuzhou, Jiangsu) the capital of his dominion. He called King Huai "Righteous Emperor", but later got rid of him while King Huai was being moved from Pengcheng to Chenxian (in present-day Hunan). Altogether, Xiang Yu named 18 princes, some of whom, however, were given territories much smaller than their former domains. With regard to Liu Bang, he ignored the promise of King Huai and accorded him, instead, the title of "Prince of Han", with a diminished fief covering Hanzhong, Ba and Shu. In making these allocations, Xiang Yu aggravated the contradiction between himself and Liu Bang, as well as the armed forces under others.

In 206 B.C., within less than six months after Xiang Yu had granted fiefdoms to the various princes, Liu Bang marched east from Hanzhong and took the Hangu Pass and the area west of it. The following year, he attacked Xiang Yu with the collaboration of other armies, with a combined force of 560,000 men. He entered Pengcheng but was thoroughly defeated when Xiang Yu counter-attacked. Liu Bang escaped with a few scores of his cavalrymen. This was followed up by fierce battles between the two sides, centring on Xingyang and Chenggao (the Hulaoguan Pass to the northwest of today's Xingyang, Henan). In 203 B.C., Liu Bang seized Chenggao and surrounded Xingyang. By then, his army had gained superioity, thanks to ample provisions and increased morale, while Xiang's army suffered from lack of supplies and decreased morale. Liu took this opportunity to make peace with his rival. An agreement was reached that Honggou ("Deep Chasm") Canal (in modern Zhongmou, Henan) be made the demarcation line, with the territory on the east going to Chu and on the west to Han. When Xiang Yu led his men back eastwards, Liu Bang ordered a surprise attack on him in Guling (northwest of modern Huaiyang, Henan), only to be routed. Later, Liu Bang joined hands with Han Xin and Peng Yue and surrounded Xiang Yu in Gaixia (southeast of modern Lingbi, Anhui). Xiang Yu's army had decreased in number and was now running out of provisions. But he managed to collect 800 cavalrymen and fight his way to a ferry named Wujiang (modern Wujiangpu northeast of Hexian, Anhui) where, in the year 202 B.C. at the age of 32, he committed suicide.

With his chief rival gone, Liu Bang proceeded to build his feudal dynasty, i.e., the feudal regime of the Western Han Dynasty. He ascended the throne two months after Xiang Yu's death, to become known posthumously as Emperor Gao Zu of the Han Dynasty. He first chose Luoyang as his capital but shortly afterwards moved it to Chang'an. Liu Bang had the valuable help of "the Three Heroes of the Early Han": Xiao He, a native of Fengxian (in modern Jiangsu), who was made Prime Minister; Zhang Liang, the chief counsellor, who was a descendant of a noble family in the former state of Han; and Grand

General Han Xin, who came from Huaiyin (also in modern Jiangsu).

During its first 60 years, the Western Han rulers took two major steps to consolidate their feudal regime. The first step was taken in the economic field, aimed to alleviate class contradictions and ensure revenue for the imperial treasury so as to strengthen the foundation of the empire. The second step was to eliminate the menace which the fiefdoms presented to the imperial court.

Fifteen years of ruthless oppression and exploitation under the Qin Dynasty, followed by eight years of incessant wars, caused a heavy toll on the common people. Population in major cities dwindled by 70-80 per cent, and people could barely make both ends meet. Even the emperor couldn't find four horses of the same colour to draw his carriage; the prime minister and generals had to travel in cars drawn by oxen. In this situation, the need for restoring and developing society's productive forces was more than obvious.

The emperors, from Emperor Gao Zu down to Emperor Jing Di, all devoted themselves to this task. In half a century or more, population in some areas doubled or even showed a five-fold increase. Life in general became easier for the peasants. Landlords gained much more and could even get official ranks according to the amount of grain they voluntarily delivered to the frontier regions and grain-deficient areas. During the reign of Emperor Wen Di, two economists, Jia Yi and Chao Cuo, developed theories which were to become the basis of the economic thinking of landlord-class statesmen for centuries. Jia Yi (200-168 B.C.), a native of Luoyang who wrote *New Political Views*, advanced the idea that agriculture was the foundation of the nation, and that only when grain was in abundant supply could an offensive or defensive war be fought with success. Chao Cuo (?-154 B.C.), a native of Yingchuan (modern Yuxian County, Henan), proposed measures against commerce in favour of agriculture. He also maintained that the peasants should be attached to the land to enable the feudal state to win their support and thus consolidate its power. The ideas of Jia Yi and Chao Cuo were clearly an advance on the thinking of Shang Yang of the Warring States Period.

After the founding of the dynasty, the Western Han ruling clique was worried about the growth of the power of the various fiefdoms, particularly seven principalities under men who were not members of the imperial Liu family. The administrative system consisted of prefectures and counties as well as fiefdoms, including principalities and marquisates. In the principalities the officials, except for the prime minister, were all appointed by the princes. Each principality might embrace from 30 to more than 100 towns, and during the early days of the Western Han, the combined territory of the seven abovementioned principalities was greater than the prefectures and counties directly under central authority. Among the princes were Han Xin, an outstanding strategist, and Peng Yue and Ying Bu, who were excellent generals. Each of them had made important contributions to the founding of the dynasty. What worried the imperial court most was that they all had armed forces of their own. In 196 B.C., Han Xin was killed by the throne, as were Peng Yue and Ying Bu afterwards. Three other princes either escaped or were displaced so that by the time immediately before Liu Bang's death in 195 B.C., principalities controlled by those not bearing the royal surnames had practically been wiped out. Only the principality of Changsha remained, but it came to an end in 157 B.C. when the prince died without issue.

Hoping to perpetuate the supremacy of the imperial court, Liu Bang installed nine princes of royal blood to head fiefdoms formerly under persons who were not members of the royal family. He regarded this as representing his ideal that "the whole empire is under one family". He commanded, "Let anyone not of the Liu family who dares proclaim himself prince suffer universal attack." But the territories of the Liu princes were also extensive and their power formidable. Their fiefdoms grew in economic strength with rises in productivity. So the principalities still posed a threat to the central government. In 177 B.C., Liu Xingju, Prince of Jibei, rebelled. In 174 B.C., Liu Zhang, Prince of Huainan, also plotted a rebellion. These events took place less than 20 years after the death of Liu Bang, during the reign of Emperor Wen Di (180-157 B.C.).

The scholar Jia Yi recommended to the court that more princes be installed in each principality to divide its strength. In regard to the powerful fiefs, Jia Yi made an analogy to the body of a person who had swollen and could hardly move because both legs had become as thick as the waist and the fingers as big as the arms. He argued that by installing more princes the central authority could control all of the principalities in the same way as a person controls his limbs. Jia Yi's proposal was accepted and put into practice, though no serious effort was ever made for its thorough implementation. During the reign of Emperor Jing Di (157-141 B.C.), Chao Cuo proposed reducing the territories of the various fiefdoms, and this was carried out. He predicted that such a measure would invite resistance on the part of the kings, but argued: "There will be revolts, whether you cut their territories or not. Cutting their territories will quickly lead to revolts which might bring smaller calamities in their wake, while not cutting them will only delay revolts which, once they occur, may entail greater calamities."

In 154 B.C. Liu Bi, Prince of Wu, in alliance with the kingdoms of Chu, Zhao, Jiaodong, Jiaoxi, Jinan and Zichuan, staged a revolt, which he had been plotting for a long time, in the name of getting rid of Chao Cuo. Emperor Jing Di responded by sending Marshal Zhou Yafu on a punitive expedition which was successful within less than three months. Taking advantage of this victory, the emperor took steps to relieve the princes of their administrative powers, reduce the number of officials in the principalities and change the title of their prime ministers to minister. These steps drastically restricted the power of the princes while strengthening the imperial government.

4. Golden Age of the Western Han Dynasty

In 139 B.C., Emperor Wu Di succeeded to the throne to rule until his death in 87 B.C., a reign that became known as the golden age of the Western Han Dynasty. Socio-economic conditions had already taken a marked change for the better, thanks to the gradual rehabilitation of the social productive forces during the preceding 60 or so years. Historical records say that in those days most people were decently fed and clad, granaries were filled to overflowing, and the state budget showed a surplus. Countless strings of cash were stored in the imperial treasury, tied by cords mildewed with age.

Emperor Wu Di took further steps to weaken the local authorities and strengthen the hands of the central government, carrying out the recommendation made by Jia Yi in the time of Emperor Wen Di. He decreed that when a prince died, his eldest son by his first wife was to succeed him, and the territory of his principality was to be divided among all of his sons who would thus be co-heirs of their father and, with the exception of the eldest son, each would be granted the status of a marquis. This meant that the power of the principalities was dispersed without their enfeoffed land being taken back by the imperial court. The emperor divided the whole country, including the prefectures and fiefdoms, into 13 regions. To tighten control over the localities, he appointed an itinerant inspector for each of these regions to keep a watchful eye on the powerful families as well as the prefects and the ministers of the various fiefdoms. At the imperial court a secretariat was set up to handle the memorials presented by court ministers. This reinforced the autocratic monarchy in that it stripped the prime minister of his power to handle such papers.

In economic matters, Emperor Wu Di enlisted the services of Sang Hongyang on whose suggestion a series of measures were adopted to increase state revenues and curtail the financial pressures put on the central government by local authorities. By law anyone could engage in minting coins, boiling salt and smelting iron without restrictions. In reality, however, these rights were monopolized by the rich, the princes and the influential ministers to victimize the peasants and disrupt social economy. Emperor Wu Di decreed a state monopoly on mintage—all five-*zhu** coins were to be made by the central government—and forbade minting by local authorities or individuals. Government offices were set up in specified places for state sales of iron and salt. Offices handling tribute from various districts were also established. They picked the goods which could easily be damaged and those involving a high cost of transportation, shipped them to needy areas, and sold them at high prices, the profit going to the state. Official departments in the capital were created to buy up certain sur-

**Zhu* was a unit of weight in ancient China. During Han Dynasty, 24 *zhu* made a *liang* (tael), and 16 *liang* made a *jin* (catty).—*Trans.*

plus commodities when prices fell and to sell them at higher prices when there was a scarcity.

In 119 B.C., Emperor Wu Di imposed a heavier property tax on merchants and usurers. Handicraftsmen were required to pay one unit of tax (120 copper coins) on every 4,000 copper coins' worth of possessions while the merchants had to pay two units of tax for the same amount. The common people paid one unit of tax for each horse-drawn cart they owned, as compared to two units for the merchants. Merchants were also ordered to send in an account on their property. Anyone giving a false report had his property confiscated and was sent to guard duty on the frontiers for two years. Huge quantities of property and large numbers of bondservants and houses belonging to merchants were expropriated.

The economic measures instituted by Emperor Wu Di helped to strengthen the autocratic monarchy. Meanwhile, he also broadened his dynasty's relations with the ethnic minorities to an extent never seen before. The Xiongnu (Hun) nomads were very powerful in the initial period of the Western Han. In 200 B.C., Liu Bang was even hemmed in by them in Pingcheng (modern Datong City, Shanxi Province) for seven days and nights and broke through only after strenuous effort. Rebellious forces within the Western Han ruling clique also allied themselves with the Xiongnu to oppose the court.

The chief policy to prevent Xiongnu invasion in the early years of the Western Han Dynasty was to try to maintain peace by arranging marriages between the royal family and the Xiongnu chieftains or sending enormous quantities of gifts. But this had been unsuccessful and Emperor Wu Di tried a new tact. He repeatedly sent Generals Wei Qing and Huo Qubing on large-scale expeditions against the Xiongnu, forcing them to move to the far north so that it became impossible for them to re-establish their rule south of the Gobi. Of course, war could not resolve the differences between the Han Dynasty and the various groups. Nevertheless, these expeditions dealt a crushing blow to the intruders from the north and thus defended the agricultural regions in the Central Plains.

To conquer the Xiongnu, Emperor Wu Di planned to form an alliance with the Dayuezhi, which would make possible a converging attack on them from the east and west. Originally living in the Gansu Corridor, the Dayuezhi had been driven to Daxia (Bactria) in the north part of modern Afghanistan. In the beginning of his reign, Emperor Wu Di sent Zhang Qian as envoy to the land of the Dayuezhi, but he was captured en route by the Xiongnu. He was kept prisoner for more than 10 years before managing to escape to make his way to his destination where, however, he failed to achieve his mission. In 119 B.C., Zhang Qian was again chosen as the Han emissary, this time to the land of the Wusun who were settled in the Ili River valley. His aim was to form a common front with this people to cut the right flank of the Xiongnu. Though Zhang Qian failed a second time, his visits promoted understanding between the Western Han Dynasty and the regions north and south of the Tianshan Mountains. The countries there began to send goodwill missions to the Han court, which on its part opened up military colonies for land reclamation along their frontiers. All this helped to spread the influence of the Han empire and to cement its links with adjoining regions.

The ethnic minorities in Sichuan, Yunnan and Guizhou provinces were then collectively known as the Southwestern Yi. Some of them—for instance, the Yelang people around modern Zunyi City in Guizhou and the Dian people near what is now Kunming City in Yunnan—already had entered a slave society. During Emperor Wu Di's reign, prefectural and county governments were set up in these regions, and the chieftain of the Dian was elevated to the status of king and given a royal seal. As a result, contacts increased further between southwest China and the interior.

The reign of Emperor Wu Di also saw new developments in China's foreign relations. Zhang Qian's journeys marked the beginning of contacts between China and some countries of Central and West Asia. He and his deputies reached the countries of Dayuan (Ferghana, in the eastern part of the Uzbekistan), Kangju (along the lower reaches of Syr Darya in Kazakhstan), Daxia (Bactria), Anxi (Parthia, or modern Iran) and Yuandu (the modern Indian Subcontinent). From then on, the Han court every year sent from five to a dozen missions to the West, each including one to several hundred members. After Zhang Qian's westward trips, many Han products, notably silks, were brought to the Western countries. And introduced to China were thoroughbreds, grape vines, pomegranates, glazed tiles, woollen carpets, etc. Sea routes were charted to link China with Korea and Japan. At the time, merchant ships sailed between China's Xuwen County (in present-day Guangdong Province) and Hepu County (in modern Guangxi) on the one hand, and India's east coast and some Southeast Asian ports on the other.

Emperor Wu Di's period witnessed significant academic and cultural achievements. It was in his time that Confucianism gained supremacy as the ideological weapon of the feudal dynasties.

Emperor Wu Di was keenly interested in literature. Among those attending to him were some famous men of letters, for example, Yan Zhu, Dongfang Shuo, Mei Gao and Sima Xiangru. Sima Xiangru (179-118 B.C.), a native of Chengdu in modern Sichuan Province, excelled in writing prose-poems which had developed out of the songs of the state of Chu. His representative prose-poems include *Zi Xu Fu* and *Shang Lin Fu,* both masterpieces in the Western Han time. During Emperor Wu Di's reign, *yuefu* poems appeared. (*Yuefu* was an official department of music whose duty was to collect and process folk songs.) These poems were composed of sentences of varying lengths, common for folk songs of the Han time, and were intended to be set to music and song at the imperial court. However, more of the folk songs of the Han Dynasty consisted of five-character lines.

Sima Qian (c. 145-90 B.C.), from Longmen (modern Hancheng County in Shaanxi Province), was a great historian in the time of Emperor Wu Di. His major work, *Records of the Historian*, is a 130-*juan*[*] general history of China which describes legends from the time of the mythical Emperor Huang Di (the Yellow Emperor), events in the Shang and Zhou dynasties, upheavals of the Spring and Autumn and Warring States periods, the rise and fall of the Qin Dynasty and the birth and consolidation of the Han Dynasty. *Records of the Historian* is unique in its accounts on different historical stages and their characteristics, its

---

[*] A traditional thread-bound volume, usually containing a much shorter text than a volume in modern book publishing.—*Trans.*

portrayal and appraisal of historical figures and its description of social conditions. Sima Qian showed originality in editing historical data and working out a style for historical writings. Though he regarded emperors, kings, generals and ministers as the creators of history, he was progressive in recognizing the role played by the people, such as in the peasant uprisings, in the making of history. He also recognized the influence of social status in determining individual consciousness. His writings had a tremendous impact on later Chinese historiography.

Despite the burning of books in the Qin Dynasty, the teachings of the various schools that had emerged in the not too distant Warring States Period continued to spread in the early Han Dynasty. In 140 B.C.—that is, not long after Emperor Wu Di's ascension—Dong Zhongshu (c. 179-104 B.C.) proposed that task of the "grand unification" of the empire in political philosophy, and consequently the institution of an ideological system serving the autocratic feudal regime. Emperor Wu Di accepted his proposal, adopted Confucianism as official philosophy, and denied scholars of all other schools the opportunity to enter the civil service. Confucian classics gradually became the main reading of scholars, and Confucianism became predominant. Comparing social to natural phenomena formalistically, Dong Zhongshu theorized that the relationship between ruler and subject was something eternal, a natural order. He advanced the doctrine of the "Three Cardinal Guides", which later Confucians summarized as "the sovereign guides the subject, the father guides the son, and the husband guides the wife". The mainstay of Confucianism, these were a severe mental constraint on the masses of people in the long years of feudal society. Dong Zhongshu, a native of Guangchuan (to the southwest of modern Jingxian County in Hebei Province), had a number of books to his credit, among them the *Chun Qiu Fan Lu* (*Spring and Autumn Studies*).

To suit the needs of building a feudal autocratic dynasty, Emperor Wu Di organized many battles and launched a series of big engineering projects. He made repeated inspection tours, gave generous gifts to his favourites and formulated harsh laws. Things became more and more intolerable for the common people until, in his late years, a number of uprisings broke out in Shandong Province. When Emperor Wu Di died in 87 B.C., he was succeeded by Emperor Zhao Di who was then only eight years old and had to be assisted by Grand General Huo Guang, Chancellor of Military Affairs.[1]

In 74 B.C., Emperor Xuan Di ascended to the throne. He paid great attention to improving the local administration and, according to historical records, "officials were competent, and the people pursued their occupations peacefully" during his reign. This period was marked by sharpening differences within the Xiongnu tribe so that in 54 B.C., it split into two sections, the northern and the southern. Huhanye, Chieftain of the Southern Xiongnu, occupied the whole tribal territory after the Han had defeated the Northern Xiongnu. Since he had pledged allegiance to the Han court the next 40 years or more were a period of rapprochement between the Han empire and the Xiongnu.

Emperor Xuan Di carried on the cause of Emperor Wu Di, maintaining the power and prosperity created by his predecessors. Though he greatly valued the services of the Confucians, he spoke his mind when he said, "The Han house knows how to rule the country, that is, by combining the hegemon's way and the king's way." He was referring to government by the Legalist method, by force and political trickery, and to government by the Confucian method, by conquering the minds of the ruled. These dual tactics were to be employed by the rulers of the succeeding feudal regimes.

5. Decline of the Western Han Dynasty; Uprisings of the Green Woodsmen and Red Eyebrows

In 48 B.C., Emperor Yuan Di came to the throne. His reign, fol-

[1] The official titles in the Western Han Dynasty were inherited from those of the Qin Dynasty, during which the prime minister, the chancellor of military affairs and the great censor were the three top officials. In the later period of the Western Han, the chancellor of military affairs who was concurrently the grand general became the top man in charge of both civil and military affairs.

lowed by those of Emperors Cheng Di, Ai Di and Ping Di, marked the beginning of the decline of the Western Han until in 6 A.D., Wang Mang, a nephew of the wife of Emperor Yuan Di, usurped the throne and three years later founded the Xin Dynasty. Not long afterwards, peasant uprisings broke out throughout the country which led to Wang Mang's downfall, the restoration of the Han regime in A.D. 25 and the period Chinese historians call the Eastern Han Dynasty.

Giving high official positions to family members of the empresses was a tradition of the Han period. From the time of Liu Bang through the reigns of Empress Lü and Emperor Wu Di to those of Emperors Zhao Di and Xuan Di, the influence of the relatives of the court women increased continuously. When Emperor Yuan Di was on the throne, palace eunuchs Hong Gong and Shi Xian collaborated with the Shis and Xus, all relatives on the empress, side, in controlling the government. Family members of Empress Wang also began to interfere in state affairs until they became a dominant group in the time of Emperor Cheng Di. During the period of Emperor Ping Di, who was only 9 years old when placed on the throne, Empress Wang assumed the reins of government as one belonging to the generation of the reigning emperor's grandmother.* As the old lady's nephew Wang Mang was appointed Chancellor of Military Affairs who was also in charge of civil administration throughout the empire. Emperor Ping Di became a puppet of Wang, who poisoned the youth to death five years later. In A.D. 6, Wang was made imperial regent and took charge of the government as "Substitute Emperor". He proclaimed himself emperor proper in A.D. 9 and named his regime the Xin Dynasty.

Wang Mang was aided by a mystical theory of the time following Emperor Yuan Di's rule which indicated some lack of confidence in the future of the Western Han Dynasty and which helped prepare public opinion for the usurping of power by a careerist. The theory held that no dynasty could exist forever because, by the mandate of Heaven, another one sooner or later would emerge to replace it. This led some

*Empress Wang was the Queen of Emperor Yuan Di and the mother of Emperor Cheng Di. As Emperor Cheng Di had no son, two nephews were chosen successively to become Emperor Ai Di and Ping Di.—*Trans.*

people to comment that the Han house was nearing its end and that it was time to hand over power to others.

After the reign of Yuan Di, the difference between rich and poor in terms of property became even more glaring than before. Appropriation of land by influential officials and nobles meant misery for the peasants who, moreover, had to shoulder many other burdens. In the first years of the rule of Emperor Yuan Di, 11 prefectures and fiefdoms suffered floods in which the common people faced starvation. But the feudal nobles, the wealthy landlords and merchants, and corrupt officials continued to lead a life of luxury and debauchery. Class contradictions intensified in the time of Emperor Cheng Di which witnessed a number of uprisings by peasants in different regions and by prisoners doing hard labour. The social crisis grew even more serious during the reign of Emperor Ai Di. Feudal oppression threatened the personal freedom and even the lives of the common people, relegating the difference between rich and poor to a secondary place. Country-wide peasant uprisings could break out any moment.

The Western Han Dynasty achieved little in the academic field during the years following Emperor Yuan Di's rule. But among the famous scholars of the time were Liu Xiang (79-8 B.C.), Liu Xin (?-A.D. 23) and Yang Xiong (53 B.C.-A.D. 18), all of whom had great achievements to their credit. When Emperor Cheng Di was on the throne, Liu Xiang, of imperial ancestry, was ordered to collate important books kept in the imperial library, such as the Confucian classics, works of the different schools of thought written in the pre-Qin period, collections of poems and prose-poems and military and medical writings. He wrote a report to the emperor about each book collated, listing its contents and giving a synopsis of it. During the period of Emperor Ai Di, Liu Xin, son of Liu Xiang, took over his father's job. He classified all the books under seven headings and briefly described the contents of each, and the summaries were later incorporated into the *Seven Categories of Writings*. The painstaking efforts of the Lius contributed to the preservation, classification and dissemination of China's ancient works. Though Liu Xiang and his son propagted the mystical theory on the non-permanence of dynasties, they took differing political stands on it. The father used mysticism as a means of remonstrating with Emperor Cheng Di on the need to guard against the ambitious family members of Empress Dowager Wang, while the son spread such views to help Wang Mang seize power from the Han house.

A native of Chengdu, Yang Xiong wrote *Tai Xuan*, a book on philosophy modelled after *The Book of Changes*, and *Fa Yan*, which was an exposition of Confucianism modelled after *The Analects*. Though his writings were not innovative, he did disagree with the theory that there was a "God" who controlled everything on earth. He was progressive in as much as he opposed the prevalent mysticism.

Having usurped the throne, Wang Mang carried out successive reforms of the officials system, currency, land tenures, taxation and state monopolies of commodities. Most of his new measures were impractical, and some were merely copied from books of antiquity. Because the reforms were too numerous and revised too frequently, general uncertainty was felt in society. This presented an opportunity for the officials to swindle and oppress the people who were liable to be declared guilty on trumped-up charges, which meant bankruptcy, imprisonment and even death. To flaunt his power and prestige, Wang Mang repeatedly organized provocative activities against the ethnic minorities in north and southwest China. Apart from worsening the friendly relations between China's various ethnic groups, this increased the burdens on the people in the Central Plains who had to do conscripted labour more and more often. Many peasants went bankrupt as a consequence.

Peasant uprisings gathered momentum in A.D. 17 when Lü Mu of Haiqu (to the west of modern Rizhao County, Shandong Province) led the local peasants in taking up arms. In Xinshi (to the northwest of modern Jingshan County, Hubei Province), peasant insurgents under Wang Kuang and Wang Feng joined forces with those in the neighbouring areas. Making Lülin (Green-Wooded) Hills (modern Dangyang County, Hubei Province) their operational base, they became one of the most well-known insurgent groups in Chinese history and are referred to in history as the Greenwood Army. The following year, Fan Chong of Langya (modern Zhucheng County, Shandong Province), led an uprising at Ju (modern Juxian County, Shandong). With its headquarters in Mt. Taishan, his contingent quickly grew to be several tens of thousands strong. Called the army of the Red Eyebrows because their brows were painted red as a mark of identification, this group, too, is well-known in Chinese history. Meanwhile, scores of big and small insurgent groups rose on the great plain in present-day Hebei and Shandong provinces north of the Huanghe River. At Yuan (modern Nanyang City, Henan Province), 7,000-8,000 peasants led by Liu Xiu and his older brother Liu Yan hoisted the banner of reconstructing the Han empire.

The armies of the Green Woodsmen and the Red Eyebrows were the largest among the peasant armed forces of the period. Later, Liu Xiu's men and a number of Lü Mu's men joined hands with the Green Woodsmen and the Red Eyebrows respectively. Among the Green Woodsmen there were some landlord elements, like Liu Xiu, a native of Caiyang County (modern Zaoyang County, Hubei) and his brother who were both scions of the Han house. On the other hand, the Red Eyebrows were simple peasants who announced, "He who kills shall pay with his own life, and he who injured others shall be dealt with accordingly." This is roughly the same law Liu Bang announced when he entered Chang'an: "Those who kill be executed, and those who inflict injuries on or rob others be punished." That the Red Eyebrows did not mention robbery but stressed personal safety and the right to survival is a refleciton of the most pressing issue concerning the peasants at the time.

In late A.D. 20, Wang Mang sent troops to attack the Red Eyebrows. Defeated after one year's fight, he tried again by mustering more than 100,000 picked men. In the winter of A.D. 22, the two hostile armies fought it out in Chengchang (west of modern Dongping County, Shandong) where Wang's forces were routed. This changed the situation on the east China front, and Wang Mang had to shift to the defensive.

On the southern front, in A.D. 21 Wang Mang attacked the Green Woodsmen with 20,000 men, but lost several thousand soldiers and all his matériel. The Green Woodsmen steadily grew stronger. In A.D. 23, Wang Mang dispatched his generals Wang Yi and Wang Xun at the head of a crack unit of 420,000 in yet another offensive on the Green

Woodsmen. Purported to be one million strong, his army made a show of force when it marched to the battlefield, with its colours and transport vehicles stretching as long as 1,000 *li* (500 kilometres). The Green Woodsmen defended their besieged city, Kunyang (modern Yexian County, Henan), with about 90,000 men while Liu Xiu went enlisting reinforcements elsewhere. He mustered all the forces he could, organized a vanguard unit of 1,000 or more, and put it under his own command. The Green Woodsmen fought bravely, pitting one against a hundred and killing large numbers of enemy soldiers. Exploiting the successive victories, Liu Xiu led a "do-or-die" unit of 3,000 men to strike at Wang Mang's main force, which was put to rout. General Wang Xun was killed. Then the Green Woodsmen defending Kunyang came out to join in a converging attack on Wang Mang's men who ran over each other in a helter-skelter retreat. A rainstorm happened to have caused the river outside Kunyang to rise, and several tens of thousands of Wang Mang's soldiers were drowned trying to cross it. Wang Yi and a few other generals escaped on horseback over the corpses of their men.

The Kunyang campaign is one of the well-known examples in the annals of war showing how a small army can overcome a big one. Dealing a crushing blow to Wang Mang both militarily and politically, it gave impetus to the anti-Wang up-risings across the country.

One month before the Kunyang campaign, the Green Woodsmen installed Liu Xuan, a member of the Han royal house, as emperor, using the reign title of Gengshi. They purposely adopted the name of the Han house for the new regime, and formally proclaimed their objective of restoring the Han Dynasty after their victory in Kunyang. This meant that some changes were taking place within the ranks of the rebellious army as well as in the character of the peasant uprisings. But in any case, the Kunyang battle added to the prestige of Liu Xiu.

The Green Woodsmen followed up their Kunyang success with attacks on the Wuguan Pass and the city of Luoyang. Aided by uprisings against Wang Mang within the city, the troops marching on the pass took it with comparative ease. Then they thrust towards Chang'an. Fishing in troubled waters, the armed forces of the landlords around Chang'an tried to enter the Han capital where people were also ready to rise in revolt. Wang Mang fled for life, but was killed en route from the capital by a merchant. His death, which marked the end of the Xin Dynasty, came only three months after the Kunyang campaign, that is, in the ninth month on the lunar calendar in the year A.D. 23. In the same month, a detachment of the Green Woodsmen took Luoyang.

Following the fall of the Xin Dynasty, the Gengshi regime made Luoyang its capital. It sent emissaries to pursuade the Red Eyebrows to surrender, asking Liu Xiu to go to Hebei with the task of enlisting the services of the rebellious armies operating there. But when Fan Chong came to Luoyang with a score of his generals, the Gengshi authorities failed to unite with them. Conflicts began to appear between Gengshi and the Red Eyebrows until they assumed serious proportions. In A.D. 25 the Gengshi government moved its capital to Chang'an, from which Liu Xuan had to flee when the Red Eyebrows captured it the next year. The downfall of his regime came shortly afterwards when he was killed by the Red Eyebrows.

Meanwhile, Liu Xiu was successful in his activities in Hebei. He gradually detached himself from Liu Xuan and extended his own influence, so that in A.D. 25 he proclaimed himself emperor in Haonan (modern Baixiang County, Hebei) and is known in history as Emperor Guang Wu. The next two years saw him defeating the Red Eyebrows and the remnant forces of the Green Woodsmen until they were basically wiped out. Thus Liu Xiu appropriated the fruits of the peasant struggle and finally restored the Han house, henceforth known as the Eastern Han Dynasty because the capital, Luoyang, was to the east of the Western Han capital of Chang'an.

6. The Establishment of the Eastern Han Dynasty, the Prolonged Turbulence, and the Yellow Turban Uprising

The opening years of the Eastern Han Dynasty (25-220) were a period of establishing relative stability through the 40 plus years between 25 and 88 when emperors Guang Wu (Liu Xiu), Ming Di and

Genealogical Table of the Western Han Dynasty*

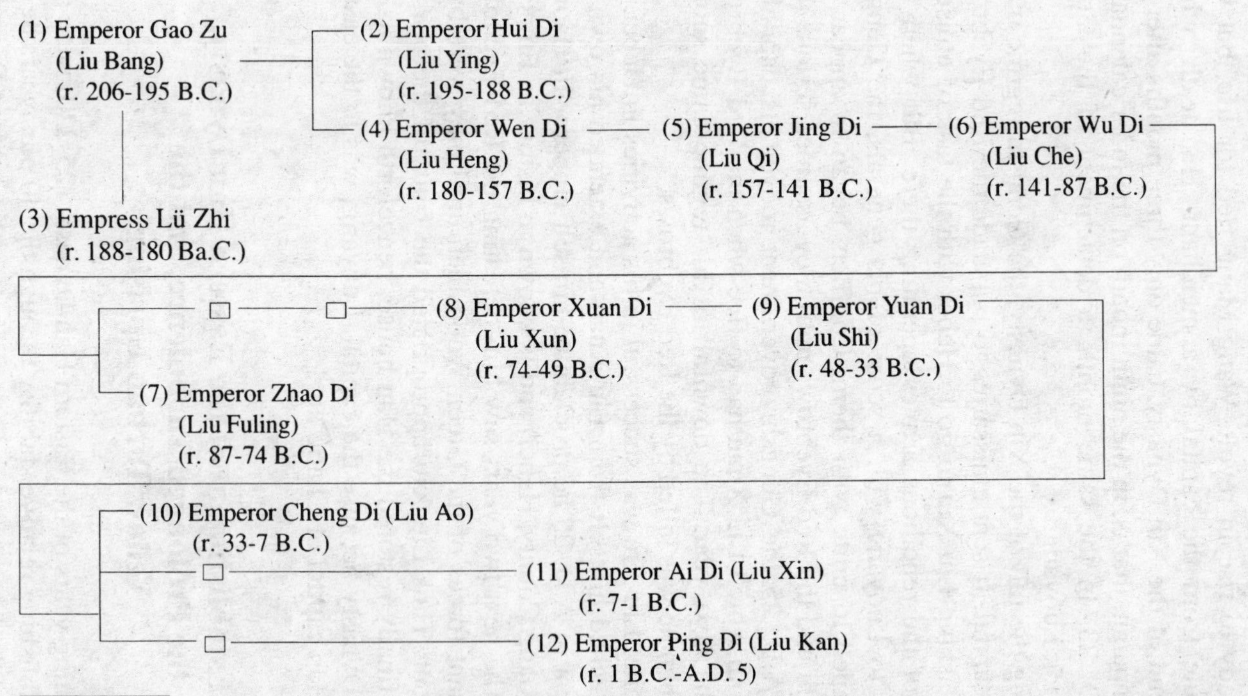

* Beginning with Emperor Wu Di of the Western Han Dynasty, each Chinese emperor used one or more propitious names, known as "reign titles", for numbering the years under his reign. When an emperor died, his successor could not change the reign title of the deceased until the next year, which would become the first year under the reign title of the new emperor. The first date used in this book for the reign of each emperor refers to the year of his actual enthronement and not the first year under his reign title.—*Trans*.

Zhang Di ruled. At the outset between A.D. 25 and A.D. 36, Liu Xiu put down the rival regimes in various localities and asserted his authority over the whole territory of the former Western Han Dynasty.

The dynasty established by Liu Xiu was even more autocratic than the Western Han. Although he gave titles and fiefs to his followers, he did not allow them to share in real power. He also took direct control of the department handling imperial documents, making it an office directed by the emperor which could decide on policy and issue orders to the whole country. The reputed three chancellors, i.e., the chancellor of civil administration, the chancellor of military affairs and the great censor, no longer had any real power, while the inspectors in the localities were empowered by Liu Xiu to watch over or impeach officials in the prefectures and counties and the lords of the fiefdoms by circumventing the chancellors and approaching the court directly. He also made use of the current Taoist practice of making prophecies, which was very popular among politicians, to add a mystical colour to his regime.

After long years of war, Liu Xiu had to pay attention to the problems of landholdings and agricultural labour which had an important bearing on state revenues. In A.D. 39, he ordered a countrywide check-up on land reclamation and census. But the local officials shielded the big landlords and cheated on figures so as to shift the tax burden onto the peasants. Liu Xiu had a dozen of the most notorious officials executed, but to no avail. Both the peasants and landlords put up a violent resistance to the order—each group having its own ax to grind, the peasants whose interests were encroached upon and the big landlords who concealed the true amount of their land. The emperor, who could do nothing effective, had to let the matter ride. Later he issued a number of rescripts decreeing the improvement of the status of bondservants before the law and the emancipation of some of them. This was also designed to increase the labour force.

After Liu Xiu died in A.D. 57, the throne was occupied first by Emperor Ming Di and then by Emperor Zhang Di, both of whom carried on and contributed to the work of the founder of the Eastern Han Dynasty. They also set store by Taoist divination, and did much to spread the already theologized Confucianism, calling themselves "prophets" to deceive the masses. In A.D. 59 Emperor Ming Di personally lectured in the imperial academy and discussed Confucian classics with scholars. Nearly 100,000 people are said to have attended. In A.D. 79 Emperor Zhang Di brought together the famous Eastern Han scholars in the White Tiger Hall in Luoyang to discuss the different versions of the Five Classics. He himself made the conclusions, which were later incorporated into *Bai Hu Tong Yi* (*Comprehensive Discussions in the White Tiger Hall*), a book serving to deify and consolidate imperial authority.

In foreign relations, the Han court received a Japanese goodwill envoy in A.D. 57, to whom Emperor Guang Wu gave a seal inscribed with a title of honour. Later, Han iron and bronze wares and silk goods found their way to Japan. The year A.D. 67 marked the beginning of the spread of Buddhism in China when the Indian monks Kasyapamatanga and Dharmaranya came to Luoyang at the invitation of the Han emissary to their country. Emperor Ming Di ordered the White Horse Monastery built in their honour and asked them to translate Buddhist sutras into Chinese. They were followed by the Parthian monk An Shigao (An Shih-kao), who came to China in A.D. 148 and stayed for more than 20 years. He became a well-known translator, rendering into Chinese 95 Buddhist works comprising 115 *juan* during his stay.

The Eastern Han period witnessed a steady rise in the export of Chinese silks to the Western world. To maintain its monopoly of the trade, Parthia kept trying to obstruct China's contacts with Daqin (the Roman Empire). In A.D. 97 the Eastern Han court dispatched an emissary, Gan Ying, to Daqin. As the most famous traveller after Zhang Qian, Gan Ying returned with a wealth of information about many regions in West Asia. However he never reached Daqin. When he reached the Persian Gulf, he was warned by the Parthains of the "insurmountable" difficulties of the voyage across it to reach Daqin. Nonetheless, Chinese silks were in great demand in the Roman Empire. In 166, the ambassador of King An Tun (thought to be the Roman Emperor Marcus Aurelius Antoninus) of Daqin arrived in China, bringing with him gifts of ivory, rhinoceros horns and tortoise shells for the reigning Han emperor.

The Eastern Han Dynasty entered its middle period when Emperor He Di, at the age of ten, ascended to the throne in A.D. 88. By then, the Xiongnu tribe had again split into two groups, the northern and the southern. But by 91, the northern group had practically been wiped out during both Han and Southern Xiongnu expeditions, and the surviving forces either migrated west or surrendered to the Chinese court. This victory over the Northern Xiongnu, a major event in the early years of Emperor He Di's reign, enabled Dou Xian, commander-in-chief of the Han forces and a relative of the empress', to take advantage of his military successes to seize power. This threw the court into prolonged turmoil.

There was nothing unusual in Emperor He Di's beginning his reign as a 10-year-old boy. Eight of the occupants of the throne after him became sovereigns when they were less than 15 years, or were even under 10. Therefore, reins of government had to be held by empress regents. As the empress mothers had more faith in their own relatives than others, power fell into the hands of their clansmen. When an emperor grew up, he tried to break away from the control of the empress' family, seeking the support of eunuchs close to him. His successor also depended on his mother for state administration and, upon attaining majority, took measures to clip the wings of the consort families with the help of his eunuch confidants. This pattern was repeated until the power of the eunuchs grew formidable. Generally speaking, the years A.D. 88-146 (between the reign of Emperor He Di and that of Emperor Zhi Di) were marked by the predominance of the families of court women. The year 146, when Emperor Huan Di came to the throne, was a turning point at which the palace eunuchs began to rise to supremacy, causing even greater upheavals in the court. The Eastern Han Dynasty entered its last stage.

For more than a century, the struggles raged between, on the one hand, an emperor and his eunuch supporters, and on the other, members of the empress' family. The court officials either attached themselves to the dominant party or resisted it, often unable to perform their normal functions and powers. Supreme imperial authority, once the objective of Liu Xiu, had now proved to be a dilemma in which the emperor was powerless to do anything significant. And this was the logical outcome of the development of the contradictions inherent in autocratic monarchy.

Between the closing years of its first period and the early part of its second period, the Eastern Han produced three outstanding scholars: the historian Ban Gu, the ideologist Wang Chong and the scientist Zhang Heng.

Ban Gu (A.D. 32-92), a native of Anling (east of present-day Xianyang County, Shaanxi Province), was the editor of *Comprehensive Discussions in the White Tiger Hall*. He theologized and systematized the teachings of Confucianism. But what earned him lasting academic fame is his *History of the Han Dynasty*. Tracing history from the peasant uprisings towards the end of the Qin Dynasty to the defeat of Wang Mang, this voluminous work follows Sima Qian's *Records of the Historian* in reflecting the official views. But it describes the various events in detail, incorporates some of the texts of the statements by important figures, and blazes a trail in the method of delineating geography, waterways, agriculture, currency, the penal code and other official documents. His prose-poem, *The Western and Eastern Capitals*, ranks among the best literary works of the Han period.

A native of modern Shangyu County in modern Zhejiang Province, Wang Chong (c. A.D. 27-97) was a militant materialist whose main work, *Lun Heng* (*Discourses Weighed in the Balance*), lashes out at orthodox theology. Regarding *yuan qi* (primordial substance) as the original material basis of all things, heaven and earth included, he took matter as the point of departure in interpreting natural phenomena and life itself. This was a criticism of the prevailing Confucian theology which took a certain mystical spirit as the dominant force in everything. Wang Chong maintained that there was no difference in human nature, and that the difference between man (kings and princes being no exception) and an inanimate thing lay in that the former possessed knowledge and wisdom while the latter did not. This repudiated the Confucian theory that there were different grades of human nature and that some persons were born sages. Wang Chong was against the view that Confucius and Mencius were above criticism, and he exposed many contradictions between what they said and what they did. His *Discourses Weighed in the Balance* was written only shortly after the completion of *Comprehensive Discussions in the White Tiger Hall*, and was, in fact, a challenge to the dominant ideology of the imperial court.

Zhang Heng (78-139), a native of Xi'e (west of modern Nanyang County, Henan), was a multi-talented scientist who invented the seismograph and was also skilled in other disciplines. In politics, he pointed to the crisis resulting from the carving up of power at the time and laid bare the absurdity of Taoist divination. In astronomy, he held that the universe was oval in shape, that the earth was like the yolk of an egg suspended in its centre, and that the universe revolved around the earth once every day. Making use of the achievements in mechanical engineering, he created an armillary sphere (celestial globe) operated by water power. It revolved at the same speed as the sun and other celestial bodies, showing their positions and the courses of their movement automatically and rather correctly. Zhang Heng's seismograph was an urn-like instrument with a central pendulum. An earth tremor would cause the pendulum to loose balance and activate a set of levers. Then, each of the eight dragons placed in eight directions on the outside of the urn would release a bronze ball held in its mouth, emitting a sound in the mean time. Thus people could know when and in which direction an earthquake had occurred. Zhang Heng wrote *Ling Xian* (*Law of the Universe*), a theoretical work on astronomy. Dealing severe blows at the official theology of the time, this book and his astronomical instruments claim an important place in the history of natural science in China.

The work of Wang Chong and Zhang Heng and the differences between their beliefs and those of Ban Gu reflected, in the realm of ideas, the ever-sharpening social contradictions of the period. In 107, not long after the death of Wang Chong and when Zhang Heng was still in his prime, peasant uprisings began to break out up and down the country. The subsequent 70-80 years saw more than 100 uprisings, each involving a few hundred or a few thousand people and some even tens of thousands. The Qiangs in northwest China and some of the tribes in the southwest also launched struggles against feudal oppression. The sustained development of these insurgent activities culminated in the Yellow Turban uprising in 184.

The leader of the Yellow Turban Army (named after the colour of their headdresses) was Zhang Jiao of Julu (south of present-day Ningjin County, Hebei), who founded a secret religious sect named "Taiping Tao" (Doctrine of Justice). His travels propagating his faith and dispensing free treatment to the sick brought him into contact with the masses. He also sent men to enlist followers in other places in present-day Hebei, Shandong, Henan, Jiangsu and Anhui. In time he built up an organization of several hundred thousand. He divided it into 36 *fang* (section), a bigger *fang* comprising more than 10,000 members and a smaller one 6,000-7,000.

Zhang Jiao spread the idea that the "Blue Heaven" (referring to the Eastern Han government) had already "passed away" and it was time for the "Yellow Heaven" (referring to the Yellow Turbans) to take over. He said that the whole country would be "blessed" in the cyclical year of Jia Zi (i.e., the year 184), an obvious call for an uprising against the Eastern Han court to establish a peasant regime. Ma Yuanyi, who was in charge of organizing the effort, travelled between the capital Luoyang and other places to see that everything was in order. He succeeded in winning the support of some court eunuchs who undertook to help the uprising from within. But shortly before the day set for joint action, the fifth day of the third month on the lunar calendar in the year 184, a turncoat informed against the Yellow Turbans. Ma was arrested and murdered, as were more than a thousand others in the capital.

Zhang Jiao, calling himself "Heavenly General", had to order the launching of the long-awaited uprising one month ahead of schedule. He was aided by his younger brothers Zhang Bao, "General of the Earth", and Zhang Liang, "General of Men".

In less than a month, the movement took hold with people responding from all over the country, and the uprising progressed rapidly. This was big shock to the Eastern Han court. Emperor Ling Di appointed He Jin, brother of the empress, commander-in-chief of the imperial army and ordered him to defend Luoyang by stationing troops in its suburbs. General Lu Zhi was sent to Hebei to fight Zhang Jiao while two other generals, Huangfu Song and Zhu Jun, proceeded to Yingchuan in Henan, leading an expeditionary army against the

Yellow Turban detachment of Bo Cai.

Bo Cai first defeated Huangfu Song and Zhu Jun. But the tables were turned when the government troops organized a joint attack during which they made use of a windstorm and set fire to the camps of the peasant army. The Yellow Turbans suffered casualties of several tens of thousands, and Bo Cai died in action.

On the Hebei front, Zhang Jiao stationed his men in Guangzong (east of modern Weixian County) and held out against the attacks by Lu Zhi's unit. The unsuccessful Lu was later replaced by Dong Zhuo, who in turn was succeeded by Huangfu Song. Having lulled the vigilance of the peasant rebels by a ruse, Huangfu sprang a surprise attack and put more than 80,000 insurgents out of action. The Yellow Turbans retreated to Xiayangqu (west of modern Jinxian County, Hebei), only to suffer more defeats in encounters with Huangfu's army there. Another 100,000 or more were killed, and Zhang Jiao and his two brothers either died of illness or in battle.

After nearly nine months of fierce battles, the main force of the Yellow Turban Army was wiped out and its chief leaders killed. But the flames of peasant uprisings were far from extinguished. Many armed insurgent units kept on fighting. By 192, there were still 300,000 or more Yellow Turbans operating in present-day Shandong. Thirteen years later, the Heishan (Black Hill) Army in central-south Hebei, an ally of the Yellow Turbans, still numbered upwards of 100,000.

Despite the failure of the Yellow Turban uprising, it shook the Eastern Han regime to its foundations. Its days were numbered.

On the death of Emperor Ling Di in 189, Emperor Shao Di ascended to the throne. Because the court continued to be plagued by eunuchs who now possessed even greater power, Grand General He Jin summoned Dong Zhuo, who was then in control of Hedong (the southwest part of modern Shanxi Province), to the capital to deal with them. However, information was leaked to the eunuchs who acted first and had He Jin killed. In retaliation, Yuan Shao, another warlord, marched with his forces into the palace, killing more than 2,000 eunuchs. Not long after that, Dong Zhuo entered Luoyang, where he deposed Emperor Shao Di and put emperor Xian Di on the throne.

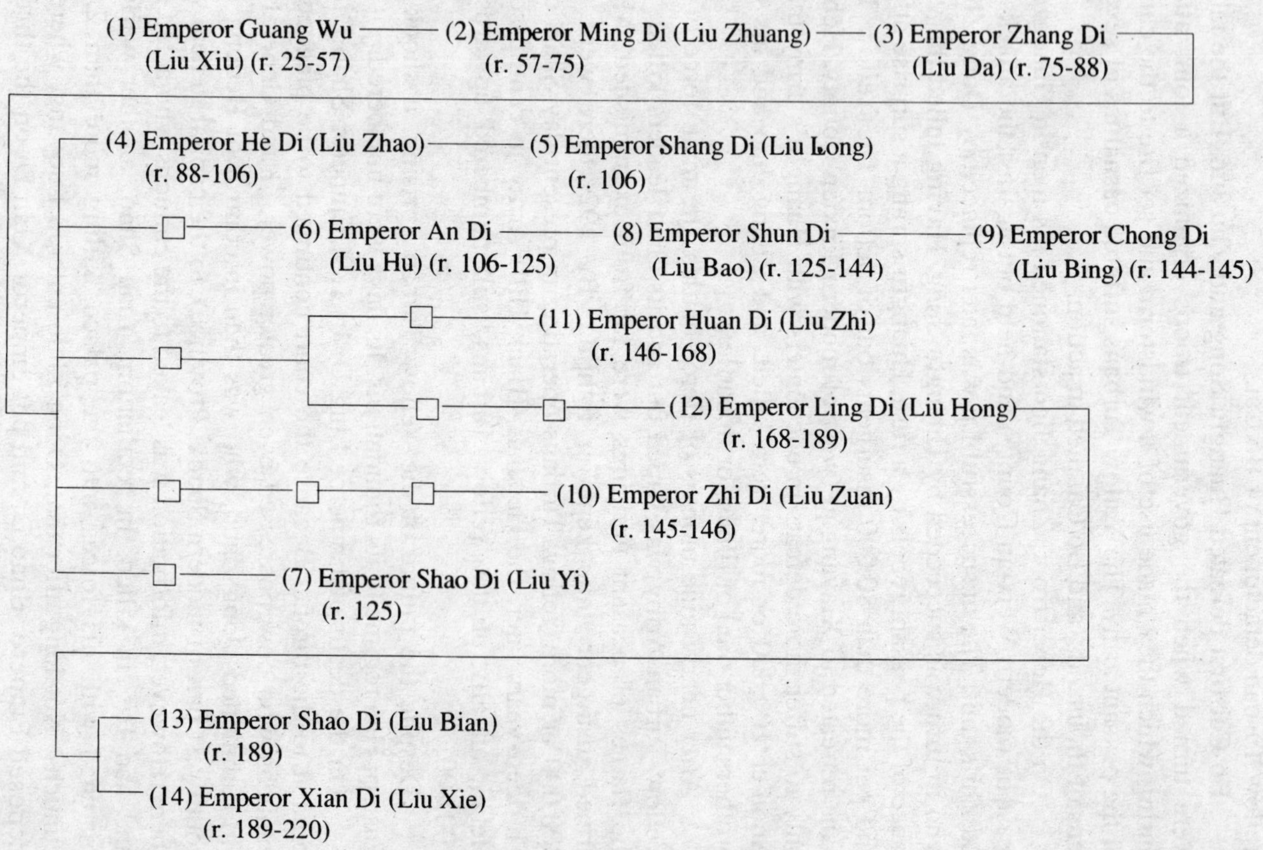

Genealogical Table of the Eastern Han Dynasty
(1) Emperor Guang Wu
(Liu Xiu) (r. 25-57)
(2) Emperor Ming Di (Liu Zhuang)
(r. 57-75)
(3) Emperor Zhang Di
(Liu Da) (r. 75-88)
(4) Emperor He Di (Liu Zhao)
(r. 88-106)
(5) Emperor Shang Di (Liu Long)
(r. 106)
(6) Emperor An Di
(Liu Hu) (r. 106-125)
(8) Emperor Shun Di
(Liu Bao) (r. 125-144)
(9) Emperor Chong Di
(Liu Bing) (r. 144-145)
(11) Emperor Huan Di (Liu Zhi)
(r. 146-168)
(12) Emperor Ling Di (Liu Hong)
(r. 168-189)
(10) Emperor Zhi Di (Liu Zuan)
(r. 145-146)
(7) Emperor Shao Di (Liu Yi)
(r. 125)
(13) Emperor Shao Di (Liu Bian)
(r. 189)
(14) Emperor Xian Di (Liu Xie)
(r. 189-220)

Dong who was extraordinarily cruel to the common people, despising the court ministers who soon came to see through his wild ambition to seize supreme power. Many careerists tried to expand their own forces and influence in the name of launching punitive expeditions against Dong. In 196, Cao Cao, one of the most powerful warlords, brought Emperor Xian Di to Xuchang, which was then made capital of the empire. From then on, Cao used the name of the puppet emperor to legalize his acts. The Eastern Han Dynasty endured only nominally, soon to give way to the Three Kingdoms.

7. The Development of Social Productive Forces

The Qin-Han period witnessed advances in many fields including agriculture, science and handicraft industry, medicine, engineering, city planning and architecture. It was a period which saw the invention of paper. Farming methods were improved through new implements like hydraulic water lifting devices; the building of canals and dams promoted irrigation and water conservation; and advanced iron-smelting techniques led to the mass-production of cheap, high-grade steel. In the meantime, physicians mastered acupuncture and the prescribing of herbal medicines, astronomers worked out a new calendar based on the formula of $365 \frac{385}{1539}$ days to a solar year and craftsmen produced exquisite wool, cotton and silk fabrics. And above all, perhaps, stands the engineering wonder of the Qin Dynasty, the Great Wall of China.

In agriculture, special treatises by Si Shengzhi reflected the level of development reached at the time by summarizing both technical and theoretical questions about farm production. To begin with, iron ploughs and ox farming were popularized and improved while a wide range of farm implements—many of them innovations—were in use. Plough frames were equipped with the main parts of animal-drawn ploughs. Already in extensive use was a plough for turning up earth, crushing stones, building up ridges between furrows and regulating the depth of ploughing. During the latter period of Emperor Wu Di, Zhao Guo, an army provisions official, invented and popularized a plough of a new type which was drawn by two oxen and operated by three people, one guiding the animals, one manipulating the plough shafts and one steering the plough itself. As time went on, the plough was adapted to fit into a team first of two oxen and one man and later of one ox and one man to save manpower and facilitate deep ploughing.

The seed plough used at the time saved labour and improved the quality of sowing through the three-fold action of furrowing, sowing and covering the furrows with earth. Besides the hydraulic water lifting devices, winnowers and water-powered mills were introduced and raised efficiency by a wide margin. Iron farm tools came into much wider use in the mid-Western Han period.

New methods of farming were also introduced, such as the "alternation method" by Zhao Guo and the "small plot method" by Si Shengzhi. In the "alternation method" the land was ploughed into furrows and the earth turned up to make ridges. Crop seeds were sown into the furrows. As the young plants grew, the earth of the ridges, together with weeds, was piled around their roots so that they grew up fast and sturdy. To maintain the fertility of the land, the ridges and furrows were alternated every year so that the ridges of this year became furrows of the next, and vice versa. This method raised the per-unit-area yield by one to two-thirds and was best suited to dry regions. In the "small plot method", deep ploughing and close planting were applied on small plots, where water and manure were used effectively and in a concentrated way and field management was intensified to ensure high crop yields.

Water conservancy projects were undertaken for agriculture, animal husbandry and navigation. The Linqu Canal built during the time of the First Emperor of the Qin Dynasty was an engineering success. Many of the water conservancy works of the Western Han period were constructed during the reign of Emperor Wu Di. The Caoqu Canal, dug in 129 B.C. by tens of thousands of people under the supervision of the noted water conservancy expert Xu Bo, channelled the Weihe River water east from the metropolis of Chang'an to the Huanghe River. This shortened the route of water transport of grain to the capital and brought irrigation to large tracts of farmland. Many more canals were dug later in present-day Shaanxi which irrigated the fields and improved the soil. Irrigation was also well developed in present-day Inner Mongolia, Gansu, Shanxi and, in particular, the Ningxia Plain. In the Eastern Han period, efforts were concentrated on repairing and rebuilding the old water conservancy works. In A.D. 69, hundreds of thousands of people were recruited to harness the Huanghe River under the supervision of the famous specialist Wang Jing. As a result, no major breaks in the dykes or change in the river course occurred through the following 800 years.

Salt-making, iron-smelting and cloth-weaving were the three principal handicraft trades. There were sea, lake and well salts. In the mid-Han period, natural gas was used to boil salt in present-day Qionglia County, Sichuan Province. Iron-smelting was well developed both in scale and technique during the Qin and Han dynasties, especially after the mid-Western Han period. Grey cast iron, which is better than white iron, appeared around the mid-Western Han period. The invention of fettling and the improvement of the repeated tempering technique, two important indications of the progress of iron-smelting in the Qin-Han period, opened the way for the mass production of cheap, high-grade steel. By the Eastern Han Dynasty, iron and steel had replaced bronze in making the principal weapons.

Cloth-weaving, the main household side-occupation in the Qin-Han period, covered silk, flax, ko-hemp and woollen fabrics. The silk fabrics used by aristocrats were of fine workmanship and exquisite design. The cotton cloth from the prefecture of Shu (Sichuan) and the silk from the prefecture of Qi (Shandong) were famous at the time. Chinese brocade, which was characteristic of the high standards of Chinese textiles, found a brisk market in Rome. The hand-operated spinning wheels, weaving looms and figured fabric weaving looms of the time had lasting influence over China's textile industry.

There was an elaborate division of labour in the making of lacquerware during the Han Dynasty. Present-day Sichuan was known for its gold-or silver-decorated lacquers. A kind of paper-like material was made for writing in the early days of the Western Han. But the type of paper we know today was not invented until the Eastern Han Dynasty, in A.D. 105, by Cai Lun who made it of rags, old fishing nets and tree bark. It was called Marquis Cai's paper in honour of the inventor. The use of these materials greatly raised the quality and efficiency of paper-making, enlarged the source of raw materials, reduced cost, put an end to the use of bamboo and silk as writing materials and created a favourable condition for the spread of culture. As techniques improved, Chinese lacquerware was introduced into Asian and European countries where it was favourably received. Chinese paper-making spread to Japan from Korea in the 7th century, to Arabia in the 8th and to Europe in the 12th, contributing greatly to the development of world culture.

The Qin-Han period witnessed new achievements in civil engineering. Besides the Great Wall, engineers during the Qin Dynasty built imperial chariot roads, the Zhidao Highway across mountains and valleys, the Epang (Efang) Palace, imperial villas, temporary imperial residences, and the Qin Shi Huang Mausoleum. With a circumference of 25 kilometres, Chang'an, the capital of Western Han, was a model of city planning. It had 160 neighbourhoods, 8 main streets where 12 carriages could run abreast, the Weiyang Palace that occupied one-fourth of the city area, and separate residential districts for dignitaries and commoners. The famous Zhandao plank road built along treacherous chiff faces during the Qin-Han period shortened the distance between Sichuan and Shaanxi. High terraces and multi-storyed buildings were designed in such a way that their wooden structure formed an intergrated whole by itself. Special components were used for beams and beam supports, bricks and tiles were of varied shapes, and new bricklaying methods were introduced. All these laid the foundation for further development in Chinese architecture.

In shipbuilding, vessels from 3.6 to 8.4 metres in width were made. In the Western Han period, the water-borne army at its strongest had 350,000 men and its vessels had two to four decks. Ten-deckers appeared later in the Eastern Han Dynasty. Han boats were equipped with rudders, sculls and cloth sails.

Development in production brought in its wake a corresponding development in astronomy, mathematics and medical science.

The "Chapter on Astronomers" in *Records of the Historian* by

Sima Qian is a systematic account of the astronomical knowledge of ancient China. On orders from Emperor Wu Di in 194 B.C., Sima Qian, Gongsun Qing and Hu Sui, basing their work on surveys by instruments and calculations by Tang Du and Luo Xiahong, developed the new Taichu Calendar, that had far-reaching influence in the history of Chinese calendrical science. The number of days of a solar year was calculated by the formula $365\frac{385}{1539}$ and that of a lunar month by the formula $29\frac{43}{81}$. The new calendar contained the 24 solar terms and reasonable arrangements of the intercalary month. The first lunar month became the beginning of the year, whereas it was the tenth in the calendar of Qin and early Han.

The *Mathematical Classic on the Gnomon*, written around late Western Han, is the earliest extant treatise of its kind in China. The *Mathematics in Nine Sections*, completed in early Eastern Han after repeated revisions over a long period, systematically summarized the important achievements in this field since the Spring and Autumn and the Warring States periods. The book contained 246 applied mathematics problems and was divided into nine sections according to the methods of solution and the fields of application. Its appearance demonstrated that mathematics in China had developed into a scientific system.

In the medical field, as early as the Warring States Period the noted physician Bian Que had mastered the methods of diagnosis of feeling the patient's pulse, observing his symptoms and listening to his voice and the methods of treatment of acupuncture, medical potions and hot compression. To consolidate his rule, Emperor Qin Shi Huang of the Qin Dynasty ordered the burning of all the books except medical classics. Another indication of the level of medical science at the time is a section in *Records of the Historian* on Chunyu Yi, a noted physician of the period of the Western Han's Emperor Wen Di. The chapter describes 25 of his cases in terms of pathology, examination of symptoms, methods of treatment, and prognosis. *The Yellow Emperor's Classics of Internal Medicine*, written in a question-and-answer form around the early Western Han period, explains the physiological signs and pathological changes of the human body, gives the earliest elucidation of its blood circulation and points out the importance of pulsefeeling in diagnosis. Apart from suggesting the methods of treatment for 311 ailments and illnesses of 44 categories, it emphasizes disease prevention and getting at the root of a disease to seek a permanent cure. *Emperor Shen Nong's Materia Medica*, a pharmaceutical work of the Eastern Han, records 365 medicines—252 medicinal herbs, 67 animal drugs and 46 mineral drugs—their functions, their time and methods of collection, their efficacy and their mixed application. The two works are monuments to the beginnings of traditional Chinese medical and pharmaceutical systems.

In the Qin-Han period agriculture with its wide areas of application continued to occupy the predominant position in the social economy. The agricultural labour force at that time was formed by individual peasants who enjoyed personal freedom to a certain degree and showed tremendous interest in production under the private economy. This labour force had two characteristics. First, the peasants were dependent upon the land, which meant a guarantee of work hands for the landlords and the use or ownership of the land for the peasants. Second, the production unit was formed by the household and combined farming and weaving, a system which, though making it hard to get separate households organized, made it possible for them to achieve self-sufficiency in food and clothing. In this way, the peasants enjoyed better working conditions than the serfs, which meant a change in the character of the labour force. This new labour force combined with the developed production tools and technique to form a new social productive force that accelerated the development of feudal relations.

8. The Growth of Feudal Relations

The Qin-Han period was one in which feudal relations reached maturity in China. The feudal landownership and the corresponding structure of the landlord class, both characterized by a hierarchy, were basically established in the middle-lower Huanghe, middle-lower Changjiang and Zhujiang river valleys.

The hierarchy in landownership was, in the order of importance, composed of the following strata:

1. The emperor
2. The landed aristocrats with hereditary titles
3. The landowners of powerful families
4. The mercantile landowners

The emperor, the supreme landowner, embodied a unity of landownership and political power. After his conquest of the six states, Qin Shi Huang had a stele erected which contained the inscriptions: "The land in all corners of the earth belongs to the emperor" and "Where there is human habitation, there is the rule of emperor." These inscriptions showed that no distinction was made between land ownership and political domination. Private ownership of land did exist, but it took the form of a hierarchy, with universal recognition of the emperor's supreme ownership. While toasting his father at a grand banquet, Emperor Gao Zu of the Western Han, i.e. Liu Bang, said to the old man, "You used to say that I was a good-for-nothing, unlike Second Brother who knew how to build up family property. Who do you think has built up more property, I or Second Brother?" The courtiers attending the banquet greeted these remarks with deafening cheers of "wan sui!" ("May the Emperor live ten thousand years!") Clearly, both the emperor and his subjects regarded the entire country as the monarch's private property. This way of merging the private with the public and the imperial household with the state also found expression in the functions of the officials. The nine ministers in both the Qin and Han dynasties mainly took care of the daily needs and property of the emperor, being responsible separately for the ancestral temples of the ruling house, the imperial palaces, the security of the ruling house, the imperial stable, the welfare of the members of the royal house, and the imperial treasury and granary. Even the highest-ranking officials, the three chancellors, were in a way retainers of the royal house. No matter who were in power, eunuchs or royal relatives on the side of the court ladies, the changes in the political situations in the Qin-Han period always took the form of internal disputes within the ruling house. This supreme authority of the emperor far exceeded the kingly authority in the Shang and Zhou dynasties and the power of the princes in the Spring and Autumn and Warring States periods.

Next to the emperor were the landed aristocrats with hereditary titles. Each of them had a fief embracing a great number of households. The powerful landlords had a deep-rooted local influence, but enjoyed no political prestige. The mercantile landlords, otherwise called "rich people", had much social influence but were discriminated against politically. As a short-lived dynasty, the Qin left few records about these ranks among the landlords, and the stratification was not so clear until the Western Han.

Among the landed aristocrats in the Qin and Han dynasties there were relatives of the royal house bearing the same surname as the emperor and those from families that had rendered outstanding service to the court. In the Han Dynasty the landed aristocracy was augmented by relatives of the emperor on the side of his mother or wife as well as some of the descendants of Confucius and well-known teachers of Confucianism. Although Qin Shi Huang granted no fiefs after his conquest of the six states, he did create a feudal aristocracy by providing descendants of the royal house with food, clothing and a regular income from land rent and tax. Also, meritorious officials could be granted the title of marquis and could request land. The Han Dynasty saw the rise of large numbers of princes, marquises, etc. among members of the ruling house and the meritorious. There were many influential families among the royal relatives on the side of the emperor's mother or wife. Liang Ji of the Eastern Han, for one, was granted territories with a total of 30,000 households. His brothers and sons were granted fiefs each with 10,000 households. In all, seven members of the Liang family were made marquises. According to *History of the Han Dynasty*, the number of households during the late Western Han Dynasty was 12,233,062 with a total population of 59,594,978, of which 23 principalities accounted for 1,343,390 households with a total population of 6,382,205. The book contains no records of the number of households in the 187 marquisates, but it was estimated at 1,51,000 with a total population exceeding 7,050,000. According to *Sequel to the History of the Han Dynasty*, the number of households during the middle period of the Eastern Han Dynasty was 9,698,630 with a total population of 49,150,220, of which 19 principalities accounted for 1,694,690 households with a total population of

10,314,523. The book makes no mention of the number of households in the 95 marquisates, but it was estimated at 930,000 with a total population of more than 4,700,000. The statistics of the two books show that the principalities and marquisates accounted for approximately one-fourth of the country's total number of households in the Western Han period and more than one-fourth in the Eastern Han period. These figures, however, did not include the labourers forced to work on the land illegally incorporated into these principalities and marquisates.

The landlords of powerful families included the descendants of the nobilities of the six states and influential local families. Although the former had lost their noble status after the fall of the six states, they remained an influential social force during the Qin and early Han periods. They also participated in the anti-Qin struggle of the late Qin peasant insurgents. Mindful of their prestige, both Qin and Han rulers moved many of these families from the east to the areas around the capitals so as to put them under control. It is hard to pinpoint the time at which these influential local families appeared in history. Around the time of the uprisings of the Red Eyebrows and Green Woodsmen, Ru Yinshi, with a clan of over 1,000 people and some protégés, and Gongsun Shu, with a clan of 10,000 people, ranked among the most powerful local landlords. Liu Xiu, founder of the Eastern Han Dynasty, was assisted by a number of generals from influential local families who later became aristocrats. During the Eastern Han period, although the powerful local families had steadily gained strength, they could not yet overshadow the feudal aristocrats. Some of the wealthy people in frontier regions were also counted among the powerful families. One of them was Ban Yi, an ancestor of the noted historian Ban Gu and a big herds-owner who possessed thousands of flocks of cattle and sheep.

The mercantile landlords generally got rich by branching out into commerce or handicraft industry. Around the Western Han period, people with wealth amounting to three million five-*zhu* coins were regarded as wealthy while those below that level were regarded as middle class. A small number of people had amassed wealth to the tune of fifty million or even a hundred million five-*zhu* coins. Some people, such as a descendant of the powerful Tian family in one of the six states, was a big landlord as well as a wealthy merchant. In the social economic conditions of the time, a rich person was invariably wedded to the land, however wealthy he might be. In the words of the famous historian Sima Qian, the practice was to "acquire fortune by attending to the non-essential and preserve it by attending to the essential." In contemporary usage, the "non-essential" meant handicraft industry and commerce and the "essential" meant farming. It was generally believed that a landowner was in a more secure position than a man with money alone. The fact that the emperor co-existed with the three categories of landlords as well as numerous medium and small landholders reflected the existence of ranks in agrarian relations. The emperor's undisputed possession of the nation's land was shared by the hereditary aristocrats, the powerful families enjoyed royal recognition of their landownership, while the mercantile landlords acquired land mainly through illegal channels, as acquisition of land through one's wealth was forbidden by law. In the stratified feudal landownership of the Qin-Han period, the hereditary aristocrats held a dominant position, second only to that of the emperor.

In addition to paying the agricultural tax in grain and different kinds of poll tax, peasants in the Qin-Han period had to perform corvée and military service. These feudal burdens were in essence land rent paid by the direct producers to the landlords, partly in kind and mostly in corvée, the poll tax being a form of the latter. State tax was identical with land rent—there were no other forms of state tax. The exploitation of peasants by hereditary aristocrats mainly consisted of a share in the rent paid to the royal house. The exploitation of peasants by powerful landlords was heavier than that by the royal house in terms of rent in kind, but was probably lighter in terms of corvée because peasants in this category did not have to perform military service and excessive corvée and the land rent they paid to landlords was not part of the state tax.

To ensure its sources of soldiers and food grain and to enforce its rule and exploitation, the feudal state organized the scattered peasants on a tithing basis. These peasants were called "registered people".

Polarization between rich and poor constantly occurred among these "registered people". Some became big or small landlords, but most of them were impoverished. Stratification of peasants took place not only through polarization but also through the practice of conferring titles of honour on them. There were twenty such titles in the Qin-Han period, each indicating a certain status of the titleholder. Peasants with certain titles were exempted from corvée. The feudal hierarchy in the Qin-Han period was complicated; it often covered up the true features of classes.

The growth of feudal relations in this period brought closer in economic life people scattered over wide areas who spoke more or less the same language and enhanced their national consciousness. It was in these historical conditions that the Han ethnic group came into existence.

Chapter VII

The Three Kingdoms, the Jin, the Southern and Northern Dynasties, the Sui and the Tang: the Earlier Period of Ascendancy of Chinese Feudalism

1. The Three Kingdoms

Feudal society developed through a period of disunity in China in the Three Kingdoms, Western Jin and Eastern Jin, the Southern and Northern Dynasties, and the short-lived Sui Dynasty to the reunification of the country in the 289-year-old Tang Dynasty, one of the most glorious eras in Chinese history. The Three Kingdoms period, in which the rival states of Wei, Shu and Wu existed side by side, dates approximately from 220 to 266 (or as far back as 196 if calculated from the time that the Wei rose as a political entity). The Western Jin, ruled by four emperors of three generations, lasted 51 years, from 266 to 316; the Eastern Jin, ruled by 11 emperors of four generations, extended over 103 years, from 317 to 420. The Southern and Northern Dynasties period, 420-589, covers 169 years, starting from the two rival dynasties of Song and Northern Wei and ending with the conquest of the Chen by the Sui, and going through the intertwining period of the Qi and the Liang in the south and the Eastern Wei, the Western Wei, the Northern Qi and the Northern Zhou in the north. The dynasty of Sui, 581-618, had just two emperors of two generations on the throne for only 37 years. The 289-year-old Tang Dynasty, 618-907, was ruled by 20 emperors and 1 empress belonging to 14 generations. The Western and Eastern Jin dynasties also saw a number of independent local regimes, known in Chinese history as the Sixteen States.

The defeat of the Yellow Turban uprising at the end of the Eastern Han Dynasty was followed by a tangled warfare of more than ten years between the various local feudal lords which was to end with the country divided and ruled by three of them. Cao Cao, who had been building up his political and military strength in the middle and lower Huanghe River valley, forced Emperor Xian Di to move his capital to Xuchang (in present-day Henan Province) in 196 and, in the emperor's name, continued to expand his influence. However, Cao Cao found a formidable obstacle in Yuan Shao who had grown strong in Jizhou and Youzhou, both in present-day Hebei Province. Cao Cao and Yuan Shao fought a decisive battle in 200 at Guandu (now Zhongmou County, Henan Province), where Cao Cao's smaller forces bested those of Yuan Shao. In the two or three years that followed, Cao Cao cleared off Yuan Shao's remaining forces and brought the entire middle and lower Huanghe River valley under his control.

Around the time of the Battle of Guandu, the southern-based Sun Quan, who had carried on the cause pioneered by his father and elder brother, was ruling in the lower Changjiang River valley. Liu Bei, who claimed to be connected with the Han royal house, was also preparing for a bid for power. He had in his brain-trust the great statesman and military strategist Zhuge Liang and the services of the renowned generals Guan Yu, Zhang Fei and Zhao Yun. However, without a stable political base, Liu Bei had to bide his time by seeking the patronage of Liu Biao, the Prefect of Jingzhou (the greater parts of modern Hubei and Hunan provinces and southwestern Henan Province).

In 208, Cao Cao led a massive force southward to capture Jingzhou, chase Liu Bei around, and pose a direct menace to Sun Quan. At Zhuge Liang's instance, Liu Bei and Sun Quan decided to put up joint resistance to Cao Cao. Sun Quan's army, led by its field marshal Zhou Yu, set fire to scores of Cao Cao's war vessels on the Changjiang River at Chibi[1]. Taking advantage of the ensuing confu-

---

[1] The site is identified as Chijishan to the west of present-day Wuchang County, Hubei, or Chibishan to the northwest of Puqi County, also in Hubei.

sion, the allied forces of Sun Quan and Liu Bei, totalling less than 50,000, launched an all-out attack and crushed the hostile army that boasted more than 200,000 men. After Cao Cao pulled back to his northern base, Sun Quan consolidated his position in the south while Liu Bei seized part of the regions under the jurisdiction of Jingzhou Prefecture and later took Yizhou (mostly in present-day Sichuan Province) in the west. And so a situation arose in which the country was divided and ruled by the three feudal lords.

After Cao Cao's death in 220, his son, Cao Pi, deposed the Eastern Han emperor Xian Di and proclaimed himself Emperor of Wei, with Luoyang as his capital. The following year, Liu Bei declared himself Emperor of Han, historically known as the Kingdom of Shu or Shu Han, and made Chengdu his capital. In 229, following the examples of Cao Pi and Liu Bei, Sun Quan called himself Emperor of Wu with the capital at Jianye (now Nanjing City, Jiangsu Province). These kingdoms—Wei, Shu and Wu—are known as the Three Kingdoms in Chinese history.

Before the Battle of Guandu, Cao Cao had introduced a land reclamation system[1] in the Xuchang area with excellent results. After setting up the Kingdom of Wei, Cao Pi enforced the system on a larger scale, had large numbers of water conservancy works built and many paddy fields opened up, quickly reviving and developing the war-torn economy in the Huanghe River valley. Politically, the Wei had many more talented people in its service than the two other states because Cao Cao promoted people to important posts on their merit rather than on their family background.

In the Kingdom of Wu the land reclamation system was also introduced extensively in the Changjiang and Huaihe river valleys. Irrigation works were built in what is now Zhejiang Province and advanced production technique was brought from the north to develop the lower Changjiang River areas. The Kingdom of Wu was also enthusiastic about forging ties with the outside world. Under orders from

---

[1] A system whereby destitute peasants placed under military officers were organized into civilian colonies to work the land while soldiers, when not fighting, were encouraged to grow crops in military colonies.—*Trans.*

Sun Quan in 230, Wei Wen and Zhuge Zhi led a large fleet with 10,000 soldiers aboard to Yizhou (now Taiwan). Three years later, another Wu fleet of the same size called at Liaodong along the northeastern coast and brought back some of the local fine-breed horses. Sun Quan also sent Kang Tai and Zhu Ying as his envoys to various states on the South China Sea. Upon their return, Kang Tai and Zhu Ying wrote books on their travels. Merchants from the Roman Empire came by the South China Sea route to trade in Wu, some of them staying as long as seven or eight years.

As Prime Minister of the Kingdom of Shu, Zhuge Liang worked hard to develop agricultural production in Sichuan. He appointed special officials in charge of the ancient Dujiang Weir and had many more water works built. To secure a peaceful environment for the kingdom, he took care to improve relations with the ethnic minorities inhabiting present-day Guizhou and Yunnan provinces and to strengthen the political, economic and cultural ties between the Han people and these ethnic minorities.

The Wei reached a higher level of cultural development than the other two states. A new sect appeared in the realm of philosophy, called *xuan xue* (a school of Taoism) which took the three books—*Lao Zi, Zhuang Zi* and the *Book of Changes*—as its "Three Classics". The founder of this school was Wang Pi (226-49), a native of Shanyang (now Jiaozuo City, Henan) and author of *Annotations to "Lao Zi", Notes on the "Book of Changes"* and *A Brief Exposition of the "Book of Changes"*. Wang Pi preached that Non-being was more important than Being and the world of Being took Non-being as its substance. This theory of objective idealism boiled down to "acting without striving" or "letting things take their natural courses". In other words, it aimed to relegate feudal moral codes to a secondary position and provided members of the feudal upper strata with excuses for their greediness and indulgence. An ideological reflection of the depraved life of the upper strata at that time, Wang Pi's works nevertheless had extensive influence in the history of Chinese philosophy. Cao Cao (155-220) and his sons Cao Pi (187-226) and Cao Zhi (192-232) were all great names in literature. Cao Cao's poems, *A Short Song* and *A Stroll Out of*

Summer Gate, written in a plaintive style at once virile and unrestrained, rank among the most famous in Chinese poetry. The *Historical Allusions and Essays* by Cao Pi is the earliest piece of literary criticism extant in China. The poems of Cao Zhi have left their mark on the development of the *wu yan shi* (poems with five characters to a line).

The relationship between the three states began with Wu and Shu joining hands against Wei. Later the two allies fell out in their scramble over Jingzhou. In 220, when Guan Yu, commander of the Shu garrison in Jingzhou, was locked in battle with the Wei forces, Wu sprang a surprise attack, captured Jingzhou and killed Guan Yu. In 222, Liu Bei led a huge force out of Shu in an expedition against Wu. A decisive battle was fought at Yiling (north of Yidu County, Hubei Province), in which the Shu troops were routed. Liu Bei died the following year, and his son, Liu Chan, succeeded to the throne with the help of Prime Minister Zhuge Liang. Zhuge Liang switched back to the earlier policy of alliance with Wu against Wei, his aim being to drive north to occupy the Central Plains and recover the cause of the Han house. But the several northern expeditions he did undertake failed. In the last expedition in 234, Zhuge Liang died on his sickbed at the front at a time when his army was fighting to a stalemate with the Wei forces under the command of Field Marshal Sima Yi at Wuzhangyuan (southwest of Meixian County, Shaanxi Province). The Shu troops then pulled back to Sichuan. From then on, Shu declined while the state power of Wei gradually passed into the hands of the Sima family. After the death of Sima Yi, his sons, Sima Shi and Sima Zhao, successively held the reins of the Wei government, relegating the Wei emperor to the status of a figurehead.

In 263, Wei vanquished Shu. Three years later, Sima Yan dethroned the Wei emperor and established the Jin Dynasty (historically known as the Western Jin), with the capital remaining at Luoyang as during the Wei Dynasty. In 280, Sima Yan, later known as Emperor Wu Di of Jin, defeated Wu and unified—though only for a short period—the China that had remained divided for scores of years after the end of the Eastern Han Dynasty.

Generalogical Table of the Three Kingdoms

1. Kingdom of Wei

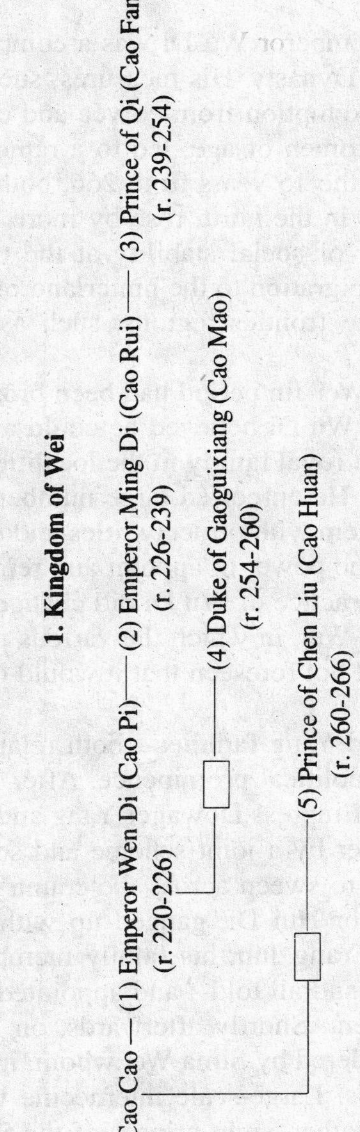

2. Kingdom of Shu

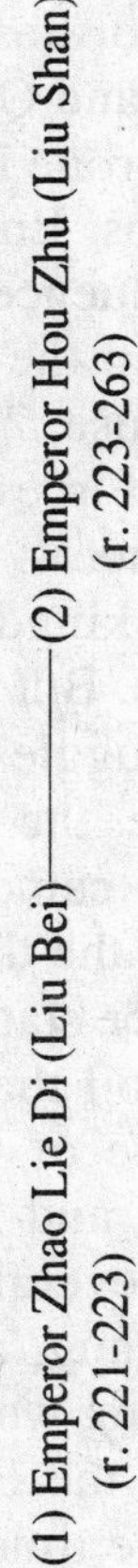

3. Kingdom of Wu

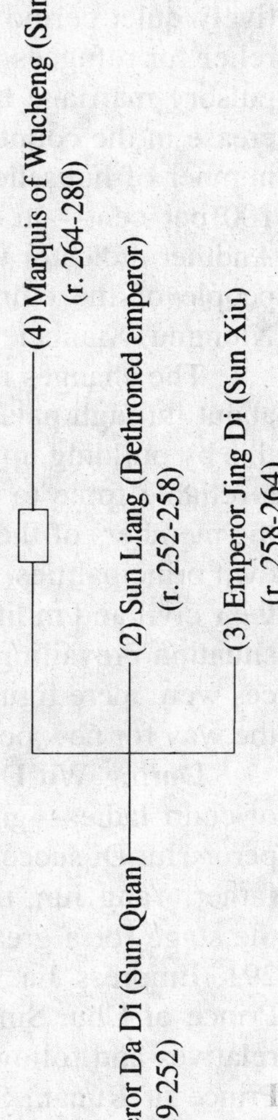

2. The Western Jin, the Eastern Jin And the Sixteen States

The 25-year reign (266-290) of Emperor Wu Di was a comparatively quiet period in the Western Jin Dynasty. His measures, such as relief for refugees, lessening of and exemption from corvée and compulsory marriage between men and women of age, led to a rapid increase in the country's population. In the 15 years from 266, both the number of households and population in the north rose by more than 100 per cent—an important indicator of social stability at the time. Another indicator was the wholesale migration to the hinterland of the people of the ethnic minorities in the frontier regions, such as the Xiongnu, Xianbei, Jie, Di and Qiang.

The changes in the throne in the Wei-Jin period had been brought about through palace coups. Emperor Wu Di believed he could avoid this by building up the influence of the royal family in the localities as a reliable force to shore up the court. He enfeoffed large numbers of the members of the Jin house, 27 of them with princely titles and their own principalities, armed forces and the power to appoint and remove their civil and military officers. This practice of Wu Di did change the situation prevailing in the kingdom of Wei, in which the various princes were mere figureheads. But he had not foreseen that it would open the way for new power struggles.

During Wu Di's time, the Jia and Yang families—both relatives of court ladies—gradually came into political prominence. After Emperor Hui Di succeeded to the throne, Empress Dowager Yang and her father, Yang Jun, took over state power by a joint scheme and so set the stage for a great turmoil that was to sweep across the country. In 291, Empress Jia, the wife of Emperor Hui Di, ganged up with the Prince of Chu, Sima Wei, and killed Yang Jun, his family members, relatives and followers—several thousand all told—and appointed the Prince of Runan, Sima Liang, as regent. Shortly afterwards, on Empress Jia's order, Sima Liang was murdered by Sima Wei whom, in his turn, was put to death by the Empress. Large-scale internecine wars then ensued, involving, one time or another, eight princes of the Sima family for a period of 16 years (291-306). These wars, known as the "Disturbances of the Eight Princes", dislocated the social economy and devastated the nation's population, rending millions homeless. The Western Jin government was paralysed.

The last few years of the "Disturbances of the Eight Princes" saw refugees and immigrants of the ethnic minorities rising against the Western Jin regime in one rebellion after another. In 301, the officials of Yizhou aroused a storm of protest when they ordered refugees to return to their home towns and villages. Led by Li Te, a Di immigrant, the refugees rebelled and occupied Guanghan (in modern Sichuan Province). In 304, Li Xiong, Li Te's son, captured Chengdu and declared himself King of Chengdu. Two years later, he proclaimed himself emperor and called his domain Kingdom of Dacheng. The Xiongnu (Hun) noble, Liu Yuan, also assumed the title of king in the same year Li Xiong claimed himself King of Chengdu. Four years later, he declared himself emperor and called his domain Kingdom of Han, with the capital at Pingyang (southwest of present-day Linfen City, Shanxi). The two independent regimes were the earliest of the Sixteen States. Beginning in 309, Liu Yuan and his son Liu Cong, launched a series of unsuccessful attacks on Luoyang, the Western Jin capital. In 311 Liu Cong occupied Luoyang, and in 316 captured Chang'an. He took prisoner both Emperor Huai Di and his successor, Emperor Min Di, which spelled the end of the Western Jin Dynasty.

Subsequently, the Kingdom of Dacheng was renamed Han, historically known as the Cheng Han. The Kingdom of Han established by Liu Yuan moved its capital to Chang'an and was renamed Zhao, historically known as the Former Zhao. In the north, there were the Later Zhao, Former Liang, Former Yan, Former Qin and other independent regimes. In the south, an Eastern Jin Dynasty was set up by Sima Rui, a member of the Jin royal house.

The Later Zhao was set up in 319 by Shi Le, a Jie tribesman and previously general in Liu Yuan's service, its capital being first at Xiangguo (southwest of present-day Xingtai City, Hebei) and then at Ye (southwest of present-day Linzhang County, Hebei). At its height, the Later Zhao occupied present-day Hebei, Shanxi, Shandong, Shaanxi and Henan provinces as well as parts of Gansu, Jiangsu, Anhui, Hubei and Liaoning provinces, making itself the largest of the Sixteen States.

The Former Liang, founded by Zhang Mao, a Han, in 320, covered northwestern Gansu, southern Xinjiang and a part of Qinghai, with its capital at Guzang (now Wuwei County, Gansu Province).

The Former Yan, established by the Xianbei noble Murong Huang in 337, dominated Hebei, Shanxi, Shandong and Henan and a part of Liaoning, with its capital first at Longcheng (now Chaoyang County, Liaoning Province) and then at Ye. A powerful state in the north the Former Yan enjoyed political stability for a time.

The Former Qin was founded in 351, with its capital in Chang'an, by the Di tribesman Fu Jiàn who was succeeded by Fu Jian a year later, in 352. Fu Jian's prime minister Wang Meng, a Han statesman, adopted a policy of restraining the big landlords and easing the burden of the people, which enabled the Former Qin to enjoy a stability virtually denied to China since the end of the Eastern Han Dynasty. Over the years, Fu Jian annexed the lands of the Later Zhao, Former Liang and Former Yan to unify the greater part of northern China.

In 317, Sima Rui proclaimed himself emperor of Eastern Jin (known in history as Emperor Yuan Di), making Jiankang (previously called Jianye, now Nanjing City) his capital. As he had little to start out with, he enlisted the support of the statesman Wang Dao, who brought together the big immigrant northern landlords and the southern landholders in a joint effort to prop up the Eastern Jin regime in southern China. Of the ranking Eastern Jin officials, Zu Di was the most insistent on a northern expedition to recover the Central Plain. With little backing from the court, he led a small expeditionary force north which, after eight years' bitter fighting, regained some of the lost territories. The expedition stopped in 321 after Zu Di's death. Twenty-six years later, the Eastern Jin general Huan Wen vanquished Cheng Han. In 354, he led a force against the Former Qin and fought his way straight to Bashang at the doorstep of its capital, Chang'an. In 369, he drove as far north as Fangtou (southwest of present-day Junxian County, Henan) in an expedition against the Former Yan. These victories, though unprecedented in the military history of the Eastern Jin, were soon followed by a series of setbacks. This, combined with Huan Wen's ambition to usurp the throne, gave rise to sharp contradictions and power struggles within the Eastern Jin ruling clique. After Huan Wen's death in 373, Xie An became the chief minister. Although peace reigned in Eastern Jin, the menace of Former Qin loomed.

In 383, the ruler of the Former Qin, Fu Jian, led an infantry force of 600,000 and a cavalry force of 270,000 in a march on the Eastern Jin. Obsessed with the desire to swallow up the Eastern Jin, Fu Jian boasted, "We can stop the flow of any river by throwing our riding whips into it!" The opposing army was much smaller, with only 80,000 men under the command of Xie Shi and Xie Xuan. But the Qin army, outwardly strong, was actually a force with low morale. Many of its men had been conscripted against their will; the Han officers and men in the ranks were half-hearted about the war and the Xianbei and Liang tribal chiefs each had his own axe to grind. Liu Laozhi, a subordinate general of Xie Xuan, led a 5,000-strong crack force in a skirmish against the Qin vanguard unit at Luojian (east of present-day Huainan County, Anhui). The Qin unit suffered 15,000 casualties. When the Jin army advanced to the east bank of the Feishui (now Feihe River south of Shouxian County, Anhui), it asked the Qin troops to move back a little for it to cross the river for a decisive battle. Fu Jian complied, hoping to strike his blow home when the Jin troops were half-way across. But when the order of withdrawal was issued, the Qin troops panicked and ran. Jumping at the opportunity, the Eastern Jin troops launched a full-scale offensive, scattering the enemy. By the time Fu Jian reached Luoyang, his army was down to only a little more than 100,000 men.

The Battle of Feishui was followed by a great change in the situation in northern China. Between 384 and 385, a number of states appeared in what had been the Former Qin's territory, such as the Later Qin set up by the Qiang tribesman Yao Chang, the Later Yan by the Xianbei tribesman Murong Chui, the Western Qin by another Xianbei tribesman Qifu Guoren, and the Later Liang by the Di tribesman Lü Guang. Fu Jian was captured and killed by Yao Chang in 385. In the 12 years between 397 and 409, six more states emerged as the Northern Liang, the Southern Liang and the Western Liang split off from the Later Liang; the Southern Yan and Northern Yan from Later

Yan; and the Xia from Later Qin. These ten states were the last independent regimes to emerge among the sixteen states. Plagued by internecine wars among these states, northern China was thrown into confusion which ended only in 439 when the Northern Wei reunified that part of the country.

Exploiting its victory in the Battle of Feishui, the Eastern Jin launched a northern expedition and regained some of the lost territories. Genreal Liu Laozhi fought all the way to the city of Ye, the former capital of Later Zhao and Former Yan. These victories, however, failed to resolve the internal contradictions of the Eastern Jin regime. After Xie An died in 385, Sima Daozi, a member of the royal house, and his son, Sima Yuanxian, were placed in power, setting off a struggle within the ruling house as well as between the royal house and the influential households. In 389, Huan Xuan, General Huan Wen's son, rebelled against the Simas and carved out his sphere of influence in Jiangzhou Prefecture (now Jiujiang City, Jiangxi), not far upstream from the Eastern Jin capital Jiankang. In 399, the people of Guiji (now Shaoxing County, Zhejiang), unable to bear the misrule of the Simas, rebelled in force and, led by Sun En, inflicted one defeat after another on the government forces. After Sun En died in 402, his cause was carried on by Lu Xun. That same year, Huan Xuan stormed into Jiankang and killed the Simas. In 404, Huan Xuan deposed Emperor An Di and proclaimed himself emperor. But three or four months later, Liu Yu, Liu Laozhi's subordinate general, drove him out of Jiankang and placed Emperor An Di back on the throne. Then Liu Yu sent an expeditionary force north against the Southern Yan and the Later Qin and another to suppress the insurgents led by Lu Xun. Having built up his own prestige, Liu Yu decided in 420 to take over the throne. He dismissed the emperor and replaced the Eastern Jin with his Song Dynasty.

During the tumultuous years from the Western Jin to the Sixteen States, the ruling classes needed something to take their minds off the harsh realities and to lull the will of the people. Buddhism with its tenets of reincarnation and transmigration enabled people to find an escape from their cares by pinning their hopes for happiness on a next life. For the time, its doctrines were more attractive than those of Confucianism and the *Xuan Xue* School. Famous Buddhist monks in this period included Zhu Fa Hu of the Western Jin and Fo Tu Cheng, Dao An, Hui Yuan and Jiu Mo Luo Shi of the Eastern Jin. Jiu Mo Luo Shi (Kumarajiva) was a well-known Buddhist author and translator. In 399, the monk Fa Xian went west in search of Buddhist scriptures. When he returned to China 14 years later, he wrote of his travels in *A Record of the Buddhist Countries* in which he described the Buddhist developments, natural landscapes and customs in India, Pakistan, Nepal and Sri Lanka. The book is the earliest detailed account of China's sea and land communications with the outside world and provides important material for historical studies. While it was an appendage to the *Xuan Xue* School during the Western Jin period, Buddhism enjoyed greater influence in the Eastern Jin Dynasty, and more so in the north than in the south.

The Western and Eastern Jin period also witnessed the spread of the *Xuan Xue* School. Its principal exponent in this period, Pei Wei (267-300), author of *On the Importance of Being*, opposed Wang Bi's doctrine of Non-being. He argued that Non-being could not produce Being, by which he meant the feudal ethical code, which was indispensable to the landlord class for maintaining its rule. Guo Xiang (252-312), author of *Annotations to "Zhuang Zi"*, identified Being (the feudal ethical code) with Non-being (real nature). According to him, the feudal distinctions between the high and the low and between the rich and the poor are only natural, and the different classes should accept things as they are. It followed that it should be taken for granted that people of rank were free to enjoy a dissipated life while the poor should suffer under feudal exploitation.

In the world of literature, Lu Ji (261-303) and Zuo Si (c. 250-305) of the Western Jin excelled in poetry. Lu Ji's special treatise, *On Poetry Writing*, contributed to the development of China's literary thought. The *Ode to the Three Capitals* (of the Three Kingdoms), written by Zuo Si in a vigorous style, created such a stir among the men of lettres that it was copied and passed from hand to hand, causing a shortage of paper supply in the capital city of Luoyang. Tao Yuanming (365-427), the poet and prose writer of the Eastern Jin, was famous for his five-character poems full of poetic imagination and the flavor of rustic life. Formerly an Eastern Jin official, Tao Yuanming resigned after becoming disillusioned with the corrupt government to lead a secluded life in the countryside. His outstanding prose piece, *Peach Blossom Stream*, a description of a Chinese Arcadia, expressed his longing for a society without power struggle, cut-throat competition, lying and cheating. During the Western and Eastern Jin period, the *pian ti wen* (a flowery antithetic style of writing) was very popular. It was gorgeous in form but lacked depth.

Calligraphy and painting reached a high level of development in the Eastern Jin. Wang Xizhi (321-379 or 306-61) absorbed the essence of calligraphy of the Han-Wei period and created a style of his own to earn his fame as the "Sage Calligrapher". Gu Kaizhi (345-406) was noted for his portraits of human figures with highly expressive eyes. The mural painting of Vimalakirti, a lay Buddhist, done for the Waguan Temple of Jiankang, impressed art-lovers with its brightly coloured and finely drawn lines. His work, *On the Art of Painting*, was a masterpiece on painting techniques.

The Western and Eastern Jin period turned out more historical works than ever. There were an outpouring of history books on the Eastern Han, the Three Kingdoms, the Jin and the Sixteen States, notably the *History of the Three Kingdoms* by Chen Shou (233-297), *An Extension of the History of the Han Dynasty* by Sima Biao (?-c. 306) and *Records of the Later Han Dynasty* by Yuan Hong (328-376). The *History of the Three Kingdoms* enjoys a fame only next to that of *Records of the Historian* and *History of the Han Dynasty*. Written in biographical form, it describes the rise, growth and fall of the Three Kingdoms. *An Extension of the History of the Han Dynasty* originally had 80 *juan* but only 30, about the institutions and statutes of the Eastern Han Dynasty, survive. *Records of the Later Han Dynasty*, annals of the Eastern Han, shows innovation in the preservation and compilation of historical material.

The period from the Western Jin to the Sixteen States, though a period of turmoil in Chinese history, established the preliminary conditions for the re-unification of China—conditions which further developed during the Southern and Northern Dynasties.

Genealogical Table of the Western Jin Dynasty

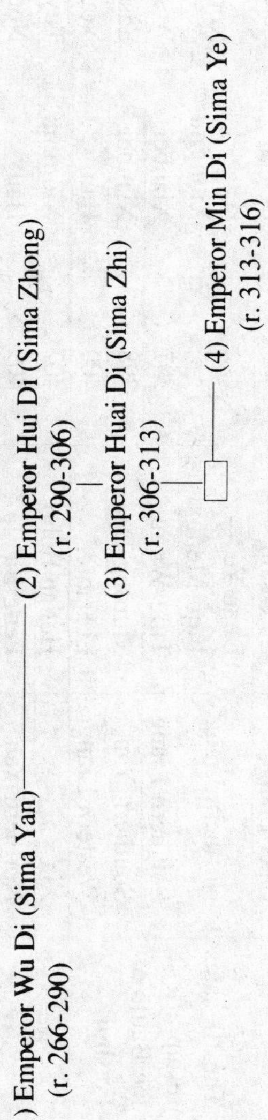

Genealogical Table of the Eastern Jin Dynasty

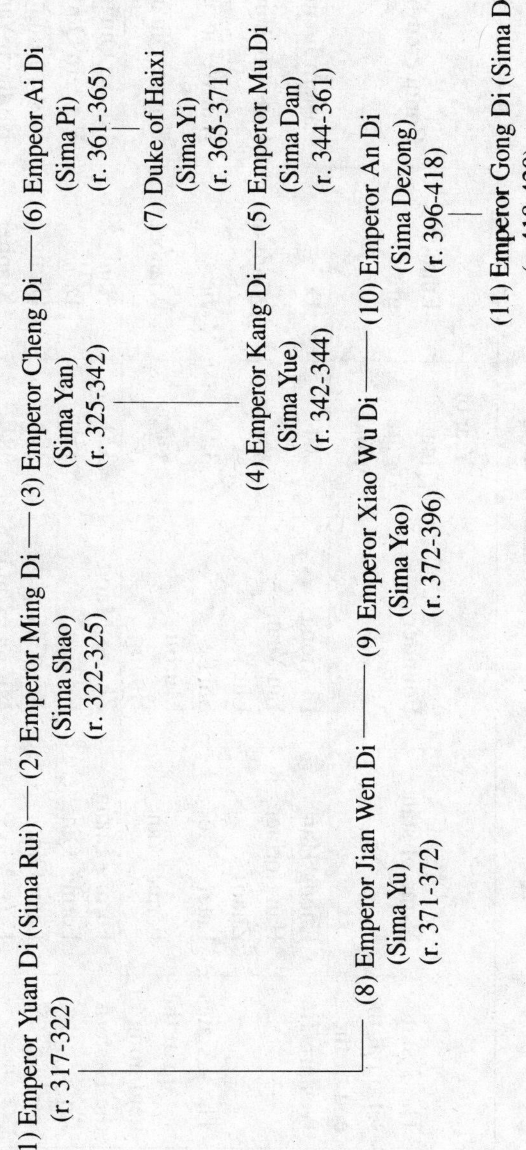

The Sixteen States

	Name of state	Founder	Year of inauguration	Ethnic group	Conquered by
The 2 states set up at the end of the Western Jin	Cheng Han	Li Xiong	304	Di	Eastern Jin in 347
	Han (former Zhao)	Liu Yuan — Liu Yao	304	Xiongnu	Later Zhao in 329
The 4 states set up at the beginning of the Eastern Jin	Later Zhao	Shi Le	319	Jie	Ran Wei in 350
	Former Yan	Murong Huang	337	Xianbei	Former Qin in 370
	Former Liang	Zhang Mao	320	Han	Former Qin in 376
	Former Qin	Fu Jiàn	351	Di	Western Qin in 394
The 10 states set up after the Battle of Feishui	Later Qin	Yao Chang	384	Qiang	Eastern Jin in 417
	Later Yan	Murong Chui	384	Xianbei	Northern Yan in 409
	Western Qin	Qifu Guoren	385	Xianbei	Xia in 431
	Later Liang	Lü Guang	385	Di	Later Qin in 403
	Northern Liang	Duan Ye — Juqu Mengxun	397	Han — Xiongnu	Northern Wei in 439
	Southern Liang	Tufa Wugu	397	Xianbei	Western Qin in 414
	Southern Yan	Murong De	398	Xianbei	Eastern Jin in 410
	Western Liang	Li Hao	400	Han	Northern Liang in 421
	Xia	Helian Bobo	407	Xiongnu	Tuyuhun in 431
	Northern Yan	Feng Ba	409	Han	Northern Wei in 436

3. The Southern and Northern Dynasties

The Song established by Liu Yu and the three successive dynasties of Southern Qi, Liang and Chen are known as the Southern Dynasties. They all had their capital at Jiankang. In its early days Song controlled a domain much larger than the other three, its northern territory stretching from Tongguan in Shaanxi in the west to Qingzhou (now Yidu County, Shandong Province) in the east. Liu Yu, later known as Emperor Wu Di, was the most powerful ruler of the South since the Eastern Jin period. After he ascended the throne in 424, Emperor Wen Di continued Liu Yu's policy and concentrated on strengthening the court, so that the economy in the Changjiang River valley enjoyed relative stability during his 30-year reign.

In the early Song period, there were five states in the north, the Western Liang, Northern Liang, Northern Yan, Western Qin and Xia. In 386, Tuoba Gui, a member of the Tuoba clan of the Xianbei tribe, set up the state of Northern Wei. In 398, he made Pingcheng (east of present Datong City, Shanxi) has capital and, the following year, proclaimed himself emperor, later known as Dao Wu Di. In 423, Emperor Ming Yuan Di of the Northern Wei crossed the Huanghe River in a march on the Song and seized Luoyang and other places south of the river. In 439, Emperor Tai Wu Di of the Northern Wei conquered Northern Liang and unified the north that had been divided and ruled by the Sixteen States.

The more than 30 years after 420 marked the early, golden period of the Southern and Northern Dynasties. In 450, a large-scale war broke out between the Song and the Northern Wei. The following year, although the Northern Wei troops had swept all the way to Guabu (now Liuhe County, Jiangsu), many of the towns and cities on the route of their march remained in the Song's hands. The war ended with tremendous losses to both sides. In 452, Emperor Tai Wu Di of the Northern Wei was murdered by the eunuch Zong Ai and the following year Emperor Wen Di of Song was killed by Liu Shao, the heir-apparent. These events were harbingers of constant turmoil and gradual decline for both the southern and northern states and marked the beginning of the middle period of the Southern and Northern Dynasties.

In the 26 years after Emperor Wen Di's death Song went through the reign of six sovereigns, three of whom were murdered. In 479, Xiao Daocheng, Commander of the Imperial Guards, usurped the power of the Song and changed its name to Qi, or the Southern Qi as historians call it. Xiao Daocheng was later known as Emperor Gao Di of Qi. The Southern Qi was the most unstable of the Southern Dynasties. In 22 years, it was ruled by seven emperors, three of whom were either deposed or murdered. In 486, Tang Yuzhi led an uprising in Fuyang (in present-day Zhejiang), which touched off a series of other uprisings. In 501, Xiao Yan, Garrison Commander of Xiangyang (near present-day Xiangfan City, Hubei Province), who had long been on the lookout for his chances, took advantage of disturbances in the Southern Qi to seize power. In one fell swoop, he renamed the dynasty Liang. Xiao Yan, later known as Emperor Wu Di, reigned for 48 years without embroiling his state in sizable wars. However, the rule of Liang, while outwardly stable, rested on a weak foundation as the peasants, ground down by ruthless exploitation, started one riot after another.

After Emperor Tai Wu Di's murder, the Northern Wei was torn by even sharper conflicts between classes and ethnic groups as well as by contradictions within the ruling class and the ruling tribe of Xianbei. In 471, when Xiao Wen Di ascended the throne as a baby, state power fell into the hands of Empress Dowager Feng. The Empress Dowager adopted a policy—a policy carried on after her death by Emperor Xiao Wen Di—that helped fuse the Xianbei with the Han people. Between 484 and 486, Emperor Xiao Wen Di carried out a number of political reforms geared to the social customs of the Han people, including the introduction of regular salaries* for government officials and the system of land equalization for peasants. After moving his capital from Pingcheng to Luoyang in 493, the emperor issued an order banning tribal languages and the wearing of tribal dress and

* The Tuoba clan of the Xianbei tribe was a backward, predatory group, and its officials had received no regular pay but lived on plunder and embezzlement.—*Trans.*

encouraging the Xianbeis to adopt Han surnames and marry the Hans. This policy helped to win the support of the Han landlords for the Northern Wei regime and consequently to consolidate the foundation of its rule. But for the Xianbei, the policy created a gap in political treatment and material benefits between the Xianbei nobles who had moved south to the Huanghe River valley and the Xianbei garrison commanders in the northern frontiers. A process of impoverishment was going on among the Xianbei soldiers guarding the northern frontiers. This, coupled with the compulsory nature of the policy of the assimilation of Han culture, sharpened the contradictions within the Xianbei tribe and tended to weaken the foundation of the Northern Wei regime. Incessant uprisings of the people took place during the reign of Emperor Xiao Wen Di and, after 497, unsuccessful wars were waged against the Southern Qi. All this showed the instability of the political situation and the flabbiness of the government.

In 523, mutinies were staged by the garrison soldiers of Woye, Huaishuo, Wuchuan, Fuming, Rouxuan (all in modern Inner Mongolia) and Huaifang (north of Zhangjiakou, Hebei), followed by many others in present-day Hebei, Shandong, Shaanxi and Gansu. The insurgent leaders included Poliuhanbaling, Du Luozhou, Xianyuxiuli and Ge Rong. Taking advantage of the turmoil, frontier commanders seized control of the Northern Wei government. In 534, Northern Wei was divided into the eastern and western parts. The Eastern Wei came under the control of General Gao Huan, a Han who had adapted himself to Xianbei customs and practices, while power in the Western Wei fell into the hands of General Yuwen Tai, a member of the Yuwen clan of the Xianbei tribe. In 550, Gao Huan's son, Gao Yang, declared himself emperor and changed the Eastern Wei to the Northern Qi. In 557, Yuwen Tai's son, Yuwen Jue, deposed the Western Wei emperor and set up the Northern Zhou. Both the Eastern Wei and the Northern Qi had their capital at Ye while both the Western Wei and the Northern Zhou had their capital at Chang'an. The areas east of Luoyang were successively held by the Eastern Wei and the Northern Qi which both controlled Luoyang itself, while those west of it by the Western Wei and the Northern Zhou.

The split of Northern Wei which marked the beginning of the

later period of the Southern and Northern Dynasties, tipped the scale in favour of the south. The rulers of the Liang Dynasty could have seized this golden opportunity to launch an expedition against the north, but they let it slip through their fingers. In 547, the Eastern Wei general Hou Jing, who was stationed south of the Huanghe River and had a personal grudge against Gao Cheng, another son of General Gao Huan, surrendered to the Liang. Emperor Wu Di of the Liang then ordered him to attack the Eastern Wei with a supporting force dispatched by the court. Defeated by the Eastern Wei, Hou Jing saw an opportunity to turn this situation to his own advantage as he pulled his army back in a southward drive. The following year, he marched on Jiankang, and laid siege to the palace city of Taicheng, where Emperor Wu Di starved to death. Hou Jing's troops ravaged Jiankang and some of the other richest places in the south, looting or burning much of the wealth accumulated from the time of the Eastern Jin. In 552, General Chen Baxian defeated Hou Jing, recovered Jiankang and, in 555, placed Xiao Fangzhi on the throne of the Liang. In 557, Chen Baxian deposed the emperor and established the Chen Dynasty. He was later known as Emperor Wu Di of the Chen. Rising from the ruins of Liang, the Chen government directed all its efforts towards the rehabilitation of the social economy in its early period. The Chen was the smallest of the Southern Dynasties, its domain smaller than all its precursors—the Song, the Qi and the Liang, and its northern border reaching only the southern bank of the Changjiang River. However, it was strong enough to resist the incursions of the Northern Qi and the Northern Zhou. In 573, it allied with the Northern Zhou in a successful expedition against the Northern Qi.

Generally speaking, neither the Liang nor the Chen of the south was in a position to make anything out of the divisions in the north. In the north, there was a negligible gap in strength between the Eastern and the Western Wei and between the Northern Qi and the Northern Zhou. But the Northern Zhou rested on sounder political ground and its military strength had grown steadily. On the other hand, the Northern Qi after the reign of Gao Yang had been ruled by tyrants, each worse than the previous one, until finally not even the ruling clique could close its own ranks. The north was reunified in 577 when Emperor Wu Di of the Northern Zhou conquered Northern Qi. Emperor Wu Di died in 578, and was succeeded by Emperor Xuan Di, a corrupt and fatuous monarch. When his son, Emperor Jing Di, succeeded to the throne at the age of eight, power fell into the hands of Yang Jian, a royal relative on the female line. In 581, Yang Jian proclaimed himself emperor and set up the Sui Dynasty in place of the Northern Zhou. In 589, Yang Jian, later known as Emperor Wen Di of the Sui, wiped out the Chen in the south and brought the whole of China under his unified control.

From the time of Emperor Wen Di of Song, many venerable Buddhist monks came to China from the west, and Buddhism of various sects flourished during the Southern and Northern Dynasties. Large numbers of Sanskrit Buddhist scriptures were translated into Chinese. Among the emperors and princes, the most devout Buddhists were Xiao Ziliang, Prince of Jingling of the Qi, and Emperor Wu Di of the Liang. Emperor Wu Di many times retired to a Buddhist temple to become a novice and each time had to be bought out of the temple by his ministers. At one time, Jiankang alone boasted more than 500 Buddhist monasteries housing upwards of 100,000 monks and nuns. Famous Buddhist monks were held in awe by people of rank and title. Monks such as Fa Yun, Zhi Cang and Seng Min drew large audiences of nobles and scholars whenever they preached Buddhist teachings.

During the Sixteen States period, the Former Liang and the Northern Liang were the Buddhist centres in the north. Buddhism lost ground for a time under Emperor Tai Wu Di of the Northern Wei, who suppressed Buddhism in favour of Taoism. But after Emperor Xiao Wen Di of the Northern Wei moved his capital to Luoyang, the Empresses Dowager of several generations believed in Buddhism, and the religion began to catch on again. During the reign of Emperor Xuan Wu Di the Venerable Bodhidharma came to Northern Wei from southern India to teach Buddhism in the north after preaching in south China. He advocated meditating, cultivating the mind, and getting rid of wishful thinking for the salvation of the soul and opposed the way famous Buddhist monks in the south lumped Buddhism and *Xuan Xue* together in their preachings. The Chan sect founded by him was an influential one, popular first in the north and later spreading to the south. Large numbers of Buddhist monasteries were built in the north, with over 1,300 in Luoyang alone and more than 30,000 throughout the domain of the Northern Wei. The rulers of the Northern Dynasties expended fabulous amounts of money, manpower and material supplies on the digging of grottoes at Yungang in Datong, Shanxi Province, and at Longmen in Luoyang, Henan Province. Each of these grottoes was bejewelled with exquisitely executed Buddhist images. The 53 existing Yungang Grottoes, completed before the Northern Wei moved its capital to Luoyang, contain over 51,000 Buddhist images, the tallest of which is 17 metres. Digging of the Longmen Grottoes started around the time when the Northern Wei made Luoyang its capital and continued down to the Tang period. During the Northern and Western Wei dynasties, work continued on the Dunhuang Grottoes dug in the Sixteen States period in Gansu Province and a host of Buddhist statues were added. Yungang, Longmen and Dunhuang are all world-famous for their engravings.

When Buddhism was gaining ground both in the south and the north, the outstanding atheist Fan Zhen (c. 450-515) voiced his opposition in his *On the Destructibility of the Soul* written at the end of the Southern Qi Dynasty. He said that the soul and the body are interdependent. According to him, the soul is to the body as sharpness is to the blade; as sharpness cannot exist independently of the blade, neither can the soul exist independently of the body. If the body dies, the soul dies too, he said. The professions about the undying soul, reincarnation, transmigration and retribution, he contended, are absurdities pure and simple. Fan Zhen's theories came as a shock to the Buddhist believers. Prince Xiao Ziliang of the Southern Qi summoned many learned Buddhist monks to debate Fan Zhen, but they were unable to demolish his arguments. In 507, Emperor Wu Di of the Liang organized more than 60 dignitaries and learned monks for another debate, and again they failed to bring Fan Zhen to his knees. During the reign of Emperor Wu Di of the Northern Zhou, the Buddhist monasteries had become a heavy drain on the sources of state revenue and soldiery. The emperor was forced to summon his ministers for a series of debates with Buddhist monks. Finally, he dealt a heavy blow to Buddhist influence by resorting to a policy of "recruiting soldiers from among

Buddhist monks and requisitioning land around Buddhist pagodas and temples".

The Southern Dynasties laid greater claim to fame in literature and historical studies than did the Northern Dynasties. In literature, poetry enjoyed popularity in the south. Xie Lingyun (385-433) was famous for his nature poems. Bao Zhao (c. 412-466) wrote many poems which gave free flow to his aspirations and longings for a better life and exerted some influence on the renowned Tang Dynasty poet Li Bai. The *Critique of Poetry* written by Zhong Rong (?-552) of the Qi-Liang period comments on 122 poets from the Han to the Liang period, at the same time analysing the various poetic trends and their origins. The 30-*juan Anthology Through the Ages*, compiled by famed scholars under the auspices of the Liang crown prince Xiao Tong (501-531), a literary enthusiast, contains the cream of literature since the pre-Qin period and exerted far-reaching influence on the literature of later generations. The 50-chapter *Wen Xin Diao Long* by Liu Xie (c. 466-c. 520) of the Liang Dynasty, one of China's famous works of literary criticism, presents a comprehensive and systematic study of literary questions and contains the author's original ideas on the relationships between content and form in literature and between the development of literature and its time. Of the literary works of the Northern Dynasties, the best-known is *The Song of Mu Lan*. This narrative poem, about a girl who disguises herself as a man to take her aging father's place in the army, was supposed to have been adapted from a folk ballad. The author, Yu Xin (513-581), who had been detained in the north during a diplomatic mission there from the southern regime of Liang, was an accomplished poet. Most of his works, notably *A Lament for the South*, expressed his nostalgia for his homeland. The 20-chapter *Family Admonitions* by Yan Zhitui (c. 531-590), covering a wide range of subjects—political, economic, cultural and educational—is notable among literary works for its easy and smooth style of writing. Readers in the old days, however, were mainly interested in its teachings about social conduct, looking upon it as a guide to the philosophy of life in feudal society. Yang Xuanzhi's *Temples and Monasteries in Luoyang*, in five *juan*, gives some idea of the political, economic, cultural and social aspects of the Northern Wei

Genealogical Table of the Southern Dynasties

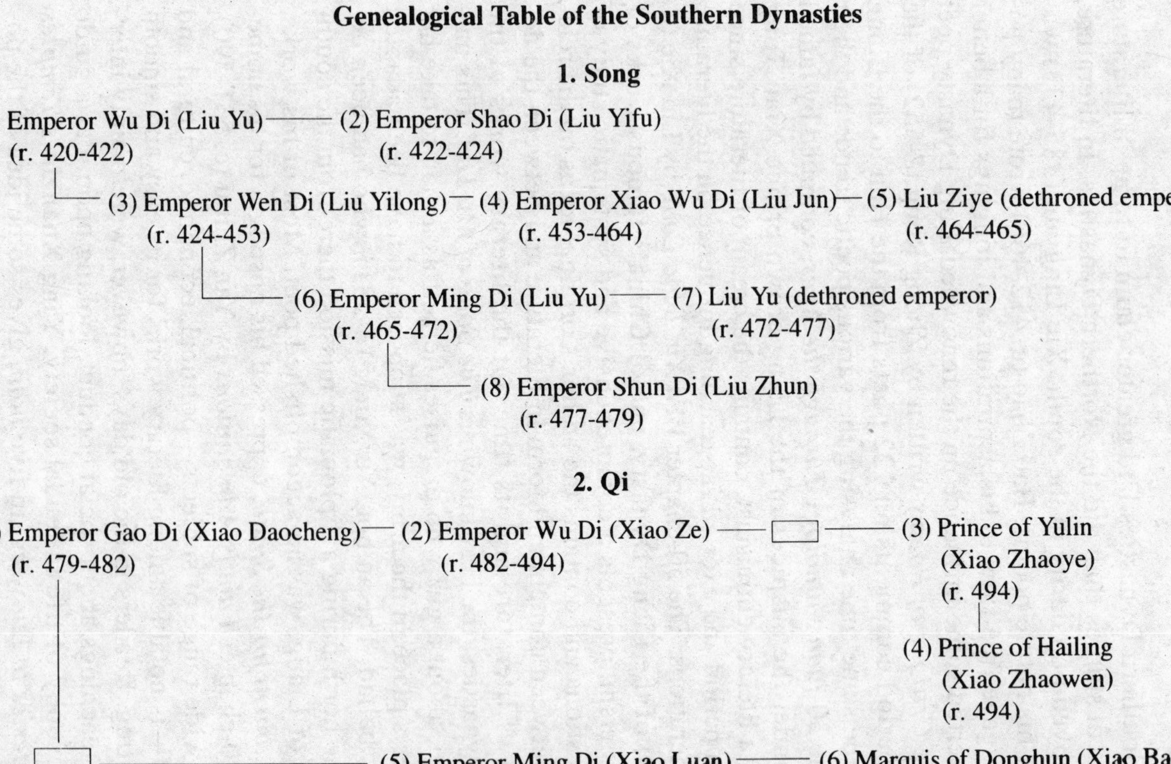
1. Song
(1) Emperor Wu Di (Liu Yu) (r. 420-422)
(2) Emperor Shao Di (Liu Yifu) (r. 422-424)
(3) Emperor Wen Di (Liu Yilong) (r. 424-453)
(4) Emperor Xiao Wu Di (Liu Jun) (r. 453-464)
(5) Liu Ziye (dethroned emperor) (r. 464-465)
(6) Emperor Ming Di (Liu Yu) (r. 465-472)
(7) Liu Yu (dethroned emperor) (r. 472-477)
(8) Emperor Shun Di (Liu Zhun) (r. 477-479)
2. Qi
(1) Emperor Gao Di (Xiao Daocheng) (r. 479-482)
(2) Emperor Wu Di (Xiao Ze) (r. 482-494)
(3) Prince of Yulin (Xiao Zhaoye) (r. 494)
(4) Prince of Hailing (Xiao Zhaowen) (r. 494)
(5) Emperor Ming Di (Xiao Luan) (r. 494-498)
(6) Marquis of Donghun (Xiao Baojuan) (r. 498-501)
(7) Emperor He Di (Xiao Baorong) (r. 501-502)

Eminent Woman (part), said to have been painted by Gu Kaizhi (346-407)

A tomb brick painting of tilling land by oxen-drawn plough
(unearthed in Jiayuguan, Gansu Province)

Model of a chariot with a south-pointing device, invented by Ma Jun

Silver container with the design of a dancing horse holding a cup in its mouth (unearthed in Hejia Village, Xi'an, Shaanxi Province)

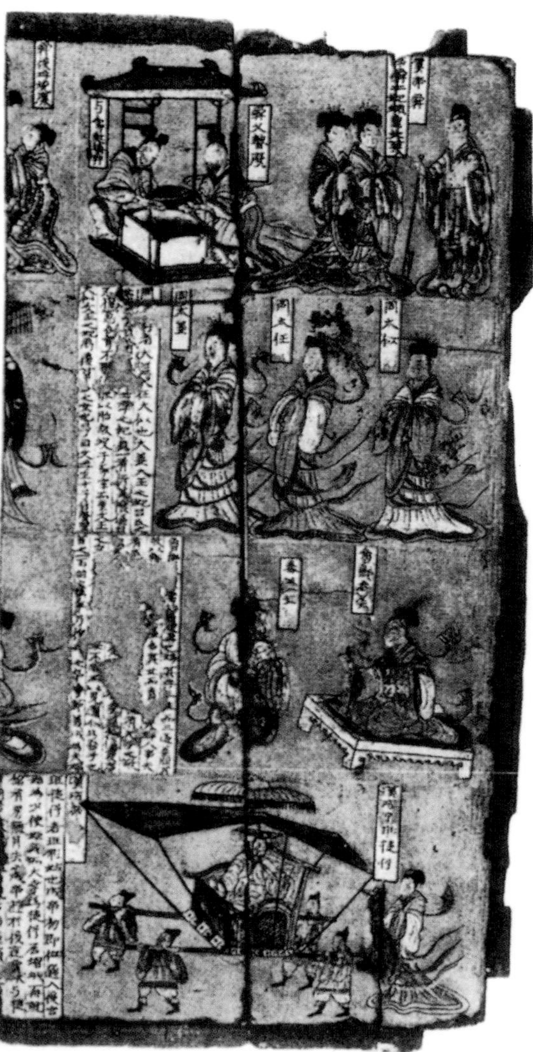

Lacquer painting on wood (unearthed in Datong, Shanxi Province)

Tablet commemorating the introduction of Nestorianism to China (in the Forest of Tablets, Xi'an, Shaanxi Province)

The Zhaozhou single-arch stone bridge, also called the Anji Bridge
(Zhaoxian County, Hebei Province)

Piebald, one of the six horses in the Zhaoling Mausoleum (Bas-relief, mounted in the west corridor of the Zhaoling Mausoleum)

Three-color glazed camel (unearthed from a Tang Dynasty tomb in Xi'an, Shaanxi Province)

Great Wild Goose Pagoda (Xi'an, Shaanxi Province)

Eight-sided flask (unearthed in the underground palace of the Temple of Famen (Dharma Gate), Fufeng County, Shaanxi Province)

Marching Chariot by Yan Liben (upper and lower pieced together)

Painting of the eminent Tang Dynasty monk Xuanzang teaching Buddhist scriptures

The Great Mosque, said to have been built in the Tang Dynasty
(Xi'an, Shaanxi Province)

Tang Dynasty infantry in armor

The Ziweiyuan Star Chart from the Dunhuang Scrolls

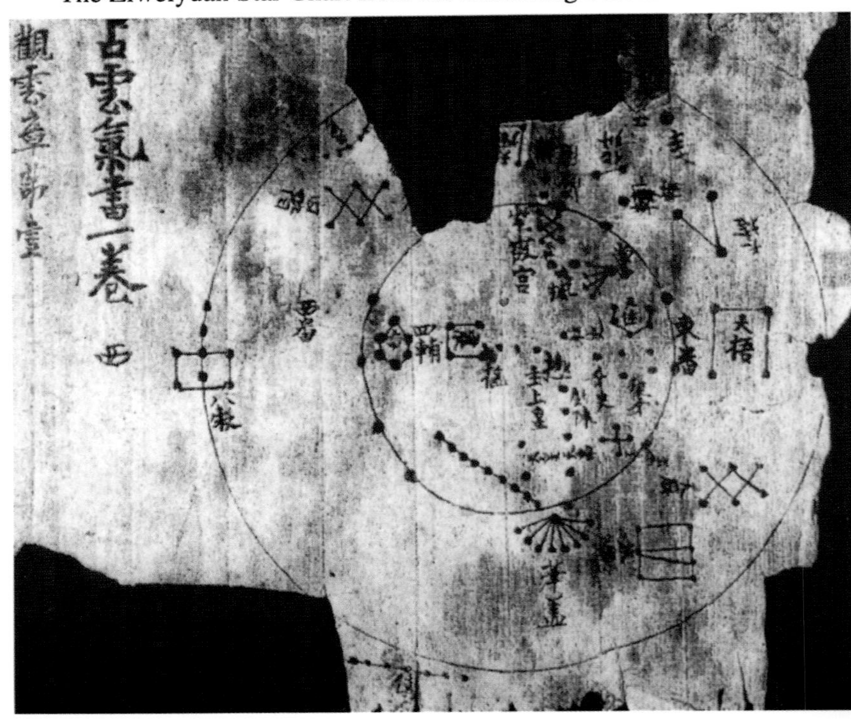

Genealogical Table of the Southern Dynasties (Continued)

3. Liang

(1) Emperor Wu Di (Xiao Yan) (r. 502-549) —— (2) Emperor Jian Wen Di (Xiao Gang) (r. 549-551)

(1) Emperor Wu Di (Xiao Yan) —— (3) Emperor Yuan Di (Xiao Yi) (r. 552-554) —— (4) Emperor Jing Di (Xiao Fangzhi) (r. 555-557)

4. Chen

(1) Emperor Wu Di (Chen Baxian) (r. 557-559)

□ —— (2) Emperor Wen Di (Chen Qian) (r. 559-566) —— (3) Chen Bozong (dethroned emperor) (r. 566-568)

(4) Emperor Xuan Di (Chen Xu) (r. 568-582) —— (5) Emperor Hou Zhu (Chen Shubao) (r. 582-589)

Genealogical Table of the Northern Dynasties

1. Northern Wei

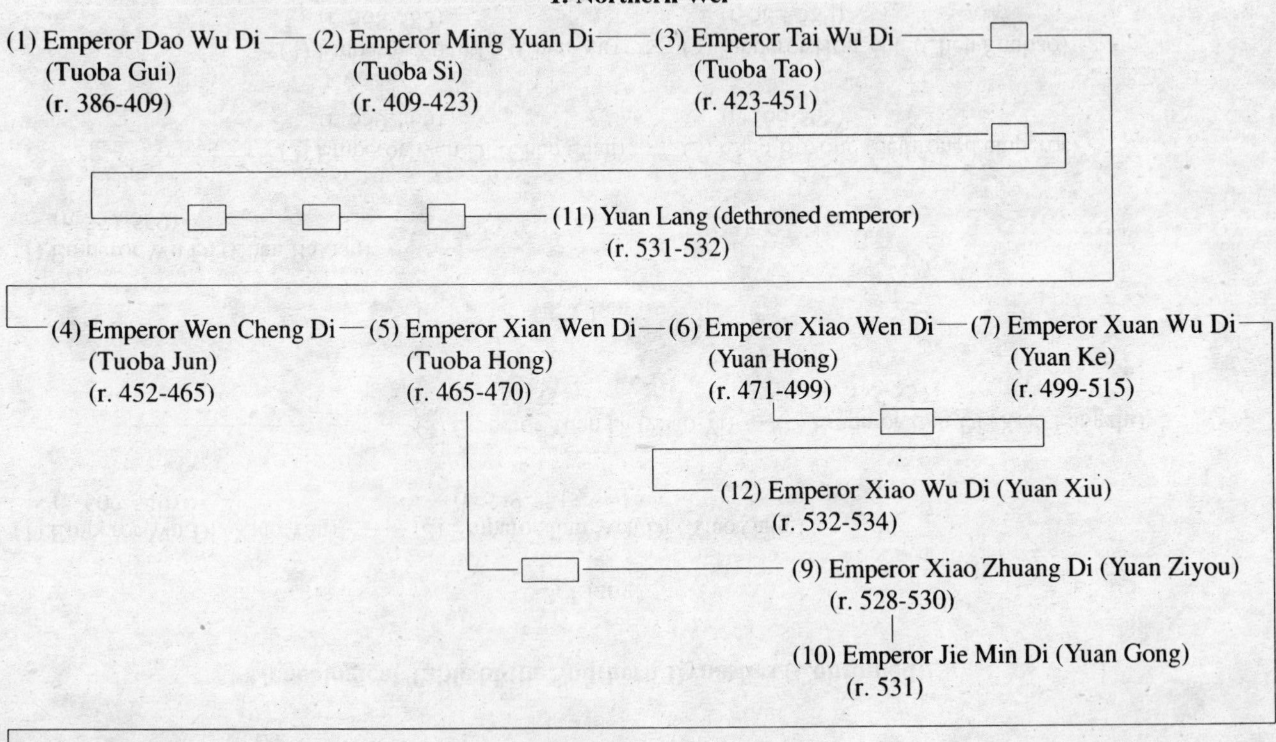

Genealogical Table of the Northern Dynasties (Continued)

2. Eastern Wei

(1) Emperor Xiao Jing Di (Yuan Shanjian)
(r. 534-550)

3. Western Wei

(1) Emperor Wen Di (Yuan Baoju) —— (2) Yuan Qin (dethroned emperor)
(r. 535-551) (r. 552-553)
|
(3) Emperor Gong Di (Yuan Kuo)
(r. 554-557)

4. Northern Qi

(1) Emperor Wen Xuan Di (Gao Yang) —— (2) Gao Yin (dethroned emperor)
(r. 550-559) (r. 560)
|
(3) Emperor Xiao Zhao Di (Gao Yan)
(r. 560-561)
|
(4) Emperor Wu Cheng Di (Gao Zhan) —— (5) Emperor Hou Zhu (Gao Wei) —— (6) Emperor You Zhu (Gao Heng)
(r. 561-565) (r. 565-576) (r. 577)

5. Northern Zhou

(1) Emperor Xiao Min Di (Yuwen Jue)
(r. 557)
|
(2) Emperor Ming Di (Yuwen Yu)
(r. 557-560)
|
(3) Emperor Wu Di (Yuwen Yong) —— (4) Emperor Xuan Di (Yuwen Yun) —— (5) Emperor Jing Di (Yuwen Chan)
(r. 561-578) (r. 579) (r. 579-581)

Dynasty. Apart from their value to historical research, these two works are also of a high literary quality.

There were many genealogical records, records of village men of virtue and biographies of famous personalities during the Southern and Northern Dynasties, but few of them survive. Important historical works in this period include *History of the Later Han Dynasty* by Fan Ye (398-445) of the Song, *History of the Song Dynasty* by Shen Yue of the Liang, *History of the Southern Qi Dynasty* by Xiao Zixian, and *History of the Wei Dynasty* by Wei Shou of the Northern Qi. The *History of the Later Han Dynasty*, well-documented, fresh in style and original in the judgement of historical facts, emerged as the most successful historical work after *History of the Han Dynasty* and *History of the Three Kingdoms*.

4. The Establishment of the Sui Dynasty and the Peasant Uprisings in Its Closing Years

Like the Qin Dynasty which united China in 221 B.C., the Sui established another feudal dynasty for the whole country, only to fall in a few decades. The Sui Dynasty had only two sovereigns. Yang Jian, later known as Emperor Wen Di of Sui, ruled for 23 years beginning with his conquest of Northern Zhou in 581, before he was slain by the heir-apparent, Yang Guang, in 604. His reign lasted only 15 years if counted from the year of the fall of the Chen Dynasty. Yang Guang, later known as Emperor Yang Di, was on the throne for only 13 years.

Immediately after the proclamation of his new state, Yang Jian reorganized his central government into three key departments—the Secretariat in charge of confidential, highly important matters and the enactment of imperial decrees; the Grand Council which examined and approved these decrees; and the Chancery responsible for the administration of the whole country. The chiefs of the three departments were equivalent to the prime minister of the Qin-Han period, whose powers and functions were now divided among these three officials who were directly accountable to the emperor. Local administrative divisions were also changed—from the three-level system (prefectures, sub-prefectures and counties) of the Northern Dynasties to a two-level system (prefectures and counties). Local officials from the ninth grade up were appointed or removed by the court and their work was reviewed and appraised annually by the Board of Civil Office. Chief local officials were transferred every three years, their deputies every four years. All these measures helped strengthen the rule of absolute monarchy.

Yang Jian also abolished the system practised since the Wei-Jin period, by which local officials were selected by prefects. He set up institutions of learning in prefectures and counties, from which candidates with fine academic records were nominated for yearly court examinations and for appointment according to the results. This opened a new channel for more people to enter upon an official career and so helped enlarge the class basis of feudal rule.

A new penal code, based on but much simpler than that of Northern Wei and Northern Qi, was adopted. It consisted of only 12 chapters, omitting more than 1,000 articles of the old code. Only five kinds of punishment were provided for—death, exile, imprisonment, heavy flogging and light flogging. Whoever considered the verdict unjust had the right to file his appeal level by level up to the emperor himself. Persons guilty of treason and other "monstrous crimes" were not to be pardoned.

Yang Jian also adopted measures to prevent persons from avoiding conscription and the payment of taxes. In 585, two strict general censuses were taken in the prefectures and counties, through which the exact ages of the inhabitants were checked on the spot and recorded in government register. Some 600,000 adult males were discovered. In the same year, measures aimed at lightening the burden of taxation and conscript labour were taken to reclassify the households into different categories according to property and size. Every year taxes were collected and labour service recruited accordingly. These measures increased the labour force available to the government by encouraging the peasant protégés of manorial lords to break away from them and entering these peasant households into the state register.

After conquering the Chen in 589, Yang Jian cracked down on

the local forces in the south. This aroused a storm of protests from the influential landlords there, who, in 590, rose in rebellions, captured towns and cities and killed government officials. General Yang Su was sent to suppress the rebels and the tense situation was taken in hand.

The political reforms initiated by Yang Jian and the quelling of the rebellions in the south created political stability in the early period of Sui and, consequently, a speedy economic growth. Abundant harvests were reaped in the first dozen years and both handicrafts and commerce flourished. Many state granaries were built, notably the Hanjia Granary at Luoyang with a capacity of 480,000 piculs (133.33 pounds to a picul); the Xingluo Granary at Luokou (modern Gongxian County, Henan) with a capacity of 24,000,000 piculs; and the Huiluo Granary north of Luoyang with a capacity of 2,400,000 piculs. During his later reign, Yang Jian reportedly had a grain reserve large enough to see the whole nation through several years.

The Sui court paid great attention to its relations with the frontier peoples. Since the Wu fleet led by Wei Wen and Zhuge Zhi called at Taiwan, an increasing number of people had migrated there from the mainland to join the local Gaoshan people in their pioneering efforts. In 607, Zhu Kuan, a cavalry commander, and He Man, a naval officer, were sent by Emperor Yang Di on an inspection tour of the island, then known as Liuqiu. The following year, Zhu Kuan again visited Taiwan, this time on a good-will mission. In 610, a Sui fleet set sail for Taiwan from Yi'an (now Chaozhou City, Guangdong Province). Mistaking the fleet for merchant ships, the Gaoshans poured out onto the waterfront bringing local products for trade. From that time, the ties between Taiwan and the mainland became closer.

The Sui Dynasty had contacts with the states set up by the ethnic minorities, such as the Qidan, Shiwei and Mohe in the Liaohe, Heilongjiang and Ergun river valleys in the Northeast; the Turks (the Tujue) south of the Altay Mountains; the Tuyuhun south of the Qilian Mountains and north of the Xueshan Mountains; as well as those inhabiting Gaochang, Quici, Yanqi and Yutian in present-day Xinjiang Uygur Autonomous Region. People from these states often came to the hinterland to barter for local products. The Sui married daughters of the royal house to the tribal chiefs of the Turks and Tuyuhun and to the king of Gaochang and had Pei Ju based in Zhangye (in modern Gansu Province) to take care of the commercial and other ties with the Western Regions.

There were three trade routes to the West during the Sui Dynasty: the northern route, from Yiwu (modern Hami, Xinjiang) via Puleihai (now Lake Barkol) and the region of the Tiele tribe to the state of Fulin (Syria); the central route, from Gaochang (now Turpan, Xinjiang) via Yanqi, Quici and Congling Range to Persia (now Iran); and the southern route, from Shanshan (near present-day Lake Lop Nur, Xinjiang) via Yutian and Congling Range to north "Poluomen" (a transliteration of the word "Brahman", now north India and Pakistan). Of the three routes, the central and the south extended even farther west.

Two major events in the Sui period were the construction of the capital Luoyang and the digging of the Grand Canal. To tighten his control of the rich middle-lower Huanghe River valley and the areas south of the Changjiang River, Yang Guang (Emperor Yang Di) launched the large-scale construction of his capital in 605, in the early period of his reign. The project involved tens of thousands of workers and cratfsmen for a duration of 12 months. The inner part of the city consisted of palace buildings, the intermediate part of government institutions, and the outer part of official residences and the dwelling houses of common people. The outer part also served as the commercial district, with well over 100 streets and alleys and three market centres. When the project was completed, the emperor ordered large numbers of the influential households and wealthy merchants to move to Luoyang. The Grand Canal project was launched at the same time as the construction of Luoyang with the participation of hundreds of thousands of workers. The canal had three sections. The first, the Tongji Channel, directed water from the Gushui and Luoshui rivers at Luoyang's West Park all the way to the Huanghe River and from the Huanghe at Banzhu east of Luoyang through the old Langdang Ditch to Shanyang (now Huai'an County, Jiangsu Province) on the south bank of the Huaihe. From Shanyang the Huaihe River water was guided through the old Han Canal dug in the time of King Fu Chai of Wu in the Spring and Autumn Period to empty into the Changjiang River at Jiangdu (now Yangzhou City, Jiangsu). The whole section, from

Luoyang to Jiangdu, was more than 1,000 kilometres long. The second section, the Yongji Channel, directed water from the Qinshui at Luokou south to the Huanghe River and north to Zhuojun (now Beijing)—also a total of more than 1,000 km. The third section, the 400-km-long Jiangnan Channel, drew its water from the Changjiang River at Jingkou to join the Qiantang River at Yuhang (now Hangzhou City, Zhejiang). In brief, the Grand Canal, totalling 2,500 km in length, extended to Zhuojun in the north and to Yuhang in the south, with Luoyang as its centre. A water transport artery, the Canal helped promote economic development and unify the country.

Both the construction of Luoyang and the digging of the Grand Canal took a heavy toll among the builders. When the Yongji Channel was being cut, the shortage of able-bodied men was made up by women. After the canal was completed, Yang Guang repeatedly went on pleasure trips to Jiangdu by boat, imposing a heavy strain on the nation's manpower and material resources.

Yang Guang was an emperor with a craze for the grandiose. To punish the Korean king for his refusal to pay respects to the Sui court, he launched three successive wars against Korea in the three years 612-14. A great deal of manpower, material and financial resources were wasted on these wars, bringing the class contradictions at home to a fever pitch.

Popular uprisings had been brewing prior to the wars against Korea, when millions of peasants were pressed into military and labour service. Many of the warship builders along the coast at Donglai in present-day Shandong Province had maggots below their waistlines from working days and nights in water. Three or four out of every ten of the labourers were literally worked to death.

The stage for the late Sui peasant revolts was set in 611, when the peasant leader Wang Bo started an uprising in the Changbai Mountains (in modern Zhangqiu County, Shandong). He rallied the peasants around him by composing a song, "Don't Go and Die in Liaodong". Wang Bo's uprising inspired others led by Dou Jiande, Du Fuwei, Fu Gongshi and Zhai Rang in Shandong, Hebei, Shaanxi, Guangdong, Zhejiang and Ningxia. These peasant forces, some of them tens of thousands while others more than a hundred thousand strong, captured towns and cities and killed corrupt officials and local tyrants.

The outbreak of the peasant rebellions caused divisions within the ruling clique. Seeing that the bulk of the government troops were pinned down by the fast-expanding peasant forces, Yang Xuangan, a Sui noble, also rose against the court in 613 with an army which quickly grew to some 100,000. He was soon defeated, but many of the rebels under him went over to swell the ranks of the peasant insurgents.

The unit led by Zhai Rang operated in Henan Province, with Wagang (near Huaxian County, Henan) as its base. In 616, Li Mi, another Sui noble who had been with Yang Xuangan in his rebellion, joined the Wagang army. He won over many lesser armed bands to the Wagang side, which swiftly expanded to become the most formidable peasant force. In 617, the Wagang army captured the Xingluo Granary and distributed the grain among the poor and destitute. This won enthusiastic mass support for the Wagang army, which by now had grown to hundreds of thousands until finally Luoyang was completely isolated from the greater part of Henan.

Meanwhile, the insurgent force led by Dou Jiande, which had been active at Gojibo (northwest of Enxian County, Shandong), fought its way to Hebei Province where, in 617, it wiped out the Sui main force under General Xue Shixiong and captured many towns and cities.

The band that had been manoeuvring in the Changjiang and Huaihe river valleys under the leadership of Du Fuwei and Fu Gongshi also defeated repeated Sui attacks and incorporated many lesser hands. By early 618, its influence had reached the areas along the Changjiang, posing a direct menace to Jiangdu where Yang Guang was enjoying himself on one of his pleasure trips.

The flames of peasant uprisings continued to rage until they engulfed the greater part of the Sui domain, leaving only Luoyang, Jiangdu and a few other secluded cities unscorched. Seeing that the situation had grown out of hand, many local officials, landlords and nobles began to look around for ways to preserve themselves or to expand their own influence in the turmoil. Some even renounced their allegiance to Sui and proclaimed themselves king or emperor. In 617,

Li Yuan, an aristocrat, led an army revolt in Taiyuan and captured Chang'an. In spring the following year, Yang Guang was assasinated in Jiangdu. Soon afterwards, Li Yuan declared himself emperor of Tang, historically known as Emperor Gao Zu of the Tang Dynasty.

5. The Golden Age of the Tang

After his ascension, with the help of his second son, Li Shimin, Li Yuan drew Li Mi and Du Fuwei into his service, suppressed Dou Jiande, wiped out the landlords' independent regimes in various places and, in 623, unified the whole of China. In 626, Li Yuan gave up the throne to Li Shimin, who became the famous Emperor Tai Zong of the Tang Dynasty.

As an outstanding statesman and military strategist, Li Shimin was exceptional among all the Chinese emperors. His assistants, such as Li Jing, Fang Xuanling, Du Ruhui, Zhangsun Wuji and Wei Zheng, were all talented administrators. Li Shimin believed that he had an important historical lesson to learn from the rapid fall of the once powerful Sui Dynasty. He often discussed with his ministers the merits and demerits of Sui politics to find better ways to consolidate his regime. He encouraged his ministers to come out with whatever differing opinions they had in mind on political questions. This style of work enhanced his political prestige and strengthened the unity of the court.

Political reforms were carried out on the basis of the Sui institutions. The three key departments of the Sui regime remained the principle organs of the central government—the Secretariat through which the emperor issued his orders, and which handled memorials to the emperor, the formulation of policies and the drafting of edicts and decrees; the Grand Council which offered advice to the emperor and examined and approved the imperial edicts and decrees; and the Chancery which was in charge of national administration and which had the Six Boards under it: the Board of Civil Office, of Revenue, of Rites, of War, of Justice and of Works. The three departments were binding on and supplementary to one another in their functions and powers. Local administrative divisions were the prefectures and counties. In important frontier regions, governors' offices were established to take care of military and civil affairs there. In addition, the country was divided into 10 circuits (*dao*). A circuit was not an administrative division and had no administrative office; it was rather an inspection area where imperial commissioners went from time to time to examine the work of local officials and learn about the grievances of the people.

In the military system, the Tang regime inherited the compulsory service of Northern Zhou and Sui. A total of 634 commanderies were set up throughout the country, each in command of 1,000 soldiers. The soldiers engaged in farming in peace time and in drills in slack seasons. They were exempted from corvée and tax but had to rotate for regular guard duties in the capital. In case of war, they responded to the call-up, taking their own weapons, clothing and provisions. When the war ended, they returned to their work behind the plough. Later, to meet the needs of massive warfare a supplementary, mercenary system was instituted, which in time outstripped the compulsory system in importance.

A new penal code was worked out under the supervision of Fang Xuanling and others. The Tang code was based on that of Sui but was simpler and shorter and contained lighter punishments. It was clarified by Zhangsun Wuji and others in the 30-*juan Exposition of the Tang Penal Code*. The Tang code together with the *Exposition* was the most complete feudal statute in Chinese history, and its influence large on all the later feudal codes.

Li Shimin was anxious to enlist talented people into his service. In the foundation period of Tang, he had won over many qualified personnel—both civil and military—from hostile political groups. After his ascension to the throne, he paid great attention to the selection of competent local officials, which he considered the key to peace and order across the land. The imperial civil examination initiated under the Sui was extended during Li Shimin's reign as an important system in selecting people of ability. During the Tang Dynasty, there were two main degrees for examination candidates, the *Ming Jing* (Senior Licentiate) and the *Jing Shi* (Advanced Scholar). Confucian classics were a must in the examination for the first degree, poetry for the second. In the course of time, the *Jing Shi* became the favoured degree.

After Li Shimin's death, Emperor Gao Zong succeeded him. His empress, Wu Ze Tian was a capable woman with political ambition. In 655, she began to participate in court affairs and, in 660, took all powers in her hands. In 690, she ascended the throne and called herself Emperor Sheng Shen. She made a point of drawing talented people into her service and successively appointed the outstanding statesmen Li Zhaode, Di Renjie and Yao Chong as prime ministers to help herself run state affairs. At the same time, she befriended some wicked and treacherous courtiers and appointed tyrannical officials notorious for their injustices, although she would not let them go too far or invest them with too much power. Wu Ze Tian's reign lasted for half a century, during which the royal power of the ruling Li house was greatly impaired, but the political situation created by Li Shimin did not end and the social economy continued to develop.

The Tang regime reached the height of its power and prosperity during the reign of Emperor Xuan Zong (712-756), who ascended the throne after seven or eight years of turmoil following the death of Empress Wu Ze Tian. Bent on making the country prosperous, he carried out political reforms and promoted competent people to premiership. He was receptive to criticism and advice from his ministers. In the first 30 years or more of his reign, the country became strong and prosperous and the population grew tremendously—a phenomenon never known before.

A number of palace coups and local peasant uprisings took place after the founding of the Tang Dynasty. In 653, a woman peasant leader, Chen Shuozhen, staged an uprising at Muzhou (modern Jiande County, Zhejiang), declared herself Emperor Wen Jia and captured some of the places in Zhejiang. These incidents, however, had no vital bearing on the country as a whole. The social economy developed continuously for over 120 years, from 618 to 741, at the height of Tang, longer than in any of the previous dynasties.

The golden age of Tang also witnessed closer relations between the various ethnic groups within China's borders, although there were also wars between them.

In the early Sui period, the Turks in the northwest split into the eastern and western branches, controlling regions north and south of the Gobi Desert and the Central Asian areas east of the Caspian Sea. In 626, the Khan of the Eastern Turks, Xieli, harassed Wugong (in modern Shaanxi Province) and pushed on to the neighbourhoods of Chang'an. In 629, on orders from Li Shimin, Xu Shiji and Li Jing led a massive counter-attack. An internal split and a sharp decrease in the livestock population after several years of blizzards weakened the fighting strength of the Eastern Turks. In 630, the Tang army won a decisive victory, conquering the Eastern Turks and capturing Xieli Khan. The Tang government resettled the officers and men of the Eastern Turks, who had pledged allegiance to the Tang, in the areas starting from Youzhou (modern Beijing) in the east to Lingzhou (modern Lingwu County, Ningxia) in the west. Four governors' offices were established there, while the Dingxiang and Yunzhong governors' offices were set up in the former territories of the Eastern Turks. The Eastern Turks rose again during the reign of Emperor Gao Zong. Ashinaguduolu, an Eastern Turki aristocrat, rebelled and made war on Tang for many years. After Pijia Khan assumed power in 716, he sued for peace, and the Tang government promised to trade with the Eastern Turks and exchange it silk for their horses. Subsequently, friendly ties were forged between the two sides. When the Khan's elder brother, Queteqin, died in 731, Emperor Xuan Zong sent an envoy to express his condolences and had a monument erected to honour his memory, which bore an inscription in both the Han and Turki languages.

The Western Turks under the rule of Shaboluo Khan broke off relations with Tang in 651. In 657, the Tang generals Su Dingfang and Xiao Siye defeated Shaboluo Khan and conquered the Western Turks. And with the states of Tuyuhun, Gaochang, Yanqi and Quici yielding their allegiance to Tang, the Tang was able to maintain its rule over the areas north and south of the Tianshan Mountains. The Tang government established the Beiting Protector-General's Office north of the Tianshan and 16 governors' offices to its south to take charge of the political and military affairs there. From then on, the economic and cultural contacts between China's hinterland and the areas north and south of the Tianshan Mountains became increasingly closer and safe traffic was ensured along the route leading to West Asia through the Tianshan Mountain area.

The Uygurs (Hui-he), a nomadic tribe inhabiting the north of the Gobi Desert, had paid allegiance successively to the Xiongnu, the Xianbei and the Turks. They had grown strong gradually in the Sui period and, in 627, made their might felt north of the Gobi when they defeated 100,000 Turki troops with a crack force of 5,000. The Uygurs had aided the Tang in its wars to conquer the Eastern and Western Turks.

The Tang Dynasty maintained close ties with the ethnic groups living in the northeast. It set up the Heishui Governor's Office there, with the chieftain of the Mohe tribe living in the lower Heilongjiang River valley as the governor, assisted by officials sent by the Tang court. The ruler of the state of Bohai established by the Sumo tribe in the Wusuli River valley was given the title Prince of Bohai by the Tang government and trade contacts were frequent between the two sides.

The Tufans, the ancestors of modern Tibetans, had made the Qinghai-Tibet Plateau their home from time immemorial. In the early Tang period, Tibet witnessed its height of prosperity under the rule of King Songzan Gambo. When Li Shimin married Princess Wen Cheng of the Tang house to Songzan Gambo, she took with her large quantities of silk fabrics, handicrafts and farm tools to Tibet. During the reign of Emperor Zhong Zong, the Tibetan king Chide Zugdan married another member of the Tang royal house, Princess Jin Cheng, who also took with her many silk fabrics and artisans as well as Confucian classics such as the *Book of Odes, Book of Rites* and *Zuo Qiuming's Commentary on the Spring and Autumn Annals*. These two marriages made it possible for the technology and culture of the Han people to find their way into Tibet.

From ancient times, many tribes had lived in present-day Yunnan Province. They were known as the Six Zhao's. In the early Tang period, the southernmost Meng She Zhao, otherwise called the Southern Zhao, grew strong. Its chieftain often sent envoys to pay his respects to the Tang court. During the reign of Emperor Xuan Zong, the chieftain of the Southern Zhao, Piluoge, secured the permission of the Tang emperor to unify the five other tribes into one state. The Tang court conferred upon him the title King Gui Yi of Yunnan. Tang culture also found its way into the Southern Zhao as bilateral trade contacts increased.

At its height, the Tang empire developed extensive ties with many countries and regions in Asia, including Korea, Japan, India, Pakistan, Afghanistan, Iran and Arabia. Japanese envoys had come to China during the Three Kingdoms and the Southern and Northern Dynasties. Many more—joined by educated monks and students—came to China in the Sui and Tang dynasties. During the reign of Emperor Gao Zong, large Japanese missions were sent to China, the biggest including some 500 members.

The growing domestic and foreign contacts made the Tang capital Chang'an not only the nation's leading city but a cosmopolitan city as well. People of the ethnic minorities in China as well as foreign emissaries, ecclesiastics and merchants came to Chang'an en masse, bringing with them exotic products, music, dance, acrobatics, customs and religions. Some of them got married and settled down in Chang'an.

With its vivid foreign flavour, culture in the golden age of the Tang Dynasty surpassed the achievements of previous dynasties. Poetry, prose, historical studies and religion all flourished. As in the Qi-Liang period, prose in early Tang emphasized parallelisms while poetry was flowery. During the reign of Emperor Gao Zong and the early period of Empress Wu Ze Tian, the famous poets Wang Bo (649-76) and Luo Binwang (c. 640-84) began to break away from the poetic style of the Qi-Liang period. By broadening subject matter and probing new rhyming schemes they were behind the development of the unique style of Tang poetry. Their prose pieces, however, remained bound by parallelisms. Chen Zi'ang (661-702) was firmly opposed in theory and in practice to the bombasts and embellishments in Qi-Liang literature. Representative of his works was *Random Thoughts*, a collection of 38 poems. He also wrote many prose pieces without parallelisms, contributing to the creation of new forms. Not long afterwards, Tang poetry attained its peak in the celebrated poets Li Bai (Li Po) and Du Fu (Tu Fu). The change in writing style in the Tang period brought further achievements through great writers like Han Yu and Liu Zongyuan.

History books compiled in biographical style were the major accomplishments in the historical studies of this period. In the first years of the Tang Dynasty, history books about the post-Three Kindoms period were not complete. There were none about the Liang, Chen, Northern Qi, Zhou and Sui dynasties although there were as many as 18 about the Jin Dynasty. On orders from Li Shimin, special people were assigned to compile a number of history books: the 56-*juan History of the Liang Dynasty* and the 36-*juan History of the Chen Dynasty*, both by Yao Silian; the 50-*juan History of the Nothern Qi Dynasty* by Li Baiyao; the 50-*juan History of the Zhou Dynasty* by Linghu Defen and others; the 85-*juan History of the Sui Dynasty* by Wei Zheng and others; the *Historical Records of the Five Dynasties* (of the Liang, Chen, Zhou, Northern Qi and Sui) by Yu Zhining and others; and the revised, 130-*juan History of the Jin Dynasty* by Fang Xuanling and others. In addition, Li Yanshou condensed the historical records of the Southern Dynasties of Song, Qi, Liang and Chen into an 80-*juan History of the Southern Dynasties* and the historical records of the Northern Dynasties of Wei, Qi, Zhou and Sui into a 100-*juan History of the Northern Dynasties*. These completed the histories of the dynasties that came after the Three Kingdoms. In 710, the historian Liu Zhiji (661-721) completed his famous 20-*juan Critique of Historical Works*, the first of its kind in Chinese history. The book reviewed the previous historical works, analysed the merits and demerits of the different styles of history writing, especially the biographical style, and pointed out the importance of historical studies. According to Liu Zhiji, a historian must have talent, knowledge and judgement in his field—a view-point much valued by contemporary and later historians.

A number of religious faiths were introduced into China during the height of Tang, such as Zoroastrianism, Manichaeism and Nestorianism from Persia and Islam from Arabia. Followers of Zoroastrianism, founded by the Persian Zoroaster, were called Fire-worshippers because they made a cult of fire as the good light spirit in the cosmic conflict between light, the good spirit, and darkness, the evil spirit. Zoroastrianism spread to north China during the Southern and Northern Dynasties. Zoroastrian temples could be found both in Chang'an and Luoyang. Manichaeism, whose followers were later known as Light-worshippers, was introduced to China in 694 and was granted permission to build temples in Chang'an in 768. Founded by another Persian named Mani, Manichaeism also revered light in the struggle between light and darkness in the world, and so the places of worship were called the Brightness Temple. Nestorianism, or Nestorian Christianity, spread to China in 635, and its first temple was built in Chang'an in 638. Muhammad, founder of Islam, was interested in Chinese culture. "Though China is far, far away," he said, "we should go there in quest of knowledge." The Islamic religion was introduced into China in 651 when an Arabian mission came to this country. From then on, religious services were frequently held by Arabian and Persian Muslims in Chang'an, Luoyang, Yangzhou and Guangzhou.

Buddhism was the most popular religion in this period. Chang'an and Luoyang were among many places where Buddhist monasteries could be formed. Among the famous Buddhist monks were Xuan Zhuang (Hsuan Tsang or Tripitaka), Dao Xuan, Yi Jing, Fa Zang, Shen Xiu and Hui Neng. Xuan Zhuang (602-64) was a learned monk. He surmounted all kinds of difficulty to go to India in search of Buddhist scriptures. After his return to China, he translated 75 Buddhist books running to 1,335 *juan*. His translations were far better than all previous ones in faithfulness and fluency. He also wrote, with the help of his disciple Bian Ji, the 12-*juan Records of Western Travels*, in which he described the geographical features, customs and religious myths of the 111 states he had visited as well as those of the 28 other states he had heard about. The book provides valuable material for the study of the history and geography of Southwest and Central Asia. In recognition of his translation of Buddhist classics, Li Shimin especially wrote "An Introduction to the Sacred Teachings of Monk Tripitaka of the Great Tang Dynasty", followed by Emperor Gao Zong's "Notes on 'An Introduction to the Sacred Teachings of Monk Tripitaka of the Great Tang Dynasty' ". Xuan Zhuang founded the Dharmalaksana sect, but it declined after a short time. Based on his interpretation of the *Avatamsaka-sutra*, Fa Zang (642-712) founded the Avatamsaka sect, which existed for a considerable length of time in China and spread to Korea and Japan. Shen Xiu (606-706) and Hui Neng (638-713) were founders respectively of the northern and southern branches of the Chan sect. The southern branch first gained ground in a few southern regions and gradually spread to the north to take the place of the northern branch and attain nationwide influence. Later, the southern branch also found its way abroad. The fourth major Buddhist sect of Tang was the Tiantai sect, named because it had originated in the Sui period from the area of Tiantai Mountain in Zhejiang Province. By the late Tang period, the Chan sect had grown so influential that it virtually became the only Buddhist sect in China. Monk Dao Xuan (596-667) was a learned Buddhist historian, who joined Xuan Zhuang in translating Buddhist scriptures and compiled the books *Extensive Teachings* and *Sequel to Biographies of Venerable Monks*. Monk Yi Jing (635-713) also made a pilgrimage to India, where he stayed for 25 years and collected 400 Sanskrit Buddhist books. On his homeward journey he wrote *The Record of the Buddhist Practices Sent Home from the Southern Sea* and *Biographies of the Venerable Monks of the Great Tang Dynasty Who Studied Buddhist Classics in the Western Regions*. After returning to China, he translated 56 Buddhist books with a total of 230 *juan*.

As a religious faith which, encouraged by royalty, had a mass following, Buddhism left a deep mark in the political, economic and cultural spheres during the height of Tang. To pray and to propagate Buddhist doctrines to fortify its own rule, the royal house had many pagodas and temples erected and grottoes dug. These were invariably embellished with sculptures and paintings, which explains the large member of Tang engravings and graphic arts to be found in Tang Dynasty temples and grottoes. Longmen Grottoes in Luoyang have 1,352 caves, 750 niches and 97,000 Buddhist images, more than half of which belong to the height of Tang. Of the carved stone statues, the most famous are housed in Fengxian Temple. In Mogao Grottoes in Dunhuang, Gansu Province, there are 492 caves with more than 2,100 coloured sculptured figures and murals covering more than 45,000 square metres, many of which date back to the golden age of Tang. These artistic gems at Longmen and Dunhuang are executed by a perfect combination of the Indian and traditional Chinese methods. Tang sculptures and paintings were not confined to Buddhist architecture alone; many of them were also found in imperial palaces and mausoleums. Great names in Tang sculpture and painting included Wu Daozi, the "sage painter"; Yang Huizhi, the "sage sculptor"; and Song Fazhi and Wu Zhimin, both of the early Tang period. The figure paintings by Yan Lide, the landscapes by Wang Wei (699-759) and Li Shixun (648-713), the portraits of women of noble birth by Zhang Xuan (early 8th century) and Zhou Fang, and the paintings of horses by Cao Ba and Han Gan (early 8th century) are all masterpieces of the golden age of Tang or a little later.

Taoism, which came into its own as a religious faith during the Southern and Northern Dynasties, won special royal favour in the Tang period, because Li Er, who was supposed to be its founder, had the same family name as the ruling house. Taoist priests were invited by Tang emperors to imperial palaces to make elixir pills for immortal life. In one of his edicts, Li Shimin explicitly said that Taoist priests and nuns should be given priority over Buddhist monks and nuns. Emperor Gao Zong conferred on Li Er the posthumous title of the Supreme Emperor of the Profound Heavens. During the reign of Emperor Xuan Zong, many temples were erected to Li Er's memory on royal order, and the Taoist classics *Lao Zi* and *Zhuang Zi* were designated as musts in imperial civil examinations. Still, Buddhism had far more influence than Taoism.

Fu Yi (555-639), an atheist scholar, and Lü Cai (600-665), a philosopher, were vocal in their opposition to religious superstition in the thick religious atmosphere of the early Tang period. In 624, Fu Yi appealed to Emperor Gao Zu to abolish Buddhism. He pointed out that life and death were natural phenomena and that it was the sovereign's business to impose penalties or act with compassion. He considered it the height of absurdity to give these powers to Buddha and argued that by doing so, Buddhism was usurping the powers of the sovereign. According to him, Buddhist monks and nuns just sat around doing nothing but evading rent and tax payment, and should be ordered to return to the laity, engage in productive efforts, get married and bear children to increase the nation's revenue and military strength. Knowledgeable about divination, astrology and astronomy, Lü Cai took advantage of Emperor Tai Zong's assigning him to collate and systematize books on divination and astrology to voice his opposition to fatalism and other superstitious beliefs. He cited a wealth of historical facts to show that one's life or death, longevity or premature death, proverty or wealth, and high or low position are determined more by one's own action than by one's horoscope or the location of one's ancestral tombs. These ideas of Fu Yi and Lü Cai are invaluable, especially in view of the context of their time.

Confucianism remained as a weapon used by the court to control people's ideology. Li Shimin authorized Yan Shigu to collate and edit the texts of the "Five Classics"—the *Book of Changes, Book of History, Book of Odes, Book of Rites* and *Zuo Qiuming's Commentary on the Spring and Autumn Annals*. Later, he entrusted Kong Yinda and others with writing explanatory notes for the Five Classics. These notes were circulated throughout the country under the title chosen by Emperor Gao Zong himself, *Annotations to the Five Classics*. With uniform interpretations stipulated by royalty of the Confucian classics, little change has ever been made in Confucian doctrines.

6. Turmoil in the Mid-Tang Period

The middle period of the Tang Dynasty, the years 742-820, was a period of disorderly government, strife between the court and independent local forces, and discord among ethnic groups. But despite the constant turmoil which brought suffering to the people and damaged the social economy, culture managed to advance.

The disorder was caused by the corrupt policies of Emperor Xuan Zong (712-56), which fostered the eight-year An Lushan-Shi Siming Rebellion. Though the rebellion was quelled in 763, it seriously hurt the rule of the Tang Dynasty. As an example of his perverted practices, Emperor Xuan Zong in 742 changed his reign title to "Tian Bao" and at the same time called himself "Emperor with Sage Literary Attainment and Godly Prowess." He also invented a story about Heaven favouring him with a divine list of attributes to hint that he enjoyed sacred protection, was deft with the writing brush and with the sword, and was both a sage and a deity. The emperor's odd behaviour indicated that he was so politically detached he believed nothing could interfere with his rule. However, inherent in his pipe-dreams were latent contradictions—contradictions which, when they surfaced, pounded the Tang regime.

Several of Emperor Xuan Zong's most trusted men began to appear in the political arena in 742 to help dig the grave of the Tang Dynasty. His prime minister, Li Linfu, was an insidious man, who used his power to persecute those with talent, who had performed meritorious services, who enjoyed high prestige or who crossed his path. He went even further to implicate his enemies' family members, relatives, friends, colleagues and subordinates. Yang Guozhong, a worse villain, took over after Li Linfu's death in 752. Also in Emperor Xuan Zong's good graces was An Lushan, who took advantage of the emperor's stupidity to acquire influence and power to the point where he was able to mount a successful rebellion against the throne in 755. An Lushan steadily came into the limelight by currying royal favour and through the good words put in for him by Li Linfu and the emperor's close attendants and favourite concubines. In 742, he was appointed the military satrap of Pinglu, which had its seat at Yingzhou (west of modern Jingzhou, Liaoning). In the following 10 years, he was concurrently appointed the military satrap of Fanyang, which had its seat at Youzhou (now Beijing), the inspector of the Hebei Circuit, and the military satrap of Hedong, which had its seat at present-day Taiyuan City, Shanxi Province. His jurisdiction covered modern Beijing, Hebei and Shanxi and parts of Liaoning, Shandong and Henan, and he had a strong, large force under his command. His political ambitions kept pace with his increasing power. Yang Yuhuan, the most favoured in Emperor Xuan Zong's harem, was connected with both Yang Guozhong, who was her cousin, and An Lushan, who was her adopted son. Her family members and relatives all held important posts and were so influential that they made no bones about openly taking bribes. Gao Lishi, a long-time eunuch close to the emperor, was also an influential personage, to whom both Li Linfu and An Lushan owed their support.

In late 755, An Lushan led a force of 150,000 in a southward march. Hebei and other places were a shambles and yet the muddle-headed Emperor Xuan Zong refused to believe army reports of An Lushan's rebellion. In early 756, the rebels crossed the Huanghe River and captured Chenliu, Xingyang and Luoyang. Having proclaimed himself Emperor of Great Yan at Luoyang. An Lushan sent a force to attack Tongguan, the gateway to the Tang capital Chang'an. After the fall of Tongguan, Emperor Xuan Zong, Yang Yuhuan and Yang Guozhong fled in panic towards Chengdu, accompanied by the heir-apparent, a small number of officials and the Imperial Guards. When the royal party reached Maweiyi west of modern Xingping County, Shaanxi Province, the soldiers in his retinue refused to go any farther unless the emperor put Yang Guozhong and Yang Yuhuan to death. Only after Yang Guozhong had been beheaded and Yang Yuhuan hanged did the party resume its trek west. Soon afterwards, Chang'an fell easily to the rebels.

The heir-apparent, Li Heng, stayed at Maweiyi to take care of military affairs. Then he went to Lingwu (northwest of present Lingwu County, Ningxia Hui Autonomous Region), where he ascended the throne to be known in history as Emperor Su Zong. Meanwhile, Li Mi, who had been on Li Heng's staff while he was heir-apparent, also arrived at Lingwu, to be followed by General Guo Ziyi with a crack force of 50,000. Both Li Mi and Guo Ziyi were great statesmen and military strategists of the mid-Tang period. Although Emperor Su Zong was not always ready to take their advice, they managed later to help him recapture Chang'an. Another military strategist, Li Guangbi, also distinguished himself in quelling the rebellion.

In 757, An Lushan was killed by his son, An Qingxu who set himself up as emperor. That same year, Guo Ziyi defeated An Qingxu and recaptured Chang'an and Luoyang. In 759, An Lushan's subordinate general, Shi Siming, murdered An Qingxu and usurped the throne of Great Yan. In his turn, Shi Siming was killed by his son, Shi Chaoyi, in 761. Two years later, Shi Chaoyi hanged himself after being defeated. This brought to an end the eight-year An Lushan-Shi Siming

Rebellion.

After the rebellion was quelled, the former subordinates of An Lushan and Shi Siming outwardly accepted court mandates while actually preserving their independent forces. From then on, it was customary for officers and men of the frontier commanderies to choose their own commanding generals, and the positions of military satraps became hereditary—a practice which the Tang court dared not change. Emperor De Zong tried to change this situation by bringing pressure to bear on the local independent forces, but to no avail.

In 805, Li Chun, historically known as Emperor Xian Zong, ascended the throne to become a politically alert sovereign. Assisted by his competent prime ministers Li Jiang and Pei Du, he succeeded in healing the splits that had lasted for long years since the An Lushan-Shi Siming Rebellion. In 806, he put down a rebellion by the Chengdu-based Liu Pi and, in 807, another by Li Qi in the areas around Zhenjiang. Beginning in 807, he changed the practice of local independent forces' choosing their own commanding generals in favour of the emperor's direct appointment of military satraps. From 815 to 817, he suppressed a rebellion by Wu Yuanji, military satrap of Zhangyi based in Caizhou (now Runan County, Henan). In 818, the satraps of Henghai (based in Cangzhou) and Youzhou filed petitions pledging their allegiance to the court. That same year, Emperor Xian Zong launched a punitive campaign against the disloyal Li Shidao, satrap of Ziqing. The following year, the expeditionary force killed Li Shidao and recovered Ziqing satrapy, which was the most powerful of all, covering almost the whole of modern Shandong Province and small parts of Henan, Anhui and Jiangsu provinces. This put an end to the separatist regimes of the military satraps and brought about a temporary national unification. At the same time, however, the power of palace eunuchs had steadily grown so that even Emperor Xian Zong himself was murdered by them the year after he suppressed the Ziqing rebellion.

The attainment of power by palace eunuchs started in the reign of Emperor Xuan Zong when he entrusted Gao Lishi with the handling of the memorials presented by his officials. Emperor Su Zong continued this policy and, on his return to Chang'an, set a precedent for giving eunuchs access to military power by putting the eunuch Li Fuguo in charge of the Imperial Guards. Li Fuguo had earlier sided with the supporters of the emperor when he acceded to the throne at Lingwu. The emperor also appointed another eunuch, Yu Chao'en, as army supervisor, for fear that he might not be able to control Guo Ziyi, Li Guangbi and other generals who had distinguished themselves in quelling the An Lushan-Shi Siming Rebellion. Emperor Su Zong died of shock in 762 when Li Fuguo and another eunuch, Cheng Yuanzhen, killed Empress Zhang Liangdi and put Heir-apparent Li Yu on the throne. Li Yu, historically known as Emperor Dai Zong, took advantage of the conflicts between the eunuchs and killed Li Fuguo. He continued, however, to place confidence in Cheng Yuanzhen and Yu Chao'en. Only because of strong opposition from his ministers did he dismiss the two eunuchs and stop appointing eunuchs as army supervisors. But palace eunuchs regained their power during the reign of Emperor De Zong when the emperor survived a mutiny with their protection, and once again appointed them as Imperial Guards superintendents and army supervisors. Emperor Xian Zong, who had ascended the throne through eunuch support, was murdered by eunuchs because he refused to allow them to manipulate him.

Discord among ethnic groups figured prominently in the mid-Tang turmoil. The Tufans stormed into Chang'an in 763, at a time when the Tang military strength was depleted by the An Lushan-Shi Siming Rebellion. After their evacuation of Chang'an under the pressure of Guo Ziyi's troops, the city was in a terrible state with many of its buildings reduced to rubble. Constant wars continued between the Tang and the Tufans until both sides were too weak to carry on.

The Southern Zhao had been on good terms with Tang during the early period of Xuan Zong's reign, and its ruler had accepted titles of honour conferred on him by the Tang emperor. During the last years of Emperor Xuan Zong, when King Geluofeng of the Southern Zhao came to the Tang Empire on a return visit, he was humiliated by a subordinate of Xianyu Zhongtong, military satrap of Jiannan, and so he shifted his allegiance to the Tufans in confrontation with the Tang. Although he had helped the Tufans attack Chang'an, King Geluofeng believed that he had done so against his original intention, and expressed his warm feelings for Tang in an inscription on a stele erected at Taihe (now Dali County, Yunnan Province). During the reign of Emperor De Zong, thanks to the good offices of Wei Gao, military satrap of Jiannan, the Southern Zhao renounced its allegiance to the Tufans and reconciled with Tang. Then it joined the Tang troops led by Wei Gao in a succession of victorious battles against the Tufans.

Poetry flourished in the mid-Tang period, with Li Bai and Du Fu as the two greatest poets of the time. Li Bai (701-762), a romanticist master, has been known for more than 10 centuries as a "poet-immortal". And Du Fu (712-70), was a master of realism whose poetry has been described as "poetic history". Li Bai liked to travel, and many of his poems sing of the beauty of the scenic areas he visited. In 742, he was summoned at the age of 42 to the capital where—held in esteem by Emperor Xuan Zong and the courtiers—his fame as a poet spread far and wide. Three years in court service broadened his poetic vision although it also brought him in touch with the corruption and decadence of official circles. Many of his works survive today, the best-known being "The Steep Road to Shu", "An Exhortation", "An Elegy" and "His Dream of the Sky-Land: A Farewell Poem". With their unrestrained feeling, rich imagination and unique style, Li Bai's poems often strike a responsive chord in readers' hearts. Speaking of Li Bai's accomplishments at the time, his contemporary Du Fu said: "His writing brush sweeps like a thunderstorm, his lines touch the hearts of ghosts and spirits." Du Fu, an erudite man of letters, lived in Chang'an around the time of An Lushan's rebellion where he was an eye-witness to the corruption of the Tang ruling group and the barbarity of the rebels. Later, his life as a wartime refugee gave him a better understanding of the sufferings of the common people with whom he was thrown during those harsh years. His poetry mirrored the times in which he lived and truthfully reflected his own concern for the destiny of his country and the plight of his people. Du Fu had a lasting influence on the development of realist Chinese poetry. Many of his poems are also extant, of which the most famous are "The Xin'an Official", "The Officer at Tongguan", "The Shihao Official", "Lament of the New Wife", "The Homeless" and "The Old Man Returns to War". Of these two great masters Li Bai and Du Fu, another noted Tang poet,

Han Yu, wrote: "The writings of Li and Du never lose their charm, radiating rays of light a hundred thousand feet high".

Han Yu (768-824) and Bai Juyi (Pai Chu-yi) (772-846) were great poets in the latter part of the mid-Tang period, each with a style of his own. Carrying on the realist tradition characteristic of Du Fu, Bai Juyi wrote a great number of satirical poems in which he drew on typical instances to expose the corruption of the official circles and the tribulations of the common people. Easy to understand and filled with realism, many of his poems were also histories in verse and filled in omissions in history books. His ten "Shaanxi Songs" and fifty "New Folk Songs" were written with realistic brushstrokes. His two narrative poems, "The Eternal Grief" and "A Singsong Girl", gained popularity for their high artistic merits. His *Anthology of Bai Juyi* is still read today. The noted poets Yuan Zhen and Wang Jian shared Bai Juyi's approach to creative writing, and the three together formed a distinguished school in their time. Yuan Zhen was as famous as Bai Juyi, their names often being mentioned at the same time. The *Anthology of Yuan Zhen* has been handed down to posterity. The poems of Han Yu are marked by profundity and compactness, quite unlike Bai Juyi's, and owe their attractiveness to a fresh and virile style. Han Yu as well as Meng Jiao, Lu Tong, Jia Dao and Li He represented another school in Tang poetry. Liu Zongyuan and Liu Yuxi were contemporary poets with Han Yu but with a different style. Both Han Yu and Liu Zongyuan (773-819) enjoyed a greater fame as prosaists than as poets.

As great prose writers, Han Yu and Liu Zongyuan contributed to changing the rhythmical prose style current since the Jin period, which was marked by parallelism and ornateness and a jumbling together of allusions and set phrases. Han Yu stood for carrying on the fine traditions of ancient prose writing, primarily substantiality and originality in content, and opposed following set rules and patterns. His prose and essays were forceful, digressive and yet lucid, the best-known being "Esteem Teachers", "On Slanders", "In Refutation of Avoidance of Using the Personal Names of People in Superior Stations", "The Scholar's Apology", "Memorial of Remonstrance Against the Worship of Buddha's Bones" and "In Memory of My Nephew". Liu Zongyuan was second in importance only to Han Yu in the reform of writing style. His prose pieces were much on the theoretical exposition side, while his travelogues were fresh and minutely descriptive, often with his gloomy mood thrown in. The work of both Han Yu and Liu Zongyuan have been in circulation to this day.

The new style of writing encouraged by Han Yu and Liu Zongyuan was closer to the vernacular than the rhythmical style. As it promoted relating events and expressing thoughts and feelings, it exerted an extensive influence over literary and cultural developments. For instance, under the new style, the *chuan qi* (tales and romances about marvels and strange phenomena, mainly love stories), which had appeared in the early Tang period, began to flourish. Many of these tales and romances were contained in the *Taiping Miscellany*. The best-known were *The Story of Liu Yi* by Li Chaowei, *The Story of Huo Xiaoyu* by Jiang Fang, *The Story of a Singsong Girl* by Bai Xinjian and *The Story of Yingying* by Yuan Zhen. *The Story of Yingying* was to be widely adapted by later writers. Some scholars believe that the new style of writing also promoted the appearance of *bian wen*. While preaching Buddhist doctrines, Buddhist monks in the Tang period often told mystic stories from Buddhist classics, which were called *bian wen* (telling a story in a popular version). Folk story-tellers at the time also adopted the *bian wen* in recounting folk tales and historical stories. Viewed in the development of literary and artistic forms, both *chuan qi* and *bian wen* were the precursors of the later *hua ben* (prompt books), popular tales, drama and fiction.

Though they were important partners in the practice and promotion of creative prose writing, Han Yu and Liu Zongyuan differed in philosophy. Han Yu held idealist philosophical concepts, much as he had opposed the worship of Buddha's bones and the preaching of Buddhist doctrines at a time when Buddhism was in full glory. Calling for the need of defending orthodox Confucianism, he spared no effort to preach the Confucian doctrines of benevolence and righteousness. He believed in the will of Heaven and held that feudal rule was dictated by Heaven. As a materialist philosopher, Liu Zongyuan believed that the universe was made of dynamic original matter and that there was nothing mysterious about heaven, earth or original matter, which were all products of nature. He held that objective trends or conditions led to human development from men's inability to feed and defend themselves at first to their being able to use certain tools for survival and then to set up sovereigns, leaders and government. Liu Zongyuan's evolutionary view of history was quite progressive in his time.

Liu Yuxi (772-842) was close to Liu Zongyuan in his thinking. In his article "On Heaven" he tried to explore the relationship between heaven and human beings and held that while both were capable of many feats, neither was omnipotent. Heaven could produce many things, he said, while humans could control many things. According to him, the relationship between heaven and human beings was that of "mutual struggle" and "mutual use". Some of Liu Yuxi's works are still available today.

There were great scholars in historical studies in the mid-Tang period, including Du You (734-813). His 200-*juan Encyclopaedia* contained data and reviews on finance, economy, selection of officials, government, military and judiciary systems, and administrative divisions of the various dynasties. Focusing on finance and economy, he chronicled the important political developments from the dawn of history—a significant innovation in Chinese historiography. Some of his views are penetrating and incisive even by modern standards. The book provides a well-documented history of the Tang Dynasty in its earlier periods. Du You gained rich experience through his service as an administrative and financial official in both central and local government. This, combined with his deep learning, made it possible for him to complete this voluminous work in little more than 30 years, ending in 801.

The Tang Dynasty produced a galaxy of calligraphers, of whom the most influential was Yan Zhenqing. Yan Zhenqing (709-785) won fame for his *zheng kai* (regular script), which was marked by elegance and majesty—a new style considered by later generations as the orthodox school in Chinese calligraphy.

7. The Decline of the Tang Empire and the Late-Tang Peasant Uprisings

The late-Tang period, or the period of decline of the Tang empire, covered 87 years, 820-907, during which palace eunuchs held sway at the court and courtiers formed coteries, the two conspiring with and struggling against each other. On the local level, each frontier commander tried to carve out his own sphere of influence, while the frontier districts themselves were each torn by internal strife. Finally, large-scale peasant uprisings brought down the Tang regime amid a continuous growth of the power of the eunuchs and frontier commanders.

After the murder of Emperor Xian Zong by eunuchs, seven out of the next eight emperors were brought to the throne through eunuch support. The only exception, Emperor Jing Zong, was killed by eunuchs. Before putting a new emperor on the throne, eunuchs invariably deposed or assassinated the legitimate successor, dismissed or murdered some of the courtiers, and killed those eunuchs who were against them. Eunuchs had gained power over the Imperial Guards since the mid-Tang period and had become a special force in the palaces. They often had their own way with the emperor, controlling him by encouraging him to indulge in dissipation and pleasure-seeking and to shun the company of his wise ministers.

In 831, Prime Minister Song Shenxi plotted to get rid of the eunuch Wang Cheng but was demoted to a local official when his scheme was exposed. Four years later, the eunuch Chou Shiliang killed the courtiers Li Xun and Zheng Zhu, who had conspired to assassinate him, as well as several thousand people who were found guilty by association. In 854, a secret plan proposed by Prime Minister Linghu Tao to the emperor for restricting eunuch power was discovered by eunuchs and further aroused their hatred for courtiers. Each setback sustained by courtiers only served to increase the power of the eunuchs and further undermine the foundation of the Tang regime.

The courtiers' coterie strife was mainly the strife between one faction headed by Niu Sengru and Li Zongmin and another headed by Li Deyu. It began when Li Deyu, out of personal grudge, tried to squeeze out Li Zongmin who then joined with Niu Sengru to attach themselves to eunuchs for protection. Li Deyu won Emperor Wu Zong's confidence in the years 840-846 when he was Prime Minister. With his help, the emperor freed the northwestern regions from harassment by certain Uygur tribes, put down a rebellion by the military satrap of Zhaoyi, weakened direct eunuch interference with certain military moves, demolished or closed down large numbers of Buddhist, Taoist, Nestorian, Zoroastrian and Manichaean temples and monasteries, and cut down unnecessary local officials. The Tang court during the reign of Emperor Wu Zong owed its rejuvenation largely to the political and military talent of Prime Minister Li Deyu. Wu Zong's successor, Emperor Xuan Zong, did exactly the opposite and removed Li Deyu to put members of the Niu Sengru faction in important posts. After being demoted four times, Li Deyu died at Yazhou (modern Qiongshan County, Guangdong) in 849. The defeat of Li Deyu's faction hastened the decline of the Tang regime.

Most prominent in the scramble for spheres of influence were the three frontier commands in modern Hebei Province, namely, Youzhou (now Beijing), Chengde (now Zhengding), and Weibo (now Daming), whose rulers were actually successors to An Lushan. They all offered their allegiance to the court during the reign of Emperor Xian Zong but declared their independence immediately after the emperor's death. The three frontier commands were themselves torn by incessant power plays involving the murder of commanding generals and the appointment of new ones of their own choice. The Tang court, being on its last legs, recognized each new general and did nothing to reassert its authority over these frontier regions. The people there fared ever worse as did those under the direct rule of the Tang court. Driven to desperation, they rose in rebellion.

In January 860, when Qiu Fu led a hundred people in revolt in eastern Zhejiang, impoverished peasants flocked to join him by the thousand. After they had taken Xiangshan and Yanxian (modern Shengxian County, Zhejiang), their ranks quickly swelled to well over 30,000. Qiu Fu was chosen as the Generalissimo Under Heaven, with Luo Ping as his reign title. The insurgent army fought for six months before it was defeated.

In 868, led by Pang Xun, the frontier guards at Yongzhou (around modern Nanning City, Guangxi) staged a mutiny and captured some prefectures and counties. On their way to Xuzhou, where they originally had come from, they were joined by poverty-stricken peasants, many of them women, to become a massive force of more than 200,000. They fought bitterly for fourteen months until they too were defeated.

These two peasant uprisings were preludes to a yet larger one in 874, when Wang Xianzhi, a native of Puzhou, rose in revolt with several thousand men at Changyuan (northeast of modern Changyuan County, Henan). Shortly after, Huang Chao, a native of Caozhou (north of modern Caoxian County, Shandong), responded by rising with several thousand men. The insurgents defeated Tang troops, took Caozhou and Puzhou and grew into a force several tens of thousands strong. From Shandong they swept into Henan, where they captured many towns and cities, extending their influence south of the Huaihe River.

After Wang Xianzhi was killed in battle in 878, Huang Chao took over the command under the name of Heaven-Storming General and led the peasant army across the Changjiang River to Zhejiang, Fujian and then to Guangzhou in the far south. In 879, under the name of Heaven-Ordained Equalization General, Huang Chao issued a proclamation denouncing the misrule of the Tang court and led his men in a northward drive. He captured many towns on his way, fighting from Guangdong, Guangxi, Hunan, Hubei, Jiangxi and Anhui to Zhejiang and swelling his ranks to hundreds of thousands.

In 880, the peasant forces took Luoyang. Marching west from Luoyang, they captured first the strategic pass of Tongguan and then Chang'an, the Tang capital. The people of Chang'an lined the streets in welcome as the well-disciplined peasant rebels marched into the city. They were told that Huang Chao had revolted to save the common people—unlike the Li royal house who cared nothing about their well-being—and that they should go about their business as usual and settle down to a peaceful life. Huang Chao proclaimed himself emperor at Chang'an and called his new regime the Great Qi.

However, being always on the move and without base areas of support, the insurgents had not been able to consolidate their gains from their many victories, nor had they wiped out the main forces of the Tang regime. Around the time of the inauguration of Huang Chao's new dynasty, the Tang government mustered reinforcements from all parts of the country to throw a tight cordon around Chang'an and cut off its food supplies.

Meanwhile, disorganization took place among the insurgent army and each of its influential commanders began to fight on his own in defiance of Huang Chao's orders. One of them, Zhu Wen, turned his back on Huang Chao and went over to the Tang side. In its fight against the peasant forces, the Tang court enlisted the support of the Shatuo* under Li Keyong. In 883, Li Keyong crossed the Huanghe River in northern Shanxi and fought his way to the vicinity of Chang'an. Huang Chao led his remnant forces east to Henan and then to Shandong. He killed himself in 884 after being cornered near Mount Taishan. The peasant war had lasted 10 solid years and had engulfed half of China, exceeding all previous peasant wars in scale. In calling himself Heaven-ordained Equalization General, Huang Chao—although not expressing this in any official slogan—did voice the insurgents' demand for equality between high and low and between rich and poor. In this sense, Huang Chao's uprising can be considered a cut above all previous peasant revolts that aimed only at opposing enslavement and striving for survival.

Both the eunuchs and frontier commanders took advantage of the chaotic situation arising from the peasant war to expand their own influence. After the peasant army had taken Tongguan, the eunuch in power, Tian Lingzi forced Emperor Xi Zong to flee to Chengdu. He took arbitrary power over everything in defiance of the emperor and put his numerous adopted sons in command of the armed forces. At the same time, he sent many of his trusted followers to spy on local officials and trumped up charges against those who refused to do his bidding. The new frontier commanders, Zhu Wen and Li Keyong, who had built up their power in the process of suppressing the peasant uprising, were more ambitious than the others who drew the line at carving out local spheres of influence.

After the defeat of Huang Chao, the frontier commanders in their scramble for independent domains began to embroil themselves in a

---

* A branch of the Western Turks which inhabited the northern part of modern Shanxi and attached itself to the Tang under Emperor De Zong.

tangled warfare, while the eunuchs and courtiers, with the sharpening of the contradictions between them, each tried to court the frontier commanders in the hope of gaining external support. The frontier commanders, on their part, all struggled to lay hold of the emperor as their political capital, and even scrambled several times for the person of Emperor Zhao Zong. Beginning in 896, Zhu Wen banded together with the prime minister Cui Yin to form a coterie. The influence of the palace eunuchs were wiped out to the last vestige in 903, when Zhu Wen and Cui Yin started a massacre of the eunuchs at Fengxiang (in modern Shaanxi Province) and Chang'an and of those sent to the various places as army supervisors. In 904, Zhu Wen murdered Emperor Zhao Zong and put Li Zhu on the throne, who was later known as Emperor Zhao Xuan Di. Three years later, he deposed Zhao Xuan Di and proclaimed himself emperor of the Liang Dynasty, ushering in the period of the Five Dynasties and Ten States. Li Keyong and a few other frontier commanders still held their own spheres of influence at the time.

In the late Tang period, when the Tufan was on the decline, it ceased to pit itself against the Tang empire. In 822, the Tufan ruler met with the emissary of the Tang emperor Mu Zong at Lhasa to discuss the alliance between the Tufan and the Tang, and a Monument of Unity was erected in front of the Jokhan Monastery the following year. Later, the Tufan was torn by a prolonged split, which ended only in the second half of the 13th century when it accepted the rule of the Yuan empire. After the Uygur Khanate was conquered by its subordinate tribe Xiajiasi in 840, the Uygurs moved west to the Tianshan Mountains area and became the ancestors of the Uygur people in present-day Xinjiang. During the late Tang period, the Southern Zhao was on very bad terms with the Tang as it frequently raided the empire's southwestern frontiers. In 830, the Southern Zhao troops stormed into Chengdu and kidnapped tens of thousands of people, many of them handicraftsmen. In 861, they attacked Yongzhou and carried off many of its inhabitants. In 870, they laid siege to Chengdu once again. In 875, the Tang government appointed Gao Pian Military Satrap of Xichuan, who, after a bitter fight, drove the Southern Zhao troops across the Dadu River. In 902, the state of the Southern Zhao was lost to one of its powerful ministers. After more than 30 years of turmoil, a noble named Duan of the Baiman tribe established the Dali Kingdom in the former domain of the Southern Zhao.

With the weakening of the empire, late Tang culture was also on the decline, with only a sprinkling of poets, notably Du Mu and Li Shangyin, lamenting over their personal misfortunes and the plight of the empire. Du Mu (803-53) was a grandson of Du You, author of *The Encyclopaedia*. Some of his poetic works reflected his worry and anger over the misrule of the government and the decline of the empire. His famous work, "Ode to the Epang (Efang) Palace", expressed his disapproval of the late Tang emperors' depraved life by castigating the misdeeds of an ancient emperor. His equally well-known poems, "Spring Comes to the South" and "Lying at Anchor on the Qinhuai River", revealed his concern for events of his day between the lines of landscape description. In his earlier days, Li Shangyin (813-58) had written a number of poems giving free flow to his personal aspirations and his discontent with the way eunuchs scrambled for power and frontier commanders for spheres of influence. In his later years, many of his poems breathed his disappointment over his unsuccessful official career. His achievements served as an epilogue of the golden age of Tang poetry.

There rose to prominence a new verse form, the *ci*, in the late Tang period when the traditional type of poetry, *shi*, was losing ground. The *ci* is a lyric with lines of irregular length set to a certain melody. The number of sentences, the number of words in each sentence, the rhyming and the tonal pattern are all governed by definite rules. The *ci* first appeared approximately in the early Tang period. Judging from the *ci* set to music in Dunhuang Grottoes, it might have developed from folk ballads. The mid-Tang poets, Liu Yuxi and Bai Juyi, were great *ci* writers, whose *ci* verses, "Yi Jiang Nan" ("Recollections of the South") and "Chang Xiang Si" ("Everlasting Love"), have become well-known *ci* melody names. Wen Tingjun (c. 812-c. 870) and Wei Zhuang (c. 836-910) were famous *ci* writers of the later Tang period, whose works, together with those of the well-known *ci* writers of the Five Dynasties and Ten States period, were contained in the *Collection of Flowers*, and they were known as the "Flowery School". The *ci*

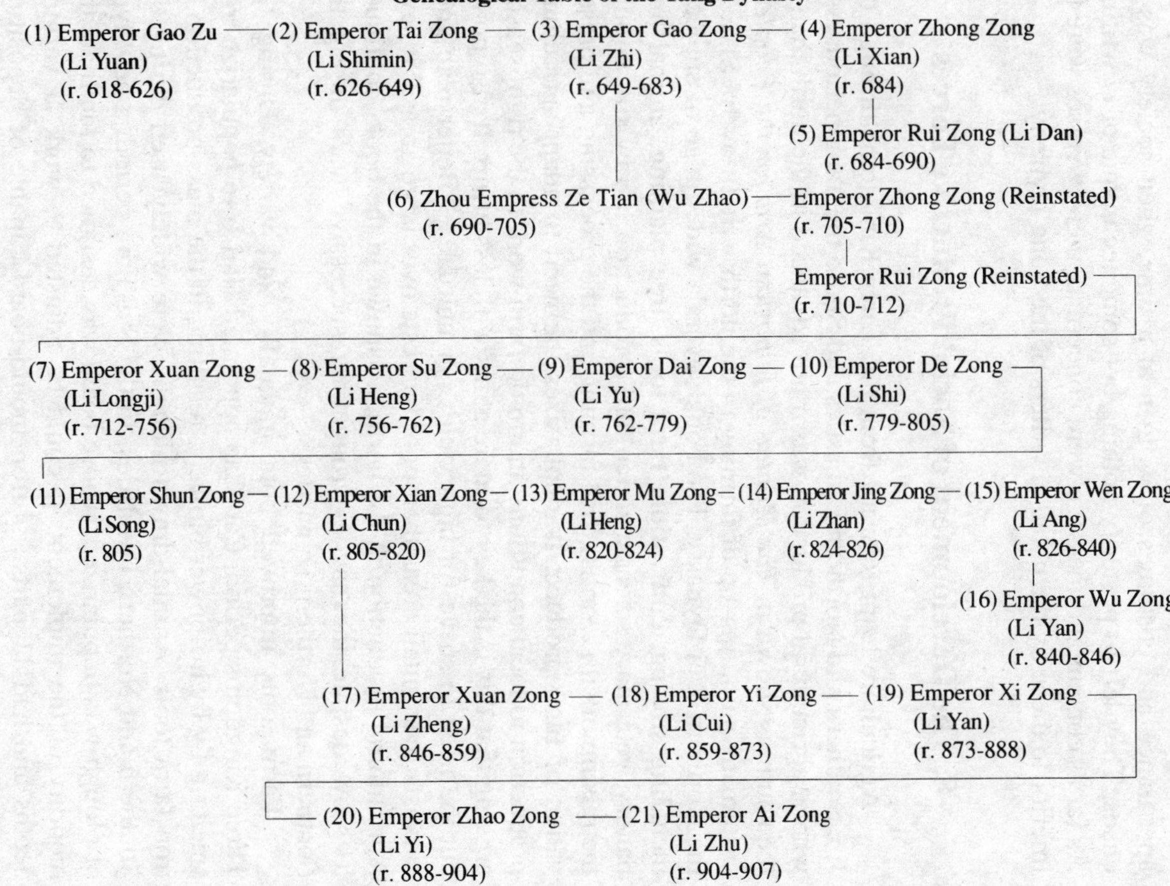
Genealogical Table of the Tang Dynasty
(1) Emperor Gao Zu (Li Yuan) (r. 618-626)
(2) Emperor Tai Zong (Li Shimin) (r. 626-649)
(3) Emperor Gao Zong (Li Zhi) (r. 649-683)
(4) Emperor Zhong Zong (Li Xian) (r. 684)
(5) Emperor Rui Zong (Li Dan) (r. 684-690)
(6) Zhou Empress Ze Tian (Wu Zhao) (r. 690-705)
Emperor Zhong Zong (Reinstated) (r. 705-710)
Emperor Rui Zong (Reinstated) (r. 710-712)
(7) Emperor Xuan Zong (Li Longji) (r. 712-756)
(8) Emperor Su Zong (Li Heng) (r. 756-762)
(9) Emperor Dai Zong (Li Yu) (r. 762-779)
(10) Emperor De Zong (Li Shi) (r. 779-805)
(11) Emperor Shun Zong (Li Song) (r. 805)
(12) Emperor Xian Zong (Li Chun) (r. 805-820)
(13) Emperor Mu Zong (Li Heng) (r. 820-824)
(14) Emperor Jing Zong (Li Zhan) (r. 824-826)
(15) Emperor Wen Zong (Li Ang) (r. 826-840)
(16) Emperor Wu Zong (Li Yan) (r. 840-846)
(17) Emperor Xuan Zong (Li Zheng) (r. 846-859)
(18) Emperor Yi Zong (Li Cui) (r. 859-873)
(19) Emperor Xi Zong (Li Yan) (r. 873-888)
(20) Emperor Zhao Zong (Li Yi) (r. 888-904)
(21) Emperor Ai Zong (Li Zhu) (r. 904-907)

writers of this school were given to florid descriptions of love and the appearance and costumes of women at a time when society was in chaos. They left to posterity nothing but some technique of *ci* writing. As far as content and message were concerned, their *ci* verses were far inferior to those by the noted *ci* writers of the Song Dynasty.

8. The Development of Social Productive Forces

Agriculture leapt forward from the Three Kingdoms through the Jin, Southern and Northern Dynasties and Sui to the Tang period. As a whole, agricultural production was more advanced in the north than in the south as shown in *The Manual of Important Arts for the People*, a systematic summing-up of farming in the north written by Jia Sixie of the Northern Wei Dynasty. The book covers a wide range of subjects, including sowing, cultivation, farm tools, tree planting, animal husbandry, veterinary science, sericulture (production of raw silk through the raising of silk worms), fish farming and the processing and preservation of farm produce. It emphasizes the need to adapt agricultural production to local conditions and to do farm work in the right season, arguing that this is the key to more gains with less effort. It also points out the need to strive for high yields per unit area. "Better reap good harvests over small areas than poor harvests over large areas," it says. Agricultural production in the north, as shown in the book, continued to grow despite the havoc wrought by successive wars during the Southern and Northern Dynasties.

Farm tools improved both in quality and variety. During the Three Kingdoms period, Cao Cao appointed Han Ji to popularize iron smelting by hydro-power blowers, resulting in the mass-production of iron farm tools. Animal-drawn ploughs were widely used during the Southern and Northern Dynasties. In the Sui-Tang period, a new type of plough was popularized, whose beam was designed to facilitate the mobility of the implement. It could be adjusted to work at varying depths and had 11 parts, its iron mould-board capable of depositing big earth clods on either side to make deep-ploughing easier. During the Northern Wei Dynasty, a new type of seeder was introduced, complete with a tool for covering the seeds with earth to promote their germination and growth. There were several kinds of implements for hoeing. By the Tang Dynasty, crescent-shaped sickles were used; they were better than the old ones which were slender at one end and thick at the other.

Progress was made in water conservation. Famous irrigation works were repaired or built during the Three Kingdoms, the Eastern Jin, the Southern Dynasties and the Sui period. According to rough estimates, 270 irrigation projects were built in the Tang period. A canal dug in the early Tang period served 40,000 hectares and another dug during the reign of Emperor Xuan Zong brought water to 20,000 hectares. The Tang government set up a special bureau for water conservation administration and promulgated decrees on river and canal control, irrigation, shipping and bridge engineering.

At the end of the Eastern Han Dynasty, a man named Bi Lan invented the *fan che* (water lifting device) and *ke wu* (pump). Ma Jun of the state of Wei in the Three Kingdoms period improved the *fan che* so that even children could handle it. During the Tang Dynasty, water-carts with wooden pails attached to them for drawing water from wells appeared in the north. In the Changjiang River valley, there were water-wheels shaped like spinning wheels, with bamboo pails attached that were turned by force of water-flow to raise water from lower to higher points.

In agricultural production, emphasis was placed on intensive farming, prevention of drought, retention of moisture, preservation and improvement of soil fertility, and the selection of seed. Cultivating was done according to the four seasons with primary and secondary ploughings in each season and vertical or transverse ploughings for different depths. Measures were developed to prevent dryness and waterlogging of the soil. One of these was constant hoeings in the course of crop growth which was considered important for increasing crop yields by preventing dryness and retaining moisture. New experience and information were gained about manure application, crop rotation and multiple cropping to preserve and raise the fertility of the soil. Farmers of the Sui and Tang periods also paid special attention to the selection of good seed strains, which was partly responsible for the many good harvests reaped at that time. During the Northern Wei Dynasty, there were 86 varieties of millet, the major food crop in the north, and 24 varieties of rice, the merits and demerits of which were well understood by the experienced peasants.

The development of handicrafts also made swift progress. Ma Jun of the Three Kingdoms period made the old damask weaving loom easier to operate by changing the number of pedals from 50 and 60 to only 12. Silk weaving was fairly well developed in the state of Shu which found brisk demand for its silk fabrics in many other parts of the country. The weft patterning technique was introduced from Persia into China during the Tang Dynasty, which was then used on silk fabrics made for export to cater to foreign tastes. There was a wide range of textiles during the Tang dynasty. Silk fabrics included brocade, pongee, gauze, damask and satin. In variety, the damask ranked first, brocade second and satin third. There was cloth made of ko-hemp, hemp, ramie and abaca (Manila hemp). In the northwest, woolen fabrics were woven from animal hair. In Gaochang in present-day Xinjiang, fine cloth was woven from cotton, which was not yet grown in the hinterland at that time.

The salt industry expanded swiftly during the Tang Dynasty under the patronage of the court, and the salt tax was an important source of government revenue in the mid-Tang period and afterwards.

During the Southern and Northern Dynasties, a new steel-making method was introduced, in which molten pig iron was poured on wrought iron to smelt it into good-quality steel by quenching with animal urine and grease. The steel produced by this process was hard but pliable, much better than that made by the previous repeated tempering method. This advanced method, which had a vital bearing on later generations, was mentioned by Tao Hongjing (456-536), a scholar in the south, and used by Qiwu Huaiwen, a metallurgist in the north, in making swords and knives—which shows that the method was adopted in both southern and northern China at the time.

Tea-making was a new industry developed in this period, although tea-growing dated back much earlier. During the Tang Dynasty, tea was grown in all the provinces in the south, with more than 20 famous varieties. The present Qimen County in Anhui Province and

Huzhou City in Zhejiang Province were major tea-growers, and the tea tax was an important source of state revenue. The *Book of Tea* by Lu Yu (733-804) of the Tang Dynasty, the world's first special primer of its kind, deals systematically with the cultivation of tea bushes and methods of tea-processing.

Porcelain-making, an important Chinese invention, reached maturity in this period. (Primitive celadon, a green porcelain, appeared as early as the Shang Dynasty.) Different kinds of porcelain ware were produced in present-day Zhejiang, Jiangxi, Anhui, Hunan, Sichuan, Fujian, Guangdong, Hebei and Henan provinces, the best-known being the celadon from the Yue Kilns in modern Shaoxing County, Zhejiang, and the white porcelain from the Xing Kilns in modern Neiqiu County, Hebei. Besides ordinary articles for daily use, porcelain was used during the Tang Dynasty to make exquisite art objects, such as the lively tribesmen on horse or camel backs and the different kinds of animals unearthed in various parts of China. The present porcelain city of Jingdezhen in Jiangxi Province was already the leading producer at that time, whose high quality products were much sought after both at home and abroad.

Paper-making technique had improved by the end of the Eastern Han Dynasty, and in the period from 220 to 907 paper was used as writing material instead of bamboo and silk. It was widely used for many other purposes, such as the paper money burned at funeral services. Paper-making reached a high level of development in the Tang period, when paper of different types and colours were produced from an abundant choice of materials, such as bast fibres, the bark of paper mulberry, common mulberry and rattan, bamboo, and stalks of wheat and rice. The paper made during the Tang Dynasty was internationally known for its even and fine texture, neatness and smoothness. The fine, white, high-quality Yu Ban Xuan paper made in Xuanzhou (modern Jingxian County, Anhui), now known as the Xuan paper, is still treasured by traditional Chinese painters and calligraphers today.

Printing from engraved wood blocks appeared in the first years of the Tang Dynasty, or even earlier. Its forerunners were oracle bone engravings of the Shang-Zhou period, the seal and stone engravings of the pre-Qin period and the brick engravings of the Jin Dynasty. These engravings usually bore inscriptions (some of which were carved in the reverse direction) and sometimes pictures. At first, wood-block printing was used in printed matter that was less voluminous but enjoyed wider circulation, such as Buddhist images and scriptures, almanacs and arithmetic booklets. Later, even the anthologies of poets like Bai Juyi and Yuan Zhen were printed by this method. There were bookshops dealing specially in printed books in Chengdu in the late Tang period. The earliest extant printed book is the *Diamond Sutra* of 868, which is 16 feet long and one foot wide and made up of seven sheets of paper to form a *juan* (roll). Both printing from engraved blocks and paper-making are great inventions attributed to China.

New advances were made in architecture and city planning. Construction of Buddhist temples and pagodas became an important architectural occupation with the spread of Buddhism. Buddhist buildings in China, which bore an Indian stamp in the beginning, quickly blended with the traditional style of Chinese architecture. The plans of the Buddhist temples, including their pavilions, eaves and embellished walls, were all eloquent with Chinese flavour, as were the tower-like wooden pagodas and multi-eave brick pagodas.

Chang'an, the capital of both the Sui and Tang dynasties and the largest city in the world at that time, is among the masterpieces of city planning in the history of Chinese architecture. Yuwen Kai (555-612), a famous architect of his time, was responsible for the city planning of Chang'an in the Sui period. Municipal construction continued during the Tang Dynasty. Chang'an in the Tang period covered an area of 84 square kilometres and consisted of a Palace City and an Imperial City. There were 14 main streets running parallel from north to south and another 11 main streets running parallel from west to east, dividing the entire urban district into 108 neighbourhoods. The Great Brightness Palace atop the Dragon Head Hill on the northeastern outskirts provided a commanding view of the city. Water supply was convenient, with four canals flowing through it from south to north. Chang'an furnished for posterity a brilliant example of city planning.

The Anji Bridge, the world's oldest open-spandrel bridge built in the early Sui period by Li Chun and other craftsmen over the Xiaohe River at Zhaozhou (now Zhaoxian County, Hebei Province) is one of the engineering feats of China. The structure, spanning 37.37 metres and made up of 28 component arches placed side by side, is 50.82 metres long and 9 metres wide, with a gentle slope to facilitate traffic. It has two minor arches at each of its two spandrels, which help lighten the weight of the main body, provide spillways for the water in time of flood and lend added majesty and grace to the bridge itself. The Anji Bridge, also known as the Zhaozhou Bridge, remains serviceable today despite the impact of the many serious floods and earthquakes of the past 1,300 years.

Shipbuilding grew with the development of transport and communications. From the Tang Dynasty onward, Chinese-built ships constantly plied between Guangzhou and the Persian Gulf.

Commerce flourished in Chang'an, Luoyang, Yangzhou, Chengdu, Guangzhou, Youzhou, Bianzhou (now Kaifeng, Henan) and Mingzhou (now Ningbo, Zhejiang). Guangzhou and Mingzhou were foreign trade ports during the Sui and Tang dynasties. Chinese commodities found a ready market in Japan, Arabia and a number of South China Sea countries, and its silk fabrics and porcelain wares were favourite luxuries of the aristocrats and rich people there. An ancient form of bill of exchange, known as *fei qian* ("flying money"), appeared during the Tang Dynasty. Merchants who sold their goods to commercial firms at Chang'an could get *fei qian* drafts with which they could draw money in other places, saving them the trouble of carrying large amounts of money with them on their trips.

New successes were achieved in fields connected with productive endeavours, such as astronomy, recording of calendar time, hydrology and health and medicine. Yu Xi, an astronomer of the Eastern Jin Dynasty, discovered the precession of the equinoxes. He held that the sun moved somewhat west from the winter solstice of one year to the winter solstice of the next, instead of returning to its original position. According to his calculations based on historical records, the sun moved one degree west every 50 years. Although his calculations missed being completely accurate. Yu Xi was the first in Chinese history to study the precession of the equinoxes. His study was carried on by He Chengtian of the Song period and Zu Chongzhi of the Song and Qi periods during the Southern Dynasties. The precession as calculated by He Chengtian was one degree every 100 years, a little less than the true figure. Zu Chongzhi (429-500) was the first to apply the precession to the recording of calendar time. The Daming Calendar worked out by him was more accurate than all previous ones, the length of its tropical year being only 50 seconds wide of the length of the modern Gregorian Calendar. What distinguished Zu Chongzhi most was that he worked out the precise figure of π to be between 3.1415926 and 3.1415927, well over one thousand years earlier than did European mathematicians. The Tang Dynasty astronomer, Monk Yi Xing (683-727), organized and directed a survey of the height of North Pole and the length of the shade of the sun—or the length of the meridian line—at 12 work centres in the country. He was the first in the world to carry out a scientific survey of the meridian.

In hydrological studies, the *Waterways Classic* written by an unknown author of the Three Kingdoms period gives a brief account of the country's 137 major waterways. During the Northern Wei Dynasty, Li Daoyuan (465- or 472-527) wrote a commentary on it, *Commentary on "Waterways Classic"*, in which he quotes from more than 430 ancient books and draws on data based on his own on-the-spot investigations. Apart from explaining the waterways mentioned in the *Waterways Classic* he filled in an outline of 1,252 others, making his book 21 times as big as the *Waterways Classic*. Written with ease and grace, the *Commentary* is also a literary work.

In medical science, *A Treatise on Fevers* by Zhang Zhongjing (Zhang Ji), a noted physician of the Three Kingdoms period, describes methods of treatment for different kinds of fevers and contains more than 100 prescriptions. His *Gold Chest Dissertations* deals with the symptoms of illnesses and ailments other than fevers as well as methods of treatment for them. Hua Tuo, a celebrated surgeon living at about the same time as Zhang Zhongjing, used an anaesthetic for abdominal operations. He also attached great importance to physical exercise as a means to keep fit and devised a set of health-building exercises called "Five Animals' Games" which consisted of imitating the movements of a tiger, deer, bear, ape and bird. During the Jin and the Southern and Northern Dynasties, Chinese medicine embraced eight branches: medical theory, acupuncture, diagnosis, pathology, herbal medicine, prescription, dietetics and veterinary science. Historical records show that surgical operations such as amputation and harelip repair were performed. The 10-*juan Treatise on the Pulse*, the earliest extant treatise of its kind in China by the noted physician of the Jin Dynasty, Wang Shuhe, analyses twenty-four types of pulse and lays the theoretical basis for diagnosis by pulse-feeling. The *Classic of Acupuncture and Moxibustion* by Huangfu Mi (215-282). The earliest treatise on this subject, still remains in use today. The *Prescriptions for Emergencies* by Ge Hong (c. 284-364) is a collection of the tested prescriptions by celebrated doctors. As a specialist in refining elixir pills for immortality, he contributed to the development of pharmaceutical science through his knowledge about the chemical properties of mercury, suphur, lead, copper and iron. The *Treatise on the Preparation and Dispensing of Medicines and Drugs* by Lei Xiao, a famous pharmacologist of the Southern and Northern Dynasties, has earned its place in China's pharmaceutic history through its presentation of 17 methods of preparing medicines. Tao Hongjing contributed to the progress of pharmacology with his *Supplement to "Prescriptions for Emergencies"* and *Annotations to "Emperor Shen Nong's Materia Medica"*, a book which added 365 drugs to the same number listed in *Emperor Shen Nong's Materia Medica* and proposed methods for pharmacological classification. The Sui government established—and the Tang Dynasty further expanded—an Academy of Imperial Physicians and an Imperial Medical Institution to take care of court medical and health affairs and the training of medical personnel. A special work in the history of Chinese medicine, the *Treatise on the Causes and Symptoms of Diseases* which runs to 50 *juan* with 1,720 articles covering 67 disciplines, written by the Sui medical academician Chao Yuanfang in 610, discusses with thorough documentation the causes, pathological changes and symptoms of the diseases as viewed within such disciplines as internal medicine, surgery, gynecology, pediatrics and the "five sense organs" (ear, eye, mouth, nose and tongue). On orders from the Tang emperor Gao Zong in 657, Su Jing, Zhangsun Wuji and others started work on the first government-authorized pharmacopoeia in the world, *A New Compendium of Materia Medica*, for which they had collected specimens and illustrations of medicines from various parts of the country. The 54-*juan* book, completed in 659, consists of a catalogue of 844 drugs, including 400 corrected and 100 added after research. The *Precious Prescriptions* and *Supplement to "Precious Prescriptions"* by the outstanding Tang pharmacologist Sun Simiao (581-682) deal exhaustively with the diagnosis, prevention and treatment of diseases, especially gynecological diseases and child care. They record the collection and preparation of over 800 common drugs. Sun Simiao was honoured as "Master of Pharmacology" and temples were erected to cherish his memory. The *Pharmacopoeia in Four Divisions*, compiled by the celebrated Tufan medical scientist Yutuo Yuandangongbu during the mid-Tang period based on Tibetan folk experience with reference to medical works by Han authors, was an important work in Tibetan medicine. It was introduced to Mongolia and contributed greatly to the development of both Tibetan and Mongolian medicines.

9. The Development of Feudal Relations and the Feudalization of Regions Inhabited by Several Ethnic Groups

Feudal relations developed in the period from the Three Kingdoms through the Tang Dynasty as private landowner ship expanded within the feudal hierarchical system and changes took place in the status of both the landlords and the peasants, while the process of feudalization began in areas where several ethnic groups lived together.

The landed aristocrats with hereditary titles of the Qin-Han period which had been decimated during the Yellow Turbans Uprising were replaced by landlords from privileged families who, like the landed aristocrats, enjoyed hereditary social status as well as economic and political privileges. But they were different in that they owned land which was not enfeoffed by the state but was handed down from generation to generation; they had under their control peasants and family servants who were not listed in government register and were therefore immune from tax payment and labour service;

and the land rent they managed to squeeze out was not part of the state tax.

Landlords from privileged families were those which developed over time from the hereditary landed aristocracy of the late-Han period or from powerful local landlords. Those who rendered meritorious service to the new dynasty also became privileged landlords, but it had taken their families a considerable length of time to build up their prestige before joining this privileged class. In 220, the kingdom of Wei created a law establishing prestigious persons in various places as *zhong zheng* to recommend talented people for classification into nine grades for government appointment. Soon, landlords from the privileged families seized this method of selecting talented people to consolidate and expand their privileges during a time of social upheaval. At the end of the Western Jin Dynasty, many of these landlords went south from the Central Plain together with their family members, relatives, family servants and fellow-villagers. Politically, they became an important force supporting the Eastern Jin court in the south, while economically they seized large tracts of land any way they could. The big native landlords also joined their ranks. After Emperor Xiao Wen Di of the Northern Wei moved his capital to Luoyang, the nobles of the different clans and branches of the Xianbei tribe settled down at Luoyang as privileged families and gradually merged with the Han people. Later, when the Northern Wei split into the eastern and western parts, the privileged families in the Central Plain were divided into the Shandong and Guanzhong groups. Among the country's privileged families, the Shandong group enjoyed high prestige for a long time. With the introduction of the civil examination system during the Sui and Tang dynasties, although the old privileged families remained a force to be reckoned with, their social status was weakened as more and more people entered into political competition with them. Both Li Shimin and Wu Ze Tian tried to rearrange the genealogical ranks of the landlord class, so as to play down landlords from the privileged families and play up the new bigwigs, but without much success.

Buddhist monks also become powerful in the landlord class. They owned large monasteries, huge amounts of monastic land and other assets, all of which passed from master to disciple. Large numbers of workers were at their service. These monasterial landlords were exempt from taxation and labour service. Each of them set up on his own account and each had his own system of imparting Buddhist learning. They did not have to respect the sovereign, and were bound by no secular laws. When Monk Xuan Zhuang (Hsuan Tsang) fell ill in 664, Emperor Gao Zong sent imperial physicians to treat him. After his death, the emperor stopped giving audience for several days and had the monk's body put in an inner coffin of gold with an outer coffin of silver. It was recorded that 1,000,000 people attended the funeral service and 30,000 mourners kept vigil around the graveyard. In the words of a memorial of the early 8th century, "Seven or eight-tenths of the wealth under the sun belong to Buddha." Much as this might exaggerate, these records throw a revealing light on the wealth and prestige enjoyed by the monasterial landlords. They were actually privileged landlords in Buddhist robes, and some of them had even more land and wielded more influence than their secular counterparts.

During the Three Kingdoms and later, so-called landlords of humble origin—landlords other than those from the privileged families, such as bureaucrat landlords, powerful local landlords and mercantile landlords—also gained status. Speaking of the compilation of the *Clan and Family Gazette*, Li Shimin gave the instruction: "Grade according to the present official ranks, with no regard to the situation generations ago." This regard only for present official ranks was precisely what set the bureaucrat landlords apart. After the kingdom of Wei made the law on classifying talented people into nine grades for government appointment, officials not from the privileged families—most of them low-ranking—also received both land and labourers from the state. With the introduction of the civil examination during the Sui and Tang dynasties, this social stratum grew to become a political rival of the landlords from privileged families, and some of its members even became prime ministers. Eunuchs grew increasingly powerful after the mid-Tang period. They held high official ranks and commandeered vast tracts of land in the metropolitan area. Being different from ordinary officials, they belonged to another category of bureaucrat landlords.

Another great local feudal force—neither from the officials nor from the privileged families—was the powerful local landlords. Some of the powerful local landlords might turn into bureaucrat landlords or privileged landlords. Each of these three kinds of landlords had its own characteristics although they were not much different in some cases. In times of social stability, powerful local landlords often tyrannized the common people; in times of social upheaval, they often mustered their own forces for self-protection or for setting up independent regimes. During the Three Kingdoms period, Li Dian, a subordinate general of Cao Cao, moved his 13,000 family servants and clansmen to the city of Ye; and Xu Chu got together neighbourhood youngsters and thousands of clansmen to resist peasant insurgent armies before he joined Cao Cao to become one of his subordinate generals. Both Wei Yan and Huo Jun, Liu Bei's subordinate generals, were powerful local landlords who took their own family servants with them when they joined Liu Bei. When peasant rebellions broke out at the end of the Sui Dynasty, many of the powerful local landlords took advantage of the situation to seize towns and cities.

Some of the bureaucrat landlords and privileged landlords used their position and power to conduct commercial activities despite the repeated imperial edicts which forbade them to do so. Officials in Guangzhou and other foreign trade ports stood a greater chance of making fabulous profits than those in other places. During the mid-Tang period and afterwards, shops were opened by military commanders in Yangzhou and other cities, which, being run in the military's name, enjoyed far greater success than others. But these people were different from the plutocrat landlords who, coming from among ordinary landlords, raked in large amounts of money from regular business deals. A man named Mi Zhu in the Three Kingdoms period boasted 10,000 servants and a fabulous fortune accumulated over generations by his merchant-ancestors. Once, he made Liu Bei a present of 2,000 servants and a large amount of gold and silver to make up his shortage of military supplies. A certain Zheng Fengzhi in the Sui-Tang period—so influential that even men of rank vied to associate with him—had warehouses, manors and residences in many parts of the country. He bragged to Emperor Gao Zu of the Tang Dynasty that he had enough pongee to go around even if each of the trees on Zhongnan Mountain was hung with one bolt. People like Mi Zhu and Zheng Fengzhi could be counted as bigshots among the plutocrat landlords. There were many specialized merchants in the Three Kingdoms period and afterwards. But none of them—from wealthy merchants to small pedlars, especially salt and tea merchants—could avoid being dependent on feudal forces.

Both the monasterial landlords and the landlords of humble origin, like those from the privileged families, had their own protégés not listed in the government register, which indicated a scramble between the landlords and the feudal state for labourers. The feudal state adopted specific measures to rebind the drifting peasants to the land. One of these was to increase the number of households in government register by a general check-up. Another was to institute a land equalization system favourable for the re-binding.

The land equalization system was practised in several forms from the Three Kingdoms period onward. In 196, Cao Cao introduced a system at Xuchang, whereby drifters were organized along military lines and given land for cultivation. Those who used government oxen in farming had to turn over six-tenths of their harvests to the government as rent while the rate was only half for those who used their own oxen. In 280, during the Western Jin Dynasty, peasants of both sexes became entitled to two types of land, the *zhan tian* (possessed field) which was rent-free, and the *ke tian* (tax field) for which land tax had to be paid, mainly in grain, pongee and cotton. In 485, under the land equalization programme of the Northern Wei Dynasty, peasants of both sexes were given a certain amount of *lu tian* (open field) for growing food grain, which could not be sold and had to be returned to the government when the recipient reached the age of 70; and a certain amount of *sang tian* (mulberry field) for growing mulberry, elm and date trees, which could be kept for good and could be sold in part. The peasants in turn were required to pay the government land rent in grain and silk. In 624, during the Tang Dynasty, land was distributed according to sex, age and health status. The *lu tian* was then known as *kou fen tian* (per capita field), which was generally unsalable and had to be returned to the government when the recipient died. The *sang tian* was called *yong ye tian* (perpetual field), which could be inherited by the recipient's heirs. Both kinds were salable in given conditions. Each adult male or female peasant was required to pay the government in grain, pongee, cotton, cloth or bast fibres and perform 20 days' labour service annually. Two points demonstrated the heightened social status of peasants under the feudal state: the classification into the tax field and possessed field, then into the open field and mulberry field, and then into the per capita field and perpetual field with their salability in given conditions which affirmed the private ownership of the peasants over part of the land they received; and, secondly, the specific number given for annual labour service days which clearly defined this burden on the peasants. Other signs of the development of the land equalization system were that, unlike the protégés of the landlords from the privileged families, the peasants had to pay land rent which formed part of the state tax, and, also, the feudal state demanded grain and pongee for the open field and mulberry field it gave the peasants, which showed government efforts to strengthen the combination of agriculture and household handicrafts to preserve the structure of the natural economy characterized by the men working on the land and the women working at the looms.

The laws and decrees of feudal states were seldom carried out to the letter. The early Tang provisions on land equalization were violated in the mid-Tang period with constant land annexations and wars. In 780, the Tang court issued a decree providing for a tax levy according to the needs of state expenditure and tax payment in proportion to the amount of one's property and land. No mention was made of the perpetual field and per capita field, nor of government distribution of land and its return to the government—which meant extensive state recognition of the private ownership of land and the existence of state tax independent of land rent. This great change pointed to the economic development of Chinese feudal society. The new decree benefited only the feudal state and the landlords, who could increase taxes or annex land at will. Consequently, from the end of the Tang Dynasty onward, the peasants rising against enslavement also had to fight for the possession of land.

The various areas where several ethnic groups lived together began their process of feudalization at one time or another from the Three Kingdoms to the Tang period. Ethnic minorities like the Xiongnu, Xianbei, Jie, Di and Qiang, who inhabited the northwestern and northern frontier regions, were at different stages of social development, some in primitive clan society and others in slave society. In the closing years of the Western Jin Dynasty, they immigrated to the Huanghe River valley where, mixing with the Han, they experienced a leap forward in their social development. During the Sixteen States period, most of the states established by ethnic minorities—such as the Han and the Former Zhao of the Xiongnu, the Later Zhao of the Jie, the Former Qin of the Di and the Later Qin of the Qiang—speeded up their process of feudalization by appointing officials of Han ethnic group, adopting the forms of government of the Han people and implementing feudal political and economic policies.

After unifying the northern part of China, the Northern Wei established by the Xianbei pressed ahead with this process in regions where several ethnic groups lived together. The process developed even further during the reign of Emperor Xiao Wen Di.

Feudalization also took place in the southern regions where several ethnic groups lived together. The chaos caused by frequent wars forced the labouring people in the north to move south en masse to Jingzhou and Yangzhou which were largely inhabited by the Shanyue and Man peoples. The Shanyues and Mans gradually accepted the advanced production techniques and social system from the north, which helped accelerate their process of feudalization.

Feudalization in regions inhabited by several ethnic groups was significant in the development of Chinese history in that the Han people and the ethnic minorities absorbed each others' positive attributes to activate the productive forces of society and bring about prosperity in the social economy.

Chapter VIII
The Five Dynasties, the Song and the Yuan: the Later Period of Ascendancy of Chinese Feudalism

1. The Five Dynasties and Ten States

Chinese feudalism experienced the later period of its ascendancy during the Five Dynasties, the Song and the Yuan. This was also a period of transition from separate feudal regimes to the establishment of a central authority over the whole country. By the Five Dynasties are meant the Later Liang, the Later Tang, the Later Jin, the Later Han and the Later Zhou. These states had all been founded at one time or another, between 907 to 960 on China's Central Plains. During this period there were altogether 13 emperors who ruled for a total of 53 years. Between 960 and 1368 there were the Northern Song and the Southern Song dynasties, jointly known as the Song Dynasty. There were 9 emperors of 7 generations during the Northern Song, covering a period from 960 to 1127. There were 7 emperors of 7 generations during the Southern Song, covering the period from 1127 to 1276. The Yuan Dynasty had 11 emperors of 6 generations between 1271 and 1368. During the Five Dynasties, there were in addition ten small kingdoms known as the Ten States and also the state of Liao established by the Qidans. During the Northern and Southern Song dynasties, there were in North China the Liao, the Xixia (Western Xia), the Jin and the Mongol regimes and, in the southern and western parts of the country, such kingdoms as Gaochang, Xiliao (Western Liao), Tufan and Dali. Though its capital was taken by the enemy as early as 1276, the Southern Song carried on its anti-Yuan struggle until 1279.

Of the Five Dynasties, the Later Liang established by Zhu Wen had the longest history of 17 years (907-923). The Later Tang established by Li Cunxu and Later Jin inaugurated by Shi Jingtang had a history of 13 (923-936) and 12 (936-947) years, respectively. The Later Han established by Liu Zhiyuan was of the shortest duration, since it had a history of only 4 years (947-950). The Later Zhou created by Guo Wei had a history of 9 years (951-960). The founders of the Later Tang, the Later Jin and the Later Han were all of Shatuo origin, while those of the Later Liang and the Later Zhou were Hans. The Later Tang had in succession five emperors of whom two were the adopted sons of the preceding monarchs. Chai Rong, a Later Zhou monarch, was the adopted son of Guo Wei.

The Later Liang had jurisdiction over an area covering the major parts of present-day Henan, Shaanxi, Shandong, and Hubei provinces, in addition to all of present-day Ningxia Hui Autonomous Region and parts of Hebei, Shanxi, Gansu, Anhui and Jiangxi provinces. The Later Tang, Later Jin and Later Han controlled wider areas. The Later Zhou occupied the largest territory, with its boundary stretching as far south as the northern banks of the Changjiang River in Hubei, Anhui and Jiangsu provinces. Notwithstanding the various sizes of their territories, these states played an important role politically, as all feudal forces in the various parts of the country, more or less, bowed to their rule. The Later Tang made Luoyang its capital, while the Later Liang and the three other dynasties all had their capital at Kaifeng.

The Ten States in the Five Dynasties period included the state of Wu founded by Yang Xingmi, the state of Wuyue by Qian Liu, the state of Southern Han by Liu Yin, the state of Chu by Ma Yin, the state of Former Shu by Wang Jian and finally, the state of Min by Wang Shenzhi. These states were established about the time when the Later Liang was founded. The founders of these states formerly had all been garrison commanders during the later part of the Tang Dynasty. Gao Jixing, a garrison commander during the period of the Later Liang, founded the state of Jingnan, also known as Nanping, after Later Liang had been exterminated. The state was the smallest among the Ten States. The state of Later Shu founded by Meng Zhixiang, the state of Southern Tang by Xu Zhigao, and the state of

Northern Han by Liu Chong appeared somewhat later than the others, as they were established, respectively, towards the end of the Later Tang, early during the Later Jin, and early during the Later Zhou.

The quick succession of dynasties after the Later Liang indicated the political confusion that existed then. Without an exception, the founder of one dynasty was a garrison commander of the preceding dynasty who then usurped the throne. Besides, members of the ruling élite fought among themselves to seize power. Zhu Wen, founder of the Later Liang, was killed by one of his sons who, in turn, met his death at the hands of his younger brother, and the latter succeeded in gaining the throne. Both the second and the fourth monarches of the Later Tang became emperors by armed force. For the seizure of power, ferocious battles were fought among rivals. On the Central Plains, people and their economy suffered as a result of wars, exorbitant taxes, severe punishments, and Draconian laws. Time and again, peasant uprisings broke out. In 920, Wu Yi and Dong Yi led peasants to stage an uprising in Chengzhou (modern Huaiyang, Henan), the best known of all the uprisings during the Five Dynasties. It dealt a heavy blow to the Later Liang regime which had to call upon the imperial army and the armies from several regions to suppress it.

Contrary to the situation on the Central Plains where one dynasty followed another in quick succession and war raged on constantly, there was relative peace lasting anywhere from 20 to 50 years in such states as the Former Shu, Later Shu, Wuyue, Southern Tang, and Southern Han. Being free from ravages of war, these states made progress in social economy. Large numbers of refugees fleeing wars from the Central Plains descended on these states. These refugees brought with them not only production technology but also academic learning and culture.

In literature, *ci* was most popular during the Five Dynasties. As a poetic form, it was highly developed during the Former Shu, Later Shu, Southern Tang. Li Yu (937-978), the last monarch of the Southern Tang, was a famous *ci* poet.

During the Five Dynasties there was in North China a Qidan tribe, later known as Liao, that, with the passage of time, became very strong. By the time when Zhu Wen founded the Later Liang, Yelü

Abaoji had accomplished the unification of the Qidan tribe. In 916, Abaoji ascended the throne. During the period of the Later Liang and Later Tang, the Qidans made frequent intrusions into present-day Hebei and Shanxi provinces for the purpose of raiding; wherever they went, they carried off people and their property. Yelü Deguang, son of Abaoji, aided Shi Jingtang in founding the Later Jin. In return, Shi Jingtang ceded to the Qidan sixteen districts located in the northern sections of modern Hebei and Shanxi provinces. He also referred to himself as a "filial emperor". After he died he was succeeded by his son Shi Chonggui, who referred to himself as the Qidan's "grandson" but not its "subject". On the ground that Shi had shown disrespect, Yelü Deguang marched his army southward and took Kaifeng in 946. After bringing an end to the Later Jin, he turned his men loose among the civilian populace, causing great havoc on the Central Plains. People, enraged, rose in resistance, in groups that were as large as "several hundred thousand men" or as small as "one thousand". In the end, they cleared the Central Plains of the invaders.

Towards the end of the Five Dynasties, Guo Wei, emperor of the Later Zhou, introduced political and economical reforms. Rents and taxes were reduced, sentences for committing crimes lightened, and corrupt officials punished. Favourable conditions for agricultural production were thus created. Hundreds of thousands of people flocked from other places to the Later Zhou for settlement. In 954, shortly after Guo Wei died, Liu Chong of the Northern Han, who had jurisdiction over present-day Shanxi Province, formed an alliance with the Qidan to attack the Later Zhou. Chai Rong took personal command of the Later Zhou's army and engaged Liu Chong at Gaoping (modern Gaoping County, Shanxi) where he exacted a heavy toll of the Northern Han army. Liu Chong fled with a hundred or so of his surviving cavalrymen. After this battle, Chai Rong began to think seriously of unifying the country. He rectified the disipline of his army. To rehabilitate the agricultural economy of the Central Plains, he paid attention to a fair exaction of rents and taxes and the construction of water conservancy projects. With his territory extending as far south as the northern bank of the Changjiang River, he succeeded in recovering a number of strategic points from Qidan, such as Ningzhou (modern

Qingxian County, Hebei), Yijinguan Pass and Yukouguan Pass (modern Baxian County, Hebei), Waqiaoguan Pass (modern Xiongxian County, Hebei), Mozhou (modern Renqiu County, Hebei), Yingzhou (modern Hejian County, Hebei). All this had paved the way for the Northern Song, during a later period, to bring to an end the prolonged division of the country and to establish a central authority over all of China.

The history of the Five Dynasties was a continuation of the history of the late part of the Tang Dynasty during which various frontier commanders maintained separatist regimes and fought among themselves. It was also a period during which the tendency towards a single central authority for the country began. It witnessed the shifting of the economic centre to the South.

2. Rise and Fall of the Northern Song; Uprisings by Wang Xiaobo and Fang La

During the period from 960 to 997, Northern Song was at its early and rising state. The emperors were then Zhao Kuangyin (Emperor Tai Zu) and Zhao Kuangyi (Emperor Tai Zong).

In 960, Zhao Kuangyin, Commander of the Later Zhou's imperial army, led a revolt against the throne with the support of his brother Zhao Kuangyi and his councillor Zhao Pu. Thus he seized the power of the Later Zhou and founded the dynasty of Northern Song. The capital remained at Kaifeng, which was renamed Dongjing (Eastern Capital). It took fifteen years for the Northern Song to conquer the four states of Jingnan, later Shu, Southern Han and Southern Tang. In 978 and 979, Zhao Kuangyi conquered the Wuyue and the Northern Han, thus bringing about national unification to a certain extent. He planned to retake areas of modern Hebei and Shanxi provinces, then occupied by the Liao. But he failed in his attempt as his army suffered disastrous defeats at Gaolianghe (around present-day Beijing) in 979 and at Qigouguan Pass (southwest of modern Zhuoxian County, Hebei) in 986. From then on, the Northern Song became defensive in its relation with the Liao.

Genealogical Table of the Five Dynasties

1. Later Liang

(1) Emperor Tai Zu (Zhu Wen) (r. 907-912) —— (2) Emperor Mo Di (Zhu Youzhen) (r. 913-923)

2. Later Tang

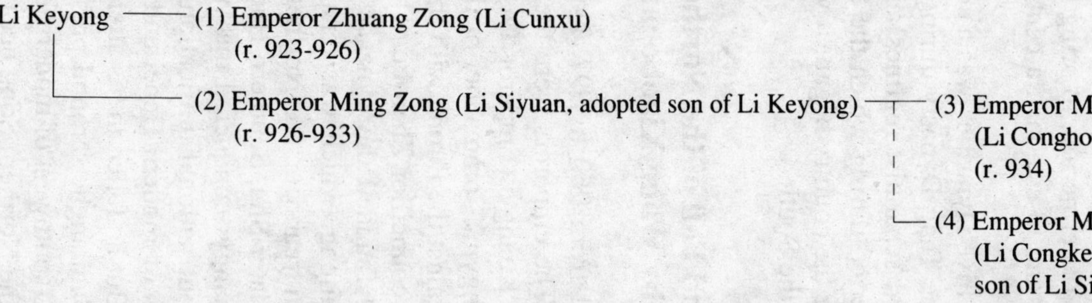

Li Keyong —— (1) Emperor Zhuang Zong (Li Cunxu) (r. 923-926)

Li Keyong —— (2) Emperor Ming Zong (Li Siyuan, adopted son of Li Keyong) (r. 926-933) —— (3) Emperor Min Di (Li Conghou) (r. 934)

(2) Emperor Ming Zong - - - (4) Emperor Mo Di (Li Congke, adopted son of Li Siyuan) (r. 934-936)

3. Later Jin

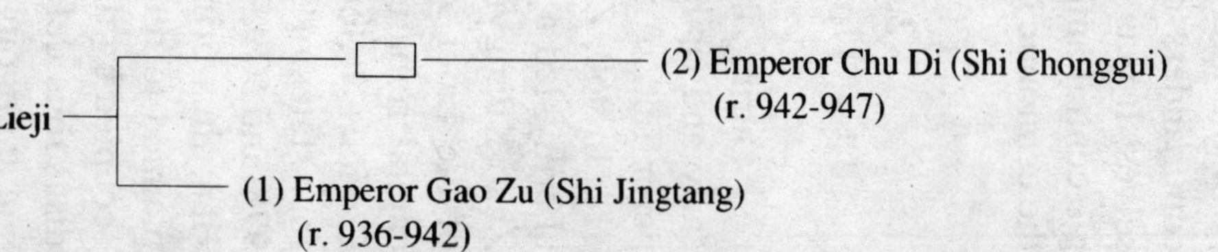

Nie Lieji —— □ —— (2) Emperor Chu Di (Shi Chonggui) (r. 942-947)

Nie Lieji —— (1) Emperor Gao Zu (Shi Jingtang) (r. 936-942)

Genealogical Table of the Five Dynasties (Continued)

4. Later Han

(1) Emperor Gao Zu (Liu Zhiyuan) (r. 947) —— (2) Emperor Yin Di (Liu Chengyou) (r. 948-950)

5. Later Zhou

(1) Emperor Tai Zu (Guo Wei) (r. 951-954) —— (2) Emperor Shi Zong (Chai Rong, adopted son of Guo Wei) (r. 954-959) —— (3) Emperor Gong Di (Chai Zongxun) (r. 959-960)

The Ten States

1. The six states that rose the earliest:

Wu (920-937) — Occupied part of modern Jiangsu, Anhui, Jiangxi and Hubei provinces. Conquered by the Southern Tang.

Wuyue (907-978) — Occupied part of modern Zhejiang and Jiangsu provinces. Conquered by the Northern Song.

Southern Han (907-971) — Occupied a major part of modern Guangdong and Guangxi provinces. Conquered by the Northern Song.

Chu (907-951) — Occupied modern Hunan Province and the northeastern section of modern Guangxi Province. Conquered by the Southern Tang.

Former Shu (907-925) — Occupied modern Sichuan Province, the southeastern section of modern Gansu and southern section of modern Shaanxi, and the western section of modern Hubei provinces. Conquered by the Later Tang.

Min (909-945) — Occupied modern Fujian Province. Conquered by the Southern Tang.

2. The state that rose comparatively late:

Jingnan (Nanping, 924-963) — Occupied present-day Jingling and Gong'an counties of Hubei Province. Conquered by the Northern Song.

3. The three states that rose the latest:

Later Shu (934-965) — Occupied modern Sichuan Province, the southeastern section of modern Gansu, the southern section of modern Shaanxi and the western section of modern Hubei provinces. Conquered by the Northern Song.

Southern Tang (937-975) — Occupied the southern sections of modern Jiangsu and Anhui provinces, Fujian Province, Jiangxi Province, Hunan Province, and the eastern section of modern Hubei Province. Conquered by the Northern Song.

Northern Han (951-979) — Occupied the northern section of modern Shanxi and part of modern Shaanxi and Hebei provinces. Conquered by the Northern Song.

Early during the Northern Song Dynasty, the rulers did their best to strengthen the feudal autocracy. High posts in various regions, formerly held by military officers, were now occupied by civil officials. Local appointments above the county level were now replaced by royal appointments. The best of local troops was incorporated into and absorbed by the central army, and there were special institutions in the central government that controlled local finance. The centralized power in the government was in turn distributed among many branches so as to make sure that no branch of government would have too much power to the detriment of the royal interest. Three central agencies, political, military and financial, were placed under the direct control of the royal house. The Secretariat took charge of political affairs, but its head, the prime minister, invested with executive power, had no control over the nation's military affairs. There was the Military Council with its chancellor invested with the power of directing all military units except the imperial army. The chancellor of the treasury handled all tax revenue and government expenditure. The imperial army was divided into three branches, each directly under the command of one marshal. There was also a Censorate, headed by a Grand Censor, with the duty of supervising all government officials. A system as described above proved to be very effective in preventing local forces from establishing separatist feudal regimes and in warding off any threat from high ministers to the throne. But over-concentration of power in the royal house, as well as those measures adopted to curb the power of high ministers, especially that of high military officers, gave rise to political corruption in the upper stratum of officialdom and weakened the fighting ability of the Northern Song when confronted with military threat from the outside.

Early during the Northern Song Dynasty, class contradictions remained acute, and peasant uprisings staged by peasants, soldiers and ethnic minorities erupted time and again. In 993, Wang Xiaobo, a poverty-stricken man, started an uprising in Qingchen (to the southwest of modern Guanxian County, Sichuan). Voicing the demand of the masses of peasants for the right to property, he openly raised the slogan of "equal distribution of wealth between the poor and the rich". This was a new development as compared to the demand for the right to existence raised by peasants during previous uprisings since the Qin and Han dynasties. The insurgent army grew fast. Early in 994, Wang Xiaobo was killed by a flying arrow. Li Shun succeeded him as commander and continued the fight. After taking Chengdu and seizing control of a vast expanse of land south of Jiange and north of Wuxia, he founded a peasant regime named the Great Shu. But he made the mistake of underestimating the strength of the enemy. Chengdu fell into the hands of the Northern Song army in the summer, and 30,000 men, including Li; were killed in action. In 995, the insurgent army collapsed.

The middle era of the Northern Song Dynasty, that covered the reigns of Emperors Zhen Zong, Ren Zong and Ying Zong (997-1967), was a period of decline. The bureaucracy, including the military bureaucracy, became more and more inflated, and political corruption went from bad to worse. While the peasants were weighted down by ever harsher exploitation, the government treasury became more and more depleted. The peasant uprisings were bigger and more frequent than those in the early period of the Northern Song. Externally, the Northern Song was threatened by the Liao and by the rising states of Xia in the northwest. In 1004, the Northern Song army routed a Liao force of many thousand that came to the south to raid Chinese borders. Yet, when the word came that the Liao troops had entered Tanzhou (modern Puyang County, Hebei) and were approaching Dongjing, Emperor Zhen Zong was so frightened that he wanted to move his capital to the south. Prime Minister Kou Zhun was strongly opposed to this and proposed instead that the emperor direct the battle. Zhen Zong took his advice. Though assuming command, he still planned to make peace. Early in 1005, he concluded a pact with the Liao, which stipulated that the Northern Song deliver an annual amount of 100,000 taels of silver and 200,000 bolts of silk to Liao. In 1044, when the Liao further threatened to use force, Emperor Ren Zong agreed to add another 100,000 taels of silver and an equal number of bolts of silk in exchange for temporary tranquillity on the northern border. During the period from 1040 to 1042, three battles were fought between the Northern Song and the Xia at, respectively, Yanzhou (modern Yan'an city, Shaanxi), Haoshuichuan (Tianshuihe, east of modern Longde

County, Gansu) and Weizhou (modern Pingliang County, Gansu). As Northern Song was decisively defeated in each of these battles, Emperor Ren Zong agreed in 1044 to present the Xia with an annual gift of silver and silk in exchange for peace on its northwestern border.

Hopeless as Emperor Zhen Zong found himself both politically and militarily, he turned his thoughts to ideological control of the people and had corresponding new measures adopted. In addition to worshipping Confucius, people were encouraged to worship Buddhist and Taoist deities. As a new method to benumb the people's will, the new measures were even more effective as compared to the worship of Confucius alone. During the middle period of the Northern Song a new school known as Neo-Confucianism came into existence. Combining Confucianism with Buddhism and Taoism, it defined the doctrines of Confucius in such a way as to serve better the interests of the landlord class. As progenitor of this school, Zhou Dunyi (1016-1073) put forward the idea of "the Absolute" which, he said, was the essence of the universe that transcended all material things. According to him, feudal order was a manifestation of "the Absolute" in social relations. Hence the eternity of the feudal system. Zhou Dunyi wrote *An Explanation of the Diagram of the Absolute (Taiji Tu Shuo)*. His philosophy falls into the category of objective idealism. A contemporary of Zhou Dunyi, Zhang Zai (1020-1077), held the view that the materialist "vitality" was the essence of all things in the universe. According to him, the interaction between the *yin* and the *yang* led to changes in the "vitality" and in the course of changes, things were formed. Proceeding from the idealist thought that men and universe were one, he believed that the people and the monarchs formed an inseparable whole. In his view, contradictions between them could be eased out.

In the period from 1067 to 1127, which covered the reigns of Emperors Shen Zong, Zhe Zong, Hui Zong, and Qin Zong, the Northern Song proceeded from decline to extinction. Early during the reign of Shen Zong, two political factions developed among the high officials. Those who proposed reforms advocated the enactment of "New Laws" that would take away part of the power from the privileged class so as to boost agricultural production and increase revenue for the government. But the conservatives were opposed to the enactment of "New Laws". According to them the "New Laws" would bring harm instead of higher production. However, under the auspices of Emperor Shen Zong the reform under the "New Laws" was carried out between 1070 and 1074. But there were difficulties. Emperor Shen Zong constantly wavered when confronted with objections to the "New Laws" raised by the conservatives. Beginning with 1085 the conservatives and the reformers took turns in winning the upper hand and thus the control of the government. It was not until the early twelfth century that struggles between the two factions finally came to an end.

The struggle between the reformers and the conservatives was also carried to the academic field. It was as acute as the political struggle and lasted much longer. The leading reformer, Wang Anshi (1021-1086), was a philosophical materialist. He maintained that "primordial vitality" was the essence of the universe, and the movement of matter was governed by natural laws. Though these laws could not be changed, men could take initiative and should not resign themselves to so-called "fate". Wang Anshi's theory of "New Learning" served as his theoretical basis in introducing the "New Laws".

Shen Kuo (1031-1095), another reformer, was also a materialist. His range as a scientist was immense. He knew mathematics, astronomy, calendar making, geography, cartography, geology, meteorology, physics, chemistry, metallurgy, the manufacture of weaponry, water conservancy, botany, zoology, agriculture, medicine, and pharmacology. He was outstanding in proposing many original ideas. As to the summation of arithematic series of second order, he also had his own method. By making a summation of circumference and height to extract the length of a curve, he proposed improvement on observatory instruments and calendar making. He went to great length in discussing the properties of the compass and found, in his own way, the difference between the true north and magnetic north.

Sima Guang (1019-86) was a leading conservative and an idealist advocating fatalism. He believed that fate was the supreme controller that determined the difference between the high and the low, between the rich and the poor, between the intelligent and the benighted, and between a long and a short life. People, therefore, should live in complete resignation to their fate. Any disobedience, he said, would augur ill. Stressing the importance of following "rites" he urged strict observance of the feudal order and its hierarchic details. He wrote *History as a Mirror* (*Zi Zhi Tong Jian*) which, consisting of 294 *juan,* took him 19 years to complete. Recording events from the beginning of the Warring States to the end of the Later Zhou, it was a work of great historic value. He also wrote a number of philosophical works.

Cheng Hao (1032-1085), from Luoyang, was a conservative theoretician. Together with his brother Cheng Yi (1033-1107) he became a principal exponent of Neo-Confucianism first advocated by Zhou Dunyi. Known as the "Cheng Brothers", they were the first to advance the idea of "reason" as the essence of the universe, which had existed before anything else. According to them, "there is only one reason under heaven", men and all material things were just one, forming an inseparable whole. Different as people were in social position, they said, each must act according to his duties and thus conform to "reason". A theory of this kind also falls into the category of objective idealism, according to which the broad masses must resign themselves to a life of poverty and humiliation, place themselves at the disposal of the feudal order, and refrain from the thought of changing things.

Amid factional strifes there was a faction led by Su Shi (1036-1101). In his early years, he had advocated political reform; later he opposed the "New Laws". Academically, he disagreed with both Wang Anshi and the Cheng Brothers. His major achievement was in literature where he took a stand against the literary style of flowery parallelisms and favoured the classic form of prose. Besides, he preferred *ci* to *shi* when writing poetry. Ouyang Xiu (1007-1072), a statesman as well as a man of letters, was the main advocate of the classic style of prose-writing. Both Sima Guang and Wang Anshi were great classic essayists. Su Shi, his father Su Xun, and his brother Su Che, jointly known as the "Three Sus", were stalwarts of classic writing. Ouyang Xiu, Liu Yong and Zhou Bangyan, as *ci* poets, were known for their description of delicate feelings of young men and young women and their portrayal of the sentiments of people parting with each other. Su Shi, however, broke through confines of this kind as he wrote in a plain and graceful style of his own.

The factional struggles during the latter part of the Northern Song, a reflection of social contradictions, showed that the rulers found themselves in a dilemma: they wanted to carry out reforms but they were unable to. The inability of Wang Anshi to implement his reform programmes entailed social disturbances. By the time of Emperor Hui Zong's reign, political struggles between various factions had temporarily stopped, but worse corruption was found among the rulers. Ruthless exploitation became intolerable to the people, especially in the southeastern section of the country. In 1120, Fang La staged a peasant uprising in Qingxi (modern Chun'an County, Zhejiang). In three months he and his men took control of six prefectures and 52 counties in modern Zhejiang and Anhui provinces, while their forces grew from one thousand to one hundred thousand men and then to a million. After establishing his peasant regime, Fang La claimed that he could unify the country in ten years. The claim frightened the rulers. They sent a large force on a southward march and defeated Fang La and his men after a bitter fight that persisted for more than one year. In 1121, Fang La himself was taken prisoner, and soon put to death. But his forces carried on the fight for another year.

Before the uprising Fang La had carried out propaganda on Manichaeism among his followers and organized their activities in a Manicaean way. Within the organization impoverished people would receive help and travellers would be provided with food and shelter. Members were organized down to the basic units, and some of them were assigned to specific tasks such as organizing religious activities and looking after funds contributed by followers. All this indicates that Fang La had done good groundwork among his forces before he started the uprising. During the uprising, he condemned the Song rulers for despoiling the peasants of their fruits of labour in order to provide themselves with all the luxuries for an extravagant life. The aim of the uprising, he declared, was to overthrow the Northern Song regime so as to bring improvement to the livelihood of the peasants. His uprising, like that led by Wang Xiaobo, was economically oriented and thus contained a new historical meaning. Before him, there was a peasant rebellion led by Song Jiang in Shandong Province. Legends about this peasant army are many and varied.

Before Fang La started his uprising, the Northern Song regime sent an emissary to the state of Jin to negotiate an agreement for a joint attack on the Liao. But, attacking Liao, the Song forces suffered repeated defeats. In 1125, following its conquest of the Liao, the Jin began an all-out attack on the Northern Song. Two years later, in 1127, it took Dongjing, capital of the Northern Song. By then Emperor Hui Zong had abdicated in favour of his son, Emperor Qin Zong. More than three thousand people, including Emperor Qin Zong and his father Hui Zong, their wives and concubines, other members of the royal family and court ministers, were taken captive and carried off northward to the Jin.

3. The Liao, the Xia and the Jin: Their Relations with the Northern Song

The Liao, the Xia, and the Jin were three regimes controlled by the aristocrats of China's ethnic minorities. Despite the various political and military contradictions among them and in their relations with the Northern Song, some compromises were made, and economic and cultural exchanges with the Northern Song developed.

The Liao was a regime where the Qidan ethnic group dominated. The ethnic group was an old one, and its activities centred on the valley of the Xar Moron River on the upper reaches of the Liaohe River in today's Liaoning Province. Rising during an unknown period in history, the Qidans consisted of eight tribes. Once every three years, they elected a Khan as their leader. In 907, Yelu Abaoji was elected. After his election, he brushed aside the electoral system and never gave up his position as the Khan till his death. In 916, he succeeded in killing the other tribal leaders and ascended to the throne, to be known later as Emperor Tai Zu of the Liao. He founded the state of Qidan and changed the electoral system to a hereditary one.

The founding of the state of Qidan coincided with a process of social changes and Sinification. During his lifetime, Yelü Abaoji had employed a number of Han people as his political advisers and

Genealogical Table of the Northern Song Dynasty

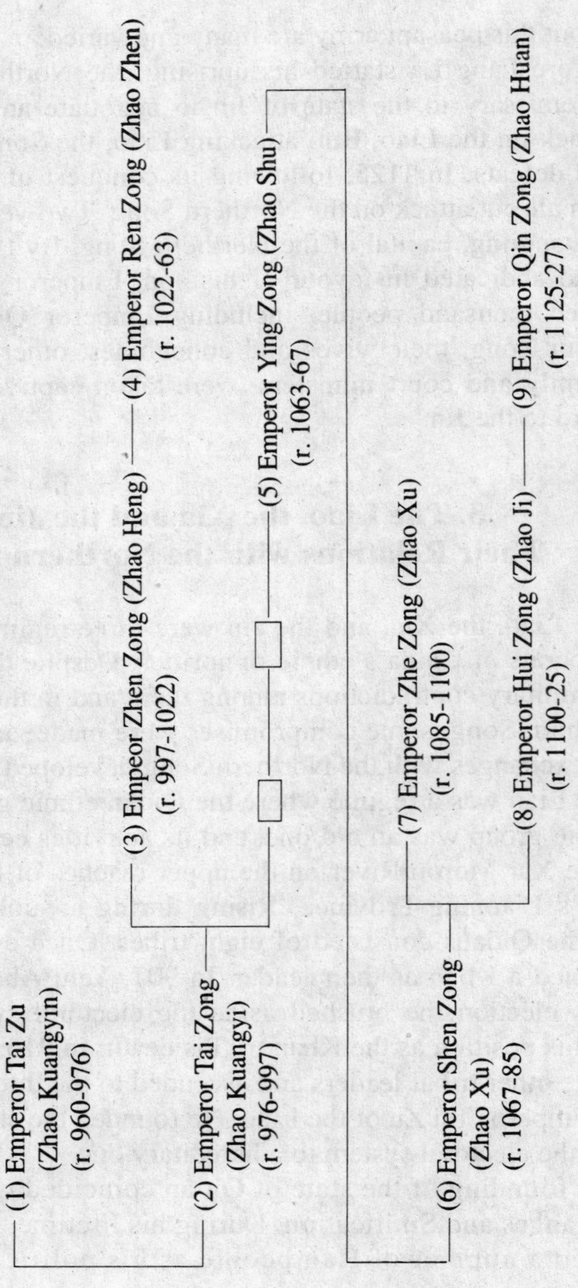

adopted, to a certain extent, the Han feudal form of production. Formerly, the Qidan people had led a nomadic life; they were also engaged in fishing and hunting. They condemned a large number of Han captives as slaves. Later, influenced by the Han Chinese, they gradually took to agriculture and learned iron-smelting and other techniques in production. Han influence brought about a change in Qidan life as well as an improvement for the life of Han captives. Towns and cities were built; in them were the emancipated former Han slaves who were now engaged in agriculture and handicraft industry, as they had been on the Central Plains before their captivity. To govern the state, the Qidan rulers adopted a dual system, the southern system for the Han Chinese and the northern system for the Qidans and ethnic groups other than the Han Chinese. The former was staffed by Han Chinese and Qidans, responsible for the collection of taxes and other exactions, and the latter was staffed by the Qidans only.

Abaoji went out to conquer, time and again, in order to expand the territory of the Qidan. At the zenith of his power, he had control over a large area extending as far east as the Sea of Japan, as far west as the Altay Mountains, as far north as the Kerulen River and as far south as modern Xiongxian County, Hebei. In 926, after the death of Abaoji, Yelü Deguang inherited the throne, known to historians as Emperor Tai Zong. In 947 he changed the title of his nation to Liao.

During the early years of the Northern Song, the Liao posed a major threat from the north. During the period between 979 and 986, having inflicted two serious defeats on the Northern Song army, the Liao became a superior power. In 1004, a peace pact was concluded at Tanzhou, under which the Liao obtained a bountiful annual gift of silver and silk from the Northern Song, while Emperor Zhen Zong had to call Empress Dowager Xiao of the Liao his aunt and take Sheng Zong of the Liao as his brother. Later, the Northern Song opened markets on its north border for trade and exchanged its tea, silk, bast-fibre fabrics, glutinous rice, porcelain, books, rhinoceros horns, ivory and spice for the Liao's sheep, horses, camels, hides, and wool. As a result, the Han Chinese strengthened their ties with the Qidan and other ethnic groups, resulting in a richer economic and cultural life for all concerned.

The Xia was a regime predominated by a Tibetan tribe named Dangxiang, the members of which formerly lived in the modern Qinghai and the northwestern section of Sichuan. Later they settled down in the adjacent area of modern Shaanxi and Gansu and Ningxia Hui Autonomous Region. Approximately in the ninth century, this tribal people began to take up agriculture in addition to stockbreeding. From the end of the Tang Dynasty to the early period of the Northern Song, the control over the area by a Dangxiang Cief had all along been recognized by the Han Chinese authorities. He accepted the surname of the Chinese royal house awarded to him. During the Tang Dynasty, his surname would be Li which was changed to Zhao at the time of the Northern Song. The Dangxiangs often made a common cause with Liao to fight against the Northern Song.

In 1032, after Zhao Yuanhao had become chief of the Dangxiang tribe, he extended his influence to the Gansu Corridor. In 1038, Yuanhao assumed the imperial title and called his new regime Da Xia or Great Xia, known to historians as Xi Xia or West Xia. The capital was Xingqing (Yingchuan, capital city of modern Ningxia Autonomous Region). His kingdom extended as far east as the Huanghe River, as far west as Yumen (to the west of modern Dunhuang County, Gansu), as far south as Xiaoguan (to the southeast of modern Guyuan County, Ningxia), and as far north as the Gobi Desert. In his kingdom were people of different ethnic groups at various stages of development, but the Dangxiangs were still at the stage of transition from slavery to feudalism.

Yuanhao knew Chinese as well as Tibetan. He had a good background in Buddhist scriptures and military and legal works by the Han Chinese. He modelled his administrative organs after those of the Tang and Song. His officials were members of ethnic minorities as well as the Han Chinese.

Following a traditional policy, Yuanhao allied himself with Liao against Song. During the period between 1040 and 1042, the Song and the Xia were three times at war, resulting in heavy economic burden on the people of both sides and a great loss of lives. Trade came to a stop; shortages of grain and daily necessities were badly felt in the Xia, creating difficulties in people's live. In 1044, the Song and Xia concluded a peace pact under which the Xia, pledging allegiance to the Song, declared itself a vassal state. In return, it received from the Song an annual gift of 72,000 taels of silver, 153,000 bolts of silk and 30,000 *jin* of tea. In addition, Song lifted its ban on trade with Xia on its border.

The Jin was a regime predominated by the Nüzhens, a tribe then living in the Songhua River valley. After the rise of the Qidans, they were subjected to the rule of the Liao. In 1114, the Nüzhens were called upon by their outstanding leader Aguda to fight for the overthrow of the rule of the Liao. In the battles at Ningjiangzhou (now Wujiazhan, Fuyu County, Jilin) and at Chuhedian (now Renjiadian, Fuyu County, Jilin), a Nüzhen force of less than 20,000 routed a Liao army of several hundred thousand. The Nüzhen force grew speedily after the victory. In 1115, Aguda, having succeeded in throwing off the yoke of the Liao, assumed the imperial title. He was known to historians as Emperor Tai Zu, and his dynastic title was Jin. Soon after the founding of the Jin, places of strategic importance to Liao, such as Huanglongfu (modern Nong'an County, Jilin), fell into the hands of the Nüzhens. Finding encouragement in this development, oppressed tribes all rose against Liao rule.

Seeing that the Liao was in a precarious state, Emperor Hui Zong of the Northern Song concluded an alliance with the Jin for a joint attack against Liao. It was agreed that after defeating the Liao, the Song would retrieve the territories previously ceded to the Qidan and that the Jin would receive from the Song the same amount of silver and silk that had been previously given to the Liao. In 1122, the war against the Liao began. Though Song troops tried more than once to take Yanjing (now Beijing), capital of Liao, they were beaten back. Later, the Jin troops took Yanjing and refused to withdraw. Emperor Hui Zong was obligated to pay the Jin 1,000,000 strings of coins each year in exchange for the return of the city of Yanjiang and a few other places.

In 1125, Emperor Tian Zuo of the Liao was captured by the Jin when he tried to flee. With his capture the Liao regime came to an end. By then the Jin ruler Aguda had died, and had been succeeded by Wuqimai, later known as Emperor Tai Zong. In the year before the Jin conquered the Liao, Yelü Dashi, a royal descendant of the Liao, had taken a part of the Liao army to the area south and north of the Tianshan Mountains and Central Asia, where he founded a new regime known as the West Liao with its capital at Husiwoerduo (near Tokmak in the U.S.S.R.). It lasted more than ninety years.

In the year of its conquest of the Liao, the Jin attacked the Song on two fronts, from the west and from the east. The western detachment was blocked at Taiyuan and could not advance further. The forces on the eastern route, however, quickly took Yanjing, crossed the Huanghe River, and reached Song's capital Dongjing. Emperor Qin Zong appointed Li Gang, who had advocated resistance, to the position of commander. Thanks to the co-operation between the military and the civilians, Li repeatedly beat back the Jin attack. But, subject to the influence of the capitulationists around him, Emperor Qin Zong showed no firm will to fight; and, to make peace with the Jin, the removed Li Gang from his command and ceded land and paid indemnities to the Jin. Headed by a student at the Imperial Academy named Chen Dong, people in the capital, exasperated, gathered in tens of thousands in front of the palace to protest against the removal of Li Gang and to demand resolute resistance against the Jin. Emperor Qin Zong yielded to popular pressure by reinstating Li Gang. Seeing the indomitable fighting will on the part of the Song people and the difficulty of taking the capital, the Jin forces withdrew. Once the enemy was gone, the Song monarch and high officials went back to their old way of life, whiling their time away in corruption. Li Gang was again dismissed. Once again, the Jin forces, in the autumn of 1126, marched southward and captured Dongjing the next year. The northern Song regime came to an end. The rise of Jin to supreme power was as fast as a summer storm. Only eleven years elapsed between Aguda's assumption of imperial title and the conquest of the Liao. The very next year after Liao was conquered, the Northern Song was subjugated too.

The Liao, the Xia, and the Jin each had its own written language employed in both private and public communication, in currencies, and in the translation of Chinese Confucian books or the translation of Chinese or Tibetan Buddhist scriptures. The written languages of the Qidan and Nüzhen peoples were a phonetic variation of the written

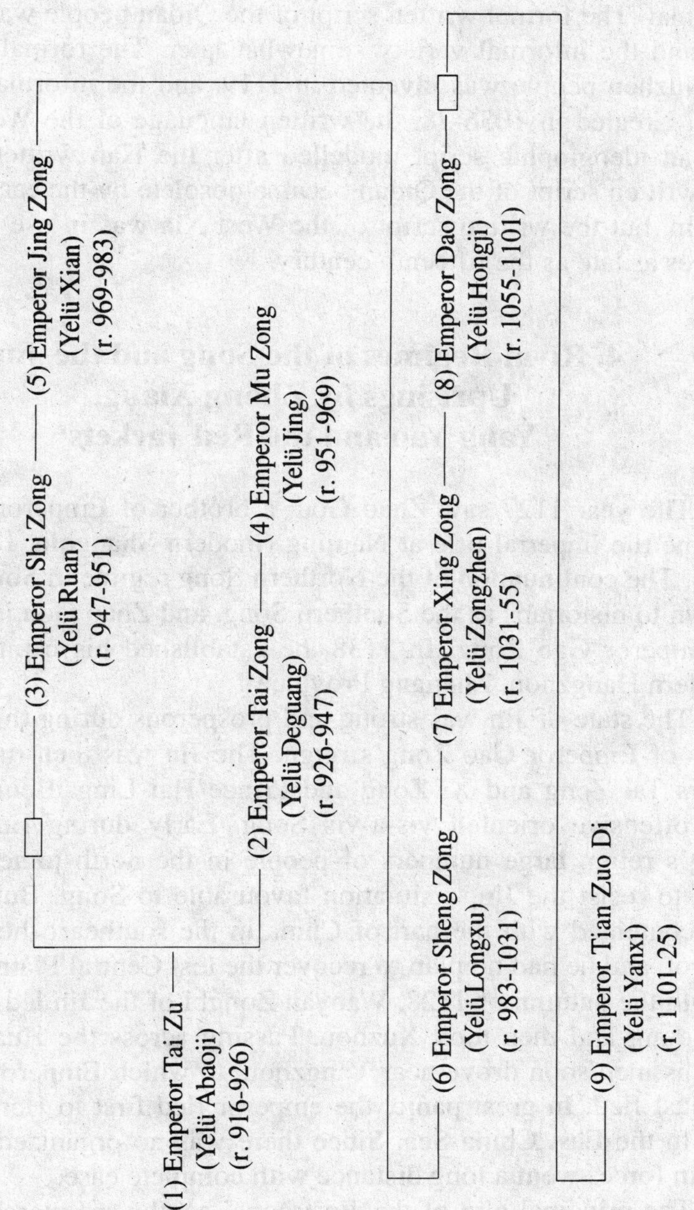
Genealogical Table of the Liao Dynasty
(1) Emperor Tai Zu
(Yelü Abaoji)
(r. 916-926)
(2) Emperor Tai Zong
(Yelü Deguang)
(r. 926-947)
(3) Emperor Shi Zong
(Yelü Ruan)
(r. 947-951)
(4) Emperor Mu Zong
(Yelü Jing)
(r. 951-969)
(5) Emperor Jing Zong
(Yelü Xian)
(r. 969-983)
(6) Emperor Sheng Zong
(Yelü Longxu)
(r. 983-1031)
(7) Emperor Xing Zong
(Yelü Zongzhen)
(r. 1031-55)
(8) Emperor Dao Zong
(Yelü Hongji)
(r. 1055-1101)
(9) Emperor Tian Zuo Di
(Yelü Yanxi)
(r. 1101-25)

script of the Han Chinese. They were of two kinds: the formal and the informal. The formal written script of the Qidan people was created in 920 and the informal variety somewhat later. The formal variety for the Nüzhen people was invented in 1119, and the informal variety in 1138. Created in 1036-38, the written language of the West Xia was also an ideographic script modelled after the Han written language. The written script of the Qidan became obsolete by the early period of the Jin, but the written script of the West Xia was in use in some localities as late as the fifteenth century.

4. Rival Regimes of the Song and the Jin; Uprisings by Zhong Xiang, Yang Yao and the Red Jackets

The year 1127 saw Zhao Gou, a brother of Emperor Qin Zong, assume the imperial title at Nanjing (modern Shangqiu, Henan Province). The continuation of the Northern Song regime in South China is known to historians as the Southern Song, and Zhao Gou is referred to as Emperor Gao Zong. In 1138, he established his capital at Linan (modern Hangzhou, Zhejiang Province).

The state of Jin was strong and prosperous during the thirty-five years of Emperor Gao Zong's reign. The Jin was then ruled by Emperors Tai Zong and Xi Zong and Prince Hai Ling. Being strong, it was offensive oriented vis-a-vis Song. Early during Emperor Gao Zong's reign, large numbers of people in the north joined organizations to resist the Jin, a situation favourable to Song. But Gao Zong was contented with the part of China in the southeast then under his control, and he had no plan to recover the lost Central Plains.

In the autumn of 1128, Wanyan Zongbi of the Jin led his army to Shandong and then took Xuzhou. Passing across the Huai River, he and his men soon drove near Yangzhou, to which Emperor Gao Zong had just fled. In great panic, the emperor fled first to Hangzhou, and then to the East China Sea. Since there was no organized resistance, the Jin forces went a long distance with complete ease.

The principal aim of the Jin troops' southward march proved to be raiding—to capture men and valuables from the rich south and take them to the north. For the time being, they had no intention of putting this vast area under their direct control. Early in 1130, satisfied with the war booty they had acquired, the Jin forces started withdrawing to the north. Wanyan Zongbi had not expected that he and his men would be intercepted on their homeward journey. At Huangtiandang (to the northeast of modern Nanjing City, Jiangsu), they were held by Han Shizhong, a Song general, for 48 days. Han and his eight thousand men inflicted heavy losses on Zongbi who claimed to have a force of several hundred thousand. When the invaders tried to ferry across the Changjiang River at Jing'anzhen, General Yue Fei intercepted them and delivered another severe blow.

In the autumn of 1130, the Jin troops attacked in Shaanxi. When arriving at Heshangyuan (to the northwest of Baoji, Shaanxi Province) in the following year, they met defeat at the hands of two Song generals named Wu Jie and Wu Lin. In the battle, Zongbi himself was injured by a flying arrow. A large number of his men were taken prisoner.

Beginning in 1133, several times the Jin forces marched southward. There were victories and defeats on both sides. The Song forces won several important battles. In 1133, Wu Jie and his men repulsed the Jin attack on Shaanxi and Sichuan. In 1134, Yue Fei recovered Xiangyang and five other prefectures in northern Hubei and southern Henan. In 1140, Liu Qi and his twenty thousand men put to flight more than one hundred thousand troops of the Jin at Shunchang (modern Fuyang County, Anhui) and effectively destroyed the cream of the Jin forces. In that same year, Yue Fei recovered Zhengzhou and Luoyang and then won a decisive battle at Yancheng (in modern Henan). From Yancheng he moved to Zhuxianzhen which was only forty to fifty *li* from Dongjing. The Jin commander Zongbi admitted that he had never met a setback like this in his whole life as a soldier. Yue Fei (1103-41) was a native of Tangyin in modern Henan Province. After joining the army as a volunteer he distinguished himself in many battles. With the passage of time, the men he led became so formidable in battle that there was a saying among the people that "it is easier to move a mountain than to defeat a Yue Fei army".

But victories on the battlefield did not change Emperor Gao Zong's determination to sue for peace. Great victories even aroused in him the suspicion that his generals might become too strong to be loyal to him. He appointed Qin Hui, a man who claimed that he had fled from the enemy camp, to be his prime minister, who took upon himself the mission of negotiating peace. Peace activities intensified even after Xiangyang and five other prefectures had been recovered by Yue Fei's army. In 1139, an imperial edict from the Jin arrived demanding of Song to pay an annual tribute of 250,000 taels of silver and 250,000 bolts of silk, and the Song accepted the demand. Soon after his triumph at Yancheng, Yue Fei was summarily called back from the front and, once back, was thrown into prison on false charges. In the winter of 1141, the Song accepted the Jin's demand for large territories. The new boundary began in the west at the Dasanguan (to the southwest of modern Baoji, Shaanxi) and ended in the east at the middle stream of the Huaishui River. The Song, from then on, had to act faithfully as a subject state to the Jin and pay annual tribute in silver and silk. Han Shizhong and other anti-Jin generals were relieved of their command; Yue Fei was put to death in compliance with the Jin's demand.

After peace had been concluded with Song, Zongbi took all the military and political power of the Jin into his hand. Meanwhile, a factional strife developed among the Jin's nobility. After 1148, when Zongbi died, the strifes became all the more pronounced. In 1149, Wanyan Liang, having murdered Emperor Xi Zong, acceded to the throne, to be known later as Prince Hai Ling. In preparation for the conquest of the Song, he carried out political reforms so as to strengthen the power of the emperor. In 1153 he moved the Jin's political centre from Huining (present-day Baichengzi, located in the southern section of Acheng County, Heilongjiang), to Yanjing, known also as Zhongdu (Middle Capital). In 1158, he ordered his ministers to build palaces in Kaifeng. In 1161, he personally led his troops of 600,000 men to march southward along four routes. The garrison forces of the Song stationed to the east and west of the Huai River collapsed without a fight. Stricken with panic, Emperor Gao Zong once again wanted to seek refuge on the sea. The situation was eased somewhat when Yu Yunwen won a resounding victory over the invaders north of the Changjiang River which Wanyan Liang attempted to pass across. Not long after his defeat, Wanyan Liang learned that Wanyan Yong, later known as Emperor Shi Zong, had started a rebellion and called himself emperor. Seeking a quick conquest of Song so he could move his forces northward to put down the rebellion, Wanyan Liang set a deadline for his troops to cross the Changjiang River. The troops responded with a mutiny and killed him with a barrage of arrows. His death put an end to his plan of seizing south China.

In 1162, Emperor Gao Zong abdicated in favour of his adopted son Zhao Shen who became known to historians as Emperor Xiao Zong. Once on the throne, Xiao Zong put General Zhang Jun in command to fight the war against the Jin. Besides, he restored all the honours due to Yue Fei posthumously. Meanwhile, he actively prepared for a northern expedition. In the following year, Zhang Jun and his men marched northward and soon gained control of a number of places. Soon internal strife broke out among the Song generals, and the strife led to their defeat when the Jin troops counter-attacked. The defeat changed Emperor Xiao Zong's mind about the war. To negotiate peace with the Jin, Tang Situi, a follower of Qin Hui, was appointed prime minister. General Zhang Jun, firm in his anti-Jin stand, was dismissed from his post as vice-prime minister. Early in 1165, Emperor Xiao Zong concluded a peace treaty with the Jin, under which Song ceded to the Jin large territories, besides promising to pay 200,000 taels of silver every year. After the conclusion of the treaty, a thirty-year peace ensued.

In 1194, Zhao Kuo, later known as Emperor Ning Zong, ascended the throne. Preparations were made for another expedition against the Jin. In 1206, war was formally declared, and the Song soon recovered several prefectures and counties. Later the capitulationists once again won political and military power. In 1208, the Song concluded another peace pact with the Jin, under which Emperor Ning Zong increased the annual tribute to 300,000 taels of silver, in addition to a lump sum payment of three million taels of silver as an award to the Jin troops. However, a powerful Mongol regime soon appeared in the rear of the Jin. Beginning in 1211, the Jin was subject to incessant attack by the Mongols, whom it could not resist. In 1234, the Mongols conquered Jin, thus bringing to a close the conflict between the Song and the Jin.

The confrontation between the Song and the Jin lasted a century's time, causing enormous sufferings to the people. Peasant uprisings broke out time and again in both states. Among the largest ones were those led by Zhong Xiang and Yang Yao in the Song and by the Red Jackets on the Shandong Peninsula under the control of the Jin.

Zhong Xiang was a native of Wuling in Dingzhou (modern Changde, Hunan). Through religion, he forged ties with the masses in the course of more than 20 years. In the spring of 1130, he led peasants to stage an armed uprising against the Song government for its excessive taxation. He raised such slogans as: "Equality between the high and the low and equal distribution of wealth between the rich and the poor." The rebels soon seized a vast amount of land around Lake Dongting and founded their own regime named Chu. Later, owing to espionage by Song agents, Zhong Xiang, together with his son, was taken prisoner at his own headquarters and subsequently executed. Yang Yao succeeded him as commander to continue the fight. Normally, Yang Yao and his men tilled the land on the lakeside but quickly they would get on boats as warriors whenever the Song troops were approaching. Time and again they defeated the Song troops, and at one time their influence reached as far as Changsha, Yueyang, and other places. Finally the Song government sent Yue Fei to suppress the insurgents, and the rebellion came to an end in 1135.

The Red Jackets uprising started in 1211, when the state of Jin was already in decline, its social economy was deteriorating, and its people having a hard time. Contradictions between various ethnic groups and classes sharpened. It was under these circumstances that Yang Aner and Li Quan staged a peasant uprising in Shandong. The rebels wore red jackets, so their army was called the Red Jackets Army. After seizing control of the major part of Shandong Peninsula, they began to build their own power. Later Yang Aner died of an illness while fighting from one place to another, and after the death of Yang Aner, some of his forces, now led by his daughter Yang Miaozhen and his son-in-law Li Quan, began to move into the areas of

Southern Song. One contingent, led by Peng Yibing, carried on their fight in Shandong and later moved into Hebei. Peng fought and defeated not only the Jin troops but also the Mongol troops then marching southward. In 1225, the rebel force led by Peng was finally crushed by the Mongols.

The period in which the Song and the Jin existed as two rival states was marked by progress made in literature, history and philosophy. The written works gave expression to the acute struggle between ethnic groups and between classes.

In the area of literature, the Southern Song Dynasty was particularly noted for its production of *ci*. Both Lu You (1125-1210) and Xin Qiji (1140-1207) were famous *ci* poets and both had participated in the anti-Jin struggle. Their works, therefore, reflected their concern for their country and their lofty sentiments and emotions. Both had their *ci* works published in anthologies. Li Qingzhao (1084-c. 1155) was a poetess who had a special place in Chinese literature. General Yue Fei, known for his military exploits, wrote good *ci*. Lu You was also an accomplished writer of the *shi* form of poetry.

In its simple form, drama or *zaju* made its appearance during the Northern Song Dynasty. Humorous and satirical, it consisted of recitations and dialogues; later, it was accompanied by songs and dances. The *zaju* of the Jin was not much different from that of the Southern Song. During the Southern Song Dynasty a most popular kind of *zaju* was the "Wenzhou drama" or "southern drama" developed in Wenzhou and other coastal regions of Zhejiang Province. Through the medium of songs, recitations, and dances, it told complicated stories with a variety of characters. In the Jin as well as in the Song, there were also dramatic ballads known as *zhugongdiao* or *gongdiao*. By songs and recitations, they told long stories. In terms of vocal style, *zhugongdiao* absorbed the characteristics of major melodies, *ci*, and folk ballads of the Tang and Song dynasties. Both *zaju* and *zhugongdiao* had contributed to the development of the Yuan drama.

Hua ben or vernacular tales consisted of two kinds: the long ones and the short ones. The short ones, known as *xiaoshuo*, or short stories, dealt with such topics as lovers, ghosts and spirits, and heroic adventures. The long ones, known as *jiang shi* or historical episodes, related historical events that occurred in a certain period. They described wars and the rise and fall of dynasties and portrayed heroes and their military exploits. Revealing the seamy side of society, they were literature of realism. By the end of the Northern Song Dynasty, vernacular tales had made considerable progress. They advanced further during the Southern Song Dynasty and served as the forerunner of the novels of the Yuan and Ming dynasties.

Books of history written during the Southern Song Dynasty were of two kinds: dynastic history dealing with changes of the time and general history covering events over a long span of time. Li Tao (1115-84), following Sima Guang's example, wrote *A Sequel to History as a Mirror* (*Xu zizhi tongjian changpian*) modelled after the latter's *History as a Mirror*. The original work had 1,036 *juan*, but today only 520 remain. Compiled by Li Xinchuan (1166-1244), *A Chronicle of the Most Important Events Since the Jianyan Reign Period* had 200 *juan*. It covered events over the 36 years of Emperor Gao Zong's reign; it could be seen as a continuation of *A Sequel*. Xu Menghua (1126-1207) wrote a 230-*juan* work entitled *A Chronicle of Three Song Emperors' Dealings with the Northern Neighbour* that recorded the Song's relationship with the Jin during the reigns of Emperors Hui Zong, Qin Zong, and Gao Zong. Rich and reliable in source materials, the three works described above chronologically recorded the events of the time. *Historical Collections* was a great work in 200 *juan* compiled by Zheng Qiao (1103-62). Centred on historical personalities, it gave a general account of the history of various dynasties prior to the late Sui Dynasty. In addition to a chronological record of historical events, it contained a historical study of various clans, cities, academic learning and bibliography. A book of history, according to him, "should locate the essence that underlies all the historical changes"; but his own book did not line up to that high standard. Based upon his own reading of *History as a Mirror*, Yuan Shu (1131-1205) wrote *Events in History as a Mirror*. It contained 239 fully accounted events in 42 *juan*. With *Events*, Yuan Shu not only introduced a new way of writing history but also demonstrated his own ability of bringing essential facts out of a confused mass of materials. Works like those described above not only reflected the political situation of the time but were also important contributions to the study of history.

In philosophy, Zhu Xi (1130-1200) inherited and developed the objective idealism pioneered by the Cheng Brothers, exerting the greatest ideological influence on Chinese feudal society after Confucius and Dong Zhongshu. He believed that "reason" in things existed before things themselves existed and all the changes in things were governed by it. As far as men were concerned, "reason" was nothing but man's nature which was inherently good; all the feudal moral standards originated in it. Blinded by the desire for material gains, man could become bad and commit violations of the feudal moral standards. The purpose of these remarks, as far as Zhu Xi was concerned, was the justification of the feudal moral standards and the necessity for people to observe them. Zhu Xi wrote many books, the most important of which were *Commentary on the Great Learning and the Doctrine of the Mean, Collected Commentaries on "The Analects" and "Mencius"*, and *Selected Writings of Master Zhu Xi*. Many books on his words and deeds were also published. *Classified Conversation of Master Zhu* was one that has survived. Lu Jiuyuan (1139-92), an ideological opponent of Zhu Xi, advocated subjective idealism. He said that "the universe lies in my mind" and that "all things are complete within me". The difference between Zhu Xi and Lu Jiuyuan was one between two schools of idealism.

As different from both Zhu Xi and Lu Jiuyuan, Chen Liang and Ye Shi were two materialists. Chen Liang (1143-94) took the view that things were objective existences from which no universal principles could be detached. He advocated the study of practical subjects as means to enrich the country and strengthen its armed strength. Firm in his anti-Jin stand, he was in favour of seeking revenge and against any compromises. Ye Shi (1150-123) maintained that man drew his knowledge from the objective world which determined the kind of knowledge he had, and that it was impossible to divorce knowledge from the objective world, not even for a moment. Benevolence and righteousness, according to him, should be based on utilitarianism, otherwise they would be meaningless. He took an active part in the armed struggle against the Jin regime.

5. The Rise of the Mongols and the Fall of the Xia, the Jin and the Southern Song

The Mongols were formerly a tribe roaming the upper reaches of the Argun River. Later they moved to live in the valleys of the Onon and Kerulen rivers. With the passage of time, they rose to become a powerful tribe. During the period from the late 12th to the early 13th century, Temujin consolidated all the Mongol tribes and placed under his leadership a centralized Khanate which brought the Mongols to a new stage of development. In 1206, he had a clan conference held on the bank of the Onon River, at which he was proclaimed the Great Khan, with the reign title of Genghis Khan. He was later known as Emperor Tai Zu of the Yuan Dynasty.

Genghis Khan organized his army and all the adults of his Mongol tribe according to a decimal system. He personally selected an élite force of 10,000 which served as a basic striking unit. He transformed customary laws into written laws so as to specify the special privileges of the nobility and to tighten the control over the herdsmen slaves. The enforcement of military discipline and the completion of written laws added to the strength of the Mongol Khanate based on slavery.

For a long period, Genghis Khan and his successors Ogdai Khan and Mangu Khan conquered and seized territories both in the south and in the western regions. In the south their attacks were directed against the Xia, the Jin, and the Song; in the western regions, their conquest extended as far as Central Europe.

Having conquered the Western Liao by 1218, the Mongols extended their influence over areas both north and south of the Tianshan Mountains and over Central Asia. In 1218, commanding 200,000 men, Genghis Khan personally led a western expedition. In five years he swept across much of Asia and Europe, with his vanguard going as far as Eastern Europe and northern Iran. During the period from 1236 to 1241, Ogdai Khan, having brought Russia to its knees, sent his forces as far as modern Poland, Hungary and other regions. In the period from 1253 to 1259, Mangu Khan sent his brother, Hulagu, to wipe out the Assassin sect in Persia. Having accomplished the mission, Hulagu and his troops sacked Xiabaoda (Bagdad) and gained control of southwestern Asia. Wherever the Mongol cavalrymen went, great devastation ensued, and people suffered serious losses.

After the successful conclusion of their western campaign, the Mongols established four Great Khanates. The Kipchak Khanate was the fief of the family of Juji, the eldest son of Genghis Khan. At the zenith of its rule, its territory extended west to the lower reaches of the Danube, east to the Irtysh River, south to Caucasus, and north to Bulgar near Kazan in Russia. The Jagatai Khanate, the former territory of the Western Liao, was now the fief of Jagatai, the second son of Genghis Khan. The Ogdai Khanate was the fief of Ogdai, the third son of Genghis Khan, covering the upper reaches of the Irtysh River and the area east of the Balkhash Lake. The Il-Khanate was the fief of Hulagu, the son of Tule, the fourth son of Genghis Khan, covering the area south of the Caucasus and the Caspian Sea. At the beginning, the four Khanates were subject to unified Mongol rule; later, they became independent states. They came to an end during the fourteenth and the fifteenth centuries.

During the period from 1205 to 1227, Genghis Khan attacked the Xia and the Jin many times. More than once he laid siege to the capital city of the Xia and the Xia ruler was forced to sue for peace by presenting him with beautiful maidens. In the end the Xia ruler had to flee for his life. Having been repeatedly defeated, the Jin ruler did likewise by presenting the Mongols with beautiful maidens so as to sue for peace. Zhongdu, which had been a capital of the Jin for more than sixty years beginning with Prince Hai Ling's reign, fell into Mongol hands in 1215. The Mongol invaders trampled over the vast territory north of the Huanghe River, burning, killing, and plundering wherever they went. In fighting a war of plunder, Genghis Khan was slow to recognize the mode of production and the way of governance under feudalism. To the ministers who had easy access to him, the Han Chinese were no more than a nuisance to be eliminated, and the Chinese farmland should be laid waste and converted into pastures. Yelü Chucai, on the other hand, maintained that the Han Chinese, instead of being a nuisance, could contribute greatly to the Mongol conquest of the south by providing military supplies and tax revenue. Yelü Chucai (1190-1244) was a learned scholar and politician of Qidan origin, active during the reigns of Genghis Khan and Ogdai Khan. He played an active role in influencing the Mongol ruling clique to adopt the Han Chinese culture. His writings are included in *Collected Works of Hermit Zhanran*.

In 1226 Genghis Khan launched his last campaign against the Xia. In the following year, the Xia ruler surrendered, and the Xia ended as an independent state. Genghis Khan died of illness in the same year. It took him only twenty-one years to start as a tribal chieftain and become a world-shaking personality.

In 1229, soon after his accession to the throne as the Great Khan, Ogdai ordered an expedition against the Jin. In the following year he personally led attacks by his troops, with only mixed result. In 1233, as soon as the Mongols took Kaifeng, Emperor Ai Zong of the Jin fled to Caizhou (modern Runan County, Henan). Following its previous agreement with the Mongols, the Southern Song sent its troops to join the Mongols in surrounding Caizhou. In 1234, Emperor Ai Zong committed suicide, and the Jin came to an end. Nevertheless, the Jin exerted a great influence on the early period of Yuan because of its cultural achievement. Yuan Haowen (1190-1257), a native of Xiuyong of Taiyuan (to the northwest of modern Xinxian County, Shanxi), was an outstanding writer during the early period of the Yuan Dynasty. After vanquishing the Jin, the Mongols aimed at the Southern Song as their main target. In 1235, the Mongols marched southward along two routes. One contingent of the Mongol troops drove into Sichuan where it met with fierce resistance. In 1236, it occupied Chengdu. Another contingent marched towards Xiangyang, which it took in 1236, after inflicting heavy losses on the Song forces. The Song general Meng Gong made a vigorous stand. In 1238, the Song forces recovered both Chengdu and Xiangyang which the Mongols had occupied only for a brief period. But the Song Emperor Li Zong was bent on coming to terms with the Mongols by making compromise. In 1241, the peace talks stopped because of the death of the Mongol ruler, Ogdai Khan.

After his succession to the throne in 1251, Mangu Khan made repeated incursions into Song territory. In 1253 Kublai, brother of the empreor, and General Uriyangqadai, driving into Yunnan, seized Dali. After inducing Tufan to surrender, they took control of China's southwest region, and succeeded in forming a ring of encirclement around the Southern Song forces in the southwest. In 1258, Mangu attacked Song on three routes. Kublai was to take Ezhou (modern Wuchang City, Hubei) and Uriyangqadai to attack Tanzhou (modern Changsha City, Hunan).

Mangu Khan himself was to lead a force to attack Sichuan. The Khan, however, met with stiff resistance at Hezhou (modern Hechuan County, Sichuan), which he could not take after six months of heavy fighting. In 1259, during the campaign to take Diaoyucheng, to the east of Hezhou, he was mortally wounded near the city wall. His death changed the war situation.

On hearing about Mangu's death while on his way to Ezhou, Kublai joined his forces with those of Uriyangqadai in a northward withdrawal. In 1260, he succeeded as Great Khan and designated Kaiping (modern Duolun County, Inner Mongolia) as Shangdu (Upper Capital) and Yanjing (modern Beijing) as Zhongdu (Middle Capital). In 1271, he called his regime Yuan. After a period of social development beginning with Genghis Khan who unified all the Mongol tribes, the Mongols had by now left slave society and entered feudal society. Kublai was later referred to as Emperor Shi Zu.

Early during his reign, Kublai found himself embroiled in the inner struggles of the nobility. In the meantime, in the Southern Song, Emperor Li Zong and his prime minister, Jia Sidao, dissolute as they were, led a life of corruption. They killed anti-Mongol generals and ruthlessly exploited the people. It was due to the hard struggle on the part of the masses of people and the military forces that Southern Song managed to secure a precarious existence in face of the constant threat of war. In the end, however, it had to collapse.

In 1267, the Mongol troops marched southward on a grand scale. Following the advice of those Southern Song generals who had surrendered, Kublai Khan concentrated his attack on Xiangyang and Fancheng, the two strategic points on the upper reaches of the Hanshui River. Six years later, the two cities fell, though Southern Song put up a strong resistance.

Genealogical Table of the Xia Dynasty

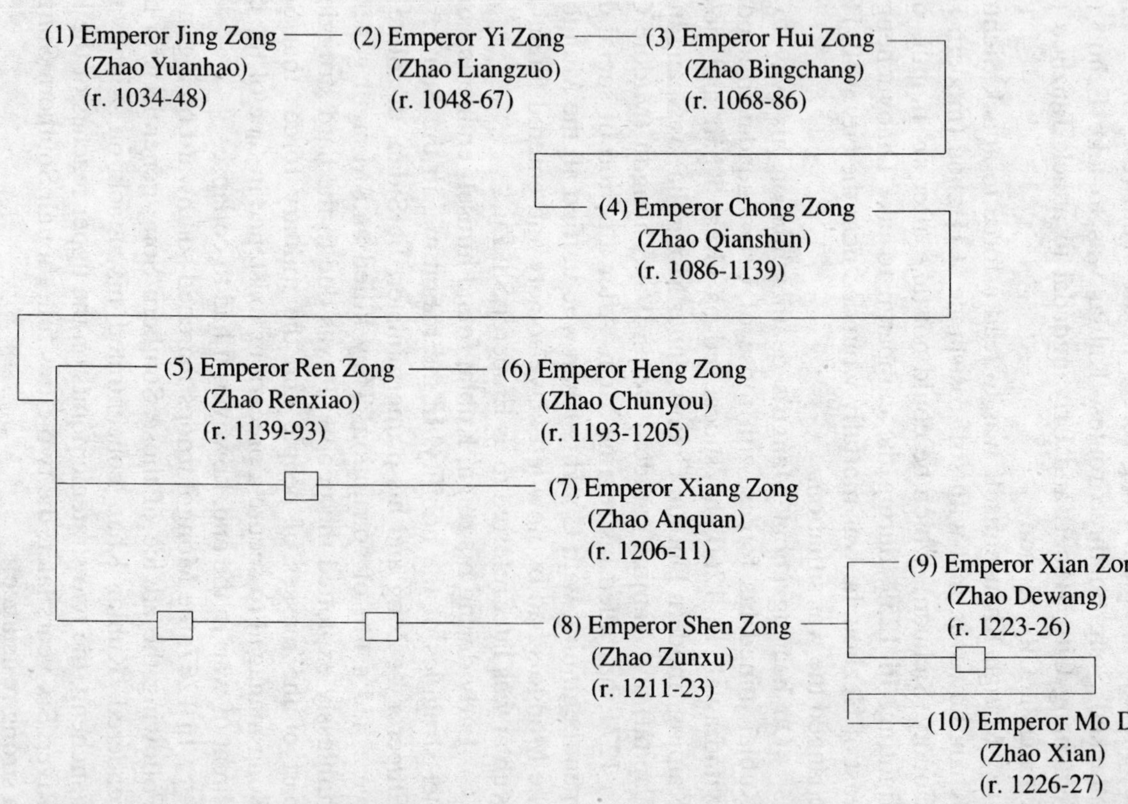
(1) Emperor Jing Zong
(Zhao Yuanhao)
(r. 1034-48)
(2) Emperor Yi Zong
(Zhao Liangzuo)
(r. 1048-67)
(3) Emperor Hui Zong
(Zhao Bingchang)
(r. 1068-86)
(4) Emperor Chong Zong
(Zhao Qianshun)
(r. 1086-1139)
(5) Emperor Ren Zong
(Zhao Renxiao)
(r. 1139-93)
(6) Emperor Heng Zong
(Zhao Chunyou)
(r. 1193-1205)
(7) Emperor Xiang Zong
(Zhao Anquan)
(r. 1206-11)
(8) Emperor Shen Zong
(Zhao Zunxu)
(r. 1211-23)
(9) Emperor Xian Zong
(Zhao Dewang)
(r. 1223-26)
(10) Emperor Mo Di
(Zhao Xian)
(r. 1226-27)

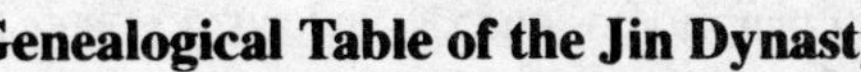

Genealogical Table of the Jin Dynasty

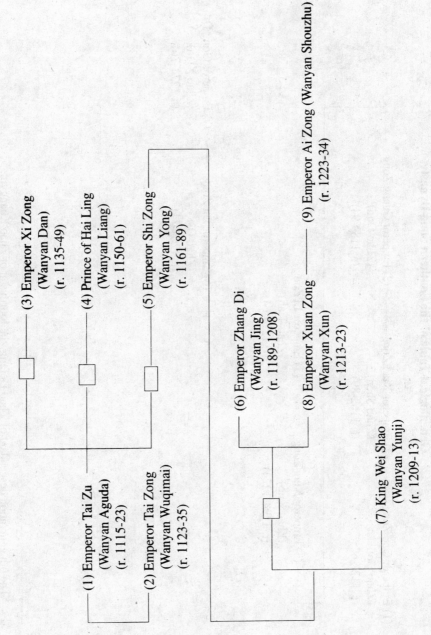

(1) Emperor Tai Zu
(Wanyan Aguda)
(r. 1115-23)

(2) Emperor Tai Zong
(Wanyan Wuqimai)
(r. 1123-35)

(3) Emperor Xi Zong
(Wanyan Dan)
(r. 1135-49)

(4) Prince of Hai Ling
(Wanyan Liang)
(r. 1150-61)

(5) Emperor Shi Zong
(Wanyan Yong)
(r. 1161-89)

(6) Emperor Zhang Di
(Wanyan Jing)
(r. 1189-1208)

(8) Emperor Xuan Zong
(Wanyan Xun)
(r. 1213-23)

(9) Emperor Ai Zong (Wanyan Shouzhu)
(r. 1223-34)

(7) King Wei Shao
(Wanyan Yunji)
(r. 1209-13)

Genealogical Table of the Southern Song Dynasty

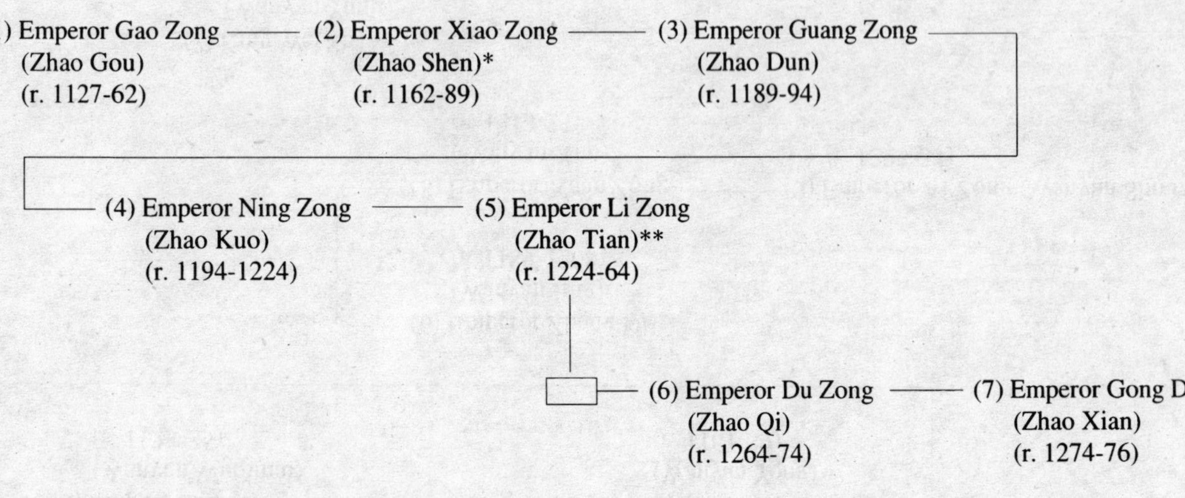

*The 6th generation descendant of Zhao Defang, the fourth son of Zhao Kuangyin.

**The 10th generation descendant of Zhao Dezhao, the second son of Zhao Kuangyin.

In 1274, a Mongol force of 200,000, led by Left Prime Minister Bayan, drove into Song territory over both land and river. In 1275, the main force of the Song disintegrated in the battle of Wuhu. Song generals and officials, led by Jia Sidao, either surrendered or fled for their lives. In 1276, Bayan and his men marched into Hangzhou, captured Emperor Gong Di, Empress Dowager Quan and Empress Dowager Xie, and carried them off to the north. Thus the Song Dynasty came to an end about forty years after Ogdai Khan launched his first campaign against it in 1235.

Though the Southern Song was exterminated by the Mongols, efforts were made by such men as Wen Tianxiang (1236-82), Lu Xiufu and Zhang Shijie to revive it despite the difficulties involved. Having been taken captive, Wen Tianxiang refused to surrender and died a martyr. Lu and Zhang also laid down their lives for their cause.

6. Founding of the Yuan Dynasty and Peasant Uprisings During the Late Yuan

After the Southern Song was exterminated in 1276, Kublai Khan made further efforts to eliminate the remnant Song forces so as to bring the country under the centralized rule of the Yuan regime. The country was governed from above via three separate organs: the Secretariat, the Military Council, and the Censorate. Though inherited from the Song, these organs had different functions under the Yuan. The Secretariat was in charge of political matters as well as "all key military problems" and also handled the country's finance. Placed under the Secretariat were the executive secretariats in various administrative regions. These were, generally speaking, headed by high officials from the central government. Institutionalized as a key organ in the government, the Secretariat under the Yuan exercised much greater power than its Song counterpart. Executive secretariats were established even in such remote areas of the country as Yunnan. In Tufan, the administrative organ was known as the Council of Buddhist Affairs. The Military Council was invested with the power to direct military activities; an executive military council would be created under its jurisdiction during a military campaign. All armed forces, excluding the Imperial Guard of the emperor, were put under the joint control of the Military Council and a central executive secretariat, or under the separate control of either. Thus the Military Council of the Yuan also enjoyed greater power than that of the Song. Executive censorates were established on local levels under the Censorate, which also directed the "clean government inspection offices". The purpose was to strengthen the supervision of local administration. From the viewpoint of strengthening feudal autonomy, the Yuan followed the philosophy of the Song in terms of administrative organizations. There was a difference in emphasis, however. The purpose of the Song system was to strengthen the power of the emperor and prevent any threat to that power from high ministers in the central government or from the local authorities. The Yuan system, on the other hand, was designed not only to strengthen the power of the emperor but also to provide local administration with enough authority to function effectively. Han Chinese like Liu Bingzhong and Xu Heng had contributed greatly to this concept.

Kublai Khan was the first Mongol ruler who attached great importance to agricultural development. Before conquering the Song, he established an agricultural promotion department headed by Yao Shu and sent people to various places to develop agriculture. He formulated a policy of "pacifying the people" and "promoting agriculture"; he distributed a pamphlet entitled *The Fundamentals of Agriculture and Sericulture* to popularize farming methods. After conquering the Song, he re-introduced China's traditional system of having the armed forces do farming and land reclamation in peace time, and organized the construction of water conservancy projects on a grand scale. Though social contradictions were still acute at the time, agricultural production was somehow restored. As a result, grain transported from the south to the north kept increasing and, in a peak year, amounted to more than 350,000,000 piculs (17,500,000 tons). As the ruler of a nomadic people, Kublai Khan distinguished himself from all previous Mongolian monarchs by his recognition of the economic and political importance of agriculture and the measures he adopted to promote its growth.

The Yuan regime paid great attention to the development of communication and transportation, including the construction of post roads and post stations. By the time of Kublai Khan a network of post roads and post stations had extended as far northeast as the Heilongjiang River and Nurkan (modern Tirin in Russia), to Yunnan in the southwest, to Hubei, Hunan, Guangdong, and Guangxi in the south, and Mongolia in the north. Among the means of transportation on the post roads were horses, cattles, donkeys, carts, sedan chairs and ferry boats. Those allowed to travel on the post roads were provided with "board and lodging", including "tents where they can stop overnight and water to quench their thirst". In water transportation, Kublai saw to it that the Grand Canal, then unfinished, be finally completed from Hangzhou to Dadu by a shift of its course from Henan to Shandong. Coastal transportation was also opened from the southeast to Dadu. It was said then that a tail wind could bring a ship from East Zhejiang to Dadu in ten days. All these achievements in transportation were possible only when the country was unified; and they helped the country's unification.

The Yuan regime adopted a policy of toleration towards all religions. Lamaism, Taoism, Christianity and Islam existed side by side. Only the White Lotus Society and the Maitreya sect were banned due to their anti-Yuan stand. Among the religions, Lamaist Buddhism received the greatest favour from the government. Kublai Khan bestowed the title "Teacher of the Nation" on the Tibetan lama Phatspa, who was instructed to create a Mongolian written script based on the Tibetan script. Known as the Phatspa Mongolian script, it replaced the one then in use, the Uygur Mongolian script. The religious activities of Lamaism were founded by the government. Taoism had many sects. By the time of Genghis Khan there was a Taoist "immortal" named Qiu Chuji who was ordered to "take good care of all the devotees who have left home for a monastic life". By the time of Kublai, the influence of Taoism had somewhat declined. Both Christianity and Islamism came to China during the Tang Dynasty. As late as the Yuan Dynasty, Nestorianism remained the only Christian sect in China, and its followers could be found in such places as Dadu, Hangzhou, and Quanzhou. Most of the *Semu* people believed in Islam, a devotee of which was Ananda, the grandson of Kublai. Amogn the 150,000 men under the grandson's command, more than one half embraced Islam. Besides the many religious faiths, the Neo-Confucianism of the Cheng-Zhu School remained popular.

During the dynasty, progress was made in science and tehcnology as well as in the humanities. Increased contacts between various ethnic groups within the country and cultural exchanges with the outside world enabled members of ethnic minorities and foreign residents in China, and also their offspring, to contribute their part in the enrichment of China's culture.

Guo Shoujing (1231-1316) was a great astronomer and an outstanding expert in water conservancy. He made improvements on astronomical equipment, built his own observatories and observed and measured heavenly bodies with great precision. He also made a land survey on an unprecedented scale. He constructed twenty-seven observatories across the country to measure latitudes. There was an observatory for the distance of every ten degrees latitude from the Xisha Archipelago to the Arctic Circle to determine the exact occurrence of summer solstice. He revised the *Time-Telling Calendar* in which he determined that 365.2425 days constituted a year and 29.530593 days amounted to a month. Both figures happened to be the most accurate in the contemporary world. Adopted in 1281, the calendar was in use for a long period of about 360 years. In water conservancy, Guo Shoujing directed the reconstruction of not only the Hanyan and Tanglai irrigation canals (in modern Ningxia) but also opened up new water resources for Dadu.

Ma Duanlin (from 1254 to early 14th century) examined what he called "the causes of historical changes". He collected a large amount of historical materials, classified them into twenty-four categories, and made his own conclusions on the events he studied. The result was *A Comprehensive Study of Civilization* in 348 *juan*. A great work on social institutions, it was richer in content than *A Comprehensive Study of History* by Du You of the Tang Dynasty. In addition, he also wrote *Comprehensive Studies* in 153 *juan*. Unfortunately, the book has been lost.

In literature, the Yuan Dynasty was best known for its achievements in *qu* or dramatic ballads. Then *qu* had two kinds, *san qu* and *za ju*. The former derived its origin from the tunes of people living in the former Jin territories: it was combined with the *shi* or *ci* form of poetry and set to the melodies of the ethnic minorities in North China. The latter, combining singing with dancing and acting, was entirely new. At the beginning, *za ju* was only popular in North China; later it spread to the south.

The two greatest dramatists of the Yuan Dynasty were Guan Hanqing and Wang Shifu.

Guan Hanqing (c. 1213-1297) wrote more than 60 pieces of drama, the most outstanding being *Snow in Midsummer*. It described a young widow who resisted the approach of a villain and put up a valiant fight against the brutality of the bureaucrats. It showed the cruel realities of the dark feudal rule. Wang Shifu, a contemporary of Guan, wrote *The Western Chamber*, which was his masterpiece. Though its main theme was love and separation, joy and sorrow, involving a scholar named Zhang Junrui and a girl named Cui Yingying, it expressed the universal hope that "those who love each other shall in the end be united in marriage". Many *za ju* writers, including Guan Hanqin, were also good at *san qu*. The Uygur poet Guan Yunshi and the Hui poet Saidula were both eminent writers of *san qu*. Late during the Yuan Dynasty, the *nan xi* or "southern drama" that had been most popular during the Southern Song Dynasty made further progress. Enriched by *za ju*, *nan xi* perfected itself and became a better form of art than *za ju*. *The Moon Worship Pavilion* by Shi Hui and *Tale of the Lute* by Gao Ming were the best known among the *nan xi*. They paved the way for the rise of *chuanqi* (operas set to southern music) during the Ming Dynasty.

The unification of China under the Yuan Dynasty ended a state of divided rule that began with the Five Dynasties. Economic and cultural successes were achieved in the unified empire. But the Yuan court maintained its rule amid acute contradictions including those between different classes, within the ruling classes and among the various ethnic groups.

Under the Yuan, the people of the country were divided into four categories. The Mongols belonged to the first or privileged class. Next were the *Semu's*, who came from both sides of the Tianshan Mountains and areas to the west of the Congling Range.* Then came the Hans, which referred to the Hans and the Nüzhens who lived in the Huanghe River valley. At the bottoms of the social scale were the "southerners", mostly Hans, who inhabited the Changjiang River valley and areas to the south and who had surrendered to the Mongols only after the fall of the Southern Song regime. The Yuan also had its armed forces classified with Mongol troops, vanguard detachemtns, Han troops, and new joiners. Strictly speaking, the Yuan regime was not purely Mongol, though it was dominated by the Mongols. With the Mongol nobles at its core, the regime was supported by the Han Chinese landlords and the upper classes of many other ethnic groups. Without such a support, the Mongol nobles would not be able to rule such a large country. The policy of national discrimination, which created discord among different ethnic groups, was merely a means to solidify Mongol rule as it prevented them from forming a unified front against the Mongols. This explains why class struggle appeared as national struggle during the Yuan Dynasty. As far as the Mongol labouring masses were concerned, they remained slaves to Mongol rulers, and some of them even became slaves to the *Semu's* and the Han Chinese.

The eighteen years after Kublai conquered the Song were the most glorious years of the Yuan Dynasty. However, in 1278, only two years after Kublai's conquest of the Southern Song, a native of Jianning (modern Jian'ou County, Fujian) named Huang Hua, in alliance with a woman leader of the She ethnic group named Madame Xu, staged an armed uprising for the overthrow of the Yuan regime. They gathered a force of several hundred thousand in a struggle that persisted for six years, taking many towns in the progress. In 1283, as many as 200 armed uprisings were reported from local officials throughout the country. In 1289, one official report said that there were more than 400 armed uprisings in the lower Changjiang River valley alone. After the death of Kublai, his grandson Emperor Cheng Zong inherited the throne. During the thirteen years of his reign (1295-1307), Kublai's

---

* Old name for the Pamirs and mountains in the western parts of the Kunlun and Karakorum ranges.—*Trans.*

accomplishments were more or less preserved. The death of Cheng Zong, however, was followed by a period of internal struggle for the throne that lasted twenty-five years, which saw the reigns of nine emperors. Peasant uprisings were then at a low ebb, but the Yuan regime had already reached the stage of decline.

By the time of Emperor Shun Di's reign (1333-68), the Yuan Dynasty had entered its last days, having become corrupt politically, economically, and militarily. Peasant uprisings occurred in many places. In 1343, the Huanghe River was breached. In 1344, following a torrential rain of more than twenty days, vast tracts of land along the river were submerged to the depth of seven metres. In 1351, to dredge the river, a labour force of 150,000 men, supervised by 20,000 soldiers, was mobilized. The mobilization increased the burden on the people in the flooded areas. Then there was the saying that "on the bed of the Huanghe River is a one-eyed stone man who calls for revolt". Sure enough, a one-eyed stone man was found on the riverbed, and the rebels took up arms in earnest.

The Red Scarves constituted the main force of the peasant uprising, and Han Shantong and Liu Futong were their earliest organizers and leaders. At the beginning, they carried out their activities under the cover of a religious sect called the White Lotus Society. In the course of preparing for the revolt, Han Shantong was arrested and subsequently executed. In 1351, Liu Futong began his uprising at Yingzhou (modern Fuyang County, Anhui). To distinguish themselves from others, the rebels tied red scarves around their heads, and from such a habit came the name of the Red Scarves army. The army, soon swelling to more than one hundred thousand men, captured a number of towns in today's Henan Province. Many places in the Huai River valley and on both sides of the Changjiang River responded.

In 1355, Liu Futong captured Bozhou (modern Boxian County, Anhui) and installed Han Linger as King Xiaoming. The new regime was called the Song. In the same year, Emperor Shun Di called upon rich people to organize forces for resistance. Those who could recruit five thousand men would receive the title of *wan hu*; those who could gather one thousand or one hundred would be titled *qian hu* and *bai* *hu* respectively.* There were then landlord forces organized by Chanquntemur, a Mongol from Shenqiu, modern Henan province, and Li Siqi, a Han Chinese from Luoshan, also in Henan. Both became inveterate enemies of Red Scarves.

In 1357 Liu Futong and his men marched northward on three separate routes. The east route army was to cross the sea from northern Jiangsu to take Shandong, from where it would enter Hebei to attack Dadu. The middle route was ordered to cross the Huanghe River to attack Shanxi, take Datong, storm the Upper Capital at Kaiping and capture Liaoyang. The west route army was supposed to enter Shaanxi and seize control of Sichuan, Gansu and Ningxia. In 1358, Liu Futong and his men captured Kaifeng whereto the Song regime moved its capital. This was the time when the Red Scarves reached the zenith of their power after they had basically destroyed the main forces of the Yuan Dynasty in the north. But the Red Scarves only fought a mobile warfare. They did not pay much attention to the reconstruction of the conquered areas or collaboration among different fighting units. They quarrelled among themselves after victory. Moreover, they were not alert enough to the newly-formed armed forces of the landlords. Their shortcomings provided their enemy with the opportunity to defeat them. By 1362, all the three route armies had encountered defeat. Once finding himself being surrounded by Chaguntemur at Kaifeng, Liu Futong and his men withdrew to Anfeng (modern Shouxian County, Anhui). He died in action in 1363. King Xiaoming received protection from Zhu Yuanzhang, later the founder of the Ming Dynasty, who took him to Chuzhou (modern Chuxian County, Anhui).

While the Red Scarves were winning one victory after another in the north, peasant insurgents in the south were doing their part to overthrow the Yuan Dynasty. Among the peasant leaders was Xu Shouhui who, having won the support of Peng Yingyu, leader of the Maitreya Sect, staged an armed uprising in 1351 at Qizhou (modern Qichun County, Hubei) and captured many places in Hubei, Hunan, Jiangxi, Zhejiang and Sichuan. In 1360, Xu Shouhui was murdered by

---

* Literally, *wan hu, qian hu* and *bai hu* mean ten thousand, a thousand and a hundred households.—*Trans.*

Genealogical Table of the Mongolian and Yuan Rulers

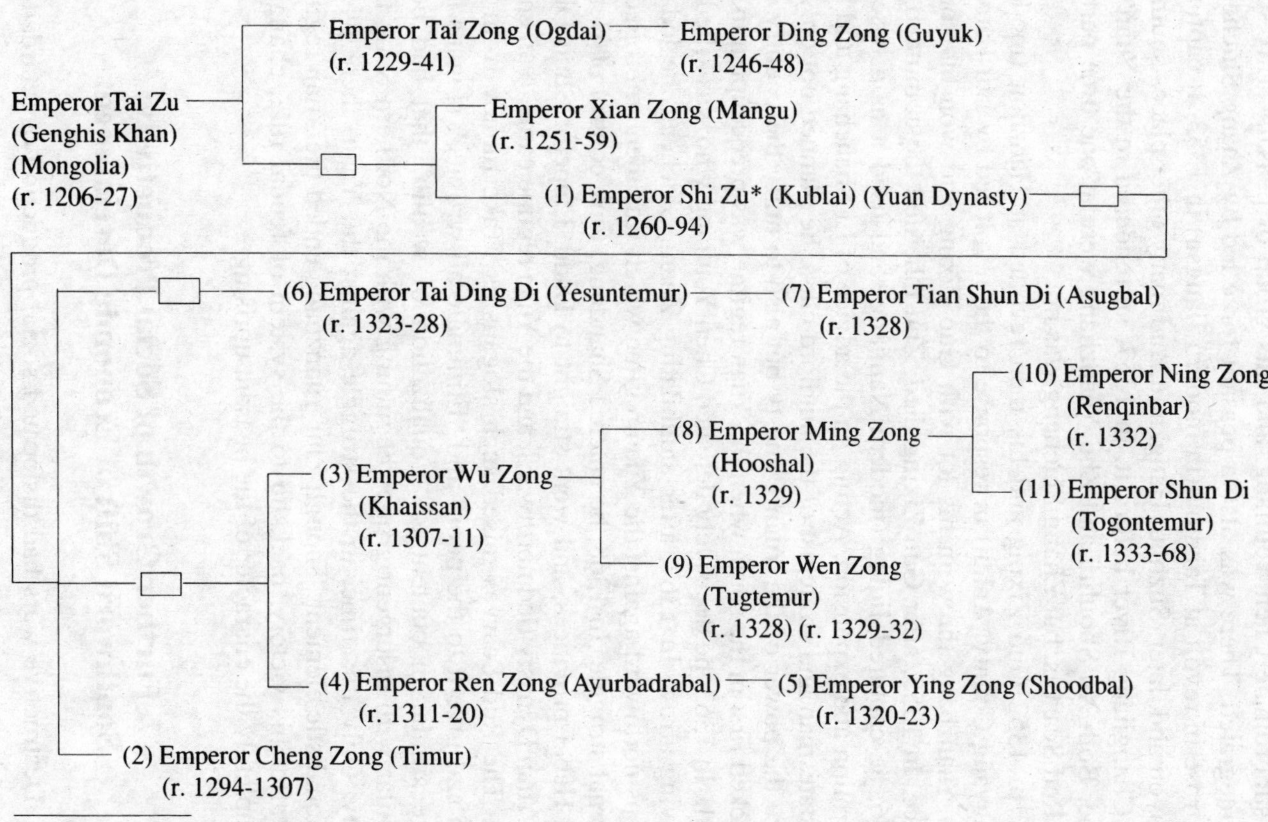

*In 1271, Kublai gave the title of "Yuan" to his dynasty; in 1276, he put an end to the Song Dynasty.

his subordinate Chen Youliang, and this group of peasant army soon disintegrated. There was also a peasant force led by Zhang Shicheng, that rose in revolt at Taizhou (in modern Jiangsu) in 1353. It captured Gaoyou and, later, Suzhou, Hangzhou, and many other places south of the Changjiang River before it, in 1357, surrendered to the Yuan regime. Both Xu Shouhui and Zhu Yuanzhang were at one time part of the Red Scarves, but Zhang Shicheng was not.

In 1352 Guo Zixing and his men revolted at Haozhou (modern Fengyang County, Anhui) in response to the revolt led by Liu Futong. Zhu Yuanzhang threw in his lot with Guo Zixing and won his confidence. In 1355, after Guo Zixing died, Zhu inherited the command. In 1356, he captured Jiqing (modern Nanjiang) and used it as a base of operation and expansion. Acting on the advice of Li Shanchang and Liu Ji, statesman and strategist of the landlord class, he planned not only to seize the power of the Yuan Dynasty but also to unify the country. He attacked first in the south when the Yuan regime was preoccupied in the north. In 1363, he decisively defeated Chen Youliang who was killed by a flying arrow. In 1367, after annihilating Zhang Shicheng, he led his troops northward against the Yuan regime which was then embroiled in internal struggle. In 1368, he entered Shandong, took control of Henan and Hebei provinces, and went straight to Dadu. Emperor Shun Di of the Yuan Dynasty fled northward, and the Yuan regime came to an end.

The Red Scarves raised such slogans as "Take money from the rich and give it to the poor" and "Eliminate all wrongs", slogans that were similar in content to "Equalization of wealth" that had been popular with insurgent groups beginning with the Northern Song Dynasty. Only this time, in the struggle against the Yuan, there was a nationalistic element. Though Zhu Yuanzhang ended the Yuan regime, he, after his victory, backslid to the system of feudal rule, changing completely the character of the peasant uprising.

7. Further Growth of Social Productivity; Southward Shift of Economic Development

Destructive wars had dislocated social production or retarded its development beginning with the Five Dynasties, Song and Yuan; malpractices innate in the backward rule of the Liao, Jin, and Yuan made things worse. When the period is viewed as a whole, however, social productive forces still made headway, though in a halting manner. This was particularly true in the south. With less destruction from wars and more time for development, the south quickly became the economic centre of the whole country in agriculture, handicraft industry and commerce.

By the time of the Five Dynasties, the Song, and the Yuan, rice, planted mostly in the south, had become the chief food crop of the country. During the Southern Song Dynasty, the number of rice strains planted in the lower Changjiang River valley was as many as two hundred. Wheat was also a major food crop. It was planted in the lower Changjiang River valley too.

Sericulture was a main sideline for those engaged in agricultural production. Cotton was planted in the south as well as in the north. By the later part of the Southern Song Dynasty, cotton acreage had increased enormously. Cotton was first grown in Fujian and then in Guangdong; its planting eventually reached the valleys of the Changjiang and the Huai rivers. In *The Fundamentals of Agriculture and Sericulture* issued by the Yuan government in 1273, there was detailed information on the technique of growing cotton, indicating that cotton planting had attracted well-deserved attention.

Attention was paid to the planting of crops in accordance with not only seasons but also local conditions. Proper arrangements were made in field building, sowing, seed-breeding, field management, fertilizing and harvesting as well as intercropping. Meticulous care was generally practised. As land was used in a planned way, different fields were designated for different purposes. *Yutian* (fields protected by dykes) were created out of lakes; to regulate waterflow, sluice gates were installed. In addition, ditches were dug to facilitate irrigation. Generally speaking, *yutian* fields were good lands that yielded bumper harvests irrespective of drought and flood. There were terraced fields built on hillsides. Land on seashore and riverside was also transformed into cropfields. All this could be seen in South China.

During the period under discussion, attention was paid to the construction of water conservancy projects for the purpose of developing agriculture. More than ten thousand of such projects were built in the latter part of the Northern Song Dynasty. A typical example was the Mulan Dyke in Xinghua and Putien of Fujian Province, a multipurpose project for water diversion, storage, irrigation, and drainage. By the time of the Southern Song, water conservancy projects were completed on an even greater scale. Works around Lake Taihu were built in such a way that all land, whether highly situated or low-lying, could be irrigated, and good harvests were thus guaranteed. As the saying went, "As soon as the crops in Suzhou and Huzhou ripen, there is enough food for everyone in China." Guo Shoujing of the Yuan Dynasty repaired and rebuilt many irrigation canals, and his efforts played a constructive role in agricultural production in Northwest China.

In 1149, Chen Fu wrote *Agriculture*, a book that described paddy field work in a systematic way. It advanced the idea that "land fertility could be permanently maintained for the production of good crops". Between 1295 and 1300, Wang Zhen wrote another book, also entitled *On Agriculture*. The book covered not only agriculture but also forestry, animal husbandry, and spinning and weaving. "Agricultural Implements Illustrated" accounted for a large portion of book. A great deal of attention was also given to the building of water conservancy projects. Both books have played a very important role in the history of Chinese agriculture.

During the Song and the Yuan dynasties, the obvious progress in the handicraft industry could be found in mining, metallurgy, shipbuilding, spinning and weaving, manufacturing of pottery and porcelain and paper making. The amount of gold, silver, copper and iron then produced had far surpassed any produced during the previous historical periods. People then could build an ocean-going ship of thirty metres long, that could accommodate 600 to 1,000 passengers and carry a freight weight of 2,000 piculs (100 tons).

Porcelains produced during the Song and the Yuan were art treasures. Among the famous kilns were those in Kaifeng, Yuzhou (modern Yuxian County, Henan), Ruzhou (modern Linru County, Henan), Dingzhou (modern Dingxian, Hebei), Yuezhou (modern Shaoxing County, Zhejiang), Geyao (modern Longquan County, Zhejiang), and Jingdezhen, Jiangxi. Different kilns produced porcelains of different forms and styles. Those produced in the northern states of Liao and Jin and in the southwestern state of Dali had their own characteristics.

The textile industry then consisted primarily of silk and ramie weaving. A gradual improvement was then made in the technique of cotton spinning and weaving; as a result, cotton cloth was produced in great quantities. In the time of Kublai Khan, offices of cotton administration were established in several provinces in South China, and they requisitioned for the government 100,000 bolts of cotton cloth per year. Early during Emperor Cheng Zong's reign, people in the lower Changjiang River valley were required to pay their summer taxes in cotton. This indicates that the cotton textile industry had made great progress by then. During the late Song and early Yuan period, a woman named Huang Daopo improved the tools as well as the technique of cotton spinning and weaving, and her contribution sped up the progress.

Progress was also made in paper making. Among the raw materials were bamboo, rattan, flax, and rice and wheat stalks. Special and high-quality paper was produced in modern Jiangsu, Sichuan, Anhui and Fujian. A thin and evenly smooth paper of about five metres long was then made in Shexian County in modern Anhui.

Commerce was flourishing throughout the Song and the Yuan dynasties. Kaifeng, Chengdu, Xingyuan (modern Hanzhong City, Shaanxi) of the Northern Song, Hangzhou, Jiankang, Yangzhou, Suzhou, Chengdu, Taiyuan, Jingzhao (modern Xi'an City, Shaanxi) and Dadu of the Southern Song and the Yuan—they were all important commercial centres. During the Northern Song Dynasty Kaifeng had more than 200,000 households. Commercial activities were carried out not only during daytime but also in some places during the night. In the Southern Song Dynasty, Hangzhou was a city of 390,000 households, or a population of 1.2 million. Trade flourished, and markets swarmed with people. More than twenty licensed paw-shops, charging high interest, were found in the city. During the Yuan Dynasty the Italian traveller Marco Polo called Dadu a most flourishing city. It was said that the silk transported into the city each day filled one thousand carts. During the Song Dynasty, trade between China's hinterland and the Liao, Jin, and West Xia was also very prosperous. As a means to facilitate exchange, the earliest paper currency made its appearance.

During the Song-Yuan periods important achievements were made in technology. Some of these achievements were closely related to social production.

During the Warring States Period, the magnetic property of lodestone was discovered. Its other property, that of pointing to the north, was also noted. The magnetic stone was then ground into an instrument that gave guidance to direction. As to the time when the compass was first employed in navigation, no one seems to be sure. However, towards the end of the Northern Song or early in the twelfth century, a person named Zhu Yu, who had lived for a long time in Guangzhou, reported that captains of ships "use stars at night, the sun during the day, and compasses during rainy days for guidance in directions". This is the earliest evidence of using compasses in navigation. Compasses used were then known as "floating needles" that were kept aloft inside bowls of water by floating wicks.

Block printing made its first appearance during the intervening years between the Sui and the Tang dynasties. At the time of the Five Dynasties it was first used in the printing of Confucian classics. During 931-953, the official version of the *Nine Classics* of Confucianism was printed in 130 *juan*. In the period 971-983, early in the Northern Song Dynasty, the official text of *The Tripitaka in Chinese* was printed in 5,048 *juan*. The technique of block printing reached its stage of maturity and flourished during the Song Dynasty. Hangzhou was then most famous for its printing plates, though Fujian and Sichuan were not too far behind. Books were exquisitely printed in large numbers. Books of Song printing are still highly valued today.

During the Northern Song period, Bi Sheng invented the movable type. Moistened clay was used as material to carve out the characters, which were hardened by fire. For each character there were several heads of type, and the number was larger for the commonly used ones. For the purpose of printing, heads of type were arranged on a plate according to the content of the book. After the printing was completed, the plate could be dismantled, and heads of type reused. Basically, the same practice is followed even today. During the Song-Yuan period, there were also tin movable type and wood movable type. Wang Zhen invented a revolving device whereby a printer could pick up the heads of type he needed without having to leave his seat.

The Chinese knew the use of gunpowder for weaponry as early as the Five Dynasties period. During the Northern Song period, a man named Zeng Gongliang wrote a book entitled *The Outline of Military Science* in which he described three kinds of explosives and many kinds of gunpowder weapons. Gunpowder could be used for its explosive power, for its smoke, and for its poisoning capacity. Towards the end of the Northern Song, an explosive device known as *pi li pao* (thunderbolt cannon) was used to defend Kaifeng and to beat back the Jin invaders. After the fall of the Northern Song regime, the Jins adopted the Song technique and invented *zhen tian lei* (sky-shaking thunder)—a gun that could inflict heavy casualties on the enemy. It was so powerful that its explosion could be heard at a great distance. Later, gunpowder was used by the Mongol troops during their western expedition. Towards the end of the Yuan Dynasty, even peasant insurgents used copper tubes filled up with gunpowder.

Other than Guo Shoujing, well known for his accomplishments in astronomy and calendar making, astronomer Su Song, who lived during the Northern Song period, wrote a book entitled *New Design for an Armillary Sphere*, in which he recorded a water-powered armillary sphere that marked the movement of the heavenly bodies. This was the earliest astronomical clock on record.

In mathematics, Liu Yi of the Northern Song Dynasty found the method of solving quadratic equation; Jia Xian then worked out the method of extracting equational roots by successive additions and multiplications. By this method not only square and cubic roots, but also roots in equations of a higher degree, could be extracted. Qin Jiushao of the Southern Song Dynasty, Li Ye, who lived during the intervening years between the Jin and the Yuan dynasties, and Zhu Shijie of the Yuan Dynasty—all three made improvements on the method of extracting equational roots. During the Song-Yuan period, mathematicians made outstanding contributions involving linear congruences and multivariate higher simultaneous equations.

In architecture, many buildings dating back to the time of the Liao, Song, Jin, and Yuan can still be found today. Li Jie, a great architect of the Northern Song period, wrote a book entitled *Building Formulas*. This was a comprehensive work on architecture in 34 *juan*, supplemented with a number of drawings. The book described every architectural requirement, as well as technical problems, that had to be dealt with in construction.

The revised edition of *Pharmacopoeia of the Kaibao* Period*, that came out early during the Northern Song period, listed 132 more herbs than its Tang predecessor. Towards the end of this period, a book entitled *Classification of Viable Herbs* by Tang Shenwei had in it the description of 1,558 individual herbs. In later years, it exerted an enormous influence on Chinese pharmacology. During the Northern Song period, an imperial physician named Wang Weiyi designed a body model made of copper over which acupuncture points were indicated. He also wrote *An Illustration of the Copper Man's Acupuncture Points* to show the correct locations of these points. Early during the Southern Song period, Song Ci compiled *The Cleansing of Wrongs*, a book of great scientific value in medical jurisprudence. During the Jin-Yuan period, there were such famous physicians as Liu Wansu, Zhang Zihe, Li Gao and Zhu Zhenheng. Jointly known as the "four authorities", they exerted a considerable amount of influence on the development of Chinese medicine.

8. Further Development of Feudal Relations; Feudalization of the Border Regions

By the Five Dynasties period, a relative change had taken place in the inner relations of feudalism. The great uprising led by Huang Chao towards the end of the Tang Dynasty had thoroughly eliminated the privileged landlord class. The rising class of bureaucrat landlords

---

* Reign title of Emperor Tai Zu of the Northern Song Dynasty, covering the years 968-976.—*Trans.*

became the most important stratum within the landlord class in the Song period.

A nine rank system was then practised in the officialdom, and the households of officials who happened to be landlords were known as "official households". On the basis of their ranks, officials were granted land; the amount to be granted varied from 5 to 50 *qing* (roughly the equivalent of 83-830 acres). The granted land was exempted from taxation and all other exactions, including corvée. Actually, the landlords seized as much land as they could while performing no obligations to the state at all. By the time of Emperor Ying Zong of the Song, the amount of land seized by the bureaucrat landlords accounted for 70 per cent of the country's land. Land concentration reached its highest point towards the end of the Southern Song period when some of the biggest landlords each owned land that covered an area of a few hundred kilometres. The bureaucrat landlords of the Song Dynasty, like their predecessors, the landlords of privileged families, enjoyed certain political status. But there was a difference. The political status of the privileged landlords was inherited, while that of the bureaucrat landlords was determined by their official ranks. When a bureaucrat landlord died, the political status of his family and the special privileges it enjoyed would come to an end if his descendants held no official posts.

During the Song period, many holding positions of authority in the government but having no official ranks made good use of their power by seizing more and more land. Enjoying great influence in local communities, their households were called "influential households". They belonged to the class of despotic landlords.

In the household register during the Song Dynasty, a household could be listed as either "host" or "guest". The former was one who owned land and had to pay taxes while the latter, owning no land, tilled land owned by others. The names of bureaucrat landlords and other despotic landlords did not appear on the household register at all.

"Host" households were divided into five categories according to the amount of land they owned. The first three categories were lanldord households. The households of the first category belonged to the biggest landlords; they were also known as "upper households". The fourth and fifth categories were "lower households", referring to independent or semi-independent small holders. The "guest" households belonged to the tenants.

According to the law, "host" households had to pay land taxes which were collected twice a year, in summer and in autumn. In addition, they had to pay a poll tax and perform a variety of duties such as corvée. But landlords, big or small, often worked hand in glove with government officials to evade taxes and other exactions, shifting most of the burden to independent or semi-independent small holders. This often bankrupted the latter and turned them into tenant farmers or refugees.

Under the system of land tenancy, there was a marked difference between tax and rent. While "host" households paid land taxes to the government, "guest" households paid rent to the landlords, also paying poll taxes to the government and performing labour services for it. The relationship between landlords and their tenants was contractual, but this did not mean that the tenants were entirely free from feudal bondage. But to a certain extent they could change their habitat as well as their landlords. They had more personal freedom than the dependent peasants of the earlier periods.

The landlord force of the Southern Song Dynasty had been, by and large, kept intact during the Yuan Dynasty. The so-called "powerful families" of the Yuan period were similar to the "official and influential households" of the Song period. Among them were the powerful households of Mongol aristocracy. These aristocrats owned land; some owned "land endowments" in addition to land. Peasants living on these "endowments" had to pay not only taxes to the government but also tribute to their Mongol lords. The monastery landlords were among the most prominent, and the most influential of the monasteries were those of Lamaism.

According to the household registration system of the Yuan Dynasty there were "upper" and "secondary" (or "middle") households that belonged to landlords. Most households were classified as "lower"; they belonged to poor people like independent or semi-independent small holders. The Yuan situation was not much different from that of the Song when landlords, big or small, tried in every way to evade taxes and other governmental obligations, leaving the burden to small farmers who were the least able to shoulder it.

Other than these households described above, there were also special households for military men, couriers, artisans, salt-miners, scholars, physicians, etc. They shouldered the feudal burden in various degrees.

Comparatively speaking, Yuan society had more slaves, derogatorily referred to as "captives". Some belonged to the government, while others were individually owned. Most slaves were former civilians captured during military campaigns. As private property, they could be bought or sold along with horses, sheep, and cattle. The human market was sometimes described as "brisk". Slaves were even sold abroad.

It must be noted that the Mongols, having entered the Central Plains, brought with them some backward practices and customs, which had a negative impact on social production. Fortunately, the bad influence was regional and temporary. Taking China or the Mongol nation as a whole, we see progress in social production. In fact, the vast borderlands were feudalized or more intensively feudalized, and the ties between various ethnic groups were strengthened. In this regard, the Mongols merely followed the footsteps of the previous regimes, like those of the Five Dynasties, the Song, the Liao, and the Jin, and achieved more than their predecessors. Important social developments could be found in the northeast where the Liao and the Jin used to be, in the area of the West Xia, and in modern Mongolia, Xinjiang, Tibet, and Yunnan.

The entry of the Liao and Jin into the Central Plains sped up the feudalization of the northeast. During the Five Dynasties, the Song, and the Yuan, an uneven pace of development was seen among the various ethnic grops living in the northeast. The Qidans and Nüzhens, who formed the bulk of the population in the Liao and the Jin respectively, had stayed for a long time at the stage of slave society. Later, under the influence of an advanced form of production in China proper, they gradually marched towards feudalism. Late during the eleventh century, the process of feudalization among the Qidans was near its completion, and the feudal system of government matured. The feudalization of the Nüzhens, on the other hand, was not completed until the middle of the twelfth century. In the process, large numbers of the slave-owning Nüzhen nobles transformed themselves into parasitic landlords who lived on rent. The Jin rulers, to practise feudal rule, followed the example of the Northern Song insofar as political administration and collection of taxes were concerned. Later, most of the Nüzhens moved to live in China proper and became completely integrated with the Han Chinese. They could not even speak their own native language. As for the remaining Nüzhens living in the northeast, their social development was still slow. It is certain, however, that when the Mongols rose in the 13th century, social feudalization had already taken place in part of the northeast. The processes continued even after the Yuan had established its unified rule over the whole country. However, some places remained in a backward state. There were some ethnic groups, including some of the Nüzhens, that, living in the remotest areas of the country, were still in the stage of a slave society or the later stage of primitive gens society.

Feudalization in the Mongol area was more or less completed when Kublai Khan established his control over all of China. By then the Mongols had made considerable progress in developing animal husbandry. Since fertile pastures had been seized by feudal owners, large numbers of herdsmen suffered from oppression and exploitation, as they grazed their animals on grounds designated by pasture owners and paid tributes and taxes. Agriculture also made progress. Han Chinese were often sent by Kublai to the Mongol area to popularize agricultural technology and to encourage the Mongols to engage in agriculture in addition to their husbandry activities. Reclamation of land was also carried out by the armed forces on a great scale. Agriculture thus made headway in Mongolia.

In the area of the West Xia, the feudalization of the Dangxiang people was obvious. They had taken the road to feudalism when Yuan Hao established the West Xia Kingdom. In economy and culture, the kingdom absorbed many new things from the Northern Song. Feudalism had already taken roots in the West Xia when Genghis Khan conquered it.

Before the appearance of the West Liao, the Uygurs who had moved westward from the Mongol grasslands to the Turpan basin of modern Xinjiang towards the end of the Tang Dynasty, established the kingdom of Gaochang. The territory of the kingdom extended eastward to Hami, westward to the Pamirs, northward to the Tianshan Range, and southward to Hotan. It occupied most of today's Uygur Autonomous Region. Harahojia, located in the eastern section of modern Turpan County, was its capital. With agriculture as their main occupation, the Uygurs had then entered the period of feudal society. Dependent on the feudal lords for their survival, serfs had to pay them tributes and taxes and could be sold at any time when the land they tilled was sold. In some places, the system of tenancy and exploitation by usury were practised. In addition to the five cereals, the kingdom produced such cash crops as cotton and grapes. Sericulture was also fairly developed. Handicraft industries such as cotton weaving, wine distilling, iron smelting, and jade carving were developed to a high level. Gaochang maintained a close political and economic tie with the Liao and the Song. Located on the route of communication and transportation between the East and the West, it was a centre of cultural and economic exchange. During the twelfth century it was subject to control by the West Liao. In 1209, Genghis Khan incorporated it as part of the Mongol empire and put it under a local satrap of his. Then it became known as Uygur instead of Gaochang. From the early period of Mongol rule to the Yuan Dynasty, the Mongols received much cultural influence from the Uygurs, who were greatly influenced by Han culture. Kublai paid great attention to the development of the Uygur area. He extended the land reclamation campaign on an even wider scale. To meet the requirements of agricultural production in the area, he established a metallurgical bureau to make farm implements and provided aid to impoverished peasants who could hardly carry on production. To develop handicraft industry, Kublai sent Han artisans to Shanshan (modern Ruoqiang County, Xinjiang) to teach local people the technique of bow making.

Tibet was, as before, inhabited by the Tufans during the Song-Yuan period. Under the impact of slave uprisings and uprisings by various ethnic groups towards the end of the Tang Dynasty, they gradually entered the stage of feudalism. The feudal lords had taken possession of all land. Serfs engaged in agriculture and stock-breeding and paid rent and tribute for using the land. During the period of the Five Dynasties, the Song, and the Yuan, there was further development of feudalism. Though living under a separate rule in Tibet, the Tufans had already been on friendly terms with the Han Chinese and other ethnic groups. Frequent contacts went on between Rgyal Sras, a Tufan who maintained an independent regime in Qinghai, and the government of the Northern Song, which bestowed upon him the title of satrap. In the name of "paying tributes" and "returning favours" to the Northern Song, oxen and horses were bartered for silk, tea and medicine. After Kublai established unified rule over China, Tibet was put under the direct administration of the Council of Buddhist Affairs, with Grand Lamas or *Di Shi* (the Emperor's Buddhist Teacher) in control. This led to a closer contact between Tibet and China proper. The Tufan people, from then on, lived in comparative peace which enabled them to engage in constructive labour and develop production. To promote trade between the Han people and the Tibetans and other ethnic groups, the Yuan government opened an official border-region market at Lizhou (modern Hanyuan County, Sichuan). Postal stations were built all the way from China proper to Tibet.

Not long before the founding of the Northern Song, a Dali regime rose in Yunnan. Controlled mainly by people of the Bai ethnic group, it came into existence more than 30 years after the fall of the Southern Zhao. It was a feudal regime, as compared to the slave rule of the Southern Zhao. It constructed water conservancy works to promote agriculture in the area of the Er Hai Lake, and in animal husbandry, it encouraged horse raising, as horses were an important export item when trading with China proper. Achievement was made in literature, history, paintings, artistic carving, and architecture. The works were marked with strong national characteristics, though benefiting from the cultural infusion with the Han Chinese. During the Yuan Dynasty, an executive secretariat replacing the Dali regime was set up, incorporating Yunnan into the civil administration of the central government. People of different ethnic groups flowed into Yunnan, including Mongols, Han Chinese, Uygurs, and the Hui. They joined hands with the native people, such as the Bai, the Yi, the Dai, the Naxi, and the Hani peoples to develop the fatherland's southwest. Sayyid Ejell, a Muslim, built water conservancy works in Yunnan, popularized the culture of the Han Chinese, and improved the relations among various ethnic groups. Zhang Lidao, a Han Chinese, fought successfully against floods in the Dian Chi Lake area, built good fields, and introduced new techniques in farming. During the period of the Yuan Dynasty many ethnic groups in Yunnan, at one time or another, entered a feudal society. The Naxi and Dai ethnic groups also began a period of transition from slavery to feudalism. There were, of course, others still remaining primitive.

9. China's Communications with the Outside World

During the period of the Five Dynasties, the Song, and especially the Yuan, the economic and cultural exchanges between China and foreign countries were greatly developed. During the Five Dynasties, the three important trading ports with the outside world were Guangzhou, Quanzhou, and Hangzhou. Following the example of the Tang, the Song and Yuan dynasties established a harbour administration in charge of foreign trade in each of the major trading ports, such as Guangzhou, Quanzhou, Hangzhou, Mingzhou, Wenzhou and Mizhou (now Jiaoxi County, Shandong). The most important trading ports during the Yuan Dynasty were Guangzhou, Quanzhou, Shanghai, Ganpu (modern Haiyan County, Zhejiang), Wenzhou, Hangzhou, and Qingyuan (modern Ningbo City, Zhejiang). Tariffs collected by various harbour administrations during the Song and Yuan dynasties constituted a very large proportion of state revenue. During the Song Dynasty, tariff was fixed at one-fifteenth to one-fifth of the value of goods; sometimes it was as high as four-tenths. During the Yuan Dynasty, the ratio was one-thirtieth to one-fifth.

During the Song-Yuan period, shipbuilding and navigation were highly developed in China. In terms of equipment, freight capacity and navigational skill China was among the most advanced in the world. Its ships sailed to Japan, Korea, Indo-China, Burma, Malaya, the Indonesian islands, the Philippines, Bangladesh, India, Pakistan, Sri Lanka, the Persian Gulf states, Arabia, Egypt, the eastern coast of Africa and the Mediterranean coast. Among the export goods from China were silk, porcelain, lacquerware, gold, silver, zinc and lead. Among the import goods were pearls, hawksbill turtle, rhinoceros horns, elephant tusk, coral, agate, frankincense, spices and medicine. The Song and Yuan governments paid great attention to foreign trade. Foreign merchants and diplomatic envoys were well received; sometimes they were granted official titles.

During the Song-Yuan period, the Silk Road once again became an important overland route between the East and the West. Merchants carried on their trade along the route, and Christian missionaries came to the East by following the same route. In 1245 Father Giovanni de Piano Carpini was sent by Pope Innocent IV of the Roman Catholic Church to Kara Korum to visit Güyük Khan. He attended the ceremony at which Güyük was made Great Khan. The Khan granted him an audience, during which Carpini requested the Khan to cultivate faith in Catholicism. In his letter to the Pope, he asked the Pope and all Christian Kings to come to China to pay homage to him. In 1253, Louis IX of France sent Father Guillaume de Rubrujuis to Kara Korum to visit with Mangu Khan, who granted an audience in the following year. As usual, Mangu Khan, in his letter to the French King, asked the latter to swear allegiance to him and pay tribute to his court. Both preachers wrote travel notes after they returned to their own countries. These notes are important materials in studying Mongol history. Among the missionaries who had come to China from the West from the beginning of the Yuan Dynasty were Giovanni de Montecorvino, Odorico de Pordenone, and Giovanni de Marignolli. In 1292 or thereabouts, Giovanni de Montecorvino came to China. Living in Dadu, he founded two churches and was made archbishop. Odorico de Pordenone arrived in China around 1325. He visited many places in China, including Guangzhou, Quanzhou, Hangzhou, Yangzhou and Dadu. While in China, he had personal contact with Giovanni de Montecorvino. In 1330 he returned to Europe. Giovanni de Marignolli arrived at Dadu in 1342. He paid respects to Emperor Shun Di, to whom he presented a white horse, called a "heavenly horse". In 1347, he left Quanzhou by the sea route.

Among the Western travellers of this period none was better known than Marco Polo. Even today, his *Travels* is still a most valuable source in studying the history of the Yuan Dynasty and its relations with the West. Marco Polo was a Venetian from Italy. In 1271, he followed his father and uncle in passing across West and Central Asia and arrived at Shangdu in 1275. He was received by Kublai Khan. He visited many places in China and wrote about important events. He described vividly the might of the Mongol empire and the prosperity of Dadu. He praised highly the courier system of China and courier stations. In 1292, after living in China for 17 years, he sailed from China's Quanzhou for Persia, wherefrom he returned to his homeland Venice. Reportedly, his book *Travels* inspired such men as Christopher Columbus and Vasco da Gama in their search for a route to the East.

In the wake of Marco Polo came Ibn Batuta, a Moroccan who journeyed to India first and then arrived in China by the sea route. While in China he visited Guangzhou, Quanzhou, Hangzhou and many other places. He returned home by sailing from Quanzhou. In his book, he wrote about people's life, customs and tradition, economic production and industrial arts in China.

During the Song-Yuan period, China maintained close cultural ties with Korea and Japan. Medically, Korea felt China's influence as early as the Tang Dynasty. During the Song-Yuan period, Chinese medical books and medicines arrived in Korea in a continuous flow, and Chinese doctors were invited to Korea. Meanwhile, such medicines as ginseng and antlers were imported from Korea, and important Korean medical works were also found in China. While learning paper making from China, Korea also manufactured its own tough and fine-grained paper made of cotton. During the Song Dynasty, it was among the items imported from Korea. Though Korea learned the making of writing brushes from China, writing brushes made of weasel hair originated in Korea. By the Song Dynasty, such Korean writing brushes had won great fame in China. Later, China manufactured its own weasel hair brushes by copying those from Korea. With the passage of time, some old Chinese books were lost in China, but they could still be found in Korea. Meanwhile, many Korean books were introduced into China. During the Song-Yuan period, many Chinese medical works, including *The Cleansing of Wrongs (Xi yuan lu)* by Song Ci found their way into Japan. Japan imported from China such medicines as musk, croton, realgar, and cinnabar. Many Japanese came to China to study medical science. Towards the end of the Southern Song Dynasty, many Japanese were sent to China to study the technology of making porcelain; meanwhile, Japanese paintings and calligraphy found their way into China and were well received.

During the Song-Yuan period, Chinese culture continued to have its influence felt in Persia and several Arab countries. The political and economical institutions of the Il-Khanate, established by the Mongols in Persia, were strongly affected by Chinese influence. Chinese medical knowledge had been long disseminated in Persia. Rashid al-Din, a Persian who served as Prime Minister of the Il-Khanate, was a great historian and an expert physician. His *Collected Histories* is an important work on Mongolian history. In 1313 he compiled a book entitled *The Il-Khanate Treasure House of Chinese Medical Science*. It covered such subject matters as pulse feeling, anatomy, embryology, gynaecology and pharmacology; it especially quoted Wang Shuhe, a well-known physician of the Jin Dynasty who wrote *Classic on Pulse*.

During the Yuan Dynasty Persian and Arab culture was introduced into China on a large scale. Great numbers of Persians and Arabs, known to the Chinese as Huihuis, arrived in China. Belonging to the *Semu* group, they later formed part of China's Muslim community. Many of these new immigrants were intellectuals who brought Persian and Arab culture into China. The Chinese attached special value to Arab astronomy, calendar-making, and medical science. During the Yuan Dynasty, a Muslim astronomical department was instituted within the government, and Arab and Persian methods were used in making astronomical observations, on the basis of which China made its calendar. In 1267 Jamal al-Din, a Muslim, made a set of astronomical apparatus by himself and used it in astronomical observations. The Ming government simultaneously used two calendars, Chinese and Muslim, and continued the Yuan practice of having a Muslim astronomical department in the administration. This remained unchanged until the early period of the Qing Dynasty. In mathematics, it was possible that the Greek mathematician Euclid's *Geometry* was translated from Arab into Chinese during the Yuan Dynasty, according to recent studies. In 1270, Kublai Khan established not only a Muslim medical department for the production of Muslim medicines, but also two Muslim pharmacological academies in two capitals (Dadu and Shangdu). Muslim physicians were especially known for their extraordinary skill in the treatment of rare diseases. During the Ming Dynasty, a book entitled *Muslim Prescriptions* was published in both Chinese and Persian. In addition, many Muslim artisans proficient in weaving were transferred to China proper and employed in the production of silk and a special kind of cloth known as *sadalaqi*. There was even a *sadalaqi* department, headed by a Muslim, in charge of the production of this kind of cloth.

The culture of Nepal was also introduced into China during the Yuan Dynasty. At the invitation of Kublai Khan, a great architect of Nepal named Arnico came to Dadu and was entrusted with the task of building palaces for the royal house. He sculptured many Buddhist statues in Dadu and Shangdu and repaired a bronze acupuncture statue. He was referred to as a genius. Moreover, he passed his unique skill to Liu Yuan of Baodi (located near modern Tianjin), who also became a famous sculptor.

The Chinese invented the compass and were the first to use it in navigation. During the Song-Yuan period, merchant ships from China, Persia, and Arabia were very active on the high seas. Ships from China were known for their speed and size, their direction being guided by compass. It was possible that Persian and Arab ships learned the use of the compass during this period in history. Later Europeans also learned its use.

The Chinese art of printing became known to Japan during the eighth century. It was introduced to Korea during the tenth century and to Egypt during the twelfth century or perhaps a little earlier. Not until the thirteenth century did the Il-Khanate of Persia learn it and then introduced it to Africa and Europe. Towards the end of the fourteenth century block printing appeared for the first time in Europe. Movable type was invented in China during the eleventh century. It was introduced into Korea during the thirteenth century and to Europe at a later date.

The introduction of firearms to the West was closely related to the Mongols' western campaign early in the thirteenth century. Nitre, indispensable to the production of gunpowder, was known as "Chinese salt" to the Persians and as "Chinese snow" to the Arabs. Persians and Arabs learned about nitrate in the eighth or ninth century. Not until the twelfth or thirteenth century did Arab merchants bring gunpowder to the Near East. During their military campaigns in Central Asia and Persia, the Mongols used weapons made of gunpowder. Fighting with the Mongols, the Arabs learned the use of firearms. The Europeans learned the use of firearms in the same fashion.

After the demise of the Qin and Han dynasties, the intercourse between China and foreign countries was most active during the Song and Yuan dynasties. It played an important role in the feudal history of China. The development of social economy and culture in China helped China's foreign relations, and the development of China's foreign relations, in turn, helped China's economic and cultural development. China then adopted an open-door policy towards people from the outside. But this policy changed during the Ming Dynasty.

Chapter IX
The Ming-Qing Period: the Twilight of Feudalism

1. Establishment of the Ming Dynasty

Feudalism declined during the Ming-Qing period. The Ming Dynasty had altogether 16 emperors of 12 generations, lasting 276 years from 1368 to 1644, and the Qing Dynasty, 10 emperors of 9 generations, lasting 268 years from 1644 to 1911. Between 1644 and 1661, after the Ming Dynasty had been terminated, four members of the Ming royal house successively established in Nanjing and elsewhere the regimes of Southern Ming, thus continuing the challenge against the Qing which by then had won firm control over the Central Plains of China. In 1840, the British imperialists invaded China and precipitated the Opium War. From then on China gradually developed from feudal into a semi-feudal and semi-colonial country.

In 1368, Zhu Yuanzhang acceded to the throne in Yingtian (modern Nanjing, Jiangsu Province) and titled his dynasty Ming. Zhu Yuanzhang's temple name was Tai Zu; he was also referred to as Emperor Hong Wu.[1] He gradually unified the whole country after taking the Yuan capital. Among his civil ministers were Li Shanchang, Liu Ji and Song Lian, and among his military commanders were Xu Da, Chang Yuchun, Tang He and Hu Dahai. All of them were instrumental

---

[1] With the exception of Emperor Ying Zong of the Ming Dynasty, every emperor of the Ming and Qing dynasties had only one reign title, by which he was customarily referred to. Zhu Yuanzhang's reign title was Hong Wu; he was therefore often referred to as Emperor Hong Wu. This custom became widespread during the Qing Dynasty.

in assisting him in the founding of the new dynasty.

Zhu Yuanzhang paid close attention to rehabilitation as a means of consolidating his regime after the country had undergone a major upheaval. "People's financial resources are stringent and inadequate, as the country has been only recently unified," he stated. "We should not pluck the feathers of an infant bird; nor is it wise to shake a newly planted tree." He instructed his officials not to exact taxes in an arbitrary manner, and forbade them to enrich themselves through corruption or cause unnecessary disturbances among the people. One constructive measure he adopted was the recruitment of peasant refugees for the reclamation of abandoned fields. The government provided these refugees with oxen to plough the fields and seeds to start the planting. They were even allowed to keep the tilled fields as their own property. No taxes would be imposed for a period of three years; in some cases tax exemption was declared to be permanent. Unemployed peasants in the lower Changjiang River valley—places like Suzhou, Songjiang, Jiaxing, Huzhou and Hangzhou—were moved to the Huai River valley where they opened up new fields for cultivation; more than once were poor peasants moved to the frontier and other sparsely populated areas for the same purpose. To solve the problem of the army's food supply, Zhu Yuanzhang promoted a system of land reclamation by soldiers. He stipulated that frontier soldiers should devote 30 per cent of their efforts to defence and 70 per cent to land cultivation, and the ratio was 2 to 8 as far as soldiers in the interior were concerned. He paid close attention to the construction of water conservancy projects, and promoted the cultivation of cash crops. The largest of such projects brought irrigation to 10,000 *qing* (approximately 160,000 acres) of paddy fields. All these measures were instrumental in the gradual recovery and development of agriculture during the early years of the Ming Dynasty. Meanwhile, handicraft industry and commerce also recovered and made progress. Population increased too.

Zhu Yuanzhang reorganized the bureaucracy so as to strengthen his rule. At the beginning be adopted the Yuan system of administration, including the Secretariat and the Offices of Left and Right Prime Ministers which administered the whole country. In 1380 he abolished the Secretariat and the Offices of the two Prime Ministers. In their place he installed the Six Boards—the Boards of Civil Office, Revenue, Rites, War, Justice and Works, and each of the Boards was headed by a minister. There were no high officials between the emperor and the ministers, who were responsible directly to the emperor. In addition to the Six Boards, there were (1) the Office of Transmission responsible for the acceptance of memorials from officials and petitions on exclusive information from ordinary citizens as well as officials, (2) the Censorate responsible for the supervision of officials, and (3) the Supreme Court responsible for reexamination of cases on appeal. The Board of Justice, the Censorate and the Supreme Court were jointly known as the "Three Justices", each of which restrained the other two in the administration of justice. In addition, there were the Grand Secretaries of the Inner Chancery who, ranking below the ministers, were the emperor's advisers responsible for his clerical work. As for military affairs, while the Board of War exercised overall leaderhsip, the recruitment, registration and training of soldiers were entrusted to five Military Commands—Left, Right, Central, Front and Rear—which had replaced the General Command established during the Yuan Dynasty. The emperor issued orders and appointed commanders whenever the army was mobilized for warfare, and officers and men returned to their garrison duties once the war was over. In local administration, the Ming Dynasty established an institution known as the Administrative Commissioner's Office in charge of civil and financial affairs of a number of prefectures, subprefectures and counties. Customarily, the area governed by such an office was referred to as a "province"—a term that has been in use since. The area of jurisdiction for each of eleven provinces—Shandong, Shanxi, Henan, Sichuan, Zhejiang, Jiangxi, Fujian, Guangdong, Guangxi, Yunnan and Guizhou—has remained approximately the same throughout the years, but the areas of jurisdiction of other provinces have undergone substantial changes. The Shaanxi Province of the Ming Dynasty was split to become Shaanxi and Gansu provinces during the early period of the Qing Dynasty; the Huguang Province was likewise split to become Hubei and Hunan provinces. By the same token, the area known as South Zhili during the Ming Dynasty became Jiangsu and Anhui provinces early in the Qing Dynasty, and the area known as North Zhili became Zhili Province that corresponded to today's Beijing Municipality, Tianjin Municipality, most areas of Hebei Province, and small parts of Henan and Shandong provinces. The Ming Dynasty had also an office known as Judicial Commissioner's Office responsible for the administration of justice in the provinces. Another office known as Military Commissioner's Office was in charge of military affairs on a local level.

Zhu Yuanzhang used severe punishment and indiscriminate killing as a means to strengthen his rule. In 1380 he killed a high official, Hu Weiyong, and the people directly or indirectly implicated exceeded 30,000, who also died as a result. In 1393 he killed General Lan Yu, and more than 15,000 persons, being implicated, were executed. Few of those who had helped him in founding the Ming Dynasty survived a normal span of life. He established an intelligence organization known as the Imperial Guard whose sole duty was to gather damaging information on officials and ordinary people alike, so as to subject each of them to the constant fear of losing not only his own life but the lives of all his family as well.

Zhu Yuanzhang stipulated that there were only two avenues to officialdom: schools and civil service examinations. The school in the nation's capital was called Imperial College; its students were recruited from children of officials who had been recommended by local schools. The subjects taught in the Imperial College included the emperor's edicts, law, and the Confucianist *Four Books* and *Five Classics*. Those who graduated with honour would receive appointment as officials. As for the civil service examination, those who had passed examinations in the provinces were referred to as *juren* or "recommended men", and all the "recommended men" could participate in the metropolitan examination in the nation's capital. Those who passed the metropolitan examination could participate in the palace examination, and the successful candidates of the palace examination, classified into three categories, would receive appointment as officials, either on the central or on the local level. The questions in the examinations at all levels were derived from the *Four Books* and the *Five Classics*, and the answers must be based upon the authorized comments and must be phrased in such a way as to reflect the speech of ancients. Later, the style of writing became gradually formalized and stereotyped, and compositions written in such a style were referred to as "eight-legged eassays". The purpose of this kind of examination was to force people to conform, happily and willingly, to the thought frame-work as determined by the royal house. Under no circumstances was independent thinking or a new style of writing allowed. Needless to say, individual view on government and politics was impossible. To strengthen thought control, Zhu Yuanzhang initiated many cases of literary inquisition. If a few words in a composition aroused his suspicion, he just might condemn its author to death.

To perpetuate the rule of China by the Zhu house, Zhu Yuanzhang, from 1369 to 1391, successively appointed his sons, nephews and grandsons to twenty-five vassalages scattered around the country, and the designed purpose of these vassalages was to protect the royal house in the capital. Meanwhile, as he was afraid that the vassals might become too powerful for the central government to control, he stipulated that a vassal in the interior regions could not command more than 3,000 personal guards and that he was not allowed to interfere with civil administration. Only the Prince of Qin at Xi'an, the Prince of Jin at Taiyuan, and the Prince of Yan at Beiping (modern Beijing) were granted military commandership. In 1398, the second year after Zhu Yuanzhang's death, a fierce struggle involving the vassalages erupted within the royal house.

Upon his death, Zhu Yuanzhang was succeeded by his grandson, who was titled Emperor Hui Di. Fearful of the expanding power of the vassalages, the new emperor, having listened to the advice of Qi Tai and Huang Zicheng, proceeded to reduce it. Hardly had he succeeded in weakening some of the vassalages before the Prince of Yan, the strongest vassal, revolted. The war between Emperor Hui Di and his uncle, the Prince of Yan, lasted four years until 1402 when Yingtian fell and Hui Di disappeared without a trace. The Prince of Yan ascended the throne and, in the very next year, changed the reign title to Yong Le. Historically he was referred to as Emperor Cheng Zu or Emperor Yong Le. Having seized the throne, he proceeded successfully with the termination of military power among all the vassalages, thus strengthening further the feudal, autocratic rule. He moved the Ming capital to Beijing and recruited approximately 250,000 artisans and nearly one million peasants to rebuild the city. Three and one-half years of intensive labour transformed Beijing into a grand, magnificent metropolis. In 1421 Beijing was formally declared to be the nation's capital, and Yingtian, the former capital, was renamed Nanjing. At the time when the capital was moved to Beijing, the emperor also mobilized a large number of peasant workers for the purpose of dredging the Grand Canal, so that grains, silks and cotton cloth produced in the south could be continually transported to the north. From Emperor Cheng Zu to his grandson, Emperor Xuan Zong, gradually the Grand Secretaries of the Inner Chancery were given more authority, as they participated more in the making of policy decisions. Yang Shiqi, Yang Rong and Yang Pu were among the most notable of the Grand Secretaries during the reigns of Emperors Ren Zong and Xuan Zong.

Beginning in the reign of Emperor Cheng Zu, the economy continued to make progress. Upon his ascension to the throne, the emperor ordered the distribution of farm implements and oxen in Shandong and other areas that had been devastated by war. Meanwhile, he continued the policy of his predecessors in opening up new fields for cultivation and in moving people to the less populated regions, thus enabling the areas around Beijing and the frontier areas in the north to be developed further. The record shows that in those years local granaries remained continually full and that grains collected as taxes were shipped to the capital in a continuous, endless flow. The annual requisition of silk and cloth by the imperial government was also very large.

As the nation's economy developed, the Ming regime strengthened its relations with the ethnic minorities, politically, economically and culturally. It established in Kaiyuan (in modern Liaoning Province) a horse market to trade with the Nüzhen tribes. In 1409 it established in Tirin, near the estuary of the Heilongjiang River, the Nurkan Commissioner's Office, with jurisdiction that extended westward to the Onon River, eastward to the Kuye (Sakhalin) Island, northward to the Oudi River, and southward to the Sea of Japan. In the northwest where the Uygurs, the Huis, and the Mongolians resided, it established garrison commands, with jurisdiction that covered all the territories to the west of Jiayuguan Pass. The jurisdiction extended westward to the Lop Nur, northward to the Barkol Mountains, and southeastward to the Qaidam Basin. In the areas where the Miao, the Yi and other minorities resided, the Ming regime designated their own leaders as government officials. It stipulated that the minorities could pay taxes with the minerals they produced, such as mercury and cinnabar. It established in modern Qinghai and Tibet (then known as "Dbus-Gtsang") six offices for administration and conferred the title of King upon the Grand Lamas. Meanwhile, it continued to trade with the ethnic minorities in the area, exchanging tea for horse. At the peak of this trade, it annually shipped out hundreds of thousands of *jin*[1] of tea in exchange for ten to twenty thousand horses.

During the reigns of Emperors Cheng Zu and Xuan Zong, the government, time and again, dispatched Zheng He, a Muslim, as an envoy to Southeast Asia and the Indian Ocean. In the summer of 1405, at the head of an armada of sixty-two ships and an army contingent of more than 27,800 men, well supplied with gold, silk and other valuables, Zheng He set to sea from the Port of Liujia near Suzhou and first landed on Fujian. He sailed again from Wuhumen, Fujian Province, and eventually reached Champa. From Champa he journeyed to Java, Sumatra, and Calicut of India, wherefrom he returned to China in the autumn of 1407. From then on until 1433, he sailed time and again. His longest voyage carried him all the way to the eastern coast of Africa, the Red Sea and Mecca. This record voyage preceded Christopher Columbus' discovery of America and Vasco da Gama's navigation around the Cape of Good Hope by more than one-half of a century. One of Zheng He's retainers named Ma Huan (also known as Ma Zongyuan) recorded his observations during the voyage in a book entitled *Vision in Triumph in a Boundless Sea*. Fei Xin also wrote a book entitled *Vision in Triumph: Ships Sail Under Starry Sky*. Both books are important source material in studying the history of inter-

[1] A *jin* by the old system of weight was equivalent to 0.6 kilogramme or 1.3 pounds.—*Trans.*

course between China and foreign countries during the Ming Dynasty.

The reigns of Zhu Yuanzhang and Emperors Hui Di, Cheng Zu, Ren Zong and Xuan Zong, totalling 67 years, marked the early and the most glorious period of the Ming Dynasty. Nevertheless, peasant uprisings continued, and Japanese pirates frequently landed on China to cause disturbances. The record shows that there were more than one hundred peasant riots and uprisings during this period, such as Sun Jipu's uprising in Shandong in 1370, the peasant uprising in Guangdong in 1381, and the peasant uprising in Sichuan in 1385. The leader of each uprising referred to himself as "King of Levellers", indicating that he wished to bring equality to society. The uprising in Sichuan had a following reported to be as large as 200,000. In 1420, a woman named Tang Sai'er, of Putai, Shandong Province, first established her base of operation in Fort Xieshipeng (located in Yidu, Shandong Province) and then attacked Ju, Jimo and Anqiu. The revolt led by her was the best known among the peasant uprisings during the early Ming period. Suspecting that she might have gone into hiding in a convent or nunnery upon her defeat, the Ming government arrested and then sent to Beijing tens of thousands of Buddhist nuns and Taoist priestesses, but nowhere could she be found.

As for the Japanese pirates, they, after 1369, repeatedly raided and pillaged the coastal areas of Shandong, Zhejiang, Fujian and Guangdong, burning and killing as they went. In some cases they even occupied cities for as long as one year. The Ming government built walled fortifications along the coast for defence; it even sent troops in hot pursuit, attempting to exterminate them. But the result was far from effective.

Both Zhu Yuanzhang and Emperor Cheng Zu did not trust their respective ministers, to a degree rarely seen among Chinese emperors. Beginning with Cheng Zu, eunuchs were entrusted with military commandership and were assigned to such important duties as the defence of the frontier. With the passage of time, they were more and more favoured and given greater and greater responsibilities, creating conditions that led, eventually, to their interference with policy decisions in the imperial government. The excessive power the eunuchs enjoyed proved to be a dangerous cancer on the body politic throughout the Ming Dynasty.

Carrying on Zhu Yuanzhang's policy of thought control, Emperor Cheng Zu ordered Hu Guang and others to edit *The Complete Works of the Five Classics* in 121 *juan, The Complete Works of the Four Books* in 30 *juan* and *The Complete Works of Neo-Confucianism* in 70 *juan*. The purpose was to promote the Neo-Confucianism of Cheng Hao, Cheng Yi and Zhu Xi, and the method was none other than a reproduction of the extant source materials. Emperor Cheng Zu also ordered Xie Jin and others to compile *The Yong Le Encyclopaedia*. The contents of the completed work, 22,937 *juan* altogether, were arranged according to phonetic rhymes, reproduced from more than 7,000 extant works. Sometimes an entire book was included. In this way the emperor kept many scholars employed and happy, demonstrating that he, the emperor, was the final authority in cultural activities. Nevertheless, the work itself was an enormous, unprecedented undertaking, preserving many precious materials which otherwise would have been lost to posterity.

The two original creations of the early Ming period were *The Romance of the Three Kingdoms* and *Outlaws of the Marsh*. *The Romance*, based on the history of the Three Kingdoms, is China's first historical novel and one of the longest novels in the history of Chinese literature. Through its poignant portrayal of different personalities, it presents vividly a political and military struggle of great complexity. As a sympathizer of Liu Bei against Cao Cao, the author describes Liu Bei and his followers as loyal, audacious and solicitous towards the people's welfare; Cao Cao and his followers, on the other hand, were characterized as devious, untrustworthy, and poisonous. In either case, the portraits were sharp and vivid, creating a deep impression upon the reader. Zhuge Liang became a personalization of wisdom, and he personally directed a spectacle of grandeur known as the Battle of Chibi. In the selection of topical materials as well as in the artistry of presentation, *The Romance* had a deep impact on the literary works of later periods. The way it judged historical personalities affected materially a reader's view of the history of the Three Kingdoms. Luo Guanzong, the author, lived between 1330 and 1400, approximately.

Outlaws of the Marsh, another novel, appeared at about the same time as *The Romance of the Three Kingdoms*. It is a masterpiece in the description of peasant uprisings. Based upon a true historical event that occurred in Liangshan Marsh during the Northern Song period, it traces the entire course of a peasant uprising in feudal China: its origin, development and final defeat. As its theme centres on the saying that "the government drives the people to revolt," this historical novel not only exposes and condemns the corruption of the ruling landlord class but also praises highly the insurgent leaders for their heroism. It successfully and poignantly sets forth not only the background of each of the Liangshan heroes but also his thought development that finally led him to climb the mountains "to join the righteous cause". From the viewpoint of characterization and development of personalities, *Outlaws of the Marsh*, artistically speaking, is much superior to *The Romance of the Three Kingdoms*. Its appearance enthused the oppressed masses; the ruling class hated it, of course. Later, other novels, dramas and popular literature in general were deeply affected by it. As for its author, he could be either Shi Naian or Luo Guanzhong. Some say that Shi started the work and Luo completed it. As for Shi, few references about his life are available.

In terms of artistic form, both *The Romance of the Three Kingdoms* and *Outlaws of the Marsh* were created out of the verbal history and vernacular tales of the Song-Yuan period. As for content, the author of *The Romance* fully utilized the materials contained in *The History of the Three Kingdoms* by Chen Shou and other works, while *Outlaws of the Marsh* absorbed many of the traditional stories long circulated among the people. Since the creation of both works had been affected by the peasant uprisings that occurred during the later part of the Yuan Dynasty, their authors were able to open up new vistas and write such masterpieces. This does not mean, however, that these two works have no shortcomings. The most obvious shortcomings are the expressed feudal concept of loyalty to the emperor and the so-called "faithfulness to friends" found among the small producers. Though *Outlaws of the Marsh* shows sympathy for, and in fact praises highly, the anti-oppression activities of the Liangshan heroes, it attributes all the hideous behaviour and atrocities to corrupt officials, thus clearing the royal house of all blame. Political situation being what it was, both books could not circulate widely during the early period of the Ming Dynasty. They had to wait until the first half of the sixteenth century when, finally, they appeared in printed form, to be handed down to posterity.

2. Decline of the Ming Dynasty; Refugee and Miner Uprisings

Emperor Ying Zong ascended the throne in 1435. From then on and for about seventy years—a period that comprises the four reigns of Ying Zong, Jing Di, Xian Zong and Xiao Zong—the Ming Dynasty declined. During this period the emperors placed their confidence in eunuchs and political instability ensued. The Mongolian tribes of Oirat and Tatar repeatedly raided and caused disturbances; the financial crisis deepened. Greater and greater in scope were the peasant uprisings in which refugees and miners played an important role.

Ying Zong was not yet nine when he was declared emperor of China. His favourite was a eunuch named Wang Zhen, a former study companion of his, whom he now elevated to become Eunuch-in-Charge-of-Rites. Wang Zhen persuaded the boy emperor to employ severe punishment to keep court ministers in line, while taking advantage of every opportunity to expand his own power. Early during the emperor's reign, the "Three Yangs" were still active in the government, and this fact deterred to some extent Wang Zhen's arbitrary exercise of power. By 1442 Yang Rong had already died, and Yang Shiqi and Yang Pu could no longer hold any office. Wang Zhen, consequently, had no more scruples in usurping power and in condemning to death, by trumped-up charges, those who disagreed with him. He became a most powerful person who could manipulate the affairs of state.

In 1449, the Oirats sent an envoy to the Ming court to present horses as tribute. The Oirats were located to the west of the Gobi, residing in the Kobdo River valley, the Ertix River valley and the Junggar Basin. Besides the Oirats there were two other Mongolian groups: the Tatars who lived in the Onon River valley, the Kerulen

River valley and the Lake Baikal region, and the Urianghads who lived in the valleys of the Liao River, the West Liao River and the Laoha River. Early during Ying Zong's reign, the Oirats, under the leadership of Esen, had grown so powerful that they actually controlled all other Mongolian tribes. In 1449 when he came to pay tribute to the Ming court, Esen felt insulted when the Ming officials deliberately forced down prices of his horses which he had brought with him. Angered, he mobilized all the Mongolian tribes and marched southward along four routes. Hoodwinked by Wang Zhen, the emperor decided to lead an army personally to meet the invaders head-on, despite the admonition of his ministers not to do so. The Ming troops were routed and the emperor was captured alive by the enemy in a place called Tumubao, outside the city of Huailai; Wang Zhen, the eunuch, was killed by rioting soldiers.

When the news of defeat arrived at Beijing, many high officials were so frightened that they wanted to move the capital and flee southward. Yu Qian, the Deputy Minister of War, resolutely proposed resistance. He took over the responsibility of defending Beijing and prepared carefully for the forthcoming confrontation. As soon as Esen's troops reached Beijing's suburbs, the defenders, under Yu Qian's command, engaged them in ferocious combat. Esen was defeated, and the safety of the capital was secured. In 1450 Esen returned Emperor Ying Zong to Beijing, and the normal relationship of trade between the Oirats and the Ming was subsequently restored. In 1455 an internal struggle developed among the Oirats, and Esen was killed by one of his subordinates. From then on the Oirats slowly declined and in its place rose the Tatars. For a long time to come, the Tatars would intermittently raid the border areas, posing a major threat to the Ming regime.

Ying Zong was returned to Beijing the year after Jing Di had become his successor as emperor. After his return, the ex-emperor was confined to the Southern Palace, cut off from outside contact. In 1457, as Jing Di became ill, Cao Jixiang, a former follower of Wang Zhen's, supported Ying Zong and succeeded in regaining the imperial position for the ex-emperor. Cao, like Wang Zhen, started his political career as Eunuch-in-Charge-of-Rites and, as his power grew, persecuted, on trumped-up charges, those who disagreed with him. Sometimes even the emperor had to put up with his arrogance. In 1461, Cao Jixiang, with the help of his adopted son Cao Qin, secretly plotted to usurp the throne by force. He was killed when the plot failed. Thus Ying Zong, by placing his confidence in eunuchs, twice ran the risk of losing his life. But he never came to see his mistakes. After his death, his descendants did not learn anything from history either. Emperor Xian Zong placed his confidence in eunuch Wang Zhi, and his successor Emperor Xiao Zong did likewise with eunuch Li Guang. The eunuchs, consequently, were able to continue to meddle in politics. Their power was as great as the emperor's, thus creating political instability. During the reigns of Ying Zong, Xian Zong and Xiao Zong, there were, of course, those who were concerned with the fate of the nation and wished to do something constructive about it; they were not afraid of opposing the eunuchs. Among them were Li Xian, Peng Shi and Shang Lu during the reigns of Ying Zong and Xian Zong; Liu Jian, Xie Qian and Li Dongyang during the reign of Xiao Zong. All of them held important positions at one time or another. They paid close attention to the recruitment of talents, the freedom of expressing ideas on current affairs, the elimination of waste in bureaucratic expenses, the dismissal of superfluous personnel in government, and the rectification of financial administration in general. They opposed and tried to suppress the arbitrary, illegal acts on the part of the eunuchs; they were brave enough to speak out what they felt in front of the emperor. From time to time, even the emperor praised their outspokenness. Thanks to their meritorious service, Ying Zong and his immediate successors were able to maintain their rule.

Nevertheless, the financial crisis gradually worsened after the reign of Ying Zong largely because of the prodigious waste at the court, the ever-increasing military expenditures, and the illegal, large-scale annexation of land by members of the royal house, eunuchs and powerful and influential landlords. Let us look at land annexation to demonstrate the case in point. Early during the Ming Dynasty, registered land under cultivation amounted to 8,507,000 *qing* (approximately 127,605,000 acres). The figure dropped to 4,228,000 *qing* in 1502. The principal cause for this drop was that land illegally annexed was no longer registered for taxation. To maintain the same income from taxation on a much smaller acreage, the Ming government had to increase the tax on peasants, namely, to shift the tax burden from the illegally annexed land to the land owned and tilled by small landowners, thus increasing the exploitation of those who could least afford it. In addition, it extorted money from peasants by invoking a variety of excuses. Yet, the larger the government's income was, the greater its expenditure seemed to grow. When the oppression and the extortion became unbearable, the peasants had no choice but to stage armed uprisings, which in turn compelled the government to increase military expenditures. Financial crisis and the increasingly large scale of peasant revolts underscored the decline of the Ming Dynasty.

The refugee problem was serious as early as Ying Zong's reign. The four districts of Taizhou, Zhejiang Province, had originally a population of 188,000 households; in 1441, only one-third of this population remained. In groups of tens or hundreds, the refugees scattered all over in different places. They ate wild herbs or elm barks boiled with water. Countless number died of hunger or cold. The Jingxiang region around Yunyang on the borders of modern Hubei, Henan and Shaanxi provinces, being comparatively affluent, became a magnet for many refugees. During the reign of Xian Zong, approximately 1.5 million refugees congregated in this region.

In 1445, Ye Zongliu, a native of Qingyuan, Zhejiang Province, led an insurrection in Shangrao, Jiangxi Province. Previously, without a means of livelihood, he followed a group of unemployed peasants to the border area of Zhejiang, Jiangxi and Fujian, where he worked in a silver mine. When the government closed the mine for good, he and his fellow miners revolted, only to be put down by the government shortly afterwards. In 1447, he rose again, and this time he was successful enough to have occupied Jinhua of Zhejiang Province, Qianshan of Jiangxi Province, and Pucheng and Jianyang of Fujian Province. In the winter of 1448, he was killed, but his followers kept on the resistance until 1450.

In 1448, a man named Deng Maoqi, of Shaxian, Fujian Province, led his fellow peasants in an armed uprising, as an opposition to the landlords' excessive extortions. Calling himself "King of Levellers", he led his men to occupy many prefectures and counties in the southwestern and northwestern sections of Fujian Province. Many peasants, financially bankrupt, came to join the revolt one after another. In fact, the peasant uprising led by Deng Maoqi and the miner uprising led by Ye Zongliu were coordinated, assisting each other. With the passage of time, their forces became greater and greater. In 1449, after Deng Maoqi had died of an arrow wound, his supporters continued the struggle.

In 1465, the refugees in Jingxiang region, under the leadership of Liu Tong and Shi Long, staged an armed uprising in Yunyang. Previously, the refugees, noting how fertile the soil was in this area, went to the mountains to open up new fields. The government said that the mountains were forbidden regions and sent troops to arrest them. Liu Tong and Shi Long reacted by calling upon their followers to resist. In Fangxian (modern Hubei Province) Liu Tong established a peasant regime and called himself "King of Han", having a following as large as several hundred thousand men. He and his men fought bravely and defeated the government's troops time and again. However, because of the lack of experience, they fell victim to the government's strategy of "divide and conquer". In 1466 he was captured alive, and subsequently executed. Six months later, Shi Long, having been betrayed by one of his followers, was also killed.

The refugees in the mountains remained where they were after the revolt was put down. In 1470 a second uprising emerged, this time led by Li Yuan, Wang Hong and Wang Biao, all of whom were Liu Tong's fromer subordinates. Li Yuan, calling himself "King of Taiping", led his men in attacking Nanzhang (modern Hubei Province), Neixiang (modern Henan Province) and other places, and his force grew quickly. In the end, however, the government was too tricky and too unscrupulous for him. Its troops surrounded the mountains, where the insurgents were active, promising the refugees the freedom to return home to their respective occupations unmolested. Altogether more than 1.4 million of these refugees bit the bait and departed, leaving Li Yuan and other leaders totally isolated. Shortly afterwards, Li Yuan and Wang Hong were captured alive upon their defeat. Though the refugee uprisings in Jingxiang, led first by Liu Tong and then by Li Yuan, failed in the end, they forced the Ming government to recognize that they, the refugees, had the right to open up abandoned fields for cultivation. In addition to the uprisings described above, there were the uprising of 1448 led by Huang Xiaoyang in Guangdong and the uprising of 1456 led by Hou Dagou in Guangxi. In the latter case the insurgents were ethnic minorities, the Yao and Zhuang peoples, and the struggle lasted a much longer time.

As for cultural activities, the reigns of Ying Zong, Xian Zong and Xiao Zong did not produce any memorable men or outstanding works. Yu Qian (1398-1457), the famous Deputy Minister of War who successfully resisted the Oirats, wrote many socially realistic poems—a rare achievement during this period. Qiu Jun (1420-95), a versatile scholar, participated in the editing of the *Documentary Records of Xian Zong* as well as the *Documentary Records of Ying Zong*. Sometimes he wrote the events as they were, regardless of contemporary opinion. Regarding the items in *Interpretations of the Great Learning* (by Zhen Dexiu of the Song Dynasty) as incomplete, he wrote his own "supplements", which comprised more than 160 *juan*. In terms of contents, the "supplements" followed the main thought of the Neo-Confucianism pioneered by Cheng Hao, Cheng Yi and Zhu Xi with special emphasis on learning from the experience of past feudal rulers. During the reign of Xiao Zong, Li Dongyang (1447-1516), an eminent minister, was also the acclaimed dean of letters whose poetry, together with that of others, constituted a new school.

3. Decay of the Ming Dynasty; Peasant Uprisings Continued

Upon his death, Xiao Zong was succeeded by Wu Zong who in turn was succeeded by Shi Zong. Wu Zong loved pleasure and indulged in dissipations while maintaining a martial appearance; he paid little attention to the running of the government. Shi Zong, a Taoist devotee, did not choose to preside over imperial meetings for years; he rarely received his ministers. These two emperors ruled China for a total of sixty-two years and lowered the Ming regime to a level of utter decadence. Later, there was some revival of vitality during the reign of Mu Zong and the early years of Shen Zong, but this revival could not in any way lessen the political crisis the regime was then facing.

Emperor Wu Zong placed his trust in Liu Jin and seven other eunuchs. Together they were referred to as "Eight Tigers" because of their brutality and ferociousness. Before a petition or memorial could be presented to the emperor via the Office of Transmission, a copy must be sent to Liu Jin first for review. The emperor's comments or decisions must also be transmitted through the eunuchs. Thus, as head of the eunuchs, Liu Jin not only controlled state secrets but could also tamper with imperial documents and edicts as he pleased. Then, outside the normal judiciary system, there were three intelligence agencies under the emperor's direct control. One agency was the Imperial Guard, established during the reign of Zhu Yuanzhang. Another agency was the Eastern Chamber that, coming into existence during the reign of Cheng Zu, had more power than the Imperial Guard. The third agency was the Western Chamber that, established during the reign of Xian Zong, was active across the country; its power was even greater than that of the Eastern Chamber. Liu Jin, the eunuch, now established a new intelligence agency called "Inner Chamber" that, operating under his personal command, watched and supervised the activities of both the Eastern and Western Chambers. Besides, he placed his own henchmen in key positions with the Imperial Guard and the two chambers. Using a variety of inducements, he persuaded Wu Zong to do nothing but pleasure-seeking so that he himself could usurp the power of the state. He employed cruel punishment, outright dismissal or killing, to suppress those who opposed him, and he openly solicited and accepted bribes. Provincial officials who sought audience with the emperor must present Liu Jin with twenty thousand taels of silver before an audience could be arranged. Imperial officials who had gone to the provinces for official business had also to bring him gifts when they returned to the capital. Finally, after he had been condemned to death for attempting a coup against the government and all of his property confiscated, it was found that he had in his possession 240,000 gold bars and 5,000,000 silver bars, plus 57,800 taels of gold and 1,583,600 taels of silver, not to mention the huge amounts of pearls and other valuables.

Having killed Liu Jin, Emperor Wu Zong transferred his trust to a military officer named Jiang Bin. Listening to the advice of Jiang Bin, many times he left Beijing for pleasure trips. At one time, while staying in a provincial town, he was besieged by hostile forces. After the invaders had been beaten off, he took the credit and began to call himself "Generalissimo Valiant". He handed over much of his authority to Jiang Bin, whose approval must be sought and obtained before any undertaking in or outside the palace, large or small, could be carried out. Jiang Bin was put to death in 1521 upon the demise of Wu Zong. Among his property confiscated, there were 70 chests of gold and 3,200 chests of silver.

Peasant uprisings continued during the reign of Wu Zong. The uprisings that had the greatest impact included one led by Lan Tingrui and Yan Benshu and another led by Liu Liu and Liu Qi. The former began in Hanzhong, Shaanxi, in 1509. The insurrectionary army moved eastward along the Hanshui River and captured Yunyang and Jingxiang. Turning westward, it entered Sichuan Province where the people enthusiastically welcomed it and responded. The peasant army expanded quickly as a result. In 1511, Lan Tingrui and Yan Benshu were captured after having fallen into a trap, but his followers continued to be active in Sichuan until 1514 when finally the struggle ended.

The uprising led by Liu Liu and Liu Qi began in 1510 at Wen'an (modern Hebei Province). The very next year it spread to Shandong, "as fast as a heavy storm". Later, the insurrectionary army marched forward along two routes to attack Shandong and Shanxi, led respectively by Liu Liu and Yang Hu. The contingent led by Yang Hu for an attack on Shanxi received welcome from the people wherever it went, and eventually rendezvoused with the contingent led by Liu Liu and Liu Qi. It then launched a ferocious attack on the western region of Shandong, and in Jining it won a great victory over the government troops, after having burned 1,218 ships which the government had used for the transport of grain. After Yang Hu was killed in action, the contingent was led by Liu Hui as commander and Zhao Sui (who had previously passed the lowest level of the civil service examination and received the degree of "licentiate") as deputy commander. The insurgents stipulated strict discipline among themselves and even planned to attack Beijing to overthrow the reigning emperor, thus posing a serious threat to the Ming regime. Later, however, they split their forces to penetrate into various areas of Henan, Hubei, South Zhili and Jiangxi. As they slowly spread and thinned out, they also became weaker, giving the Ming government the opportunity to defeat them one by one. In 1512 the insurrection collapsed.

In the spring of 1511, peasants in various parts of Jiangxi revolted. They repulsed the government troops that had come to exterminate them. In 1513, the various insurgent groups collapsed, having suffered suppression and trickery at the hands of the Ming government. Having won the victory, the Ming officials in Jiangxi increased their oppression of the people, especially the peasants who had chosen to surrender themselves to the government. In 1517, peasants revolted again in Nan'an, Dayu and other areas. Meanwhile peasant insurgents were also active in Lechang, Guangdong Province, in Chenzhou (modern Chenxian County, Hunan), Huguang Province, and in Damaoshan, Fujian Province. Governor Wang Shouren of South Jiangxi responded by adopting a dual policy in dealing with the insurgents. On the one hand, he sowed discord among the insurgents and concentrated all his forces for attacks. On the other hand, he controlled the peasants through the tightening of the *bao-jia* system* and through an efficient reorganization of the troops under his command. In 1518 he reported to Beijing that the whole province of Jiangxi had been pacified.

Wang Shouren (1472-1528) was often referred to as Master Yangming. He was responsible for suppressing not only the peasant uprisings but also a rebellion launched by a member of the royal house, the Prince of Ning, Zhu Chenhao. Furthermore, he was a theoretician who defended the feudal rule. Suffering at the hands of the eunuchs,

---

* The *bao* and *jia* were organized on the basis of households; ten households made up a *jia* and ten *jia* made up a *bao*. The *bao* and *jia* chiefs watched all the households under their administration—*Trans*.

he, during a period of sorrow and anguish, developed a philosophical system of subjective idealism. He advocated the theory of "innate knowledge" and "agreement between knowledge and action". Innate knowledge, according to him, is none other than the ability to differentiate right from wrong, a knowledge that is a priori and born with man. Why, then, do people differ in their concept of right and wrong? The reason, he said, is that some people, led astray by selfish desire, can no longer tell right from wrong. We must eliminate selfish desire, he concluded, so we can preserve the innate knowledge born with us. Benevolence, righteousness, loyalty, filial piety, and all other feudal virtues are part of innate knowledge, and only by extending innate knowledge can these virtues grow and develop. By "agreement between knowledge and action" Wang Shouren meant that innate knowledge must manifest itself in action. In other words, man's action is governed by innate knowledge, which cannot be tested by practice. All in all, the emphasis is on knowledge. The ideology of Wang Shouren is an extension of Lu Jiuyuan's philosophy, and its real meaning is to demonstrate the inherent, unshakable nature of feudal order. It served only as a cardiac stimulant to the dying Ming Dynasty. Among Wang Shouren's works, the most important is *The Complete Works of Wang Shouren,* 38 *juan* altogether. Two treatises in this book, "Record of Learning" and "Questions on the Great Learning" are his major contribution to philosophical studies. His student Wang Gen (1483-1540), a native of Taizhou, spread and developed the philosophy further, until it became known as the Taizhou School. Contemporary with Wang Shouren were two other philosophers, namely, Luo Qinshun (1465-1547) and Wang Tingxiang (1474-1544). Luo Qinshun wrote *Knowledge Through Hardship*, and Wang Tingxiang was known for his *Careful Speech, Elegant Narrative* and *Discourse on Human Nature*. More progressive than their contemporaries, they opposed the subjective idealism advocated by Wang Shouren, and proposed a materialistic point of view. But their influence was not great at that time.

Shortly after he ascended to the throne, Emperor Shi Zong corrected some of the political abuses which he had inherited from his predecessor Wu Zong. Basically he was just as decadent, though in a different way. Beginning in 1523, he set inside the palace altars to worship Taoist deities, praying for good fortune and long life. He believed in the use of charms and holy water as a means of avoiding evil spirits and banishing devils and demons. He placed confidence in Taoist priests, some of whom were appointed to high positions in the government. The imperial government had a rear court as well as a front court. While memorials from regular ministers were submitted through the front court, those from Taoist priests were transmitted by the rear court. None of the regular ministers knew the contents of the Taoist memorials. One day in 1542, Emperor Shi Zong, while soundly asleep, was almost choked to death by one of his lady attendants. From then on he no longer dared to live inside the palace; he moved to the Western Gardens instead, where he spent all his time praying for a long life, and his ministers had a difficult time seeing him. Those who admonished him against his obsession with Taoism could suffer either outright dismissal or some other form of punishment. Among the ministers he trusted no one except Yan Song, who not only acted piously when he prayed but also knew how to write good prayers. Yan served as Prime Minister for twenty years, a long tenure that enabled him to build up his own political clique and practise corruption on a large scale. He was the most powerful and also the most treacherous premier during the Ming Dynasty.

There were two difficult problems the ruling oligarchy faced during the reign of Emperor Shi Zong. One was the Tatars' southern march. In 1550 the Tatars marched towards Datong. The garrison commander presented the invaders with heavy bribes and asked them to bypass the city and attack somewhere else. The invaders then marched towards Beijing. Yan Song, the Prime Minister, would not allow the defenders of Beijing to resist, and the invaders, consequently, could do whatever they pleased in the city's suburbs, raiding and pillaging as they went. Another difficult problem was the raiding and pillaging by Japanese pirates. In the spring of 1547, the invaders, in alliance with China's own powerful gentry, unscrupulous merchants and local pirates, landed on the coastal areas of Zhejiang and Fujian where they stepped up their lawless activities. Zhu Wan, then responsible for coastal defence, rectified the situation by arresting and putting to death those Chinese who had collaborated with the Japanese and guided their invasions. By doing this, he antagonized many high officials and members of the gentry who had been collaborating with the Japanese. He was forced to commit suicide. After Zhu Wan's death, all officials, high or low, no longer dared to speak candidly on coastal defence, and the Japanese pirates became more and more unscrupulous. In 1555, Qi Jiguang (1528-1587), having been appointed lieutenant colonel of Zhejiang, proceeded urgently with the preparation of defence against Japanese invaders. Not only did he succeed in training a crack army, but he also introduced new tactics in conducting warfare. Backed by local inhabitants and civil officials, he won great victories against the Japanese pirates successively in Zhejiang, Fujian and Guangdong, thus materially changing the defence situation for the better along China's southeastern coast. Qi Jiguang summarized his military experience in two books: *A Treatise on Efficiency* and *A True Record of the Training of Soldiers*.

The financial crisis accelerated during the reign of Emperor Shi Zong. Annual revenue from regular taxes did not exceed 2,000,000 taels of silver, but expenditures, in the year 1551, reached 5,950,000 taels. From then on, annual expenditures fluctuated between three and five million taels; often annual revenue was less than half of annual income. Shi Zong loved construction, on which he spent an annual amount of six to seven million taels during the first fifteen years of his rule. Later, because of his obsession with Taoism, he spent anywhere between two and three million taels on Taoist buildings annually. Since tax revenue from regular sources was obviously inadequate, he invented a variety of excuses in extorting money from his subjects, thus continuing to increase their burden.

During the reign of Shi Zong, uprisings rose and fell, only to rise again. Among the participants were peasants, miners, ethnic minorities and soldier mutineers. In Guangdong there was a peasant uprising led by Li Wenji; in Ganzhou there was another one led by Lai Qinggui. The insurgents either forcibly took land away from the landlords or went to the mountains to appropriate land for themselves. They continued the tradition of demanding land for themselves, a tradition that went back to the Jingxiang uprising in the early fifteenth century.

During the period of Mu Zong's reign and the early years of Shen

Zong, Zhang Juzheng (1525-1582) was a most able political figure, and most political developments of importance during this period had something to do with him. He became a member of the Inner Chancery upon Mu Zong's ascension to the throne; by the time Shen Zong became the emperor, he had been head of the Inner Chancery for ten years. Being respected and highly regarded by both Shen Zong and the Empress Dowager, he had a golden opportunity of carrying out his political proposals.

At the time of Mu Zong's reign, Qi Jiguang, the general famous for his victory over the Japanese pirates, was transferred to the north as a garrison commander in Jizhou, a strategically important city outside of Beijing. He was supported by Zhang Juzheng in the construction of defence fortifications; many times he repulsed the Tatars' attack. In 1571, Altan Khan of the Tatars expressed the desire for friendship, and the Ming government, at the suggestion of Zhang Juzheng, conferred upon him the title of the Prince of Shunyi. Markets were opened for trade, and fields on the frontier were put into cultivation. The economic and cultural exchange between Hans and Mongolians prospered as a result.

During the early years of Shen Zong's reign, Zhang Juzheng, as head of the Inner Chancery, streamlined and revitalized the administration, unified the government's command, and made sure that every order was strictly obeyed. He took a variety of measures to ease the financial crisis the government was facing. He strove to reduce the loss of grain when it was shipped to Beijing from the south through the Grand Canal, so that "the imperial granary was so full that the grain it contained could last ten years". He charged Pan Jixun (1521-95) with the duty of supervising the water conservancy works along the Huanghe River. Pan was an expert in water control. His two books, *My Humble View of the Two Rivers* and *An Outline of River Control*, were, for a long time, outstanding works in the field. As superintendent of water conservancy works, he corrected the situation that had, previously, led to the frequent breaching of dykes along the Huanghe and Huai Rivers and the interruption of grain transport through the Grand Canal. His efforts helped agricultural production enormously and "transformed abandoned fields of several decades into paddy fields and mulberry groves". As a government official, Zhang Juzheng's most important achievements were two: surveying and registration of cultivated land and adoption of a single tax system. In 1578, having ordered a survey of cultivated acreage across the country, he found that a large amount of land was hidden from taxation, as it was never registered. As a result of this survey, taxable land was increased from 4,228,000 *qing* in 1502 to 7,013,000 *qing* in 1578, an increase by 2,785,000 *qing* (approximately 41,775,000 acres). In 1581, the tax system underwent a drastic change for the better when all levies and impositions, including the corvées, were converted into one single tax to be paid in silver. This reform not only simplified tax collection but also forestalled any excuse that tax collectors might use in extorting money from taxpayers. Besides, paying tax in silver would free peasants from the difficulty of having to transport grain and other harvests over a long distance. This does not mean, however, that the single tax system did not have shortcomings. It was true that the hitherto irregular, miscellaneous requisitions became a regular tax under the new system. But since the tax must be paid in silver, the peasants' selling of grain for silver gave the middlemen another opportunity of exploiting them. Furthermore, the single tax system itself could not prevent government officials from imposing extra levies. While the new tax system simplified tax collection, reduced illegal takes by tax collectors, and therefore helped the increase of government revenue, it did not in any way lessen the burden on taxpayers. Nevertheless, the measures taken by Zhang Juzheng were a change for the better, in view of the widespread corruption in the government; as a means of reform, they were, of course, incompatible with the personal interests of many powerful men. Those whose interests were adversely affected launched a ferocious attack against him. Meanwhile, Shen Zong also became increasingly annoyed with a man who constantly found something to criticize in connection with the emperor's personal life and activities. In 1582, Zhang Juzheng died. His death was like the lifting of a heavy burden as far as the emperor was concerned.

From the time Emperor Wu Zong ascended the throne to the early years of Shen Zong, there had been indeed much achievement in literature. There were influential writers who made contributions in the fields of essays, dramas and novels. In different artistic forms and in a variety of ways of expression, these writers and their works reflect certain aspects of life during this period of decadence in Chinese history.

In essay writing, writers like Li Mengyang (1472-1527), Li Panlong (1514-70) and Wang Shizhen (1528-90) advocated that "good prose should read like the works of the Qin and the Han, and good poetry should be a replica of the golden years of the Tang Dynasty". In other words, they advocated a formalism whereby writers would return to ancient times in terms of writing style. They opposed the eight-legged style most popular with government officials, and they had nothing to do with the kind of literature aimed to please and flatter those in power. Later, such writers as Tang Shunzhi (1507-60), Mao Kun (1512-1601) and Gui Youguang (1506-71) opposed Li and Wang, promoting instead the writing style that characterized the great writers of both the Tang and the Song dynasties. They stated that "the purpose of writing is to express honestly what one really feels" and that "good writing is a successful communication between the mind and the events outside of it". In his description of daily life, Gui Youguang was good at revealing the intimate feelings that were both true and moving. His famous works include *A Brief Account of My Deceased Mother* and *A Record of the Xiangji Pavilion*.

In the field of drama, the representative works were *The Ape with Four Voices* by Xu Wei (1521-93), *The Girl Who Washes Silk* by Liang Chenyu (1510-80), and *The Story of Mingfeng*. *The Ape with Four Voices* actually contains four plays. One of them, *The Three Songs of Yuyang*, uses Cao Cao as an example to show how selfish and hypocritical powerful ministers really are when they sacrifice other people's flesh and blood for their own pleasure. Two others, *A Girl Named Mulan* and *A Woman Who Passes the Metropolitan Examination as Number One*, subject to criticism the feudal concept of sexual inequality when they point out that women can be as able and talented as men. In the former play, a girl, impersonating a man, substitutes her father as a draftee and eventually leads an army and wins great victories on the battlefield. In the latter, a young woman who disguises herself as a man takes the metropolitan examination and emerges as number one. Both plays are meant as a satire against those high officials and military commanders—all males—who are incompetent and cowardly. In *The Girl Who Washes Silk*, Liang Chenyu describes the tragic love between the silk-washing girl Xishi and a minister in the Kingdom of Yue named Fan Li. It is a story of how two persons in love sacrifice their own happiness in order to avenge the shame of their own country. *The Story of Mingfeng*, according to tradition, was written by either Wang Shizhen or one of his students. It describes the struggle between Yan Song and his political enemies during the reign of Shi Zong and, in the process, reveals the cruelty and corruption of politics at that time. About the time of Shi Zong, there was a musician in Kunshan named Wei Liangfu who worked on improving the popular songs of his native city. The improved version, sung with the accompaniment of flute, pipa and moon guitar, was later known as the Kunshan tune. *The Story of Mingfeng* was the first opera that adopted the Kunshan tune and helped to popularize it.

As for novels, the most outstanding creation was *Journey to the West.* Its author Wu Chengen (c. 1500-82) came from Huai'an (modern Jiangsu Province). The novel, 100 chapters altogether, is based upon the popular, traditional tales about a Tang monk named Xuan Zhuang (Hsuan Tsang or Tripitaka) who went to India to procure Buddhist scriptures. Writing in a romantic, imaginative style, the author artistically creates a Monkey King named Sun Wukong. Courageous and fearless, the Monkey King turns the Palace of Heaven upside down, challenging the authority of all the Taoist deities, such as the Jade Emperor, the Immortals, and the Star Kings, to whom wide publicity was given during the Ming Dynasty. Poking fun at them, he views them with contempt when they try to buy him over. Because of his resoluteness and alertness, he is able to overcome eighty-one ordeals, defeating all the deities and demons each and every time. In the end he reaches nirvana with his master Xuan Zhuang and two fellow monks, attaining Buddhahood. The author's description of the Monkey King reflects the wishes of the labouring masses of his time, who, like the Monkey King, dared to challenge the established authority, and hoped that they would become totally free after all the ordeals they had gone through. But the Monkey King wears on his head a golden band that automatically tightens up and causes enormous pain if he chooses to disobey his master Xuan Zhuang. No matter what wonders he may work, he cannot jump out of Buddha's palm. All this shows Wu Chengen's fatalistic point of view: peasant uprisings come and go, bearing little hope for the future. The limitations of the Monkey King reflect the tragedy that all men have to suffer. The deities and demons the author depicts have as many social implications as they are supernatural. Besides, he attributes to some of the characters an animal characteristic and places them in a special realm of fairy tales where they perform all kinds of magic. The depiction looks natural and harmonious, full of wonder and fun. *Journey to the West* pioneered a new way of novel writing which was unprecedented and unique. Later novels of this genre fell far behind, in terms of artistic skill as well as content.

The works of literature as described above contrast sharply with the corruption in politics at that time, indicating unmistakably the intensity of social contradictions. The force of reform was marching forward, relentlessly, to attack the force of corruption. But social contradictions of this kind would continue; they could not find a resolution in a short space of time.

4. Rise of the Manchus; Peasant Uprisings Towards the End of the Ming; Fall of the Ming Dynasty

After the death of Zhang Juzheng, Emperor Shen Zong did whatever he wished in the pursuit of pleasure and paid little attention to state affairs. This was the time when the Manchus rose steadily as a military power in the Northeast, and their aristocracy, in a short period of sixty years, replaced the Ming Dynasty as sovereign of China.

The forerunner of the Manchus was the Nüzhen. At one time, one group of the Nüzhen named Wanyan moved from the Northeast to the Huanghe River valley and founded the Kingdom of Jin, leaving behind many other tribes that continued the primitive life characterizing the later stage of a gentile society. After the Kingdom of Jin was conquered, the various tribes of Nüzhen lived under the jurisdiction of first the

Yuan and then the Ming Dynasty. During the Ming Dynasty, the Nüzhen had three major groups: Jianzhou, Haixi and Donghai. They lived in, respectively, the upper reaches of the Hun and the Suzi rivers, the middle and lower reaches of the Songhuajiang River and the valley of the Huifa River (located to the north of Kaiyuan, modern Liaoning Province), and, finally, the lower reaches of the Songhuajiang River and the vast area where the Heilongjiang River pours into the sea. The region where the Jianzhou inhabited was fertile in soil, and it grew practically all the drought-resistant crops. The Jianzhou group traded regularly with the Mongolians and the Koreans, as well as the Hans. It exported horses, cattle, pelts of marten and ginseng, in exchange for iron tools and daily necessities. In terms of economic development, it was much more advanced than any of the other Nüzhen groups. In 1583, Nurhachi of the Aisin Gioro clan was elected chief of the Jianzhou group. With Hetuala (modern Xinbin, Liaoning Province) as his base of operation, he annexed neighbouring tribes one by one. In 1593, Yehe (located in the area to the north of Kaiyuan), Hada (located in the area to the east of Kaiyuan) and other Haixi tribes attacked Nurhachi, in alliance with such Mongolian tribes as Horqin. Nurhachi defeated them all and became more powerful as a result. From then on and for more than twenty years, his power increased steadily until he controlled practically all the Nüzhen territories. In 1616 he, having won great victories in a war of unification, declared himself Great Khan, established his capital at Hetuala, renamed Xingjing, and called his regime Great Jin, known as Later Jin to historians. Later Jin was then a local, independent regime within the territory of China other than the Ming regime. At this time the Nüzhen had not yet acquired the name of "Manchu".

While expanding his power and influence, Nurhachi adopted such measures as registration and organization of civilian population, construction of city walls for defence, invention of a written language and enactment of statutes. Based upon the tribal *niulu* system, he developed an Eight Banner organization. In the past, whenever the Nüzhen marched as a military group or went out hunting, every ten participants were organized to form a basic unit known as *niulu*. Now, under Nurhachi's Eight Banner system, each *niulu* was expanded to include 300 persons; 5 *niulu* or 1,500 persons formed a *jiala*, and 5 *jiala* or 7,500 persons became a banner. There were altogether eight banners, each of which was identified by a specific colour of its flag: yellow, red, blue, white, yellow-bordered, red-bordered, blue-bordered and white-bordered. Appointed by Nurhachi, the head of a banner was one of his sons or nephews. The purpose of the Eight Banner system was to organize all the Nüzhen people in a military fashion, so that they could become more efficient as producers and as warriors. As a result of introducing this system, the military strength of the Nüzhen increased; so did their economic production. The system sped up the Nüzhen's social development; it also strengthened Nurhachi's position as their ruler.

Interestingly, this enormous development in the northeastern section of China did not attract the attention of the Ming government at all. At the time when Nurhachi was busy with the establishment of a new regime, Shen Zong, the Ming emperor, squandered money even though the treasury was virtually empty; he sent out eunuchs across the country to extort more and more even though his subjects had little for their own livelihood. Besides, he waged three wars in Ningxia, Korea and Guizhou.

For the investiture of the crown prince and other princes, plus their respective weddings, Shen Zong spent 9,340,000 taels of silver, not to mention the 2,700,000 taels spent on their costumes. For the purpose of collecting pearls and other valuables, he spent 24,000,000 taels more. At that time, the annual revenue from land taxation totalled about 4,000,000 taels. In other words, it would require six years' collection of land tax to come up with this enormous sum, provided, of course, that this collection was not used for any other purpose. He sent eunuchs to open up gold and silver mines, stipulating the amount of gold and silver that they had to produce, regardless of whether the mines had or had not gold or silver, or whatever amount the mines could actually produce. He also dispatched eunuchs to Guangdong to search for pearls and other valuables, to Lianghuai* to

---

* The name of one of the regions designated for the collection of gabelle in the Yuan Dynasty. During the Ming and Qing dynasties, it covered most of the districts in present-day Jiangsu, Anhui, Jiangxi, Hubei and Hunan provinces and part of Henan Province.

extort money from gabelle, and to all the commercial regions to set up tariff barriers so as to collect more. These eunuchs, by invoking the authority of the emperor, blackmailed as they wished. Not only did they rob people of their property and punish local officials under various excuses, they also arrested and killed people at will. In the end they could not but provoke the people's vigorous resistance. In 1599, the merchants in Linqing (modern Shandong Province), in protest against tax superintendent Ma Tang's ruthlessness, called a strike. They burned his office and nearly beat him to death. Chen Feng, who was sent to Huguang as a mine superintendent, simultaneously serving as a tax superintendent, suffered a similar fate. When collecting taxes at Wuchang, he was besieged in his residence by local inhabitants who, subsequently, arrested six of his henchmen and threw them into the Changjiang River. For more than a month, the tax superintendent did not dare to show up outside of his residence. In Suzhou, tax superintendent Sun Long wanted to increase taxes on looms, only to see many workers call a strike and close the workshops. Those workers who had lost their jobs because of the strike, under the leadership of a man named Ge Xian, surrounded Sun Long's office, beat to death several of his retainers, and burned to the ground the residence of Tang Xin, a local bully who had collaborated with the tax superintendent. In 1603, the workers in the Xishan Coal Mine went in groups to Beijing to demonstrate against mine superintendent Wang Chao. In 1606, the miners in Yunnan burned the office of the tax collector as a protest against mine superintendent Yang Rong. Yang Rong retaliated by suppression and killed more than one thousand miners in the process. More miners joined the struggle and, in alliance with the people in the area, burned Yang Rong's residence, killed its owner and threw his body into the fire, besides killing more than two hundred of his followers. The struggle waged by workers and merchants against mine and tax superintendents was a new class struggle, at a time when the feudal society of China had entered a period of decline.

Three wars were waged by Shen Zong, beginning in 1592. In that year, Bobai, the former deputy commander in Ningxia, made an alliance with the Tatars to challenge the authority of the Ming regime.

Jiaozi, the earliest paper money in the world

Flourishing Nanjing (part), showing the commercial prosperity of the capital city

Farming scene (part)

Mongolian cavalry in battle (part)

Ming Emperor Wanli's crown made of gold and silk (in Dingling Museum)

The earliest, biggest and best ancient Chinese woodcut, depicting the nine star gods (discovered in the Wood Tower in Zhuangxian County, Shanxi Province)

The Imperial Palace

A mural depicting *zaju*, poetic drama set tomusic, which flourished during the Yuan Dynasty (1271-1368)

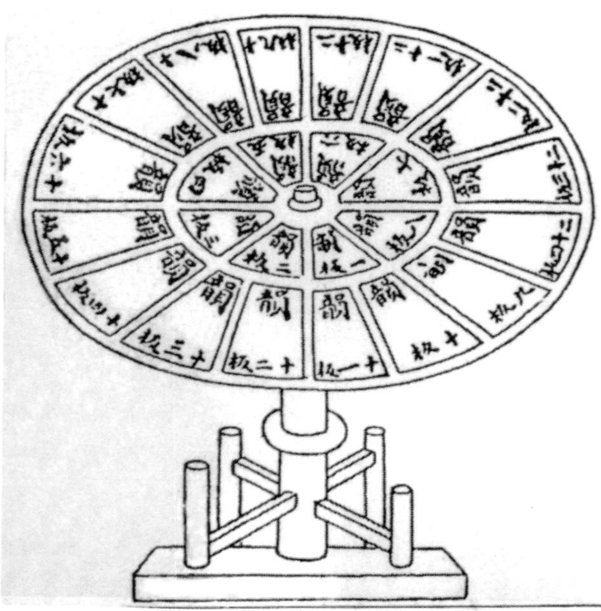

Typesetting frame with a revolving wheel, invented by Wang Zhen

The Terrace for Observing Stars (Dengfeng County, Henan Province)

The Badaling section of the Great Wall, built in the Ming Dynasty

The Kaifeng market, part of the *Riverside Scene at Qingming Festival*

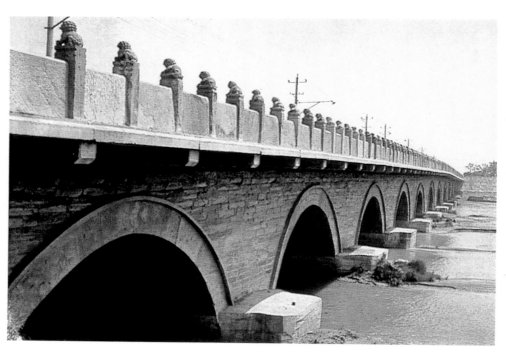

Lugouqiao (Marco Polo Bridge) in Beijing

A picture of the fifth Dalai Lama meeting the Qing Emperor Shunzhi

Zheng Chenggong accepting the surrender of Dutch colonialists in Tainan, Taiwan

A simple astronomical instrument invented by Guo Shoujing

The latter sent an expeditionary army to crush him and succeeded only after more than six months of fighting. In the same year, Hideyoshi of Japan, invaded Korea, which the Ming government dispatched troops to support. The war persisted for six years before it finally ended. In 1594, Yang Yinglong, a native officer in Bozhou (modern Zunyi County, Guizhou), refused to obey any more orders from the Ming government, and the latter responded by sending an expeditionary army. Almost six years had to elapse before the war came to an end. The enormous outlay in manpower and financial resources occasioned by the three wars further weakened the Ming regime.

During Shen Zong's reign, many key posts in the government were left vacant, and factional strifes among officials remained serious. For more than twenty years, the emperor did not grant audience to his ministers; too often were there no responsible officials in charge of this or that office, on both the central and the local levels. In 1611, the Six Boards of the Inner Chancery, the Censorate, the Supreme Court, the Office of Transmission and many organs on the local level were inadequately supplied with administrative officials. But this administrative paralysis did not prevent top officials from engaging in factional strifes. In 1594, Gu Xiancheng, a former senior secretary of the Board of Civil Office, joined with such eminent scholars as Gao Panlong and Qian Yiben to lecture at the Donglin Academy in Wuxi. Not only did these scholars speak candidly on current affairs, but they criticized contemporary leaders as well. They wanted reforms to be carried out in government, tax collection rationalized and rectified, and the power of high officials and influential gentry curtailed. Their proposals had an enormous impact, and they, therefore, were resented and ostracized by those in power, who called them "Men of the Donglin Party" and instigated political groups on the local level to suppress them. A factional strife ensued, leading to political disturbance and instability.

Political anarchy and costly military campaigns on the part of the Ming government provided Nurhachi with opportunities to attack it. In 1618, at the head of twenty thousand men of a combination of cavelry and infantry, Nurhachi captured the strategic Fushun (modern Liaoning Province) and the nearby fortifications. Shortly afterwards, he attacked Yaguguan (located to the southeast of Fushun) and captured Qinghecheng. Only then did the Ming government realize how serious the situation was. Quickly it ordered Yang Gao to take command and prepare for offensive action. But there were difficulties involving the raising of funds and the gathering of troops. Ten months had to elapse before Yang Gao succeeded in bringing together an army of 90,000 men. This army, plus a supporting unit of 10,000 men from Korea, marched towards Xingjing along four routes. Nurhachi responded with all of his Eight Banners—60,000 men altogether—for the confrontation. In the summer of 1619, the two sides fought a ferocious battle at Sarhu (to the southeast of Fushun), and the Ming army was decisively defeated, losing 310 commanders and 45,800 men. This battle proved to be a turning point, as it enhanced the morale of the Nüzhen, while reducing sharply the strength of the Ming regime.

The Ming government deteriorated further during Emperor Xi Zong's reign (1620-27). The emperor placed confidence in a eunuch named Wei Zhongxian, who was in charge of not only the Eastern Chamber but all the incoming petitions and memorials as well. He was given a free hand to place his diehard followers in the Six Boards and the offices of the governors and governors-general. Altogether they formed a eunuch clique. They ruthlessly persecuted persons whose names they had on a list—those who held high positions but refused to collaborate with them, or those whom they simply disliked. At this time Gu Xiancheng, the leader of the Donglin Party, was already dead, and other leaders like Zhao Nanxing, Zou Yuanbiao and Gao Panlong were either exiled, compelled to resign, or forced to commit suicide. In 1626, Wei Zhongxian sent a man to Suzhou to arrest a member of the Donglin Party named Zhou Shunchang. The people in Suzhou responded by storming into the governor's office, and governor Mao Yilu fled in panic.

A corrupt regime like this was face to face with an energetic, newly-arising power known as the Later Jin; it could not do much even if it had the best military commanders. Commanders who succeeded Yang Gao, such as Xiong Tingbi and Sun Chengzong, were all able and talented in military affairs; they were good organizers capable of putting up stiff resistance. But all of them were dismissed from their respective commands after only a brief tenure of office. At the time when Sun Chengzong was in charge, he, assisted by his chief lieutenant Yuan Chonghuan, strengthened the city wall of Ningyuan and other fortifications, in preparation for the defence of the key line between Jinzhou and Ningyuan, so as to make sure that the Shanhaiguan Pass would be safe. But his successor, a member of the eunuch clique named Gao Di, had no understanding whatsoever of the measures hitherto undertaken. In the spring of 1626, Nurhachi attacked at the head of 130,000 men. Gao Di wanted to abandon all the areas in the Northeast and retreat southward to defend the Shanhaiguan Pass. He ordered garrison troops in Jinzhou, Xingshan, Songshan, and other places to destroy all the defence fortifications, discard the military supplies, and force the inhabitants to move southward by way of the Shanhaiguan Pass. Yuan Chonghuan defied the order by insisting on defending Ningyuan and in the end succeeded in defeating the enemy. Unfortunately, an able general like him soon became a target of jealousy and resentment and was dismissed from office.

In 1625 Nurhachi moved his capital to Shenyang, known as Shengjing from then on. Having suffered serious injuries in the battle of Ningyuan, he withdrew to Aiyangbao (approximately forty *li* from Shenyang) where he died. Nurhachi was succeeded by Huangtaiji who, in 1627, renewed the attack on Ningyuan and lay siege on Jinzhou. Then Yuan Chonghuan was still Ningyuan's defender, and Huangtaiji, having suffered reverses on a large scale, decided to withdraw. Two months after the battle, the Ming emperor Xi Zong died and was succeeded by Si Zong. The new sovereign was also known as Emperor Chong Zhen, coming to the throne at a time when the situation had become critical. He had to face not only a threat posed by the Later Jin but also peasant uprisings of great intensity, against which he had to devote most of his energy.

Emperor Chong Zhen reinstated Yuan Chonghuan who had been dismissed from his office previously. Yuan was appointed Minister of War with special responsibility for the military campaign in the Northeast. He adopted a long-range plan for defence, strengthened the line between Jinzhou and Ningyuan, and strove to recover those territories that the Ming forces had lost in the battle of Sarhu. In 1629 Huangtaiji, having bypassed the defence line established by Yuan Chonghuan, crossed the Great Wall via Inner Mongolia, and captured Zunhua in North Zhili. Quickly Yuan Chonghuan led his troops to reinforce the defence. But Emperor Chong Zhen, falling into a trap set up by Huangtaiji to sow discord and distrust among the Ming camp, arrested Yuan Chonghuan and condemned him to death. Meanwhile, Huangtaiji continued the offensive and succeeded in capturing Yongping, Qian'an and Luanzhou. However, as Sun Chengzong was reinstated to the commandership, the Later Jin forces could not break the defence at the Shanhaiguan Pass. Shortly afterwards, Sun Chengzong recovered Yongping and other cities, and the Later Jin forces had to withdraw.

In 1636 Huangtaiji changed his title from "Great Khan" to "Emperor" and named his new regime "Great Qing". The Jianzhou group of Nüzhen was, from then on, known as "Manchu". Shortly afterwards, new organs of government were added, such as the Six Boards, the Censorate, and the Board of Minorities Affairs. In 1636 and again in 1638, Huangtaiji sent troops to breach Xifengkou, a pass of the Great Wall, and launched attacks against the Ming regime. In their first campaign, the attacking Qing forces captured Changping and went as far as the area outside the west city gate of Beijing. In their second campaign, they went as far as Shandong Province. Having been dismissed from office, Sun Chengzong lived in his native city of Gaoyang at the time; he committed suicide when the city fell to the invaders. The Qing troops retreated northward only after they had captured large numbers of people and animals, plus gold and silver. They devastated many cities and towns that they did not wish to occupy.

In 1639 the Ming government ordered Hong Chengchou to defend all the areas to the north of the Shanhaiguan Pass. Huangtaiji, meanwhile, was determined to destroy the defence line between Jinzhou and Ningyuan as a prelude to the seizure of the Shanhaiguan Pass. In 1641 he dispatched large forces to besiege Jinzhou, and Hong Chengchou personally led his men to that city for defence. The battle lasted more than six months, and in the end the Ming forces were decisively defeated. Many generals heroically sacrificed their lives, but Hong Chengchou, the top commander, surrendered after he had been captured alive. Now that Jinzhou was lost to the enemy, all the defence lines north of the Shanhaiguan Pass were breached, and the invading Qing forces began to knock at the pass itself.

In 1642 the Qing forces again crossed the Great Wall in force, capturing many cities in Zhili and Shandong. As before, the invaders took into possession large numbers of people and animals, plus gold and silver, before they retreated to the Northeast.

Both Nurhachi and Huangtaiji were outstanding leaders in military affairs. The latter was an outstanding statesman besides. By repeatedly penetrating deep into North China, he swept aside all the obstacles beyond the Shanhaiguan Pass. He organized for the purpose of production those Han people who had surrendered to him; he recruited able-bodied Mongolians and Hans to form Mongolian Eight Banners and Han Eight Banners, respectively. He treated well the Ming generals who had switched their loyalty to him, such as Hong Chengchou, Kong Youde, Geng Zhongming and Shang Kexi, all of whom helped the Manchus militarily and made no small contributions to the establishment of the Qing Dynasty.

Huangtaiji died in the fall of 1643 and was succeeded by his third son Fu Lin. Fu Lin, after the Qing forces had entered North China, was known as Emperor Shun Zhi. Six months after he ascended the throne, peasant insurgents led by Li Zicheng entered Beijing. The situation in China changed drastically.

The peasant uprisings towards the end of the Ming Dynasty began in Shaanxi Province. They were the net result of a gradual development that had persisted for a long time. In 1627, Shaanxi suffered a severe drought, and acres of land could not yield one kernel of grain. But the government continued to put pressure on the peasants to pay rent and taxes, and such pressure precipitated a rebellion. Peasant Wang Er gathered several hundred hungry men to attack Chengcheng and killed the magistrate. The very next year, Wang Jiayin staged an uprising at Fugu, and Gao Yingxiang, Wang

Zuogua and Zhang Xianzhong did likewise in Ansai, Yichuan and Yan'an, respectively. In a short period of time, several dozen uprisings erupted, and thousands of hungry peasants participated in the battle for survival.

In 1631 the Ming government dispatched troops to suppress the widespread revolts. The insurgents moved from Shaanxi to Shanxi and fought on both sides of the Huanghe River. As each of the insurgent groups fought alone without coordination, they were easily defeated by the government troops one by one, and many important leaders lost their lives as a result. Gao Yingxiang, in alliance with Zhang Xianzhong, Ma Shouying and Luo Rucai, broke through the government encirclement, crossed the Huanghe River at Mianchi, and then, after passing through western Henan and northern Huguang, reached southern Shaanxi. Once again, they were surrounded. Mistakenly Gao Yingxiang led his men into the Chexiangxia Gorge, Xing'an (modern Antang, Shaanxi Province), wherefrom they could not escape. Li Zicheng feigned surrender and, by bribing government troops, was allowed to leave. Shortly afterwards, the insurrectionary army expanded to become a powerful force of several hundred thousand men.

In 1635 the peasant army led by Gao Yingxiang, Zhang Xianzhong and Li Zicheng, fought its way towards Fengyang, original home of the royal house of the Ming, where it burned and destroyed the tombs of the reigning emperor's ancestors. This action indicated the rebel leaders' determination to overthrow the Ming Dynasty. Later, Zhang Xianzhong led his army eastward and captured Luzhou (modern Hefei City, Anhui) and Anqing. Gao Yingxiang and Li Zicheng, on the other hand, returned to southern Shaanxi, where they repeatedly defeated the Ming army sent to exterminate them. The next year, Gao was captured in an ambush and subsequently executed. The remainder of his forces supported Li Zicheng as their leader who, from then on, took over the title "Dashing King" which had been Gao's. Li's forces fought in various places in Shaanxi and Sichuan until, in 1638, they were defeated at Zitong, northern Sichuan. Only Li Zicheng and eighteen of his close followers managed to escape on horseback, while the rest was dispersed. To forestall the government's attack, Li and his close followers hid themselves in the Shangluo Mountains, Shaanxi Province. Previously, Zhang Xianzhong, having been defeated, feigned surrender to the government in Huguang. The tide of peasant uprisings reached a low ebb.

In the summer of 1639 Zhang Xianzhong rose again at Gucheng (in modern Hubei), Huguang Province. Meanwhile, Li Zicheng emerged from the mountains, once again gathering followers to stage another uprising. Zhang Xianzhong, having fought for several years in Huguang, Shaanxi, and Sichuan, declared himself emperor at Chengdu, Sichuan Province, in 1643. He called his regime "Da Xi" ("Great West"). Li Zicheng, while marching through the Yaohan mountains, was once again defeated by the Ming forces. With fifty of his followers, he broke through the encirclement on horseback and entered Henan. Then a severe famine occurred in Henan, and thousands of hungry people joined him. Many intellectuals, who had been ostracized by the corrupt Ming regime, also enlisted under Li Zicheng's banner, helping in planning strategy. From then on, the insurrectionary army raised such slogans as "equalization of landownership" and "freedom from taxation". It declared that "virtuous scholars will be respected", "despots will be eliminated and the people protected", and "there will be no violation of people's lives and property". These slogans indicated that the warfare waged by the peasants had made a qualitative jump.

In 1641, while the Ming forces were concentrating on attacking Zhang Xianzhong in Sichuan, Li Zicheng, taking advantage of the void in Henan, attacked and seized Luoyang. The Prince of Fu—Zhu Changxun—was killed, and all the grain, gold, silver and other valuables were taken from his mansion and then distributed among hungry people, who enthusiastically supported Li's forces. In 1642, after his army had captured Xiangyang, Li Zicheng declared himself King of Xinshun and established positions for civil and military officials. In 1643, the insurrectionary army left Xiangyang and marched northward; it passed through Henan and then captured Xi'an. Early in 1644 Li Zicheng changed the name of Xi'an to Xijing. He called his regime the Great Shun and himself the King of Great Shun. He conferred ranks and titles on those who had performed meritorious deeds; he introduced the civil service examination system as a means to elevate scholars. Shortly afterwards, he left Xi'an and marched his army towards Beijing. There was little resistance from the Ming forces, and in a little more than one month, he and his men reached the suburbs of Beijing. On the 18th day of the 3rd lunar month, Li's army succeeded in seizing the outer city of Beijing. Early next morning Emperor Chong Zhen hung himself at the foot of the Coal Hill (known as Jing Hill today) behind the imperial palace. Li Zicheng personally led his army into the city, and the Ming Dynasty perished in the storm of peasant uprisings.

As the corruption of the feudal system, feudal governance and feudal rulers—especially the hypocritical and cruel aspect of it—was revealed unmistakable for the world to see towards the end of the Ming Dynasty, there were philosophers, men of letters and historians who exposed or criticized the social evils they saw, in various degrees and, in some cases, in a highly concentrated form.

Li Zhi (1527-1602), also known as Li Zhuowu, was a prolific writer, his representative works being *Book Burning, Book Holding, Supplement to Book Burning* and *Supplement to Book Holding*. He was a fighter who dared to oppose feudalism openly. He satirized not only those self-styled Neo-Confucians but also powerful officials. He criticized the viw of "heavenly reason" vis-a-vis "human desire"—a view that was held by Cheng Hao, Cheng Yi, Zhu Xi, Lu Jiuyuan and Wang Shouren. He exposed the hypocrisy of speaking loudly about "benevolence" and "righteousness" while paying no attention to the life or death of common men. He said that scholars, beginning with the Tang-Song period, only echoed Confucius regarding what was right or wrong without making their own judgement. He criticized all those who elevated the sayings of Confucius to the level of infallible feudal canon, and he wanted nothing better than to pull down the tablet of Confucius from the altar of feudal ideology. He opposed the condemnation of Qin Shi Huang by all the Confucians throughout history; he, instead, praised the Qin monarch as the "most unique emperor" since history began. He admired Zhuo Wenjun for her foresightedness when she selected Sima Xiangru as her husband, even though the self-righteous, diehard pedants had characterized her behaviour as a violation of good customs.* Nevertheless, Li Zhi was an idealist. He did not have the courage to oppose the feudal concept of a subject's obligation to be loyal to the sovereign, and he did not provide a new ideal as a substitute for feudal ethics. His contribution lies in the fact that he exposed the ugly side of feudal rulers, and dealt a crushing blow to feudal ethics. Frightened, these feudal rulers put him to death on trumped-up charges when he was seventy-six years old. After his death, repeated orders were issued to burn all his books, but somehow his works survived. Later, other writers invoked his name for their own works, believing that a book bearing his name would enjoy greater prestige.

Tang Xianzu (1550-1616) was one of China's best dramatists. Among his works were *Peony Pavilion, Purple Hairpin, The Dream of Handan* and *The Southern Tributary State*; together they are referred to as *Four Dreams of Linchuan.* Of the four, *Peony Pavilion* is his most representative work. It is a story of a young woman named Du Liniang who, shackled by feudal ethics, resolutely struggles for romantic love and happiness. As the only daughter of Du Bao, Prefect of Nan'an, she lived in her father's official mansion for three years without even visiting the garden, being so enslaved by the feudal concept of "proper behaviour". Living under such lonely, joyless circumstances, she, as a girl of adolescence, cannot but feel sorrowful and unhappy. One day, she ventures into the garden and the bright, beautiful spring suddenly wakes her up to her youth. She does not actually meet any young man, of course; the young man only appears in her

---

* Zhuo Wenjun, a native of Linqiong (present Qionglai County in Sichuan Province) and a granddaughter of the Prince of Zhou, was widowed as a young woman. A cultured and unorthodox woman who was musically gifted, she fell in love with a famous man of letters named Sima Xiangru (179-117 B.C.) and married him after they eloped to Chengdu. Her actions were unusual in several respects. Customarily in feudal China, widows did not remarry; in any case, women did not choose their own husbands; and princesses did not marry commoners. After some time, the couple returned to Linqiong where they reportedly lived happily after opening a wineshop where Zhuo Wenjun stood behind the counter to sell wine—again, an unusual occupation for a princess. The romance is a famous one in China.—*Trans.*

dream. She grasps the young man and will not let him go, only to wake up and see him disappear. From then on, she suffers a love sickness, of which she eventually dies. As a spirit, she finds the young man in her dream, who turns out to be a scholar named Liu Mengmei. She takes the initiative and expresses to him her love, and they are married as soon as her spirit reenters her body and she becomes alive again. In this story, the author, through the use of romanticism and imagination, made possible what in real life could not be realized. The struggle of a young woman for love, unchangeable through life and death despite all the obstacles, was a sharp and poignant challenge to feudal ethics. The story reveals not just the difficulty involving a young woman's search for love. It reflects the kind of ordeal people have to undergo just to enjoy the rights that are inherently theirs. It shows that even under the harshest circumstances people do not lose hope for a bright future. Subtly and in fine detail, the author presents a psychological drama as he reveals a young woman's innermost feelings in the way of a lyrical poem. Completed in 1598, the play was performed on stage across the country shortly afterwards. It has had an enduring influence on Chinese theatre for more than three hundred years.

Flowering Plum in a Golden Vase, a novel of considerable length, appeared sometime during Shen Zong's reign. Since the author referred to himself as "A Laughing Man from Lanling", probably he was a native of Lanling (modern Yixian, Shandong Province). Unfortunately, there is no way we can find out about his real name. Unlike *The Romance of the Three Kingdoms,* which was based on history, or *Outlaws of the Marsh* and *Journey to the West* which owed their sources to long-standing popular tales, *Flowering Plum* was the creation of one man who wrote about society as he saw it. Tracing the rise and fall of a powerful family that belongs to a man named Ximen Qing, the author describes the evil-doings of influential officials, despicable members of the gentry, local scoundrels and dishonest merchants—how they secretly plot with one another to kill people in order to obtain their wealth, illicitly appropriate other people's wives and daughters, and wheel and deal in litigation. These people are not hypocrites who wear Neo-Confucian masks; they have torn off the mask of feudal ethics; and they openly live a corrupt life and conduct criminal activities. In exposing the rotten life of the landlord class, the novel is certainly a success. Still, while exposing the seamy side of society, the author does not reveal his personal likes or dislikes: he does not make value judgement. Besides, he devotes a sizable space to homilies by Buddhist nuns, obscene songs by prostitutes, and ponographic details. All this mars the artistic achievement of the novel itself.

Shortly after the appearance on the market of *Flowering Plum in a Golden Vase*, three other books, all by Feng Menglong (1574-1646), were also in circulation. The three books are: *Stories to Enlighten Men, Stories to Warn Men* and *Stories to Awaken Men*, each of which has 40 stories. These books contain the vernacular tales of the Song-Yuan period and their imitations written during the Ming Dynasty, all of which were edited or rewritten before incorporated into the new volumes. Some of the stories deal with internal struggle among the feudal ruling class, exposing its cruelty and hypocrisy; others describe the true feelings of men and women in love and the oppression that women suffer under feudalism. They often express a fatalistic point of view, and sometimes describe sex in a vulgar way. An admirer of Li Zhi, the author was a progressive in his thinking. Through the three books he edited, he contributed to the popularity of vernacular tales and similar stories.

During the reigns of Emperor Xi Zong and Emperor Chong Zhen, three voluminous works on history made their appearance. One was *A Record of Military Affairs* by Mao Yuanyi. Consisting of 240 *juan*, it was completed in 1621. It is a collection of all relevant materials on war theories, military strategies, battle tactics and war supplies throughout Chinese history. It is in fact a military history rich in source materials; it might be regarded as a military encyclopaedia of its time. The second book is a chronological history of the Ming Dynasty entitled *National Deliberations*, which has 100 *juan*. Tan Qian (1593-1657), the author, began work on this book in 1621. Written in the form of annals, it is one of the most important works on Chinese history. The third book was *A Collection of Essays on National Affairs During the Ming Dynasty*, edited by Chen Zilong (1608-47) and

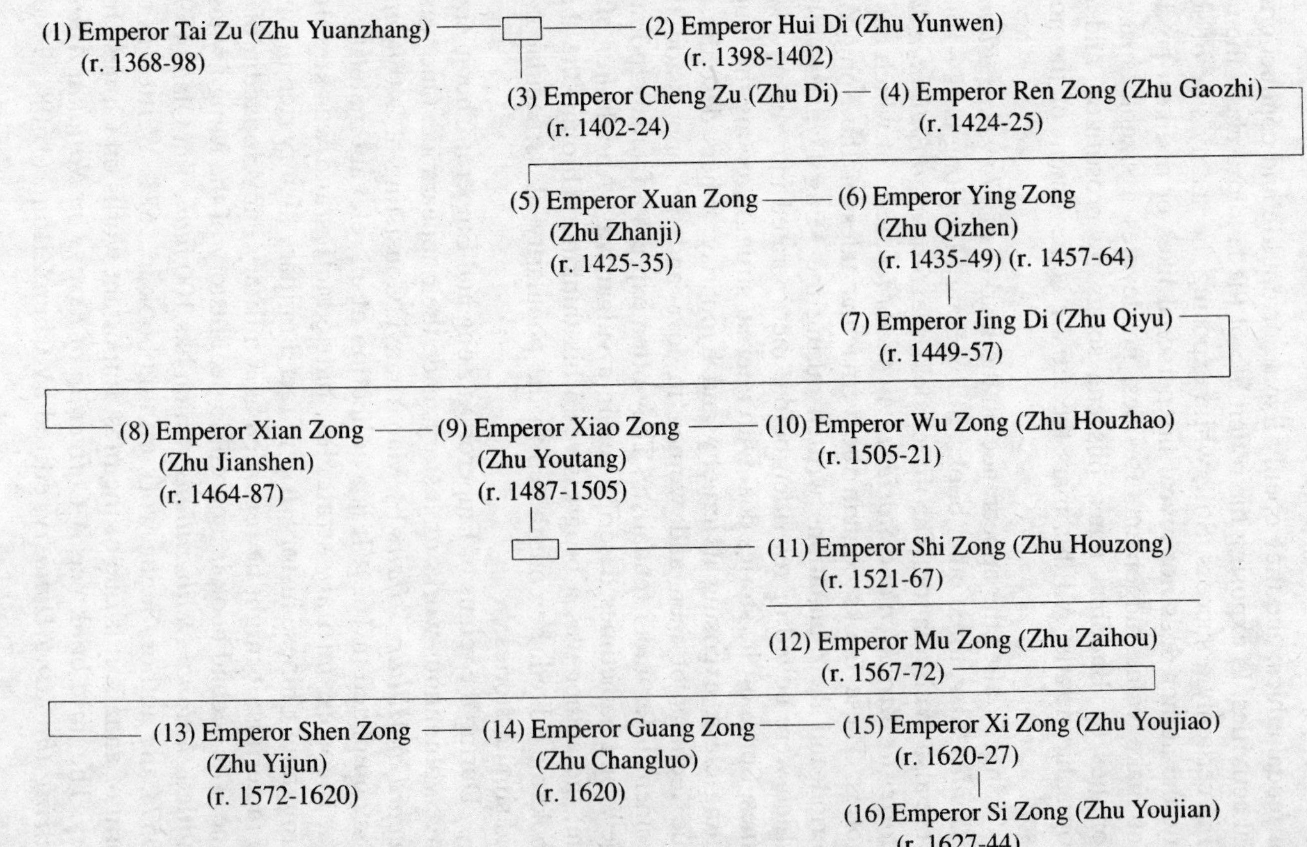
Genealogical Table of the Ming Dynasty
(1) Emperor Tai Zu (Zhu Yuanzhang)
(r. 1368-98)
(2) Emperor Hui Di (Zhu Yunwen)
(r. 1398-1402)
(3) Emperor Cheng Zu (Zhu Di)
(r. 1402-24)
(4) Emperor Ren Zong (Zhu Gaozhi)
(r. 1424-25)
(5) Emperor Xuan Zong
(Zhu Zhanji)
(r. 1425-35)
(6) Emperor Ying Zong
(Zhu Qizhen)
(r. 1435-49) (r. 1457-64)
(7) Emperor Jing Di (Zhu Qiyu)
(r. 1449-57)
(8) Emperor Xian Zong
(Zhu Jianshen)
(r. 1464-87)
(9) Emperor Xiao Zong
(Zhu Youtang)
(r. 1487-1505)
(10) Emperor Wu Zong (Zhu Houzhao)
(r. 1505-21)
(11) Emperor Shi Zong (Zhu Houzong)
(r. 1521-67)
(12) Emperor Mu Zong (Zhu Zaihou)
(r. 1567-72)
(13) Emperor Shen Zong
(Zhu Yijun)
(r. 1572-1620)
(14) Emperor Guang Zong
(Zhu Changluo)
(r. 1620)
(15) Emperor Xi Zong (Zhu Youjiao)
(r. 1620-27)
(16) Emperor Si Zong (Zhu Youjian)
(r. 1627-44)

others who completed the work in 1638. Consisting of 508 *juan*, it contains all the important works on national affairs, dating back to the very beginning of the Ming Dynasty. It is a collection of source materials on Ming politics and economics. In its own way, each of the three books attempted to rescue the Ming Dynasty from the crisis it faced. But the trend towards demise had gone too far for these books to do any good.

5. Peasant Regime of the Great Shun; Princes of the Southern Ming; Unification Activities During the Early Qing Dynasty

Upon entering Beijing late in the spring of 1644, Li Zicheng further developed his political regime, known as the Great Shun, that had its beginning in Xi'an. The key personnel in his government consisted of the peasant commanders who had fought with him, but he also brought in some of the ex-Ming officials. In the areas within his control, he carried out a policy of "taking money away from the rich and giving it to the poor". He opened the granaries and distributed their contents among the needy; he also encouraged peasants to recover the land which the landlords had illegally occupied. By means of this kind, he intended to carry out his policy of "equalization of landownership" and "exemption from rent and taxation". In addition, he took such measures as the cultivation of abandoned fields by unemployed peasants, besides forcing the corrupt Ming officials to hand over their illegal gains for military expenditures. However, he underestimated the strength of the Ming forces that remained, as he did not choose to take them on in hot pursuit, certainly not in an organized fashion. The measures he took in defence against the Qing forces to the north of the Shanhaiguan Pass were also inadequate. Meanwhile, the peasant regime itself, due to the rapid development of the revolution, underwent a change. The moment he entered Beijing, Li Zicheng wanted to be inaugurated as an emperor as early as possible. His chief adviser, Niu Jinxing, gathered around himself a large number of ex-Ming officials and busily prepared for Li's inauguration so that he himself could quickly assume the position of a prime minister and thus enjoy the power of the state. Outstanding generals like Liu Zongmin and Li Guo, who had fought hundreds of battles, were now only thinking of pleasure and comfort; their militancy wanted.

Bad policy and adverse internal development caused the peasant regime of Great Shun to lose the opportunity to strengthen itself. At the time when the peasant army entered Beijing, Wu Sangui, the Ming garrison commander at the Shanhaiguan Pass, had not decided what course to follow: his attitude was that of wait-and-see. Then, when he saw how the peasant army put pressure on the corrupt Ming officials to hand over their illegal gains and how the remainder of the Ming forces planned to counterattack, he decided to surrender to the Qing army and lead it into China proper by the route of Shanhaiguan. Jointly they would defeat the peasant regime, so he hoped. The Qing army, stationed north of Shanhaiguan and only waiting for an opportunity to attack, accepted Wu's surrender. Immediately it moved southward in two columns.

As Li Zicheng had no information about Wu Sangui's surrender to the Qing, he personally led an army of 60,000 men eastward from Beijing, attempting to force the Shanhaiguan commander to surrender to himself. While he was engaged in heavy fighting against Wu Sangui at Yipianshi near Shanhaiguan, a cavalry unit of the Qing army suddenly attacked him, a move that was totally unexpected. Unable to take any counter measures, he hurriedly withdrew and returned to Beijing. Meanwhile, the Qing army, led by the turncoat generals Wu Sangui, Shang Kexi and Kong Youde, crossed the Great Wall in force.

After returning to Beijing, Li Zicheng was most anxious to be inaugurated as emperor despite the military crisis. He left Beijing in a hurry the very next day after the inauguration, as he moved his army westward towards Shaanxi. The Prince of Rui (Dorgon) of the Qing followed in the wake and soon entered Beijing. In marching his army against Li Zicheng, Wu Sangui raised the slogan of "avenging our sovereign and fathers", a slogan that was meant to cover up his own capitulation to the Qing regime. After entering Beijing, the Qing regime itself also declared that it sought to "avenge the sovereign and fathers" on behalf of the Ming subjects. Through measures like this, it wished to ingratiate itself with the Han landlords, and win them over.

As the Qing regime became more or less stabilized, Dorgon proposed that the capital be moved to Beijing. Emperor Shun Zhi was invited to enter North China, as thanks were offered to Heaven and Earth, suggesting that the emperor was the sole sovereign of all of China. Dorgon, the emperor's uncle, was appointed regent who wielded the real power of the state, politically as well as militarily. It was then decided that Ajige, or the Prince of Ying, was to lead an army to attack Li Zicheng, while Duoduo, or the Prince of Yu, was to march southward to conquer South China.

After retreating from Beijing, the Great Shun army led by Li Zicheng suffered a series of internal dissensions, and its morale also went from bad to worse. In defending Tongguan and in the ensuing battle against the Qing attackers, it suffered reverses; it had no choice but to move to the Xiangyang region, Huguang Province. During the early summer of 1645, Li Zicheng retreated to Wuchang. Shortly afterwards, he went to the Jiugong Mountains, Tongshan County, where he was killed by the enemy in an ambush. Among the remainder of his following, the group led by Li Jin and Li Laiheng continued to fight for the next twenty years. Zhang Xianzhong, who had established the Great West regime in Sichuan, was defeated by the Qing forces in a battle fought in 1646. He was killed in action in the Fenghuang Mountains, Xichong. His surviving lieutenants, like Sun Kewang and Li Dingguo, realized that the Qing army was a much more dangerous enemy than the Ming regime and therefore decided to make an alliance with the Southern Ming to face the common foe.

The term "Southern Ming" comprises several ephemeral regimes in South China. In 1644, one month after Li Zicheng had entered Beijing, Ma Shiying, the Ming governor of Fengyang, and Shi Kefa, Minister of War in Nanjing, supported Zhu Yousong, or the Prince of Fu, to assume the imperial title in Nanjing. This was the first regime of the Southern Ming. Real power was in the hands of Ma Shiying and Ruan Dacheng who, at one time, were members of Wei Zhongxian's eunuch clique. They indulged in bribery and corruption and did their best to ostracize Shi Kefa. Furthermore, they induced the Prince of Fu to indulge in pleasure-seeking, paying no attention to the affairs of the state. There was also dissension among the generals who defended the Changjiang River, and the defence was weakened considerably as a result. When the Qing army, under the command of the Prince of Yu (Duoduo), marched southward, Shi Kefa put up a heroical resistance at Yangzhou. Being totally isolated from any support, he was captured when the city fell. He refused to surrender and was executed. In the summer of 1645, the Qing army entered Nanjing, and the first Southern Ming regime came to an end after only one year of existence.

Two months after the fall of Nanjing, two other Southern Ming regimes emerged in Fujian and Zhejiang, respectively. Huang Daozhou and Zheng Zhilong supported the Prince of Tang (Zhu Yujian) as emperor in Fujian, and Qian Suyue and Zhang Huangyan supported the Prince of Lu (Zhu Yihai) as "National Supervisor" in Shaoxing, Zhejiang. Zheng Zhilong, the real power behind the Prince of Tang's regime, only knew how to exploit people and nothing else; consequently there was not much hope here. In the summer of 1646, the Qing army attacked Fujian, and Zheng Zhilong surrendered. The Prince of Tang retreated to Tingzhou where he was captured and died shortly afterwards. As for the Prince of Lu's regime, it had at one time repulsed a Qing attack. However, its military commanders were arrogant and disobedient, and the power of the state fell into the hands of the prince's relatives and eunuchs. It suffered defeat when the Qing army attacked again. The Prince of Lu retreated first to Zhoushan and then to Jinmen Island. Eventually he went to Taiwan.

In the winter of 1646, Qu Shisi, the high-ranking Ming official then in charge of the defence of Guangdong and Guangxi, supported the Prince of Yongming (Zhu Youlang) as emperor at Zhaoqing (modern Gaoyao, Guangdong Province), with the reign title of Yongli. Though he was as incompetent as other Ming princes who had failed, Emperor Yongli's regime lasted for a period of fifteen years, thanks to the co-operation given to it by the remainder of the peasant army and the heroism of such generals as Qu Shisi and He Tengjiao. Li Dingguo, a former subordinate of Zhang Xianzhong's and Li Jin and Li Laiheng, Li Zicheng's former lieutenants—all of them had fought on the side of Emperor Yongli against the Qing forces. Early in 1662, Emperor Yongli was captured, and the last regime of Southern Ming came to an end. At this time the Qing Emperor Shun Zhi had already died, and Emperor Kang Xi had been in power for almost one year.

While fighting against the peasant army and the various regimes of Southern Ming, the Qing Dynasty stressed the importance of bringing about harmony among the ethnic minorities in China's border areas. In 1647, the Mongolian group of Chigin and the Uygurs in Xinjiang sent envoys to pay tribute, indicating their fealty to the new regime. In the same year, the two leaders in Tibet, Dalai Lama and Panchen Lama, also sent envoys to present native products. In 1651, the Qing court dispatched officials to invite Dalai Lama to Beijing where he lived for many years. In 1655, the Mongolian group of Khalkha sent envoys to pay tribute and pledge fealty. After the successful suppression of the peasant uprisings and the extermination of the various Southern Ming regimes, there were only two obstacles to the unification of China. One involved Yunnan, Guizhou, Guangdong and Fujian, and the other concerned Taiwan.

Because of his contribution to the anti-Ming campaigns, the turncoat general Wu Sangui was titled Prince of Pingxi, who had under his jurisdiction the provinces of Yunnan and Guizhou. The three generations of Geng Zhongming, Geng Jimao and Geng Jinzhong, each titled Prince of Jingnan, controlled Fujian. Shang Kexi and his son Shang Zhixin, successively titled Prince of Pingnan, occupied Guangdong. Over any of these territories the Qing government had no effective control. Wu Sangui could appoint and dismiss his own officials, organize and train his own army; the Boards of Civil Office and War in Beijing had no say on these matters at all. In fact, Wu Sangui and others had become separatist regimes in direct confrontation with Beijing. In 1673, when Emperor Kang Xi decided to take back their fiefs, they revolted. For a while, they seemed to be powerful and mighty, and the rebellion was not crushed until 1681. Yunnan and the other provinces were finally brought under the Qing Dynasty's direct control.

Taiwan was Zheng Chenggong's base of operation against the Qing regime. Zheng Chenggong was the son of Zheng Zhilong but held a different political view from that of his father. After the father had surrendered to the Qing, the son led more than ninety of his followers to Nan'ao, Guangdong Province, where he began his anti-Qing activities. The small number of his initial followers quickly grew to scores of thousands. First, he established the anti-Qing bases in Jinmen and Xiamen; and then, in coordination with Zhang Huangyan who supported the Prince of Lu, he thrice moved northward to attack the coastal areas of Zhejiang and the lower Changjiang. For the purpose of conducting a protracted war, he, in 1661, sailed across the sea to Taiwan where he expelled the Dutch colonialists who then illegally occupied the island. On the island of Taiwan, he proceeded with political, economic and cultural reconstruction. Not until 1683 when his grandson Zheng Keshuang was in charge did Taiwan finally succumb to the Qing forces. Taiwan and the mainland were once again united, and the unification effort of the Qing government was crowned with success.

The political chaos prevalent during the dynastic change from the Ming to the Qing was long and intense. From a historical perspective, it presented a series of important questions. To answer these questions, a number of great thinkers emerged, such as Fang Yizhi, Wang Fuzhi, Gu Yanwu, Huang Zongxi, Tang Zhen and Yan Yuan.

Both Fang Yizhi (1611-71) and Wang Fuzhi (1619-92) had personally participated in the anti-Qing movement. Both were outstanding thinkers of the materialist school. Besides, Fang was a scientist, and Wang a historian. Both believe that the universe consists of matter, and it has not been created by God or man's consciousness. Following traditional phraseology, they call matter "*qi*", or "vitality", which, says Fang Yizhi, is none other than "fire". According to Fang, "fire" itself contains contradictions that are in fact the source of motion in the material world. As nature and society are in a continual process of motion, man's knowledge, which is based upon man's continuous observation of the laws that govern things, will also increase. The gathering and dispersion of "vitality", says Wang Fuzhi, is in itself a revelation of the objective laws that govern the motion of matter. The motion of things becomes richer and richer with the passage of time; in the process of development, a new stage is reached, only to be replaced by a newer one. Though the water in a river flows continuously and endlessly, today's water in the river is no longer yesterday's. Society continues to make progress, and the new things of today have grown out of certain aspects of the old things of yesterday. Wang Fuzhi is eloquent in historical criticism; sometimes he combines knowledge of history with personal observation to reach independent judgements of his own. He says, "Land should not be appropriated by the ruler of the country as his private property," indicating that the tiller should own the land he tills. A viewpoint of this kind was indeed very progressive for its time. Fang Yizhi wrote several books, his representative works being *Understanding the Literary Expositor* and *Yaodipao Village*. Wang Fuzhi was often referred to as Master Chuanshan. Among his works were *Yellow Book, Nightmare, Unauthorized Commentary on the "Book of Changes", Thought and Question, Comments on "History as a Mirror"* and *Comments on the History of the Song Dynasty*.

Gu Yanwu (1613-82) was often referred to as Master Tinglin. Actively opposing the Qing regime all his life, he was an outstanding historian who stood for "learning for the purpose of utilization". "Every individual is responsible for the rise or fall of his country," he says, and the individual should regard the affairs of the state as his own. Gu Yanwu had nothing but contempt for those who, like a slave or servant, pledged fealty only to one family or one dynasty. Through the study of history, plus his own observation of geography, customs and products of different regions in China, he analyses past and contemporary reforms, criticizing obsolete social systems, and points out the problems existing in society, and expresses his own social ideals. In 1639, he began the writing of *Zhaocheng Gazette* and *The Merits and Drawbacks of Different Regions in China*. He describes each region's geographical conditions, mountains, rivers and natural fortresses, irrigation and water conservancy, products, taxation and military defence. *The Daily Accumulated Knowledge* is his representative work which, he says, "would be hidden in a famous mountain, waiting to be discovered by those who want to change the world for the better". "It would be circulated," he continues, "when a true, benign ruler emerges." He also makes concrete proposals for political reform. In philosophy, he believes that "vitality permeates throughout the universe", or in other words, consciousness derives its origin from matter.

Though he had materialist leanings, he was not systematic in his presentation. Contemporary with Gu Yanwu was Gu Zuyu (1631-92), also a historian who believed in "learning for the purpose of utilization". He devoted more than thirty years of his life to the writing of a book entitled *Essentials of Historical Geography*, consisting of 130 *juan*. It has remained an outstanding work on the military history of China and historical geography. Another contemporary of Gu Yanwu's was Ma Su (1621-73). He was also a historian interested in the betterment of the world. His work, *An Interpretation of History*, consists of 160 *juan*. It is detailed on the rise and fall of different kingdoms during the pre-Qin period; it is also detailed on the similarities and differences between different schools of philosophy during the same period. In the use of historical materials, the author views Confucian classics, history and philosophy with impartiality. As for the organization of his book, he combines different forms in history writing and comes out with a composite form of his own. The book has remained a most useful work on pre-Qin history.

Huang Zongxi (1610-95), often referred to as Master Lizhou, was a great political thinker as well as a historian. During his early years, he fought uncompromisingly against Wei Zhongxian's eunuch clique. He fought against the Qing army too when the latter marched southward to annex South China. Later, he summarized his political thought in a brilliant, anti-feudal work entitled *A Ming Barbarian Waiting for a Visitor*. In this book he condemns feudal monarchs for their attempt to "appropriate for themselves all the good things in the world, while leaving to others all the harmful things in the world". It is this kind of attitude, he says, that really brings harm to the world. He criticizes feudal laws as "laws of a single family" rather than "universal laws" because they are intended to satisfy the selfish desires of monarchs at the expense of the people's interests. He wants politics to be what it ought to be, namely, an instrument for public good. He regards the division between sovereign and subject, between officials and common men, as no more than a division of labour. Political administration should be in the hands of a powerful, virtuous premier, he says, and schools, serving as a forum of public opinion, should have the added function of supervising governmental activities. All in all, this book amounts to a declaration of human rights at a time of feudal decline; it remained a source of inspiration to Chinese youth when a movement for democracy developed two hundred years later. Later in his life, Huang Zongxi worked diligently on the history of the Ming. He wrote *Cases in the History of the Ming* (244 *juan*) and *Ming Literature* (482 *juan*). Another book, *The Ideological Controversy During the Ming Dynasty* (62 *juan*), was a pioneer work in its field. He also wrote *The Ideological Controversy of the Song-Yuan Period*, but the book was never completed. Tang Zhen (1630-1704) wrote a book entitled *Private Thoughts*, in which he courageously condemns the entire feudal system, going as far as saying that "all the monarchs for the past two thousand years were none better than bandits and thieves". In many respects, his political thought is similar to Huang Zongxi's.

Yan Yuan (1635-1704), also known as Yan Xizhai, advocated the acquirement of practical knowledge through practice and action rather than through the mere reading of books. He pointed out the contrast between two worlds, the world of "fancy" and the world of "matter" or "reality". In the former world, people speak for the sake of speech, believe in superstition, and employ rigid dogma to smother people's creativity. In the latter world, farmers till the fields, tailors make clothes, workers construct roads, physicians take care of patients, etc.—it is a world full of life and work, as each of the participants makes his own contribution to society. The author predicts that the former world will fall and will in due course be replaced by the latter world. As for his thought on social economy, he believes that a land system will develop, in which "all land in the world will be enjoyed by all the people in the world". Philosophically, he regards "vitality" as the essence of all the objects in the universe, and "reason" as the law that exists a priori in all objects and things. "Reason" cannot exist independent of objects and things, he says. Thus he severely criticizes the Neo-Confucianism of the Song and Ming dynasties and, from the beginning to the end, regards himself as an ideological opponent of such philosophers as Cheng Hao, Cheng Yi, Zhu Xi, Lu Jiuyuan and Wang Shouren.

Amid the tide of progressive thought, there was, in the field of literature, a book entitled *Strange Tales from a Lonely Studio*. Pu

Songling (1640-1715), the author, was also known as Pu Liuxian who hailed from Zichuan (modern Zibo, Shandong Province). Consisting of nearly 500 tales, the book was, basically speaking, completed in 1680. Most of the tales describe the violent interference with young people's love affairs by feudal ethics and the resistance young people put up in quest of their own happiness. They also describe the cruel oppression people suffer under feudal governance and the stifling of talents under the civil service examination system. The author uses a combination of the literary language of classical beauty and refined vernacular of his day to portray lively characters in his stories. Thus in content as well as in artistic form, the book is a great accomplishment.

Among the men of letters early during the Qing Dynasty were Qu Dajun (1629-96) and Wei Xi (1624-80). The former's poetry and the latter's prose, which reflect the reality of their time, are characterized by an artistic skill of the highest quality. Wu Weiye (1609-71), also known as Wu Meicun, was a famous poet, particularly noted for his seven-character lines.

In conclusion, it might be said that the progressive thought as expressed by Fang Yizhi and others was the major contribution to culture during the period of later Ming and early Qing. The contribution was particularly significant in view of its opposition to what the feudal rulers stood for at that time. It is true that the thought as expressed by Fang Yizhi and others had its limitations and, due to the immaturity of historical conditions, could not develop further. Nevertheless, it heralded the inevitable change that was forthcoming. As the history of the Qing proves, the change was a change for the worse, certainly not a change for the better.

6. Qing Rule Strengthened

Beginning in 1683 when it finally unified China, the Qing regime took various measures to strengthen its rule. Not until 1774 when Wang Lun staged an armed uprising did anything eventful take place.

The various Qing institutions were fairly well established at the time when it moved its capital to Beijing. Slowly and gradually they became more complete upon China's unification. Government institutions included the Inner Chancery, the Six Boards, the Censorate and the Supreme Court, all of which were inherited from the Ming Dynasty and adopted with some modifications. In the Innr Chencery there were Grand Secretaries, Assistant Grand Secretaries and Secretaries, who could be either Manchu or Han, but the Manchus held the real power. Hans as well as Manchus were appointed ministers, vice-ministers and censors. Only in the organs below the level of the Inner Chancery and the Six Boards was there the provision that some Mongolians may be also employed. The Inner Chancery held a higher position than its Ming counterpart, but it was not the highest policy-making organ in the government. During the early Qing period, the highest organ of the government was the Conference of Princes Regent, established before the Manchus entered Beijing. It consisted of members of the Manchu aristocracy who were charged with the responsibility of presenting policy options for the emperor to act upon. The Privy Chamber was established in 1729; not until 1732 was it formally named the Privy Council. Emperor Yong Zheng established the organ as a means to strengthen his personal rule at the expense of the power of the Manchu aristocracy, as the newly created organ was meant to replace the Conference of Princes Regent. Serving in the Privy Council was a Grand Minister of the emperor's own choice who could act or issue orders upon the emperor's personal command. Whenever an important event of military nature ensued, a specially selected Grand Minsiter, normally a Manchu, would be put in charge. The paramount position of the Manchus in matters military and their privileged position in politics characterized the Qing rule. It cannot be denied, however, that while maintaining the privileged position of the Manchu aristocracy, the Qing regime also found it necessary to consider the interests of Chinese landlords and leaders of the ethnic minorities. Essentially it was a regime that, using the Manchu aristocracy as the core, united the ruling classes of all the ethnic groups in China.

The governor-general was the highest official on the local level, at the head of one, two or three provinces. The governor headed only one province, and his position was a little below the governor-general's. Legally, however, their positions were parallel, as the governor-general had no jurisdictional control over the governor. Each was in charge of the military as well as civil affairs within his jurisdiction. Under each were the administrative commissioner and the judicial commissioner, in charge of the administrative and the judicial functions, respectively. Below a province were prefectures and counties, headed by prefects and magistrates, respectively. Early during the Qing Dynasty, all the governors-general were Manchu, but the governors could be either Manchu or Han, at a ratio of approximately fifty-fifty. Later, however, some Han people were appointed governors-general, and more as governors. Most of the prefects and magistrates were Han.

On the lowest level of territorial administration, the Qing regime put into practice a *bao-jia* system. According to the *bao-jia* law promulgated in 1757, every ten households were organized as a *pai*; every ten *pai* formed a *jia*, and every ten *jia* became a *bao*. The leaders of the *pai, jia,* and *bao* were chosen from local landlords or heads of large clans. Their responsibility was to watch all the inhabitants within their respective jurisdictions. A tablet was posted on the front door of each household, and on the tablet were written the name of the household head, his occupation, and the number of people in the household. Whenever a member departed from the household or moved to live in another residence, such fact must be reported to relevant authorities. The registration and organization of inhabitants in groups of ten and five had their beginning as early as the Qin-Han period and were enforced throughout subsequent dynasties. The purpose was the organization of all the available labour force for governmental duties. As far as the *bao-jia* system of the Qing Dynasty was concerned, the emphasis was on the "prevention of banditry". This marked a very important change.

At the beginning, the Qing Dynasty enforced the Ming statutes. In 1646, the *Code of the Great Qing* was completed; it was repeatedly revised during the reigns of Kang Xi and Yong Zheng. In 1740, during the reign of Emperor Qian Long, the *Statutes of the Great Qing*, consisting of 47 *juan* and 226 categories, was completed. In addition to the regulations normally found in the legal codes of the previous feudal dynasties, the Qing document contained elements of oppression based upon the difference in ethnic groups. For instance, the Manchus were leniently treated whenever punishments were imposed for crimes committed. In the case of the Manchus, there were such leniencies as "substitute pnishment" and "deferred punishment"—leniencies that were denied to other ethnic groups. There were specially constructed jails for the Manchus, and the living conditions in these jails were generally better than those in other jails.

As for the recruitment of governmental officials, the Qing Dynasty followed the Ming example by putting into practice the civil service examination system. In addition, it had the so-called contribution system and the special examination system. Under the former system, a person could make contributions to the government, in the form of either cash or grain, and would then be rewarded with a promotion or a governmental post to hold. Under the special examination system there were three categories: scholarship and literature, government, and virtuous conduct. The examination for scholarship and literature was given twice, one in 1679 and one in 1736. Candidates for the examination had to be recommended either by officials in the nation's capital whose ranks were third degree or above, or by the highest officials in the local government, namely, governors-general and governors. Only those who were outstanding in learning and personal conduct, besides being talented in writing, would have a chance to be recommended. Having passed the examination, the recommendee would be rewarded with an official appointment.

In military matters, the main force for fighting was still the Manchu, Mongolian and Han Eight Banners even after the Qing had entered China proper. Meanwhile, the government began to organize new military units, known as Green Battalions in the provinces, and the Green Battalions were staffed by Han Chinese, with Manchus as commanders in some cases. The soldiers of the Eight Banners and the Green Battalions were stationed across the country, from the nation's capital to small cities and towns, but the soldiers of the Eight Banners soon became corrupt after they entered China proper. Thus, beginning at the time when Wu Sangui's rebellion was suppressed, the Green Battalions became more and more important as the nation's fighting force. Besides the Eight Banners and the Green Battalions, there were military units temporarily organized for a specific campaign, and they were dissolved as soon as the campaign was over. As an instrument of controlling the people, the military organization was more emphasized during the Qing Dynasty than it had been during any of the previous dynasties.

Having succeeded in securing the control of the areas where the Han people lived, the Qing regime began to take steps to strengthen its control over the ethnic minorities. During the early Qing Dynasty, the Mongolians who lived in the northwestern region of China appeared in three separate groups. The three groups were Southern Mongolians, Northern Mongolians (Khalkhas), and Western Mongolians (Eleuts or Oirats). During the reign of Emperor Kang Xi, the Jungar tribe of the Eleut Mongolian group became more and more powerful, and eventually it annexed all of the four tribes of the Eleut group. It threatened Tibet and harassed the Khalkha Mongolians. In 1690, the Jungar army, under the commandership of Galdan, moved to the Ujumqin area of today's Inner Mongolia, only 900 *li* from Gubeikou, a narrow pass at the Great Wall to the northeast of Beijing. The Qing government was greatly alarmed. Emperor Kang Xi personally led troops to meet the invader and, at Ulanbutung (modern Chifeng, Inner Mongolia Autonomous Region), decisively defeated him. In 1696 and again in 1697, the emperor moved against Galdan who, having been defeated and feeling hopeless, committed suicide. In 1717, Tsi-wang Arabtan, a nephew of Galdan's, led his Jungar tribe towards Tibet and captured Lhasa. In 1720, the Qing government sent an expeditionary army to Tibet where it succeeded not only in expelling Tsi-wang Arabtan but also in installing Dalai Lama VI as ruler of Tibet. In 1727, it placed two ministers-in-residence in Tibet and thus greatly strengthened its control. During the reign of Kang Xi, the Uygurs who lived on both sides of the Tianshan Mountains had been, at one time, under Galdan's control. After Galdan's defeat, a religious leader named Huojizhan gathered troops south of the Tianshan Mountains and set up a separatist regime. In 1758, Emperor Qian Long sent an expeditionary army westward and, the very next year, pacified the areas south of the Tianshan Mountains. In Kashgar and other cities, the government, to administer the pacified areas, created new offices of assistant ministers, pioneer ministers, and managing ministers, all under the jurisdiction of the General of Ili. As for such ethnic minorities as Miao, Yao and Yi who inhabited China's southeastern region, the government, beginning in 1726 (during the reign of Emperor Yong Zheng), promoted the policy of "replacing tribal chiefs with government officials" on a large scale. The hereditary system whereby tribal chiefs succeeded one another was abolished, and the tribal areas were converted to prefectures and counties, the heads of which were appointed by the central government. The measures taken by the Qing government in China's border regions helped strengthen national defence and stabilize local communities in terms of social order. Naturally, while employing military force to achieve the intended purpose, the government also brought sorrow and misfortune to the local populace.

During the reign of Kang Xi, the government proceeded with the struggle against the Tzarist expansionists who were committing aggression against China. Towards the end of the Ming and early during the Qing Dynasty when China was plunged into chaos, Tzarist Russia continued to nibble away Chinese territories on the upper valley of the Heilongjiang River. In 1649, the Cossacks of Russia forcibly occupied Yacsa and built the Albazin fortress. In 1658, Tzarist Russia constructed the city of Nerchinsk at the mouth of the Nibuchu (Nerchinsk) River, besides dispatching troops to invade the valley of the Songhuajiang River. After China was unified, Emperor Kang Xi, in 1685, ordered an counterattack. The Qing forces defeated the Russians at Yacsa and then destroyed the city of Albazin. Tzarist Russia sent reinforcements the next year and rebuilt the city of Yacsa. Chinese troops counterattacked again and once more defeated the Russians. The Tzarist expansionists, knowing that the trend was working against them, expressed the desire for peace. The result was the Sino-Russian Treaty of Nerchinsk of 1689, which fixed the boundary between the two countries at the Ergun River (a tributary of the upper Heilongjiang), the Geerbiqi River, and the Outer Hinggan Mountains up to the sea. The areas to the south of the rivers and the mountains, including the Kuye (Sakhalin) Island, were Chinese, and the areas to their north were Russian. The treaty legally delimited the eastern section of the Sino-Russian border and curbed Tzarist Russia's greed and aggression.

It was an important victory for Chinese diplomacy.

Social order returned upon the unification of China. In 1712, the government declared that the 1711 revenue from poll tax be made permanent and that no additional poll tax be levied, no matter how fast the population was to increase from then on. This measure was publicized as "no increase in tax during a prosperous era when population increases". In 1716, an experiment was introduced in Guangdong, whereby "poll tax is incorporated into land tax". In 1724, the same measure was put into practice in the Beijing area. Later it was adopted nationwide. This programme of incorporating poll tax into land tax meant the abolition of the poll tax de facto, and those who did not own land would not have to pay poll tax. It was a good programme which helped the restoration of social order. From then on people did not have to hide themselves from census-takers in order to evade taxes, and population figures, as reported by local governments to Beijing, also became more accurate. In 1711, the reported population of China was 24,620,000; in 1774, it was 221,020,000.

Generally speaking, administrative efficiency during the best years of the Qing was higher than that of the Ming Dynasty. The Qing regime not only adopted the Ming institutions on a large scale but also learned a lesson from its predecessor's failures. In other words, it did not exploit people in such a ruthless fashion as the Ming had done. During the Qing Dynasty there was no emperor who favoured and trusted eunuchs to such an extent that he would not attend to the affairs of the state for years. The relationship between a Qing emperor and his Privy Council was also much closer than that between a Ming emperor and his Inner Chancery. Not surprisingly, the Qing regime could maintain the appearance of being powerful for a considerable length of time, while the Ming regime could not. Beneath the surface there was, of course, all kinds of contradictions, which would some day break through the cover and emerge to the surface.

As for cultural activities, the Qing regime adopted various measures to control them as soon as it had succeeded in consolidating its conquest of China. First, it continued to promote the eight-legged essays and the honouring of Confucius and the Neo-Confucian scholars so as to freeze people's thought. During the reign of Kang Xi, *The*

Complete Works of Neo Confucianism was reprinted, and *The Complete Works of Master Zhu Xi* and *The Essence of Neo-Confucianism* were also compiled and published. Scholars like Li Guangdi and Tang Bin were placed in high position and praised highly as the so-called "famous ministers of Neo-Confucianism". In 1684, Emperor Kang Xi personally went to Qufu to pay homage to Confucius. During his reign, Emperor Qian Long did the same nine times. Second, the Qing regime prohibited the circulation of books deemed unfriendly or harmful to itself. Third, it carried out literary inquisition, the most notorious of which occurred in 1711-13 and involved a book entitled *A Collection of Nanshan*. The book was considered to have anti-Qing contents and the author violated a taboo by proposing to use the reign titles of Southern Ming princes; he and more than one hundred implicated persons were executed as a result, while several hundred others were punished by exile. Fourth, in the name of editing books, the Qing authorities censored them. During the reigns of Yong Zheng and Qian Long, the government sponsored the compilation of two giant works. One was *A Collection of Books of Ancient and Modern Times,* completed in 1725. Consisting of 10,000 *juan* and rich in source materials, it was divided into 6 major parts and 6,109 individual items. This was the greatest undertaking since the compilation of *The Yong Le Encyclopaedia*. With the materials classified according to their characteristics, *A Collection of Books* was superior to *The Yong Le Encyclopaedia*, which had a classification based upon the difference in phonetic rhymes. Another literary undertaking, entitled *The Complete Library of the Four Treasuries*, had its beginning in 1772 and was completed ten years later. Consisting of more than 89,000 *juan* that were bound into more than 36,000 volumes, it was the largest collection of books in all of China's history. The purpose of compiling *A Collection of Books* was to take scholars' minds away from such thought as "learning for the purpose of bettering the world"; when busy with a literary undertaking of such a gigantic size, scholars would have little time for anything else. Still, there was no obvious attempt to censor books in the name of editing them. The compilation of *The Four Treasuries*, on the other hand, was a different matter. In the name of collecting books, the government burned and destroyed those which it did not like. In the name of editing books, it arbitrarily deleted or changed their content. While the compilation of *The Four Treasuries* helped the preservation of many books which otherwise could have been lost, it also changed and made less authentic many books it helped preserve.

After the reign of Kang Xi, the government could not control the development of culture despite its attempt. Li Gong (1659-1733), a student of Yan Yuan's, promoted his teacher's ideas until he became as famous as his mentor. Their philosophy was known as the School of Yan-Li. Li Gong wrote *The Collected Works of Shugu*. Wan Sitong (1638-1702), a student of Huang Zongxi's, wrote *A Chronological Chart According to Dynasties*, which has 64 *juan*. To trace the events towards the end of the Song Dynasty and the rise and fall of the Ming Dynasty, he wrote *Loyal and Righteous Men Towards the End of the Song Dynasty* (16 *juan*) and *A Draft History of the Ming* (500 *juan*). To understand a historical figure, he says, one must evaluate the time he lives in and must know the inside of him as well as the outside. What he says reflects the thought of many scholars of the late Ming and the early Qing period who wanted to use learning as a means to better the world. Later, influenced by Wan Sitong, Quan Zuwang (1705-55) studied the history of the Southern Song and the history of the Southern Ming. He wrote biographies for many distinguished scholars and outstanding persons who lived during the late Ming and the early Qing period. By reading his book, *The Collected Works of the Jiqi Pavilion*, one senses his dissatisfaction with the Qing regime.

In the area of literature, the outstanding works were dramas by Hong Sheng and Kong Shangren and novels by Wu Jingzi and Cao Xueqin.

Hong Sheng (1645-1704) completed a drama entitled *Palace of Eternal Youth* in 1688. It describes the Tang emperor Xuan Zong's exodus to Sichuan upon the outbreak of An Lushan's rebellion and the death of his favourite concubine Yang Yuhuan, who was forced to commit suicide. Later, the emperor thought of her constantly, and his devotion to her moved Heaven who agreed to let the lovers become an eternal, inseparable twosome in the Palace of Heaven. Kong Shangren (1648-1718) wrote *Peach Blossom Fan* which was completed in 1699. It describes a story of love between Li Xiangjun, a songstress, and

Hou Fangyu, a well-known man of letters. It praises the true, unshakable love, which she feels for him, and which enables her to resist all kinds of threats and temptations from the feudal elements. Moreover, it describes Li Xiangjun as a resolute, uncompromising fighter. Both books use stories of love to reveal the important events that accompany a dynasty's rise and fall; they present to their readers not only the broad vistas of social contradictions but also the lessons to be learned from history. They have a deep, practical meaning.

Wu Jingzi (1701-55) wrote *The Scholars*, a long novel satirizing the civil service examination system. He describes how the system attracts those intellectuals who have on their minds only fame and wealth which they pursue like a mad man. He also describes the unsavoury behaviour of those who have passed and those who have failed to pass the examination. While depicting the harmful effect of this system upon society, he in fact reveals the deep roots of corruption that existed during even the most glorious era of the Qing Dynasty. The book is as realistic as it is profound. Though there are no major characters in the book, a reader does not feel that it is loosely organized, since its main point is always clear and refreshing. The language used in the book is precise and yet rich in symbolism, and the poignancy of its caricature is both humorous and real. All in all, it is an outstanding novel of satire. It had a strong impact at the time of its publication, and it laid a solid foundation for similar novels that appeared in later years.

Cao Xueqin's real name was Cao Zhan (c. 1715-64), born into a Han Banner family in Nanjing. He later moved to live in Beijing. His novel, *The Dream of Red Mansions*, is a great realist work. The main thread of the story concerns the love between Jia Baoyu and his two cousins, Lin Daiyu and Xue Baochai. In the process of describing the tragedy of love and marriage among the main characters and the decline of the feudal, aristocratic Jia family, the author reveals the evils that accompany the life of a feudal clan. Because of the unconquerable contradictions within the family itself, it is a foregone conclusion that sooner or later it will decline. The novel approves the rebel spirit of Jia Baoyu and Lin Daiyu who oppose feudal ethics; it speaks positively of their feelings towards each others, feelings that are built upon a common ideal. It only regrets that in the end they cannot escape the yoke of feudal influence. After the death of Lin Daiyu, Jia Baoyu is duped to marry Xue Baochai, but there is no happiness in the marriage. The novel reveals the author's awareness of contemporary failings and his broad understanding of the pulse of his time. He feels that the society of his day will certainly collapse, even though the old influence is still strong enough to drag down the new force and thus creates tragedy. Through this novel the author ably crystalizes China's fine tradition of artistic expression; using vivid and rich language, he creates a great number of characters of various types. On the positive side are such characters as Jia Baoyu, Lin Daiyu, Qingwen, Yuanyang; on the negative side appear Xue Baochai, Wang Xifeng, Jia Zheng and Xiren. Each person, while appearing as a model in a given category, also possesses his or her own characteristics. Like a roll of painting that slowly unfolds its content, each character in the novel develops his or her own bent while going through the life process. The novel's construction is seamless; encompassing a broad vista, it is sheer beauty on a massive scale. It marks the peak in the history of Chinese novel. The book was hand-copied for circulation even before it was completed. From the viewpoint of content, artistic skill, and treatment of subject matter, its beneficial impact on Chinese literature—not only on novels but also on dramas, poetry and films—has been long and obvious.

As for academic studies, the area that had been most affected by the Qing's cultural policy and been used for the realization of its political purpose was collation in the field of Confucian classics and history. During the reign of Kang Xi, Yan Ruoqu (1636-1704) and Hu Wei (1633-1714) studied the texts of the *Book of History* and the *Tribute of Yu* and made important contributions. Thus began the academic vogue of collation for the sake of collation. The emphasis on "learning for the purpose of bettering the world" that characterized scholars of the early Qing period was abandoned altogether. As the new academic style could in no way violate the Qing regime's taboos, it was happily encouraged by the government. During the reign of Qian Long, two schools of textual criticism developed, the Wu and the Wan. The former school was headed by Hui Dong (1697-1758), and the latter by

Dai Zhen (1723-77). Dai Zhen, also known as Dai Dongyuan, had a tendency towards materialism, as he strongly opposed Neo-Confucianism. "A man might be saved if he were to be killed by law," said he. "He is doomed if he were to be killed by Neo-Confucianism." Dai's contribution to philosophy was overshadowed by his contribution to textual criticism, and his philosophy did not exercise the same kind of influence as his study of collation did. In doing textual research, he covered a large ground, including phonology, etymology, study of institutions as well as textual evaluation, to all of which he made contributions. However, in terms of the development of social thought, these contributions, as compared to those made by scholars of the early Qing period, were a step backward.

7. Decline of the Qing; Uprisings of Different Ethnic Groups

People' resistance activities did not stop even after the Qing had unified China. For one thing, the secret White Lotus Society, historically eminent, continued to be active. In 1721, Zhu Yigui staged an armed uprising in Taiwan and, at one time, had a following of as many as 300,000 men. But the anti-Qing uprising, being crushed six months later, did not have a chance to be developed into something more challenging. Half a century later, in 1774, Wang Lun, a leader of one of the White Lotus sects, raised the standard of revolt in western Shandong Province. He attacked and captured Shouzhang, Tangyi, Yanggu, and the old city of Linqing. As Linqing, located on the bank of the Grand Canal, was the place where ships bearing grains and other materials must pass through on their way northward to Beijing, the Qing government immediately dispatched troops to exterminate the rebels. Wang Lun, surrounded and outnumbered, ascended to the top of his residence where he burned himself to death. Later, uprisings against the Qing government continued throughout the later part of Qian Long's reign and the reigns of Jia Qing and Dao Guang.

In 1761, a Muslim in Gansu named Ma Mingxin founded a new sect of Islam. This event marked the beginning of Islam being divided into the Old and the New Sect. The division provided the Qing government with the opportunity of sowing dissension among the Muslims, as it supported one sect against the other. In 1781, it threw Ma Mingxin, leader of the New Sect, into a prison in Lanzhou, and such an action generated strong resentment on the part of all the Muslims and the Salars. Under the leadership of Su Sishisan and Han Er, both from Xunhuating (modern Salar Autonomous District, Xunhua County, Qinghai), the Muslims attacked and occupied Hezhou (modern Linxia, Gansu). They proceeded to march towards Lanzhou. The Qing government ordered Ma Mingxin to be killed and dispatched General Agui, at the head of a crack division from the capital, to attack the Muslim rebels. Though Su Sishisan and many of his followers made the heroic and ultimate sacrifice, the Muslims of the New Sect and the Salars did not submit themselves meekly to the suppression, as they, under the new leadership of Tian Wu, continued to propagate the teachings of the New Sect. In 1783, once again they raised the standard of revolt, this time in Fuqiang (modern Gangu, Gansu). Once again, the Qing government dispatched General Agui, at the head of troops from the capital, to suppress them. Tian Wu was killed in action, but his followers, commanded by Zhang Wenqing and Ma Siwa, continued the attack and captured such cities as Tongwei and Jingyuan. In 1784, the uprising collapsed.

In 1786, Lin Shuangwen staged an armed uprising in Taiwan. Previously, he had been a leader of the Heaven and Earth Society in Zhanghua, Taiwan. The organization was also known as the Triad Society, a popular, secret group that had its beginning during the reign of Kang Xi. It opposed the Qing regime and was most active in South China. The background of its members was complex, but most of them were poor, hard-working peasants. Lin Shuangwen raised such slogans as "winning people's hearts" and "protecting agriculture" to protest against the Qing government's ruthless exploitation. After capturing Zhanghua, he was declared "Marshal of Obedience to Heaven". Meanwhile, another man named Zhuang Datian, having raised the standard of revolt in Fengshan (modern Gaoxiong), attacked and captured Fengshan. Marching northward, he rendezvoused with Lin Shuangwen to attack the capital of Taiwan (modern Tainan). The

Qing government summoned a combined force of army and navy from seven coastal provinces to suppress the insurgents. Early in 1788, Lin Shuangwen was captured, and the uprising ended.

In 1795, Shi Liudeng, a Miao leader in Tongren Prefecture (modern Tongren County, Guizhou), led his people to stage an armed uprising in Dazhaiying, as a protest against excessive corvée and ruthless exploitation on the part of the Qing government. Subsequently, a Miao man named Shi Sanbao, who hailed from Yongsuiting (modern Huayuan), Hunan Province, and another Miao man named Wu Bayue, who hailed from Qianzhouting (modern Jishou), Hunan, led other Miao people in response. The insurgent army quickly won over large areas in Hunan, Guizhou and Sichuan, after having killed Fu Kangan, the Governor-general of Yunnan and Guizhou. The Qing government then dispatched several hundred thousand troops from Yunnan, Guizhou, Hunan and Guangdong to suppress the rebellion. Meanwhile, it sowed dissension among the insurgents so as to achieve its goal of "divide and conquer". Shi Liudeng was killed in action after having been defeated, and Wu Bayue and Shi Sanbao were captured. But the remainder of the insurgent army did not submit readily, as it reemerged in 1799 to challenge the Qing authority in the various areas of Hunan and Guizhou. It persisted in its struggle until 1806.

In 1796, members of the White Lotus Society revolted in a variety of areas: Nie Jieren at Zhijiang, Hubei Province and Wang Conger (female) and Yao Zhifu at Xiangyang. Fellow members in Dazhou, Dongxiang, Taiping, Bazhou and Tongjiang responded one after another. Refugees and poor people in Jingxiang, salt workers in the Changjiang River valley, and army deserters in eastern Sichuan—all of them participated in the struggle. The insurgent army fought in various areas of Henan, Shaanxi and Sichuan, tiring to exhaustion the Qing army that had been dispatched to crush it. Later, the Qing government put in good use the militias controlled by local landlords, that were coordinated with the regular army to fight against the insurgents. In the meantime, it mobilized several hundred thousand troops from various provinces for the effort. In 1798, the insurgent unit led by Wang Conger and Yao Zhifu was surrounded on all sides in the mountainous area of Yunxi. Unable to break through the encirclement, both leaders jumped from a cliff and committed suicide. In 1799, the insurgent unit that had its beginning in Dongxiang, Sichuan Province, was compelled to retreat to Gansu and subsequently fought at Qinzhou, Mianzhou and other places. After Leng Tianlu, its leader, was killed in action, his followers quickly dispersed. Towards the insurgents who continued to resist, the Qing government adopted a scorch-the-earth policy, as it built fortifications and castles into which it evicted all the peasants. The purpose was to cut off the link between the insurgents and the masses so as to isolate and entrap the former. In 1801, after the death of its leader Xu Tiande, the insurgent contingent that had raised its standard of revolt in Dazhou, Sichuan Province, became several small units active in different areas. In 1804, the uprising led by the White Lotus Society formally came to an end, having persisted for a period of nine years. To suppress it, the Qing government had to mobilize forces from a dozen provinces and spend more than 220,000,000 taels of silver in military expenditure.

The Sect of Heavenly Reason was an offshoot of the White Lotus Society. Earlier it had proselytized in Zhili, Shandong, Shanxi and Henan provinces. Its members were mostly poor peasants, domestic servants and slaves, hired hands and small peddlers. Lin Qing, its leader, had been proselytizing in Daxing County near Beijing for a long time. By attending to the needs of the sick and organizing poor people for mutual assistance, he became a leader of many. Meanwhile, another man named Li Wencheng was proselytizing in Huaxian, Henan Province. Lin and Li made an agreement with the followers of the Heavenly Reason Sect in Shandong and Zhili that they would simultaneously rise in rebellion on the fifteenth day of the ninth lunar month, 1813. Unfortunately, the news of the attempted uprising was leaked before it could be carried out. As Li Wencheng was thrown into jail, Zhang, Li's wife, led the sect's adherents in revolt ahead of schedule. On the seventh day of the ninth lunar month, Zhang and her followers successfully broke into Huaxian. They not only rescued Li Wencheng but, subsequently, also occupied Junxian (Henan Province). The sect's adherents in Dingtao and Jinxiang, Shandong Province, and in Changyuan, modern Henan, responded positively to the uprising one after another. Lin Qing, however, had no inkling that the uprising would take place ahead of schedule. On the fifteenth day of the ninth lunar month, he led two hundred of his followers into Beijing and then attacked the imperial palace. Quickly the Qing government sent its Rifle Battalion to the scene to counterattack, and Lin Qing, having been captured was subsequently executed. Meanwhile, the insurgent army in Henan was surrounded by the Qing forces, and Li Wencheng and many of his followers burned themselves to death. But Zhang, Li Wencheng's wife, continued the defence of Huaxian; thrice she and her men attacked the Qing army at night. Early in 1814, the Qing army attacked and entered the city. Wielding a sword, Zhang fought from street to street. Overcome by exhaustion, she finally killed herself.

In 1835, Cao Shun staged an armed uprising in Zhaocheng (modern Hongdong County, Shanxi). Cao was a member of a secret society named First Heaven. In 1834, upon assuming the leadership of this society, he began to organize peasants and manufacture weapons. The next year, he attacked Zhaocheng and killed its magistrate. Later, he divided his army to attack Huoxian, Linfen and several other places. As his force was thinned out, it became an easy target for the Qing army. The uprising failed as a result.

There were numerous armed uprisings against the Qing authority towards the end of Emperor Qian Long's reign. Facing them, the Qing government not only dispatched troops to suppress them but also promoted or strengthened the *bao-jia* system, so as to tighten its control of the people. Meanwhile, Emperor Qian Long himself lived a corrupt life of self-indulgence as usual. After his accession to the throne, he went to South China time and again for pleasure; the tours of pleasure were repeated between 1780 and 1784. Earlier, during Kang Xi's reign, summer palaces were built in Chengde. The construction was continued during Qian Long's reign. In 1790, the last of Qian Long's seventy-two summer villas was finally completed. Like corrupt members of the ruling classes during other dynasties, the officials of the Qing Dynasty used a variety of methods, including blackmail, to extort money from the people, and greedy landlords exploited peasants likewise, so as to enrich themselves. Heshen, a Grand Minister of the Privy Council, amassed a huge fortune towards the end of Qian

Long's reign, a fortune that consisted of 8,000 *qing* (approximately 120,000 acres) of farmland, 84,000 taels of gold, and 55,000 silver bars, not to mention, in the underground vault, 1,000,000 taels of silver, pearls and other valuables worth 8,000,000 taels of silver, silk and leather worth another 1,000,000 taels of silver, and six hundred *jin* of ginseng. In addition, he owned forty money stores and seventy-five pawnshops. Towards the end of Qian Long's reign, corruption and bribery were open secret among local officials. Among the higher posts, the Superintendency of Water Control yielded the largest reward in terms of bribery that could be collected. Emperor Jia Qing said in 1811 that more than half of the annual budget of 30,000,000 taels of silver appropriated for water control was lost in corruption. Many superintendents of water control deliberately broke dykes to create an emergency, so they would be able to request huge funds to repair them. Then they siphoned off for their own use large sums from the appropriated funds.

Corruption among officials reduced the government's income. Besides, there were huge outlays occasioned by the suppression of people's uprisings. As a result, the government had a difficult time to make ends meet. Towards the end of Qian Long's reign, the government each year had only about two million taels of silver at its disposal after payment of the salaries of officials and administrative expenses. Towards the end of Jia Qing's reign, only five provinces were able to fulfil their tax quotas and hand over the receipts to the national treasury. As a result, the budget could not be balanced, as total revenue could not match the huge expenditure. To solve the financial problem, the Qing government, time and again, introduced miscellaneous, oppressive taxes. Besides, it expanded the so-called tribute system. Not only offices but also nominal titles, such as the degree of *jiansheng* (imperial college student) could be bought and sold. Those who had bought such titles were not entitled to the holding of an office, of course; they were, however, to enjoy higher social positions that enabled them to bully others. From 1816 to 1830, the selling of the *jiansheng* degree alone netted the government as much as 2,270,000 taels of silver. As revenue increased, so did waste. Besides, much of the revenue which should have gone to the national treasury was intercepted for personal use by officials at various levels. It was said then that if a magistrate wished to become rich by one thousand taels of silver, his subordinates, who handled the bribery for him, would acquire for themselves ten times as much; if a governor wished to become richer by ten thousand taels of silver, the magistrates, who handled the bribery for him, would use the opportunity to obtain for themselves one hundred thousand taels of silver. The seriousness in financial difficulties in the government and the widespread corruption among the officials indicated nothing but the utter rottenness on the part of the ruling oligarchy.

As for cultural activities, there were a number of outstanding scholars during the later part of the Qian Long period and thereafter. They continued the work pioneered by Hui Dong and Dai Zhen and made important contributions in the textual study of Confucian classics and history. Fearful of antagonizing the ruling elite, they avoided reality as much as possible. The research scholar Qian Daxin (1728-1804) was as much noted for his versatility as for his specialization. In his books, such as *The Study of Differences in the Twenty-two Dynastic Histories* and *The Record of New Discoveries by Shijiazhai*, he was discriminating in his selection of materials and objective in his judgement. Both books were important works on historical studies. Sometimes he assumed the role of a lecturer when he spoke of the corrupt practices in politics of his time. In this regard, he was much more progressive than his fellow textual researchers.

Contemporary with Qian Daxin and independent of the vogue of textual criticism were Wang Zhong and Zhang Xuecheng. Wang Zhong (1744-94) was a supperior writer, an eminent historian and an outstanding philosopher and, in his own words, "a man who, ashamed of pursuing useless studies, was most interested in being of practical use to the world. He studied institutional changes from ancient to modern times and also the measures adopted which were beneficial or detrimental to the people's livelihood. He learned about all of them and studied thoroughly each, in the hope that someday he might be able to use the knowledge he had acquired." A scholarly interest of this kind was most unusual at this time since it was contrary to the general trend. He believed that only by studying history could one understand the implications of academic changes. The academic successor to Confucius, said he, was Xun Zi rather than Mencius; Confucianism and Mohism were equally outstanding, and Mohism should not be discriminated against. He was, in fact, criticizing the popular, time-honoured orthodoxy and proposing a new attitude towards different schools of thought. This attitude of freeing oneself from the bondage of feudal culture and of pursuing historical truth as one saw it was highly praiseworthy since it was very rare at the time. He wrote *On Learning* that, because of its huge size, was not yet completed when he died.

Zhang Xuecheng (1738-1801) was an outstanding critic on historical science. Against the academic trend of his time, he pointed out that textual research, being only a means to an end, should not be an academic discipline by itself. Textual research to a scholar, said he, was like a vehicle or a boat to a traveller. Just as a traveller could not be satisfied with sitting in a vehicle or a boat without knowing where he was going, a scholar should not study textual criticism for its own sake. He proposed that a scholar should not just follow the vogue and should instead oppose it if it were wrong. In defining a good historian, he emphasized a systematic and objective assessment of cultural and academic developments, as well as faithfulness to historical reality. In other words, a historian should not distort historical facts and should avoid being blinded by his own prejudice. Speaking of the ancient history of China, he regarded Confucian classics as historical records, proposing that the developments of all schools of thought be studied. He believed that social development followed an objective, inevitable course, and this belief was contrary to the scholastic approach adopted by scholars of textual criticism and research. His historical point of view contained in it elements of materialism, but his main interest was confined to the history of culture. Besides, his views were heavily coloured by a cyclic approach to history. His works, compiled by later scholars, were known as *The Posthumous Works of Zhang Xuecheng*, the most important of which was *The General Meaning of Literature and History*.

Both Wang Zhong and Zhang Xuecheng were unorthodox in the sense that they did not choose to follow the popular trend. As a result, they did not exercise as much influence on scholarship as they should have. The presence of their works, nevertheless, indicated a new demand, a new trend in academic studies.

After Wang Zhong and Zhang Xuecheng came Gong Zizhen (1792-1841) who, also known as Gong Ding'an, was an essayist, a poet, a historian and a philosopher. He compared the society of his days to a sick body covered with scabs and scars, stating that its sickness was so advanced as to be beyond cure. He pointed out the corruption of officials at all levels, the shamelessness of those who exploited others through blackmail and oppression in order to live a materially more enjoyable life. The male tillers and the female weavers, on the other hand, lived a life of slavery. He believed that there was no law that could not be changed or no precedent that could not be broken. Sooner or later, changes had to be made. He wrote a well-known poem which read as follows:

The vitality of China cannot come about
Until storm sweeps and thunder roars.
Ten thousand horses are mute:
How tragic it is!
May Heaven arouse itself—I plead:
Send us talents—all kinds of talents!

The poet felt sad in view of the deathly situation he faced. He called for the storms and thunders so that necessary changes could be made and a new situation created. One year before his death, the Opium War broke out, and China entered a new historical period. The new period did not bring to the Chinese people good fortunes. Instead, it brought nothing but greater misfortunes.

8. The Decline of Feudalism and the Emergence of Sprouts of Capitalism

The Ming-Qing period was marked by the decline of feudalism. During this period, the social economy continued to develop, the nature of labour power underwent a considerable change, and the feudal relations of production imposed shackles on production development. Sprouts of capitalism slowly emerged in certain areas and in certain industries. It could not grow normally, however, since it could not yet free itself from the prevalent feudal influence.

In agriculture, cultivated acreage increased at a fast rate during the early part of the Ming Dynasty. In 1383, the newly cultivated acreage was as much as 1,800,000 *qing* (27,000,000 acres), about one-half of the total cultivated land. In 1393, total cultivated land for the nation as a whole reached 8,500,000 *qing* (127,500,000 acres). The principal cause for the speedy increase of cultivated acreage was peace and stability after a long period of war. However, the figure declined to 7,010,000 *qing* (105,150,000 acres) in 1581—a figure that stood as the largest during the later part of the Ming Dynasty. In 1661, early during the Qing Dynasty, total land under cultivation amounted to 5,490,000 *qing* (82,350,000 acres). The amount steadily increased until by 1812 it reached 7,900,000 *qing* (118,500,000 acres), or 900,000 *qing* (13,500,000 acres) above the 1581 figure. Still, it was less by 600,000 *qing* (9,000,000 acres) compared to the 1393 figure. The reason was that the Qing government designated the Northeast as a forbidden region to which Han people were not allowed to emigrate for the purpose of opening up new acreage for cultivation. There were, of course, newly cultivated fields in Mongolia and in the areas south and north of the Tianshan Mountains, but the amount was rather limited.

The development of agriculture during the Ming-Qing period centred on the production of paddy rice and of cash crops, as well as the development of new varieties of crops. During the Ming Dynasty, Fujian and Zhejiang discovered a new strain of paddy rice that could bring two harvests per year. In Guangdong, three harvests of paddy rice per year were not uncommon. Paddy rice fields appeared as north as Zhili Province. During the Ming Dynasty, the most productive areas were the provinces of Jiangsu, Hunan, Hubei and Sichuan and the areas along the southeast coast. Such cash crops as cotton were grown across the country. Mulberry trees, tea bushes, sugar canes, fruit trees, dye plants like indigo, safflower and scholartree, sesame, peanut, dragon spruce, tun tree, and other oil-yielding plants—the cultivation of these plants was continually promoted until it reached larger and larger areas. The same thing could be also said about medicine herbs. Maize, imported into China early in the sixteenth century, was grown in virtually all regions of China by the eighteenth century. Sweet potato, introduced to China from Luzon towards the end of the sixteenth century, was grown experimentally first in Fujian; later, its planting spread to Zhejiang, Shandong and Henan. As planting skill continued to improve, it could be found, eventually, in North China where winter was noticeably colder. Both maize and sweet potato are highly productive plants, and sweet potato can be planted even in sandy soil. The expansion of cotton planting over large areas and the introduction to China of maize and sweet potato were important events in the history of Chinese agriculture, as they were closely related to the livelihood of the people. Tobacco was also introduced to China during the sixteenth century. At the beginning, its cultivation was confined to the provinces of Fujian and Guangdong. After the Qian Long period, it could be found in Zhejiang, Jiangsu, Shandong, Zhili, Shanxi, Shaanxi and Sichuan provinces. Meanwhile, several famous strains of the same tobacco were produced. Tobacco was a cash crop; its cultivation had a direct bearing on the rural economy.

As for the handicraft industry, spinning and weaving remained a major vocation among the peasants in a self-sufficient economy. Spinning and weaving involved all kinds of raw materials, such as silk, cotton and hemp; in Northwest China, wool was also an important raw material. After the middle decades of the Ming Dynasty, the industry created solely for the manufacturing of marketable textiles slowly developed, and it thrived as an independent enterprise in several regions. Silk produced in Huzhou, cotton cloth produced in Songjiang, and satin produced in Nanjing and Suzhou were famous throughout the country. As for the agricultural processing industry, including tea making, sugar refining, and oil pressing, it was more advanced than it had ever been. Besides, tea was an important item for export.

The porcelain industry reached a high stage of development during the Ming-Qing period. Jingdezhen, Jiangxi Province, remained the most famous place for the nation's porcelain industry. Innovations were continually made in glazing and in multicoloured drawing. The blue vase and the multicoloured vase were then among the industry's most famous products. Meanwhile, paper making and printing also made progress. Printing could be done by moveable type made of wood, copper, lead or tin, in addition to printing by wooden block. Other than the regular printing plate, there were the multi-printing plate and the flower-relief plate. The multi-printing plate actually consisted of two or more plates, each of which printed a specific colour according to design. A page was completed after all the plates had been applied to it one after another. The flower-relief plate bore no ink. When a sheet of paper was pressed upon it, the reliefs on the plate would appear on the sheet in convex form.

During the Ming-Qing period, the salt-making and the iron-smelting industries grew to considerable size in terms of their production. One salt-making plant in Sichuan employed tens of thousands of workers, directly or indirectly. Even a small plant employed ten thousand persons or thereabouts. As for iron-smelting, coke was used as fuel as early as the Ming Dynasty, during which bellows with valves were invented. Bellows of this kind generated strong wind under heavy pressure. The production of cast iron and wrought iron in a continuous process, in addition to a new method of making steel, was also invented during the Ming period. All these achievements were indeed very advanced for their time. The smelting of zinc was considered a most difficult process throughout the world, but the record shows that it was done in China as early as the first decades of the fifteenth century. In the eighteenth century, the Chinese method of smelting zinc spread to Europe. The record also shows that the Chinese used "explosives" for mining. It seems that the skill of using dynamite had already been acquired at this time.

The shipbuilding industry of the Ming-Qing period, especially the building of seagoing ships, had had a long tradition. The very fact that Zheng He could lead a fleet of large ships to pass across the Indian Ocean and reach as far as the eastern coast of Africa speaks loudly of the advanced level of China's shipbuilding and navigational skill. During the reign of Kang Xi, the city of Suzhou built more than one thousand seagoing ships every year, and most of these ships, once abroad, were purchased by foreign countries. This indicates that Chinese ships had a good reception abroad. The government, however, often subjected the shipbuilding industry to arbitrary intervention. The industry, therefore, could not enjoy a normal development.

As for the building industry during the Ming-Qing period, among the largest constructions were those of the royal palaces in Beijing, the royal summer palace in Rehe, and the Great Wall. Numerous gardens were also constructed, especially in Beijing and Suzhou.

As for special handicrafts, there were tapestry embroidery in silk, lacquer carvings, jade carvings, and cloisonne enamel, all of which commanded high price and prestige. Cloisonne enamel was a new art form developed during the reign of Emperor Jing Tai of the Ming Dynasty. As for the others, they had had a long history.

Commerce thrived in the Ming-Qing period, and such cities as Beijing, Nanjing, Chengdu, Hankou, Suzhou, Hangzhou and Songjiang were its major centres. After the Wanli period of the Ming Dynasty, trade and commerce were particularly brisk in the lower valley of the Changjiang River, and many places, because of commercial prosperity, developed quickly from small hamlets of several hundred households to towns or cities of thousands of households. During the Qing Dynasty, the newly developed but nationally known centres of commerce included Foshan of Guangdong Province, Hankou of Hubei Province, Zhuxian of Henan Province, and Jingde of Jiangxi Province. Jointly they were referred to as the four famous towns of China.

Side by side with the development of agriculture, handicrafts and commerce, there were important written works on science and technology.

In 1578, Li Shizhen (1518-93) completed his *Outline of Herb Medicine* which consists of fifty-two *juan*. In the *Outline*, he recorded 1,892 herbs, listed more than 11,000 prescriptions, and included more than 1,100 illustrations. Though much of the materials in the book were available elsewhere, he did a lot of work verifying them. There were other materials which he collected himself. The *Outline* was a definitive work on Chinese medicine and pharmacology, summarizing all the knowledge on these subjects up to the sixteenth century. It was an important work on botany as well, and it contained much experience in the raising of different plants. Its influence persisted for about four hundred years. It has been translated into various foreign languages. A Chinese physician, who was Li Shizhen's contemporary, discovered the prevention of smallpox by vaccination. One generation younger than Li Shizhen was another man named Chen Shigong (c. 1555-1636) who wrote *Principles of Surgery*, a summary of all knowledge on the subject matter.

About fifty years after the appearance of *Outline of Herb Medicine*, Xu Guangqi (1562-1633) wrote *A Complete Treatise on Agriculture*. In his book, he discussed all aspects of agriculture, from the planting of food crops, mulberry trees, cotton, vegetables, fruits, bamboo, trees, and medicine herbs to the manufacturing and maintenance of farm implements. He also discussed animal husbandry. Still, he devoted comparatively more space to water control and the prevention of drought. In the book could be found relevant historical materials as well as his personal observations. He believed that man could conquer nature and proposed the promotion of more and better crops. The author did not have time to complete the book, and the present version, consisting of sixty *juan*, was edited by Chen Zilong. It was published in 1639.

Geographer Xu Hongzu (1586-1641) was also known as Xu Xiake. Beginning at a time when he was only twenty-two, he travelled across China. For more than thirty years, he recorded each of the areas he had visited—its geography, its rivers and streams, its geology, its vegetation, and the living conditions of its people. His most important contribution, however, was his observation and recording of the karst landscape in China's southwest. The topography created through the dissolution of lime in running water took a variety of forms, strange but interesting, and the presence of such a topography indicated a most complex subterranean water system. A study of this kind was, of course, of enormous value to land cultivation and construction. Xu Hongzu's discovery was two hundred years earlier than that of Europeans. His work, *Travels,* is available today.

Song Yingxing (1587-c. 1660) wrote *Expositions of the Works of Nature* which, consisting of eighteen treaties, was completed in 1637. First, the book discussed the production of food and clothing, including the cultivation of food crops, cotton and hemp, the raising of silkworms and the reeling of silk, the making of dyes, the processing of food, the making of salt and the refining of sugar. Second, it elaborated on the manufacture of such usable items as bricks and tiles, porcelain and pottery, vessels, boats and vehicles, the making of paper and candles, the pressing of oil, and the mining and manufacture of lime. Lastly, it discussed the mining and smelting of metals, the manufacture of military weapons and gunpowder, the making of red, black and other dyes, and, finally, the harvesting and processing of pearls and jade. The author went to great detail in describing the raw materials to be used and the process of production for each item elaborated in this book. The book was a definitive work on agriculture and handicraft industry of sixteenth-century China, as it paid particular attention to the advanced experience in production at that time. Almost as soon as it was published in China, it was reprinted in Japan. Later it was translated into several foreign languages.

The accomplishments in science and technology indicated the high level of social production and its possible development. But these accomplishments, in a feudal society like the Ming-Qing China, might not be applied to production at all, largely because of the small scale on which production could be conducted and of the limitations imposed by political conditions. Even if they could be used in production, they, nevertheless, could not be promoted over a wide area. Beginning with the late Ming period, while science and technology continued to make progress, major written works, such as those described above, became much more scarce.

The development of social production and the continuance of class struggle during the Ming-Qing period gave rise to certain changes in the nature of labour power. First, as the single tax was put into practice and as the poll tax was absorbed by the land tax, not only did the land tax take the form of a property tax which was separated from rent, but the peasants themselves were also exempted from corvée, the poll tax and other oppressive taxes. Such an exemption, of course, reduced the degree of the peasants' dependence upon the government. Second, the craftsmen of the Ming Dynasty were different from their predecessors of the Yuan Dynasty, whose position was close to that of a slave. Other than the obligation of having to work for the government at a specific time, they had personal freedom. During the Jia Jing period, the obligation to work for the government was compounded into a cash levy. During the Wan Li period, the government paid for the services rendered by the craftsmen, and the system of employing labour via pay was soon institutionalized. Early during the Qing Dynasty, the separate identification of "craftsmen households" was abolished altogether, thus freeing the craftsmen from the feudal bondage that had tied them to the government. Third, changes also took place in the relationship between landlords and peasants. During the Ming Dynasty, a new kind of tenant households appeared, the kind that did not have a master-servant relationship with the landlords. The Qing law particularly forbade the use of corporal punishment against tenants by landlords, and the forcible taking over a peasant's daughter as concubine or slave was punishable by hanging. During the Ming Dynasty, there also appeared large numbers of hired labourers who worked for landlords on a yearly, seasonal, monthly, or daily basis. Most of these labourers, owning their own farming tools, had not yet been completely separated from the means of production; there were, of course, a few who owned absolutely nothing. On the other hand, they were not simple freemen who sold their labour power, as their relationship with the landlords was still that between a superior and an inferior. But they were less dependent upon the landlords, compared to tenant peasants. During the Ming-Qing period, a big landlord might have as many as one hundred or more hired labourers. We know that this kind of development was not uniform across China, and there were extralegal expropriations that had persisted for a long period during the feudal era. Nevertheless, the nature of the labour force did change during the Ming-Qing period, as it slowly freed itself from feudal control. This new trend of development must be duly noticed by historians.

Early during the Ming Dynasty, the sprouts of capitalism first appeared in the textile industry. At this time, a wealthy man in Hangzhou provided looms and hired a dozen weavers to work for him. This must be the first handicraft workshop in China organized in the capitalist fashion. During the Wan Li period, "craftsmen in Hangzhou, having their own employers, were paid wages on a daily basis. Those who had no regular employers stood on a bridge early in the morning, waiting for their names to be called." Among the craftsmen were cotton weavers and spinners as well as silk weavers. They gathered in groups of tens or hundreds and would disperse of their own accord if, on a given day, no work was available. Regardless of the purpose of production, for profit in the market place or on orders of the government, these workers had all been separated from the means of production and had become independent workers selling their labour power. This meant that a market for free labour power had finally appeared.

Towards the end of the Ming Dynasty, many weavers in Suzhou, Hangzhou and Songjiang, realizing that there was profit to be made, gradually increased the number of looms so as to hire other weavers for increased production, while they themselves no longer worked at the looms, even though they started as self-employed workers, buying their own raw materials and personally labouring to transform these raw materials into finished products. There were also cloth merchants who distributed raw materials among the weavers, the dyers, and the stampers who processed the materials that had been given to them. Step by step, the final product materialized. People of the former group—the weavers—were separated from small commodity producers to become owners of handicraft workshops, and people of the second group—the cloth merchants—possessed certain characteristics of a contractor, as they organized different sections of production into a handicraft workshop. Both groups had in them capitalistic characteristics in terms of production relationship. Still, their existence was confined to southeastern China and to a limited number of industries. All we can say is that they represented only the bare beginning of Chinese capitalism.

During the Qing government's unification of China, southeastern China suffered enormous damages, and the nascent capitalism, as described above, was virtually destroyed. Only after peace was restored did the sprouts of capitalism reappear, growing so steadily as to spread to areas outside southeastern China. Nascent capitalism could be found in the textile industry of Suzhou and Nanjing, in the porcelain industry of Jiangxi, in the sugar-refining industry of Guangdong, in the paper-making industry of Jiangxi, Zhejiang and Shaanxi, in the copper-mining industry of Yunnan, and in the coal industry of Beijing and other areas. During the Dao Guang period, some of the silk workshops in Nanjing each had five to six hundred silk looms, and a mine in Yunnan might employ several thousand workers.

Though nascent capitalism made its appearance during the late Ming and early Qing period, it never had a chance to grow normally for several centuries. The reason was complex. First, there was this inertia of a self-sufficient economy that had prevailed in feudal China for a long, long period. The basic unit of this self-sufficient or natural economy was the family where men tilled and women wove, and there was no need for marketable goods to satisfy the daily demand. An average peasant had no way of improving his livelihood, as he was exploited and oppressed by his government and his landlord. Whenever productivity increased, the benefit of such an increase would first go to the landlord, and the peasant received little or nothing. Peasant uprisings struck hard at the landlords, but basically they did not change the economic well-being of the peasants. After a major uprising, certain changes occurred as far as the peasants' status was concerned; yet they must return to the land and reestablish the traditional household where men tilled and women wove. This structure of a natural economy, namely the traditional household, limited the expansion of a commercial market and prevented industrial capitalism from opening up its own avenue for expansion.

Second, the guilds of the handicraftsmen limited capitalist development. Handicraft guilds existed as early as the Tang-Song period. A guild was not organized for the protection of the toilers; instead, it was organized to enable the feudal government to control the handicraftsmen. By the Ming-Qing period, the guild had been long established as a customary organization that became a force binding the handicraftsmen. According to the rules of the guild, the distribution of raw materials, the grading of finished products, the numbers of apprentices and journeymen, the marketing of goods produced, and the prices of goods to be sold in the market—all this was carefully regulated. The regulation was designed to limit development and forestall competition, presenting an insurmountable obstacle to capitalist development.

Third, the oppression of commerce and the handicraft industry by the feudal government also prevented a capitalist form of production from developing. A feudal government was only interested in tying peasants to the land they tilled in order to control them. It did not want toilers to leave the land, and it was most afraid of their assembly. During the Ming-Qing period, a mine was sometimes opened and sometimes closed, and the government strictly forbade individuals to operate mines on their own. Why? Despite the profit to be realized when the mine was open, the government was most concerned with the troubles that might arise when so many miners gathered for a considerable length of time. As for certain industries that showed promise of further development, such as the textile and mining industries, the Qing government often imposed limitation on production and forcibly purchased finished products at a low price. In the name of governmental monopoly, it levied heavy taxes upon the manufacturing of salt, tea and liquor. As for other products, it charged a broker's fee when the products were traded, a tariff when the products were transported from one place to another, and a local tax after the products had arrived in the market. Besides, there were extortions on the part of local officials. All this could not but hinder a nascent capitalism from developing further.

Fourth, the handicraftsmen and merchants, operating under risky conditions, could not compete with landowners and moneylenders in terms of the safety of investment as well as the size of financial returns. Wishing to acquire more land, the landlords lent money at high interest. Wealthy merchants bought land too, besides opening pawnshops. In short, land was considered the most reliable assent and usury the most profitable line of business. All this prevented social wealth from being transformed into industrial capital. Capitalism, consequently, could not grow.

Fifth, both the Qing and the Ming government imposed strict limitations on foreign trade. Sometimes they went as far as forbidding merchants to go out to sea. This self-defeating policy of preventing one's own goods from being sold abroad did not help the development of commodity production, of course.

In conclusion, it can be said that the main reason why capitalism could not develop normally in China was the strong and stubborn resistance on the part of feudal influence, which capitalism, in its initial stage of development, could not overcome. The feudal production relationship of the Ming-Qing period not only failed to help the development of the productive forces, but was also able to counteract any development and make social production stand still. In other words, the feudal system, aging and corrupt though it was, was still strong enough to prevent the emergence of a new social system. This, one might say, was the most important characteristic of the declining stage of Chinese feudalism.

The landlord class of the Ming-Qing period was among the most corrupt on record, and the royal house formed the highest echelon of this class. During the Ming Dynasty, members of the royal house controlled directly large landholdings, known as royal plantations. Feudatory princes of the Ming Dynasty and Manchu dukes and counts of the Qing Dynasty were all granted large landholdings by their respective sovereigns. Nevertheless, the group that had the largest landholdings and the greatest influence on society as a whole was a group known as "the official gentry". As a result of the often-repeated peasant war of the Song and Ming dynasties, the degree-holding bureaucrat landlords with official ranks were by and large overthrown, and the official gentry took their place. Among the official gentry were also bureaucrats with official ranks but, as a separate class, official gentry of the Ming-Qing period differed from the bureaucrat landlords of the earlier dynasties in many respects. First, their constituents were much wider in scope than the bureaucrats. They included incumbent officials, retired officials, and prospective officials—the last-mentioned being those who had already passed the civil service examinations but had not yet been rewarded with official posts. The word "gentry" was applicable only to the last two groups: a man might be an incumbent official in one place, but he remained a member of the gentry in his hometown. While the official gentry, as a class, were lower in political status when compared to the bureaucrats with official ranks, their capacity of doing evil, such as exploitation of others and corruption, increased nevertheless. Second, incumbent officials protected the gentry, and the gentry supported incumbent officials. Together they formed the local power elite. Thus the official gentry was actually a class of landowning despots. Third, members of the official gentry were interchangeable with "mercantile landlords". Once an official, a man would start a business of his own or open a pawnshop; this was referred to as "a normal process of proceeding from official to businessman". Salt merchants, tea merchants and import-and-export businessmen—they were conducting business in the name of the royal house, and some of them even acquired official titles. This was referred to as "a normal process of proceeding from businessman to official". Besides, one could always become an official by making financial contribution to the government. In that case, all wealthy businessmen could become government officials, or at least acquire official titles. An important reason why the government of the Ming-Qing period, corrupt though it was, could continue to rule and rule for such a long time was that it was supported by the powerful but corrupt official gentry. Amid widespread, pervasive influence of corruption, new industries could not develop and grow in a normal fashion.

In short, the Ming-Qing period saw a change from progressiveness to backwardness in China. The period from the early sixteenth to the middle decades of the seventeenth century was an important one in world history: it was a period that marked Western Europe's transition from feudalism to nascent capitalism. In 1640, while a bourgeois revolution broke out in England, Chinese peasants, led by Li Zicheng, were waging a bloody warfare. In 1784, the steam engine was invented, and the invention paved the way for the Industrial Revolution and ushered in the era of modern industry in Western Europe. In China the same year marked the unsuccessful amred uprising led by Tian Wu. Later, a series of people's anti-feudal uprisings occurred, but none succeeded. While the feudal forces of the Ming-Qing period remained strong enough to win temporary victories against the people, it created such backwardness that it could in no way resist Western colonial aggression against China. The end result was that Chinese people of all ethnic groups had to experience an ill fate sadder than ever.

9. Arrival of Western Colonialism

The relationship between China and foreign countries underwent a drastic change during the Ming-Qing period. For two centuries beginning in the early years of the Ming Dynasty, pirates from Japan invaded and caused disturbances on the coastal areas of China. During the late Ming and early Qing period, Tsarist Russia forcibly occupied Chinese territories, an aggressive action that eventually led to a Sino-Russian war fought at Yacsa. All this was unprecedented in the history of China's foreign relations. In 1498, Vasco da Gama discovered a new route to the Orient, and this discovery was followed by the arrival of Portuguese colonialists in China. In the wake of the Portuguese came the Spaniards, the Dutch, the Englishmen, the Frenchmen and the Americans. All of them employed a variety of methods—commerce, gunboats, and missionary activities—to plunder China in a savage manner.

In 1511, Portugal conquered Malacca. In 1513, its commercial ships arrived in China for the first time. In 1516-17, Portugal sent more ships to Guangdong to sell such products as spices and, in the process, illegally occupied the island of Tunmen, part of Dongguan, Guangdong Province. Later, it dispatched George Mascarenhas to Zhangzhou, Fujian Province, where he, at the head of a fleet, clandestinely surveyed the coastline. In 1521, the Ming government forcibly evicted the Portuguese from China's territorial waters after they had refused to leave the island of Tunmen of their own accord. In 1523, 1547 and 1549, the Portuguese invaded and caused disturbances at Xicaowan (Xinhui, Guangdong Province), Zhangzhou (Fujian Province) and Zhaoan (Fujian Province), but they were repulsed by the Ming forces in each case. Many of them continued to reside in Macao, however, beginning in 1535. In 1553, by bribing local officials, the Portuguese occupied part of Macao in the name of having obtained a lease. In 1557, they illegally enlarged the territories they had occupied, built forts and installed governmental organs. They, in fact, viewed Macao as their colony. Macao turned out to be the first of many territories illegally occupied by Western colonialists on a sustained basis. Still, the Chinese government had its own offices in Macao, the sovereignty of which belonged to China.

In 1565, Spain occupied the Philippines. In 1571, it built the city of Manila. In 1575, Spanish merchants arrived in China. Later, with the permission of the Ming government, they traded in Xiamen, the designated port of trade. The Spanish colonialists deliberately mistreated Chinese residents in the Philippines and, between 1603 and 1639, initiated three massacres. In 1626, they forcibly occupied Jilong, Taiwan.

The Dutch emerged as a major power towards the end of the sixteenth century when they occupied Java, Sumatra and other islands in Southeast Asia. In 1602, the Dutch East India Company was formed. In 1619, the Dutch built the city of Batavia in Java, known today as Djakarta, capital of modern Indonesia. From then on, they intensified their evil scheme of plundering China. In 1601, a Dutch merchant fleet, well-armed, arrived in Guangzhou for the first time. They did not dare to resort to reckless behaviour, however, thanks to the strict surveillance conducted by local governments and people. In 1604, they attacked Penghu Islands. In 1622, they forcibly occupied the islands on which they built fortifications. They intended to use Penghu as a base of operation to further their aggression against China itself. Subsequently, they raided the coastal areas of Fujian for plunder, piracy and the kidnapping of people to be sold as slaves. In 1623, they occupied Taiwan and built Fort Anping (Fort Zeelandia). In 1624, the Ming forces chased them out from Penghu; nevertheless, they built Fort Chiqian (Providentia) in Taiwan during the same year. In 1641, the two colonial powers, Holland and Spain, fought over the control of Taiwan. The Dutch emerged victorious, took over Jilong, and occupied all of Taiwan.

The Dutch realized enormous profits once the trade route to China became open to them. They sold to China spices, sandalwood and other native products of Southeast Asia. They imported from China gold, copper-nickel alloy, raw silk and silk products. They sold most of the raw silk and silk products to Japan in exchange for silver. Using gold and copper-nickel alloy from China and silver from Japan, they purchased cotton textiles from India and then exchanged these cotton textiles for spices from Java and other islands. Besides, they imposed poll and other oppressive taxes on the Taiwan people and then, using these tax revenues and the profits they realized in the intramural Asian trade, purchased Asian goods to be shipped to Europe. The revenues and the profits were also employed to equip or expand fortifications, fleets and warehouses in the territories which they had occupied.

Unable to stand the cruel rule imposed upon them by the Dutch colonialists, the Taiwan people revolted time and again. In 1652, more than 16,000 people participated in an armed uprising led by Guo Huaiyi. They attacked the city of Chiqian and fought for fifteen days. Though they were defeated in the end, a severe blow was nevertheless delivered to the Dutch colonialists. Nine years later, the famous anti-Qing general Zheng Chenggong, determined to recover the island, led several hundred ships and 25,000 men to sail from Jinmen to attack the city of Chiqian, which he subsequently captured, thanks to the support given to him by the people of all ethnic groups on Taiwan. In the spring of 1662, the head of the Dutch colonialists, a man named Frederik Coyett, surrendered, and once again Taiwan was returned to the Chinese people.

But the Dutch colonialists did not concede after their defeat. Furthermore, they were afraid that the defeat might affect adversely their position in the Orient. They, therefore, expressed the desire to cooperate with the Qing government for a joint attack on Zheng Chenggong. In 1663, they, in alliance with the Qing forces, took from Zheng Jing, Zheng Chenggong's son and successor, the islands of Xiamen and Jinmen. By then Zheng Chenggong had already died. In the fall of 1664, the Dutch attacked and once again occupied Jilong. In the fall of 1668, Zheng Jing recovered Jilong and forced the Dutch to withdraw to Batavia. From then on, the Dutch colonialists were not able to realize the kind of profits they used to make.

The British colonialists formed the British East India Company in 1600. From then on, they fought against the Dutch over the hegemony of the sea and succeeded in attaining their goal in the middle decades of the seventeenth century. In 1637, an Englishman named John Weddell, at the head of four warships, sailed towards Guangzhou and, ignoring the warnings by Chinese garrison troops, bombarded Humen and forcibly occupied its battery. His purpose was to use force to compel China to trade with England. He was forced to leave Humen, however, after the Chinese had put up a strong resistance. In 1670, the British began to trade with Taiwan, then controlled by Zheng Jing. Later, they also traded at Xiamen. In 1680, shortly after Zheng Jing had lost Xiamen to the Qing authorities, the British stopped trading with Taiwan. In 1699, they obtained permission from the Qing government to open commercial offices in Guangzhou. But they continued to request the opening of more ports for trade, while conducting a variety of illegal activities.

Between 1802 and 1809, the British repeatedly used force in their attempt to seize Macao from the Portuguese, as they hoped to use Macao as a base of operation in committing aggression against China. In 1811 and again in 1821, they opened fire along the coastal areas of Guangdong, killing and wounding Chinese peasants. During the 1830s they time and again sent ships to conduct survey among China's sea lanes, make maps, and gather military intelligence in Xiamen, Fuzhou, Ningbo, Shanghai and other places.

During the early period of Anglo-Chinese trade, the British colonialists shipped to China woollens and spices in exchange for tea, medicine and porcelain. As late as the 1820s, the major British export to China was still cotton textiles. Since England could not sell its products well in China, under normal circumstances, she would have a deficit in her trade with China. Between 1781 and 1790, the total amount of tea China shipped to England was valued at 96,267,833 *yuan*. Meanwhile, between 1781 and 1793, the total amount of woollens and spices that China imported from England was valued at only 16,871,592 *yuan*, or one-sixth of what China sold to England. To eliminate the deficit, England began to ship large quantities of opium to China. The shipment was 200 chests in 1787, 2,000 chests in 1800, 5,147 chests in 1820, 7,000 chests in 1821, 12,639 chests in 1824, 21,785 chests in 1834 and 39,000 chess in 1837. In 1815, the Qing government enacted regulations governing the search of opium in foreign ships, but the British colonialists, violating Chinese law at will, resorted to bribery and smuggling to continue the shipment. Precisely because opium was banned, the profit it brought was also enormous. While the British colonialists were busy selling opium, not only did millions of Chinese lose their health or their will to live a constructive life, but large quantities of silver also flowed out of the country. The continuous outflow of silver brought damage to national finance as well as the government's treasury. From the Chinese point of view, a situation of this kind should not be allowed to continue. From the British point of view, however, a financial resource of this kind had to be maintained at all costs. The sharp contradiction led to a war that exploded in 1840.

The French colonialists began trading with China as early as 1640. In 1728, they, like the British, opened commercial offices in Guangzhou. Though the volume of their trade was far below that of the British, they brought with them Catholic missionaries who went to work in China's interior regions without authorization from the Chinese government. In due course, missionary activities became another form of aggression on the part of the colonialists.

The American colonialists did not trade with China until 1784, but the development of Sino-American trade was very rapid after that date. In 1789, altogether 86 Western ships arrived in China; of the 86, 61 ships belonged to the British and 15 were American. In 1832, the number of American ships arriving in China was 62. Besides trading in normal items, the Americans were powerful as opium peddlers.

Beginning in 1579, the Jesuits of the Roman Catholic Church arrived in commercial ships one after another. During the late Ming and early Qing period, they opened churches in thirteen provinces of China. In 1610, the total number of Chinese Catholics was about 2,500; the number rose to 13,000 in 1617, 38,200 in 1636, and 150,000 in 1650. Such political figures as Xu Guangqi and Li Zhizao and such eunuchs as Pang Tianshou and Ruo Se were all Catholic converts. Emperor Yong Li of Southern Ming, his empress, his mother the empress dowager, and his crown prince were also Catholic converts. This indicates that Roman Catholicism was widespread towards the end of the Ming Dynasty. Early during the Qing dynasty, some Western missionaries were employed as government officials; but the government, regarding them as technicians, imposed restrictions on their missionary activities. At one time, Emperor Kang Xi ordered a ban on the construction of Catholic churches as well as the promotion of Christianity, but the Pope, ignoring the ban, instructed Chinese coverts not to worship Heaven, ancestors and Confucius. A papal envoy arrived in Beijing in 1720, requesting an audience with Emperor Kang Xi. He wanted himself to be regarded as chief of all the missionaries in China; he also wanted all the Chinese converts to be governed according to the rules of Rome. Demands of this kind reflected the Pope's intention to violate the sovereignty of China. Emperor Kang Xi scolded the papal envoy severely as he told him: "China is not a place for Roman Catholicism which must be prohibited!" Nevertheless, the Qing government's ban against missionary activities was sometimes strict and sometimes lax. In any event, the missionaries were not so successful in promoting Christianity during the Qing as they had been during the late Ming period.

The missionary activities of the Roman Catholic Church in China began in 1583 when an Italian named Matteo Ricci started to work in Zhaoqing, Guangdong Province. From then on and until 1775, the missionary work in China was practically monopolized by the Society of Jesus. Because of their written works, more than seventy Jesuit missionaries can be identified today. Besides Matteo Ricci (1552-1610), there were Julio Aleni (Italian, 182-1649), Francesco Sambiaso (Italian, 1582-1649), Nicolas Trigault (Frenchman, 1577-1628), Johann Adam Schall von Bell (German, 1591-1666), and Ferdinand Verbiest (Belgian, 1623-1688). They were the most outstanding among the Jesuits.

The Society of Jesus was a diehard, anti-reform organization within the Roman Catholic Church, that came about in response to the Protestant Reformation of the sixteenth century. It advocated none but the orthodox theology of medieval time. It believed that God, the creator of the universe and everything in it, was the source of all power and morality in the world. God was the Father in Heaven, and kings, as God's representatives to govern nations, were people's fathers on earth. The people, therefore, must obey the laws of kings as they must obey the teachings of the church. Thus the Jesuits confirmed the correctness of Confucian ethics. However, since Confucian philosophers did not speak of a Heavenly God, the Jesuits maintained that Confucian ethics was incomplete. Only Catholic ethics, they concluded, was complete. A theory of this kind not only strengthened feudal rule and feudal ethics but also, by inventing the so-called blessings of God, glorified Catholic nations and individuals. Holding tightly the key to the Heavenly Kingdom of God, the Jesuits trampled on the earthly kingdom of man. Their thinking coincided well with the thinking of the colonialists who brought to China gunboats and opium. It contrasted sharply with the progressive thought among Chinese scholars during the late Ming and early Qing period.

The Jesuits have been praised as the importer of Western science to China, a praise they did not deserve. We know that modern science came about as a result of liberating man's mind from theology and that the Roman Catcholic Church was a deadly enemy of modern science and a brutal persecutor of scientists. Naturally, the Society of Jesus would stand on the front line against science and scientists, and it is unthinkable that its members would bring modern science to China. In fact, they tried their utmost in preventing Chinese scholars from learning about the latest developments in modern science. For instance, they chose not to provide adequate information on the great accomplishments of such men as Nicholas Copernicus, Johannes Kepler, Galileo and Issac Newton. Instead, they singled out for praise such men as Euclid in geometry, Peolemy in astronomy, and Aristotles in mechanics. Peolemy, as one recalls, believed that the sun circles around the earth. Aristotles and those who followed him maintained that "the speed of a falling object is in direct proportion to its weight". In other words, as their own knowledge of science remained as the level of ancient Greece, what the Jesuits had brought to China was not really modern science; it was none other than the antithesis of modern science. Besides, they wanted to subject scientific knowledge to the control by theology which remained the master. Speaking of human anatomy, they asked questions like: "How was this part divinely inspired? How was that part pre-arranged?" Speaking of earthquake, they stated: "Earthquake, like drought, flood, war, fire and disease, is controlled by God. Though it is caused by man, God, as the creator of all things over which He has absolute control, has the final word on its occurrence." Speaking of astronomy, they maintained that "the change in the movement of stars and planets affects the fortunes or misfortunes of man". Was this really modern science? The Jesuits castrated modern science of which they made a mockery.

Tsarist Russia, meanwhile, had its own tool of aggression against China, which was the Eastern Orthodox Church. In 1732, the Qing government gave permission for Tsarist Russia to establish churches in Beijing and, later, allowed Russian missionaries in China to be rotated once every ten years. Using churches as a cover and a base of operation, the Russians were in fact engaged in evil schemes against China. Before the Opium War, their rotation as missionaries in China had occurred eleven times. Most of these so-called missionaries were intelligence agents, gathering information on China's politics, economics and culture. They even secretly mapped certain areas of China and then brought the detailed maps back to Russia. These maps would be subsequently used by their government for aggression against China.

Two more points need to be mentioned in connection with the missionary activities in China. One involves geography, and the other concerns the making of calendar. In geography, Matteo Ricci's *Atlas of the World* was followed by Julio Aleni's *On World Geography* and Ferdinand Verbiest's *Complete Atlas of the World* and *Explanations of the World Atlas*. One of the reasons for making the world atlas was to arouse the curiosity of Chinese intellectuals about the non-Chinese world so as to foster with them a personal relationship. It cannot be denied, however, that the effort did help Chinese intellectuals in broadening their world outlook. As for the Chinese calendar used during the Ming Dynasty, it had not been accurate due to the lack of revision for a long period. Under the Ming law, individuals were not allowed to study calendar-making; consequently, few knew what calendar-making was all about. Then Xu Guangqi petitioned the government for calendar revision; under his leadrship, such Jesuits as Johann Adam Schall von Bell were invited to make contributions. The result was the *Chong Zhen Calendar* that consisted of approximately 100 *juan*. It was never put into practice, however. During the reigns of Shun Zhi and Kang Xi, Jesuits like Schall von Bell and Verbiest were once again invited to revise the calendar. The result of their work, completed in the seventeenth year of Kang Xi, was entitled *Yongnian Calen-*

dar that comprised 32 *juan*. The Jesuits' major contribution to calendar-making was accuracy; in devising the *Chong Zhen Calendar*, for instance, they quoted the works of Copernicus, Kepler and Galileo. Still, they chose too ignore the essence of Copernicus' contribution by insisting on the correctness of the geocentric theory. The progressive scholars of the late Ming and early Qing period, such as Fang Yizhi, described these Jesuits as "detailed in computation but inadequate in over-all understanding". He added that the Jesuits were inadequate even in computation.

Emperor Kang Xi promoted science, and it was during his reign that the two major scientific works, *The Essence of Mathematics and Physics* and *A Study of Universal Phenomena*, were compiled. Both works syncretized the existing knowledge from the West and the East. In 1708, he ordered a geographical survey of all regions in China, and the result, completed in 1718, was known as *The Complete Atlas of the Empire*. No country in the world had undertaken a geographical survey on such a large scale. In this survey French missionaries like Joachim Bouvet (1656-1730), Joannes B. Régis (1637-1738), and Petrus Jartoux (1668-1720) made important contributions. As a result of participating in the survey, the missionaries brought to their own countries valuable geographical materials about China that were subsequently circulated in Europe. The final work itself, namely the atlas, was kept inside the imperial palace, and it had little impact on the development of Chinese cartography.

Wang Xichan (1628-82) wrote *The Surviving Works of Xiaoan*. Mei Wending (1633-1721) wrote more than eighty books. Both scholars were outstanding mathematicians and astronomers of the Qing period, and they did thorough research on the scientific knowledge imported by the missionaries. They were able to merge this imported knowledge with the scientific knowledge of traditional China, so each would be in a position to correct or substantiate the othre. Wang Xichan deplored the attitude of missionaries towards science, an attitude which, he said, should not be taken by anyone with a broad, unbiased mind. He believed that the purpose of studying mathematics and astronomy was "to find out about reality and all its mysteries through the mastery of numbers". In other words, he was searching for a natural philosophy embodied in mathematical principles, totally different from the theology as advocated by the missionaries.

Taking advantage of their contacts with Chinese officials and ordinary people alike, the missionaries were able to gather information about China and help the colonialists in their aggression against China. At the time of the Opium War (1840), there were in China Protestant as well as Catholic missionaries, and the Protestant missionaries lent a helping hand to the aggression by England, the United States and other countries against China. Freedom of religion is a wonderful thing, but committing aggression under the cloak of religion is a different matter altogether.

Chapter X
Semi-Colonial and Semi-Feudal Society; the Old Democratic Revolution

1. The Opium War

The Opium War (1840-42) marks a significant turning point in China's history and ushered in the era of semi-colonial and semi-feudal society in China. Before the war, China had been an independent feudal country with the Qing court exercising full sovereign rights without outside interference. After the Qing rulers submitted to the British on August 29, 1842 by signing the unequal Treaty of Nanking, China turned step by step into a semi-colonial and semi-feudal country dominated—with the help of the Qing regime—by foreign power.

The era of semi-colonial and semi-feudal society in China's history includes two periods: the old democratic revolution from 1840 to the May 4th Movement in 1919 during which the Republic of China was founded after the fall of the Qing Dynasty; and the new-democratic revolution after the May 4th Movement led by the Chinese Communist Party.

To protect her lucrative opium trade, England had been preparing for war against China for some time before 1840. The Qing regime had become concerned about the social problems created by the importing of large quantities of opium and the rapid drain of silver from China. In 1838 Emperor Dao Guang appointed a strong advocate of opium prohibition, Lin Zexu, Governor-General of Hunan and Hubei provinces, as imperial commissioner in charge of banning the drug. Lin Zexu took firm action the next year when, on his arrival in Guangzhou in March, he arrested the opium dealers, punished officials who accepted bribes and ordered foreign merchants to hand over their opium. Foreign traders were also required to sign a bond guaranteeing they would never again bring opium into China. Charles Elliot, British Superintendant of Trade in China, did what he could to undermine the ban, including trying to prevent the British merchants from surrendering opium and signing the bond, and ordered foreign vessels anchored off the estuary of the Zhujiang River (Pearl River) to flee. He then prepared for battle. Countering Elliot, Liu Zexu ordered a halt to Sino-British trade and sent troops to keep under surveillance the foreign community where British merchants stayed. These actions compelled Elliot to order British merchants to surrender more than 20,000 chests of opium. Under the direction of Lin Zexu, from June 3 to 25 this lot of opium was burned in public on the Humen beach. Then Lin announced the restoration of normal trade—with the provision that opium be strictly forbidden—between China and Britain. Meanwhile, Elliot continued to try to undermine Lin Zexu's policy while urging the British government to launch a war in retaliation. In April 1840 the British Parliament formally passed a resolution to start a war against China and in June, a British fleet carrying 4,000 soldiers reached the seacoast of Guangdong.

Lin Zexu repaired and strengthened the fortifications at Humen and added more cannon. He also directed officers and men in training, recruited others among the boat dwellers and fishermen to form a marine force of "water braves" and generally intensified defence preparations. Having blockaded the Zhujiang River, the main British forces sailed north. They captured Dinghai of Zhejiang Province. In August the British fleet reached the port of Tianjin and threatened Beijing. At this point, Chief Grand Councillor Muchanga, who had opposed the opium ban in the first place, took the opportunity to attack Lin Zexu and advocate compromise with the British. Qishan, Governor-General of Zhili (present Hebei) Province, told the British invaders that if they withdrew to Guangdong, all outstanding issues would be settled to their satisfaction. The British agreed to negotiate at Guangdong. Emperor Dao Guang then appointed Qishan imperial envoy and sent him to Guangzhou to conduct negotiations. Lin Zexu was ordered dismissed and put under investigation.

On arrival at Guangzhou, Qishan dismantled the coastal defences and disbanded those armed men Lin Zexu had organized to resist the British. In January 1841, while negotiations were going on, British forces suddenly attacked and captured the fortress outside Humen. Qishan then agreed to the draft convention of Chuanbi[1] which required China to cede Hong Kong to the British and pay indemnities for the destroyed opium. Then British forces outrageously occupied Hong Kong, a part of China's territory.

However, Emperor Dao Guang considered those terms both excessive and damaging to the ruling position of the Qing court. He dismissed Qishan and declared war on Britain, sending Yishan, a member of the royal house who represented the most corrupt forces of feudal rule, to Guangzhou to direct military operations. But before his arrival, the British attacked the Humen fortress defended by Admiral Guang Tianpei and 400 greatly outnumbered men.

Qishan refused to send reinforcements, and after a brave fight, all officers and men in the fortress were killed by the British. Arriving at Guangzhou, Yishan failed to prepare for defence, but instead slandered the Guangdong people as "traitors". In May, when the British threatened Guangzhou, Yishan sued for peace and concluded the Convention of Guangzhou with the enemy, agreeing to pay an indemnity of six million silver dollars.

The Chinese people, meanwhile, were outraged by the actions of the British troops and the capitulation of the Qing officials. On May 29, they struck back on their own when the people in Sanyuanli outside the city of Guangzhou killed several British soldiers who had come there to plunder. Then the villagers organized, joining with people from neighbouring villages in a common fight against the British. Taking a three-star flag as their standard, they pledged "to advance as it advanced and retreat as it retreated, with no fear of death". On May 30, a force of 1,000 British soldiers invading Sanyuanli were greeted by peasants from 103 villages armed with the raised three-star flag, swords, spears, hoes and spades. The villagers surrounded the British in circles and in hand-to-hand combat killed and wounded many of the

---

[1] Chuanbiyang, outside Humen.

enemy. This was the earliest known spontaneous struggle by the Chinese people against foreign aggression in modern history.

In April 1841, the British government received a report on the draft convention of Chuanbi and, not satisfied with its provisions, decided to expand its invasion of China. In August British forces captured Xiamen (Amoy) of Fujian Province and in October Dinghai, Zhenhai and Ningbo of Zhejiang. Everywhere they went, Chinese soldiers and civilians resisted. The peasants of eastern Zhejiang Province voluntarily organized themselves for struggle against the enemy. They used small boats in an effective campaign to attack and harass the British at night. About the same time, the British attacked Taiwan of Fujian Province twice. Chinese soldiers and civilians there sank enemy ships and captured 183 invaders.

With the loss of three cities in Zhejiang Province, Emperor Dao Guang decided again to take military action. This time he sent Yijing of the royal house to Zhejiang to direct the war. Like Yishan, Yijing also represented that most corrupt forces of fedual rule. In March 1842, he foolishly started attacks by dividing his forces into three routes in an attempt to recover Dinghai, Zhenhai and Ningbo at one strike. His serious defeats discouraged him from fighting again.

In June, Admiral Chen Huacheng and the garrison troops resisted gallantly as the British attacked Wusong on the estuary of the Changjiang River. They managed to shell and damage some enemy ships but finally the whole garrison died heroically.

After occupying Shanghai the British advanced to Zhenjiang of Jiangsu Province, where 2,400 Chinese officers and men fought street battles with the enemy, killing and wounding some 180. In August British warships arrived at the Changjiang River off Nanjing (Nanking). The Opium War then came to an end when the Qing rulers submitted to the invaders.

Despite the courageous resistance of the people and the patriotic officers and men, the war ended with defeat for China because of the Qing court's domestic policy of hostility to the people and its foreign policy of compromise with and capitulation to the invaders.

On August 29, 1842 the representatives of the Qing court signed the humiliating Treaty of Nanking with England on a British warship off Nanjing. The treaty provided for the cession of Hong Kong, opening of five trading ports—Guangzhou (Canton), Xiamen (Amoy), Fuzhou (Foochow), Ningbo (Ningpo) and Shanghai where British consulates could be set up; indemnity of twenty-one million silver dollars; and tariff on export and import customs and other dues on British goods to be fixed by mutual agreement. In the following year, Britain forced the Qing government to sign the General Regulations under which British trade is to be conducted at the five ports of Canton, Amoy, Foochow, Ningpo, and Shanghai and the Supplementary Treaty of Hoomun Chai (The Bogue) as supplements to the Treaty of Nanking, giving Britain the privileges of consular jurisdiction and a unilateral most-favoured-nation treatment in China.

The first unequal treaty in modern Chinese history, the Treaty of Nanking was followed up by other treaties like it with other capitalist nations. The United States, a helping partner to Britain during the Opium War, had sent supporting naval units to China's coastal waters, and in 1844 the United States, backed by arms, forced the Qing court to conclude the Treaty of Wang-hea. In the same year the Qing court signed the Treaty of Whampoa with France. The United States and France both gained all the privileges of the Treaty of Nanking and its supplementary regulations, except the acquisition of territory and indemnities.

With these unequal treaties which infringed on her sovereignty and territorial integrity, China began to lose her political independence. Besides representing the interests of the landlord class, the Qing court now gradually also became the instrument of the foreign bourgeoisie in ruling over the Chinese people. Economically, China had been a feudal country with self-sufficient small farming combined with domestic handicrafts. After the Opium War, this economy gradually disintegrated with the penetration of foreign capital as the country was swept into the capitalist world market.

Class struggle changed with these fundamental political and economic changes in society. Besides the contradiction between feudalism and the masses of people, now there was the contradiction between foreign capitalism and the Chinese nation, and this became the most important of all contradictions. From the time of the Opium

War on, the Chinese people shouldered the double task of opposing domestic feudalism and foreign capitalism.

2. The Taiping Peasant War

In the aftermath of the Opium War treaties favouring the foreign powers, Chinese handicraft production dwindled in the coastal trade ports and nearby areas with the influx of cotton textiles and other industrial goods from Britain and other Western capitalist countries. At the same time, opium addiction became even more widespread—50,000 chests by 1850—under the rampant British opium smuggling which also aggravated the silver drain from China as reflected in the saying, "silver is dear, and copper cash cheap".

These burdens were made even heavier by the Qing government's increasing taxes on the peasants to pay for war expenses and indemnities. The landlords, too, took their toll on the people by intensifying land annexation so that in Jintian Village, Guiping County, Guangxi Province, landlords owned 88.3 per cent of the land, peasants only 11.7 per cent. On top of this, working people faced starvation under a famine that continued several years during this period. The people rebelled. In the decade after the Opium War over one hundred uprisings were staged by various ethnic groups: Han, Miao, Hui, Yao, Zhuang, Yi and Tibetan. By 1851 the people's rebellion had grown into a full revolutionary movement known as the Taiping Heavenly Kingdom led by Hong Xiuquan.

Hong Xiuquan (1814-64) was a rural intellectual, a school teacher born into a peasant family in Huaxian County, Guangdong Province, who sympathized early on with the plight of the people. Having several times failed the official examination given in Guangzhou for *xiucai* (a low degree in the imperial examination system), he increasingly became aroused by the misery of the people and the country's defeat in the Opium War. He began to join in the upsurge of popular struggle for challenging the authority of the local feudal forces by smashing the ancestral tablets of Confucius set up for worship in schools. Hong Xiuquan had been particularly inspired by a book he had come across in 1843, *Good Words for Exhorting the Age*, which propagated Christianity but to which Hong Xiuquan gave his own interpretation. Through his reading of the book, Hong Xiuquan claimed to have received a "mandate of Heaven" from God to come to earth to save mankind. Advising people to worship only God, not the "demons", he began to organize followers behind the *Bai Shang Di Hui* (Society for the Worship of God), the earliest of whom were his schoolmate, Feng Yunshan, and his cousin, Hong Rengan.

In 1844, Hong Xiuquan and Feng Yunshan left their home village to conduct propaganda and organize in Guangxi. Later, Hong returned to Huaxian County where he wrote *Doctrines on Salvation, Doctrines on Awakening the World, Doctrines on Arousing the World* and other articles to demand equality and oppose oppression. He said: "All men under Heaven are brothers and all women are sisters." Hong Xiuquan urged people to fight against the feudal emperor, officials, landlords and all such "demons" and to fight for making "the world one family to enjoy peace in common". About the same time, Feng Yunshan set up the *Bai Shang Di Hui* in Zijingshan District, Guiping County, Guangxi Province, taking in more than 2,000 members including poor peasants and handicraftsmen of the Han, Zhuang, and Yao ethnic groups. In 1847 Hong Xiuquan returned to Zijingshan to join Feng Yunshan and develop the *Bai Shang Di Hui's* struggle against local feudal forces. The movement's core centred on Hong Xiuquan as leader and Feng Yunshan, Yang Xiuqing, Xiao Chaogui, Wei Changhui and Shi Dakai as members.

In 1850, the year Empreor Xian Feng succeeded Dao Guang, the struggle of the *Bai Shang Di Hui* against the landlord forces became more intense. In the midst of a great famine, Guangxi Province was shaken by peasant rebellions and the time was ripe for the *Bai Shang Di Hui* to stage an uprising. On January 11, 1851 Hong Xiuquan led the *Bai Shang Di Hui* in an insurrection in Jintian Village. He organized the Taiping Army, called his organization the Heavenly Kingdom of Taiping and named himself Heavenly King. In September the Taiping Army captured Yong'anzhou (present Mengshan County, Guangxi Zhuang Autonomous Region). Hong then further established military and political systems and gave titles to several leaders: Yang

Xiuqing, Eastern Prince; Xiao Chaogui, Western Prince; Feng Yunshan, Southern Prince; Wei Changhui, Northern Prince; and Shi Dakai, Prince Wing. The Eastern Prince was placed in charge of all the other princes.

The Qing government reacted by sending large forces to encircle the city of Yong'an. In April 1852, the Taiping Army broke through and advanced northward. Feng Yunshan, the Southern Prince, and Xiao Chaogui, the Western Prince, died heroically in the course of march and battles across Guangxi, Hunan and Hubei. Along the way, the Taiping Army killed or drove away Qing officials, local gentry and landlords, burned title deeds and loan papers and distributed grain, money and goods to the impoverished peasants who enthusiastically received the army, many joining its forces.

In January 1853 the Taiping Army captured Wuchang, capital of Hubei Province, evacuated it the following month and advanced eastward along the Changjiang River. The Qing forces collapsed without putting up a fight. A month later the Taiping Army captured Nanjing, renamed it Tianjing (the Heavenly Capital), made it the capital of a formally established revolutionary force of peasants in opposition to the feudal power of the Qing Dynasty.

The Taiping Heavenly Kingdom proclaimed the Heavenly Land System, which stated: "All the land under Heaven should be cultivated by all the people under Heaven." The system called for land to be divided into nine grades depending on yields to be distributed evenly regardless of sex. A share was given to those above the age of sixteen and half a share to those up to fifteen. Twenty-five households were to compose a basic unit, and a system of village officials was to be set up for primary state power. The income from farm and side-occupations of each family, besides the part for consumption, was to be turned over to the "state treasury" to pay extra expenses of the family such as weddings or funerals according to a grade system. By practising this system, the Heavenly Kingdom hoped to establish an ideal society in which "land, food, clothing and money should all be shared equally, and all under Heaven should be well fed and clad".

The Heavenly Land System was significant in that it greatly expanded the idea of equalizing rich and poor and land-owning which the peasant wars had put forward in the past. It also reflected the peasants' urgent demand to abolish feudal landownership. However, the measures were not practical. To abolish private ownership and create equality on the basis of small production was only an illusion. The Heavenly Land System, as an ideal, could not be realized and was not realized. But conditions within the territory controlled by the Taipings did improve as the peasants who had worked for landlords who had fled or were killed no longer paid rent. And the few landlords still left lost their influence, so that many tenant peasants either refused to pay rent or paid less.

Another important aspect of the Heavenly Kingdom was its policy of respecting women. The Heavenly Land System provided that women be given land the same as men and that "under Heaven marriage should have nothing to do with property". Orders were issued to prohibit prostitution and the buying and selling of slave girls. A women's army was formed and women officials were appointed, and women took part in social productive labour and enjoyed the right to take official examinations.

In foreign relations, the Heavenly Kingdom opposed unequal treaties and foreign aggression and strictly prohibited the importing of opium. Between April 1853 and June 1854, ministers sent by Britain, France and the United States to Tianjing failed in their efforts to get the Taipings to recognize the unequal treaties.

In May 1853, the Heavenly Kingdom sent an army commanded by Lin Fengxiang and Li Kaifang on a northern expedition. Given support by peasants along the way, it swept across Jiangsu, Anhui, Henan and Shanxi provinces and into Zhili, and by October threatened Tianjin. But troops sent by Emperor Xian Feng succeeded in blocking the Taipings' advance, and since they lacked grain and winter clothing, they had to withdraw to Shandong. After another year of courageous fighting, lack of grain and reinforcements caused the northern expedition to fail in 1855.

At the same time the northern expedition began in 1853, a western expedition was started to safeguard the capital Tianjing. The troops marched along the Changjiang River up to Hankou and Hanyang of Hubei Province. When they came to Hunan Province, they were strongly opposed by the "Hunan army" organized by the Qing official Zeng Guofan with the Hunan landlords as the core.

After suffering setbacks the Taipings withdrew from Hunan and Hubei. In early 1855, with reinforcements under Shi Dakai, Prince Wing, the western expeditionary army scored a great victory over the Hunan army at Hukou and Jiujiang of Jiangxi Province, burning more than forty of its gunboats. After three years of struggles the Taipings won another important victory in early 1856, putting eastern Hubei and most parts of Jiangxi and Anhui under their control.

Soon after the Taipings established their capital at Tianjin the Qing forces set up the Great Southern Camp outside the city gates of the Heavenly Capital and the Great Northern Camp in the vicinity of Yangzhou. In early 1856 the Taipings removed the threat to the capital by crushing these two camps. At this point the Heavenly Kingdom reached the height of its military power.

Anti-Qing revolts by many ethnic groups spread in the wake of the Taipings' revolutionary victory. The principal ones were: the *Tian Di Hui* (Heaven and Earth Society) and its branches south of the Changjiang basin and along the southeastern seacoast; the Nians in North China and the ethnic minorities in the Southwest; the *Xiao Dao Hui* (Small Sword Society) of Shanghai; and those under the *Tian Di Hui* organization led by Chen Kai and Li Wenmao of Foshan, Guangdong Province. In September 1853 the Small Sword Society led by Liu Lichuan occupied the Shanghai county seat and nearby counties. But in February 1855 this group was defeated under the joint attack by the Qing and the invading British-French forces. The rebels under Chen Kai and others who rose at Foshan in 1854 laid seige to Guangzhou and in the following year went into Guangxi where, in Xunzhou (present Guiping County, Guangxi), they set up the Da Cheng Kingdom. In 1861 they also failed.

The Nians, composed mainly of bankrupt peasants and drifters, were active in Anhui, Henan, southwestern Shandong and northern Jiangsu. First a few dozens then hundreds formed the Nian forces which started an insurrection after people were left destitute following a Huanghe River flood in the area in 1851. The movement grew under the impact of the Taipings' northern expedition in 1853. In 1855 Nians from different routes met at Zhiheji, Mengcheng (present Woyang County), Anhui Province, and elected Zhang Luoxing to head the allied forces under the regime of "Da Han" (Great Han). This became the main force in the anti-Qing struggle in North China. After the failure of the Heavenly Kingdom, the Nians and the remaining Taipings continued together to fight Qing rule in eitht provinces until 1868.

In the Southwest, the Miao people led by the farmhand Zhang Xiumei staged an uprising in Guizhou Province in 1855. People of various ethnic groups—Han, Bouyei, Dong and Shui—joined the revolt. In 1856 the Yi people of the Ailao Mountains, Yunnan Province, led by the Yi farm-hand Li Wenxue and the Han labourer Wang Taijie, rebelled and established political power. Joining the ranks were people of the Han, Hui, Miao, Lisu, Dai, Bai, Hani and other ethnic groups. In the same year the Hui people in Yunnan led by Du Wenxiu revolted, capturing Dali and establishing a government. People of several ethnic groups—Han, Bai, Yi, Dai and Jingpo—joined this army. All of these various troops, fighting either singly or jointly, repeatedly defeated the Qing forces. Some persisted in fighting until 1876.

Though not a united movement, these anti-Qing rebellions encouraged and supported one another. With the Taiping Heavenly Kingdom as the centre, they did form a great revolutionary upsurge.

3. The Second Opium War; Russia's Occupation of Chinese Territory

At the height of the Taiping revolutionary movement, Britain and France, with the support of Russia and the United States, launched a new war of aggression against China. Taking advantage of China's civil war, they tried to force the Qing government to agree to complete revision of the treaties to extend the privileges obtained from the Opium War of 1840. This new war was, therefore, a continuation of the first Opium War, and so was called the Second Opium War.

On October 8, 1856 the Chiense navy captured some pirates from a Chiense vessel, the lorcha *Arrow*, off Guangzhou. To start provocations, the British claimed the ship as one of theirs, saying that Chinese soldiers had insulted the British flag flown on the vessel. On the 23rd British warships attacked Guangzhou and on the 29th British troops entered the city, followed by wild looting. The local people and soldiers rose to resist the invaders who withdrew because of inadequate strength.

After the *Arrow* incident, Britain decided to enlarge its war of aggression and asked France, the United States and Russia also to send troops. Using the killing of a French Catholic priest in Guangxi as an excuse, France joined Britain. Russia and the United States gave active support. Thus a united front of Britain, France, the United States and Russia was formed in a war of aggression against China.

In December 1857 some 5,000 Anglo-French forces attacked Guangzhou. Since the Qing government was then fully engaged in suppressing the Taiping Revolution, it offered practically no resistance and Guangzhou quickly fell.

In this grave situation, the people of Guangdong began a vigorous struggle. Once again the residents of Sanyuanli and other villagers took up arms against the invaders. In Hong Kong over 20,000 workers staged strikes, bringing the business there to a standstill.

After the capture of Guangzhou, the Anglo-French forces, leaving a small force to guard the city, sailed north. In April 1858 they reached the sea off Dagu. The ministers of Russia and the United States also arrived, ostensibly to act as "mediators" but actually as advisors to the British and French. In May the Anglo-French forces took Dagu fort, approached Tianjin, and threatened they would advance to Beijing. The corrupt Qing court sent negotiators to Tianjin to sue for peace. On June 26 and 27 the treaties of Tientsin were concluded with Britain and France. In November Britain and France forced the Qing government to sign the agreement containing rules of trade. These unequal treaties established residence for foreign ministers in Beijing and opened additional trade ports: Niuzhuang (later Yingkou), Dengzhou (later Yantai), Taiwan (Tainan), Danshui, Chaozhou (later Shantou), Qiongzhou, Hankou, Jiujiang, Nanjing and Zhenjiang. They also allowed foreign warships and vessels to freely navigate to the ports on the Changjiang River and foreigners to travel, trade and carry on missionary activities in China's inland. They provided for legalization of the opium trade; China's Customs tariff to be fixed with the assistance of foreigners; import and export duties set at 5 per cent *ad valorem* and the transit tax of foreign goods to the inland at 2.5 per cent. Four million taels of silver were to be paid to Britain and two million to France as indemnity.

Before the conclusion of the Sino-British and Sino-French treaties at Tianjin, Russia and the United States had persuaded the Qing government to sign Sino-Russian and Sino-American treaties at Tianjin by which they obtained many privileges. The treaty with Russia specially provided that the two countries appoint men to study the "uncharted" border. In doing this Russia hoped to occupy more Chinese territory.

Russia had always aspired after China's territory, and since the Opium War she had stepped up her armed aggression against China's Heilongjiang basin. At the end of May, 1858, two weeks before the conclusion of the Sino-Russian Treaty of Tientsin, N. Muraviev-Amursky, Russian Governor-General of Eastern Siberia, taking advantage of the Anglo-French attack on Tianjin, forced Yishan,[1] Chinese general in Heilongjiang, to sign the unequal Treaty of Aigun, through which Russia carved off over 600,000 square kilometres of China's territory south of the Outer Hinggan Range and north of the Heilongjiang River, and which designated about 400,000 square kilometres of China's territory from the eastern side of the Wusuli River to the sea as being under "Sino-Russian joint control". According to Engels, Russia deprived "China of a country as large as France and Germany put together, and of a river as large as the Danube".[2]

The treaties of Tientsin still did not satisfy the Anglo-French aggressors. In June 1859, under the pretext of exchanging ratifications of the treaties, the British and French ministers came to Dagu on warships. The Qing government notified them to land at Beitang on their way to Beijing. The notice was ignored. Their warships—with the

---

[1] The same Yishan who directed the war in Guangzhou in the first Opium War.

[2] Engels, "Russia's Successes in the Far East," *Karl Marx/Frederick Engels, Collected Works*, Eng. ed., Progress Publishers, Moscow, 1980, Vol. 16, p. 83.

warships of the United States giving support—bombarded the Dagu fortress. The Chinese garrison returned the fire, sinking and damaging many enemy ships and inflicting some 500 casualties. The Anglo-French invaders fled.

Threatening a large-scale retaliation, Britain and France sent a joint force of 16,000 men to Dagu in July 1860. The Russian minister followed and supplied the British and French with the intelligence that Beitang could be attacked as it was not on the alert. In August the invading forces landed at Beitang and occupied Dagu and Tianjin. In the following month they continued their advance to threaten Beijing. Emperor Xian Feng fled to Rehe (present Chengde, Hebei) with a group of officials, leaving his brother Yixin (Prince Gong) in Beijing to negotiate peace. On the eve of the Anglo-French attack on Beijing, the Russian minister contributed a map of Beijing which the Russian legation had drawn from secret surveillance, showing the weak points in the city's defence. With this information the Anglo-French forces in October entered the Andingmen gate and controlled the city. Along their way the invaders looted, burned and killed. After a wanton looting of the Yuan Ming Yuan Summer Palace, a magnificent palace combining Western and Chinese architectural art rarely seen in the world, housing many valuable artistic and cultural objects, they set this palace on fire and reduced it to ruins, inflicting inestimable loss on China's cultural achievement. Charles George Gordon who led the expedition admitted his troops had committed the outrage by "destroying in a vandal-like manner most valuable property".[1]

Submitting in late October, the Qing government exchanged ratifications of the treaties of Tientsin and signed the unequal treaty, Convention of Peking. Through these treaties, Tianjin became a trade port and Chinese labourers were "allowed to go abroad", which in fact legalized trafficking in Chinese labourers; a portion of Kowloon was ceded to Britain; French missionaries were permitted "to buy or rent land and to construct as they wish",[2] and the war indemnity to be paid

[1] A. E. Hake: *Gordon in China and the Soudan*, London, 1896, p. 18.

[2] This clause was secretly added to the treaty by J. M. Mouly, a Catholic missionary who acted as an interpreter for the French army.

to Britain and France prescribed in the treaties of Tientsin was increased to eight million taels of silver each.

In November 1860 Russia, again taking advantage of the Anglo-French attack and occupation of Beijing, by claiming that it had been a successful "mediator" and warning that war might again come, forced the Qing government to sign the Sino-Russian Additional Treaty of Peking. Besides reaffirming the Treaty of Aigun, the new treaty gave Russia about 400,000 square kilometres of China's territory east of the Wusuli River and many other privileges.

Through the Sino-Russian Additional Treaty of Peking and the later Sino-Russian Protocol of Chuguchak (which Russia forced the Qing government to sign in October 1864), Russia also seized 440,000 square kilometres of China's territory east and south of Lake Balkhash.

The amount of Chinese territory seized by foreign aggressors through the Second Opium War was unprecedented. They grabbed more and more rights and interests and stepped up political and economic control over China. Through their envoys stationed in Beijing, the capitalist countries were able to pressure the Qing government and dominate its internal and external affairs. The opening of more trade ports—extending from the southeast coast to seven coastal provinces and the middle reaches of the Changjiang River—furthered capitalist economic penetration. Foreign administration of Chinese Customs also tightened foreign control of the Qing court.

After the Second Opium War, domestic and foreign reactionary forces began to work in collusion as the pace of China's being turned into a colony quickened. In January 1861 the Qing government set up the Zongli Yamen under Prince Gong to deal with foreign affairs. It became an agency through which the Qing government betrayed the country by allowing foreign aggressors to carry out many-sided control over the Qing court. No sooner had the Zongli Yamen been established than a British citizen was appointed Inspector-General of Customs with full power of customs administration, including appointment of its personnel. As March went by, Britain, France and Russia set up their missions in Beijing. From then on their diplomats fostered Prince Gong and other Qing officials as their agents.

In August 1861 Emperor Xian Feng died of illness in Rehe and was succeeded by his son, Zai Chun, who was still under age and whose mother, Nala, was honoured with the name Empress Dowager Ci Xi. But power fell into the hands of Zai Yuan, Prince Yi; Duan Hua, Prince Zheng; and Su Shun, Minister of the Board of Revenue. Empress Dowager Ci Xi then collaborated with Prince Gong, who had the support of the foreign aggressors, to plan a coup d'etat. In November she returned to Beijing from Rehe and took charge of state affairs "behind the screen". She had Zai Yuan, Duan Hua and Su Shun executed, made Prince Gong the Prince Regent and put him in charge of the Privy Council, and changed the name of the reign "Qi Xiang" which had been proposed by Zai Yuan and others into "Tong Zhi" (joint reign), meaning that the Dowager and the Emperor ruled together. The foreign envoys were pleased with the rise to power of Ci Xi and Prince Gong. F. W. A. Bruce, British minister to China, reported to his government, stating that in the previous 12 months a faction which favoured and believed in the possibility of having friendly intercourse with foreign countries had been formed. It was an extraordinary success to have effectively helped these people to come to power. He went on to say that in Beijing, satisfactory relations had been established and to a certain extent he had become a Qing government advisor.

In other words, Qing rule and the foreign powers became collaborators. And one area in which the Qing rulers found their foreign advisors more than willing to help was in supplying arms and troops to suppress the Taiping Revolution, a movement which blocked the British, French, Russians and Americans from enjoying their full privileges under the treaties of Tientsin and the Convention of Peking.

4. The Later Period of the Taiping Peasant War

After the establishment of the capital at Tianjing, Weaknesses began to surface in the revolutionary ranks. In the first place, a complicated feudal system of rank and grade—from the Heavenly King on down to the ordinary soldier—began to corrode the Taipings' original simple idea of equality. Ceremonial rules became strict and insurmountable. Some leaders began to indulge in luxury and extravagance. Factionalism developed within the leading cliques. And some landlords and merchants—a few secret agents but mostly opportunists—managed to infiltrate the revolutionary ranks, trying to create contradictions and waiting for an opportunity to sabotage the revolution with the ideas and practices of the exploiting class.

In September 1856, at the height of its military success, the leading core of the Taipings openly split.

Yang Xiuqing, the Eastern Prince, had been of great service in the establishment of the Taiping Heavenly Kingdom. But as the revolution progressed, he became arrogant. In August 1856 he demanded that Hong Xiuquan give him the title of "Wan Sui" (His Majesty). Hong Xiuquan put him off and secretly ordered Wei Changhui, the Northern Prince, to return to the capital with troops to deal with Yang Xiuqing. Wei responded by not only killing Yang Xiuqing but also his whole family and all of his followers, over 20,000 people in all. Wei's arbitrary exercise of power created a reign of terror in Tianjing. Shi Dakai, Prince Wing, returned to the capital to denounce Wei for his massacre, which only led to Wei's wanting to kill Shi. Shi escaped to Anqing, Anhui Province, to prepare to lead troops against Wei. But, meanwhile, officers and soldiers in Tianjing took matters into their own hands and killed Wei. Hong Xiuquan then called Shi Dakai back to the capital to administer state affairs but also appointed two of his own brothers to share the same post to watch him. In June 1857, Shi Dakai, sensing that Hong did not trust him, left Tianjing with his crack troops to fight alone. In 1863 he was surrounded by the Qing troops at the Dadu River in Sichuan, and he and his entire army were destroyed.

Wei Changhui's violence and Shi Dakai's departure gravely weakened the strength of the Taipings and became the turning point from the rise to the decline of the revolution. As a serious crisis appeared in the Heavenly Kingdom, the Qing forces launched counterattacks, occupying many places on the middle and lower reaches of the Changjiang River, rebuilding the Great Northern Camp and the Great Southern Camp which had been destroyed by the Taipings before and laying siege to Tianjin. In his efforts to avert the crisis, Hong

Xiuquan promoted young commanders such as Chen Yucheng and Li Xiucheng to responsible positions in military affairs. In September 1858, Chen Yucheng and Li Xiucheng, joined by the Taiping forces from different routes, crushed the Qing's Great Northern Camp. In November they annihilated 6,000 crack troops of the Hunan army at Sanhe Town, Shucheng, Anhui Province, and forced the Qing troops, who were besieging Anqing, to flee. These victories stabilized the war situation on the Changjiang River upstream from Tianjing.

In April 1859 Hong Rengan, Hong Xiuquan's cousin, came to Tianjing. He had lived in Hong Kong many years, where he had some contact with the conditions of Western capitalist countries. Given the title of Prince Gan, he was placed in charge of the kingdom's state affairs. A little latr Hong Xiuquan gave the titles of Prince Ying to Chen Yucheng and Prince Zhong to Li Xiucheng. Hong Rengan wrote *New Guide to Government*, advocating political reform by following the example of the Western countries in building railways and establishing post offices, factories, mines, banks, etc. Hong Xiuquan approved these proposals, but as the conditions for their realization did not exist, they could not be carried out.

In March 1860, Li Xiucheng was sent to Hangzhou to spring a surprise attack to distract the attention of the enemy's forces at the Great Southern Camp. Then his troops returned from Hangzhou and joined Chen Yucheng to attack the Great Southern Camp, crushing it in May and raising the siege of Tianjing. Following this victory, the Taipings advanced eastward and by the end of 1861 occupied virtually the whole of Zhejiang and southern Jiangsu.

While the Taipings marched to the southeast, Zeng Guofan's Hunan army besieged Anqing. To lift the siege, Tianjing decided to send Chen Yucheng and Li Xiucheng by two routes to attack Wuchang in order to prevent the Hunan army from sending reinforcements. Chen Yucheng, leading the northern route troops from Anhui, approached Wuchang in March 1861. Li Xiucheng, leading the southern route troops, wasted so much time recruiting soldiers along the way that he failed to meet up with Cheng Yucheng in time, upsetting the whole plan. Since Anqing was in danger Cheng Yucheng first returned to rescue it, but failed when Anqing fell in September and Tianjing lost its protective screen. Withdrawing to Luzhou (present Hefei, Anhui) to prepare a counterattack, Chen Yucheng was captured by the Qing troops. He died in 1862, a still defiant hero at the age of 26.

The Qing court and foreign aggressors had collaborated from 1860 on to suppress the Taiping Revolution. The American adventurer Frederick T. Ward, conspiring with the Qing officials and their agents in Shanghai, recruited foreign mercenaries and organized them into a "Foreign Rifle Detachment". Britain and France also sent troops to join the Qing campaign, while Russia supplied the Qing government with 10,000 rifles and fifty cannon along with troops to intercept the Taipings in their attack against Shanghai. The Taipings fought the foreign aggressor troops with great courage. In May-June 1862, in battles around Shanghai, they repeatedly defeated the British, French and the Foreign Rifles. They killed the French naval commander, A. L. Protet, wounded the British naval commander, James Hope, and captured the American deputy leader of the Foreign Rifles, Edward Forrester. They recovered Jiading and Qingpu and were approaching the city wall of Shanghai County. The domestic and foreign counter-revolutionary forces there gained a reprieve as the Taiping army had to back off and return to defend Tianjing which the Qing troops had again besieged.

From the spring of 1862 on, Zeng Guofan, a large landowner in Hunan who as early as 1853 organized a militia under an edict from the emperor to fight the Taipings, began offensives against the Taipings along three routes: Zeng Guoquan leading the Hunan army's main force from Anqing against Tianjing; Zuo Zongtang leading the Hunan army from Jiangxi against Zhejiang; and Li Hongzhang leading the Anhui army—organized similarly to the Hunan army under the Anhui landlords—from Shanghai against Suzhou and Changzhou. In June, Zeng Guoquan's branch of the Hunan army laid siege to Tianjing, threatening Yuhuatai in its outskirts. The Taipings fought the Hunan army for over forty days but could not break the siege. In the meantime, the other foreign and Qing reactionary troops intensified their attacks on Jiangsu and Zhejiang. In Zhejiang, the British and French troops helped the Qing forces capture Ningbo. At Cixi the Taipings engaged the British and French troops and Ward's

Foreign Rifles in pitched battles, killing Ward. Then Zuo Zongtang's branch of the Hunan army, joined by the British and French at Shaoxing, attacked Hangzhou and nearby cities. Hangzhou fell in March 1864, and the Taiping forces in Zhejiang disintegrated. In May, Suzhou and Changzhou also fell under the joint attack of Li Hongzhang's Anhui army and the Foreign Rifles, now led by the British officer Charles Gordon. The Taipings' southern Jiangsu front also collapsed.

The situation at the capital became increasingly critical and in the last stages of the Taiping Heavenly Kingdom's struggle, its outstanding leader, Hong Xiuquan died on June 1, 1864. In July the Hunan army dynamited the city wall, and Tianjing fell after fierce street fighting. The Hunan army committed all kinds of atrocities as it plundered and burned the whole city.

Li Xiucheng managed to break through the encirclement but was taken prisoner outside Tianjing. He wrote a confession but Zeng executed him.

Hong Rengan was captured in Jiangxi. He refused to surrender and was killed. The Taipings' remaining forces continued armed struggle north and south of the Changjiang until 1868.

The failure of the Heavenly Kingdom gave the Qing government a free hand to suppress the revolts of the Nians and the various ethnic groups in the Southwest. In the Shaanxi-Gansu area the Huis rose in 1862 and kept fighting for eleven years until they were defeated in 1873.

The glorious Taiping Revolution in semi-colonial and semi-feudal China failed for the lack of proletarian leadership. But having failed in its fight against feudalism and foreign aggression, it nevertheless was the largest peasant revolution in China's history. It established a revolutionary political power, put forward a clear-cut anti-feudal programme, engaged the greater part of the country in struggle for fourteen years and dealt heavy blows against Qing feudal rule and foreign capitalist forces of aggression. Its magnificent struggles and historic achievements will always be remembered for propelling the forward advance of history and stimulating the revolutionary will of the Chinese people.

5. Culture and Learning After the Opium War

Academic and cultural circles after the Opium War also witnessed a period of change and struggle. Some of the enlightened officials and educated people of the landlord class—like Lin Zexu (1785-1850) and Wei Yuan (1794-1857)—developed the Ming-Qing tradition of stressing the practical application of learning. They turned their attention to real problems such as critically examining China's relations with foreign countries and exploring the use of new technologies and theories to develop production.

Lin Zexu, who so strongly opposed the British importation of opium, was farsighted on the question of China's relations with other countries. He sought out information about conditions in foreign countries as well as their views on China. While in Guangzhou, he organized people for translation of foreign newspapers and books, and sponsored the publication of the books, *Four Continents* and *China's Affairs in the Words of Foreigners.* At the height of British aggression, he took note of the question of defence of the northern border by saying, "Russia is the country that will give trouble to China!" Lin Zexu was also concerned with water conservation. In his later years, he helped agricultural development in Xinjiang by building canals and ditches and cultivating 37,000 *qing* (755,000 acres) of farmland there. His writings were compiled into the *Works of Lin Zexu*.

Wei Yuan helped Lin Zexu draft proposals on water transport of grain to the capital, irrigation and salt revenue administration. Before the Opium War, he edited *Imperial Collection of Essays on Government.* At the outbreak of the war, he participated in planning the resistance against the British on the Zhejiang front. Later he wrote *Records of Warrior Sages,* a history of the military operations of the Qing emperors, as a contrast to the military incompetency of the time. He also wrote *Illustrated Records of the Maritime Nations* in one hundred *juan* on the history and geography of foreign countreis and the policies China should adopt towards them.

Like Gong Zizhen who advocated political reform, Wei Yuan believed that "any change, whatever the extent may be, brings good order, and the more thoroughly the old ways are changed the greater the benefit to the people". He advanced the idea of "learning from the foreigner to restrain the foreigner" and criticized those in power for refusing to adopt superior Western technology and looking down at machinery as a "strange trick". In other words, he advocated China's learning the advanced technology of the Western capitalist countries and their methods of organizing and training armed forces for defence against foreign aggression.

Wei Yuan's idea of political reform was based on the view of historical evolution. He said: "There is no law which does not change over hundreds of years, and there is no law which is limitless and unchangeable." Believing that "knowing" comes from "doing", he opposed the idealistic theory of knowledge of "knowing before doing". He believed knowledge originates from direct experience and denied there was any innate, supra-experience knowledge. His principal works also included *Collected Works of the Guweitang Study*.

The raising of border region questions helped bring about study in the area of history and geography. Zhang Mu (1805-49) of Pingdingzhou (present Pingding County), Shanxi Province, investigated the geography of Mongolia and the activities there by previous regimes. His famous work *Shepherding in Mongolia* was, after his death, supplemented, proofread and printed by He Qiutao. It consisted of sixteen *juan*.

He Qiutao (1824-62) of Guangze County, Fujian Province, saw that there had been no special books written on the question of the Sino-Russian border and so he, having studied the history and geography of China's Mongolia, Xinjiang and the Northeast and Sino-Russian relations, wrote *Collected Articles on the Northern Frontier Question* in eighty *juan*.

Lin Zexu, Wei Yuan, Zhang Mu and He Qiutao sponsored new academic research, widening the area of scholarly investigation and reflecting changes in the cultural field. They all were greatly influential.

In literature, many patriotic works after the Opium War praised the anti-aggression struggle of the Chinese people and condemned British invasion and the Qing rulers' capitulation to foreigners. Famous poems included *World Seas* by Wei Yuan, which denounced the

Qing officials' shameful surrender to invaders, and *Sanyuanli* by Zhang Weiping, which portrayed the patriotic anti-British struggle of Sanyuanli villagers and described the plight of the terrified intruders under the blows of the Chinese people, and expressed the popular indignation against the decadent Qing rule. Posters and folk songs, in simple popular language, by denouncing foreign invaders and Qing rulers, also aroused the militancy and resistance of the masses.

In science and technology, Wu Qixun, Zou Boqi and Zheng Fuguang made contributions. Wu Qixun (1789-1847) compiled ancient essays on plants into the twenty-two-*juan Compendium of Illustrated Investigation of the Names and Natures of Plants*, which contains 838 varieties of plants. Reporting on his own observations and investigations, he compiled the thirty-eight-*juan Illustrated Investigation of the Names and Natures of Plants*, which contains 1,714 varieties. These two are among the important works on plants published in modern China. Zou Boqi (1819-69) was a scholar in astronomy, calendar-making, mathematics, geography and surveying. Based on a synthesis of the country's knowledge about geometric optics he further explained the basic principles of the reflecting mirror, transparent mirror, spectacles, telescope, magnifier and other optical instruments.

Zheng Fuguang (?-1846) wrote *Summary of Knowledge of Optics*, systematizing the basic principles of Chinese and Western knowledge of optics and of the structure and application of the telescope, magnifier and other glasses. He wrote articles on the principles of the structure of the steamship with illustrations. This was the beginning of the study of the modern steamship by the Chinese.

The reactionary landlord class did not forget to try to dominate the academic and cultural field. This class was represented by Zeng Guofan (1811-72) who, while ruthlessly suppressing the Taiping Revolution, propagated feudal ethics, claiming that relations between the emperor and minister, father and son, and superior and subordinate were like hats and shoes which could not change places. He thought foreign aggression was "Heaven's doing" and maintained there was no way to defend against foreigners and the only way to deal with them was through courtesy and retreat. Foreign cultural activities in China included Britain, the United States and other countries beginning to establish churches, run newspapers, and open hospitals and museums. In 1858, the British Royal Asiatic Society set up a branch in Shanghai. These activities were actually cultural aggression carried on under the protection of guns. Sharp struggles went on in the academic and cultural field after the Opium War, as in the political field.

6. Foreign Economic Aggression and the Official "Westernization" Drive

Relying on privileges extorted from China after the two Opium Wars, foreign capitalists continued to make inroads into China's economy, turning China into a dumping-ground for their goods and a base for their industrial raw materials. They shipped and sold to China cotton textiles, kerosene, dyes and sewing needles, with the quantity of cotton goods increasing the most quickly. During the twenty years from 1873 to 1893, cotton yarn shipped and sold to China increased from 4.1 million kilogrammes to 59.3 million kilogrammes. Foreign capitalists also controlled China's traditional exports of tea and silk and shipped from China enormous quantities of cotton, soybean and other farm produce and raw materials. The transformation of China into a market for world capitalism under imperialist control, which was an indication of the semi-colonial nature of her economy, brought about a depression in agriculture and handicrafts and the impoverishment of Chinese peasants and other producers.

Apart from dumping industrial goods and seizing China's raw materials, foreign capitalists continued to open banks and factories in China. By the time of the Sino-Japanese War of 1894, more than a dozen foreign banks had illegally opened in China. Prominent among them were the British Hongkong and Shanghai Banking Corporation (1865), the German Deutsche-Asiatische Bank (1889) and the Japanese Yokohama Shokin Bank (1893): they accepted money deposits, issued paper currencies, handled inland and overseas remittances and extended loans to the Qing government, and were important instruments for foreign encroachments upon China's economy.

In total disregard of China's sovereignty, foreign aggressors began to set up factories in many Chinese cities soon after the Opium Wars, and factories with foreign investment grew steadily in number from the 1860s on. The majority were either ship-repairing dockyards, serving the rapid development of inland navigation, or processing factories for making brick tea, reeling silk, ginning cotton and refining sugar with local raw materials. There were also other light industries such as match factories, paper mills and soap factories, which exploited cheap Chinese labour and the easily accessible local market. By 1894, there were more than a hundred foreign-owned factories on Chinese territory, with a total investment amounting to twenty-eight million Chinese yuan, embodying a force that suppressed and hindered the growth of China's national industry. Foreign export of capital and the establishment of banks and factories in China were further indications of the semi-colonial nature of the Chinese economy.

Confronted with intensified foreign aggression, some of the Qing officials advocated "making the country strong and rich" by the establishment of "Western-style factories". They realized the importance of learning military and industrial technology from Western capitalism so as to buttress their rule in the face of the Taiping Revolution and in contacts with foreign aggressors in the 1860s. Unlike Lin Zexu, Wei Yuan and others who wished to learn about foreign countries to resist aggression, the "Westernization group" studied Western technology in order to build up their military and civilian industries and a modern navy and army, relying on despotic rule and foreign assistance. Represented by Yixin (Prince Gong), Zeng Guofan, Li Hongzhang, Zuo Zongtang, Zhang Zhidong and others, the Westernization group can be distinguished from members of landlord class who had little contact with foreign capitalism and were blindly anti-foreign.

The Westernization group devoted the greatest effort to establishing war industries. In the course of suppressing the Taiping uprising, Zeng Guofan had an arsenal set up in Anqing, Anhui, in 1861. Li Hongzhang patronized the founding of the Kiangnan Machine Building Works in Shanghai in 1865 for making rifles, guns and ammunition. Zuo Zongtang had the Fukien Dockyard built in Fuzhou, the biggest of its kind at the time, in 1866; and Chonghou sponsored the establishment of a machinery factory, which was in effect an arsenal, in Tianjin in 1867. It later came under Li Hongzhang's charge and was further expanded. More and more weapon and ammunition factories were set up in the 1870s in many cities. These factories were financed by the Qing government, managed by officials appointed by the court, and manned in part by soldiers. The products were directly issued to the armies. Not capitalist but government-owned enterprises, they depended completely on foreign personnel from establishment to management and were under their sole control.

To provide the necessary raw materials, fuels and means of transport for the war industries, and envying the large and profitable sale of foreign goods in China, the Westernization group began to open up factories, mines and transport and communication facilities of a capitalist nature in the 1870s. The earliest and largest among these was the China Merchants Steamship Navigation Company organized by Li Hongzhang in Shanghai in 1872. In 1876, he developed a mine in Kaiping, Zhili and prepared to open up a machine-weaving textile mill in Shanghai. Then in 1877 Zuo Zongtang projected to set up a machine-weaving worsted mill in Lanzhou, Gansu. And in 1890, Zuo Zongtang promoted the setting up of an ironworks in Hanyang. By 1894, more than twenty enterprises of this kind had been built up. In the form of "government-supervised and merchant-managed" enterprises or "co-management by government and merchants", they absorbed capital from landlords, merchants and officials and were controlled mainly by the latter. An embryonic form of bureaucrat-capitalism, these officially-authorized enterprises monopolized production, and fettered the activities and development of national capital. Civilian industries similarly relied on foreign capital and were branded with a feudal birthmark.

In the 1870s, the Westernization group planned to build up two navies, the Beiyang (North China coast) and the Nanyang (South China coast) fleets. In the 80s, Li Hongzhang founded a military academy in Tianjin, had a dockyard built in Lüshun and a navy port in Weihaiwei, and bought warships and cannon from abroad for the Beiyang Fleet.

7. The Proletariat and the National Bourgeoisie in the Early Days; the Spread of Modern Western Science

With the appearance of modern industry in China, the first generation of modern industrial workers, the early Chinese proletariat, emerged. National capitalism engendered a national bourgeoisie. With modern industry came modern Western science.

From the 1870s onward, groups of officials, landlords and merchants invested in modern industries of a capitalist nature, mainly filatures, textile mills, flour mills, match factories and coal mines. Among those established were Fachang Machinery Plant, Shanghai, 1869; Jichanglong Filature of Nanhai, Guangdong, 1873; Chizhou Coal Mine, Guichi, Anhui, 1877; Yilaimou Flour Mill, Tianjin, 1878; Gongheyong Silk Factory, Shanghai, 1881; Liguoyi Coal and Iron Mines, Xuzhou, Jiangsu, 1882; Tongjiuyuan Cotton-Ginning Plant, Ningbo, Zhejiang, 1887; and Yuyuan Cotton Mill, Shanghai, 1894. Between 1869 and 1894, more than a hundred enterprises of this kind came into operation, their total investment amounting to six million yuan, with about thirty thousand employees on their payroll. Most of these enterprises were rather small with a slender capital of less than 100,000 yuan, or even only a few thousand yuan. Though they were weak compared with the foreign-owned and the officially-managed enterprises, their very existence indicated the presence of national capitalism and consequently a national bourgeoisie in China.

However, national capitalism could barely survive in a semi-colonial and semi-feudal society. Competition was intense. Whereas foreign countries and their factories and mines in China could sell products and get hold of raw materials due to their special privileges, the native industries, in addition to difficulties in obtaining raw materials and securing markets, were constantly faced with the danger of annexation by foreign capital. Instead of helping native industries, the Qing government levied heavy taxes on them and fettered their growth in every way. Chinese national industries relied on foreign countries for machinery, technology and even "protection" and had to turn to the feudal government for support as well, though the latter was more nominal than real. Many of the industrialists themselves were originally officials, landlords or merchants, and some still possessed land and collected land rent from peasants. They, therefore, were on the one hand in constant and inevitable conflict with foreign capitalism and domestic feudalism, and on the other were bound closely to them. From its very first days, the Chinese bourgeoisie had a dual character; it opposed foreign capitalism and domestic feudalism, while at the same time it tried to compromise with them.

With the emergence of national capitalism, the initial demand voiced by reformists within the landlord class for political reform and learning from the West for self-defence developed into a trend towards bourgeois reformism in society at large in the 1870s. Early representatives of this trend were Wang Tao (1828-97) of Suzhou, Jiangsu; Xue Fucheng (1838-94) of Wuxi, Jiangsu, Ma Jianzhong (1844-1900) of Dantu, Jiangsu, and Zheng Guanying(1842-1921) of Xiangshan (present Zhongshan), Guangdong.

The gist of their ideas was as follows:

1. Opposition to foreign aggression, a serious and constant danger to the country. They pointed out that the unilateral most-favoured-nation treatment, consular jurisdiction, tariff rates on Chinese imports and exports and other such provisions in the unequal treaties were sources of endless damage to China and demanded their revision.

2. Development of national capitalism and opposition to the Qing policy of restricting national industry and commerce. They criticized the Westernization-group sponsored enterprises where the officials had sole control while the merchants had no say. They demanded that effective government support be given to national industry and commerce and a protective customs tariff adopted, so that Chinese capitalism would have the ability to compete with foreign rivals. Zheng Guanying criticized the feudal policy of "promoting agriculture, restricting commerce" and called for "a trade war". He said: "To check Western forces and strengthen the country, no measures are more effective than the stimulation and promotion of commerce." The development of capitalism, he believed, was the only way out for China if she wanted to become independent and prosperous. His demand of

waging a trade war had anti-imperialist and patriotic significance.

3. Institution of a constitutional monarchy. Wang Tao, Zheng Guanying and others recommended various Western political systems and the substitution of feudal autocratic monarchism with parliamentarianism, as practised in certain foreign countries. Arguing that "it is not strong warships and powerful cannon alone that end chaos and bring prosperity, but the establishment of a parliament", they considered that the institution of a political organ like parliament could unite the whole country for resistance to foreign aggression. This shows that the early reformists differed not only from the Westernization group but was also more advanced than the landlordclass reformists who called on people to learn the foreigners' skills just for the purpose of resisting them.

The early reformists, however, neither established any systematic theories nor brought about any political movement, showing that the Chinese national bourgeoisie was still very weak. Separated only recently from the Westernization group, they could not free themselves from the latter's influence either politically or ideologically.

China's early proletariat arose in the 1840s when dockyards and factories were opened up by British, U.S. and French merchants in coastal port cities. Most of the workers were originally destitute peasants and handicraftsmen. The number of industrial workers increased in the 60s and 70s when military and civilian industries were set up by the Westernization group and the Chinese national bourgeoisie. By the 70s, apart from dockers whose number fluctuated, the Chiense industrial workforce amounted to 10,000 strong. The number rose to more than 40,000 by the beginning of 80s and to 100,000 by 1894.

The proletariat in semi-colonial and semi-feudal China was subjected to the threefold oppression and exploitation by foreign capitalism, national capitalism and feudalism, with a harshness and ruthlessness seldom known elsewhere. Their meagre pay was often deferred. With their wages forfeited and deducted under various false pretences, they could hardly eke out a living. They were beaten and abused by supervisors and overseers. Working conditions were deplorable, and injuries and accidents were daily occurrences. Without any freedom or rights, the Chinese workers led a miserable life.

Suffering economic and political oppression, the Chinese proletariat had to fight for its survival. The earliest strikes against foreign exploitation were staged by workers of Farnham & Co. in Shanghai in 1868 and again in 1879 against the embezzlement of workers' pay by overseers. In 1879, workers of Boyd & Co. demonstrated against the beating of a Chinese worker by a foreign overseer. In 1883 and 1890, workers of the Kiangnan Machine Building Works laid down their tools in protest against extensions of their working hours. In 1891, Kaiping miners protested against a foreign engineer's abuse of Chinese workers, forcing the engineer to leave the mine temporarily. Workers' struggles of this period, however, were mainly economic, as the Chinese proletariat was still very young.

The propagation of Western science by the Jesuits at the end of the Ming and the beginning of the Qing dynasties had very little impact on Chinese society as a whole. The real job was done by Chinese scholars like Li Shanlan (1810-82), who spread Western science by their systematic studies in the 1860s and 70s. Modern science had progressed rapidly in the West after the discovery of the solar system by Copernicus. The subsequent initiation of analytical geometry by Descartes, of logarithms by Napier and of calculus by Leibniz and Newton supplied the most important mathematical methods for scientific development. Basing his theory of rigid body mechanics on Kepler's laws of planetary motion, Newton summarized the law governing the motion of matter in general and advanced the law of universal gravitation. China lagged far behind foreign countries in the study of natural sciences in the Ming and Qing dynasties. Li Shanlan's translations and articles were of great significance in the history of development of modern science in China. A mathematician of considerable stature, he arrived independently at the fundamental concept of calculus in his works. His stress on the importance of an objective study of nature in contradistinction to wishful thinking shows his scientific, materialist approach.

Li's contemporaries included Hua Hengfang (1833-1902), who wrote a 23-*juan* work on mathematics and translated more than 60 *juan* of works on algebra, trigonometry, calculus, the theory of probability and so on, and Xu Shou (1818-84) who was well versed in physics, chemistry and mechanics. Together with Hua Hengfang, Xu Shou compiled and translated many scientific works. The two also built a 50-foot-long timber steamboat, the *Yellow Crane*, which could cover more than 20 kilometres an hour. This was the first steamboat ever built by the Chinese. Around 1875, Xu Shou founded the Academy of Natural Sciences in Shanghai and gave demonstrations of chemical activity in laboratory experiments. He was a pioneer in propagating modern chemistry in China. A firm materialist, Xu was opposed to superstitious beliefs and adhered to the principle of "enlightening students by experiments and demonstration of facts".

Though a few outstanding scientists appeared in China in the last quarter of the nineteenth century, they exerted little influence since semi-colonial and semi-feudal China had no developed modern industries to sustain their efforts. Moreover, they were hampered ideologically by China's feudal culture.

8. Foreign Aggression and China's Border Crises

The last few decades of the nineteenth century saw a transition to imperialism in major capitalist countries. These countries were locked in an increasingly acute struggle over markets, sources of raw materials and areas for capital investment in colonies and the territories of other countries. The Far East was a bone of contention. The United States, Japan, Britain, Russia, France and Germany extended their aggression to China's vast border regions, creating a critical situation.

The United States had long coveted Taiwan. On the pretext that the crew of the *Rover*, a wrecked ship, had been killed in Taiwan, it sent warships to invade the island and landed its troops in Langqiao (present Hengchun) on the southwest tip of the island in 1867. The native Gaoshan people drove the invaders away.

In 1874, encouraged by the United States, Japan invaded Taiwan with 3,000 troops. The local people, both Gaoshans and Hans, resisted the aggressors from strategic positions. The Japanese invaders suffered casualties and were unable to advance further. Through the "mediation" of the U.S. and Britain, however, the corrupt Qing government agreed to pay the Japanese 500,000 taels of silver as indemnity as a condition for them to withdraw.

From the 60s to the 70s, Britain constantly sent men to Tibet for espionage in the guise of travellers or explorers. When Emperor Guang Xu succeeded Empror Tong Zhi in 1875, the British interpreter Augustus Raymoond Margary, at the head of 200 armed men, crossed China's southwest border and intruded into Yunnan Province from Burma. When the local Jingpo people tried to stop them, Margary opened fire, and the Chinese killed Margary and drove out the invaders. Seizing this excuse, Britain forced on the Qing court the 1876 Agreement of Chefoo which stipulated that Britain could send men to Yunnan to "investigate" trade, or to India from China's hinterland via Tibet or back from India by the same route. This opened the way for Britain to enter Yunnan and Tibet.

After the signing of the Agreement of Chefoo, Britain sent people to Tibet for aggression. The Tibetans and some local officials refused them entry. In 1888, Britain launched an aggressive war against Tibet, but met with stubborn resistance from the Tibetan army and civilians. More than a hundred of the aggressor troops were killed or wounded. The corrupt Qing government, however, forbade the Tibetan people to resist the invaders who continued with their aggression. In 1890, the Qing government negotiated with Britain on the border issue and signed the Sikkim-Tibet Convention. In 1893, the Qing government agreed to Britain's request to open a trading city in Tibet, and British influence infiltrated Tibet as a result.

While the United States and Japan landed their troops in Taiwan and Britain made inroads on China's southwestern frontier, Russia extended its aggression to Xinjiang. In 1865, Yakub Beg, an army officer from Khohand in Central Asia, took advantage of internal strife in Xinjiang to occupy Kaxgar. By 1870, Yakub Beg had occupied most of the areas north and south of the Tianshan Mountains. Since Britain and Russia both had plans for extending their influence to Xinjiang, they were in fierce competition over collaboration with Beg. In 1871, Russia sent troops to occupy the Ili region and imposed colonial rule on the people of different ethnic groups there.

Aggression perpetrated by Russia and Beg stiffened the Xinjiang people's resistance, who organized themselves for struggle in anticipation of Qing government action to restore the lost territories. In 1876 the Qing government ordered Zuo Zongtang to lead an army into Xinjiang. With the people of the different ethnic minorities arming themselves and fighting in co-ordination with the Qing army, the Beg bandits were eventually vanquished, and the lost territories were recovered in early 1878. However, the Russians remained in occupation of the Ili area.

The Qing government repeatedly made representations to the Russian government, demanding the return of Ili. Russia refused and instead advanced a series of unreasonable requests. In February 1881, it forced the Qing government to sign the unequal Treaty of St. Petersburg. Though China recovered Ili as a result, it lost large tracts of territory west of the Khorgos River. Through this and other boundary treaties concluded later, Russia exacted more than 70,000 square kilometres of territory and enormous political and economic prerogatives from China.

After concluding the Treaty of St. Petersburg, Russia further intensified its encroachment upon China's Pamir area. In 1892, violating the 1884 "protocol on the Sino-Russian boundary in the Kaxgar region", a treaty on the Sino-Russian boundary in the Pamir area, Russia occupied more than 20,000 square kilometres of Chinese territory west of the Sarykol Range. The Qing government declared explicitly that it would not yield its sovereignty over territories in the Pamirs which were situated beyond the positions occupied at the time by the Chinese troops. However, in 1895 Russia and Britain concluded an agreement and partitioned between themselves China's Pamir territories west of the Sarykol Range.

In the mid-nineteenth century, France followed its occupation of the southern part of Viet Nam with invasion of the north. Using Viet Nam as a foothold, it made inroads into China. The Black Flag Army, a former peasant rebel force led by Liu Yongfu, active on the Sino-Vietnamese border and the middle section of the Honghe River, fought in co-operation with the Vietnamese army and civilians against the French invaders, and repeatedly repulsed their advance. However, China's military and diplomatic power was then in the hands of Li

Hongzhang who only knew how to appease the aggressors and who had time and again yielded to them. His appeasement only encouraged the French colonialists and the flames of war spread to China.

In August 1884, France used warships to attack Jilong Fort, Taiwan, and landed its troops on the island. The Taiwan garrison troops counter-attacked, killing and wounding more than a hundred of the invading troops and driving away the rest. The routed French invaders turned to attack Fuzhou, Fujian. The administrative officials in Fujian, abiding by Li Hongzhang's policy, made no preparations against attack and went so far as to forbid the Fujian Squadron under penalty of death to fire at the enemy. When the French warships bombarded the Chinese squadron, it acted in a hurry; some of its warships were hit and sunk even before weighing anchor. The Chinese officers and crew faced up to the enemy under very unfavourable conditions. The flag ship *Yangwu*, though badly damaged by enemy cannonade, hit the enemy flag ship with its stern gun and killed many of the enemy. The *Zhenwei* came under crossfire and was pierced through by enemy cannon balls, its bow and stern all aflame. Still the ship's company fought to the end and just before submerging fired a last cannon at a French ship, seriously wounding its captain and some of its crew. The *Fuxing* engaged the enemy ships in their midst and repeatedly gunned the enemy flag ship with unerring aim. Its company fought courageously and died heroically when the armoury was hit and exploded.

In the sea battle, nine of the eleven ships of the Fujian Squadron were sunk and more than 700 officers and crew members died or were wounded. This revealed the worthlessness of the "regeneration" policy of the Westernization group.

The Chinese people were incensed by the French aggression. In the coastal areas, struggles against French aggression culminated in the destruction of churches and expulsion of missionaries. Overseas Chinese pledged their support by contributions of money to the popular movements at home, while Chinese workers in Hong Kong went on strike in protest.

In October of the same year, French warships once again invaded Taiwan. Meeting with resistance from the Taiwan army and civilians, they suffered a serious defeat at Danshui, northwestern Taiwan;

dozens of the invaders died or were wounded and the rest beat a hasty retreat to the sea. In March 1885, French warships again harassed Zhenhai, Zhejiang, but were repulsed by Chinese garrison troops there.

While invading Zhejiang, the French aggressors also attacked Zhennanguan Pass (present Youyiguan Pass), Guangxi, on the Sino-Vietnamese border. General Feng Zicai, who was then nearly 70, led his men to the front, deployed his forces and saw to the building of the defence works there, in preparation for the coming battle. Near the end of March, French troops charged at the long defence wall on the Chinese side of the battlefield, and some leaped over it. Feng Zicai, a spear in hand, appeared from behind the wall to fight the invaders. His men, inspired by their commander's courage, plunged into the enemy ranks and engaged them in hand-to-hand fight. Faced with local people of the Zhuang, Yao, Bai, Yi and Han ethnic groups and more than 1,000 Vietnamese people joining in the battle, the French troops were defeated and fled. General Feng followed this victory with a hot pursuit and the French invaders self-admittedly suffered "a disastrous defeat".

When news of the defeat reached Paris, the French cabinet resigned, and France found itself in political and military chaos. The situation was favourable for Chinese resistance to French aggression. Nonetheless, the Qing government negotiated cease-fire terms with the aggressors despite its own winning position. In April 1885, James Duncan Campbell, a British customs commissioner, signed on behalf of the Qing government a cease-fire agreement with the French government in Paris. In June, Li Hongzhang and a French delegate signed the Treaty of Tientsin which stipulated that France could open trading cities, in Yunnan and Guangxi provinces bordering on View Nam and that China was obliged to consult France if it wished to build railways there. The gate to China's Southwest was thus further opened to aggression.

9. The Sino-Japanese War and Imperialist Partition of China

The Sino-Japanese War of 1894-95 was launched by Japan to annex Korea and extend Japanese influence into China.

Japan had invaded Korea on several occasions since the 1870s, and exacted from it privileges in regard to trading and stationing troops there, turning Korea gradually into its semicolony.

The United States helped Japan to invade Korea and Britain also abetted Japanese aggression; since Japanese and Russian interests in East Asia were often in collision, Britain supported Japan in order to counter Russia.

A large-scale peasant uprising occurred in Korea in the spring of 1894. Panic-stricken, the Korean feudal rulers appealed to the Qing government to send troops and help it suppress the revolt. Taking advantage of the strife in Korea, Japan deployed nearly all its naval force and more than 10,000 infantry at Seoul and around Inchun. When 1,500 Chinese troops reached Asan in June, the uprising had already subsided. The Qing government proposed to Japan that both countries withdraw their troops from Korea. Japan refused, however, saying that it was helping Korea in its internal reform.

Towards the end of July, the Japanese fleet near Pong Island off Asan suddenly attacked Chinese warships, sinking a transport ship leased from Britain and causing the deaths of more than 700 Chinese soldiers on board. Then the Japanese army attacked the Chinese army at Asan, forcing it to retreat to Pyongyang. On September 15, the Japanese mustered a strong force and stormed Pyongyang, but the Chinese troops supported by the Korean people fought back. Commander Zuo Baogui of Field headquarters mounted the city wall to give orders and was killed at his post. General Ye Zhichao on the other hand carried out Li Hongzhang's non-resistance policy, fleeing from Pyongyang and crossing the Yalu River in the latter half of September.

Two days after the battle of Pyongyang, the Beiyang Fleet under the command of Admiral Ding Ruchang fought a fierce battle with the Japanese fleet on the Yellow Sea. Inexperienced at sea battle, the Beiyang Fleet was surrounded by Japanese warships, but it fought courageously. Captain Deng Shichang of the *Zhiyuan* intended to dash his badly damaged ship at the enemy *Yoshino*, but the *Zhiyuan* was sunk by an enemy torpedo, and Deng and two hundred of the ship's company lost their lives. When Captain Lin Yongsheng of the *Jingyuan* died in the battle, the other officers and crew fought on until the ship submerged. The battle lasted five hours. Five ships were lost on the Chinese side, and the Japanese flag ship *Matsushima* was also badly damaged. After the battle, Li Hongzhang instructed the Beiyang Fleet to anchor in Weihaiwei Harbour and not to engage the enemy under any circumstances. As a result, the fleet could only wait in harbour for its doom.

At the end of October, the Japanese army began a doublepronged invasion of China: one force was to cross the Yalu River and capture Jiulian and Andong (present Dandong, Liaoning); the other was to land troops at Liaodong Peninsula, occupy Jinzhou, and eventually take Dalian and Lüshun.

The People of Shengjing (present Liaoning Province) rose up in arms against Japanese invasion. When the Japanese attacked Xiuyan, local coal-miners joined with peasants from dozens of villages to offer resistance against aggression. They killed and wounded many of the enemy. Peasants from around Liaoyang repulsed four successive advances by the enemy within a month, and the people of Lüshun similarly refused to submit to the enemy's slaughter.

In mid-January 1895, the Japanese landed on the Shandong Peninsula, assaulting the Weihaiwei Harbour from behind and blockading its entrance. Attacked from both front and back, the Beiyang Fleet was paralyzed, and in February was completely destroyed. The enemy troops that entered from Korea occupied Niuzhuang, Yingkou and other places. Panic-stricken, the Qing government sued for peace.

This defeat proved that the new policy of Westernization could not make China independent and prosperous.

In March 1895, Li Hongzhang, accompanied by his American advisor John Watson Foster, negotiated peace with Japan at Shimonoseki. Browbeaten by Japan and the United States, he signed the humiliating Treaty of Shimonoseki, which stipulated that China was to cede to Japan the Liaodong Peninsula, Taiwan and the Penghu Islands;[1] pay an indemnity of 200 million taels of silver; open Shashi, Chongqing, Suzhou and Hangzhou to foreign trade; and give Japan

---

[1] Taiwan was proclaimed a province by the Qing government in October 1885, with the affiliated islands and the Penghu Islands under its jurisdiction.

the right to open factories in all trading cities. The occupation of the Liaodong Peninsula by Japan on the conclusion of the treaty prevented Russia from extending its influence in the Northeast. It therefore aligned with France and Germany to request that China "redeem" the Liaodong Peninsula from Japan with 30 million taels of silver.

The Treaty of Shimonoseki marked a new stage of foreign aggression in China. The provisions that allowed foreign powers to invest in factories in China satisfied their urgent need to export capital. China's status as a semi-colony was further confirmed.

However, the Chinese people were indignant over the treaty. They condemned the crimes of the aggressors, denounced the Qing government for its treasonable conduct, opposed the cession of Taiwan and payment of indemnity and demanded resistance to aggression. When the news of the annexation of Taiwan reached the island province, the Taibei people beat gongs and stopped business in protest. They posted denunciations pledging to execute traitors like Li Hongzhang and others. The local gentry sent telegrams to the Qing court opposing the cession of territories.

In May, the Japanese army landed in Jilong, on the north end of Taiwan. The governor, Tang Jingsong, fled back to the mainland and Taibei was lost without so much as a shot. The local Han and Gaoshan people organized themselves into a volunteer army headed by Xu Xiang and others. Together with the Black Flag Army led by Liu Yongfu who now commanded the Taiwan garrison, they put up a defence at Xinzhu, Taizhong and Zhanghua. The defence of Zhanghua was the largest engagement with the main enemy force, which suffered heavy casualties, but the Chinese volunteers and the Black Flag Army also sustained heavy losses. During the fighting near Tainan in October, Japanese marines landed near Tainan and entered the battle in support of the Japanese infantry, while the Chinese garrison troops had to fight single-handed. With their supplies exhausted and no reinforcements, they eventually lost the city. In their defence of the island the army and civilians inflicted 30,000 casualties on the enemy in less than five months, and during the half century of Japanese occupation, the various ethnic groups in Taiwan continued their unremitting resistance. After the conclusion of the Sino-Japanese War, Britain, Russia, the United States, Japan, France and Germany competed for bigger shares in the partition of China. The imperialist partition of China occurred at the time when the chief capitalist countries reached the stage of imperialism.

In addition to dumping merchandise and seizing raw materials, the powers were also in competition in investing capital in China. They also lent money to the Qing government and opened more banks, including the French Banque de l'Indo-Chine, the Russo-Chinese Bank and later the U.S. International Banking Corporation. They opened up factories, built railways and operated mines, monopolizing and controlling Chinese finance and economy.

The imperialist powers also grabbed "leased land" and divided China into spheres of influence. In November 1897, Germany supported by Russia sent troops to occupy Jiaozhou Bay in Shandong. In 1898, there was a series of moves by imperialist powers to capture seaports and claim spheres of influence in China. Germany leased Jiaozhou Bay and obtained the right to build two railways in Shandong as well as to open up mines within 15 kilometres along them, making Shandong its sphere of influence. Russia had in 1896 forced the Qing government to sign the Contract for the Construction and Work of the Chinese Eastern Railway, gaining the right to build the Chinese Eastern Railway in Heilongjiang and Jilin. Now it leased Lüshun and Dalian, thereby obtaining at the same time the right to construct and manage a branch of the Chinese Eastern Railway to Dalian. The Northeast, therefore, became its sphere of influence. France took Guangzhou Bay (present Zhanjiang area, Guangdong) on lease, claimed the right of building a railway from Viet Nam to Yunnan, and demanded that Yunnan, Guangdong and Guangxi not be ceded to any third country, so that the three provinces constituted a French sphere of influence. Britain had for sometime taken the Changjiang valley as its sphere of influence. Now it leased the Kowloon Peninsula and the Weihaiwei Harbour to offset French and Russian influence as well as to maintain a dominant position in the Changjiang valley. In addition to appropriating Taiwan, Japan carved out Fujian as its sphere of influence.

While the other imperialist powers were staking out their spheres of influence in China, the United States was engaged in preparations for war against Spain over the Philippines and missed its opportunity. It therefore advanced in 1899 the "open-door" policy, which recognized the spheres of influence of the different powers and their privileges in China, and requested the powers to open their leased land and spheres of influence to the United States, which would thus share equal benefits and opportunities. Britain was the first to agree; the other powers followed suit. The United States then expanded its aggression in China.

The violent contention between the powers brought China closer to dismemberment, and posed an unprecedentedly grave crisis for the whole nation.

10. The Modernization Movement of the Bourgeois Reformists

Defeat in the war against Japan and the serious crisis of partition by imperialists awakened the Chinese people. In 1898, bourgeois reformists initiated a modernization movement for reform and national revival.

A wave of factory establishment swept the whole country after the Sino-Japanese War, with the result that national capitalism began to thrive in China. Between 1895 and 1898, more than 50 enterprises, including textile mills, filatures, flour mills and other light industries, were established by Chinese merchants, their capital of about 12 million yuan exceeding the total Chinese investments in the twenty years prior to the Sino-Japanese War. The influence of the national bourgeoisie grew. The most powerful element in this class was its upper stratum which was composed mainly of former officials, former landlords and rich merchants who had close ties with the imperialists and feudal forces. They wanted to develop capitalism as a means of averting the national crisis and chose the reformist road of institutional change and modernization.

The reformism of the 1870s and 80s, which aimed at changing China's status quo, grew into a popular political movement after the

Sino-Japanese war. At the head of this movement were the bourgeois reformists Kang Youwei, Liang Qichao, Yan Fu and Tan Sitong, who advocated an institutional reform and modernization in China, and were hence known as the modernization group.

Kang Youwei (1858-1927), from Nanhai, Guangdong petitioned Empror Guang Xu in 1888 for reform. When the Treaty of Shimonoseki was signed in 1895, he led 1,300 scholars who had passed the provincial examination and were now in Beijing for the metropolitan examination to submit a memorial to the emperor, opposing the treaty and requesting immediate political reform. Kang Youwei maintained that the basis for reform and modernization was the substitution of bourgeois constitutional monarchy for feudal autocracy. His works *A Study of the Forged Classics* and *An Inquiry into Confucius' Reform* supplied a theoretical basis for reformism. He blended Western evolutionism with the Confucian idea of the "Triple World", alleging that a society invariably developed along a sequence of chaos, peace and eventually "great harmony". Current Chinese society, governed by an autocratic monarchy, he contended, was in the stage of chaos. To attain great harmony, the social system of a bourgeois democratic republic, it was imperative to reform first the chaotic world and set up the peaceful world of a constitutional monarchy. His idea of historical evolution was progressive in combating feudal conservatism at the time.

Though Kang's memorial was intercepted and failed to reach the emperor, his activities produced a great impact on society at large. He himself as a result became a well-known leader of the reformist group. Hereafter he sent in memorial after memorial, reiterating his proposal for reform. He urged the Qing government, in order to avert the national crisis, to replace feudal autocracy with constitutional monarchy, encourage civilians to establish modern industries, develop national capitalism, abrogate the civil service examination system of selecting officials through the stereotyped "eight-legged essay" writing and encourage the study of Western bourgeois culture. Both the diehard clique in the court headed by Empress Dowager Ci Xi and the Westernization group resolutely upheld the feudal order in opposition to any political reform. Kang Youwei's petitions were intercepted by them and failed to reach the emperor. Nevertheless, the petitions appeared in printed pamphlets and were widely read by the public.

In August 1895, Kang Youwei and Liang Qichao published in Beijing the *Zhong Wai Ji Wen* (*World Bulletin*), a paper published every other day reporting on current affairs and calling for reform. In September they formed the *Qiang Xue Hui* (Learn-to-Be-Strong Society), which gave regular lectures and published and distributed books and periodicals recommending Western learning, also known an new learning to China. (Western learning here refers to European bourgeois democratic culture, including socio-ideology, sciences and technology, recommended to China in the mid-nineteenth century by progressive Chinese intellectuals.) In this way, the *Qiang Xue Hui*, moulded public opinion and accumulated strength for reform. A branch society was organized in Shanghai, which put out the *Qiang Xue Bao*, a paper published every five days. In the court, the conflict between Emperor Guang Xu's faction and that of Empress Dowager Ci Xi intensified. Weng Tonghe, Grand Minister of the Privy Council and Minister of the Board of Revenue, and others who rallied round Emperor Guang Xu supported the *Qiang Xue Hui*, while the feudal diehards and the Westernization group attaching themselves to Empress Dowager Ci Xi attacked the other faction in force. Subsequently, the *Qiang Xue Hui* and its Shanghai branch were forced to disband and the *Zhong Wai Ji Wen* and *Qiang Xue Bao* were banned at the beginning of 1896.

However, discussion of current affairs had become widespread: the tide of reform was surging forward irreversibly. From 1896 to 1898, more than 300 study societies, modern schools and newspapers mushroomed in Beijing, Shanghai, Zhili, Hunan, Guangdong and Guangxi. Among the most influential were the *Shi Wu Bao* (*Contemporary Affairs*) in Shanghai under the editorship of Liang Qichao, the *Nan Xue Hui* (Southern Society) and the *Shi Wu Tang* (School for Contemporary Learning) founded by Tan Sitong in Hunan, and the *Guo Wen Bao* (*National News*) in Tianjin edited by Yan Fu. Liang Qichao (1873-1929), from Xinhui, Guangdong, was Kang Youwei's student and close collaborator. His "Exposition on Institutional Reform" published in *Shi Wu Bao* advocated institutional reform and the doctrine of popular rights. This article exerted great influence at the time. Yan Fu (1854-1921) from Houguan, Fujian, had studied in England and had a relatively comprehensive understanding of the socio-political doctrines of the Western bourgeoisie. After the Sino-Japanese War, he translated the first two articles of Huxley's *Evolution and Ethics*, adding to the translated version some of his own interpretations. He laid great emphasis on such biological evolutionist ideas as "organic evolution and natural selection" and "the victory of the strong over the weak". He believed in social development—"the ways of the world improve invariably and posterity will be better than its predecessor". These ideas became powerful weapons against the ossified ideas of the feudal diehards and stimulated people's demand for institutional reform and national revival. Yan Fu also wrote *A Refutation of Han Yu* and other articles, in which he criticized feudal monarchy on the basis of Western concepts of popular rights. He pointed out that according to the principle of the social division of labour, the king should be elected by the whole populace and be recalled by them if necessary. He denounced all the Chinese emperors from the Qin Dynasty down as "arch usurpers of state power". Tan Sitong (1865-98), from Liuyang, Hunan, wrote *On Benevolence*, in which he called for the breaking off of all feudal trammels, censured feudal ethics, denounced all emperors as "despots and traitors to the people" and characterized autocratic monarchy as rule by bandits. Nonetheless, like Yan Fu, he did not call for the abrogation of monarchism, believing in the establishment of a constitutional monarchy.

To propagate the need for institutional reform, Liang Qichao advocated changes in literary style. In his own essays, which were clear, fluent, colloquial and easy to understand, he broke away from the classical style, and created what was known as "the new style". Liang Qichao, Tan Sitong and others also launched a "revolution in poetry circles", demanding that poetry mirror current political and social reality without violating the traditional poetic style. On this score, Huang Zunxian (1848-1905), from Jiaying (present Meixian), Guangdong, broke fresh ground. He was opposed to treading in the ancients' footsteps, holding that poetry should express one's own ideas and feelings. His poems described foreign lands and people and gave expression to new ideology and culture, opening a new and wide range of subject matter in poetry. More importantly, he wrote many poems in ordinary language and with great feeling during the wars against aggression, especially the Sino-Japanese War. The most widely recited was the "Ballad of Taiwan" which opposed the cession of Taiwan, with lines such as the following:

All pledge to die resisting the foe,
The people united are indomitable.

The grave situation brought about by Germany's annexation of Jiaozhou Bay aroused popular anger at the corruption of the Qing court. Kang Youwei once again petitioned the emperor, pointing out that only institutional reform could avert the danger of partition and restrain the popular rebellious activities that threatened Qing rule. To avert national crisis, free himself from Empress Dowager Ci Xi's clutches and seize real power, Emperor Guang Xu instructed Kang Youwei to plan the reform. In January 1898 Kang presented his "Memorial on Policy Concerning the General Situation", asking the emperor to use his imperial authority to carry out institutional reform, bring the reformists into the government, and reform the political system by establishing a constitutional monarchy which would in effect be based on the alliance of the bourgeoisie and the landlord class. In April Kang Youwei, Liang Qichao and others organized the *Bao Guo Hui* (Protect-the-Country Society) in Beijing and sponsored the establishment of branches at provincial, prefectural and county levels. They gave lectures to the society, adopting the slogan "protect the state, the race and the teaching (Confucianism)". The call for institutional reform reached a new high.

On June 11, 1898, Emperor Guang Xu declared an institutional reform, appointed Kang Youwei reform counsellor and Tan Sitong, Liu Guangdi, Yang Rui and Lin Xu to help in the Privy Council on matters relating to institutional reform. In the 103 days from June 11 to September 21, the reformists, on the authority of the emperor, issued a series of decrees to effect institutional reform. This is known in history as the Hundred Day Reform. The main features of the reform edicts were: to set up a bureau of agriculture, industry and commerce to protect and encourage industry and commerce; to establish a bureau of mines and railways to construct railways and extract ores; to reform the administrative organs and dismiss unnecessary staffs; to reform the civil service examination system and abolish the stereotyped "eight-legged essay"; to establish a modern school system for the study of Western learning; to permit the publication of newspapers and founding of study societies; to encourage the expression of opinions through memorials to the throne; and to encourage new inventions.

There was no mention whatsoever in these measures of instituting a parliament or adopting a constitution, or of any other act that might lead to substantial political changes. They were only a few changes in the original system, favourable to the further development of national capitalism. Nonetheless, the diehards and the Westernization group frustrated the reformists in their attempt to effect the new policies. Among the provincial officials, only the governor of Hunan supported the reform. The struggle between the reformists and their opposition was very acute. Three days after the reform edict was issued, Empress Dowager Ci Xi compelled the emperor to dismiss Weng Tonghe, the Grand Minister of the Privy Council, from all his other posts, and appointed her trusted follower Ronglu as Viceroy of Zhili and Supreme Commander of the Beiyang Army. In this way she took control over both Beijing and Tianjin, and awaited the opportunity to destroy the reform movement. In early September, the two cities were full of rumours that Ci Xi and Ronglu were conspiring to coerce the emperor to abdicate during a military review in Tianjin. Sensing the gravity of the situation, Emperor Guang Xu secretly instructed Kang Youwei and his group to devise plans against the conspiracy. As the reformists did not rely on the masses, they had no real strength. And at this critical juncture, they thought they could rely on Yuan Shikai's army, kill Ronglu during the military review, and avert the crisis. Yuan Shikai had organized and trained a modern army in Xiaozhan (near Tianjin), which was the embryo of the later Beiyang warlord army, and was Ronglu's trusted subordinate. But as a skilled political opportunist he was also a member of the Learning-to-Be-Strong Society. When Tan Sitong paid him a secret visit he was very eloquent in his support but after the visit, he immediately informed Ronglu about the secrets of the reformists. On September 21, Empress Dowager Ci Xi staged a coup d'etat, imprisoned Emperor Guang Xu and arrested the reformist leaders. The reform movement ended in defeat.

During the movement, the reformists harboured the illusion that the imperialist powers would help them. At that time, Britain, the United States, and Japan were in frequent conflict with Russia, and since the latter supported the Empress Dowager, the former tried to befriend the emperor and the reformists in order to counter their common adversary. The reformists were also in favour of contacting Britain and Japan to enlist their support. After the coup d'etat, Kang Youwei and Liang Qichao escaped abroad with the help of Britain and Japan. Tan Sitong was unwilling to escape, saying: "No country in the world as yet has had a successful reform without blood being shed. In China no one has ever heard of someone shedding blood for the sake of reform. If this will happen now, let it begin with me." At the end of September, Tan Sitong, Liu Guangdi, Yang Rui, Lin Xu, Yang Shenxiu and Kang Guangren (Kang Youwei's brother) were executed, and the officials who had supported the reform were dismissed. All of the new policies were abolished, except the establishment of a Metropolitan College.

With their hopes of changing existing conditions in China to ward off a national crisis and enable China to develop capitalism through a political reform, the bourgeois reformists were progressive in the given historic conditions of their time. Their promotion of the new learning proved to be a heavy blow to the rule of feudal ideology. However, the reformists were completely alienated from the masses and even attempted to counter the popular revolutionary movement through reform. They were opposed to a revolution to bring radical changes to China, believing that reform from the top down through the authority of a feudal emperor would make China a strong capitalist country. Moreover, they were under the illusion that if China would only learn from the West the imperialist powers would give up their aggressive schemes. All this determined their inevitable defeat.

11. The Anti-Imperialist Patriotic Movement of the *Yi He Tuan*

The year following the defeat of the reform movement saw the outbreak of the *Yi He Tuan* movement (known to the West as the Boxers), which was mainly composed of peasants and which had international repercussions. It was the product of intensified foreign aggression and an unprecedentedly grave national disaster, and was a development of the struggle against the imperialist partition of China following the Sino-Japanese War. It was also the culmination of decades of popular upheavals all over the country against aggression perpetrated by the missionaries and churches.

The movement originated in Shandong. In 1899, the section of the *Yi He Tuan* led by Zhu Hongdeng rose in armed revolt in the northwestern part of Shandong. The insurgents destroyed churches and drove away the missionaries and defeated the Qing army which was sent to suppress them. Other contingents of the *Yi He Tuan* rose in response, and the movement gained enormous momentum.

The rapid development of the *Yi He Tuan* anti-imperialist and patriotic movement frightened the aggressors. The United States and the British plenipotentiaries in Beijing pressed the Qing government to crush it. They even compelled the Qing government to replace the governor of Shandong with Yuan Shikai. Yuan Shikai led 7,000 men of his New Army from Zhili to Shandong and, in collaboration with the local armed forces, ruthlessly suppressed the insurgents. In early 1900, part of the *Yi He Tuan* insurgent army moved from Shandong to Zhili and merged with the local *Yi He Tuan* to form a stronger force. In May, one of its detachments occupied Zhuozhou (about 50 kilometres to the southwest of Beijing), threatening the capital; another detachment manoeuvred near Tianjin, trying to gain entrance to the city.

The *Yi He Tuan's* struggle against aggression won support from the whole country and people joined up with great enthusiasm. Its flag was hoisted in many of the townships and villages of Zhili. However, with people from the landlord class joining in the movement at its high tide, including even conservative members of the gentry and small or medium landlords who had old grievances against the churches, the composition of the insurgent army grew more and more complicated. These people whipped up retrogressive tendencies such as general xenophobia and rejection of modern industry, science and technology, which were inherent in a peasant army.

The momentum of the *Yi He Tuan* movement shocked the Qing court, which then sought to use it to its own advantage. At that time, the Qing government was at loggerheads with the foreign aggressors. Empress Dowager Ci Xi bore a grudge to Britain and Japan for allowing Kang Youwei and Liang Qichao to continue their activities abroad and opposing her plan of dethroning Emperor Guang Xu. After formulating secret plans, the Qing court decided to recognize the legal status of the *Yi He Tuan* and covertly agreed to its entry into the capital. The combination of the local Beijing movement and the newcomers greatly magnified the influence of the *Yi He Tuan* movement. Thousands of the urban populace, including even Manchu and Han soldiers in the Qing army, flocked to join the *Yi He Tuan* within a matter of a few days. They set fire to churches in Beijing, attacked the foreign aggressors and held continuous demonstrations in the streets. At the same time, the *Yi He Tuan* detachment that was active around Tianjin entered the city, exercised administrative functions in some areas of the city and struggled against the foreign aggressors there.

The expansion of the *Yi He Tuan* movement in Beijing and Tianjin encouraged the people of the whole country. Soon the movement spread from Shandong and Zhili to other northern provinces—Shanxi, Shaanxi, Henan and Inner Mongolia, and even to the northeastern provinces. Before long, mass action against the aggression of the churches flared up in the southern provinces as well, echoing the movement in the north. Anti-imperialist upheavals swept the country.

To crush the *Yi He Tuan*, the imperialist powers joined forces and launched a war of aggression against China. In June 1900, Britain, Russia, Japan, the United States, Germany, France, Italy and Austria organized an army of 2,000 men, which landed at Dagu, a harbour on Bohai Bay some 60 kilometres to the southeast of Tianjin, and advanced towards Beijing under the pretext of "rescuing the envoys". The insurgents and the Qing army engaged the aggressors in a battle at

Luofa and Langfang, about 50 kilometres to the southeast of Beijing, causing heavy casualties to the enemy troops. The allied army retreated hastily to the foreign settlement in Tianjin.

At this time, the foreign warships off Dagu Harbour attacked and occupied Dagu Fort under the command of a Russian naval officer. More invading troops landed at Dagu and advanced towards Tianjin. As soon as the 2,000 Russian troops arrived at the Tianjin railway station, they fired cannon at the *Yi He Tuan* positions. The joint forces of the *Yi He Tuan* insurgents and the Qing army led by Cao Futian killed and wounded more than 500 Russians, winning a splendid victory. Another contingent of joint forces led by Zhang Decheng beleaguered the foreign settlement in Tianjin. The Red Lantern Detachment, composed mainly of young women, also took part in the battle.

In Beijing, the foreign officials and troops in the Legation Quarter provoked the *Yi He Tuan* insurgents and shot Chinese inhabitants at sight. This roused the indignation of the Chinese civilians and the Qing troops. On June 20, the Chinese joint forces laid siege to the foreign legations to strike at the aggressors. They broke through the enemy defence lines, killing and wounding enormous numbers of enemy troops.

Bowing to the pressure of circumstances, the Qing court declared war on the imperialist powers on June 21, but this was no more than a devious trick. While rewarding the *Yi He Tuan* with silver and grain and praising its members as "righteous subjects", the Qing court appointed officials as their commanding officers to lead them so as the better to cheat and control them, and at the same time surreptitiously engaged in capitulationist manoeuvres, getting ready to come to terms with the imperialists. Four days after the declaration of war, Empress Dowager Ci Xi decreed the lifting of the siege of the legations and preparations for truce talks.

In late June, several thousand of additional foreign troops advanced towards Tianjin. The joint forces of the *Yi He Tuan* and part of the Qing army resisted the enemy, annihilating about 1,000 of them. However, some of the Qing army commanders, carrying out secret orders from the Qing court, attacked the *Yi He Tuan* from behind.

Fighting on two fronts against foreign and domestic counter-revolutionaries, the *Yi He Tuan* insurgents suffered terrible casualties. Its strength seriously sapped, it lost Tianjin on July 14.

Even more eager to capitulate to the enemy now that Tianjin had fallen, the Qing court sent envoys to the Legation Quarter to inquire after the well-being of the foreign diplomatic staff, saying that it was willing to apologize, pay an indemnity and punish the culprits. The imperialists ignored these as they planned to extort greater gains from their aggression. On August 4, the 20,000-strong eight-power allied forces set out from Tianjin towards Beijing. As the *Yi He Tuan* insurgent army and part of the Qing army repulsed the enemy, the Qing court sent Li Hongzhang as plenipotentiary to sue for peace. On August 14, the allied army occupied Beijing. Empress Dowager Ci Xi fled to Xi'an, taking Emperor Guang Xu with her. On her way there, she instructed Li Hongzhang to beg the aggressors for a hasty peace, and decreed that local officials should extirpate the *Yi He Tuan*. The allied forces on their way from Tianjin to Beijing committed arson, murder, robbery and rape, razing entire villages. After they occupied Beijing, the troops were allowed to loot for three days in the capital. They plundered and destroyed the literary and artistic treasures of past dynasties and people's property, and insulted and slaughtered the inhabitants.

While joining in the allied army, Russian independently occupied China's Northeast. In July 1900 when the *Yi He Tuan* movement spread to the Northeast, Russia mustered 150,000 troops and invaded Heilongjiang, Jilin and Shengjing (present Liaoning) by several routes under the pretext of protecting the Chinese Eastern Railway. By October, the whole of the Northeast was under Russian control. Everywhere the Russian aggressors went, they set fire to people's houses and plundered and murdered the inhabitants. More than 7,000 people of Hailanpao and the sixty-four villages east of the Heilongjiang River were murdered, burned to death or drowned in the river. The ancient and historical city of Aihui (Aigun) was reduced to a heap of rubble. Lenin at the time denounced the Russian aggressors for "burning down whole villages, shooting, bayoneting, and drowning in the Amur River (Heilongjiang) unarmed inhabitants, their wives, and their children".[1]

In face of the savage Russian aggression, the *Yi He Tuan* and people of various local ethnic minorities in the Northeast launched an armed resistance against the invading enemy. The popular armed forces soon grew into a contingent 200,000 strong. With the motto "Resist the Russian bandits! Restore our lost territory!" they assaulted the enemy repeatedly, so that it could not relax its guard for a moment.

The imperialist powers each strove against the other to seize the maximum gains from their aggression in China after the occupation of Beijing. The conflict between them became so acute that they were on the verge of an armed clash. Under such circumstances, they accepted the second "open-door" policy put forward by the United States: to continue to maintain Qing rule under Empress Dowager Ci Xi and outwardly guarantee China's "territorial and administrative integrity", while in reality setting up a condominium over China. On this basis, they opened peace negotiations with Li Hongzhang, forcing the International Protocol of 1901 on the Qing court in the ninth lunar month of 1901. By the terms of the unequal treaty, the Qing court would apologize to the powers and punish the officials who had "offended" them; pay an indemnity of 450 million taels of silver by 39-year instalments which amounted to about a billion taels of silver with interest; allow the imperialist powers to control China's maritime customs and salt gabelle so as to provide for the payment of the indemnity; establish in Beijing a "legation quarter" where foreign troops were to be stationed and Chinese barred from residence; dismantle the fort at Dagu and allow foreign troops to be stationed in strategic areas along the railway line from Beijing to Tianjin and to Shanhaiguan; and ban forever any popular anti-imperialist activities under penalty of death. The protocol was a heavy manacle forced on the Chinese people, which further strengthened imperialist rule over China. Empress Dowager Ci Xi, however, was very satisfied with it, since it ensured the continuation of her dominance. She declared herself willing "to win the good graces of the powers, to the full extent of China's re-

[1] V. I. Lenin, *Collected Works*, Foreign Languages Publishing House, Moscow, 1960, Vol. 4, P. 374.

sources", and was fully determined to rule China as a faithful servant of imperialist powers.

The momentous *Yi He Tuan* anti-imperialist and patriotic movement failed under the concerted suppression of the imperialist powers and their flunkey, the Qing court. Nevertheless, the tenacious struggle frustrated the foreign powers in their attempt to dismember China and demonstrated the potential strength of the Chinese People.

12. The Rise of the Bourgeois Revolutionary Movement

After the signing of the unequal International Protocol in 1901, the imperialist countries intensified their plunder and domination of China. In addition to continuing to establish factories in China, they further seized for themselves the right to open mines and gained control of China's railways by means of direct investment and high-interest loans. The continued forfeiture of railways and mining rights became an extremely grave problem for China in the early twentieth century.

The imperialist powers were engaged in fierce struggles in their contention for rights and interests in China, and the Northeast was the focus for their contention. After Russia invaded and occupied the Northeast, it nourished vain hopes of establishing a "yellow Russia" there and refused to withdraw its troops. Japan had long harboured ambitions in regard to this area and secured the support of the United States and Britain. In 1904, an imperialist war finally broke out between Russia and Japan on Chinese territory over their contention for China's Northeast. In 1905, with the United States as mediator, they concluded a treaty for a division of the spoils, which provided that Russia should wholly "cede" to Japan its leased territories of Lüshun and Dalian, the Changchun-Dalian (Southern Manchurian) railway and other related rights. When the conflict broke out, the Qing court proclaimed its "neutrality" and delineated the area east of the Liaohe River as the battlefield; after the war it recognized the spoils-sharing provisions of the treaty. Thus Russian influence withdrew to the northern part of the Northeast and Japanese influence penetrated the south.

Since the latter half of the nineteenth century, Britain and Russia had been engaged in fierce contention over Tibet. At the end of 1903, taking advantage of Russian preoccupation in the Northeast, Britain launched an invasion of Tibet. The local Tibetan army and people resisted British aggression, putting up a particularly heroic defence at the battle of Gyangze (Gyantse) in southern Tibet. The British army occupied and looted Lhasa in August 1905, and in 1906 Britain forced the Qing court to sign an unequal treaty (Convention Between Great Britain and China Respecting Tibet, 1906), opening Gyantse and Gartok as trading towns.

The Qing court's betrayal of the *Yi He Tuan* and its capitulation to the imperialist powers confronted its rule with serious difficulties. In 1901, the court promulgated some "institutional reforms" and for some years carried out a "new administration". Some of the measures of the "new administration", such as promoting national industry, abolishing the imperial examination system, establishing schools and sending students abroad, were for the purpose of mitigating the contradictions between the rulers and the national bourgeoisie. A major part of the "new administration" was training troops and raising funds for their support. In 1903, a military training office was established in Beijing, and a reform of the military administration was undertaken. In 1905, an ambitious plan was drawn up for a national New Army of thirty-six *zhen* (garrisons or divisions). In the same year, a police department was set up and police were trained. All these measures aimed at strengthening its rule over the people. All items in the court's "new administration" were financed by increasing old taxes and levies or adding new ones. Apart from this, the intention of the "new administration" was also to win further favour from the imperialist powers. In 1901, in accordance with the demands of the imperialist powers, the court changed the Zongli Yamen to a Ministry of Foreign Affairs. Later, also answering to their needs, express provisions were made for the protection of foreign investment in building railways and opening mines in China.

The aggression of the imperialist powers and the treachery and oppression of the Qing court brought increased hardship to the life of the labouring people. People in every part of the country staged an unremitting resistance. In 1902, peasant uprisings in the Zhili Province raised anew the banner of "overthrow the Qing, destroy the foreigner". On a larger scale were the armed uprisings of the Han, Zhuang, Miao, Yao and other ethnic groups in Guangxi, where the flames of battle raged throughout the whole province for altogether three years. The movement to restore rights and oppose imperialist control of railways and mines developed gradually after 1903. In 1905, in opposition to American imperialism's maltreatment of Chinese migrant workers, a movement to boycott American goods swept the country. This movement, initiated by the national bourgeoisie, was also supported by workers, peasants, students and other urban residents. Spontaneous popular resistance increased rapidly after 1905. The records show that in 1909 there were more than 130 outbreaks of popular resistance in different regions, and the figure rose to over 290 in 1910. Struggles to resist taxes and levies and to seize rice were widespread throughout each province; two large-scale movements were the "rice raids" in Changsha, Hunan, and the anti-tax struggles in Laiyang, Shandong. In 1910, there were floods and droughts in the Changjiang River basin, and the famine refugees of Hunan lived on bark and grass. The gentry, landlords and Chinese and foreign merchants took this opportunity to hoard grain for profiteering. Starving people from Changsha and surrounding districts demanded that local authorities reduce the price at which grain was sold, but their protest was crushed and dozens were killed or wounded. The starving people rose in force against the Qing army, and in the end tens of thousands were drawn into the movement. They raided grain shops and banks, burned down yamen and tax bureau, and smashed up consular residences, foreign firms and churches, pointing the spearhead of their struggle at the feudal rulers and imperialist aggressors. Finally the court was forced to agree to official control of the sale of rice. In the same year, the peasants of Laiyang demanded that the rice stored in preparation against disaster, which had been misappropriated by officials and the gentry, be released to tide people over the famine and to pay taxes. Their demands were refused by the officials and their representatives arrested. Tens of thousands surrounded the county town of Laiyang and many fierce battles took place. The spontaneous resistance of the masses dealt a heavy blow against Qing feudal rule and at the same time promoted the development of the bourgeois democratic revolution.

The anti-imperialist, anti-feudal Chinese bourgeois democratic revolution, in a strict sense, was started by Dr. Sun Yat-sen. Sun Yat-sen (1866-1925, also known as Sun Wen or Sun Zhongshan) was born into a peasant family in the village of Cuiheng in Xiangshan (present-day Zhongshan City), Guangdong Province (near Macao). As a teenager he went to Honolulu where he received a Western education. After he returned to China in 1885, he studied medicine in Guangzhou and Hong Kong, and began to practise in Macao and Guangzhou. During this period he got to know some patriotic young men and secret society members who met regularly to assail the oppressive rule of the Qing court. He had a strong admiration for the Taiping Revolution, and called himself "Hong Xiuquan the Second". He was also influenced by reformist thinking. In 1894, he wrote a letter to Li Hongzhang, hoping to see some capitalist reforms, but was met with rejection. Not long after this, the Sino-Japanese War broke out. Sun Yat-sen felt that the crisis confronting the country was very grave, and considered that under Qing rule it would be impossible to make the country rich and powerful. The only way for national salvation was to take the path of revolution and over-throw Qing feudal rule.

In November 1894, Sun Yat-sen assembled many Chinese living in Honolulu to establish the *Xing Zhong Hui* (Society for the Revival of China), the first bourgeois revolutionary organization. The next year, he returned to Hong Kong and called together his comrades to establish the General Headquarters of the *Xing Zhong Hui*. The *Xing Zhong Hui* put forth in clear and definite terms the revolutionary aim of "establishing a government for the people".

Immediately after its establishment, the *Xing Zhong Hui* prepared for an armed uprising, deciding to begin in Guangzhou in 1895. But because the plan was leaked, the uprising was crushed before it began. Sun Yat-sen, under order of arrest by the Qing court, fled abroad. In Japan, Europe and America, he came into contact with many bourgeois revolutionary theories; he also developed a revolutionary organization and made preparations for another armed uprising. During the *Yi He Tuan* movement, the *Xing Zhong Hui* under Sun Yat-sen's leadership took advantage of the opportunity to stage an armed uprising in Huizhou (Waichow), Guangdong. Within a fortnight its forces grew to over twenty thousand, and it repeatedly defeated the Qing army. Afterwards, under siege by superior forces, they ran out of ammunition and were cut off from aid, and the uprising was defeted. Sun Yat-sen did not lose heart but persevered in the revolutionary struggle, continuing to seek the path of national slavation.

The initial development of Chinese capitalism took place in the early years of the twentieth century, as the middle and lower strata of the national bourgeoisie grew in strength. Thanks to the newly popular practice of going abroad to study and the opening of new schools at home, large numbers of intellectuals were trained for this class. Learning from the failure of the reformist movement and also from the peasants' anti-imperialist patriotic movement, they began to feel that if the oppression of imperialism and feudalism were to be cast off, they would have to overthrow Qing rule. At home and abroad they organized many revolutionary groups, published newspapers and magazines, and spread bourgeois democratic revolutionary ideas. Shanghai and Tokyo were the centres of their activities.

The influence of Zhang Taiyan in the area of propaganda was very great. Zhang Taiyan (1869-1936), also known as Zhang Binglin, was from Yuhang in Zhejiang. At that time, reformists like Kang Youwei and Liang Qichao had fled abroad, but they adhered to their reformist ideas, promoting constitutional monarchy and opposing revolution. In 1903 Zhang Binglin published his famous "Letter in Refutation of Kang Youwei's Views on Revolution" in the newspaper *Su Bao* (*Jiangsu News*), denouncing the mistaken notion spread by Kang Youwei that "China must have a constitution, but we cannot have revolution". Pointing out that only through revolution can democratic freedom be attained, Zhang Taiyan expressed clearly the bourgeois democratic revolutionary viewpoint. In the same year, Zou Rong, a young man still in his teens, published in Shanghai his pamphlet *The Revolutionary Army*, which had a tremendous impact. Zou

Rong (1885-1905) was from Baxian (present Chongqing) in Sichuan. He raised the solgan for the establishment of a bourgeois "Republic of China", demanded the eternal eradication of the monarchical autocratic form of government and opposed foreign intervention in China's revolution and independence. *The Reovlutionary Army* was reviewed and recommended by Zhang Taiyan in *Su Bao*, went through more than twenty printings and sold a million copies. The Qing court, in great fear and hatred of these activities and in collusion with the imperialist powers in Shanghai, closed down *Su Bao* and arrested Zhang Taiyan and Zou Rong. Zou Rong died in jail after suffering two years' imprisonment. Another propagandist was Chen Tianhua (1875-1905), from Xinhua in Hunan, who had been a fellow-student of Zou Rong in Japan. In 1904 he published two pamphlets, *About Face!* And *Alarm Bell*, exposing in simple language the aggressive acts of imperialism and calling on people to arise and fight against imperialism. He also pointed out that the Qing court was in fact a "foreigners' court", and "if we want to resist the foreigners we must preach revolution and independence". These two pamphlets also aroused a strong response.

At the same time that the bourgeois revolutionary groups were spreading democratic revolutionary ideas, new revolutionary organizations were being formed. In 1904, Huang Xing, together with Chen Tianhua, Song Jiaoren and others, set up the *Hua Xing Hui* (Society for the Revival of the Chinese Nation) in Changsha, and Cai Yuanpei, Zhang Taiyan, Tao Chengzhang and others organized the *Guang Fu Hui* (Restoration Society) in Shanghai. Revolutionary youth in Hubei also established the *Kexue Buxi Suo* (Science Study Group). All of these bodies organized armed uprisings, but none was successful.

The *Xing Zhong Hui* was still carrying out activities abroad under the leadership of Sun Yat-sen, developing organizations among overseas Chinese, advocating revolution and waging a struggle against reformists like Kang Youwei and Liang Qichao. In 1904 Sun Yat-sen published *A Message to My Compatriots*, exposing the true nature of Liang Qichao's pseudo-revolution and his actual wish to protect the emperor, pointing out that revolution and protection of the emperor were two different courses which were mutually exclusive and repulsing the reformists' onslaughts. In *The True Solution of the Chinese Question*, he also made the following points: Qing rule "is speedily approaching its doom", "China is just now on the eve of a great national movement", "this time is now ripe for a nationwide revolution" and "once our great aim of transforming China is achieved, not only will the dawn of a new age appear in our beautiful country, but the whole of mankind will attain through shared prosperity a more glorious future".

13. The Founding of the *Tong Meng Hui*

The rapid development of the revolutionary situation required a national, unified political party to lead the revolutionary movement. At this point, Sun Yat-sen and Huang Xing amalgamated part of the membership of the *Xing Zhong Hui, Hua Xing Hui, Guang Fu Hui, Kexue Buxi Suo* and other revolutionary bodies to form the *Zhongguo Tong Meng Hui* (Chinese Revolutionary League) in Tokyo in August 1905. It elected Sun Yat-sen as president, set up an executive group and adopted the programme proposed by Sun Yat-sen to "drive out the Manchus, restore China, establish a republic and equalize landownership". This programme was spelled out in the manifesto written by Sun Yat-sen for the first issue of the *Tong Meng Hui's* journal, the *Min Bao* (*People's Journal*) as the Three People's Principles—the Principle of Nationalism, the Principle of Democracy, and the Principle of People's Livelihood. The Principle of Nationalism was to overthrow the government of the Manchu aristocracy. The Principle of Democracy was to overthrow the monarchical autocratic system and establish a republican government. The Principle of People's Livelihood was to appraise and fix land prices, and to apportion to the state the increase in land prices that would result from the development of the social economy after the revolution, and gradually let the state purchase land from landowners. The Three People's Principles was a political programme which embodied the hopes of the Chinese bourgeoisie for the establishment of a republic and the development of capitalism, and was a great rallying cry for the revolution at that time.

The founding of the *Tong Meng Hui* and the formation of its programme indicated that the Chinese bourgeois democratic revolutionary movement had entered a new stage. However, this programme did not raise in clear and definite terms the solgan of anti-imperialist, anti-feudal struggle, and did not include a thoroughgoing land programme. Hence it was a non-thoroughgoing national democratic revolutionary programme reflecting the weak and compromising character of the Chinese national bourgeoisie.

The activities of the *Tong Meng Hui* had two main aspects, the debates with the reformists on political ideology and the development of a series of armed uprisings.

The reformists, headed by Kang Youwei and Liang Qichao and with the journal *Xin Min Congbao* (*New People's Journal*) published in Japan as their fortress, praised constitutional monarchy and vilified revolution. They said that it was not necessary to overthrow the Qing to make China rich and powerful, that it would be enough to persuade it to reform and demand that it practice a form of constitutional monarchy. They attacked armed revolution, claiming that it would lead to an internecine war and the partitioning of the country by foreign powers, and that it was not an expression of patriotism but an invitation to disaster for the country. With *Min Bao* as their stronghold, the revolutionists pointed out, to the contrary, that the court had not the slightest intention of renouncing its position, and would not function as a constitutional monarchy at all. They also pointed out that the court had already become a flunkey of the imperialists and unless this traitorous government was overthrown, China would be totally forfeited, so that the only way out for China was to "promote popular rights and establish democracy". They considered that the "patriotism" paraded by the reformists was in fact love for a traitorous government which acted as the foreigners' slave, and that the reformists' support for a monarchy and opposition to a republic was really "a criminal act against China". This great debate fully exposed the reformists' pro-Qing stance and opposition to revolution. By their defeat of the reformists on the theoretical front, the revolutionists took over the ideological leadership, winning over people to their side and heightening the revolutionary atmosphere of the time.

The first armed uprisings led by the *Tong Meng Hui* were those staged in 1906 by peasants and miners in the areas around Pingxiang in Jiangxi and Liuyang and Liling in Hunan. Members of the *Tong Meng Hui* were active in the uprisings, spreading revolutionary messages on the political programme of the society to rally the masses to their forces. The troops of the uprising quickly grew to about thirty thousand men and rapidly gained control over four or five counties, defeating the Qing army time after time. Only after the court had reinforced its army with troops from several provinces was it able to crush them. From 1907 to 1908 the *Tong Meng Hui* lauched six uprisings in succession in Guangdong, Guangxi and Yunnan. Sun Yat-sen personally took part in the fighting in Zhennanguan in Guangxi. Xu Xilin, a member of the *Guang Fu Hui*, and the revolutionary Qiu Jin (1877-1907), from Shanyin (modern Shaoxing), also launched uprisings in Anhui and Zhejiang in 1907.

On April 27, 1911, after six months of preparation, Sun Yat-sen and Huang Xing launched the Guangzhou Uprising which sent a tremor through the whole country. The revolutionists attacked from different directions. After more than a hundred men led by Huang Xing attacked the yamen of the governor-general of Guangdong and Guangxi, fighting broke out in the streets between them and a large Qing army which had come to suppress them. Since the isolated force was numerically weak, it was defeated after a night of fierce battle, and Huang Xing and the other survivors escaped with their wounds. More than eighty died in battle or were executed after their capture. Disregarding the danger to themselves, the people of Guangzhou collected the remains of seventy-two of the martyrs which they found and buried them at Huanghuagang on the city outskirts.

Because of the weakness in their mass base and the purely military adventuristic tactic of surprise attack they usually adopted, the repeated *Tong Meng Hui* uprisings ended in defeat. However, each delivered a blow to Qing rule. The selfless heroism of the revolutionists aroused a nation-wide spirit of resistance and inspired more people to join the anti-Qing campaign.

Confronted with the growing trend towards revolution, the Qing court looked for support from the upper strata of the bourgeoisie to prevent revolution and announced—to secure "eternal imperial stability"—a policy of "preparing for constitutional government" in 1906. Its first step was to reform the official system, that is, to concentrate political power in the hands of the Manchu aristocracy and reduce the power of the local governors. It recalled to court Zhang Zhidong, the Governor-General of Hubei and Hunan, and Yuan Shikai, the Governor-General of Zhili, the most powerful of the local governors, and gave them titles of Grand Ministers of the Privy Council while depriving them of actual power.

After the Qing court announced its constitutional preparations, reformists in places like Jiangsu, Zhejiang, Hubei, Hunan and Guangdong organized bodies to prepare for setting up a constitution. Their plan was to demand by kowtowing and petitioning tactics that the court practise a constitutional monarchy, thus checking the development of revolution and also giving themselves an opportunity to join the government. Known as "constitutionalits", their chief representatives were Kang Youwei and Liang Qichao abroad, and Zhang Jian, Tang Hualong, Tang Shouqian and Tan Yankai at home.

In August 1908, the court issued an "Imperial Constitution" stipulating a nine-year preparatory period for setting up constitutional government, which revealed their lack of sincerity. The Empress Dowager, Ci Xi, died soon after in November, one day after the death of Emperor Guang Xu. Puyi then succeeded to the throne with the reign title Xuan Tong, but because he was still a child, the political and military power devolved upon the regent, his father Zai Feng. Soon after coming to power, Zai Feng forced Yuan Shikai to retire.

Between 1909 and 1911, provincial consultative councils were established one after the other and a National Consultative Assembly was convened in Beijing in 1910, with constitutionalists playing a dominant role. The constitutionalists continuously presented petitions for a constitution, but the court only issued strict prohibitions against them. The court set up a new cabinet in May 1911, but nine of the thirteen ministers were Manchu nobles and five were members of the imperial clan, so that the political and military power was further concentrated in the hands of the imperial clan. This revealed the fraudulence of "constitutional preparation", arousing universal dissatisfaction among the warlords, high officials and constitutionalists who represented the upper strata of the bourgeoisie, and isolating the court.

For the sake of loans from the imperialist powers, the court issued a policy of the "nationalization" of trunk railway lines in May 1911, seizing the Guangzhou-Hankou and Sichuan-Hankou railways to be built by local private investment and selling the rights to build the two railways to the foreign powers. Upon this a mass movmeent to protect railway rights promptly broke out in the four provinces immediately concerned, Sichuan, Hunan, Hubei and Guangdong. The movement was particularly vigorous in Sichuan. In June, associations for the protection of railway rights were set up everywhere in Sichuan with hundreds of thousands taking part, and in Chengdu, tens of thousands attended a meeting for railway rights protection in August, calling for strikes among workers and students and refusal to pay taxes. The constitutionalists sought to control the movement but found themselves incapable. In September, Zhao Erfeng, Governor-General of Sichuan, ordered the massacre of several dozen petitioners in Chengdu. This only promoted further popular outrage. Wu Yongshan (also known as Wu Yuzhang) and other members of the *Tong Meng Hui* established revolutionary political power in Rongxian after an uprising. The railway rights protection movement developed into an armed uprising, which furiously assailed Qing rule in Sichuan. The overthrow of the Qing Dynasty was drawing near.

14. The Wuchang Uprising; the Founding of the Republic of China and the Fall of the Qing Dynasty

The Wuchang Uprising broke out on October 10, 1911. The driving force behind it included two *Tong Meng Hui* associates, the *Wen Xue She* (Literary Association) and the *Gong Jin Hui* (March Together League), which had been carrying out revolutionary propaganda and organizational work in the Hubei New Army and the secret societies for some time, drawing into their orgnaizations more than five thousand officers and soldiers or approximately one-third of the provincial army. Encouraged by the armed uprising which developed out of the railway rights protection movement in Sichuan, they decided to stage an armed uprising on October 11. But due to the accidental explosion of a bomb on October 9 which alerted the authorities, the plans for the uprising were discovered and the uprising headquarters was raided. A large number of the revolutionary leaders were arrested and executed by Ruicheng, Governor-General of Hubei and Hunan. The revolutionaries in the New Army, seeing that the situation was critical, decided to go ahead with the uprising earlier than planned. On the night of October 10, the first shots in the revolution rang out: the Wuchang Uprising had begun. The revolutionary army attacked the governor-general's yamen, sending Ruicheng and his officials fleeing in confusion. Wuchang was occupied after one night's fighting. On the 12th, the revolutionary army also occupied Hanyang and Hankou, the other two towns which with Wuchang make up the city of Wuhan.

The victory of the Wuchang Uprising quickly aroused a high tide of revolutionary enthusiasm throughout the whole country. Revolutionaries launched New Army and secret society uprisings in every province, and spontaneous struggles by peasants, workers, artisans and the urban poor took place. By early November, thirteen provinces had declared independence from the Qing court, and the disintegration of Qing rule was under way.

On the day after the Wuchang Uprising, the revolutionaries immediately began preparations to set up a government. On the recommendation of the constitutionalists, Li Yuanhong, former brigade commander of the New Army, was chose as military governor, and a Hubei Military Government was set up. On the 12th, Tang Hualong, a well-known constitutional monarchist, was chosen as minister of civil affairs in the government. Then, the abrogation of the Xuan Tong reign was announced and the name of the country changed to the Republic of China (Zhonghua Minguo). The revolutionaries forgot that Li Yuanhong was an extremely hostile opponent of the revolution and, even worse, failed to realize that they should keep political power in their own hands. Instead they considered that it was necessary for people who had some social standing to come forward to form a government so that it would have mass appeal, and therefore handed over lightly the political power they had won in battle to the feudal officials. Following the victories of the provincial uprisings, the representatives of the constitutionalists and the old bureaucrat politicians, taking advantage of the compromising and conciliatory nature of the bourgeois revolutionaries, infiltrated the revolutionary regime and usurped the leadership. The Jiangsu Governor, Cheng Dequan, merely hung a signboard over the yamen saying "Military Government" and changed his title to military governor, while keeping everything else exactly as it had been. Ten days after Hunan had declared its independence from the Qing court, the constitutionalist party headed by the leader of the Advisory Bureau, Tan Yankai, executed the revolutionary military governor, Jiao Dafeng, and usurped political power in Hunan.

In November, the Hubei Military Government invited delegates from the other independent provinces to Wuhan to discuss the formation of a central government. On December 2, the Jiangsu-Zhejiang revolutionary army attacked and took Nanjing. The convention of provincial delegates then decided to make Nanjing the seat of the provisional government of the republic, where the provincial delegates soon assembled. Sun Yat-sen returned to China on December 25 and the convention of provincial delegates elected him Provisional President of the republic four days later. On January 1, 1912, Sun Yat-sen took the oath of office and proclaimed the establishment of the Republic of China; with the adoption of the Gregorian calendar, 1912 was declared as the first year of the republic. Next, Li Yuanhong was elected Vice-President, and a Provisional Senate was set up in Nanjing to act as a legislature. A bourgeois republican regime came into being.

The Provisional Government at Nanjing headed by Sun Yat-sen was the product of a bourgeois democratic revolution. Owing to the weakness and compromise of the bourgeois revolutionaries, it was actually a coalition government of revolutionaries, constitutionalists and former officials. Although the revolutionaries predominated in the government, the constitutionalists and former officials headed the ministries of internal affairs, industry, and communications, possessing considerable power. Most of the provincial military governors, were also manipulated by the constitutionalists and former officials, but the Provisional Government in fact could not exercise central government authority over them.

The Provisional Government at Nanjing issued many laws relating to political, social and economic reform. The major ones, like the abolition of torture, prohibition against traffic in Chinese labourers abroad, abolition of slavery, prohibition against the cultivation and smoking of opium, and encouragement of the initiation of industrial and commercial enterprises and overseas Chinese investment in their homeland, were for the benefit of democratic politics and the development of capitalism. But because the government did not touch the basis of the semi-colonial, semi-feudal society, it could not resolve the immediate concerns of the people, especially the peasants' demand for land, and so its mass base was very weak.

The imperialist powers both feared and hated the Chinese revolution, and after the Wuchang Uprising they went to great lengths to support the Qing court and smash the revolution. In mid-October 1911, over a dozen British, American, Japanese, German and French warships assembled opposite Wuhan awaiting orders, threatening the revolutionary army. Because of the speedy development of the revolution, the imperialist powers were forced to declare "neutrality", but in fact they actively intervened. They continued to send customs duties to Beijing, and the Four-Power Consortium of British, French, German and American banks granted loans to the Qing court amounting to more than three million taels of silver. They hoped by these means to maintain Qing rule. Russia also tried to destroy the Chinese revolution, hoping to take this opportunity to divide China. It instigated a few princes of the Mongols to declare the "independence" of Outer Mongolia, and sent troops to occupy Hulun Circuit (modern Hailar), Manzhouli and other areas in Heilongjiang Province.

With the rapid disintegration of the Qing, the imperialist powers then sought a new flunkey. Their choice fell upon Yuan Shikai, a representative of landlord and comprador forces, and they put pressure on the Qing court to appoint him to an important position. The court first hastily appointed him Governor-General of Hubei and Hunan on October 14, and then as Imperial Commissioner in charge of all China's armies on October 22, with orders to suppress the revolution. Yuan Shikai delayed his acceptance to gain further powers. In November, the court was forced to appoint him Premier of the cabinet at Beijing, and the old cabinet of the imperial clan resigned. After he had gathered the military and political power in his hands, Yuan Shikai dispatched troops to attack the revolutionary army at Wuhan, capturing Hanyang. The imperialist powers further supported Yuan Shikai, helping to engineer negotiations between the north and the revolutionaries in the south. When peace talks began in Shanghai on December 18, the British, American, Russian, Japanese, French and German consuls presented a note to both sides asking them "to establish a peaceful resolution at all speed", to force the revolutionists to hand over political power. The constitutionalists who had infiltrated the revolutionary ranks also gave support to Yuan Shikai and actively exerted pressure from within the revolution, creating an atmosphere of compromise and destroying the revolution.

Under pressure from reactionary forces inside and outside, the revolutionists compromised and on January 15 agreed, on condition that the Qing emperor abdicate and Yuan Shikai support the republic, to hand over political power to Yuan. On February 12, 1912, Emperor Puyi abdicated, bringing to an end two thousand years of feudal monarchy in China. Next day, Sun Yat-sen resigned as Provisional President, and on February 15 the Provisional Senate elected Yuan Shikai Provisional President of the republic. A few days later, Li Yuanhong was elected Vice-President. On March 10, Yuan Shikai formally assumed office in Beijing and established an anti-revolutionary regime representing the big landlords and comprador class. The fruits of victory of the revolution had been usurped by Yuan Shikai, an agent of the imperialist powers, and thus began the rule of China by Beiyang warlords.

The day after Yuan Shikai assumed office, Sun Yat-sen proclaimed a Provisional Constitution which had been hastily drawn up by the Provisional Senate in Nanjing. The Provisional Constitution stipulated that sovereign rights belonged to the whole people in the Republic of China, and that the people uniformly enjoyed freedom of speech, publication, assembly and association, and the right to petition, elect and be elected. It had the character of a bourgeois republican constitution with a revolutionary and democratic character.

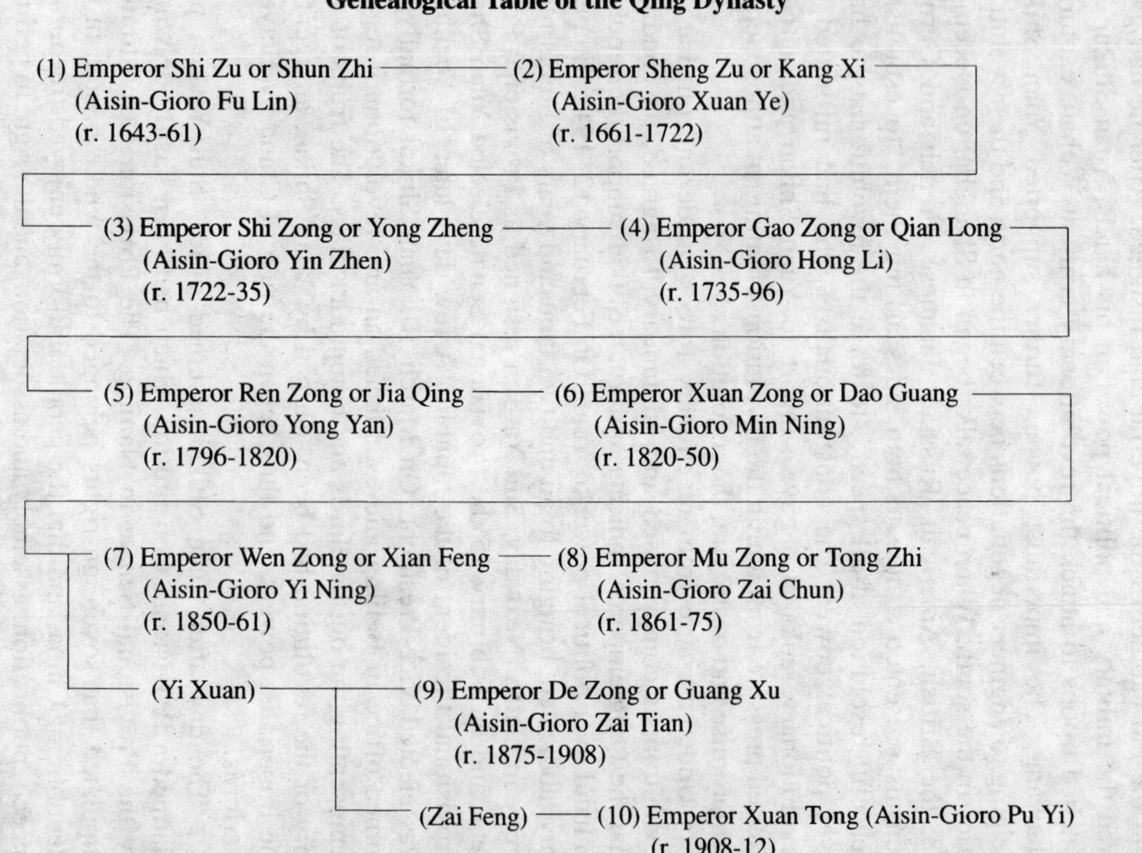
Genealogical Table of the Qing Dynasty
(1) Emperor Shi Zu or Shun Zhi (Aisin-Gioro Fu Lin) (r. 1643-61)
(2) Emperor Sheng Zu or Kang Xi (Aisin-Gioro Xuan Ye) (r. 1661-1722)
(3) Emperor Shi Zong or Yong Zheng (Aisin-Gioro Yin Zhen) (r. 1722-35)
(4) Emperor Gao Zong or Qian Long (Aisin-Gioro Hong Li) (r. 1735-96)
(5) Emperor Ren Zong or Jia Qing (Aisin-Gioro Yong Yan) (r. 1796-1820)
(6) Emperor Xuan Zong or Dao Guang (Aisin-Gioro Min Ning) (r. 1820-50)
(7) Emperor Wen Zong or Xian Feng (Aisin-Gioro Yi Ning) (r. 1850-61)
(8) Emperor Mu Zong or Tong Zhi (Aisin-Gioro Zai Chun) (r. 1861-75)
(Yi Xuan)
(9) Emperor De Zong or Guang Xu (Aisin-Gioro Zai Tian) (r. 1875-1908)
(Zai Feng)
(10) Emperor Xuan Tong (Aisin-Gioro Pu Yi) (r. 1908-12)

As a bourgeois democratic republic, the Republic of China made only a brief appearance in history. The bourgeois democratic revolution of 1911 had been strangled by Chinese and foreign reactionary forces. It only overthrew a feudal emperor, but did not overthrow the exploitation and oppression by imperialism and feudalism. China was still a semi-colonial, semi-feudal society. Imperialist and feudal forces continued to rule China, and the Chinese people's anti-imperialist, anti-feudal democratic revolution was still far from being completed.

15. The Period of Beiyang Warlord Rule

After usurping the position of Provisional President, Yuan Shikai gradually established autocratic rule by suppressing the democratic forces. A group of *Tong Meng Hui* members headed by Song Jiaoren hoped to wage a parliamentary struggle against Yuan Shikai on the basis of the Provisional Constitution to bring into effect a bourgeois democratic government. In order to win the national parliamentary elections and to have the parliament organized along party lines, that is, on the basis of political parties rather than individuals or provincial associations, Song Jiaoren and others formed the Kuomintang (Nationalist Party) in August 1912 from a central core of *Tong Meng Hui* members together with some small political parties. Its platform called for political unity, development of local autonomy and attention to people's livelihood. This was a considerable retreat from the old *Tong Meng Hui* platform.

The Kuomintang won the majority of seats in the national parliamentary elections, which were held between the end of 1912 and the beginning of 1913. In the position of a majority party, Song Jiaoren and other Kuomintang leaders hoped to form a cabinet, so as to restrict the power held by Yuan Shikai. But on March 20, 1913, Song Jiaoren was assassinated at the Shanghai railway station by Yuan Shikai's agents.

The assassination provoked different reactions from the revolutionists. Sun Yat-sen called for the immediate overthrow of Yuan Shikai, but Huang Xing, supported by the majority of Kuomintang parliamentarians, opposed the use of military force on the grounds that it stood little chance of success; instead, they argued for a peaceful solution by legal means in parliament. However, Yuan Shikai issued orders to exterminate Kuomintang power in several of the southern provinces by military force. Yuan Shikai received substantial support from the imperialist powers: he was granted loans amounting to 25 million pounds sterling from the Five-Power Consortium formed by Britain, France, Germany, Japan and Russia, and gained U.S. recognition for his regime. In June 1913 he ordered the dismissal of the Kuomintang military governors of Jiangxi, Anhui and Guangdong. Faced with this new challenge, the Kuomintang finally took up arms in the uprising known as the "Second Revolution". In July 1913, Li Liejun, military governor of Jiangxi, and Huang Xing declared war on Yuan from their bases in Hukou and Nanjing respectively. Anhui, Hunan, Guangdong, Fujian and Sichuan also declared their independence. Because of internal laxness within the Kuomintang, the anti-Yuan forces were weak and the Second Revolution was completely defeated in less than two months. The provinces in the south thus came under the control of Yuan Shikai, and Sun Yat-sen and Huang Xing were forced once again to flee to Japan.

After having crushed his opposition in the Second Revolution, Yuan Shikai turned his attention to gaining the formal presidency. On October 6, the day set for the election of President, he sent self-proclaimed "citizens' groups", consisting of several thousand plain-clothes military police and hooligans, to surround the parliament, not allowing the members of parliament to leave until Yuan had been elected. The following day Li Yuanhong was elected Vice-President. Britain, France, Russia, Japan, Germany and other imperialist powers simultaneously declared recognition of Yuan Shikai's regime.

On becoming President, Yuan Shikai declared the Kuomintang illegal in November and then in January 1914 ordered the dissolution of parliament. In April he annulled the Provisional Constitution and proclaimed his reactionary Constitution of the Republic of China, substituting presidential for cabinet rule and expanding presidential power to the maximum to carry out a dictatorship.

All that was left of the republic was an empty name, but Yuan

Shikai even wanted to discard that name and start his own imperial dynasty. The imperialist countries continued to support his ambitions, thinking that thereby they could extend their own influence in China. In August 1914 World War I broke out in Europe. Taking advantage of the diversion of European interest to the war at home, the Japanese made plans to invade China, sending troops to occupy Qingdao (Tsingtao) and the Jiaozhou-Jinan railway. As a condition of their support for Yuan Shikai's imperial ambitions, they put forward in January 1915 the "Twenty-One Demands". The main items were that China transfer German rights in Shandong to Japan and also open other parts of the peninsula to Japan; recognize the special interests of Japan in Liaoning, Jilin and eastern Inner Mongolia; extend the lease on Lüshun and Dalian and on the related railway; operate jointly with Japan the Hanyeping Iron and Steel Works; not lease or cede to other powers China's coastal ports, harbours or off-shore islands; engage Japanese advisors on political, financial and military affairs; and operate jointly with Japan China's police departments and arsenals. Apart from a few individual items reserved for further negotiation, Yuan Shikai in strict secrecy accepted these demands on May 25, 1915. With the support of Japan, the United States and other powers, Yuan Shikai declared himself "Emperor of the Chinese Empire" in December 1915.

Yuan Shikai's reactionary rule caused a great deal of hardship among the Chinese people, and spontaneous mass movements broke out all over the country in protest. The largest was the Bailang Uprising, which broke out in Henan in 1912 spread to other parts of Henan, Anhui, Hubei, Shaanxi and Guangxi, and continued against Yuan Shikai's forces for more than two years. After the news came out that Yuan had accepted the Twenty-One Demands, a movement for the boycott of Japanese goods immediately broke out in Shanghai, Beijing, Shenyang, Changsha, Hankou and elsewhere. Students went on strike, making speeches and distributing leaflets. Workers were also on strike in opposition to Japanese aggression and Yuan's treachery, and patriotic businessmen organized alliances for the exclusion of Japanese goods.

In July 1914 Sun Yat-sen organized the *Zhong Hua Ge Ming*

Dang (Chinese Revolutionary Party) in Japan, whose aims were to "wipe out autocratic politics and establish a full republic" and to carry out the struggle against Yuan Shikai. After Yuan announced the restoration of the empire, Sun Yat-sen issued a proclamation calling for the people to rise against him.

When the anti-Yuan movement was at its height, Cai E, former military governor of Yunnan, formed the *Hu Guo Jun* (Republic Protection Army) and announced the independence of Yunnan on December 25, 1915. Other provinces responded with similar moves. On New Year's Day, 1916, Yuan Shikai announced 1916 as the first year of his dynasty with the reign title Hong Xian (Great Constitution), and dispatched over one hundred thousand troops to Yunnan to exterminate the *Hu Guo Jun*. But Yuan's army was low in morale and suffered one defeat after the other. Yuan's trusted associates, such as Feng Guozhang and Duan Qirui, were alarmed at the disintegration of central control, and sent a joint telegram urging Yuan to abandon his attempt at imperials rule. Noting Yuan Shikai's isolation, Japan, the United States and other powers also withdrew their support for him. Beset with difficulties internally and externally, Yuan was forced to abrogate his dynasty on March 22, 1916. He still hoped to retain his position as President, but hostility towards him continued to mount, and he was unable to remain in power. He died on June 6 in despair.

After Yuan's death, the situation deteriorated rapidly as the warlords, each backed by an imperialist power, ought for control of the country. China then saw separatist warlord regimes and tangled warfare among warlords. In the south, the main warlord forces were the Yunnan clique headed by Tang Jiyao, and the Guangxi clique headed by Lu Rongting; both were formed in the anti-Yuan war waged by the *Hu Guo Jun* and had close ties to the British and Americans. The Yunnan clique occupied Yunnan and Guizhou, and the Guangxi clique occupied Guangdong and Guangxi. The Beiyang warlords split into two groups, the Anhui clique headed by Duan Qirui, and the Zhili clique headed by Feng Guozhang. The Anhui clique had Japanese backing and controlled the Beijing government as well as Anhui, Shaanxi, Shandong, Zhejiang, Fujian and other provinces. The Zhili clique had the support of Britain and the United States and was based in Jiangsu, Jiangxi and Hubei. In the Northeast, Zhang Zuolin with Japanese support expanded his territory to form the Fengtian clique in Liaoning, which held the balance of power between the Anhui and Zhili cliques. Minor warlords also staked out their own territory.

In June 1916, Li Yuanhong succeeded as President and resurrected the Provisional Constitution; parliament was reconvened in August 1916. Duan Qirui was appointed Premier with the real power of the government in his hand. He attempted to crush Li Yuanhong and the anti-Anhui opposition, while Li Yuanhong and the Zhili clique headed by Feng Guozhang for their part strove to resist the Anhui clique. The struggle between them broke out on the question of whether China should take part in World War I. The Zhili clique with the backing of the United States opposed a declaration of war against Germany, but Duan Qirui's Anhui clique with the backing of Japan forced the parliament and Li Yuanhong to agree. In May 1917, with the backing of forces close to Britain and the United States, Li Yuanhong dismissed Duan Qirui as Premier. Deciding to retain his political power by military force, Duan incited warlords in Zhili, Fengtian (Liaoning), Shandong, Henan and other provinces to declare independence, organized a "General Headquarters for the Independent Provinces" in Tianjin and announced that he was dispatching troops to Beijing. With no military force of his own, Li Yuanhong was completely helpless, and invited the military governor of Anhui, Zhang Xun, to act as mediator.

Zhang Xun had hitherto been a supporter of Qing restoration. With the secret backing of Duan Qirui, he first forced Li Yuanhong to dissolve the parliament, then led his army into Beijing, coercing Li Yuanhong into resignation. On July 1, he restored Puyi to the throne. The whole country was immediately up in arms. Most of the newspapers in Beijing closed down as a gesture of resistance. A rally of more than ten thousand people was held in Changsha, calling for troops to be dispatched against him. In Shanghai, Sun Yat-sen called a joint meeting of revolutionists and military and political figures, and issued a statement condemning the restorationist forces. Seeing that the aim of driving out Li Yuanhong and dissolving parliament had been achieved, Duan Qirui immediately about-faced and denounced the restoration, sending troops into Beijing to drive out Zhang Xun. Puyi abdicated for the second time and the twelve-day restoration thus came to an end. Duan Qirui consequently resumed his post as Premier.

In conformity with the ambitions of Japanese imperialism, Duan Qirui declared war on Germany in August. At home, he did not revive the Provisional Constitution and parliament, but tried to unify the country by force. In order to expand his real power, he raised a Japanese loan of 380,000,000 yen, mortgaging railways, the telecommunications system, mines, forests and so on, selling national sovereignty with a free hand.

Sun Yat-sen strongly condemned Duan Qirui for "assuming the face of a republican while actually running an autocracy", and advocated upholding the Provisional Constitution and restoring parliament. In September he called an extraordinary session of the parliament in Guangzhou, and set up a military government to uphold the constitution. Sun Yat-sen was elected Generalissimo and Lu Rongting and Tang Jiyao were its marshals. The slogan "protect the constitution" had by that time lost its appeal and lacked a mass basis, and Sun Yat-sen was relying on local warlords. The warlords in the southwest appeared to support the constitution but in reality they were anxious to maintain their own territory. In order to get rid of Sun Yat-sen, they collaborated with some officials and politicians to manipulate the extraordinary parliament, and in May 1918 reorganized the military government. Sun was forced to resign and left Guangzhou. The failure of the movement to protect the constitution made Sun Yat-sen realize that warlords north and south were "jackals of the same lair", and that he could not carry out the revolution by relying on them.

16. Ideology and Culture During the Period of Bourgeois Revolution

The main ideological trend in the learning and culture of the early twentieth century was the ideology of the bourgeois democratic revolution. Compared with the reformists, the revolutionists led by Sun Yat-sen were even more conscientious in seeking truth from the West. They introduced a broad range of political theories, history philosophy and so on from the Western bourgeois revolutionary period, with Rousseau's *Social Contract* as their gospel and the French Revolution and the American War of Independence as their models. Thus equipped they criticized feudalism and reformism, raised the banner of the "democratic republic" and took the road to "bloody revolution". The doctrine of the Three People's Principles advocated by Sun Yat-sen became the political programme of the old democratic revolution led by the bourgeoisie.

Sun Yat-sen believed in the Western theory of evolution, but was opposed to the anti-revolutionary, vulgar theory of evolution held by the reformists. He held that the process whereby the old gave way to the new was an incontrovertible law of nature. Hence, the progress of civilization in human society and changes in political systems were unavoidable and necessary historical trends, which is also to say that democratic revolution was a historical necessity. Sun Yat-sen opposed the theories of the reformists that one must "proceed in an orderly way and in proper sequence" and not "skip the necessary steps"—hence, that reform, not revolution, was what was needed. He believed that the evolution of civilization was a consistent development from a lower stage to a higher stage. Opposing the tendency to crawl behind in other people's footsteps by imitating every move, he foresaw, from a positive and progressive evolutionary view, the historical prospect in which "the newcomers surpass their elders". In 1905, he predicted that a great leap forward would appear in the development of Chinese history, in which China would overtake and surpass Japan and the Western capitalist countries in a few decades. His outlook was bourgeois and there were inevitably idealist and metaphysical mistakes in his evolutionary views. Nevertheless, from beginning to end he always stood at the forefront of the trend of the age, and realized that the struggle for national independence and liberation was an irresistible worldwide trend in the twentieth century.

In regard to epistemology, Sun Yat-sen held that "knowledge follows practice" and "facts precede theories", and expressed in simple terms a materialist theory of knowledge which was directly opposed to the idealistic apriorism of "knowledge precedes practice". He emphasized the function of "practice" and upheld the doctrine that "knowledge is hard, practice is easy", stating that revolutionists should "be fearless and enjoy practising". However, he was basically an empiricist, content to enumerate perceptual facts in a simple synthesis; he ignored scientific summarization and could not advance to the stage of seeking the intrinsic nature of phenomena. "Practice", as he spoke of it, was an independent individual act that went beyond class, not considered as social practice. He separated knowledge from practice, and sometimes stressed the function of rational knowledge in isolation. Also, he divided people into categories according to their relative degree of "innate ability", such as "the foresighted" and "the ignorant". He thus abandoned the viewpoint of "practice" and fell into the trap of the theory of genius. This contradiction in his theory of knowledge, which reflected his class bias as a bourgeois revolutionist, made him unable to perceive correctly the historical function of the popular masses.

The bourgeois revolutionist and propagandist, Zhang Taiyan, was also an influential thinker. In works such as *Book of Grievances,* he expressed a materialist and atheistic thinking. He opposed religion and theology, and denied the existence of gods and ghosts. He pointed out that there were no gods, and that after death people did not turn into ghosts but became "dry bones", their flesh being transformed into inorganic matter or another form of organic matter. He also explained the origin of mankind according to Darwin's theory of biological evolution, holding that man was not created by gods but evolved from the ape who had in turn evolved from marine life. After the failure of the 1911 Revolution, however, he did not further develop his materialistic views but on the contrary turned to Buddhist philosophy and dreamed of establishing a new religion in a compromise with idealism.

In the early twentieth century, the histories of foreign countries were introduced into China through translations and commentaries to propagate bourgeois democratic revolutionary thinking. Chief among them were the histories of the English and French revolutions and the independence movements in America, Italy, Greece and other countries.

In this period, Liang Qichao, along with others, made critiques of traditional Chinese historiography from the evolutionary viewpoint, pointing out that the old histories were only collections of biographies of emperors, kings, generals and ministers, and could not explain trends in historical evolution and causal relations in historical events. He advocated a bourgeois "new history", demanding that historians "describe the phenomenon of the evolution of the masses and seek its general rules". Zhang Taiyan put forward similar views. Also along the same lines was Xia Zengyou's *A Textbook History of China*, published in 1904. In his own words, Xia hoped to explain in this book "the main principle of the evolution of the masses from ancient times to the present". Proceeding from an idealist point of view, Xia was unable to expound the laws of historical development and made unscientific judgements on important historical problems.

Education was also taken very seriously by the bourgeois revolutionists. Zou Rong stated that widespread "revolutionary education" should be conducted in order to let people know of the revolutionary cause and struggle for the overthrow of Qing rule, and of opposition to the system of monarchical rule "to restore our natural human rights". Chen Tianhua advocated "the establishment of schools and spread of education". In his view, in order to withstand imperialist aggression, "we must first study the strong points of foreigners", and "if we want to study them, we must have more schools and also send students abroad". In order to raise new recruits for the revolution, and also to provide a base for revolutionary activity, the bourgeois revolutionists founded several new schools. The most well-known was the Patriotic School founded in Shanghai in 1902 by Cai Yuanpei, which propagated the idea of popular rights and anti-Qing revolution among the students and carried out military training. In Shaoxing, Xu Xilin established in succession the Recheng Primary School, the Yuequn Public School and the Datong School. The Datong School concentrated on military training for the students. Qiu Jin (1875-1907), also known as Jianxiong or Woman Warrior of Jianhu Lake and from Shaoxing, Zhejiang, was the administrative inspector of the school. She made it the centre of preparations for an uprising. Qiu Jin had also been one of the founders of the Chinese Public Institute in Shanghai in 1906, which provided education for Chinese students who had returned from

Japan.

In the first years of the twentieth century, the Qing court under Empress Dowager Ci Xi, with deceptive intent, converted the old style academies in the provincial capitals into colleges and established a universal system of middle and primary schools. A Committee on Education was appointed to run the Metropolitan College and to administer national school affairs; a Ministry of Education was established in 1905. The Qing court's educational reforms were changes in form only and the substance of education was still based on "self-cultivation and classical studies" with the primary stress given to rote learning the Confucian classics and observing feudal morality. In 1906, the Qing court decreed that the aim of education was to be the diffusion of "loyalty to the ruler" and "respect for Confucianism"; this clearly revealed the purpose of its educational reforms.

Many schools as well as churches were founded by Western missionaries to serve the cultural aggression on China. By the end of the nineteenth century, there were more than five hundred middle and primary schools run by the Catholic Church in Zhili, Shandong, Shanxi and Henan alone. By 1898, there were more than 1,100 American missionary schools in China. The missionaries also established colleges and universities in China, such as the Huiwen University in Beijing, the Wenhua University in Wuchang, the Qilu University in Jinna and St. John's University in Shanghai, by the early twentieth century.

The large-scale translation of Western literary works was an important feature of this period. The most productive translator was Lin Shu (1852-1924, also known as Lin Qinnan), from Minghou, Fujian; his first and most popular translation, *La Dame aux camélias* by Dumas fils, was published in Fuzhou in 1899. The quantity of translations grew rapidly in the early years of the twentieth century. By 1911, several hundred novels had been translated, and the range of translated material also grew wider with translations, mostly the work of Lin Shu, from Shakespeare, Dickens, Balzac, Hugo, Pushkin, Tolstoy and others. At the peak of the movement in protest against American mistreatment of Chinese migrant labour in 1905, Lin Shu translated Harriet Beecher Stowe's *Uncle Tom's Cabin,* arousing Chinese patriotism with this story of American mistreatment of black slaves. Lu Xun (1881-1936), the famous writer, also translated fiction from foreign countries in the early twentieth century.

The reformists advocated reform in Chinese fiction, stressing the role of fiction in reforming politics and society in defiance of the low esteem in which fiction was held by the orthodox feudal literati. Among the large number of novels reflecting reformist political demands and denouncing the sordid reality around them, the most famous were Li Baojia's *Exposure of the Official World,* Wu Woyao's *Strange Events Seen in the Past Twenty Years* and Zeng Pu's *The Flower in the Sea of Sin*. The novels were written in a popular and easily understandable vernacular, making extensive use of satire and exaggeration to expose the criminal activities of the feudal ruling class and foreign aggressors. However, at their best these novels are still far below earlier works such as *A Dream of the Red Mansions* and *The Scholars*.

The revolutionary intellectuals consciously disseminated revolutionary thinking through poetry and other popular literary forms. Qiu Jin, a poet as well as revolutionary, wrote many poems expressing her resolute revolutionary will and fervent patriotism. The lines:

> *We will shed if we must the blood of a hundred*
> *thousand heads*
> *For the sake of bringing about radical changes on*
> *our land,*

show her readiness to dedicate her life to the revolution. An association of poets who were mainly *Tong Meng Hui* members founded the Southern Club in 1909 to publish poetry advocating revolution in its journal, *Southern Club*.

The dominant form of theatre in China from the second half of the nineteenth century until well into the twentieth was Peking opera. An amalgamation of several different kinds of local opera, it was deeply rooted in popular culture. In singing, acting, recitation and stage fighting, it gradually surpassed the other forms of opera or drama then prevalent, and attracted a very wide audience from all sections of society. Seeking temporary diversion after the suppression of the Taiping Revolution, the Qing court turned Beijing into a centre for operatic performers from all over the country, giving Peking opera further opportunity to profit from a diversity or regional opera styles. In the last thirty years of the nineteenth century, the repertoire of Peking opera was greatly enlarged, with a wide variety of subjects. Many famous actors took the stage, creating excellent and lively artistic forms, and Peking opera began to exert a great influence throughout the country. The actors who made the greatest contribution to the formation and development of Peking opera were Cheng Changgeng and Tan Xinpei. Cheng Changgeng (18911-80), from Qianshan, Anhui, had a unique artistic accomplishment. His most famous roles include Lu Su in *Meeting of the Heroes* and Wu Zixu in *Wenzhao Pass*. Tan Xinpei (1847-1917) was from Jiangxia (modern Wuchang County), Hubei. He did not confine himself to one model of acting but blended together characteristics of different styles to form his own school. The development of the bourgeois revolutionary movement in the early twentieth century had an effect on Peking opera. After the siege of Beijing by the Eight-Power Allied Forces, the famous actor Wang Xiaonong (1858-1918) wrote *Weeping at the Ancestral Temple*, based on the story of Liu Chen, king of Northern Shu (in modern Sichuan) at the end of the Three Kingdoms period who was opposed to surrendering to the enemy and wept as he made a sacrifice at his ancestral temple, to stir up patriotism and attack the corruption of the Qing court. Some actors tried to stage operas in contemporary costumes to satirize the government. Some Peking opera actors in Shanghai took part in the attack on the Jiangnan Machine Building Works after the outbreak of the 1911 Revolution. However, the imperial patrons of Peking opera, such as the Empress Dowager, exerted considerable influence on the development of Peking opera by using it as an instrument to protect their reactionary rule and for their own diversion, so that the repertoire came to include many inferior works which preached feudal morality, superstition and sexual license.

Western-style modern drama made its appearance in the early twentieth century, closely associated from its inception with the revolution. A group of Chinese students in Tokyo founded the Spring Willow Society in 1907. As part of the protest against American mistreatment of Chinese migrant labour, they put on a five-act play of *Uncle Tom's Cabin. Plays like Qiu Jin* and *Xu Xilin* were staged in Shanghai. Two professional companies, the Progress Troupe and the New Drama Association, were founded in 1910 and 1912 respectively. Their performances such as *Long Live the Republic! Huanghuagang* (about the seventy-two martyrs) and *About Face!* Played an important role in the bourgeois revolutionary movement.

Early twentieth-century China was very backward in science and technology. Nevertheless, there were still some notable achievements. In 1905, a locally-run railway from Beijing to Zhangjiakou was constructed under the supervision of Zhan Tianyou as chief engineer. The two-hundred kilometre railway was not very long, but as it passed through the Yanshan mountain range the terrain was complex and there were many difficulties in construction. Some imperialist elements sneered at this undertaking, claiming that a Chinese engineer capable of constructing such a railway "had yet to be born" and that China must be dreaming if it wants to build a railway on its own without foreign assistance; even if it could it would be at least fifty years before it got to that stage." Zhan Tianyou (1861-1919), from Wuyuan in Anhui (today in Jiangxi), assumed the responsibility for building this railway to bring credit to his country. He and his workers conquered repeated difficulties, reducing the length of track to half that in the original European and American blueprints, and using two engines to pull and push on winding tracks to solve the problems of a steep ascent. The railway went into full operation in October 1909, ahead of schedule and with a surplus of funds.

At the same time, Feng Ru also achieved outstanding results in the design and manufacture of aeroplanes. Feng Ru, a Chinese resident in the United States, built his first plane in 1908, one of the earliest in the world, with the assistance of other local Chinese. After many experiments, he finally built a plane in 1910 which could reach a speed of 104 kilometres per hour and an altitude of more than 230 metres. This plane won first prize in an international aviation competition in October the same year. He returned to China in February 1911, bringing his monoplane and biplane with him and three assistants. After the Wuchang Uprising he organized together with some other revolutionaries the Northern Airforce Reconnaissance Squad. Unfortunately, he was killed in a plane crash in Guangzhou while testing a plane in 1912.

The achievements of Zhan Tianyou and Feng Ru won under difficult circumstances are highly commendable, once again demonstrating the creative and inventive genius of the Chinese people. However, the repression and devastation by the imperialist powers and the reactionary regime at home retarded for decades the development of science and technology in China's semi-colonial, semi-feudal society.

17. The Dawn of the Chinese Revolution

The 1911 Revolution was followed by an upsurge in industrial growth. The period of World War I provided an opportunity for the development of Chinese capitalism. The import of British goods in 1918 was nearly reduced by half compared with 1913, French imports were reduced by one-third, and German imports almost came to a complete halt. The mass anti-imperialist struggle, especially the movement to boycott Japanese goods, also gave a strong impetus to the development of national capitalism. In the period 1912-19, national capital financed the construction of more than 470 new factories and mines, plus the expansion of existing enterprises, bringing the total amount of new capital to at least 130 million yuan, which exceeded the total capital investment of the previous fifty years.

The development of national industry found expression mainly in the textile and flour mills in the light industrial sector. In 1913 there were only 16 cotton mills, with a total of about 500,000 spindles; by 1918 this had increased to 35 mills and about 650,000 spindles. The growth in flour milling was even greater, with 40 mills in 1911 increasing to more than 123 in 1921, among them 105 managed by national capital, and an increase in capital investment from more than 6 million yuan to about 42.1 million yuan. Other branches of light industry which also developed greatly in this period included match factories, woollen and paper mills, tanneries and the manufacture of cigarettes and soap. Although there was some degree of increase in heavy industry, it was chiefly under the control of the imperialist powers.

World War I also provided Japan and the United States with the opportunity to step up their aggression against China. In 1917 and 1918, the United States imports in China were worth about 60 million taels of silver, about 60 per cent of the total value of British imports in 1913. Japanese investment in Chinese enterprises increased from more than 380 million yen in 1913 to more than 880 million yen in 1919. Almost the entire production of pig iron and iron ore was controlled by Japanese capital, and one-third of coal production. Over one quarter of the equipment in operation in the cotton spinning industry was in Japanese enterprises. The economic expansion of Japan in China was a new source of pressure on Chinese capitalism forming an obstacle to its development.

The gradual development of Chinese capitalism did not change the semi-colonial, semi-feudal nature of Chinese society. National industry still could not break imperialist control over heavy industry or its dominance of light industry. The development of national capitalism was also unable to affect the outstandingly superior position of the feudal economy in the national economy as a whole. High feudal land rents, usury and commercial profit all restricted the formation and expansion of industrial capital. Chinese capitalism was in conflict with Chinese feudalism and at the same time dependent on it.

Nevertheless capitalism developed to some extent and the ranks of the Chinese proletariat were correspondingly strengthened. Before the 1911 Revolution, industrial workers in China numbered about 500,000 to 6000,000, but by 1919 this number had increased to more than 2,000,000. China's industrial workers were mostly concentrated in mines, railways, and textile, match, cigarette and steamship enterprises, in a dozen or more large cities such as Shanghai, Wuhan, Tianjin, Guangzhou, Qingdao, Dalian and Harbin; 300,000 to 400,000 industrial workers were concentrated in Shanghai alone. This high degree of concentration was a special characteristic of the Chinese proletariat, which enabled them to form alliances and unite at a comparatively early stage and become a powerful fighting force. The 1911 Revolution failed to bring changes to the political and economic position of the Chinese proletariat. The life of the workers became even more difficult under warlord rule, and workers had no democratic rights whatsoever, being deprived of the freedom of assembly and discussion and the right to strike. Yuan Shikai's Regulations Rgarding Public Security and Police of 1912 and Public Security and Police Law of 1914 defined strikes as a criminal act obstructing "social order and peace" and openly proclaimed the need "to adopt police powers to prevent workers' associations and activities". The triple yoke of imperialist, feudal and capitalist exploitation and oppression of the Chinese proletariat became heavier. This led to a rising wave of resistance and an increasing number of strikes. From 1912 to May 1919, there were more than 130 strikes, more than double the total of the previous seven years. These years saw notable advances in the scale of strikes and the level of the struggle.

The role played by the Chinese proletariat in the political struggle to oppose imperialism and warlord treachery also became increasingly evident. When opposition arose to the Russian policy of "independence" for Outer Mongolia in 1912, the Chinese workers at the Russian-owned brick tea factories in Hankou held a spontaneous strike. In the 1915 patriotic movement to oppose the signing of the Twenty-One Demands between Japan and Yuan Shikai, Shanghai dock workers were the first to strike, and Chinese workers in Japanese-owned enterprises in Shanghai, Changsha and elsewhere also took part in the struggle. In 1916, the workers in French-owned enterprises in Tianjin went on strike in opposition to the forcible occupation by France of Laoxikai to enlarge its concession in Tianjin. Under the impetus of the workers' strike, the Tianjin students also went on strike and merchants closed shop. Workers in Beijing and elsewhere held strikes in support, and the struggle against imperialism reached new heights. Workers from each branch of industry in Tianjin got organized to lead the strike and hold demonstrations. The struggle lasted five or six months, and the aggressive act of French imperialism was finally defeated. These struggles showed that the Chinese proletariat had become a powerful force.

Phenomena such as supportive strikes and joint strikes show that by this stage in the Chinese labour movement, the scattered and spontaneous economic struggles for better living conditions were giving way to unified and organized anti-imperialist, anti-feudal political struggles. From January 1912 to April 1919, there were six or seven large-scale joint strikes by industrial workers. Modern trade unions to replace the old trade associations were founded in the course of the strike movement. The strike at the Shanghai Commercial Press in 1917 demanding non-interference in union activities was led by a trade union. The development of the Chinese labour movement at this time shows the Chinese proletariat in the process of change from a class-in-itself to a class-for-itself, a precondition for the birth of the Chinese Communist Party.

The new cultural movement to modernize Chinese culture dates from the foundation of *Youth Magazine* in Shanghai in 1915. The magazine's first editor was Chen Duxiu who played a leading role in the new movement. In 1916, the magazine, now called *New Youth*, moved to Beijing, where it soon became the centre of the gradually unfolding movement. *New Youth* brought together a number of progressive intellectuals: among the earliest and most prominent editors and contributors were Li Dazhao and Lu Xun.

The chief concern of the new cultural movement was the promotion of democracy and science. By democracy was meant a French-style bourgeois democratic government. The proponents of democracy at this time believed that the 1911 Revolution had not established true democracy in China. It was their hope to bring about, by promoting bourgeois democratic ideas and opposing autocratic rule, a bourgeois republic in fact as well as in name. Li Dazhao pointed out that "the people" and "the ruler" and "freedom" and "autocracy" were irreconcilable concepts, and that "monarchy is death to a republic, autocracy is the destruction of liberty". He urged resolute struggle against "the restorationists who are traitors to their country and enemies of the republic", saying that no leniency should be shown towards them, but they should be "permanently uprooted so they cannot grow and spread". Although such proposals could not be realized, they exposed and attacked the reactionary rule of the feudal landlords.

The proponents of democracy promoted the study of science in order to combat superstition and blind obedience to authority, using modern knowledge of natural sciences to undermine belief in gods and ghosts. They also criticized theories of the divine sanction of rulers and predestination, upheld atheistic views and introduced bourgeois materialist philosophy from the West.

As the new cultural movement developed, the proponents of democracy directed the spearhead of their attack against the doctrines of Confucius, which had been developed by Confucianists throughout the centuries as a bulwark for feudal autocracy. Li Dazhao pointed out that autocratic monarchs made Confucius an idol, and Confucius in turn became "an idol for the protection of monarchical rule" and "a screen to provide shelter for imperial autocracy". Hence the destruction of the idol was at the same time criticism of the spirit of monarchical autocracy. Lu Xun's attacks on the "cannibalism" in feudal ethics were particularly acute, and he expressed the hope that young people would unloosen the bonds of the feudal system and thinking. Such deep-going and powerful attacks as Lu Xun's were unprecedented and played a great role in mobilizing people for the struggle.

New Youth also called for the promotion of literature in the modern vernacular language and opposition to writings in classical language, the promotion of new literature and opposition to old literature. This was the start of a revolution in literature. Its commander-general was Lu Xun, whose "A Madman's Diary", published in *New Youth* in May 1918, was the first short story in the new literary movement, followed by stories such as "Kong Yiji" and "Medicine". Lu Xun was also famous for his short satirical essays on all aspects of society. His stories and essays, with their combination of revolutionary content and modern artistic form, established outstanding models for the new literature.

The new cultural movement from 1915 to 1919 had serious shortcomings due to the bourgeois outlook of its leaders. It did not reach into the masses, was not closely united with the political movements of its time and treated cultural problems formalistically. However, in its attacks on feudalism the new cultural movement went far beyond any previous movement. It played a major role in helping young intellectuals to cast off the bonds of the old thinking, encouraged people to intensify their search for a means by which the country and its people could be saved from foreign aggression, was the pioneer in thinking for the May 4 Movement and paved the way for the spread of Marxism-Leninism in China.

"The salvoes of the October Revolution brought us Marxism-Leninism."[1] The success of the 1917 October Revolution in Russia was welcomed enthusiastically by progressive people in China, who took up the study of Marxism-Leninism and reevaluated China's problems in its light. The process of propagation of Marxism-Leninism produced the first group of Chinese intellectuals with an elementary knowledge of communist ideology. In "A Comparison Between the French and Russian Revolutions", published in July 1918, Li Dazhao pointed out the socialist nature of the October Revolution and called on the Chinese people to greet the new tide of revolution. In "The Victory of Bolshevism", published in November, he proclaimed that "we can see that the future of the universe is a world of the red flag".

From the beginning of the spread of Marxism-Leninism in China, Mao Zedong represented the correct direction in the combination of the universal truth of Marxism-Leninism and the concrete practice of the Chinese revolution.

As the new cultural movement quickly developed into a movement for the study and dissemination of Marxism-Leninism, the Chinese revolution also changed into a new-democratic revolution. On May 4, 1919, an anti-imperialist, anti-feudal demonstration was held by students in Beijing, which grew into a large-scale nation-wide movement of students, workers and others known as the May 4 Movement. The May 4 Movement marked the end of the old democratic revolution led by the bourgeoisie and the beginning of the new-democratic revolution led by the proletariat.

---

[1] Mao Zedong, "On the People's Democratic Dictatorship", *Selected Works*, Vol. IV, p. 413, Foreign Languages Press, Beijing, 1975.

Chapter XI
The Continuation of the Semi-Colonial and Semi-Feudal Society and the New-democratic Revolution

1. The May 4th Movement and the Beginning of the New-democratic Revolution

The May 4th Movement which broke out in 1919 was a great anti-imperialist, anti-feudal revolutionary movement. It marked the beginning of the new-democratic revolution in China.

After the Beiyang (Northern) warlords replaced the rule of the Qing Dynasty, contradictions in Chinese society deepened.

Japanese imperialists seized the chance of World War I, when the European powers were too busy with wars among themselves to interfere in China, to quicken their pace in their attempt to occupy China. In late August of 1914, Japan declared war on Germany, and subsequently sent troops to Shandong, China, occupied the Jiaozhou-Jinan Railway in October and Qingdao in November, and seized all the special rights that Germany had possessed in Shandong Province. In May 1915, Japan compelled Yuan Shikai to recognize its "Twenty-one Demands", a secret document attempting to destroy China, by way of ultimatum. In 1917 Japan concluded an agreement with the United States, in which the United States consented to the special rights Japan enjoyed in China. From 1917 to 1918, Japan gained further control of Chinese railways, tax revenue, mines and forest resources, and rights of army training through huge loans. In 1918 it signed the "Military Agreement of Joint Defence Against Enemies" with the Duan Qirui government and sent troops, tens of thousands strong, to occupy

China's northeast. During the world war period, the Japanese economic influence rapidly expanded in China. Between 1913 and 1919, the enterprises run by Japan in China increased from 36 to 178; banks, from 21 to 38 in China's northeast. The intensified aggression of Japanese imperialism aggravated the crisis of the Chinese nation. In September 1918, Zhang Zongxiang, then the Chinese Minister to Japan, went so far as to express "ready agreement," in an exchange of letters on the Shandong issue between China and Japan, to Japan's seizing of Germany's former special rights in Shandong. After coming to power Duan Qirui, continued selling out the country's sovereignty externally and carrying out autocratic rule internally in the name of the republic. In 1917, after warlord Zhang Xun engineered the restoration of Xuan Tong, the Manchu boy emperor, to the throne, Duan abrogated the 1912 Constitution of the Republic, organized a parliament under his control, unified the country by force and created a succession of civil wars, thus dragging China into an even darker abyss.

The May 4th Movement took place as a result of deepening contradictions between the Chinese people on the one hand and imperialism and feudal warlords on the other, and under the influence of the October Socialist Revolution in Russia and the subsequent upsurge of world revolution. Its direct fuse, however, was the failure of China in the Paris Peace Conference.

In November 1918 World War I, which had lasted for four years and three months, ended in the defeat of Germany, Austria, etc. In the following January, the victor countries held a peace conference at Paris for the purpose of drawing up a peace treaty with Germany. Participated in by more than 20 countries, the conference was actually manipulated by the United States, Britain and France. The U.S. president Woodrow Wilson, the British prime minister David Lloyd George and the French premier Georges Clemenceau were the three policy makers. China sent a five-member delegation composed of Lu Zhengxiang, foreign minister of the Beijing government, Gu Weijun, minister to the United States, Shi Zhaoji, minister to Britain, Wei Chenzu, minister to Belgium, and Wang Zhengting, representative of south China's military government. Lu was the first delegate, but it was Wang and Gu who attended the conference regularly. Chinese delegates began by submitting an appeal to the conference of seven "hopeful conditions" and demanding the abrogation of the "Twenty-one Demands," The seven conditions were abolition of foreign spheres of influence; withdrawal of foreign troops and policemen stationed in China; dismantling foreign post, wire and wireless telegram offices; annulment of consular jurisdiction; return of leased territory; removal of foreign concessions; and restoration of Chinese authority over the Customs administration. The conference's manipulators refused to discuss China's demands on the excuse of their being "beyond the scope of the peace conference." Then the Chinese delegation brought up the Shandong issue and asked for the return of the former German leased territories in Jiaozhou Bay, the Jiaozhou-Jinan Railway and other privileges directly to China. Despite Gu Weijun and Wang Zhengting's strong protests, China's demands were again turned down, due to the pressure of international power politics. On April 30 the articles about the Shandong issue in the Paris Peace Treaty were decided by Britain, the United States and France in a meeting to which the Japanese delegates were invited and the Chinese delegates were not allowed to attend. It was laid down in the treaty that all the former German interests in Shandong were to be taken over by Japan. On May 1, the British foreign minister notified the Chinese delegation of this decision.

When World War I came to an end, the Chinese people, having long suffered from imperialist aggression and full of hopes for national independence, had hailed "the victory of truth over might" and the "14 Articles of Peace" put forward by the U.S. president Wilson. But the method of dealing with the Shandong issue at the Paris Peace Conference rid the Chinese people of their illusion and made them realize the need for themselves to "take direct action." The May 4th Movement thus broke out.

Before May 4, activities for national sovereignty had been launched among people from all walks of life. The natives of Shandong in Beijing organized a diplomatic support society. More than 100,000 people held a petition rally in Jinan expressing their determination to "fight to the death" for the restoration of Shandong sovereignty. Over 10,000 college students in Beijing published an open telegram to the nation and the Chinese delegates to the Paris Peace Conference demanding "abolish the Chinese-Japanese secret treaty" and "safeguard national rights." Personages from political circles like Xiong Xiling, Lin Changmin and Wang Daxie set up a Chinese People's Diplomatic Association in Beijing, and published open telegrams on several occasions for restoring national sovereignty. Students', workers' and merchants' organizations in Shanghai and hundreds of parliament members in Guangzhou also sent open telegrams to voice their appeal.

On May 1 Lu Zhengxiang secretly cabled the Beijing government, reporting the Chinese diplomatic failure in the Paris Peace Conference. On May 2, after Lin Changmin received confirmation of the failure from a telegram sent by Liang Qichao from Paris, he published an article entitled "A Diplomatic Warning to the Nation" in Beijing's *Morning News*. On the same day, Cai Yuanpei told the news to representatives of Beijing University students. The failure only stimulated the Chinese to take more vigorous actions. A general meeting of the Diplomatic Association was held in the afternoon of May 3. It decided a mass rally be held on May 7 at Central Park, and cabled popular organizations in the provinces to hold similar rallies on the same day. On the evening of May 3, a mass rally of Beijing University students was held, and they decided to stage a demonstration in Tiananmen Square the following day. On the same day, students of Beijing Teachers College also held a rally and determined to take stronger action the following day.

On the afternoon of May 4, more than 3,000 students from 13 colleges and universities gathered in Tiananmen Square. Holding aloft banners, distributing leaflets and making speeches, they demanded "upholding China's sovereignty," "punishing traitors," "abolishing the Twenty-one Demands," "recovering Qingdao," "refusing to sign the Paris Peace Treaty," and "punishing the three pro-Japanese national traitors Cao Rulin, Zhang Zhongxiang and Lu Zongyu." They swore, "Better die in glory than live in dishonour...the land of China can be conquered, but will not be forfeited...the Chinese people can be killed but they will not bow their heads!" After the rally, students marched to the Legation Quarters at Dongjiaominxiang. When they reached the west entrance, the way was obstructed by foreign policemen and they could not pass through. The enraged students, headed by Kuang Husheng, then went straight to Cao Rulin's house where they beat Zhang Zongxiang, who was found there, and set fire to the house. They were suppressed by the reactionary government and 32 students were arrested.

After the May 4th demonstration, college students in Beijing twice organized general classroom strikes to protest against the suppression and to launch patriotic activities. They organized into "10-people groups," making speeches on the streets, calling for the use of Chinese goods and the boycotting of Japanese goods, formed "protect-Shandong volunteers' teams" and carried out military training. The Beijing government did its utmost to absolve Cao Rulin and other traitors from blame and slandered the students' action as "transgression" and "unlawfulness." It proclaimed that they should be punished to the extent of the "sanction of law". On June 3 and 4 the reactionary government arrested as many as 900 students making speeches on the streets, and turned Beijing University buildings into prison houses.

The patriotic movement in Beijing rapidly swept over the whole country. Students in Tianjin, Jinan, Taiyuan, Shanghai, Wuhan, Changsha, Xi'an, Guangzhou, Nanjing, Hangzhou, Nanchang, Kaifeng, Fuzhou, Hefei, and Baoding also went on classroom strikes and held demonstrations. Activities such as making speeches and boycotting Japanese goods were held one after another. Many cities and counties held mass rallies in support of the students. The Shanghai rally ended with the setting up of a permanent office. Shandong, apart from a mass rally attended by 100,000 people, organized a delegation composed of the provincial assembly, educational society, peasant society, press association, student federation and diplomatic discussion federation. It went to Beijing to petition to the government to refuse to sign the Peace Treaty and to punish the traitors. Thus a nationwide patriotic movement took place. The mass round-up of the Beijing students by the warlord government enraged many people in China.

After June 5, the movement entered a new stage. The struggle centre shifted from Beijing to Shanghai, where masses of workers, merchants and salesmen plunged into the movement. On June 5, Shanghai workers put down their tools to support the arrested students. Merchants, under the slogans of "students and merchants act in unison" and "suspension of business to save the country," closed shops and stopped business. Over 20,000 college and middle school students had held classroom strikes before the workers' and merchants' actions. Shanghai thus became the first city to realize "three strikes" (of students, workers and shopkeepers). On June 6, the Shanghai Federation of All Circles was established. In a week, over 50 factories and enterprises with some 70,000 workers in Shanghai joined in strikes. Merchants in other cities, like Tianjin, Jinan, Nanjing, Wuhan, Ningbo, Xiamen, Suzhou and Jiujiang followed the example of Shanghai's merchants; and workers in Tangshan, Changxindian and Jiujiang also launched strikes. Plans for strikes were brewing among workers in Tianjin and on the Tianjin-Pukou Railway. Statistics showed that over 150 cities in 22 provinces in China were involved in the suspension of business, factory walkouts and classroom strikes. The May 4th Movement grew from a mainly intellectual movement to a revolutionary one joined by the masses of the proletariat, petty bourgeoisie, national bourgeoisie and other patriotic persons. Under the pressure of the mass movement, the Beijing government was compelled, on June 10, to dismiss Cao Rulin, Zhang Zongxiang and Lu Zongyu. The Chinese delegation was not present at the meeting on June 28 in which delegates signed the Paris Peace Treaty. Thus the movement attained its two immediate objectives of punishing the traitors and refusing to sign the Peace Treaty.

The resolute and uncompromising anti-imperialist and anti-feudal spirit as displayed by the Chinese people in the May 4th Movement forced the Chinese delegates of the Beijing government to refuse to sign the treaty. It was an unprecedented action in Chinese diplomatic history. In the May 4th Movement the working class held political strikes as an independent force instead of following the bourgeois and petty bourgeois classes in revolutionary struggles as they had done in the past. The new Chinese intellectuals, armed with rudimentary ideas of communism after the October Revolution, played a leading role in the movement. The movement rapidly expanded the rank of the progressive intellectuals and also promoted the dissemination of Marxism-Leninism and its integration with the workers' movement in China, thus preparing ideologically and nurturing the necessary cadres for the founding of the proletarian party, the Chinese Communist Party. All these illustrated that the May 4th Movement had pushed the anti-imperialist and anti-feudal bourgeois democratic revolution to a new stage—the new-democratic revolution.

The May 4th Movement was at once a patriotic political movement and a new cultural movement. The former began from May 4 to June 28, the latter from September 1915, when Chen Duxiu published the first issue of *Youth Magazine*, to July 1921, when the Chinese Communist Party was founded, lasting for 5 years and 10 months. The cultural movement before the May 4th Movement had prepared ideological conditions for the breakout of the patriotic movement and, in the meantime, the rising patriotism also pushed forward the cultural movement, transforming it from a cultural movement characteristic of old democracy into one characteristic of new democracy with the dissemination of Marxism as its main current.

The May 4th Movement gave the Chinese people a new awakening. The wave of social reform reached a new high after it. Most intellectuals worked anxiously in search of the truth for the salvation of the country and people. In such circumstances philosophic theories of the West poured into China and became widespread, and a situation in which a hundred schools of thought contended appeared in the Chinese ideological field. Statistics showed that one year after the May 4th Movement over 400 new publications came out. There were, to name a few, "Awakening" (a supplement to *Republican Daily*), *Weekly Review* and *Construction* in Shanghai; *Young China, Liberation and Reform, New Society,* and *Student Weekly of Beijing University* in Beijing; *Xiangjiang Review* in Changsha; *Awareness* in Tianjin; and *Zhejiang New Trends* in Hangzhou. New mass organizations were set up by the hundreds. Both organizations and publications took up the tasks of popularizing new ideologies and researching the issues of reforming society, forming a wide-spread and vigorous ideological trend. The new ideological trend was then a rather complicated conception, including both proletarian ideology and various bourgeois and petty bourgeois ideologies. All those Western ideological trends different from Chinese traditional feudal culture were regarded as new ideological trends. Among them the most popular and widespread were: Marxism, pragmatism, guild socialism, new village and work-study mutual help doctrines, as well as anarchism. Besides these, were cooperationism, pan-labourism, parliamentarism and the philosophies of Immanuel Kant, Ernst Mach, Henri Bergson, Friedrich Nietzsche, etc.

A number of intellectuals armed with rudimentary ideas of communism under the influence of the October Revolution grew up after the May 4th Movement. Their efforts made it possible to disseminate Marxism widely in China. Li Dazhao, one of the founders of the Chinese Communist Party, contributed greatly to the dissemination of Marxism in China. Li Dazhao (1889-1927) came from Hebei Province. In 1918 he wrote articles such as "Comparison Between the French and Russian Revolutions" and "Victory of Bolshevism," praising the October Revolution. In May 1919 he published a long article entitled "My Understanding of Marxism" in a special issue on Marxist study in *New Youth.* He was the first person to systematically introduce Marxism to China. He helped the influential, Beijing-based *Morning News* to open a special column ("Marxist Study") in its supplement. He also translated Marx's works and works about Marxism, and initiated curriculums in Beijing's colleges to popularize the materialist conception of history and socialism. In March 1920 the Marxist Study Society was founded to guide young people in the study of Marxist theory. Many publications which started around the May 4th Movement contributed, to varying degrees, to the popularization of Marxism. The *Weekly Review* published an abridged translation of the *Manifesto of the Communist Party,* with editor's notes that emphasized the *Manifesto's* ideas on "class struggle" and "unity of workers." *New Youth* developed into the main magazine to spread Marxism. *Citizens* translated and printed the full text of the first chapter of the *Manifesto of the Communist Party.* "Awakening," a supplement to *Republican Daily, Sunday Review*, and *Construction* carried many articles on Marxism, the October Revolution and labour problems.

Xiangjiang Review issued articles in praise of the October Revolution. *New Society* propagated the viewpoints of "direct action of the Marxists," "thorough transformation," etc. In August 1920 the complete Chinese edition of *Manifesto of the Communist Party* was published. Apart from Li Dazhao, there were Chen Duxiu, Li Da, Li Hanjun, Chen Wangdao, Mao Zedong, Cai Hesen, Yang Pao'an, Qu Qiubai and Zhou Enlai, who were all devoted propagators of Marxism and the October Revolution.

Pragmatism, which originated in the late 19th century in the United States, was introduced to China by Hu Shi (1891-1962) on the eve of the May 4th Movement. It holds that the objective world is "like an extremely docile girl," or "a piece of marble," which can be fashioned and embellished at one's will; that truth is "man-made," and it is in the service of the people as a "supposition" and a "tool"; that whether a conception can be crowned with the beautiful name of "truth" lies in whether it has "wide usage." When dealing with a political or social issue, it advocates making certain reform and opposes social revolution. In early May 1919 when the most influential U.S. pragmatist philosopher and educator, John Dewey, came to teach in China, he further disseminated pragmatic philosophy in education, sociology and political science. In July, Hu Shi put forward the slogan "More about problems, less about-isms," voicing the main views of the Chinese pragmatists on the question of social reform. The propagation of the pragmatists played a role in opposing feudal ethical codes, but it hampered the dissemination of Marxism in China.

Guild socialism, which originated in Britain, was an ideological trend of bourgeois reformism in the early 20th century. It advocated establishing "industrial autonomy" by following the guild system's certain spirit and method of the Middle Ages so as to eliminate exploitation and realize the labourer's emancipation, while maintaining the existing state of affairs. It opposed proletarian revolution and proletarian dictatorship. After the May 4th Movement, Liang Qichao (1873-1929), a well-known statesman and scholar, and Zhang Dongsun (1886-1973) propagated this doctrine in *Liberation and Reform*, a publication run by them. After the death of Yuan Shikai, Liang Qichao and some others, under the signboard of carrying out constitutional government, organized a Constitution Research Association, so they were also called the Research Group. In October 1920 the British bourgeois philosopher Bertrand Russell came to teach in China. He opposed Russian Bolshevism and maintained that the urgent task in China was to run industry and education, and that guild socialism was most suitable for China. Liang Qichao, Zhang Dongsun and others, taking advantage of Russell's lecturing tour, issued a series of articles to propagate capitalism and guild socialism. Later the Research Group opened a special column "Socialist Study" in their journal popularizing guild socialism, which they proclaimed "the most thorough theory of social reform" and the "most appropriate 'road to freedom'" for China.

The new village doctrine was advocated by Japanese writer Mushyakoji Saneatsu, who came from a noble family, and was introduced to China by Zhou Zuoren. Mushyakoji Saneatsu cherished building up a "reasonable society" with equality for all people through the "new village." In the winter of 1918 he set up the first new village at Hiuga in Kyushu. Zhou Zuoren went to Hiuga for an investigation and held that what Mushyakoji Saneatsu advocated was "really a practical ideal." While propagating it, Zhou organized a "Beijing branch of the New Village." Many young intellectuals were influenced by the doctrine, and some of them proposed to build up a "young China" through setting up new villages. But this was nothing but a Utopia which could never be realized. The exponents of the new village doctrine took the countryside as their base, while the work-study mutual help doctrine's base was in the cities. Wang Guangqi, head of the executive department of Young China Society, during the May 4th Movement, was the first to advocate the organization of "work-study mutual help groups" in the cities. His advocacy won the support of many famous persons like Cai Yuanpei, Hu Shi, Li Dazhao and Chen Duxiu. From late 1919 to early 1920, four such groups were organized in Beijing, including a women's group. Later similar groups appeared in Shanghai, Tianjin, Wuhan, Nanjing, Guangzhou, and Yangzhou. The work-study mutual help doctrine was a synthesis of the then popular anarchism, the "labourers sacred" idea and the new village doctrine. Its main principles were: Everybody works and studies; from each according to his ability, to each according to his needs; and the establishment of a work-study mutual help society covering all mankind through popularizing work-study mutual help groups. Although its advocacy and practice manifested the young intellectuals' earnest desire to reform China, its Utopian nature decided its eventual failure. The work-study mutual help groups in Beijing and other places existed only for a few months and then broke up.

Anarchism, a petty bourgeois ideological trend, was introduced to China in the early 20th century. Liu Shifu actively disseminated anarchism for several years after the 1911 Revolution, and anarchist associations such as Huiming Society and Xin Society were set up under his guidance and published their own journals, such as *Huiming Records* and *People's Voice*. His successors included Beijing University students Huang Lingshuang, Ou Shengbai, etc. They merged several such small groups into an Evolution Association in early 1919. From 1919 to 1920 the number of anarchist associations amounted to 50, putting out over 70 publications. The earliest Chinese anarchists played a positive part in lashing feudal politics and ethical codes. At the time of the rapid dissemination and expansion of Marxism in China, they turned to take Marxism as their main target of attack.

"Absolute freedom" is the basic viewpoint of anarchism. In politics they oppose any state and might and advocate immediate overthrow of the state. In economics they maintain "free organization" of workers and immediate implementation of the principle of giving to everyone according to his needs. Anarchism was the most widespread ideologic trend among the intellectuals during the May 4th Movement. In the beginning the Communist Party organizations in Shanghai, Beijing, and Guangzhou all had some anarchists. Not long afterwards they all withdrew because they disfavoured proletarian dictatorship and organizational discipline.

The above-mentioned ideological trends all had, then, anti-feudal significance. Struggle between Marxism and anti-Marxist ideological trends such as pragmatism, guild socialism and anarchism was inevitable, when they co-existed and fought to disseminate, so during the two years after the May 4th Movement ideological debates were going on between Marxists, bourgeois reformists and petty bourgeois anarchists. There were three major debates:

The first was the debate on "problems and –isms." It was carried on mainly between Marxist Li Dazhao and pragmatist Hu Shi in the second half of 1919. Hu Shi advocated studying more problems and less –isms, and opposed the "thorough solution" of social problems. Li Dazhao argued that to study problems was inseparable from propagating –isms. To solve China's problems required –isms as guidance. The "-ism" was Marxist scientific socialism, or Russian Bolshevism. China's problems required a "thorough solution," i.e. transformation of the economic system through class struggle.

The second debate was about socialism. It was carried on between communists and members of the Research Group, such as Liang Qichao and Zhang Dongsun, from late 1920 to the first half of 1921. Liang and Zhang held that the only way to save China was to rely on the "gentry and businessmen class" to develop industry and increase national strength by adopting the capitalist method. They thought that China had no labouring class, so it could not develop a socialist movement, and had also no conditions for establishing a Communist Party. Communists Chen Duxiu (1879-1942) and Li Da (1890-1966) argued that only socialism could save China and only through the "direct action of the workers and peasants" could the goal of social revolution be reached, and that it was necessary to build up communist organization to act as a guide to revolution.

The third debate was on anarchism. It was carried on between communists and anarchists headed by Ou Shengbai and Huang Lingshuang between the second half of 1920 and 1921. In this debate the communists correctly expounded the relationship between freedom and discipline, freedom and union, and freedom and obedience. They criticized the erroneous anarchist viewpoint of negating any state with the Marxist theory of proletarian dictatorship. Through the three debates, more and more progressive intellectuals began to accept taking the revolutionary road of scientific socialism, thus establishing the position of Marxism in the political and ideological field.

The ideological emancipation movement after the May 4th Movement was the dissemination of Marxism and growth of the Chinese first-generation communists in terms of content and influence;

also including the spread of various other new ideological trends, the popularization of the ideas of freedom and democracy, scientific concepts and methods, as well as the emergence of new-type bourgeois and petty bourgeois intellectuals. Mass organizations and groups of different trades emerged in large numbers; national assemblies were often held; movements for women's rights were launched; proposals for reforming society and saving the country through industry, education, science, literature, constitutionalism and disarmament were put forward; and an increasing number of students were going to the West to study. Many thinkers, politicians, scientists, educators, writers, artists and scholars who afterwards made outstanding contributions had gone through the baptism of the "May 4th spirit" and been influenced by new ideological trends. Sun Yat-sen, pioneer of bourgeois democratic revolution, enlightened by the May 4th Movement, realized that integration with the masses would produce a strong force. It had a significant impact on his later ideological transformation.

However, the great achievement of the May 4th Movement was its preparation of conditions for the founding of the Chinese Communist Party. The communist intellectuals who grew up after the movement came to realize the strength of the working class. Through their propaganda and organizational work among the workers, Marxism began to integrate with the Chinese workers' movement. The Chinese Communist Party was just the product of this integration.

Early in 1920 Li Dazhao and Chen Duxiu started to work for the founding of the Chinese Communist Party. In March of the same year, representatives of the Communist International led by Lenin came to China. They discussed the establishment of Communist organizations in China with Li Dazhao and Chen Duxiu in Beijing and Shanghai. On the May the First International Labour Day that year, celebrations led by communist intellectuals were held in Beijing and Shanghai. They were important manifestations of Marxism integrating with the Chinese worker movement. Starting from the summer of 1920, early Communist groups were successively set up in Shanghai, Beijing, Wuhan, Jinan, Changsha and Guangzhou, as well as among Chinese students in Japan and France.

In August 1920, China's first Communist group was set up in

Shanghai and Chen Duxiu was elected its secretary. The group played a leading and liaison role for the early Communist groups in other places in China. The Beijing Communist branch was set up in October 1920 with Li Dazhao as secretary. It also contributed greatly to the preparatory work for the founding of the Chinese Communist Party. Li kept in close touch with Chen Duxiu and sent comrades to Jinan to help set up a Party group there. The establishment of the Wuhan branch in autumn 1920 was directly helped by the Party organization in Shanghai, and was led by Dong Biwu (1886-1975), Chen Tanqiu and Bao Huiseng. In the winter of 1920, the Jinan group came into being. Activities for the founding of the Communist group in Changsha were led by Mao Zedong (1893-1976). He had exchanged opinions with Cai Hesen (1895-1931) who was then studying in France, and had made a clear explanation for the necessity of founding the Party and the Party's guiding ideology. The New People's Society they set up in Changsha in 1918 played an important role in the founding of the Communist organization in Hunan. The Guangzhou Communist group, set up in the autumn of 1920, included many anarchists in the beginning. In March 1921 they withdrew from it. Chen Duxiu and some others helped Tan Pingshan and Chen Gongbo reorganize the Guangzhou Communist group. The Chinese Students' Communist Group in Japan was formed by Shi Cuntong and Zhou Fohai, both of whom had joined the Communist group in Shanghai during their home leave. The student Communist group in Paris was organized and set up in the spring of 1921, composed mainly of Zhang Shenfu and Zhou Enlai. Zhang went to Paris after he had joined in the Party-founding activities in China. Later he admitted many others into the group.

These early Communist groups did much work to disseminate Marxism and organized members to go deep among the workers, thus further promoting the integration of the Chinese workers' movement with Marxism. The Shanghai Communist group took *New Youth* as its open theoretic publication and put out an inner-Party monthly, *Communist Party*. Marxist study societies were set up in many places, and popular publications for workers were put out, such as *Labour World* in Shanghai, *Labourer's Voice* in Beijing, and *Laboures* in Guangzhou. Workers' night schools, new-type trade unions and workers' clubs and the Socialist Youth League were set up. The appearance of the local Communist groups and their effective work prepared for the convention of the First National Congress of the Chinese Communist Party.

On July 23, 1921, the Chinese Communist Party held its First National Congress in Shanghai. Thirteen delegates attended. They were Mao Zedong, He Shuheng, Dong Biwu, Chen Tanqiu, Wang Jinmei, Deng Enming, Li Da, Li Hanjun, Zhang Guotao, Liu Renjing, Chen Gongbo, Zhou Fohai, and Bao Huiseng, representing over 50 Communists in China. Two representatives from the Communist International also attended. The chief founders of the Party, Chen Duxiu and Li Dazhao, were both absent because of a crowded work schedule. In the middle of the congress it was raided by French policemen, so the last session of the congress was held on a painted pleasure boat in the Nanhu Lake in Jiaxing County, Zhejiang Province.

The congress adopted the first Party constitution and resolution. The constitution stipulated that the Party was named the Chinese Communist Party and its aim was to overthrow the capitalist regime by a proletarian revolutionary army; to adopt proletarian dictatorship; to abolish capitalist private ownership and to attain the final goal of eliminating classes. The resolution announced the Party's central task: get the workers organized. The congress elected a Central Bureau composed of Chen Duxiu, Zhang Guotao and Li Da, with Chen Duxiu as the secretary.

The founding of the Chinese Communist Party was an epoch-making event in Chinese history. Thereafter, the Chinese revolution had a new leading centre and underwent a basic change. After the establishment of the Chinese Communist Party, it plunged into the revolutionary struggle of the Chinese people with its characteristic proletarian spirit.

2. The Development of the National Capitalist Economy and the Formation of the Programme of the Chinese Communist Party in the Democratic Revolution

During World War I, the imperialist countries, with the exception of Japan, temporarily relaxed their aggression in China. This provided conditions for the development of China's national capitalism. For a period after the conclusion of the war national industry not only continued to advance but at a pace faster than during the war period. The reasons were as follows: Firstly, the European imperialist countries, exhausted shortly after the war, were occupied by working to restore their economies, thus affording favourable conditions for China's national industry to grow. Secondly, during the war period Chinese national capitalists increased their capital, which could be invested in building up new factories for several years after the war. Thirdly, before and after the May 4th Movement, two campaigns of boycotting Japanese goods had affected the import of Japanese goods, thus benefiting the development of national industry. Fourthly, the world war and the May 4th Movement stimulated the Chinese national capitalists and intensified their desire to develop industries. These reasons provided a "golden time" for developing Chinese national industry during the war period and several years after it.

The most important sector of national capital was the cotton textile industry. Between 1920 and 1922 an upsurge of factory building took place; production capacity made great headway. Before 1910 there were a total of 21 cotton mills with investments by national capital. From 1910 to 1919, 13 new cotton mills were added. But from 1920 to 1922 the mills increased by 32, close to the total number of cotton mills built up in the previous decades. The number of spindles in Chinese-owned cotton mills was over 650,000 in 1919, an increase of 20 percent compared with 1914; in 1922 it rose to over 1,500,000, an increase of 129 percent compared with 1919. In 1919 the number of looms was 2,650, an increase of 15 percent compared with 1914 and in 1922 it jumped to 6,767, an increase of 155 percent compared with 1919.

The flour industry, another important field of national capital, also developed conspicuously. There were 61 flour mills before 1913 and 53 new flour mills were set up from 1914 to 1918, 39 of which had a total capital of 9.53 million yuan. Forty-seven mills were added between 1919 and 1922; the total amount of capital in 34 factories was 15.19 million yuan, a big increase in the total amount of investment.

Shanghai, the largest industrial city in China, had a total of 78 cotton, raw silk, flour and tobacco mills in 1914. The number increased to 102 in 1919 and 120 in 1922.

China's largest national capitalists, the Rong brothers, rapidly expanded their industries in the few years after World War I. The Rong family started to invest in the flour industry in 1902 and owned nine flour mills of the Maoxin and Fuxin systems, and 128 flour grinders in 1918. They increased by three flour mills in 1919. The grinders increased to 301 in 1921 with a daily production capacity of 76,000 sacks, making up 31 percent of the whole productive capacity of the country's national capitalist flour mills. The family began investing in the textile industry in 1907, initiated Shenxin Cotton Mill in 1916 and added Shenxin Nos. 2, 3 and 4 mills from 1919 to 1921. The spindles they owned increased from more than 12,900 in 1918 to over 134,900 in 1922, increasing about 11 times.

During the years before and after World War I, a number of outstanding national capitalists appeared. The Rong brothers stood out in their engagement in the flour and textile industries in Shanghai, Wuxi and other places. They were known as "flour bigshots." In the textile industry they possessed the largest ammount of capital and the bigest productive capacity. By 1923 the Rong family owned a total capital of more than 10 million yuan. Liu Hongsheng, from Zhejiang Province, started the Hongsheng Match Factory and the Dazhonghua Match Company in Shanghai, their output constituting a quarter of the country's total. Their matches outshone those from Sweden and Japan on the home markets, so they were honoured as "matches bigshots." Fan Xudong, from Hunan, started to run the Jiuda Salt Industrial Corporation in 1914 in Dagukou and then opened the Yongli Soda Factory in Tanggu after the world war. After several years' effort the factory began to turn out sodas, and crushed the monopoly of the British Brunner Mond & Co. Ltd on the home market. He also initiated the Huanghai Chemical Industry Research Society to do scientific research. Jian Zhaonan and his brother Jian Yujie from Guangdong set up the Nanyang Brothers Tobacco Company in the late Qing Dynasty and moved its head-office from Hong Kong to Shanghai after the world war. Its capital increased from 100,000 to 15 million yuan and its products were sold throughout the country and on the Southeast Asian markets. Nie Yuntai from Hunan initiated the Dazhonghua Textile Mill in Shanghai in 1919, and owned 45,000 spindles and nearly 3 million taels of silvers' worth of share money. He was once the president of the Huashang Cotton Mill Federation and the Shanghai General Chamber of Commerce. Guo Le and his brother Guo Shun from Guangdong did business first in Australia, and later transferred their capital back to China. They started Yongan Department Store first in Hong Kong, then in Shanghai, and opened Yongan Cotton Mill in Shanghai in 1921. Their capital in the national textile industry was second only to the Rong family. Mu Ouchu, from Shanghai, was founder of Deda, Housheng and Yufeng Cotton mills and Shanghai Huashang Yarn and Cloth Trading Company, and owned more than 100,000 spindles. All these capitalists were national industrialists who hoped to save China through industry. They managed to adopt the then up-to-date administrative methods, and made great contributions to the development of China's national industry and commerce.

Although making some headway, the national industry also faced a mountain of difficulties and obstacles, chiefly from imperialists. During the years when the building of textile mills reached their climax, the Japanese-owned textile mills and spindles increased much more rapidly than Chinese mills. Between 1918 and 1922 the spindles in the Chinese textile mills increased by 132 percent, while those of Japanese-owned mills increased by 158 percent. Imperialists also controlled Chinese heavy industry, finance and banking. In 1922, 78 percent of the total volume of the Chinese raw coal machinery exploitation and 52 percent of the total raw coal exploitation, as well as nearly 100 percent of the iron ore and pig iron output were under the control of the imperialists. They also controlled over 90 percent of China's railway transport. From 1921 to 1922 China's imported machinery, 60 percent of it textile machinery, was worth 50 million *haikuan* taels (the customs scale for silver). Although it illustrated the development of China's textile industry, it was also a serious blow to China's machine-building industry. Imperialist-owned banks rose from 21 before 1914 to 65 in 1930, not including many branches and offices. In a word, they controlled China's economic lifeline. The

Washington Conference held from November 1921 to February 1922 ended Japan's monopoly in China and reaffirmed the United States' "open-door policy" and "equal opportunities" in China for all powers. Henceforth the imperialists further intensified their economic aggression against China. Take the textile industry again as an example: Between 1922 and 1925 the spindles and looms of Chinese-owned mills rose by 23 percent and 64 percent respectively while those of foreign mills rose by 67 and 65 percent respectively. By 1925 the number of spindles and looms in foreign-owned mills made up 44 and 46 percent respectively of the whole number of spindles and looms in China's textile mills. Relying on capital superiority and the protection of the unequal treaties, foreign businessmen manipulated the cotton and yarn markets. They rushed to purchase raw materials or dumped their products, thus creating a situation of "expensive cotton and cheap yarn in China," inflicting a fatal blow on the national textile industry.

Since 1923 Chinese national industry had developed to a certain level, but faced a lot of difficulties because of the imperialists' oppression, the destruction caused by the warlords' wars, and the pressure of exorbitant taxes and levies as well as poor agricultural production and transportation. As a result of running at a loss, quite a number of factories were reorganized, stopped production, went bankrupt or were annexed by foreign capital. Between 1923 and 1931, 25 new textile mills were set up by the national capitalists, but the mills which had been reorganized, rented, taken over by creditors or closed down were more than double that number. Several large machinery factories in Shanghai went bankrupt or kept going with difficulties. The Shanghai Qiuxin Machinery Works, the largest machinery factory in China, which had once turned out 3,500-ton ships, was annexed by French capital in 1919 because of the rising price of iron and steel and for lack of ability to cope with losses of capital. The Daxiao Machinery Works stopped production in 1926. The Zhongguo Ironworks Factory, which went into operation in 1922, collapsed in 1927 due to losses of capital for several years in succession. The Dalong Machinery Factory, the only one that tried hard to keep going, faced severe trouble with unsalable goods. Facts showed that in a semi-colonial and semi-feudal society, it was impossible for national capitalist economy to get along smoothly.

The development of national industry further strengthened the national bourgeoisie and working class. Becoming active in political activities, and discontented with the unequal treatment and the political darkness under the warlord rule, the national bourgeoisie began to lodge their protests. Nevertheless, they could not sever their link with the imperialists and disagreed to reforming the extant society through revolutionary violence. They merely hoped to stop the warlord wars, improve domestic politics, and create favourable conditions for expanding the national capitalist economy. Owing to their mounting dissatisfaction with the domestic political situation, various reformist ideological trends emerged in Chinese society during the early 1920s. The following were representative trends:

Hu Shi and Cai Yuanpei printed an article entitled "Our Political Views" which put forward the "good government" doctrine. They thought that "the outstanding people in society" were "good people." If they came out to fight against evil forces and organized a "good government ... it would be a good start for China's political reform." Meantime, in order to maintain and expand their own forces, local warlords and politicians then made a big cry for "provincial autonomy" and "confederation of autonomous provinces." Some bourgeois representatives also actively popularized this view or directly joined in the "local autonomy" activities. They attributed the chaotic political situation to the central government's power being too high, thus causing the scramble for power. They proposed to weaken the central power and to grant more power to the local governments, and through "provincial autonomy" or "confederation of autonomous provinces" to reduce the central government to a position of "only existing in name" and turn China into a "federation." As a result nobody would compete for the central power and put an end to the warlord strife.

Another proposal was for "drawing up a constitution to save the country." The only way, the proponents said, would be to frame a constitution, so as to "eradicate the source of chaos and consolidate the foundation of the state." *Dongfang* magazine issued two special issues on "Constitutional Study" in 1922, which widely propagated this proposal.

Still another proposal was to "abolish military governors, cut down on soldiers, and turn them into workers." More than 20 mass organizations in Shanghai such as the Shanghai-based China National Industrial and Commercial Association and the China National Goods Maintenance Association, jointly issued a declaration to this effect. Many places held meetings for the same demand and many people wrote down concrete proposals. Sun Yat-sen had also advocated cutting down on soldiers and turning them into workers. However these proposals were no way to save China, nor a thorough way to solve the basic issue of overthrowing the imperialist and feudal rule in China.

The growth of the Chinese working class and its fighting strength was beyond compare with the national bourgeoisie. Since it had accepted Marxism and organized its own Party, the working class had appeared on the political stage as an active force. In order to gain political rights and improve their lot, the working class led by the Chinese Communist Party launched a nationwide strike from January 1922 to February 1923. During the 13 months, over 100 strikes broke out involving 300,000 workers in China's big cities. The strike upsurge began with the Hong Kong Seamen's Strike asking for a wage increase in January 1922. In March a general strike of workers of all trades was held involving some 100,000 workers. It came to a victorious end with the British authorities in Hong Kong agreeing to a wage increase of 15 to 30 percent, and the recovery of the closed trade unions.

In May 1922 the Communist Party, through the Chinese Trade Union Secretariat which engaged in open workers' movements, sponsored the First National Labour Congress. It was attended by delegates from more than 100 trade unions in 12 cities and led by the Kuomintang, the Communist Party, the anarchists and other political organizations. The congress adopted the slogans raised by the Communist Party: "Down with imperialism" and "down with warlords," passed a resolution on support for the strikes and another on making the Chinese Trade Union Secretariat the national liaison centre pending the establishment of an All-China Federation of Trade Unions. This showed that the working class had taken on the road of national solidarity against imperialism and warlords. During the two months of July and August, the Chinese Trade Union Secretariat led the movement for labour legislation and proposed a 19-article Outline Labour Law. This marked the beginning of the legislative activities for protecting the political rights and economic benefits of the working class in Chinese history. In mid-September a strike of the miners at Anyuan Colliery in Jiangxi took place with over 17,000 workers involved. The strike ended victoriously with an increase in workers' wages and recognition of the lawful rights of the workers' club by the mining authorities. In late October a big strike of over 50,000 Kailuan coal miners followed the Anyuan strike, but it was suppressed by the British capitalists and Chinese reactionary authorities. On February 4, 1923, the Beijing-Hankou Railway workers inaugurated a general strike. It was occasioned by the warlord sabotage of the Beijing-Hankou Railway Trade Union. On February 7, warlord Wu Peifu ordered his troops to slaughter the strikers. This incident came to be known as the "February 7th Massacre." Henceforth the workers movement sunk from a high tide to a temporary low ebb. The upsurge of the strikes, lasting for a year, demonstrated the strength of the Chinese working class and raised the political prestige of the Communist Party in the country. It also further disclosed the ruthlessness of imperialists and Chinese warlords.

During the period when the workers' movement was running high, the bourgeois reformist trend also became popular. In July 1922, the Chinese Communist Party held its Second National Congress in Shanghai, attended by Chen Duxiu, Zhang Guotao, Cai Hesen, Deng Zhongxia and eight other delegates. It worked out the Party's programme of democratic revolution.

The imperialist aggression and feudal oppression were the root cause of China's poor and backward economy and the constant political strife since the Opium War in 1840. Nevertheless, before the birth of the Chinese Communist Party, revolutionaries and reformers of all classes had been unable to make a scientific analysis and to put forward a clear-cut anti-imperialist and anti-feudal revolutionary programme. Only one year after its founding, the Chinese Communist Party, assisted by the Communist International, completed this task.

The Second National Congress of the Chinese Communist Party, in accordance with Lenin's theory on national and colonial revolutions, analysed Chinese society and the Chinese revolution and pointed out that after 80 years' aggression by imperialist powers, "China had practically become their colony." Both China's economy and politics were manipulated by the imperialists, and in the meantime China's economy remained based on a semi-primitive household agriculture and handicraft industry. As China was still under the feudal oppression of warlords and bureaucrats politically, it was still a far cry from the period of industrial capitalism. "The greatest oppression that the bourgeoisie, workers and peasants suffered was that imposed by the imperialists, warlord and the bureaucrat feudal forces, therefore the democratic revolutionary movement against the two forces was very significant." It was the earliest scientific analysis about the character of the semi-colonial, semi-feudal society and the democratic revolution in China. The congress pointed out that the struggle of the Chinese proletariat should be divided into two steps. The first step was to support and join the bourgeois democratic revolution; the second was to carry out a revolution against the bourgeois class. With this recognition, the congress designated the maximum and minimum programmes of the Communist Party. The maximum programme, namely, the final goal of struggle, was to organize the proletariat and build up the politics of worker-peasant dictatorship by means of class struggle, and to get rid of private property ownership and gradually develop a communist society. The minimum programme, or the immediate goal of the democratic revolution, was to depose the warlords, ensure domestic peace, overthrow the international imperialist oppression, attain the complete independence of the Chinese national and set up a "genuine democratic republic." To accomplish the tasks of the anti-imperialist and anti-feudal democratic revolution, the congress passed the decision to form a "democratic united front" with the Kuomintang and other democratic forces.

The democratic revolutionary programme of the Chinese Communist Party disclosed the basic contradiction of Chinese society and the objective law of Chinese revolution, and pointed out the direction of the struggle. The mapping out of the programme was an important step in the integration of Marxism-Leninism with the practice of Chinese revolution. After its Second Congress, the Communist Party made a widespread popularization of the democratic revolutionary programme, issued the *Guide Weekly* criticizing the then-popular reformist ideas, and put forward "national revolution" as the general political slogan, which had been used in the early period of the China Revolutionary League (Tong Meng Hui). Henceforth "national revolution" became the banner in the common struggle of the Kuomintang, the Chinese Communist Party and the revolutionary classes. The people throughout China were rapidly mobilized under the militant call for the overthrow of imperialists and warlords.

3. The Evolution of the Beiyang Warlord Forces and the Rise of the National Revolutionary Movement

After the May 4th Movement China continued to be ruled by the Beiyang warlords. There was constant strife among them. In July 1920, the war between the warlords of the Zhili (Hebei) and Anhui cliques broke out. At that time, the warlords of the Anhui clique headed by Duan Qirui (1865-1936) had seized control of Beijing's central government for four years. During the May 4th Movement the Anhui clique had become the target of public attack, as its reactionary nature had been laid bare through its selling out China and suppressing the people. The Zhili clique warlords backed by the British and American imperialists intensified their scheme of overthrowing the Anhui clique. Wu Peifu (1874-1939), commander of the Third Division and strong man of the Hebei clique, even published an open telegram to oppose the signing of the Paris Peace Treaty and support the student movement for the purpose of winning the hearts of the people. After the death of Feng Guozhang in December, 1919, Cao Kun (1862-1938) became the leader of the Zhili clique. In April 1920, Cao Kun and some other warlords formed an anti-Anhui alliance of eight provinces (Hebei, Anhui, Jiangxi, Hubei, Henan, Liaoning, Jilin and Heilongjiang). In July, the war between the Zhili and Anhui warlords broke out in places around Gaobeidian and Yangcun along the Beijing-

Hankou and Beijing-Tianjin railway lines. After several days of battle the Zhili clique, supported by the Fengtian (Liaoning) clique, came out victorious. Then Duan Qirui resigned, and the Zhili and Fengtian cliques came into joint control of the Beijing government.

After defeating the Anhui clique, the tensions between the Zhili and Fengtian cliques, each with its own imperialist backing, became acute. In late 1920 Zhang Zuolin (1875-1928), a Fengtian clique warlord, entered Beijing and overthrew the pro-Zhili cabinet, and made the pro-Japanese Liang Shiyi responsible for the formation of a new cabinet. Wu Peifu took advantage of the situation to order his troops to attack Liang, and forced him to leave office. In late April of 1922 their conflict culminated in the Zhili-Fengtian War. After a week of fierce battle along the Beijing-Hankou and Tianjin-Pukou railway lines, the Fengtian clique was defeated and its troops retreated to the north side of the Shanhaiguan Pass. The Zhili clique thus took complete control of the Beijing government. To make a pretence of lawfulness, Cao Kun and Wu Peifu began with the swindle of "restoration of the legally constituted authority" by reopening the old parliament that had existed in 1917, and restoring the old presidential post to Li Yuanhong. When they thought their rule was stabilized, they drove Li out of office. In October 1923, Cao Kun was elected as President of the Republic of China through bribery.

Cao Kun's election and Wu Peifu's policy of unifying China by armed force and excluding outsiders met with nationwide opposition. Zhang Zuolin, Sun Yat-sen and Lu Yongxiang, governor of Zhejiang of the Anhui clique, formed an anti-Zhili triangular alliance. Wu Peifu schemed to ask Sun Chuanfang, military governor of Fujian, in coordination with Guangdong worlord Chen Jiongming, to attack the Guangdong revolutionary government and to defeat Lu Yongxiang with the help of the Jiangsu military governor Qi Xieyuan. Wu himself prepared for war against Zhang Zuolin. In early September 1924, the Jiangsu-Zhejiang war between Qi Xieyuan and Lu Yongxiang broke out first. It ended in the defeat of Lu after over one month of fighting. In mid-September when Qi and Lu were locked in battle, the second Zhili-Fengtian war broke out. While the troops of the two sides were fighting desperately in Chaoyang and Shanhaiguan, Feng Yuxiang

(1882-1948), the Zhili general who had been sent to command the battle in Rehe, changed sides in the war and staged a Beijing coup d'état. On the night of October 22, Feng Yuxiang's troops returned to Beijing, encircled the president's residence and put Cao Kun in custody. Feng reorganized his troops into the National Army of the Republic of China and broke away from the Zhili warlord clique. In early November and National Army drove the last Qing Dynasty emperor Pu Yi out of the Imperial Palace. As a result of Feng's changing sides, the Zhili troops were defeated by the Fengtian troops. Wu Peifu escaped to south China aboard a warship.

After the Beijing coup d'état, the political situation in the north underwent a big change. The influence of the Zhili clique in the north was eradicated; the National Army controlled Beijing; large numbers of Fengtian troops entered the Shanhaiguan Pass, occupied Tianjin and went south along the Tianjin-Pukou Railway line; the tension between Feng Yuxiang and Zhang Zuolin sharpened; Duan Qirui wanted to stage a comeback and regain political power. In face of the complicated political and military situation, Feng Yuxiang cabled an invitation to Sun Yat-sen to come to the north to exchange views on the current affairs. In the meantime, he held a meeting with Zhang Zuolin and Duan Qirui and supported Duan temporarily presiding over the government of the Republic. Although the Beijing coup d'état had overthrown the rule of the Zhili clique, the Beijing government was still in the hands of warlord bureaucrats. Nevertheless it created a situation favourable for revolution.

After receiving Feng's cabled invitation, Sun Yat-sen issued a "Declaration on the Current Political Situation," in which he proposed convening a national assembly to solve the problems. Duan Qirui insisted on holding an "aftermath conference" with the aim of maintaining warlord rule in opposition to the rising national assembly movement. In April 1925, Duan Qirui's government signed an agreement with France, in which it recognized the "gold Franc case" that had been debated for several years and agreed to pay indemnity to France in "gold Francs" for the events of 1901. This made China pay 62 million more taels of Customs silver. In March 1926 Duan Qirui directed the "March 18 Massacre," ruthlessly suppressing the anti-imperialist and anti-warlord struggle of the people. Duan Qirui's government's domestic and foreign policies met with the opposition of the whole nation.

Wu Peifu, who had escaped to the south after defeat in the second Zhili-Fengtian war, gained control of Hubei in 1925. In October he declared the founding of the 14-province united army with its headquarters in Hankou. In the meantime the Zhili clique general Sun Chuanfang (1885-1935) developed a coterie of his own and expanded it. In the name of the commander-in-chief of the Zhejiang-Fujian-Jiangsu-Anhui-Jiangxi United Army, he issued a circular telegram denouncing the Fengtian clique. Through war and by making use of the nationwide anti-Fengtian situation after the May 30th Movement, he captured Shanghai and drove the Fengtian forces out of Jiangsu and Anhui provinces, thus becoming the ruler of the five provinces.

In November 1925 an incident known as "Guo Songling's Mutiny" broke out within the Fengtian clique. Guo was a powerful general in the Fengtian armed forces. Because he disagreed with certain measures taken by Zhang Zuolin and was depressed by the factional strifes within the Fengtian clique, he signed a secret agreement with Feng Yuxiang and others, and determined to turn his coat and overthrow Zhang Zuolin. In late November Guo led an army from Luanzhou in Hebei and fought his way to Xinmin, some 50 kilometres from Shenyang. Due to intervention by Japanese troops, he was defeated and killed. This mutiny formed a component part of the nationwide anti-Fengtian struggle, dealing the Fengtian warlords a heavy blow.

Guo's mutiny caused a new change in the relations between Feng Yuxiang, Zhang Zuolin and Wu Peifu. After Guo Songlin's mutiny began, Feng's National Army occupied Rehe, and then Tianjin under the guise of leaving Shanhaiguan Pass to support Guo. Li Jinglin's Fengtian troops stationed in Zhili retreated to Shandong, joined forces with Zhang Zongchang in Shandong, and formed a Zhili-Shandong United Army. Wu Peifu "reconciled" with Zhang Zuolin and the two determined jointly to attack Feng Yuxiang. In the spring of 1926, a joint force composed of Fengtian troops, Zhili-Shandong United Army and Zhili troops was formed to attack the National Army. Feng

Yuxiang retired from his post, handing his troops and area to his subordinates and preparing for an investigation of the Soviet Union. In March Fengtian troops occupied Luanzhou and Tangshan, while the Zhili-Shandong United Army occupied Tianjin and Fengtai. In April the Fengtian army occupied Rehe, while the National Army stationed in Beijing overthrew Duan Qirui's government and then retreated to Nankou. The United Army entered Beijing.

While the Beiyang warlords' internecine strife brought about chaos in China, the national revolutionary movement in the south was gaining momentum. The national revolutionary movement started with the First National Congress of the Kuomintang and the formal establishment of Communist-Kuomintang cooperation.

After the Revolution of 1911, Sun Yat-sen (1866-1925) had insisted on the standpoint of democratic revolution and struggled persistently to set up a genuine democratic republic. Not finding a correct revolutionary road, he adopted the measure of using the warlords' mutual strife and cherished the idea of seeking foreigners' help. His struggles all ended in failure. Two revolutions launched by Sun in 1913 were suppressed by Yuan Shikai. The campaign of protecting the constitution miscarried in 1917 because of the southwest warlords' disruption. In November 1920 Sun Yat-sen returned to Guangzhou, reorganized the military government, and launched the second protect-the-constitution campaign. In April 1921 he assumed the post of Provisional President of the Republic. While Sun was preparing for the Northern Expedition, Chen Jiongming, the governor of Guangdong Province and commander-in-chief of the Guangdong Army, who had been groomed by Sun, betrayed him. Chen Jiongming (1878-1933) staged a mutiny in June 1922, and surrounded and attacked the president's house in an attempt to get rid of Sun. Sun Yat-sen was compelled to move to a gunboat where he kept on struggling for over 50 days. Arriving at Shanghai in August and greatly worried, he came to understand that the realization of the Three People's Principles could not "solely rely on the soldiers' struggle," and that he should rely on the strength of the party. But what condition was the party in? After his Chinese Revolutionary Party was reorganized and renamed the Kuomintang in October 1919, the party did not achieve regeneration.

Its members were complicated and its discipline was lax. The party badly needed consolidation and reorganization.

The Communist International and Soviet Russian Government led by Lenin had supported the oppressed nations in their struggle for emancipation and upheld the coordination of the proletariat and the bourgeois democrats in the colonial and backward countries into a revolutionary union. The Communist International sent delegates to hold talks with Sun Yat-sen on several occasions and suggested that he should have more connections with Soviet Russia and cooperate with the Chinese Communist Party. Helped by the Communist International, the Chinese Communist Party at its Second National Congress of July 1922 passed a resolution on the establishment of a democratic united front. It convened a meeting in Hangzhou in August, 1922, at which it was decided that Communist Party members join the Kuomintang as individuals and realize cooperation between the two parties. Sun Yat-sen rapidly accepted the suggestion of the Communist International and the Chinese Communist Party, and agreed to admit the Communists to the Kuomintang while they maintained their Communist membership.

In September 1922 Sun Yat-sen started reorganizing the Kuomintang. In January 1923 Sun Yat-sen and the Soviet representative, Adolph Joffe, issued a joint statement, in which Joffe expressed Russia's earnest desire to support the revolutionary cause of the Chinese people. In June 1923 the Communist Party at its Third National Congress formally passed the resolution establishing cooperation between the Chinese Communist Party and the Kuomintang. It decided that its Party members join the Kuomintang and make efforts to enlarge the Kuomintang organization throughout China. In August of the same year Sun Yat-sen the "Dr. Sun Yat-sen Delegation," headed by Chiang Kai-shek (1887-1975) and joined by Communists, to the Soviet Union for an investigation on military and party affairs. In October, Soviet representative, Michael Borodin, arrived in Guangzhou and was appointed by Sun Yat-sen as organization adviser. At the end of 1923 Li Dazhao, leader of the Communist Party, was invited to go to Guangdong to assist Sun in preparation for the convention of the First National Congress of the Kuomintang.

The First National Congress of the Kuomintang was held in Guangzhou in January 1924. Sun Yat-sen chaired the congress in the capacity of the Party's director-general and designated Hu Hanmin, Wang Jingwei, Lin Sen, Xie Chi and Li Dazhao to form a presidium. There were a total of 165 delegates, among whom were Liao Zhongkai, Tan Yankai, Dai Jitao, Sun Ke (Sun Fo) and other Kuomintang members, and Communists Li Dazhao, Mao Zedong, Lin Boqu, and Tan Pingshan, who were also members of the Kuomintang. The congress adopted the manisfesto laid down jointly by Communist and Kuomintang members. It confirmed the Three Cardinal Policies worked out by Sun Yat-sen: "alliance with Soviet Russia, cooperation with the Communist Party and assistance to the peasants and workers"; agreed to absorb individual Communists into the Kuomintang, and organized the Kuomintang Central Executive Committee, composed also of Communists. This congress marked the formal establishment of cooperation between the Communist Party and the Kuomintang.

The manifesto passed in the congress reinterpreted the Three People's Principles. The New Principle of Nationalism advocated "self-emancipation of the Chinese nation," "freedom from imperialist aggression" and "full equality for all the ethnic groups within China." The Principle of Democracy now stipulated that "democratic rights should be shared by the common people, instead of the monopoly of a few people," and those who were loyal agents of imperialists and warlords should not enjoy freedom and rights. The Principle of People's Livelihood was reinterpreted as follows: Firstly, equalization of landownership—preventing a small group of people from manipulating landownership, and the state giving land to landless peasants to till; secondly, the regulation of capital and turning over to state administration large enterprises or those of monopolistic nature so as to prevent private capital from manipulating people's livelihood. As the political principles of the Three People's Principles after reinterpretation were largely identical with the political programme of the Communist Party in its democratic revolutionary stage, they thus became the political basis of cooperpation between the two parties and also between the revoluionary classes. Following the constitution of the Kuomintang, Sun Yat-sen, as the director-general, acted as President of the National Congress and Chairman of the Central Executive Committee without another election. The director-general had the power to "make a reconsideration" of the decision of the National Congress and to "make the final decision" on the resolutions of the Central Executive Committee. From the congress period to August of the same year, Sun Yat-sen made many speeches about the Three People's Principles for which he had fought for many years, and finally completed the theoretic system of these principles.

In May 1924 the Kuomintang established the Huangpu (Whampoa) Military Academy near Guangzhou (renamed the Central Military and Political Academy in the spring of 1926). It was a school training military cadets, set up jointly with the Communist Party, with Chiang Kai-shek as commandant, Liao Zhongkai (1877-1925) as party representative, and Communist Zhou Znlai (1898-1976) also holding a leading post in the academy.

After the establishment of the cooperation between the two parties, a national revolutionary movement including the majority of the people of China's various ethnic groups rapidly gained momentum. The worker-peasant movement, patriotic anti-imperialist movement, anti-warlord and democratic movements as well as the fight to unite the Guangdong revolutionary base areas all forged ahead, giving impetus to one another.

In July 1924, the workers in the British concession of Shamian in Guangzhou staged a big strike against the new police regulations laid down by the British and French imperialists, which requested the Chinese to produce their identification cards on entering or leaving the district. The strike lasted for over a month and eventually gained victory. That was a beginning of a new upsurge of the worker movement after the February 7th Massacre. In the same month, Communists such as Peng Pai started a peasant movement institute. In two years they ran six terms and trained over 800 peasant movement leading cadres. The sixth term, the largest in scale, was presided over by Mao Zedong. On the first of May, 1925, the first provincial peasant association in China was set up in Guangdong Province. From the winter of 1925 to 1927 Wei Baqun (Zhuang ethnic group) ran three terms of a peasant movement institute in Donglan, Gaungxi Province, training several hundred cadres for the peasant movement.

In May 1924 the "Agreement of General Principles for the Settlement of Outstanding Questions Between the Republic of China and the U.S.S.R." was signed in Beijing. In it the Soviet side promised to relinquish all tsarist Russian privileges in China. This was the first equal agreement that China had signed with a foreign country since the Opium War in 1840. Consequently, mass movements to abrogate unequal treaties were launched throughout China. After the Beijing coup d'état, Sun Yat-sen, invited by Feng Yuxiang, left Guangdong for the north in November 1924. Before that time, in July 1923, the Communist Party had called for the convening of a national assembly to solve political problems. Along with Sun Yat-sen's arrival in the north, a nationwide movement to convene a national assembly arose in China. Although the movement failed to get a direct result, it was the earliest people's democratic movement during the new-democratic revolutionary period. It widely propagated democratic ideas through the combination of leadership and the masses.

On March 12, 1925, Sun Yat-sen, the great predecessor of the Chinese revolution, died in Beijing. Sun Yat-sen had made great contributions to the founding of the Republic of China and the establishment of the first cooperation between the Communist Party and the Kuomintang. His death was mourned by people throughout the country and an extensive campaign to propagate the Three People's Principles was launched.

The May 30 Movement of 1925 marked the beginning of the high tide of the National Revolution. In January 1925, the Chinese Communist Party called the Fourth National Congress, in which the leadership of the proletarian class over the democratic revolution was raised and resolutions to develop the revolution were worked out, thus preparing for the oncoming revolutionary upsurge. In February, workers in a Japanese-owned cotton mill held a big strike to maintain their work and political rights. On May 15, a Japanese factory guard opened fire on the strikers, killing a worker named Gu Zhenghong and wounding a dozen others. The Gu Zhenghong Incident lit the fuse of the May 30th Movement. After the incident, while students in Shanghai were raising funds for the workers' families and holding a memorial service in honour of Gu Zhenghong, several students were arrested. The imperialists fixed the date of their trial on a charge of "disturbing public order." In the meantime the imperialists wanted the passage of the "four proposals," which included regulations on the press, an increase of wharfage dues, registration of the stock exchange, and a ban on child labour. These enraged the people in Shanghai all the more. On May 30 2,000 students made public speeches along the streets in the International Settlement, disclosing the imperialists' crime of firing on workers and arresting students, and opposing the "four proposals." Some of them were arrested. Thousands of paraders marched down Nanjing Road, shouted "down with imperialism," and demanded the immediate release of the students. The British policemen fired into the crowd of unarmed demonstrators, killing four on the spot and nine who died shortly afterwards; scores of students were seriously wounded. This came to be known as the "May 30th Massacre."

Following the massacre, the Central Committee of the Chinese Communist Party called on people from all social starta to oppose imperialism and broaden the movement by forming a united front. It called on workers to down tools, students to stop attending classes, and merchants to close shops. The students plunged into the struggle with high patriotism, with 50,000 students ceasing to attend class. They also urged the merchants to close shops. The merchants' federations representing the interests of the middle and small merchants warmly favoured closing shops. The Shanghai Central Chamber of Commerce, mainly representing the interests of big capitalists, influenced by the anti-imperialist wave, also joined in closing shops. Although the bourgeoisie and petty bourgeoisie had participated in the struggle, the working class remained the backbone force. On June 1, the Shanghai Federation of Trade Unions was established and issued as its first order the call for a general strike. Taking part in it were a total of 113 factories and enterprises involving 150,000 workers. Among them were over 120,000 strikers from 102 foreign-owned factories and enterprises. Subsequently a Federation of Workers, Merchants and Students was founded on June 4. It was an organization comprising the Shanghai Federation of Trade Unions, merchants' federations, the All-China Students' Federation and the Shanghai Students' Federation. Only the Shanghai General Chamber of Commerce refused to join and changed its 17 demands into 13, leaving out those demands for abrogating consular jurisdiction, withdrawing British and Japanese land and naval forces and recognizing the right of workers to hold strikes and organize trade unions. But the General Chamber of Commerce played an active part in boycotting British and Japanese goods and donation activities. The imperialists continued to adopt the policy of slaughtering the people in Shanghai. From May 30 to June 10 they killed more than 60 and seriously wounded over 70 people. In the meantime they adopted measures to split the anti-imperialist united front. They decoyed the bourgeoisie in Shanghai to compromise through proposals of a "judicial investigation" and a "customs duty conference" on the one hand, and on the other threatened them with the stopping of loans, international remittance, transport and power supply. On June 26 merchants resumed business. Soon summer vacation began and students left school one after another. In view of this situation the Communist Party decided to change tactics of the worker struggle, from the general strike to an economic struggle and partial solution. In August and September the workers gradually went back to work.

After the "May 30th Movement", revolutionary storm spread to the whole country. Masses in dozens of cities such as Guangzhou, Beijing, Nanjing, Hankou, Tianjin, Changsha, Jinan, Xuzhou and Qingdao, gathered to hold meetings, parades, demonstrations and strikes as well as boycotting class and closing shops to oppose imperialists' atrocities. Peasants in some places also joined the ranks of the struggle. The anti-imperialist struggle involved about 1.2 million people in the country, forming a second anti-imperialist upsurge since the May 4th Movement. It demonstrated the strength of working class leadership and the function of the revolutionary united front. Experience in this movement produced a great impact on the revolution in later years.

Among the strikes in support of the Shanghai people's anti-imperialist movement, the Guangzhou-Hong Kong strike on June 19, 1925, was the biggest both in scale and influence. It involved over

200,000 workers from Shamian, the foreign concessions and Hong Kong. The strike turned Hong Kong into a "dead port," dealing a heavy blow to the British imperialists. The strike did not end until 16 months later. The Guangzhou-Hong Kong Strike Committee was its leading body. It and the armed picket corps composed of over 2,000 workers became a backbone force in the Guangdong revolutionary government.

The May 30th Movement gave a powerful impetus to the Mongolian ethnic group's popular revolutionary movement. In 1925, under the leadership of the Communist Party, the Inner Mongolian People's Revolutionary Party and the Inner Mongolian People's Revolutionary Army were founded, both being united fronts in nature. The People's Revolutionary Army led by Xini Lama defeated the warlord troops several times. He also led a popular movement in Uxin Banner and finally abrogated the system of rule by the feudal nobility and set up people's revolutionary regimes in 19 townships. Xini Lama was murdered in 1929; thus the revolution suffered a setback.

After the downfall of the Zhili clique's Beijing regime, Duan Qirui and the Fengtian warlords became the chief enemies of the Chinese people. In October 1925 a war between the Zhili clique led by Sun Chuanfang and the Fengtian clique broke out. The warlord battle provided a very good opportunity for opposing the Fengtian clique. Using this situation, the Chinese Communist Party led a struggle to oppose the Fengtian clique and overthrow Duan Qirui. By the end of November a mass demonstration of several tens of thousands of people including student dare-to-die corps and worker-defenders teams was held in Beijing. It aimed to overthrow the Duan Qirui government through an uprising and to establish a national government. But the struggle, known as "capital revolution," failed. In March 1926, the "March 18th Massacre" took place. On March 12, a Japanese destroyer shielded the Fengtian army's warship's entry to Port Dagu and fired on the National Army stationed at Fort Dagu. The enraged National Army fought back and drove the Japanese destroyer out. Then the Japanese imperialists, on the pretext of abiding by the Protocol of 1901, gathered eight countries such as Britain, the United States, France and Italy, issued an ultimatum to the Duan Qirui government, raised unreasonable demands, and asked for a reply at a fixed date. The Port Dagu Incident caused great indignation among the Chinese people. Led by the North Regional Committee of the Chinese Communist Party and the Kuomintang Beijing Executive Department, over 30,000 people in Beijing held a demonstration at Tiananmen on March 18 to protest against the eight-nation ultimatum. After it, a petition corps of over 2,000 people was organized and went to petition the Duan Qirui government. The Duan Qirui government ordered the suppression of the patriotic people, killing 47 and wounding over 100. After the slaughter a huge revolutionary wave against the traitorous government and in support of the people in Beijing was launched throughout the country. The masses in various places and overseas Chinese and students studying abroad held meetings in protest. Nevertheless, after the petition was put down, the revolutionary movement in the north was reduced to a low ebb.

During the nationwide revolutionary upsurge, the Guangdong revolutionary bases became gradually consolidated. In October 1924, the Guangdong revolutionary government, relying on the cadets of the Huangpu Military Academy and a section of the revolutionary armed forces, and supported by the workers and peasants, crushed the counter-revolutionary armed rebellion of the Guangdong Merchant Volunteers. In February and March, 1925, the revolutionary army launched the First Eastern Expedition to fight against warlord Chen Jiongming, who attempted to attack Guangzhou and overthrow the revolutionary government. The revolutionary army with the support of the peasants in the Dongjiang river valley routed Chen's main force, over 30,000 strong, and occupied Chaozhou, Meixian County, etc. In June the Eastern Expeditionary Army returned to Guangzhou and put down the rebellion of the Yunnan and Guangxi warlords. On July 1, the Guangdong revolutionary government was reorganized from one dominated by a generalissimo into the National Government of the Republic of China under a committee member system with Wang Jingwei as chairman. In August, the National Government unified all its armies into the National Revolutionary Army. In October, the National Government ordered the army to launch the Second Eastern Expedition against Chen Jiongming. It crushed all of the warlord's troops and quickly recovered the whole Dongjiang valley. It also launched a Southern Expedition and wiped out the warlord troops on Hainan Island in February 1926. The whole of Guangdong now came under the power of the revolutionary government. In March, Li Zongren (1891-1969) and Bai Chongxi (1893-1966), who was in control of Guangxi, accepted the leadership of the National Government, and the unification of Guangdong and Guangxi was thus realized. The unification and consolidation of the revolutionary base in Guangdong paved the way for the Northern Expedition.

While the revolutionary situation gained momentum, the struggle inside the revolutionary united front also intensified. When Sun Yat-sen defined his Three Cardinal Policies, he met with the opposition of landlords, compradors and the Right wing of the bourgeoisie inside the Kuomintang. After his death, they threw all caution to the winds. In August 1925 Liao Zhongkai, a loyal friend of the Communist Party and a Kuomintang Leftist, was assassinated. This was a major move in the Kuomintang Right wing's attack on the Left and opposition to the cooperation between the two parties. The Communist Party pushed the Kuomintang central authorities to resolutely attack the Right-wing forces. Hu Hanmin, acting generalissimo and governor of Guangdong, was held in custody for a time under suspicion of involvement in Liao's assassination, and later left Guangzhou.

In the summer of 1925 Dai Jitao-ism made its appearance. Dai Jitao (1891-1949) was a Kuomintang Right-wing theorist. In June and July of 1925 he wrote two pamphlets, *The Philosophical Foundation of the Doctrines of Dr. Sun Yat-sen* and *The National Revolution and the Chinese Kuomintang*. In them he explained Sun Yat-sen's thinking, using Confucianist ideas and ethics. He used the philosophy of people's livelihood to oppose the Marxist class struggle theory, national struggle to negate class struggle, and the so-called exclusiveness of groups to oppose Kuomintang-Communist cooperation. Dai Jitao-ism reflected the political tendency of the bourgeoisie to seize revolutionary leadership from the proletarian class, so it became the theoretical basis of the Kuomintang Rightists to oppose the Communist Party and to usurp power. Communists Chen Duxiu and Qu Qiubai (1899-1935) wrote articles refuting Dai's reactionary viewpoints, and defending the cooperation between the two parties and the national revolution.

In November 1925, the Western Hills Conference clique was formed. It was so called because a section of the Right-wing Kuomintang Central Executive Committee and Supervisory Committee members had held the so-called fourth plenum of the First Central Executive Committee, in the Biyun Temple in Beijing's Western Hills, at which they openly opposed the Three Cardinal Policies and the Kuomintang-Communist cooperation. They passed a resolution to deprive the Communists of their Kuomintang membership, dismissed Borodin from his advisory post, and expelled Communists from the Central Executive Committee. Later they held a bogus second national congress of the Kuomintang in Shanghai and established a bogus second central executive and supervisory committees. The Kuomintang Central Executive Committee carried out a firm struggle against the Western Hills Conference clique. The *Political Weekly*, the official central organ of the Kuomintang edited by Mao Zedong, made a major counter-attack against the Rightists.

In January 1926, the Kuomintang called its Second National Congress. It decided to carry out the testament of Sun Yat-sen and the political programme designated by the First National Congress: Down with imperialists, and down with warlords, the bureaucrat-comprador class and the local tyrants. In order to accomplish the revolutionary task, the congress thought it necessary to sincerely cooperate with Soviet Russia and admit Communists to the Kuomintang, so as to jointly complete the national revolution and the campaign of helping workers and peasants. The congress passed a resolution on impeaching the "Western Hills Conference" and "punishing party members violating Party discipline." It also took disciplinary measures against the members of the Western Hills Conference clique. The congress elected 36 members and 24 alternate members to the Central Executive Committee. Both groups had seven Communists. After the Congress, Communists Tan Pingshan (1886-1956) and Lin Boqu (1886-1960) continued, respectively, to head the Central Organization Department and Peasant Department. Mao Zedong was acting director of the Propaganda Department. The secretaries of the various central departments were mostly Communists and the local Party committees were also led by Communists. The Kuomintang Second National Congress had pushed forward the Chinese revolutionary cause.

When the anti-Communist forces in the Kuomintang saw the growing strength of the Communist Party in the revolutionary camp, they looked for an opportunity to attack it. In March 1926 Chiang Kai-shek engineered the "Cruiser *Zhongshan* Incident." Chiang's position in the Kuomintang had been raised after the founding of the Huangpu Military Academy and the two Eastern Expeditions. After the National Revolutionary Army was organized, Chiang was appointed as the commander of the First Corps. At the Kuomintang Second Congress he was elected a Central Executive Committee member, and after the congress he was appointed general supervisor of the National Revolutionary Army. The increase of Chiang's political power strengthened his political ambition and aggravated his contention with the Communists and the Wang Jingwei bloc in the Kuomintang. Knowing the importance of military power, he attacked the Communists first militarily. On March 18 the provincial office of the Huangpu Military Academy notified the Naval Bureau that Chiang Kai-shek had ordered them to dispatch two cruisers to Port Huangpu. This the bureau did including the cruiser *Zhongshan*. After the cruisers reached Huangpu, Chiang claimed that he had not ordered their dispatch. After the *Zhongshan* returned to Guangzhou, Chiang, on the pretext of guarding against "political turmoil" caused by the cruiser on the morning of the 20th declared martial law without authorization and arrested Li Zhilong (then a Communist), the leader of the Naval Bureau, occupied the *Zhongshan* and the Naval Bureau, put the Communists in the academy and the First Corps in custody, and surrounded the lodgings of the Soviet advisory group and the office of the Guangzhou-Hong Kong Strike Committee. Responding to Chiang's attack, the Communist Party Central Committee and the Soviet advisory group adopted a policy of compromise and concession. This resulted in the withdrawal of the Communists from the First Corps and dismissal of some Soviet advisers, who returned to the Soviet Union according to Chiang's wishes. Chiang also dismissed Wang Jingwei from his post as the latter's position was higher than Chiang's. Wang later went abroad. In May 1926 at a plenary session of the Second Kuomintang Central

Executive Committee, Chiang, under the pretext of "dispelling suspicions and stopping disputes," submitted a "Bill on Reorganizing the Party's Affairs." It included clauses not only to restrict Communists from taking official posts in the KMT organizations but also to limit their activities. For instance, Communists were not allowed to occupy more than one-third of the executive committee in the central, provincial and city party departments, or to take posts as heads of department in Kuomintang central organizations. Because the Communist Party Central Committee continued to adopt a policy of compromise and concession, Chiang's bill was adopted. It and the *Zhongshan* Incident were two important steps taken by Chiang to expand his power.

In revolutionary practice, the Chinese Communist Party had gradually evolved its basic ideas on the new-democratic revolution. The Second National Congress of the Party held in 1922 specified that the Chinese revolution had to go through two stages: democratic revolution and socialist revolution. Thereafter, many Communist Party documents and articles written by Party leaders analysed the conditions of the various classes in Chinese society. Qu Qiubai and Deng Zhongxia first put forward the question of proletarian leadership in the democratic revolution. The Fourth National Congress of the Chinese Communist Party, held in January 1925, not only confirmed the importance of the proletarian leadership in the democratic revolution but also connected it with the question of alliance with the peasants. At the congress Mao Zedong made it clear, "After the overthrow of the imperialists, warlords, comprador and landlord classes, a united rule, namely the rule of revolutionary masses, composed of the proletariat, the petty bourgeoisie and the Left wing of the middle bourgeoisie, should be established." This was the concept of the united regime of the masses. These ideas later developed into a complete theory of the new-democratic revolution. At that time, as the Communist Party did not recognize the importance of directly controlling the revolutionary armed forces and political power, this hindered the real solution of the proletarian leadership question. This was a reflection of the fact that the Communist Party was still in its infancy, and also a chief reason for the failure in its later revolution.

4. Northern Expeditionary War and Failure of the National Revolution

The upsurge of the mass revolutionary movement propelled the outbreak of a revolutionary war. In July 1926 the Northern Expeditionary War, waged jointly by the Communist Party and the Kuomintang, started. This was a war aimed at overthrowing both the reactionary rule of the Beiyang warlords and the imperialist power in China. It was a significant event in the political situation in China.

The Northern Expeditionary Army encountered enemies from three columns: The first was Wu Peifu who controlled Henan, Hunan, Hubei and southern Zhili with a force of 200,000; the second was Sun Chuanfang with an armed force of 200,000 in Jiangsu, Zhejiang, Anhui, Fujian and Jiangxi provinces; the third was Zhang Zuolin who, with 350,000 troops, occupied the northeast, Shandong, Zhili, Rehe and Qahar and held the political power in Beijing. The joint forces of the Fengtian clique and Wu Peifu were now fiercely attacking the National Army commanded by Feng Yuxiang around Nankou. According to their plan, after winning the battle against the National Army, Wu's troops would concentrate on attacking Guangdong, thus eliminating the Guangdong revolutionary political power. Sun Chuanfang took a temporary wait-and-see attitude and declared that "for the sake of the security of the five provinces and their residents" he would not join in any battle. In fact he wanted to reap the rewards after both sides had weakened themselves.

The National Army had eight corps with 100,000 troops, and with Chiang Kai-shek as its commander-in-chief, Li Jishen (1885-1959) as chief of the general staff, and Deng Yanda (1895-1931) as director of the General Political Department.

A part of the Fourth Corps and most of the Fifth Corps led by Li Jishen stayed behind in Guangdong and a part of the Seventh Corps remained in Guangxi for garrison duty, while other troops started their Northern Expedition. The Northern Expeditionary Army, in light of the relative strength between it and its enemies, and their internal divisions, decided to adopt a policy of concentrating a superior force to destroy the enemy forces one by one. It first sent the Fourth, Seventh and Eighth corps, 50,000 strong, to the Hunan-Hubei front; at the same time ordered the Second, Third and Sixth corps, some 30,000 strong, to enter southern and eastern Hunan to guard against enemy troops from Jiangxi, and the First Corps to garrison at Chaozhou and Meixian to guard against enemy troops from Fujian. After destroying Wu Peifu's forces, the Northern Expeditionary Army would concentrate the main force on the southeast provinces and crush Sun Chuanfang's forces, finally sending troops to the north of the Changjiang (Yangtze) River to wipe out Zhang Zuolin's forces.

Before the start of the Northern Expedition, the Hunan warlords split, thus creating favourable conditions for the march of the Northern Expeditionary Army. Hunan warlord Zhao Hengti, acting in the name of "provincial autonomy," was actually serving the interests of Wu Peifu. In March 1926, Tang Shengzhi (1889-1970), commander of the Fourth Division of the Hunan Provincial Defence Force, ordered his troops to drive Zhao out and occupied Changsha, declared himself acting provincial governor and then went over to the side of the Guangdong National Government. Wu Peifu appointed Ye Kaixin, commander of the Third Division of the Hunan Provincial Defence Force, as the commander-in-chief of the Hunan troops, and in the meantime sent troops to attack Tang Shengzhi in Hunan. Defeated, Tang retreated to south Hunan and asked for help from the National Government. In May the National Government appointed Tang commander of the Eighth Corps of the National Revolutionary Army and the frontline commander-in-chief of the Northern Expeditionary Army, and sent two divisions and the Independent Regiment of the Fourth Corps, and a section of the Seventh Corps to enter Hunan first to help Tang Shengzhi in the battle, thus raising the curtain on the Northern Expeditionary War. On July 9, 1926, the National Revolutionary Army held an oath-taking rally in Guangzhou and then the Northern Expeditionary War officially began. The worker and peasant masses, enthusiastically supporting the expedition, launched a large-scale movement to support the front. The Guangzhou-Hong Kong strikers organized 3,000 people into transport, propaganda and medical teams to go with the army. Tens of thousands of peasants and workers from

Qujiang and other places came to help the army with transport or to serve as scouts, messengers or guides.

Upon their arrival in Hunan, the Expeditionary Army rapidly stabilized the war situation in south Hunan and gained one victory after another in the front. On July 10 it occupied Xiangtan and Liling, and Changsha on July 11. After a month's rest and reorganization it launched attacks again, taking Pingjiang on August 19 and Yuezhou on the 22nd and then entering Hubei. Wu Peifu rushed from the north to the south and ordered his 20,000-strong main force to defend to the last the Dingsiqiao Bridge, an important strategic point along the Guangzhou-Hankou Railway. The Fourth, Seventh and Eighth Corps of the Northern Expeditionary Army were divided into four columns to launch joint offensives on the Dingsiqiao Bridge. After fierce battles, on August 29 they eventually routed Wu Peifu's army. On the strength of this victory, the Expeditionary Army attacked and occupied another strategic point, Heshengqiao Bridge, in south Hubei on August 30. The Dingsiqiao and Heshengqiao battles were two key battles the Expeditionary Army fought in its war against Wu Peifu. Although Wu had thrown in his crack forces and supervised the battles in person, he had not been able to resist the Expeditionary Army's powerful offensives. After capturing two bridges, the gateway to the triple city of Wuhan was swung open. In early September the Expeditionary Army launched a general offensive on Wuhan and rapidly captured Hanyang, then Hankou after a month of fierce fighting. It occupied Wuchang on October 10. Wu Peifu's main forces were basically annihilated and the Northern Expeditionary Army won victory on the Hunan-Hubei front. The Independent Regiment of the Fourth Corps, led by Ye Ting (1896-1946) with Communists as the backbone, fought bravely and repeatedly rendered outstanding service, earning the name "Ironsides" for the Fourth Corps.

After the defeat of Wu Peifu's forces, the major front shifted to Jiangxi. In late August 1926, Sun Chuanfang called a military conference, at which it was decided to send some 100,000 troops from Jiangsu, Zhejiang and Anhui provinces to Jiangxi to prepare to face the Expeditionary Army. Early in September the Second, Third, and Sixth corps and part of the First and Fifth corps as well as the new recruits of the National Revolutionary Army took advantage of the time when Sun Chuanfang's troops were not yet concentrated, launched a massive offensive in Jiangxi and quickly occupied over 20 counties and the important city Ganzhou. By early October the Seventh Corps entered north Jiangxi from south Hubei, defeated Sun Chuanfang's main force, and cut off the Jiujiang-Nanchang Railway. In mid-October the Zhejiang provincial governor, Xia Chao, declared Zhejiang autonomous, but not long afterwards he was defeated and killed. In late October when the Fourth Corps entered Jiangxi, the Expeditionary Army mounted an attack on Nanchang on three fronts. It took Jiujiang on November 5 and entered Nanchang on November 8. Most of Sun's main forces were wiped out.

The victory on the Jiangxi battlefront was soon followed by victory on the Fujian battlefront. In early October the First Corps garrisoned in Chaozhou and Meixian launched an attack on the Fujian border, and took Yongding on October 10. Later, thanks to the rapid split and mutiny of the Fujian warlords' forces, the Northern Expeditionary Army occupied many places in southern Fujian without fighting major battles, and captured Fuzhou on December 9.

In the process of the Northern Expedition, Feng Yuxiang's National Army officially joined the revolutionary camp. In May 1926, Feng visited the Soviet Union and returned to China three months later. On September 17, he took the post of commander-in-chief of the United National Army in Wuyuan County, Suiyuan, and declared his support for the Northern Expedition, and the whole army joined the Kuomintang. Subsequently the National Army marched through Gansu and occupied the whole of Shaanxi Province at the end of 1926.

As the troops of Wu Peifu and Sun Chuanfang were defeated by the National Revolutionary Army, Zhang Zuolin was further expanding his influence. Sun had persisted in uniting with Feng Yuxiang to oppose the Fengtian clique, but now he suddenly changed his attitude and sought refuge with Zhang Zuolin. With the support of Sun Chuanfang and Zhang Zongchang, in early December, Zhang Zuolin styled himself commander-in-chief of the "National Pacification Army." Thereafter, Zhang Zuolin sent armed forces to the south in the name of assisting Sun Chuanfang and Wu Peifu. The Zhili-Shandong United

Army entered Nanjing and Shanghai, and Fengtian troops entered Henan.

In January 1927 the National Government moved north to Wuhan. The National Revolutionary Army continued to march forward in three columns: The eastern column was to enter Zhejiang from eastern Jiangxi and northern Fujian, and march directly to Hangzhou and Shanghai; the middle column was to drive towards Jiangsu and Anhui along the Yangtze River and attack Nanjing together with the eastern column; the western column was to enter southern Henan and contact the National Army in Shaanxi, for an opportunity to jointly enter central Henan. The central task of the campaign was to seize Nanjing and Shanghai. In mid-February the Expeditionary Army entered Hangzhou. In mid-March it arrived at the Shanghai suburbs. Yang Shuzhuang, commander-in-chief of the Navy of the Beijing government stationed in Shanghai, crossed over to the side of the Northern Expeditionary Army, and was appointed commander-in-chief of the Navy of the National Revolutionary Army. On March 22, the Shanghai working class captured Shanghai in its third armed uprising, and the Expeditionary Army occupied Nanjing on March 24.

The Northern Expeditionary Army in less than 10 months, from July 1926 to March 1927, annihilated the main forces of two chief warlords, fought from Guangdong to Wuhan, Nanjing and Shanghai, and expanded the revolutionary area from the Zhujiang valley to the Yangtze valley.

The victorious march of the Northern Expeditionary Army pushed forward the vigorous development of the nationwide anti-imperialist movement and the worker-peasant movement.

In January 1927, because the British aggressors in Hankou and Jiujiang sent troops to disrupt a mass rally to celebrate the victory of the Northern Expedition, killing and wounding many, the enraged Chinese people rose in a wave of opposition to the British imperialists. The National Government, with the support of the workers and local people, took back the British concessions in the two cities. It was a great victory won by the Chinese people in the history of the anti-imperialist struggle.

Between October 1926 and March 1927, the working class in

Shanghai, in coordination with the Northern Expeditionary War, held three armed uprisings. The third uprising, under the leadership of the Central Special Committee composed of Chen Duxiu, Zhou Enlai, Zhao Shiyan and Luo Yinong, shattered the warlord troops garrisoned in Shanghai and occupied the city after 30 hours' hard fighting. It wrote a brilliant page in the history of the Chinese revolution. By March 1927 the trade union membership in China had increased from 1.2 million before the Northern Expedition to two million. Many trade unions in Shanghai, Hubei, Hunan and many other places set up armed workers' picket corps which became backbone forces in suppressing counter-revolution and safeguarding the interests of the working class.

Wherever the Expeditionary Army went, the peasants were mobilized to organize themselves. In May 1927 the membership of the peasant associations rose to five million. Under the leadership of Mao Zedong, secretary of the Peasant Committee of the Party Central Committee, and others, a great revolutionary situation prevailed in the countryside in Hunan, Hubei, Jiangxi and other provinces. The peasant masses rose to overthrow the landlord regimes and disarm their forces, and set up their own political power and armed forces. They struggled for reduction of rent, interest and deposit, dealing an economic blow to the landlords. They also strongly opposed the feudal patriarchal clan system and the three authorities—clan, religious and male. To support the vigorous movement, Mao Zedong investigated the peasant movement in five counties including Xiangtan and Changsha in Hunan, and wrote his important work *Report on an Investigation of the Peasant Movement in Hunan.* In it he gave his full recognition to the big change in the rural areas, warmly praised the peasant movement as something "very good indeed," and hoped that revolutionaries would place themselves firmly at the head of the peasant movement, leading the peasants' struggle. He refuted with facts the denunciation and attack on the peasant movement. The KMT Leftwinger Deng Yanda, director of the Peasant Department of the Kuomintang Central Executive Committee and head of the General Political Department of the National Revolutionary Army, actively supported the peasant movement.

In the spring of 1927 the political situation in China was in the process of upheaval and disintegration. On the one hand, the rapidly developing revolutionary situation formed the first upsurge of a great people's revolution in China's modern history, and on the other, factors that endangered the revolution grew swiftly giving rise to a new counter-revolutionary alliance.

With the progress of the Northern Expeditionary War, the imperialists intensified their interference with the Chinese revolution. It was inevitable that the imperialists would act to maintain their interests in China. The British, American, Japanese and French imperialists all reinforced their troops and warships in China. In March 1927 there were imperialist armed forces over 30,000 strong in Shanghai, and 60 warships anchored near the city. The Shanghai consular corps decided after discussion to organize a joint marine corps composed of 5,000 seamen from Britain, the United States, France, Italy and Japan in preparation for a landing operation at any time. When the Northern Expeditionary Army occupied Nanjing, the escaping Zhili-Shandong United Army and part of the warlord troops recruited by the National Army attacked, and plundered foreign consulates, foreign institutions and residential quarters, and killed several foreigners. Responding to this, the British and American imperialists bombarded Nanjing on March 24, killing and wounding many Northern Expeditionary Army soldiers and Nanjing residents. This was called the "Nanjing Massacre." It was a severe step taken by the imperialists to interfere with the Chinese revolution by armed force.

While the imperialists were carrying out their gunboat policy, they adopted various sinister means to split the revolutionary camp and incited the "moderates" to break with the "extremists." After the Nanjing incident, the Japanese foreign minister Shigehare also used this ploy. After repeated consultations, Britain gave up "armed sanctions" against Chiang Kai-shek and instead urged Chiang to "organize the moderates" so as to oppose "extremists in the National Government." In so doing, the imperialists of various countries reached the same view on the question of supporting Chiang Kai-shek and suppressing the Communist Party.

With the advance of the Northern Expeditionary War and the

disintegration of the revolutionary camp, it became more apparent that Chiang Kai-shek was heading for military dictatorship and gradually identifying himself with the imperialists and China's big bourgeoisie. After the start of the Northern Expedition, as the commander-in-chief of the National Revolutionary Army, Chiang arrogated all power. On the forward march of the Northern Expedition, he rapidly expanded his military strength. By the end of 1926 he raised the dispute of "moving the capital," wanting to change the resolution of the Kuomintang Central Executive Committee and to move the Kuomintang Party Centre and the National Government to Nanchang, where the headquarters of the National Revolutionary Army was located, so as to administer the party and government with military force. However, the Communists and Kuomintang Left-wingers in Wuhan attacked Chiang on this issue. They tried to restrict Chiang's power and dictatorship by various means, but in vain. In February 1927, Chiang claimed that as "the leader of the national revolution" he had the responsibility and right to "intervene and sanction" the Communists. After the Nanjing incident, Chiang hurriedly sent a representative to the Japanese consulate to express his "apology," at the same time claiming that the Nanjing plunder was "created by the Communist Party deliberately," and that he had ordered the break-up of the Nanjing Communist Party branch. Arriving in Shanghai on February 26, Chiang made it clear that he would "never change the status quo of the concessions by armed force." Urged by the Japanese government, Chiang "determined to reorganize the internal structure of the National Government," by disarming the Shanghai workers, "replacing the Wuhan clique with members of the Kuomintang Central Executive and Supervisory committees in Shanghai, seizing the Kuomintang Party Centre and dispelling the Communists." In the meantime Chiang promised the Shanghai capitalists that on the labour-capital issue, "Shanghai would never adopt the attitude of Wuhan." The big capitalists in Shanghai now promised financial support to Chiang and immediately collected three million yuan for him. The gangsters in Shanghai organized the "China Mutual Progress Society" armed force and put it at the disposal of Chiang. The Chiang Kai-shek clique thus collaborated with the imperialists and big bourgeois in their common desire to suppress the Communist Party and smother the Chinese revolution.

Beginning from the end of March, Chiang Kai-shek and others called secret conferences, discussing the issue of "purging the party" and opposing the Communist Party. Wu Zhihui proposed "impeachment" of the Communist Party and asked "extremely urgent handling" of the Communist leaders. At this critical moment, Chen Duxiu adopted a serious Reight-deviationist attitude. Chen together with Wang Jingwei, who had just come back from abroad, issued a "joint statement" on April 5. It claimed that the Kuomintang "had never done anything to drive out members of friendly parties and shatter the trade unions," and asked people to "ignore rumours." After all preparations for his reactionary plot were completed, Chiang left Shanghai for Nanjing. The Shanghai reactionary coup d'état would be carried out by the Guangxi clique's Bai Chongxi.

Before dawn on April 12, armed gangsters disguised as workers rushed out from foreign concessions to attack the workers' pickets. The workers' pickets rose in counter-attack. The reactionary troops, on the pretext of "mediating internal dissension among the workers," disarmed their pickets. In the course of the action, over 1,700 guns were seized and more than 300 workers and Communists were killed or wounded. To protest against this bloody massacre, 200,000 Shanghai workers staged a strike on the 13th and the Shanghai Federation of Trade Unions called a mass meeting. After it the masses held a parade in the rain. When they passed through Baoshan Road, they were attacked from all directions by ambushing troops. Over 100 paraders were killed outright and many were wounded. This was followed by an order to ban strikes and parades, to dissolve the Shanghai Federation of Trade Unions, to close down the revolutionary organizations, and to arrest and kill the Communists and revolutionary masses. According to incomplete statistics, three days after the coup more than 300 Communists and revolutionary masses were killed; over 500 were arrested and more than 5,000 disappeared. Wang Shouhua, head of the Shanghai Federation of Trade Unions, had been secretly murdered on April 9. Leaders of the Jiangsu Provincial Committee of the Communist Party like Chen Yannian and Zhao Shiyan were killed one after another after the April 12 coup. On April 18 Chiang Kai-shek established another "National Government" in Nanjing against Wuhan's National Government. In the meantime, Chiang ordered the reactionaries to "purge the party."

After the April 12 counter-revolutionary coup, the Kuomintang reactionaries in Guangzhou followed suit on April 15. Over 2,000 Communists and workers were arrested, and some 200 trade unions and other mass bodies were closed down. In June the second party purge took place. In two or three months some 2,100 revolutionaries were killed, including well-known Communists and worker leaders Xiao Chunü, Xiong Xiong, Deng Pei and Li Qihan. Besides Shanghai and Guangzhou, party purges were also carried out in Guangxi, Jiangsu, Zhejiang, Fujian and Sichuan. At the same time, the Fengtian warlords arrested and killed Li Dazhao and other Communists. A large number of Communists and revolutionary masses were slaughtered.

The April 12 coup marked a great change in class relationships and the revolutionary situation. The Chiang Kai-shek Right-wing clique, who had military power inside the Kuomintang, openly went over to the side of the big landlord and capitalist classes and became a ferocious enemy of the revolution. In areas controlled by Chiang, the national bourgeoisie also issued statements, upholding Chiang's policy of opposing the Communists and "purging the party." The revolution suffered great failure in some areas.

Meanwhile, the mass revolutionary movement in Hunan, Hubei and Jiangxi provinces under the administration of the Wuhan government continued to develop. After his arrival in Wuhan on April 11, Wang Jingwei continued to pose himself as "a leader of the Left wing." A mammoth movement against Chiang Kai-shek was launched in Wuhan. The Kuomintang Central Executive Committee issued an order to expel Chiang from the party and dismiss him from all his posts. The Central Committee of the Communists Party issued a statement pointing out that Chiang Kai-shek had become the open enemy of the national revolution and a lackey of the imperialists. Workers, peasants, townspeople and students held rallies and published open telegrams against Chiang. The worker and peasant movements in Hunan and Hubei further expanded and deepened. A workers' picket corps of 5,000 people and 3,000 guns was established in Wuhan. In June the membership of trade unions throughout the country increased to 2.9 million, and that of the peasant associations swelled to 9.15 million, with Hunan having 4.51 million and Hubei 2.5 million. The peasants in some villages in Hunan and Hubei provinces began to launch the struggle for redistribution of land.

But the Wuhan government was already encircled by counter-revolutionary forces and faced deepening economic and political crisis. Warlords of the Nanjing, Guangdong, Sichuan and Fengtian cliques surrounded Wuhan militarily and established an economic blockade, making Wuhan, the gateway to nine provinces, almost an isolated island. The British and Japanese imperialists sent warships to threaten the Wuhan government by force, and in the meantime closed down all their enterprises in Wuhan, creating economic difficulties for the Wuhan government. The comprador and bureaucratic capitalists seized the opportunity to extract cash and close down factories; the national capitalists followed their example and intensified the economic crisis in Wuhan. The city of Wuhan found itself in a state of shortage of commodities and war materials, soaring prices, workers' unemployment and insecurity of people's livelihood. It is true that the situation was a result of the oppression of imperialists and encirdement of reactionary forces, but the "left" polices towards the capitalists adopted by the Chinese Communist Party also played a role. On April 19, the Wuhan government started the second stage of the Northern Expedition and dispatched troops to Henan. In early June the Northern Expeditionary Army joined hands with the forces of Feng Yuxiang in Zhengzhou, which had marched eastward from Shaanxi. The occupation of Henan was another victory gained by the Northern Expeditionary Army. However it could not avert the dangerous situation of Wuhan.

During the second stage of the Northern Expedition, the Wuhan government, under the control of Wang Jingwei, turned gradually to the Right and began openly suppressing worker and peasant movements and attacking the Communist Party. Reactionary officers who had sought to cash in on the revolution, now turned their back on it one after another. At the end of April He Jian. commander of the 35th

Corps, called a secret conference to conspire in an anti-Communist military coup. In Mid-May Xia Douyin, commander of the Independent 14th Division, colluded with Yang Sen, a Sichuan warlord, and staged a revolt in south Hubei. They were routed by Ye Ting's troops at Zhifang, 20 kilometres from Wuchang. On the night of May 21, Xu Kexiang, commander of the 33rd Regiment of the 35th Corps stationed in Changsha, staged a coup d'état at the instigation of He Jian. The provincial trade union federation, peasant association, peasant movement institute, special court and other revolutionary organizations and institutions were destroyed overnight, and more than 100 Communists and mass movement leaders were killed. In late May and early June Zhu Peide, the Jiangxi Provincial governor, twice "deported" Communists and ordered the peasant and worker movements in the province to stop their activities. In mid-June Feng Yuxiang called Zhengzhou and Xuzhou conferences attended by Wang Jingwei, Chiang Kai-shek, etc. The results of the Zhengzhou Conference inflated the anti-Communists arrogance on the side of Wuhan and also caused the fruits of the second-stage Northern Expedition to fall entirely onto the lap of Feng Yuxiang. The conference made this decision: The Northern Expeditionary Army led by Tang Shengzhi would withdraw from Henan to Wuhan and the tasks unfinished in Henan would be handled by Feng Yuxiang. After the Xuzhou conference Feng Yuxiang and Chiang Kai-shek reached agreement over such issues as Nanjing-Wuhan collaboration, "purging the party" and opposition to the Communist Party, and driving Borodin out of China. After the conference, Feng sent a telegram to Wang Jingwei and company urging them to quickly decide to unite with Chiang in opposition to the Communists. Feng expelled the Communists from the army and the areas under his administration. In the first half of June, Shanxi warlord Yan Xishan (1883-1960) changed his army's name to the National Revolutionary Army, appointed himself commander-in-chief of the National Revolutionary Army in North China, sent an open telegram in support of the Nanjing government, and carried out a "purge of the party" in Shanxi Province.

At this critical moment, the Communist Party should have adopted a correct policy and action, stabilized the allies, launched a counter-attack against the reactionaries, continued to push the revolution forward and kept the revolution's losses to a minimum. But the leading organ of the Party had sunk deeply into the Right opportunist mire, and failed to give the revolution correct guidance. In December of 1926, the Communist Party Central Committee held a special conference in Hankou. It decided to adopt a Right deviationist general policy of supporting Wang Jingwei, restricting the worker and peasant movements, and winning Chiang Kai-shek to the Left. As a result Chiang, instead of turning to the Left, eventually betrayed the revolution openly. After the April 12 coup, the Central Committee of the Communist Party failed to realize its error from the setbacks and to change its method of over-believing in and relying on some Kuomintang leaders to that of winning army support. Its only change was from seeking the support of Chiang Kai-shek to an attempt to win Wang Jingwei over to the revolutionary side. In late April and early May, 1927, the Chinese Communist Party held its Fifth National Congress. Although the congress criticized Chen Duxiu's viewpoint in his report that only "expanding the revolution" suited the present situation instead of "deepening the revolution," and discussed a series of important problems in the revolution, it failed to work out practical and effective methods to save the revolution. Moreover, while the Right-deviationist mistake continued to exist, the "Left" mistake emerged. The congress assumed that the Chinese revolution had developed to "the stage of democratic dictatorship by workers, peasants and the petty bourgeois class," and that "a powerful offensive should be launched on the bourgeoisie both politically and economically." The Fifth National Congress failed to undertake the task of saving the revolution at that critical juncture. After the congress even Chen Duxiu, the General Party Secretary, and Michael Borodin, the Soviet adviser, took the relationship with the "Left wing" as the most important of all the issues. In order to ensure that the self-claimed "Left-wing leader" Wang Jingwei and the "Left-wing armyman" Tang Shengzhi would not break with the Communist Party, Chen and Borodin went so far as to adopt repressive measures against workers and peasants and sacrifice the interests of the revolution. In May the Communist International sent an emergency instruction to the CPC to the effect that every effort should be made to help the worker and peasant movements and "to genuinely seize land from the bottom level," to "renovate" the Kuomintang Centre and to expand the Kuomintang local branches by relying on worker and peasant strength; to mobilize 20,000 Communists and 50,000 workers and peasants to establish a new revolutionary army, to organize a revolutionary military court led by influential Kuomintang members to punish the reactionary officers, etc. Chen Duxiu and some others considered that there was no way to carry out these measures. The representative of the Communist International, Roy, relayed this instruction to Wang Jingwei to express his confidence in Wang. As a result it later served as an excuse for Wang's "splitting the Communist Party."

On June 29, the reactionary officer He Jian gave his subordinates anti-Communist instructions, demanding that the National Government order a "split with the Communist Party." He Jian moved his 35th Corps to Hankou and prepared to slaughter the revolutionaries. On July 12 the CPC Central Committee, in accordance with the instruction of the Communist International, reorganized and established a Provisional Central Standing Committee. Chen Duxiu was compelled to leave his leading post. Then the Central Committee published a declaration on the current situation, disclosing that the Wang Jingwei bloc "had openly prepared for a coup d'état," and announcing its decision to withdraw the Communists from the National Government. Deng Yanda, a Left-wing Kuomintang member, published a declaration of resignation (Deng by then had left Wuhan), condemning Wang Jingwei's bloc for distorting Sun Yat-sen's Three People's Principles and betraying his Three Cardinal Policies. Soong Ching Ling published a statement, expressing her determination to uphold the Three Cardinal Policies. On July 15, Wang Jingwei called an enlarged meeting of the Standing Committee of the Kuomintang Centre. It decided to "sanction the Communists" for any violation in words or actions of the Kuomintang's policy and principles. The holding of the July 15 meeting indicated Wang Jingwei's open betrayal of the revolution.

The July 15 coup marked the final break of the first cooperation between the Communist Party and the Kuomintang and the failure of the national revolution. By now the nature of the Kuomintang, the National Government and the National Revolutionary Army had changed. The Kuomintang was no longer an organization of alliance of all revolutionary classes and had become a reactionary political party representing the interests of the landlord and comprador classes; the National Government was no longer a united political power of all revolutionary classes and had turned into a counter-revolutionary dictatorship of the landlord and comprador classes; and the National Revolutionary Army was no longer a revolutionary army, but a tool to maintain the rule of the landlord and comprador classes. Both the revolutionary and counter-revolutionary camps had undergone a great change. The revolution faced a new situation and a new enemy.

5. Establishment of Kuomintang Rule and the Beginning of the Soviet Revolution

After the Northern Expeditionary War from 1926 to 1927, China's warlord forces underwent great changes. With the exception of Zhang Zuolin's Fengtian army, all other old warlord forces had either been eliminated or come under the jurisdiction of the Kuomintang. The old Beiyang warlord rule gradually changed to the rule of the new Kuomintang warlords.

The Kuomintang had divided into many factions. In military affairs Chiang Kai-shek, Tang Shengzhi, Li Zongren, Li Jishen, Feng Yuxiang and Yan Xishan all had their own armed forces. In politics, Wang Jingwei, Chiang Kai-shek, Hu Hanmin and the Western Hills Conference clique each formed a faction. The warlord forces ganged up with the political groups, creating intense struggles. For a period of time a major struggle was that between Nanjing and Wuhan.

Both Nanjing and Wuhan had set up a Kuomintang Centre and a National Government, and confronted each other militarily. Feng Yuxiang mediated between the two sides and proposed to solve their disputes through negotiations. Due to opposition from the Wang Jingwei bloc in Wuhan and the Guangxi clique led by Li Zongren inside the Nanjing faction, as well as the failure in the war along the Tianjin-

Pukou Railway line, Chiang Kai-shek declared his resignation from the post of commander-in-chief of the National Revolutionary Army in August 1927. His resignation promoted the merging of the Nanjing and Wuhan sides. In mid-September Nanjing, Wuhan and Shanghai (Western Hills Conference clique) organized the Kuomintang Central Special Committee, and reorganized the National Government and the Military Commission. However, because the Special Committee was under the control of the Guangxi clique, Wang Jingwei and Chen Gongbo could realize their desire to control central power, so they returned to Wuhan and resisted the Special Committee, relying on Tang Shengzhi's forces. The cooperation between Nanjing and Wuhan was thus replaced by their confrontation. Not long afterwards the confrontation developed into war between Li Zongren and Tang Shengzhi, which ended in the defeat of Tang Shengzhi and the expansion of the Guangxi clique's influence to Wuhan. Thereafter, the Wang Jingwei clique was further pushed out by other factions and for a long period of time was out of office. Later they founded the Kuomintang "reorganization" faction and continued the scramble for power. Chiang Kai-shek paid a visit to Japan between late September and early November. He resumed his post as commander-in-chief of the National Revolutionary Army in January 1928.

In February 1928 the Kuomintang called the Fourth Plenary Session of its Second Central Executive Committee. The session passed resolutions on rearranging party affairs, reorganizing the National Government, stopping the Communist Party's "conspiracy" and concentrating revolutionary forces to complete the Northern Expedition within a definite time. It elected Chiang Kai-shek, Tan Yankai and seven other members of the Standing Committee of the Kuomintang Central Executive Committee. Tan Yankai (1880-1930) was president of the National Government, and Chiang chairman of the Military Commission. In March Chiang was appointed Chairman of the Central Political Conference. Chiang thus again concentrated party, military and political power in his own hands.

After the Fourth Plenary Session, the four group armies headed respectively by Chiang Kai-shek, Feng Yuxiang, Yan Xishan and Li Zongren, launched another "Northern Expedition," this time against

Zhang Zuolin, in a scramble for the rule of the whole country. However, the Kuomintang's "Northern Expedition" was interfered with by the Japanese imperialists. On May 3, 1928, Japan even launched an armed attack on Jinan, which had already been occupied by Kuomintang troops, in order to obstruct the latter's northward march. This was followed by a slaughter, with more than 10,000 soldiers and civilians being killed or wounded in a week. Chiang Kai-shek ordered the troops to withdraw from Jinan and take a circuitous route to the north. On June 3, Zhang Zuolin, seeing that the situation was unfavorable to him, left Beijing secretly and retreated to the northeast. The following day he was killed in an explosion on a train at Huanggu Village near Shenyang by the Japanese imperialists. Then Yan Xishan's troops occupied Beijing and Tianjin. The Nanjing government declared on June 15 the "accomplishment of unification." The name of Zhili Province was changed to Hebei Province and Beijing to Beiping (Peiping).

After Zhang Zuolin died, his son, Zhang Xueliang, succeeded him as commander-in-chief of the Peace Preservation Army of the three northeast provinces. Regardless of the obstruction of the Japanese imperialists, Zhang Xueliang sent an open telegram on December 29, 1928, declaring he would "obey the Three People's Principles and the National Government." Before his declaration, Yang Zengxin in Xinjiang and Tang Yulin in Rehe had also declared a "change of banner." Thus the Kuomintang expanded its rule to the whole country.

In July 1928 the Kuomintang announced the conclusion of "the period of military government" and the beginning of the "period of political tutelage." In October it published the "Programme of Political Tutelage." It provided that the Kuomintang National Congress and the Kuomintang Central Executive Committee would exercise the functions and powers of the National Assembly; the Kuomintang would be responsible for "training" the citizens to exercise the four rights of election, recall, policy formulation and redecision; the Kuomintang Centre would "guide and supervise" the National Government in the exercise of administrative power; and the Kuomintang "alone would hold the full responsibility" for "the exercise of political and administrative power of the Republic of China." This "programme" proved that the Kuomintang's "political tutelage" was the dictatorship of one party depriving the people's rights. While publishing the "Programme of Political Tutelage," the Kuomintang also published the "Organization Law of the National Government." It divided the National Government into the Executive, Legislative, Judicial, Examination and Control Yuan, headed respectively by Tan Yankai, Hu Hanmin, Wang Chonghui, Dai Jitao and Cai Yuanpei. Chiang was president of the National Government and concurrently commander-in-chief of the army, navy and air force. The establishment of the five Yuan manifested the complete formation of the Kuomintang regime.

In the name of "political tutelage," the Kuomintang implemented a high-handed rule over the people, ruthlessly suppressed the worker-peasant movement, and ferociously slaughtered Communists and revolutionaries. The Kuomintang's documents directed that all Communist theories, methods, organs and movements "should be eradicated thoroughly or be prevented." According to the criminal law designed by the Nanjing government: "Those who attempt to subvert the government, forcibly seize land and bring disorder to the National Constitution should be sentenced to death, life imprisonment, or at least seven years of imprisonment." Between 1927 and 1932 more than one million Communists and other people were killed.

After the Kuomintang army occupied Beijing, the Nanjing government launched a campaign "to draw up new pacts," and demanded that relevant countries abrogate the old pacts and draw up new ones with China. The new pacts were to include tariff autonomy and abrogation of consular jurisdiction. In July 1928 the Nanjing government concluded with America the Sino-U.S. Treaty of Tariff Relations, and similar trade and tariff treaties were concluded with other countries. In accordance with these "new pacts," tax rates of some imported commodities were raised by China, but China did not acquire genuine tariff autonomy. As for the abolition of consular jurisdiction, it remained unsolved for a long period of time, because the major imperialist countries disagreed. "Concluding new pacts," an unprecedented action in the history of modern China, was certainly significant. However, it did not deprive the imperialists of special rights in China, and fell far short of making China a country maintaining independence and keeping the initiative in its own hands. Through this action, the Nanjing government received recognition from various foreign countries.

Under the rule of the National Government the feudal relation of landlords exploiting the peasants did not change. The interests of the comprador-bourgeoisie were protected. The Kuomintang began to organize an economic monopoly of bureaucrat-capitalism, represented by Song Ziwen (T.V. Soong) and Kong Xiangxi (H. H. Kung). Workers, peasants, and even the national bourgeoisie received no emancipation, either economically or politically. Thus, this political power, in terms of class nature, still maintained the rule of the urban comprador class and rural gentry. It practised "administration of the country by the party" under the slogan of Sun Yat-sen's Three People's Principles, its only difference from the Beiyang regime being that it was less feudal and strongly comprador in character. China was still semi-colonial and semi-feudal in social nature, so all class contradictions remained unsolved in Chinese society. China still faced the task of anti-imperialist and anti-feudal bourgeois democratic revolution. Overthrowing the National Government thus became the main revolutionary target during that period.

After the defeat of the national revolution, the Chinese Communist Party summed up its experiences and lessons, continued to hold high the revolutionary banner, and pushed the Chinese revolution to a new stage.

On August 1, 1927, Zhou Enlai, Zhu De (1886-1976), He Long (1896-1969), Ye Ting and Liu Bocheng led a unit of the Northern Expeditionary Army over 30,000 strong, which had been under the leadership and influence of the Chinese Communist Party, in an uprising at Nanchang, Jiangxi Province. This uprising continued under the Kuomintang Left-wing banner and in the name of the National Revolutionary Army. The army occupied the city of Nanchang on the first day and then set up a leading organ called "The Revolutionary Committee of the Chinese Kuomintang." Then the troops marched south towards Guangdong, where they planned to rally their forces for another northern expedition. In early October they were defeated around Chaozhou by the numerically superior Kuomintang forces. The Nanchang Uprising fired the first shot against the Kuomintang reactionaries. It was the start of the building of an army and an armed struggle led independently by the Chinese Communist Party. The insurgents, instead of joining forces with the local peasant movement, carrying out local agrarian revolution and setting up a rural revolutionary regime, adopted the strategy of marching southward in isolation. This was the main reason for their defeat.

On August 7, 1927, a week after the Nanchang Uprising, the CPC Central Committee called an emergency conference at Hankou. This important conference, held at the critical juncture when the revolution had suffered defeat, aimed at reviewing and correcting past mistakes and defining the future revolutionary policy. It published the well-known "Letter to the Communists," which made an all-round criticism of the Right opportunist mistakes represented by Chen Duxiu during the period of national revolution, and decided on the general policy of agrarian revolution and armed resistance against the Kuomintang reactionaries. It decided to mobilize the peasants in the four provinces of Hunan, Hubei, Jiangxi and Guangdong for an Autumn-Harvest Uprising. Mao Zedong made a speech, pointing out that "political power grows out of the barrel of a gun." The meeting marked the change of the strategic policy of the Chinese Communist Party. From that time onward the Party guided the Chinese revolution to a new stage based on armed struggle and agrarian revolution. Because the meeting neglected the struggle against and prevention of the "Left" tendency while correcting the Right opportunist tendency, it thus opened the gate for "Left" adventurism.

Early in September 1927, Mao Zedong and Lu Deming led the Autumn Harvest Uprising on the Hunan-Jiangxi border, in the name of the Workers' and Peasants' Revolutionary Army instead of the National Revolutionary Army. They had originally planned to attack Changsha in three columns, but soon after the outbreak of the uprising, the army suffered serious losses. Seeing that in such a situation it would be impossible to occupy the central city, after the forces of various columns assembled at Wenjiashi in Liuyang, Mao Zedong abandoned the plan to attack, led the forces along the Luoxiao Mountain range southward towards the countryside. At the end of September the forces were reorganized at Sanwan Village in Yongxin County, Jiangxi Province, where they streamlined the organizational system, and established the principle of Communist Party leadership over the army. In October these forces reached the middle section of the Luoxiao Mountain range—Ciping, the central area of the Jinggang Mountains. The march of the Autumn Harvest Uprising forces to the Jinggang Mountains opened up a new and correct way for continuing the revolutionary struggle after the defeat of the Great Revolution of 1925-27.

In September 1927, the Communist Party Central Committee made an important decision: instead of taking the name of the Left-wing Kuomintang in the uprising, it would hold up the banner of the "worker-peasant Soviet." In early November the enlarged meeting of the Political Bureau of the CPC Central Committee clearly pointed out that the Kuomintang's rule "had become a White terror," that at the current stage of revolution, "the main slogan of the Party was Soviet." It was an important change. In November the peasant uprising in the Haifeng-Lufeng area in Guangdong brought about the establishment of the first Soviet political power in China. For nearly a decade thereafter, the Chinese revolution marched forward under the Soviet banner.

On December 11, Zhang Tailei (1898-1927), Ye Ting, and Ye Jianying led an uprising in Guangzhou. The city of Guangzhou was occupied on the very first day of the uprising and the founding of the Guangzhou Soviet Government was declared. For the first time, the army was named the Workers' and Peasants' Red Army. The Guangzhou Uprising was held at a time when Guangdong and Guangxi warlords were locked in a war in Wuzhou and Zhaoqing. After the outbreak of the uprising, the warlords stopped their war immediately and concentrated 50,000 armed forces to attack Guangzhou. After three days and nights of brave fighting, the insurgents fell to the enemy's persecution. Zhang Tailei and many officers and soldiers were killed in action, and some 8,000 revolutionary people were murdered. Although the Communist Party and revolutionary people displayed a brave fighting spirit, failure to evacuate the armed forces to the countryside in time made the revolutionary forces suffer great losses.

Besides the above-mentioned three major uprisings, over 100 uprisings took place in Hunan, Hubei, Jiangxi, Guangdong, Jiangsu, Fujian, Hebei, Shaanxi, Henan and Sichuan between autumn 1927 and 1928. The major ones included the Haifeng-Lufeng Uprising, Qiongya Uprising (Guangdong), Huang'an-Macheng Uprising (Hubei), Weinan-Huaxian Uprising (Shaanxi), Pingjiang Uprising (Hunan), and the peasant armed struggles in Honghu Lake and western Hunan and Hubei.

These armed uprisings were all courageous counter-attacks against the Kuomintang's policy of slaughter, dealt by the people who were led by the Communist Party, and concrete illustrations of the Communist Party's persistence in revolutionary struggle. They expanded the Communist Party's influence among the masses, popularized the slogan of agrarian revolution among the peasants and preserved a part of the revolutionary armed forces. These prepared the conditions for continued armed struggle and establishment and development of rural revolutionary bases.

In the early days of the Soviet revolution, there were rapid changes in class relations of the country, hatred for the Kuomintang reactionaries' policy of massacre, and indignation at the Right opportunism represented by Chen Duxiu and "Left" putschism represented by Qu Qiubai inside the Party. After the enlarged meeting of the Provisional Central Political Bureau in November 1927, "Left" putschism dominated the central leading body of the Party. The putschists confused bourgeois democratic revolution with socialist revolution and thought that in order to overthrow the gentry and landlord class, "the bourgeois class must also be overthrown." Believing that the tide of revolution was "rising" rather than ebbing, they opposed any retreat and demanded continuous attack. In armed uprisings they carried out a policy of burning and killing and in some places even raised such erroneous slogans as "exterminating landed gentry," "burning the cities," "reducing the petty bourgeoisie into proletarians and then compelling them to make revolution." Because "Left" putschism caused loss of work, the Communist International also criticized the erroneous tendency. The implementation of these policies was stopped after several months.

In July 1928 the Sixth National Congress of the Communist Party was held in Moscow, in which over 100 delegates including Zhou Enlia, Cai Hesen, Qu Qiubai, Li Lisan, Zhang Guotao and Xiang Zhongfa took part. The congress continued to criticize the Right opportunist mistakes represented by Chen Duxiu and the "Left" putschism, and stressed that putschism and commandism were the main current dangerous tendencies. It reaffirmed that the Chinese revolution at present stage was still a bourgeois democratic revolution against imperialism and feudalism, and pointed out that the political situation being then in a trough between two revolutionary upsurges, the central task of the Party was to win over the masses. It put forward a 10-point political programme for the Chinese democratic revolution, which included overthrowing the rule of imperialism and the Kuomintang warlord government, setting up a worker-peasant-soldier congress (Soviet) government, confiscating the landlords' land for distribution among the peasants, etc. The line laid down by the Sixth National Congress of the Communist Party played a positive role in pushing the Chinese revolution forward. Its shortcomings lay in failure to correctly estimate the role of the intermediate classes and the internal contradictions among the reactionary forces, and in its consideration of the national bourgeoisie as "one of the most dangerous enemies" and "all factions of the Kuomintang as reactionaries." These views did not conform to the reality of Chinese society. Besides, the Congress failed to have an adequate understanding of the importance of rural revolutionary bases and the protraction of democratic revolution. The overemphasis on working-class origin in the election of the Central Committee members also showed a deviation of taking into account class origin alone. Xiang Zhongfa, a worker was elected chairman of the Political Bureau and the Standing Committee of the CPC Central Committee at the 1st Plenary Session of the 6th Central Committee. However, he actually played no role in the leadership.

6. Growth and Decline of the Kuomintang Factions and Setting-up of the Soviet Areas

After the four factions of the Kuomintang warlords (Chiang Kai-shek, Feng Yuxiang, Yan Xishan and Li Zongren-Bai Chongxi) gained victory in the battle against the Fengtian clique, contradictions between them became acute immediately. Domain was the foundation of warlords' existence and the army their lifeline, so struggles between warlords were first manifested in these two aspects.

Chiang Kai-shek then occupied Nanjing, Shanghai, Jiangsu and Zhejiang provinces; Feng Yuxiang, Shaanxi, Gansu, Ningxia and Henan provinces; Yan Xishan, Shanxi, Hebei, Suiyuan and Qahar provinces as well as Beijing and Tianjin; Li Zongren and Bai Chongxi (Guangxi clique), Hunan, Hubei and Guangxi provinces; and Li Jishen who supported the Guangxi clique, occupied Guangdong. Feng Yuxiang was discontent with such a distribution. Although large in territory, his domains were mostly barren areas. He had contributed greatly to the war against the Fengtian warlord clique, but Chiang Kai-shek had place Hebei, Beiping and Tianjin under the control of Yan Xishan. Li Zongren and Bai Chongxi were also displeased with their domains, which were not only small but had no outlets to the sea. As Yan controlled Hebei, Beiping and Tianjin, he took all the levies and taxes into his own pockets. This caused Chiang's discontent. The warlords of the four factions all sought an opportunity to expand their spheres of influence.

After the conclusion of the war against the Fengtian clique, Chiang Kai-shek proposed to reorganize and discharge the nation's two-million-strong army. The reason he gave was to reduce military expenses and use the money for economic construction. Actually he wanted to weaken the forces of the Feng, Yan and Guangxi factions and to further strengthen his own position. In January 1929, a meeting to reorganize and discharge the army was held in Nanjing, attended by leaders of different Kuomintang military factions. It passed an outline of the procedure for the reorganization and discharge of the army. It provided the cancellation of the general headquarters of the National Revolutionary Army, the group armies, and the navy; the classification of the country into six areas for the reorganization and discharge of the armies of Chiang Kai-shek, Feng Yuxiang, Yan Xishan, the Guangxi clique, the northeast and the northwest. The army of the country would not exceed 800,000 and the provinces would be divided into pacification areas with garrisoned divisions or brigades. They failed to reach an agreement on a concrete plan for the reorganization and discharge. Chiang Kai-shek demanded every group army hand over "power to the central authority," but the leaders of the group armies found every reason to obtain more troops and to discharge fewer. Feng proposed a plan favouring his own troops, but it was turned down by Chiang and Yan. Pretending to be sick, Feng left Nanjing. The meeting further deepened the contradictions among the four warlord factions, and in its wake large-scale warlord wars broke out.

In March 1929, a war between the Chiang and Guangxi cliques was the first to break out. To control the Guangxi clique, Chiang secretly sent ammunition to the governor of Hunan, Lu Diping, and urged Lu to oppose the Guangxi clique. When the Guangxi clique fought back and dismissed Lu from his post in the name of the Wuhan branch of the Kuomintang Central Political Conference and sent soldiers to attack Changsha, Chiang ordered "a thorough investigation of the Guangxi troops invading Hunan"; meanwhile he cajoled Li Jishen, who supported the Guangxi clique, to go to Nanjing and then put Li under house arrest. On March 26, the war broke out. Due to Chiang's bribery, a section of the Guangxi troops mutinied at the front. This made the Guangxi troops retreat in a hurry from the Wuhan area; they were entirely defeated in April. Chiang's influence thus extended to Hunan and Hubei. In the second half of 1929, a war between Chiang and Feng, the second war between Chiang and the Guangxi clique, and a war between Chiang and Tang Shengzhi broke out one after another, each time with Chiang coming out the winner.

In May 1930s, the Central Plain War between Chiang Kai-shek on the one side and Feng Yuxiang and Yan Xishan on the other, the largest of its kind in modern Chinese history, broke out. In the spring of that year the three warlord cliques of Feng, Yan and Guangxi and the two political blocs—the Kuomintang reorganizing faction and Western Hills Conference faction, formed a large combined force to oppose Chiang. In early April, Yan Xishan was chosen as Commander-in-Chief of the naval, land and air forces of the Republic of China and Feng Yuxiang and Li Zongren Vice Commanders-in-Chief. In mid-May Chiang Kai-shek ordered the launching of a general offensive against Yan and Feng. The Central Plain War between Chiang on the one side and Feng and Yan on the other thus began. The two sides each employed some one million soldiers and the battlefront extended over a thousand kilometres along Henan, Shandong, Anhui and other provinces. The fighting along the Longhai (Lanzhou-Lianyungang) Railway Line was the most furious. In the early period, Feng and Yan fought some victorious battles. Later, because Feng's troops were too fatigued after repeated furious battles, and short of grain and ammunition, they were unable to sustain their offensive. In May and June, after the outbreak of the war, the Guangxi troops entered Hunan to attack Chiang's troops, and occupied Changsha and Yuezhou. In early July the Guangxi clique suffered great losses and retreated to Guangxi. While the warlord war continued, the Wang Jingwei bloc called an enlarged meeting of the Kuomintang Centre in Beiping. With the reorganization clique as the main force, it was attended by representatives of the Western Hills Conference clique, as well as the Yan and Feng cliques. On September 9, a "National Government" was set up in Beiping with Yan Xishan as its president, in opposition to Chiang's Nanjing government. In mid-September, Chiang won over Zhang Xueliang in the northeast, who then published an open telegram expressing his support for Chiang, and ordered his troops to enter Shanhaiguan Pass and occupy Tianjin and Beiping. Chiang cut off Feng Yuxiang's route of retreat, thus making a rapid change in the war situation. Yan Xishan, Wang Jingwei and others withdrew to Taiyuan. In October Yan, Feng and Wang were completely defeated. The majority of Feng's troops went over to Chiang and the rest was reorganized by the Northeast Army. Yan's troops were reorganized in name by the Northeast Army, but suffered little loss. Feng was forced to relinquish power and Yan temporarily took refuge in Dalian. After the "enlarged meeting" published a "provisional constitution," it vanished like mist and smoke. The Central Plain War, lasting for five months, brought great disaster to the people. There were 300,000 soldiers killed, countless wounded, and extensive property losses.

After several wars, especially the Central Plain War, great changes occurred in the balance of various warlords' strength. Chiang

Kai-shek, by relying on the support of the U.S and British imperialists and financial magnates of Jiangsu and Zhejiang provinces, taking advantage of the contradictions among the anti-Chiang factions, and adopting a policy of bribing and sowing dissension, defeated all his opponents and gained obvious superiority over the other Kuomintang warlord forces. Although other warlords still existed and some continued to wage an anti-Chiang struggle, they had not enough strength to defeat Chiang Kai-shek.

After Chiang Kai-shek defeated his opponents militarily, he started to consolidate his position politically. Sun Yat-sen had struggled in his lifetime for the convention of a National Assembly. The "enlarged meeting" chaired by Wang Jingwei had also held out the banner of calling a National Assembly and working out a "provisional constitution" so as to win the initiative politically. In order to stop his opponents' criticism and create legal ground for his rule, Chiang decided to call a National Assembly.

The National Assembly was held in Nanjing in May 1931. It was not the National Assembly that Sun Yat-sen had advocated, one that would oppose warlord rule and give people the right to exercise democracy, but a false one which would oppose the people, maintaining the one-party dictatorship of the Kuomintang and the personal dictatorship of Chiang Kai-shek. In his opening speech Chiang publicly praised fascism. He said that communism advocated class struggle with "ruthless means" and would not be "suitable for the industrially backward China and its inherent morality." He asserted that "China does not need it." According to him, the people's administration practised in the West was "putting stress on individual freedom," but China had no such historical and social background for carrying out this policy. He believed that only under fascism "the state is considered the most lofty entity... its rule is the most effective." He vilified the Communist warlords for "feathering their nests in the Central Plain area" and claimed that carrying out effective rule was "what the people in the country demand today." The meeting passed "the provisional constitution for the political tutelage period." An embodiment of the "political tutelage programme" of 1928, it affirmed the political system of the Kuomintang's one-party dictatorship in the form of a state constitution. The meeting passed a resolution on "suppressing the Red bandits," and determined "to encircle and suppress" the Red Army on a large scale. It illustrated the strengthening of Chiang's rule and the transition from Kuomintang internal struggles to "suppression of the Communist Party." It was an important reactionary meeting in Kuomintang history.

The Kuomintang warlord wars weakened the reactionary camp and offered favourable conditions for the recovery and development of revolution. On the basis of the local armed uprisings throughout the country, Soviets were set up in many areas and developed during this period.

The earliest revolutionary base was in the Jinggang Mountains. In October 1927, Mao Zedong led the reorganized Autumn Harvest Uprising contingent to the Jinggang Mountains, where he reorganized the local armed forces, attacked and seized county towns, liberated rural areas, set up workers' and peasants' regimes, and re-established Communist Party organizations. By the spring of 1928 preliminary base areas had been set up. By the end of April, Zhu De and Chen Yi (1901-1972) led the Nanchang Uprising troops and the contingent of southern Hunan armed peasants to the Jinggang Mountains and joined forces with the revolutionary army led by Mao Zedong. On May 4, the Fourth Corps of the Chinese Workers' and Peasants' Revolutionary Army (later changed to the Fourth Corps of the Chinese Workers' and Peasants' Red Army) was formed, with Zhu De as commander and Mao Zedong as Party representative. The Red Army created the famous guerrilla tactics as follows: "The enemy advances, we retreat; the enemy camps, we harass; the enemy tires, we attack; the enemy retreats, we pursue." Victories were achieved in many battles by using these tactics. A Hunan-Jiangxi Border Soviet Government was established in May. The Jinggang Mountains base area first covered the three counties of Ninggang, Yongxin and Lianhua and parts of Ji'an, Anfu, Suichuan and Lengxian counties and later developed into the Hunan-Jiangxi base area.

Besides the Jinggang Mountains base area, from 1928 to 1930 the Communist Party led and set up the following six base areas:

Southern Jiangxi-Western Fujian base area: In January 1929, in order to break through the "joint suppression" campaign against the Jinggang Mountains launched by the enemies in Hunan and Jiangxi and to solve the problem of provisions for the Red Army, Mao Zedong and Zhu De led the main force of the Fourth Corps to attack southern Jiangxi. The Fifth and part of the Fourth corps, which had just entered the Jingang Mountains and were led by Peng Dehuai (1898-1974), were assigned to defend the Jinggang mountain area. The Fourth Corps fought in southern Jiangxi and western Fujian, coordinated with the local Party organizations and armed forces, and opened up the southern Jiangxi and western Fujian base areas. In the spring of 1930, the western Fujian and Jiangxi Soviet governments were established. In June the First Army of the Workers' and Peasants' Red Army was formed with Zhu De as commander and Mao Zedong as political commissar. During this period, 17 Soviet governments at the county level were set up in southern Jiangxi and western Fujian, thus laying the foundation for the later central revolutionary base area. In August the First Red Army and the Third Red Army led by Peng Dehuai were combined into the First Front Red Army, with Mao Zedong as general secretary of the Front Committee and general political commissar, Zhu De as commander-in-chief, and Peng Dehuai as deputy commander-in-chief.

Hunan-Hubei-Jiangxi base area: In July 1928 Peng Dehuai, Teng Daiyuan and others led a part of the Kuomintang's Fifth Independent Division, stationed in Hunan, in a revolt in Pingjiang and organized themselves as the Fifth Corps, with Peng as commander and Teng as Party representative. After the uprising, the Fifth Corps waged guerrilla warfare in the counties on the border of the three provinces of Hunan, Hubei and Jiangxi, and set up a Soviet government. In December Peng and Teng led the main force of the Fifth Corps and entered the Jinggang Mountains; Huang Gonglue led the remaining force to continue the struggle in the Hunan-Hubei-Jiangxi area. In 1930 the two areas of Hunan-Hubei-Jiangxi and Hunan-Jiangxi were linked together. The Fifth Córps then expanded and was organized into the Third Red Army with Peng and Teng as commander and political commissar respectively. At this time the Hunan-Hubei-Jiangxi area already covered about a dozen counties around the border of the three provinces, and a Hunan-Hubei-Jiangxi Soviet Government was founded.

Fujian-Zhejiang-Jiangxi base area: In January 1928, Fang Zhimin (1899-1935) and other leaders led a peasant uprising in Yiyang and Hengfeng counties in northeast Jiangxi, set up the Agrarian Revolutionary Army and carried out guerrilla warfare. In December 1928, the Xinjiang Speical Area Soviet Government was set up, covering northeastern Jiangxi's eight counties. In the same winter the Communist Party led a peasant uprising in Chongan, northern Fujian. In the summer of 1930 the Xinjiang Soviet Government changed its name to the Northeastern Jiangxi Soviet Government with Fang Zhimin as the chairman. The Red Army troops in northeastern Jiangxi and northern Fujian were organized into the 10th Corps with Zhou Jianping as commander and Shao Shiping as political commissar. In the spring of 1931, the northeastern Jiangxi base area developed into the Fujian-Zhejiang-Jiangxi base area comprising over 20 counties.

Hubei-Henan-Anhui base area: In November 1927, a peasant uprising in northeastern Hubei's Huang'an (today's Hongan) and Macheng broke out. Then a Workers' and Peasants' Revolutionary Army was established and a base area founded. In 1929 the Communist Party launched uprisings in Shangcheng of Henan, and Liuan and Huoshan of Anhui, and organized a Red Army unit, laying the foundation of the southeastern Henan and Western Anhui base areas. In 1930 the troops of the three areas were combined to form the First Corps with Xu Jishen as commander. It took advantage of the Kuomintang warlords' Central Plain War to launch a big attack, expanding the base areas to over 30 counties, linked together as the Hubei-Henan-Anhui base area. In early 1931 the First Corps changed its name to the Fourth Corps, and later developed into the Fourth Front Red Army.

Honghu Lake-Hunan-western Hubei base area: In the winter of 1927 and the spring of 1928, He Long, Zhou Yiqun and Duan Dechang mobilized the peasants in the Honghu Lake area and Sangzhi and Hefeng in Hunan and western Hubei to carry out armed struggle, and organized the Workers' and Peasants' Revolutionary Army. In the spring of 1929, the Hunan and Western Hubei Workers' and Peasants'

Revolutionary Army, led by He Long, was organized into the Fourth Corps and opened the Hunan-western Hubei base area. In the spring of 1930 the guerrillas, led by Duan Dechang, were organized as the Sixth Corps, opening up the Honghu Lake base area. In the summer the two corps joined forces in Gongan. The Fourth Corps changed its name to the Second Corps with the Sixth Corps becoming the Second Red Army, with He Long as commander and Zhou Yiqun (later replaced by Deng Zhongxia) as political commissar. Later the two base areas were linked together as one.

Youjiang base area: In December 1929, Deng Xiaoping and Zhang Yunyi led a part of the Kuomintang's Guangxi garrison forces and local peasant army to launch an uprising in Baise, and established the Seventh Corps and the Youjiang Soviet Government, opening up the Youjiang base area. In February 1930, Li Mingrui led another part of the Guangxi garrison forces in an uprising in Longzhou and set up the Eighth Corps. Soon it was defeated by its enemies and merged into the Seventh Corps. In October the Seventh Corps was ordered to move to the north. Wei Baqun led the people to carry on the struggle in the Youjiang area.

In addition to these major base areas, the Communist Party also set up base areas in Guangdong's Haifeng and Lufeng counties and Hainan Island. After being suppressed by the enemy, the Red Army transferred to the mountain areas to continue armed struggle. By 1930 a dozen large and small rural base areas had been established in many provinces such as Jiangxi, Fujian, Hunan, Hubei, Guangxi, Guangdong, Henan, Anhui, and Zhejiang. The Red Army expanded to a dozen corps, over 70,000 strong, and local armed forces with about 30,000 people and over 60,000 guns.

The widely-opened Soviet area and the expansion of the Red Army indicated that the Chinese revolution had taken the road of a rural, armed, independent regime. From October 1928 to January 1930, Mao Zedong wrote articles such as "Why Is It That Red Political Power Can Exist in China?" "The Struggle in the Jinggang Mountains," "A Single Spark Can Start a Prairie Fire." In these works he expounded theoretically such issues as the possibility and necessity of setting up rural base areas, summarized the experience of the Communist Party in leading the armed uprisings and setting up rural base areas, and analysed the characteristics of Chinese society. He pointed out that China was a large semi-colonial country with an imbalanced economic and political development, and this, plus the divisions inside the counter-revolutionary camp and its various contradictions, made possible the emergence, existence and development of one or more small areas under Red political power. The establishment and expansion of the Red Army and the Red areas were the highest form and the logical outcome of the peasant struggle under the proletarian leadership, as well as the most important factors in promoting a nationwide revolutionary upsurge. The Communist Party must have the idea of "workers' and peasants' armed independent regime," and adopt the policy of setting up base areas, systematically founding political power, deepening agrarian revolution, and gradually expanding people's armed forces. These ideas laid the theoretical foundation for the Chinese revolution to take the road of occupying the villages first and then the cities, and encircling the cities from the villages.

In September 1929 the letter of instructions issued by the Military Commission of the CPC Central Committee to the Fourth Corps and the subsequent Ninth Party Congress of the Fourth Corps, namely the "Gutian Conference," both indicated the direction for building a people's army. The letter of instructions, written at the suggestion of Zhou Enlai, affirmed the "great significance" of the Red Army's struggle and gave comprehensive explanations and profound analysis of the basic tasks of the Red Army and the various erroneous ideas existing inside the Party organization of the Fourth Corps. The letter pointed out that founding of Red Army units in rural areas predating the establishment of political power in cities was characteristic of the Chinese revolution and the outcome of China's economic foundation. The basic tasks of the Red Army were to mobilize the masses to wage struggle, carry out agrarian revolution and set up the Soviet regime; to wage guerrilla warfare, arm the peasants and expand its own organizations; to expand the guerrilla areas and spread their political influence all over the country.

The Ninth Party Congress of the Fourth Corps was convened in December 1929 at Gutian in Shanghang County, Fujian Province. It passed a resolution drawn up by Mao Zedong. Its first part, "On Correcting Mistaken Ideas in the Party," pointed out the manifestations of various non-proletarian ideas in the Communist Party organization in the Fourth Corps, their source and the methods of correcting them and called upon the whole army to rectify them thoroughly. The major erroneous ideas were manifested as follows: taking purely a military viewpoint, ultra-democracy, disregard of organizational discipline, absolute egalitarianism, subjectivism, individualism, ideology of roving rebel bands, remnants of putschism, etc. The main methods of correcting them were to intensify ideological education inside the Party and to strengthen discipline. The letter of instructions and the Gutian Conference resolution were two important documents in the history of building the people's army.

The basic task of the Communist Party and the Soviet government in the rural revolutionary base areas was to lead the peasants to solve the land problem. It was one of the main tasks of the bourgeois democratic revolution in China. The peasants in the base areas waged struggle by burning land deeds and distributing farmland. Several million peasants with little or no land won back their land from landlords. In western Fujian some 600,000 peasants got land in a short period of time in 1929. The agrarian revolution boosted the growth of agricultural production in the base areas and offered a mass foundation for the war of the Red Army. In the practice of struggle, the Communist Party gradually solved the problems of line and policy in the agrarian revolution. The first problem was who should be the target of land confiscation. In the beginning of the agrarian revolution, the Communist Party stipulated the confiscation of the land of only the big and medium landlords, not that of small landlords (owning about three hectares of land each). Later it supported the confiscation of all privately-owned land.

The Sixth CPC National Congress further stipulated the confiscation of the land of only the landlord class. Secondly, it laid down the principle and method of land distribution. Generally, the township was taken as the unit for land distribution, which was to be carried out on a per capita basis, that is, men and women, old and young, should receive an equal amount of land. The original amount of arable land should be taken as the basis and the principle adopted of taking from those who had too much and giving to those who had too little. Thirdly, the congress settled the ownership rights of the land after distribution. In the beginning years, the base areas carried out the principle of public ownerhsip of land (ownership by the Soviet government); the peasants could use the land but were not allowed to sell or buy it. By the spring of 1931 a change was made, that the land after distribution would be owned by the peasants. They also had the right to rent, borrow, sell or buy. Fourthly, the class line was determined, namely, who to rely upon in the agrarian revolution; who to unite with and who to attack. The Sixth Party Congress basically stipulated the correct class line and policy. Reliance should be placed upon the poor peasants and farm labourers, while uniting with the middle peasants, neutralizing the rich peasants and eliminating the landlord class. The policy towards the rich peasants underwent a change in 1929, when the Communist Party, in accordance with the instructions of the Communist International, demanded adoption of the policy of "resolutely opposing the rich peasants." Actually it was a policy of eliminating the rich peasants. It brought a harmful influence to the agrarian revolution.

As the revolutionary forces made headway and the "Left" ideas and sentiment remained after the Party's August 7 conference, the Party Centre was, from June to September 1930, ruled for the second time by the "Left" opportunists represented by Li Lisan. He was then a member of the Standing Committee of the Central Political Bureau and Director of Propaganda, and his line was known historically as the "Lisan line." Li Lisan (1899-1967) said impractically that "the time of an unprecedented big world change and world revolution" was pressing on towards us and the situation of class struggle in China was much more acute than that in Russia before the October Revolution. He maintained that any problem could lead to a revolutionary upsurge. In his opinion, once the workers' struggle in industrial areas was mobilized, a nationwide revolutionary upsurge would take shape, and it would inevitably be followed by an upsurge of world revolution. Li Lisan opposed the viewpoint of "encircling the cities from the rural areas," criticized it many times as an "extremely mistaken viewpoint," and thought that the Party should take the mobilization of urban workers' struggle as "the first important tactic." In accordance with his erroneous estimation of the situation and the "taking the city as the centre" theory, Li Lisan mapped out his adventurist plan of launching a nationwide general uprising and concentrating the Red Army attacks on central cities. He raised the slogan "joining forces in Wuhan and watering the battle steeds by the Yangtze." The implementation of the Lisan line caused to the revolution heavy losses. As a result of attacking central cities, the numbers of the Red Army were reduced by over 30,000 and a number of base areas lost. Because of organizing armed uprisings in central cities, the Communist Party organizations and the revolutionary mass bodies in the White areas suffered great damage. In September 1930, the Sixth Central Committee of the Party held its Third Plenary Session and put a stop to Li Lisan's adventurist plan, ending the reign of the second "Left" opportunist line in the Party Centre.

Three months after the Third Plenary Session of the Sixth Party Central Committee, as a result of the intervention and support of the Communist International, the "Left" opportunists headed by Wang Ming ruled the Party Central Committee after its Fourth Plenary Session held in January 1931. After the Third Plenary Session, Wang Ming (1904-1974) wrote a booklet entitled *Two Lines*, later revised and renamed *Struggle for a More Bolshevik Communist Party of China.* In it, he gave a systematic explanation of his "Left" opportunist theory and viewpoints. Instead of criticizing Li Lisan's "Left" mistakes, he held that the Li Lisan line was a sort of "Right opportunism under the cloak of Leftist' cliché." He criticized Li Lisan's ideas in his recognition of the existence of "the third group" or "the intermediate camp," assuming that the upper stratum of the petty bourgeoisie had turned to the reactionary camp in the post-Wuhan period and that any bourgeois reformist group "formed a wing of the reactionary camp." Just like Li Lisan, he placed the struggle against the bourgeoisie on an equal footing with the anti-imperialist and anti-feudal struggle. He maintained that the reason the present-stage revolution was bourgeois-democratic by nature was because the struggle of the working class against capitalism was lower both in proportion and status, as compared with national emancipation and agrarian revolution. This was giving theoretic explanation to the "Left" deviationist viewpoint on the issue of the character of the revolution. Wang Ming stressed that the nationwide revolutionary upsurge had appeared, so he proposed carrying out an "offensive line" on a nationwide scale. He criticized the Third Plenary Session for having "failed to give the least disclosure of and attack on Li Lisan's consistent Right opportunist line," and demanded the assignment of cadres who "actively uphold and carry out the international line to remould and replenish the Party leading bodies at different levels" and "resolutely implement the two-line struggle in the whole Party ... especially to oppose the most dangerous Right opportunism." Wang Ming's opportunism was more "Leftist" than Li Lisan's line and more complete in form. After the Fourth Plenary Session, Wang Ming and his followers gained control of the leadership of the Party Central Committee for as long as four years. The emergence of Wang Ming's "Left" opportunism had brought danger to the revolution, but its implementation had undergone a process. Therefore, after 1931 the Soviet areas continued to make progress, thanks to the brave struggle of the broad masses of soldiers and people.

The expansion of the Soviet areas was achieved in an environment of hard armed struggle. The birth of the Red Army and the Soviet areas was followed immediately by constant attacks from the Kuomintang reactionaries. After the Central Plain War, Chiang Kai-shek immediately concentrated forces to "encircle and suppress" the Red Army. Backed by the people of the base areas, the Red Army waged "anti-encirclement and suppression" wars. Repeated "encirclement and suppression" campaigns and "anti-encirclement and suppression" campaigns formed the main pattern of China's civil war. From December 1930 to May 1931, the Red Army in the Hubei-Henan-Anhui base area smashed the Kuomintang's first and second "encirclement and suppression" campaigns with the enemy casualties amounting to over 20,000. From late December 1930 to September 1931, the First Front Red Army crushed the three "encirclement and suppression" campaigns launched by Kuomintang troops against the central revolutionary base area, killing and wounding more than

70,000 enemies. These resulted in the linking together of the southern Jiangxi and western Fujian base areas, thus expanding the base areas to over 20 counties with a total population of three million. When the Kuomintang army concentrated its forces to attack the southern Jiangxi and western Fujian areas, the Red Army in the Hubei-Henan-Anhui base area took advantage of this to launch offensives to enlarge the base areas. In November 1931, the Fourth Corps of the Hubei-Henan-Anhui area and the newly founded 25th Corps were merged into the Fourth Front Red Army with Xu Xiangqian as commander and Chen Changhao as political commissar. From that time to May of the following year, the Fourth Front Red Army initiated four battles, wiped out 60,000 enemies, and disrupted the Kuomintang troops' plan for a third "encirclement and suppression" campaign against the Hubei-Henan-Anhui area. The Sujiafu Battle alone wiped out over 30,000 enemies. By now the population of the Hubei-Henan-Anhui base area amounted to 3.5 million. The Honghu Lake base area, which had suffered great losses because of the implementation of the Li Lisan line, had recovered by the spring of 1931. The main force of the Red Army, which had retreated to the Hunan-Hubei border area, returned to the Honghu Lake area in October. From the winter of 1930 to the spring of 1932 the northeastern Jiangxi, Hunan-Jiangxi, Hunan-Hubei-Jiangxi, and Shaanxi-Gansu base areas all launched struggles against the Kuomintang's "encirclement and suppression." Mao Zedong was the chief Communist to lead the Red Army in wars against the Kuomintang's "encirclement and suppression." He developed the simple principle of the Red Army's guerrilla warfare in the Jinggang Mountains period and raised a complete set of scientific principles in strategy and tactics: affirm active defence, oppose passive defence; lure the enemy in deep; concentrate troops to wage mobile wars, wars of quick decision and wars of annihilation. These strategic and tactical principles became a magic weapon of the Red Army for defeating the enemy and constituted an important part of Mao Zedong Thought.

While the workers and peasants led by the Communist Party were taking the road of armed revolution, a number of people were engaged either in anti-Chiang activities or in demanding democracy and reform. They were neither satisfied with the Kuomintang's dictatorship and warlord wars nor in favour of the Communist armed struggle and agrarian revolution, so they formed a third force outside the Kuomintang and the Communist Party. They were mainly national capitalists, the upper stratum of petty bourgeois intellectuals, and reformists from other classes. They formed the following major political parties and factions: the third party, the reorganization group, the human rights group, and the rural development group.

The third party, headed by the noted Kuomintang Left-winger Deng Yanda in the period of national revolution, was formally called "Provisional Operation Committee of the Chinese Kuomintang." It was a revolutionary democratic faction splitting off from the Kuomintang. It advocated carrying out the revolution of the common people, overthrowing the Kuomintang Nanjing government and setting up the political power of the common people, abolishing unequal treaties, implementing land to the tillers, developing state capitalism and then realizing socialism. All these were revolutionary propositions, but they opposed the Party-led workers' and peasants' armed revolution. They regarded such revolution as putchism and rash action, and that the idea of setting up a Soviet regime was merely utopian. Their so-called revolution of the common people would be realized by holding a National Assembly and instigating the mutiny of the Kuomintang army against Chiang Kai-shek. In November 1931 Deng Yanda was secretly murdered by Chiang Kai-shek. The third party thus suffered great setback.

The reorganization group, headed by Wang Jingwei and Chen Gongbo (1890-1946), was formally called the "Society of Comrades for Reorganization of the Chinese Kuomintang." It was an opposition faction, not in office, within the Kuomintang. Their main slogan was to recover the reorganization spirit of the Kuomintang in 1924 and to reestablish an alliance of peasants, workers and petty bourgeoisie. They opposed both Chiang and the Communist Party. Among its members there were a great number of intellectuals and young students who could not find a correct way out. The upper stratum of the group, except a small number of anti-Chiang democrats, were mostly speculative politicians. To seize power from the persons in authority in the Kuomintang was the main objective they sought to attain. In 1929 they actively engaged in anti-Chiang activities, but were suppressed by Chiang. After

1930 only a small number of the upper stratum were left; they speculated politically by attaching themselves to warlords. After the September 18th Incident, the cooperation between Wang Jingwei and Chiang Kai-shek ended the existence of the reorganization group.

The human rights group was headed by Hu Shi and Luo Longji (1898-1965). Their basic stand was to uphold reform and to oppose violent revolution. They demanded the realization of Western bourgeois democratic politics in China and upheld the extinguishing communism and the Communist Party by way of ideological competition. They were dissatisfied with the one-party dictatorship of the Kuomintang, so they raised the slogan of "fighting for human rights." They cherished the illusion that the Kuomintang would open up its regime, so they could join in the government to reform China's politics in accordance with the British and American political system. They failed to realize their hope.

The rural development group was headed by Liang Shuming. Yan Yangchu was one of the chief figures in the group. He had engaged in the education of the common people and the rural development work in the early 1920's. However, the group's composition was very complicated, including capitalists and landlord-class reformists, Kuomintang officials, and progressive scholars and youth keen on national salvation. For a period of time, there were several hundred institutions and organizations engaged in rural development work, in addition to over one thousand experimental centres. Three nationwide seminars on this work were held. Some of these institutions and organizations put stress on common people's education and vocational education; others on social services and disaster relief; still others on agricultural technical amelioration and popularization of agricultural cooperation, on village self-defence and autonomy, or on creation of "new-type social organization." Representative bodies were: the Shandong Rural Development Academy led by Liang Shuming, the China Society for Promotion of Common People's Education led by Yan Yangchu, the Jiangsu Provincial Education Academy led by Gao Jiansi, etc. The rural development group aimed at saving the bankrupt countryside and taking China onto the road of national self-salvation through the above-mentioned activities. They would not do anything to challenge the Kuomintang reactionary rule; some of them clearly expressed their opposition to revolution, class struggle and the Communist Party. The rural reformist movement launched by the rural development group had a certain impact upon Chinese society. Some of the organizations had done useful work in popularizing rural education and agricultural technical amelioration, but this movement could not save China, just like the others.

There existed a Trotskyite faction among the political forces in China at that time. It was directly guided by Trotsky himself. Its official name was "The Left Opposition of the Chinese Communist Party," or the "Lenin Faction of Chinese Bolsheviks." The faction first appeared among Chinese students in Moscow. After these students returned to China, they urged some old Right opportunists to take the Trotskyite road. In May 1931, several small Trotskyite groups jointly organized into a central leading organ with Chen Duxiu as the general secretary. Although China's Trotskyites opposed Kuomintang rule, they were also sharply antagonistic to the CPC Centre. They considered that since the bourgeoisie gained victory in the 1925-1927 revolution, the feudal forces had become "remnants of remnants," that China had become a capitalist society and bourgeois democratic revolution had already been completed. The central task at present, they said, was to struggle for the convention of a "National Assembly," and the socialist revolution should be carried out after capitalism had further developed. Some of them cursed the Red Army and opposed the armed struggle led by the Communist Party. The Trotskyite centre after unification was rapidly disrupted by the Kuomintang. China's Trotskite faction remained, from start to finish, a small group with few members, full of contradictions.

7. The September 18th Incident and the Upsurge of the Nationwide Anti-Japanese Democratic Movement. The Kuomintang Policy of "Internal Pacification Before Resistance to Foreign Invasion"

The September 18th Incident broke out at a time when Chiang Kai-shek was employing every military and political means to strengthen his own rule in China, the Chinese revolution was making rapid headway on the tortuous road and the intermediate political factions were making new political explorations. It changed to a great extent China's political situation and concrete historical process.

On the night of September 18, 1931, the Japanese troops dynamited a section of the South Manchuria Railway in Shenyang's northern suburb and falsely accused Chinese troops of the act. On this pretext the Japanese troops suddenly attacked Beidaying, where the Chinese Northeast Army was stationed, and Shenyang. The army withdrew without fighting while the major officers and officials quickly took refuge in other places, thus making it possible for the Japanese troops to occupy such important cities as Shenyang, Changchun, Yingkou, Liaoyang, Anshan, Benxi, Fushun, Siping and Andong (today's Dandong) on the second day. The Japanese troops stationed in Korea also crossed the border to intrude on China's northeast provinces. By the end of September the Japanese troops occupied Liaoning (excluding Liaoxi) and Jilin provinces, and in November took the larger part of Heilongjiang Province. In January 1932, the Japanese troops attacked Jinzhou and seized the Liaoxi areas and on February 5, occupied Harbin. The three northeast provinces thus fell into the enemy's hands in less than five months. In March 1932 the puppet state of "Manchukuo" was set up under the Japanese imperialists' direction. Pu Yi became its "chief executive." Pu Yi (1906-1967) was the banished Qing Dynasty emperor Xuan Tong, of Manchu ethnic group, whose surname was Aisin-Gioro. In September Japan officially proclaimed its recognition of the state of "Manchukuo" and a protocol of alliance was signed between Japan and "Manchukuo." "Manchukuo" was a puppet state entirely under the control of the Japanese Kwantung Army. In March 1934 it changed its name to the "Manchu Empire" under the Japanese imperialists' direction, and Pu Yi was called emperor in place of the "chief executive," The commanding officer of the Kwantung Army, as the representative of the Japanese Mikado (emperor), acted as Pu Yi's "instructor" and "guardian" and concurrently as the Japanese ambassador plenipotentiary to "Manchukuo." He was actually the overlord who held sway in northeast China. The Japanese imperialists ruthlessly carried out military occupation and colonial rule through the puppet power.

After the September 18th Incident, the Japanese imperialists turned northeast China into a colony under Japan's exclusive control, then began the second step of colonizing all of China under its sole domination, thus changing the Versailles-Washington world pattern formed after World War I and deepening the tension in China between the United States and Britain on the one side, and Japan on the other. Thereafter a great change took place in China's internal political situation and class relations. The threat from Japan became the most important issue so anti-Japanese aggression became the common demand of the whole Chinese people. A partial anti-Japanese war waged by the Chinese people began.

The Kuomintang government adopted a non-resistance policy towards Japanese imperialist aggression. Chiang Kai-shek asked the whole nation to "submit temporarily to oppression and await the judgement of acknowledged international justice." The Kuomintang government many times accused the Japanese troops of aggression in Chinese territory before the League of Nations and asked it to uphold justice, in the hope of compelling Japan to withdraw its troops from the northeast. The League of Nations, however, was then recognized as powerless to impose sanctions against Japan. Disillusioned, Chiang attempted to make direct negotiations with Japan, but to no avail as there was opposition from many sides.

The people throughout China were indignant at the Japanese imperialists' armed aggression and the Kuomintang's non-resistance, and all demanded resistance. A nationwide wave of feeling against Japanese aggression, unprecedented in scale, was thus launched. The Chinese Communist Party, the Soviet government and the Workers' and Peasants' Red Army issued many statements and made decisions calling upon the Red Army and the oppressed masses "to wage a national revolutionary war to drive the Japanese imperialists out of China." Open telegrams were issued from all over China to protest against the Japanese imperialists' atrocities and to demand resistance to the Japanese aggressors. In large and medium cities, meetings, demonstrations and petitions were held, unprecedented both in popularity and scale. Workers in Shanghai and Beiping held strikes one after another. Students played a vanguard role in the anti-Japanese movement. They held assemblies and parades, issued open telegrams, produced propaganda, set up anti-Japanese organizations and organized anti-Japanese volunteers, and demanded that the Kuomintang government stop the civil war, arm the civilians and send soldiers to fight the Japanese aggressors. Students in Shanghai, Beiping, Jinan, Wuhan and Guangzhou sent delegates or went in groups to Nanjing to present petitions. On September 28 the petitioning students in Nanjing and Shanghai beat the foreign minister, Wang Zhengting, and smashed Wang's office. In late November students in Nanjing and other places launched the "send Chiang to the north to resist the Japanese aggressors" movement. Early in December as the petitioning students to Nanjing kept increasing, the Kuomintang authorities formally ordered the prohibition of student groups coming to Nanjing to petition. On December 17, over 30,000 students went to demonstrate and petition around the offices of the Kuomintang central headquarters and the National Government in Nanjing. The Kuomintang troops and armed policemen suppressed them near the Zhenzhu Bridge, killing over 30, wounding over 100, and arresting another 100. The Zhenzhu Bridge massacre sparked off protester in many places. Students, workers and other people in Shanghai, carrying the coffins of the student victims, held a 100,000-person demonstration. Patriotic industrialists and merchants in many cities launched a campaign to boycott Japanese goods and demanded that economic relations with Japan suspended. Public figures and newspapers representing the national bourgeoisie made speeches and carried commentaries demanding for an immediate end to civil and union against the Japanese imperialists, criticizing the Kuomintang government's non-resistance and internal policy, and calling for reorganization of the government and for a government of national defence. Splits and vacillation also occurred inside the Kuomintang and among its troops. In November when the Japanese troops attacked Heilongjiang Province, Ma Zhanshan, acting governor of Heilongjiang and the commander-in-chief of the province's garrison, led his troops in resistance at the Nenjiang Bridge. Donations were sent from all sections of society in support of Ma in the resistance war. In December the 26th Route Army, over 17,000 strong, which had been sent by Chiang to Jiangxi to attack the Red Army, revolted in Ningdu under the leadership of Zhao Bosheng and Dong Zhentang, and went over to the Red Army. To sum up, from the September 18th Incident, a resistance upsurge against Japanese invaders appeared among the workers, peasants, students and urban petty bourgeoisie. The national bourgeoisie also took an active attitude towards resistance against Japan. Even some of the Kuomintang members and troops, in defiance of the Kuomintang Centre's order, rose in resistance. The patriotic anti-Japanese movement became an irresistible historical trend.

The September 18th Incident brought about a strong international response. The peace-loving and justice-upholding people around the globe unanimously condemned the Japanese imperialists' aggressive conduct. The governments of the Soviet Union, the United States and Britain reacted differently with their varying standpoints. The Soviet government sympathized with and supported China morally, but it adopted a "neutral" attitude of non-interference in its foreign policy. The American government adopted a wait-and-see attitude at the beginning and only after the Japanese troops had occupied Jinzhou did the U.S. Secretary of State Henry Lewis Stimson deliver notes of "nonrecognition" to the Chinese and Japanese governments, declaring that the United States would not recognize the changed status quo in China's northeast. Taking a wavering attitude, the British government did nothing practical. This was manifested through activities in the League of Nations. Although the League of Nations made a decision asking Japan to withdraw its troops within the set time, Japan simply ignored the demand. The League did nothing about it. Later it appointed an investigation group. It was formally set up in January 1932 with British representative V. L. George Robert Lytton as its head. After over six months' "investigation," in October it published a "documented report of the group." This document recognized some basic facts such as "the three northeast provinces being part of China," made certain disclosures of the Japanese imperialists' aggressive actions, and pointed out that their military action in the "September 18th Incident" could not be regarded as "legal self-defence methods" and "Manchukuo" was a puppet state rigged up entirely by Japan. However, the document excused the aggressors in many respects and proposed placing northeast China under "international control," which would have infringed upon China's sovereignty. In February 1933 the League of Nations Assembly passed a resolution which basically accepted the opinions and suggestions of Lytton's investigative report. It declared that no factual and legal recognition would be given to "Manchukuo," but this was only a scrap of paper.

In May 1931, after Chiang Kai-shek had held the "National Assembly," the anti-Chiang faction members such as Wang Jingwei, Sun Ke, Chen Jitang and Li Zongren set up the Kuomintang Central Executive and Supervisory Committee Conference and the National Government in Guangzhou in armed confrontation with Chiang's Nanjing government. After the September 18th Incident both the Nanjing and Guangzhou governments took a conciliatory attitude. The Nanjing side asked its opponent to cancel the "Guangzhou national government," "unite and take concerted action immediately to cope with national calamity," while the Guangzhou side asked Chiang to leave office and organize a "united national government," to "stop internal contention and resist foreign aggression." Actually what they did was scramble for power under the pretense of "united action against national calamity." After some contention, a "peace and unity conference" was held in Shanghai, attended by delegates of both sides, in late October. Both sides cast "united resistance against Japan" to the wind. Their talk centred around the distribution of party, political and military power.

The Guangzhou delegates put forward "a reform programme of the central political system," which aimed at destroying the dictatorship system set up by Chiang Kai-shek and seizing central power. The Nanjing delegates insisted that the party's rule and the constitution could not be changed. What this really meant was that they were refusing to abandon control of central power. As both sides attacked each other, the conference came to a deadlock. Later they reached an agreement after the mediation of many people. They decided the Kuomintang Fourth National Congress would be held by both sides at their locales to choose their own Central Committee members, and then the Fourth Plenary Session of the Fourth Central Committee would be held in Nanjing to deal with the proposals raised by both sides and also with the issue of reorganizing the government. The Nanjing Kuomintang Fourth National Congress was held on November 12, at which Chiang Kai-shek talked loudly about strengthening "internal unity" so as to "resist foreign aggression," but proposed no concrete measures of resisting foreign aggressors. What he wanted was to hold fast to central power. The Guangzhou Kuomintang Fourth National Congress was held on November 18. Because of the scramble for power between the anti-Chiang cliques, no compromise was reached. The Guangzhou congress members were split into the Hu Hanmin clique of Guangzhou and the Wang Jingwei clique of Shanghai. Hu Hanmin (1879-1936) claimed the congress' aims were to sincerely unite against foreign aggression, "overthrow dictatorship and implement democratic politics." His intention was to force Chiang Kai-shek to leave office and reorganize the Nanjing government. After the congress, the party central headquarters of the Hu clique was formally set up in Guangzhou. In such a situation Chiang Kai-shek considered that it would be disadvantageous to him to hold out tenaciously; so he decided to make concessions in order to gain advantage. He handed in his resignation as the president of the Kuomintang National Government and the head of the Executive Yuan on December 15.

After Chiang's resignation, Lin Sen (1867-1943) was appointed president of the National Government and Sun Ke (1891-1973) head of the Executive Yuan by the First Plenary Session of the Fourth Kuomintang Central Committee. The Nanjing and Guangzhou sides thus organized a "united government." Actually Chiang, Wang and Hu did not cooperate, but they all manipulated the political situation behind the scenes. Sun Ke, without real power, could do nothing. In January 1932 the Japanese troops occupied Jinzhou without much effort. This aroused a nationwide denunciation of Sun Ke's government. The Kuomintang government kept up the policy of nonresistance and no negotiations. Making use of the situation, Chiang's close followers in the Kuomintang raised a cry for Chiang's resumption of office. Chiang made a speech at Fenghua's Wuling School on the "Northeast Problem and the Policy Towards Japan" on January 11,

1932. He tried hard to explain the nonresistance of the Kuomintang government and attacked the patriotic anti-Japanese movement. He asked the citizens to obey the government in everything. He opposed declaring war on and breaking off relations with Japan. His policy towards Japan was to continue relations, avoid a declaration of war and refuse to conclude and sign any treaty ceding territory and surrendering China's sovereign rights. At that time collaboration between Chiang Kai-shek and Wang Jingwei was brewing. After delivering his speech, Chiang went to Hangzhou to meet with Wang and the two reached an agreement on the division of power, whereby Wang was to take charge of domestic and foreign affairs and Chiang military affairs. The Chiang and Wang cliques thus jointly held the power of the Kuomintang central government and pushed the Hu Hanmin clique out of the government.

On the night of January 28, 1932, the Japanese troops launched an attack on Shanghai. The 19th Route Army stationed in Shanghai, influenced by the anti-Japanese enthusiasm of the patriotic Chinese people, started resisting the Japanese invasion under the leadership of its commanding generals Cai Tingkai (1892-1968) and Jiang Guangnai (1887-1967). After the January 28 Incident, the people of all circles in Shanghai launched a big movement to support the 19th Route Army's anti-Japanese fighting. In mid-February 1932, Zhang Zhizhong led the Fifth Corps with Chiang's agreement to participate in the fighting. Thanks to the 19th Route Army and the Fifth Corps' heroic resistance and the active participation of the broad masses, Shanghai held off the aggressors for over one month, killing and wounding over 10,000 Japanese troops. The Japanese army was forced to change its commanding general three times, but was still unable to make any headway. However, after the 19th Routh Army suffered heavy casualties and was badly in need of support and help, Chiang Kai-shek refused to send reinforcements, and his Ministry of Military and Political Affairs even pocketed a portion of the soldiers' pay and held up the people's donations. The Japanese aggressors organized additional troops in Shanghai, launched a general attack and landed at Liuhe. Outflanked, the 19th Route Army was forced to withdraw from the city. On March 14, through the British envoy

Lampson's mediation, both the Kuomintang and Japanese troops stopped military actions and engaged in armistice negotiations. On May 5, an armistice agreement of national betrayal and humiliation was signed.

After that, Chiang Kai-shek formally affirmed the reactionary policy of "internal pacification before resistance to foreign invasion" as his basic norms of handling internal and foreign affairs. This policy was aimed actually at "pacification," rather than "resistance." Under the reactionary state policy, the anti-Japanese democratic movement upsurge after the September 18th Incident was suppressed. In the meantime the country's territory and sovereign rights were continuously encroached upon by the Japanese imperialists. China's national disaster deepened day by day.

On New Year's Day of 1933 when the Japanese troops launched an attack on Shanhaiguan Pass, the Chinese army stationed there rose in counter-attack, thus raising the curtain on resistance on the Great Wall. On January 3, Shanhaiguan Pass fell into the Japanese hands. Then the Japanese invaders attacked Rehe in three columns. The Rehe provincial governor, Tang Yulin, and 200,000 soldiers fled without fighting. The Japanese vanguard, 128 strong, occupied Chengde, the provincial capital, on March 4. This caused a nationwide denunciation of Zhang Xueliang and demand for the punishment of Tang Yulin. Chiang Kai-shek decided to have Zhang Xueliang resign and appointed He Yingqin to replace him and act concurrently as chairman of the Beiping branch of the Military Commission.

After the Japanese aggressors occupied Shanhaiguan Pass and Rehe, they launched attacks on the militarily important location of Xifengkuo, Lengkou and Gubeikou along the Great Wall. The Kuomintang Northwest Army led by Song Zheyuan, the Shanxi Army led by Shang Zhen, the Northeast Army led by Wang Yizhe and the Central Army reinforcements led by Guan Linzheng, all heroically resisted the offensive of the Japanese troops. The Great Wall resistance battle dealt the arrogant Japanese aggressors a heavy blow. When the Japanese invaders suffered setbacks at the important passes on the Great Wall, they pushed forward through Shanhaiguan Pass towards the east of the Luanhe River. The Kuomintang troops at these passes withdrew one by one after being attacked front and rear. While the Japanese troops were penetrating to the east of the Luanhe River, the British government began to worry that this action would endanger British interests and rights in this area. It then lodged a serious protest to the Japanese government. Afraid of incurring international disputes, the Japanese government ordered the withdrawal of the Japanese troops from east Luanhe River back to the Great Wall line in mid-April. It adopted a method of instigating rebellion internally through buying over agents in an attempt to create a second "Manchukuo" in north China. Early in May, seeing that their instigation could not come to effect quickly, the Japanese troops launched another offensive to the east of the Luanhe River and forged across the river to make a surprise attack on the river's west. Over 20 counties of eastern Hebei Province were occupied by the invaders, placing Beiping and Tianjin in imminent danger. At this critical juncture, on May 3, 1933, the national government published an order to establish the Beiping Government Affairs Rearrangement Committee of the Executive Yuan and appointed Huang Fu as its chairman. Huang was then sent to north China to negotiate with Japan about armistice issues. Huang held secret negotiations with the Japanese in Beiping and reached an agreement in principle. On May 31, 1933, He Yingqin, acting chairman of the Beiping branch of the Military Commission of the national government, with the agreement of Chiang Kai-shek and Wang Jingwei, sent Xiong Bin to sign the Tanggu Agreement with the Japanese army's delegate, Yasuji Okamura. This agreement virtually acquiesced in the "lawfulness" of the Japanese occupation of the three northeastern provinces and Rehe, and recognized eastern Hebei as a "demilitarized zone."

Although the anti-Japanese democratic movement of the Chinese people had met with ruthless suppression by the Kuomintang government, it continued to grow in momentum in face of the deepening aggression of the Japanese imperialists and the sharpening national crisis consequent upon Chiang's policy of "internal pacification before resistance to foreign invasion." The public opinions centred on condemning the Kuomintang government and Chiang's nonresistance policy, and called upon the Kuomintang to change its "suppress the

Communists" policy, stop civil war and unite against foreign aggression. Newspapers and magazines such as *Shen Bao* (*Shanghai Daily*), *Da Gong Bao* (*Impartial Daily*), *Xin Wen Bao* (*News Daily*), and *Dongfang* (*The East*) carried commentaries, criticizing the Kuomintang's domestic and foreign policies, urging the Kuomintang government to "change its attitude" and castigating Chiang Kai-shek and his followers. These commentaries expressed the discontent of the people of the whole country, who were more and more dissatisfied with the Kuomintang's rule and its policy. The progressive intellectuals, agitated by the national crisis, demanded an anti-Japanese policy, as well as democracy and unity.

In December 1932 the China League for Defence of Civil Rights was formally established, with Soong Ching Ling (1893-1981) as president and Cai Yuanpei (1868-1940) as vice-president. The aims of the league were to save all patriotic revolutionary "political prisoners," and fight for freedom of speech, the press, assembly and association.

In the spring of 1933 the Japanese troops extended their aggression to south of the Great Wall threatening north China. Open telegrams from people's organizations in various provinces and municipalities were sent to Feng Yuxiang, asking him to put up resistance against Japan. With the encouragement and help of the Chinese Communist Party, Feng Yuxiang organized the Qahar People's Anti-Japanese Allied Army in Zhangjiakou on May 26, with himself as the commander-in-chief. The First Congress of the Anti-Japanese Allied Army was held in Zhangjiakou in June. It passed a resolution on the programme of the People's Anti-Japanese Allied Army. After the congress the army was divided into three columns to fight the approaching enemy. They recaptured Dolon Nor in July, and drove the Japanese and puppet troops out of Qahar. Chiang Kai-shek used every means to attack the allied army. The allied army, under the converging attack of the Japanese invaders and Chiang's troops, was in a difficult position. When the Japanese troops reoccupied Dolon Nor in August, Feng Yuxiang was compelled to abolish the general headquarters of the Allied Army and left the army. Subsequently Ji Hongchang and Fang Zhenwu declared by open telegram that the name of the Anti-Japanese

Allied Army was now changed to Quell-the-Aggressors Army. The army continued its resistance against Japan in Rehe and around the Great Wall. However it suffered defeat due to the joint attacks of the Chiang and Japanese troops in September.

In November 1933, the Kuomintang 19th Route Army under the command of Cai Tingkai, Chen Mingshu (1889-1965) and Jiang Guangnai, and part of the Kuomintang anti-Chiang forces headed by Li Jishen launched the "Fujian Incident." They held the Chinese People's Interim Congress in Fuzhou, published "The Manifesto of People's Rights," and established the People's Revolutionary Government. They advocated eliminating the imperialist forces in China, abolishing unequal treaties, overthrowing the counter-revolutionary, traitorous government, getting rid of all feudal forces, distributing farmland on a per capita basis, developing national capital, improving the livelihood of the workers and peasants, ensuring that the working people enjoy absolute freedom and equality, etc. These reflected the political and economic demands of the middle stratum. The Chinese Soviet Provisional Central Government and the Workers' and Peasants' Red Army concluded an agreement with the Fujian People's Government for resistance to Japanese aggression and struggle against Chiang Kai-shek. The establishment of the Fujian People's Government marked the breaking-up of the Kuomintang camp. Chiang made every effort to eliminate the Fujian People's Government. By the end of 1933, Chiang made himself commander-in-chief of the "Suppress-the-Bandit Army" and mustered large numbers of troops to attack Fujian. Meanwhile he sent people to sneak into Fujian and buy the officers of the 19th Route Army with money and official posts. The Japanese, British and American naval vessels and gunboats, under the pretext of protecting their nationals in Fujian, coordinated with Chiang's troops to threaten the Fujian People's Government. In January the following year, due to the fierce assault and siege of Chiang's troops and some officers within its own ranks crossing over to Chiang's side, the Fujian People's Government collapsed. The CPC Central Committee under the rule of the "Left" opportunist line failed to give adequate support to the Fujian People's Government.

On April 20, 1934, the "Basic Programme of the Chinese People's War Against Japan" proposed by the Chinese Communist Party and signed by 1,779 people including Soong Ching Ling, He Xiangning and Li Du was published. It called on the Chinese people to rise and arm themselves to drive the Japanese imperialists out of China, and to set up a general leading body of the nation's armed resistance against Japan. In May the General Committee of the Chinese Nation for Armed Self-Defence was set up in Shanghai. This programme, though expressing the just demand of the Chinese people for resistance against Japan and for national salvation, could never be realized under the Kuomintang reactionary rule.

8. Fascist Rule of the Kuomintang Government. The Deepening and Expansion of the Soviet Revolution and the Long March of the Red Army

After the September 18th and January 28th incidents, while pursuing a policy of compromise with Japan, Chiang Kai-shek used every means to strengthen his reactionary state apparatus, tighten the rule over the people and the suppression of the anti-Japanese democratic movement, and consolidate his autocratic rule and the KMT one-party dictatorship.

In January 1932, the KMT government decided to re-establish the Military Commission with Chiang Kai-shek as its chairman. In June, the Military Commission issued an order to organize the KMT troops into 48 corps to found a massive Central Army. At the same time, the local armed forces—Peace Preservation Corps of all provinces—were unified and augmented. All these armies served as a major prop for the KMT regime.

Within the KMT party and government Chiang Kai-shek set up huge spy organizations. As far back as the end of 1927, instructed by Chiang, Chen Guofu (1892-1951) had formed the "Central Club," the origin of the so-called CC clique. During the Third National Congress of the KMT in 1929, Chen Lifu was appointed secretary-general of the KMT Central Executive Committee. The influence of the two Chens therefore gradually spread into the organizational sections and grassroots units under the KMT party departments of various cities and provinces. There was a saying, "The state belongs to the Chiang family and the party to the Chens." Early in 1933, the KMT Faithful Comrades Association came into being with the two Chens at the centre and Chiang Kai-shek as its president. Under the KMT Central Organization Department, which was controlled by Chen Guofu, there was an organ called "Party Affairs Investigation Section" (later, expanded and named "Party Affairs Investigation Department"), which was actually a spy organization. This was the predecessor of the KMT Central Investigation and Statistics Bureau (CISB). In March 1932, Chiang Kai-shek instructed He Zhonghan, Dai Li, Kang Ze and others to set up the Zhong Hua Fu Xing She (China Rejuvenation Society, or CRS for short), in the name of "national revival," with Chiang as its president. Soon afterwards, an inner and more secret organization called Li Xing She (Earnest Practice Society) was founded within it, and its peripheral organizations were also formed. Initially CRS mainly operated in the KMT military system, then it extended to other fields. CRS included a Secret Service Department (headed by Dai Li) and a Special Detachment (headed by Kang Ze). Later this spy system came under the command of the Military Commission, and was called "Investigation and Statistics Bureau of the Military Commission" (ISBMC). With the secret organizations extended into military, political, economic and cultural systems, China was thrown into a rule of spy terror. On July 17, 1932, the Conference of the Shanghai Anti-Imperialist League was destroyed by special agents and over 80 people were arrested. On April 23, 1933, when a public funeral for Li Dazhao, who had been executed by the warlord government, was held by Beiping's educational circles, the reactionary army, police and special agents rushed to suppress it on the spot. People arrested and killed that day and afterwards numbered over 400. On June 18, Yang Xingfu (1893-1933), chief secretary of both the Central Academy and the China League for Defence of Civil Rights, was assassinated in Shanghai by KMT special agents. Soong Ching Ling, Lu Xun and Cai Yuanpei were all given warning of assassination. On November 13, 1934, Shi Liangcai (1878-1934), general manager of the *Shanghai Daily*, was murdered on the highway from Shanghai to Hangzhou. In addition, the KMT special agents infiltrated through various channels into the Communist Party and other revolutionary or progressive organizations, and even into the Communist-led revolutionary bases.

To strengthen its rule over the people, the KMT government set up the *Bao-Jia* system in the areas around the revolutionary bases from August 1932. In 1934, this system was further practised all over the country. The *Bao-Jia* system stipulated that each county should be divided into a number of districts which should establish this kind of organization within a definite time, that this system be organized on a household basis; each *Jia* being made up of 10 households, and each *Bao* of 10 *Jia*; and each *Jia* or *Bao* must have a head. Households should keep watch on the movements of one another, and report offences if they took place. Punishment would go to those related to somebody regarded as an offender. *Bao* and *Jia* heads were usually landlords or members of the gentry. Corvée, such as building fortifications, was organized through this system. Thus a tight network of reactionary rule was formed from the central government down to the localities.

Apart from strengthening its military, political and spy forces, the KMT used all means of reactionary propaganda in the fields of culture and ideology. Chiang Kai-shek gave enormous publicity to China's inherent feudal ethics such as the "Four Social Bonds" (manners, justice, integrity and honour) and the "Eight Virtues" (loyalty, filial piety, benevolence, love, faith, righteousness, harmony and peace), as well as the philosophy of "attaining intuitive knowledge" advocated by Wang Yangming (1472-1528). At the same time, he stealthily peddled fascism from abroad. When propagating fascist "activism," he said, "In the universe since ancient times, only by action can everything be created." The integration of both led to the formation of China's reactionary ideology which was called "philosophy of earnest practice" or "philosophy of honesty." Chen Lifu followed it up with the publication of his book *Vitalism*, which preached idealism and fascist anti-rationalism. The KMT newspapers and publications at that time raised a hue and cry about "carrying out the KMT's fascistization" and "only blook-and-iron fascism can save China," etc. In July 1933, Chiang Kai-shek conducted the Officers' Training Corps at Mt. Lushan in

Jiangxi Province. He appointed himself head of the corps and gave his high-ranking officers "spiritual training," imbuing them with his reactionary ideas and the policy of "internal pacification before resistance to foreign invasion." In August, he set up an institute especially for training high-ranking party and government officials. Later on, the Lushan Training Corps was expanded for training party, government, military and educational personnel. In August 1935, the "Emei Military Training Corps" was formed.

In February 1934, Chiang Kai-shek started the "New Life Movement" in Nanchang, the base of launching his "encirclement and suppression" campaign against the Communists. According to Chiang, the New Life Movement was a movement to bring the whole life (clothing, eating, housing and travelling) of the entire people up to the standards of the nation's traditional virtues—manners, justice, integrity and honour. This movement was aimed at "organizing the life of the people along military, productive and artistic lines," and at carrying out "social transformation and national rejuvenation." However, this was only for the sake of appearances. Chiang's real intention was to control public feeling with feudal ethics so as to shackle people's words and deeds, and make them submissively endure the KMT's feudal, comprador and fascist dictatorship. With the promulgation of the "Outline of the New Life Movement" and the "Points for Attention in the New Life Movement" the Association for Promotion of the New Life Movement came into being. Headed by Chiang Kai-shek, it enforced the movement throughout the country. By 1936, counties under the KMT rule with branches of the association numbered 1,355.

To propagate feudal-comprador ideas and fascism, the KMT initiated a "Cultural Construction Movement" in 1934, and founded the Chinese Cultural Construction Association with Chen Lifu as its director-general. The association published a magazine entitled *Cultural Construction*, advertising the so-called China-oriented cultural construction, which meant a "new culture" based on China's traditional feudal culture mixed with that from the West. In January 1935, Tao Xisheng and nine other professors jointly issued a "Manifesto on China-oriented Cultural Construction." A great number of articles on this topic appeared in newspapers and journals, which were later compiled and published as a special collection.

As stated above, after the September 18th Incident, the threat from Japan had become the main problem for China, and had brought about tremendous changes in China's situation. As a decisive factor in China's political situation, the Chinese Communist Party and the revolutionary forces under its leadership were also experiencing great changes.

In late September 1931, the CPC Provisional Central Political Bureau was formed with Bo Gu (also known as Qin Bangxian, 1907-1946) as its head. The Provisional Central Political Bureau advocated resolutely resisting Japanese imperialist aggression, strongly attacked the nonresistance policy of the KMT government, called on the whole Party to integrate themselves with the lower stratum of the petty bourgeoisie to form a united front against Japan and Chiang Kai-shek, and mobilized and led the masses to wage armed struggle against Japanese aggression and the Kuomintang reactionary regime. However, the line and policies adopted by the Party Central Committee in this period were mainly wrong. This line held that the September 18th Incident would "touch off a world war, especially an anti-USSR war," and that "opposition to the USSR has become the fundamental and immediate danger." So it raised the call to "defend the USSR with armed force," which was completely divorced from the people's desire to resist Japanese invasion. It over-emphasized the unity of imperialist powers in suppressing the Chinese revolution after the September 18th Incident, so it maintained that it was necessary to oppose "all kinds of imperialism" when struggling against Japan. It only emphasized that Japan's aim was to suppress the Chinese revolution, and ignored the national crisis and the danger of national extinction consequent upon Japan's aggression. It only noticed the KMT government's moves of compromise and capitulation, but completely denied the contradictions between the Japanese invaders and the Chinese authorities. So it time and again stressed that while opposing Japanese imperialism, the struggle to overthrow the KMT's rule must be carried out, and that "overthrowing the KMT government is a precondition for successfully waging the national revolutionary war." It regarded the KMT as a monolithic bloc and all the anti-Chiang factions within the KMT as "reactionary factions not in office," and wanted to put them all down. It failed to see the change of the political attitude of the national bourgeoisie since the September 18th Incident and refused the slogan of a "National Defence Government." It denied the existence of the moderate camp and the middle classes' demand for democracy and resistance against Japan, and even concluded that the moderates were "the most dangerous enemies," who ... "should be struck at with the main force." Consequently, it not only failed to give correct guidance to the movement for resistance and democracy at that period, but also made itself extremely isolated.

In addition, the Left-deviationist Party Centre refused to carry out necessary retreats from the cities where enemy forces were strong or take any defensive action in those places, and refused to make use of every available legal condition. It adopted a form of attack which was totally unsuited to the situation at that time, set up huge Party organs without mass cover and Red mass organizations which were divorced from the people. It frequently called for or organized political strikes, league strikes, students' strikes, shopkeepers' strikes, demonstrations, etc. All of these brought great losses to the work in White areas. But, because Wang Ming's "Left" adventurist policy had not yet been put into practice in the Soviet areas at that time, the workers' and peasants' revolution there continued to deepen and expand.

In November 1931, the First National Congress of the Chinese Soviet was convened in Ruijin of Jiangxi Province. The congress proclaimed the Provisional Central Government of the Chinese Soviet Republic and adopted an "Outline of the Constitution of the Chinese Soviet Republic." The Outline stipulated: "The state founded by the Chinese Soviet power is a state of the workers' and peasants' democratic dictatorship." The congress approved a series of important documents such as a labour law, land law, and economic policies. These documents had been discussed and jointly drafted by the CPC Central Political Bureau and the Far East Bureau of the Communist International after the Fourth Plenary Session of the Sixth Party Central Committee before they were submitted to the congress. Many of the policies formulated in them were erroneous "Left" ones. The congress elected Mao Zedong and others members of the Central Executive Committee. The Central Executive Committee elected Mao Zedong chairman of the Provisional Central Government of the Chinese Soviet Republic, and Xiang Ying and Zhang Guotao vice-chairmen. At the same time, the Military Commission of the Chinese Soviet Republic was formed with Zhu De as chairman and Wang Jiaxiang and Peng Dehuai as vice-chairmen. The founding of the Provisional Central Government of the Chinese Soviet Republic marked the existence in China of two political powers which were completely different in nature. The Chinese Soviet Republic was of the broad exploited and oppressed masses of workers and peasants.

The birth of the Chinese Soviet Republic aroused the deepest hostility of the KMT reactionaries. After putting down the movement for resistance and democracy, Chiang Kai-shek convened a conference to "suppress the bandits", held on Mt. Lushan of Jiangxi Province in June 1932, attended by the leading personnel concerned from the five provinces of Henan, Hubei, Anhui, Hunan and Jiangxi. This conference decided the principle for attacking the Red Army—"paying equal attention to military and political affairs," and the policy to be put into practice—"30 percent military force and 70 percent political work." Late that month, the "General Headquarters for Suppressing Bandits" was set up in Wuhan, with Chiang Kai-shek himself as commander-in-chief. He now mustered 630,000 troops for the fourth "encirclement and suppression" campaign against the Soviet areas. The KMT main force first attacked the Hubei-Henan-Anhui and Hunan-Western Hubei Soviet areas. Due to wrong guidance by Zhang Guotao, secretary of the Hubei-Henan-Anhui sub-bureau of the CPC Central Committee and chairman of its Military Commission, the main force of the Red Army was obliged to retreat from the Hubei-Henan-Anhui Soviet area and move to southern Shaanxi and northern Sichuan. Soon afterwards they opened up the Sichuan-Shaanxi Soviet area. In the Hunan-Western Hubei Soviet area, because Xia Xi, secretary of the Hunan-Western Hubei sub-bureau of the CPC Central Committee, faithfully carried out the "Left" adventurist policy of the Provisional Central Committee, the Red Army lost the chance to defeat the enemy's "encirclement and suppression" campaign and was forced to give up the Soviet area and move to the Hunan-Hubei-Sichuan-Guizhou border.

After his success in the "encirclement and suppression" campaigns, Chiang Kai-shek concentrated his main force—about 400,000 troops—early in 1933 and launched the fourth "encirclement and suppression" campaign against the central Soviet area. When the enemy started an all-out offensive, Mao Zedong was no longer in the leading position in the Red Army. At the time, Zhou Enlia, and Zhu De, respectively general political commissar and commander-in-chief of both the Red Army and its First Front Army, and others who were responsible for directing the campaign against the "encirclement and suppression," adhered to the correct operational principles. By adopting ambush tactics by large formations and concentrating superior forces, they won two battles in February and March, annihilating almost three enemy divisions and capturing over 10,000 enemy troops and over 10,000 weapons. This victory led to the expansion of the Soviet area to Hunan, Jiangxi, Fujian and Guangdong, of the First Front Army to 100,000 troops, and of the Red Guards to 200,000. This was the heyday of the central Soviet area. In 1933, the Red Army grew to 300,000 in total, its highest level during the Second Revolutionary Civil War.

Not resigned to the defeat of his fourth "encirclement and suppression" campaign, Chiang Kai-shek actively made preparations for another attempt, at the same time intensifying the economic blockade against the Soviet areas. In summer 1933, Chiang once again convened a conference to discuss how to further implement the policy of "30 percent military force and 70 percent political work." The Field Headquarters of the Chairman of the KMT Military Commission in Nanchang issued the "Measures for Blocking Bandit Areas" and the "Additional Measures," which stipulated that transportation of all military supplies, articles of daily use, seeds and draught animals into the revolutionary bases was strictly prohibited, that export of goods and products of revolutionary bases was absolutely forbidden, and that a blockade on post and telecommunications as well as transportation was to be enforced. Apart from these, there were stipulations as follows: "Daily necessities for residents who are close to a bandit zone or a semi-bandit zone should be bought by the head of the *Bao* on their behalf according to the exact amount needed by the exact population of the *Bao* community"; and "Within the blockade period, anyone providing bandits with information, or making a deal with them privately, or secretly shipping goods to them for gains, or attempting to line his pockets with discovered and seized goods for aiding bandits by concealing the facts and not reporting to the leadership, or failing in his duty on blockade, should be shot." Later on, additional concrete measures for examining post and telecommunications as well as for selling salt and kerosene were put into practice. Salt rations ranged from 20 to 25 grams per person per day. "In the areas near bandit zones, the amount of salt or kerosene purchased by each household each time should not exceed the need for five days." People buying salt and kerosene should show certificates with *Bao* and *Jia* heads' signatures and seals. Certificates of this kind were prepared and issued by county governments. Violation of these stipulations would incur execution by shooting or other severe punishments according to the seriousness of the case. Chiang Kai-shek's plan of enforcing the economic blockade was to make it impossible for the troops and people in the revolutionary bases to "keep a single grain of rice, a spoonful of salt and a ladleful of water," so as to make them unable to live there. Launching an "encirclement and suppression" campaign in coordination would then destroy the revolutionary bases and wipe out the Red Army.

The situation of long-term struggle against "encirclement and suppression" required the mobilization of all forces in the Soviet areas to go in for necessary and possible construction. To break the KMT's economic blockade and correct the "Left" mistakes in economic work in the central Soviet area, Mao Zedong went into the midst of the masses and deep into the realities of life in Changgang Township in Xingguo County of Jiangxi Province and Caixi Township in Shanghang County of Fujian Province. There he made investigations, summarized experiences, and guided both economic and political construction in the revolutionary bases. In July 1933, the Provisional Central Government of the Chinese Soviet Republic decided to convene a meeting on economic construction in the central Soviet area to discuss how to develop economic work. In August, a meeting on economic construction of 17 counties in the southern part of the central Soviet area was held in Ruijin. In that same month a meeting on the economic construction of 11 counties north of the central Soviet area was convened in Bosheng County. After these two meetings, economic construction in the revolutionary bases gradually progressed. In January 1934, economic work was discussed at the Second National Congress of the Chinese Soviet. Mao Zedong gave a report and made a summary. Summarizing the experiences and lessons from economic construction in the revolutionary bases under the conditions of warfare and of besiegement by the White political power, the congress advanced the theory and policies for economic construction in the revolutionary bases, and the conception of a new-democratic economy was thus initially shaped.

The Communist Party paid great attention to the building of political power in the Soviet areas. After the First National Soviet Congress, elections were held in all the Soviet areas. These admitted a great number of advanced elements from among workers and peasants into organs of political power at all levels. In January 1934 the Second National Congress of the Chinese Soviet was held in Ruijin. Having summed up the experiences of the Chinese Soviet movement of the past two years, the congress put forward the current tasks and discussed such important questions as the building of Soviet political power, the Red Army, and the economy. In addition, the congress adopted the amended Soviet constitution and resolutions on these questions. The congress elected the new Central Executive Committee, while the presidium elected by the First Session of the Central Executive Committee served as the supreme organ of political power after the session. Mao Zedong was elected chairman of the Central Executive Committee, and Xiang Ying and Zhang Guotao as vice-chairmen. Zhang Wentian was the chairman of the People's Council. The People's Council and the 11 departments under it served as the central administrative organs.

While the Soviet areas and Red Army were rapidly expanding, the revolution was confronted with new, grave problems. In the summer of 1933, after signing the Tanggu Agreement and crushing the anti-Japanese allied forces in Qahar, Chiang Kai-shek launched the fifth "encirclement and suppression" campaign against the Soviet areas. Before this campaign, Chiang had made preparations in many respects, including setting up a "Field Headquarters of the Chairman of the Military Commission" in Nanchang; convening a military conference on "suppressing bandits" attended by personnel in authority from the five provinces of Jiangxi, Guangdong, Fujian, Hunan, and Hubei; sponsoring the Officers Training Corps at Lushan; inviting military specialists from Germany as advisers to work out operational plans and research new strategies and tactics; purchasing munitions from the United States, Britain and other countries and increasing modern military equipment; and building economic blockade lines and thousands of blockhouses around the Soviet areas. To launch this campaign, the KMT government mustered one million troops and 200 planes, with Chiang Kai-shek as the commander-in-chief. Directed by Chiang, 500,000 KMT troops took four routes to attack the central Soviet area. At that time, there were over 80,000 Red Army troops in the area, stronger than before. But there existed a most unfavourable factor—the erroneous guidance by the Provisional Party Centre in struggling against this campaign. Under the wrong direction of Bo Gu and Otto Braun, a military adviser sent by the Communist International, the Red Army was first adventurist in its offense and then conservative in its defense consequently landing itself in a completely passive position. In November 1933, when Chiang Kai-shek was compelled to transfer part of his main force attacking the Red Army to suppress the Fujian Incident, the Red Army should have seized this chance to move quickly to the Jiangsu-Zhejiang-Anhui-Jiangxi area with Zhejiang as its centre, and to turn the strategic defensive to the strategic offensive. But the leaders of the Provisional Party Centre did not take advantage of this favourable opportunity. So, after suppressing the People's Government in Fujian Province, Chiang Kai-shek again concentrated his armed forces on a continuous drive to the central Soviet Area. In January 1934, the Fifth Plenary Session of the CPC Sixth Central Committee was held in Ruijin. This session made an absolutely wrong assessment of the current situation. It concluded that victory in the struggle against the fifth "encirclement and suppression" campaign "would lead to the victory of the Soviet revolution in one province or several provinces and therefore lay a firm foundation for the victory of the Soviet revolution all over China," and that this struggle would decide "who will win in the struggle between taking the Soviet road or taking the colonial road." The session's decisions on strategies and tactics were also incorrect. All this led to the inevitable defeat of the struggle against the fifth "encirclement and suppression" campaign.

Early in 1934, the Red Army and enemy troops were locked in a stalemate for several months in the Jianning areas. Later on, the Red Army troops were obliged to retreat because of their inability to win battles. After the fall of Guangchang, the Red Army divided its forces into six columns and assumed the defensive on all fronts, and continued using the erroneous short-swifthrust tactics. This brought greater losses. By October the entire war situation was becoming more and more unfavourable to the Red Army, and it was obviously impossible to break the "encirclement and suppression" campaign. Bo Gu and other Party Central Committee leaders now decided that the main force of the Red Army should leave the central Soviet area and break through the encirclement to move away. In the middle of October, the Central Red Army and personnel of its rear organs, numbering over 86,000, set out from Changding and Ninghua of Fujian, and Ruijin and Yudu of Jiangxi for western Hunan, where the Second and Sixth corps of the Red Army were stationed. The Red Army's historic Long March now began. But after the beginning of the Long March, the Party Central Committee leaders committed the military mistake of fleeing from difficulties. Battling very hard, the Red Army troops broke through the enemy's four blockade lines in succession and crossed the Xiangjiang River. But the forces suffered heavy losses, with personnel reduced to around 30,000.

At this critical juncture, Mao Zedong suggested that the Party Central Committee give up the plan of joining forces with the Second and Sixth corps and move straight forward to Guizhou where the enemy's strength was relatively weak. Most of the Central Committee leaders were for Mao's suggestion. The Red Army entered Guizhou from Hunan, forged across the Wujiang River and captured Zunyi. There the CPC Central Committee convened an enlarged meeting of the Political Bureau from January 15 to 17, 1935. The Zunyi Meeting focused its attention on correcting military errors—this was of decisive significance at that time, and adopted the "Resolution of the Central Committee on the Summary of the Struggle Against the Enemy's Five 'Encirclement and Suppression' Campaigns." The resolution affirmed the basic strategic and tactical principles Mao Zedong and others had employed in directing the Red Army to defeat the enemy's four "encirclement and suppression" campaigns, and clearly pointed out, "The main reason for our being unable to crush the enemy's fifth encirclement and suppression campaign is that we followed a mere defensive military line," and that Bo Gu and Otto Braun should take the main responsibility. This meeting decided to reorganize the central leading body, elect Mao Zedong to the Standing Committee of the Political Bureau, and disband the "three-person group" composed of Bo Gu, Otto Braun and Zhou Enlai, which had been in charge of political and military affairs. It also decided that Zhou Enlai and Zhu De, the principal leaders of the Central Military Commission, be responsible for directing military work. After the meeting, the Standing Committee of the Political Bureau appointed Luo Fu (also known as Zhang Wentian (1900-1976), to replace Bo Gu as the top leader of the Party. Later on, the Central Military Commission resolved to set up the Front Headquarters with Zhu De as commander-in-chief and Mao Zedong as political commissar, and a group consisting of Mao Zedong, Zhou Enlai and Wang Jiaxiang, 1906-1974) to be responsible for military direction and action. The Zunyi Meeting was held as a critical war time, so it could not discuss political problems from all sides. The resolution of the meeting only generally affirmed the Party Central Committee's political line and did not go into the political causes of the erroneous military direction. But, it solved the pressing military issue at that time and ended the "Left" dogmatist domination over the Party Central Committee. In fact, the Zunyi Meeting established the correct leadership of the new Party Central Committee represented by Mao Zedong, saved the Party and the Red Army, and was a turning-point at the moment of life and death in the history of the Chinese Communist Party. It opened the way for the Chinese revolution to advance to victory and marked the fact that the Communist Party of China was developing from infancy towards maturity.

After the Zunyi Meeting, the Central Red Army crossed the Chishui River four times and got across the Wujiang River in the south, as if it were planning to press on to Guiyang. This forced Chiang Kai-shek to send in reinforcements from Yunnan Province. Taking advantage of this opportunity, the Red Army penetrated into Yunnan and crossed the Jinsha River. In this way, the Red Army steered clear of the encirclement, pursuit, interception and attack by hundreds of thousands of enemy troops, and took the initiative in its own hands. Having crossed the Jinsha, the Central Red Army smoothly passed through the Daliangshan Yi ethnic group area because it carried out the Party's correct policy towards ethnic groups and were helped by the Yi people. Then, forcing its way across the Luding Bridge on the Dadu River and climbing over the perennially snow-clad Jiajin Mountain, the Central Red Army arrived at Maogong of Sichuan Province in June 1935 and joined forces with the Fourth Front Army there. Now the troops totalled 100,000. In that same month, the Central Political Bureau held a meeting at Lianghekou and decided to march northward to set up a revolutionary base on the Sichuan-Shaanxi-Gansu border. But Zhang Guotao (1897-1979) ran counter to this decision. He advocated going to the minority areas bordering on Sichuan and Xikang. In July the Red Army arrived at Maoergai. Here the Party Central Committee convened a Politburo conference, deciding to reorganize the First and Fourth Front armies into the Right Route Army and the Left Route Army. Then the two armies continued marching to the north. Led by Mao Zedong and others, the Right Route Army reached Baxi in northern Sichuan after passing through desolate and uninhabited marshlands. When the Left Route Army got to Aba, Zhang Guotao telegrammed the Party Central Committee to oppose marching north and ask the Right Route Army to advance south. He even attempted to harm the Party Centre by force. Finding out Zhang's scheme, the Party Central Committee resolved to leave the dangerous areas as quickly as possible. In September, the Right Route Army, numbering about 8,000, continued its northward march. They captured the natural barrier Lazikou, climbed over Minshan Mountain and broke through the Weishui River blockade line. In October, after crossing over Liupan Mountain, they arrived at Wuqizhen in northern Shaanxi to join the forces of the 15th Corps. In November, the Red Army under the leadership of the Party Central Committee and Mao Zedong annihilated a division plus a regiment of enemy troops at Zhiluozhen, destroying the KMT army's third "encirclement and suppression" campaign against the northern Shaanxi revolutionary base and laying the foundation for the establishment of the national revolutionary headquarters in the northwest.

In October 1935 at Zhuomudiao, Zhang Guotao illegally proclaimed the founding of another "Central Committee," "Central Political Bureau," "Central Secretariat," and "Central Revolutionary Military Commission," and styled himself "chairman" of the Central Committee. In a difficult situation, Zhu De, Liu Bocheng and others unremittingly struggled against Zhang Guotao's anti-Party divisive action, which was also unpopular in the Fourth Front Army. In June 1936, Zhang was obliged to declare the disbandment of his bogus central committee. In November 1935, the Second and Sixth Corps set out from the revolutionary bases in Hunan, Hubei, Sichuan and Guizhou to start the Long March and joined the forces of the Fourth Front Army in Ganzi, Xikang in June 1936. Early in July, the two corps were reorganized into the Second Front Army with He Long as commander-in-chief and Ren Bishi (1904-1950) as political commissar. The joining of the two Red Army units greatly strengthened the forces against Zhang Guotao. Though Zhang had cancelled his bogus central committee, he still acted independently and defiantly. At the insistence of Zhu De, Ren Bishi, He Long and others a meeting was held in Ganzi. After a hot debate with Zhang Guotao, the meeting decided that the army should advance north to meet the Central Committee, and Zhang's actions ended in failure. In October 1936 when the Second and Fourth Front armies joined forces with the First Front Army at Huining in Gansu Province, the great Long March ended triumphantly. After the joining of the three main forces of the Red Army, the main forces of the Fourth Front Army and the Fifth Corps, numbering over 20,000, were formed into the Western Route Army on November 10. Making their way westward, they crossed the Huanghe

(Yellow River) and headed for the Hexi Corridor. During their progress, they fought heroically. But, attacked by the enemy's superior forces from all sides, they finally lost the battle in March 1937. In December 1936, a new Central Military Commission was formed, with Mao Zedong as chairman. In March 1937, the Party Central Committee convened an enlarged Politburo meeting in Yan'an to criticize Zhang Guotao, and summarized his opportunist mistakes and splittist anti-Party activities. In April 1938 Zhang betrayed the revolution, joining the KMT's spy organization, and was then expelled from the Party.

After the Long March of the Central Red Army, a sub-bureau of the Party Central Committee (later changed to the Southeast Sub-bureau) with Xiang Ying as its head was established in the central Soviet areas and an Office of the Central Government of the Chinese Soviet Republic with Chen Yi as its director was set up to lead the Red Army and guerrilla forces in the revolutionary bases in the south to keep up the struggle. The Red guerrilla forces in the 14 areas of the eight provinces in the south persisted in guerrilla war for three years, contributing much to the Chinese revolution.

The armed forces under the Chinese Communist Party included the revolutionary troops fighting the Japanese invaders in the forefront of the northeast, as well as the Red Army forces concentrated in the northwest and those conducting guerrilla war in the old revolutionary bases in the south. By the end of 1933, detachments under the leadership of the Chinese Communist Party had already become the main force in the guerrilla war against Japanese invasion in the northeast. In 1936, the various armed forces resisting Japan in the northeast were reorganized into the Anti-Japanese Allied Army. From early 1936 to summer 1937, the Northeast Anti-Japanese Allied Army waged guerrilla war in the vast areas between the Lesser Hinggan Mountains in the north and the Changbai Mountains in the south as well as the Wusuli River in the east and the Liaohe River in the west. They engaged the Japanese and puppet armies in thousands of battles and crushed their numerous "expeditions." Their heroic fighting struck heavy blows at Japan's colonial domination in the northeast.

9. The Birth of New-democratic Economy. Economic Changes in the Kuomintang Area

The economy in the revolutionary bases, which was born with the establishment and development of the rural revolutionary bases, was a new-democratic economy. It was the foundation for the existence and development of Soviet political power in the revolutionary bases and represented the future of the development of China's economy. The economy in the revolutionary bases had three main characteristics: (1) It emerged and developed in a war environment in which the revolutionary bases were carved up and encircled by the enemy. (2) It came into being and grew in the backward agricultural areas, so it was mainly agricultural, with very little industry, most of which was handicraft industry. (3) It was a new-democratic economy, including state-owned, cooperative and private economies. This was decided by China's economic situation, and the nature and tasks of the Chinese revolution.

The birth and initial development of the economy in the revolutionary bases was, first of all, the result of carrying out the agrarian revolution and changing the ownership of land by feudal landlords to that by peasants. Early in 1931, following a clear solution to the question of peasant land ownership in the agrarian revolution, peasants' enthusiasm for production increased dramatically. But, due to the desperate launch of "encirclement and suppression" campaigns by the KMT against the revolutionary bases and the fact that large numbers of young and able-bodied people had joined the army to defend Red political power, agricultural production in the revolutionary bases faced many difficulties, especially a shortage of manpower and oxen to till the land. To rehabilitate and develop agricultural production, the Communist Party organizations and Soviet governments in the revolutionary bases tried every means to solve these difficulties. The most fundamental of these was to organize the peasants to help one another in production (including mutual aid in labour, and the use of oxen and tools). Hence the provisional central government issued such documents as the "Organizational Programme of Mutual-aid Groups in

Farm Work," "Measures on Setting up Farm Cattle Stations," and "Instructions on Organizing Farm Cattle Cooperatives". There were slight differences in names and forms of the mutual-aid labour organizations in various revolutionary base areas. Some were called farming teams, some mutual-aid labour groups, some labour cooperatives, some mutual-aid corps, and some mobile production teams. The mutual-aid labour organizations now were a kind of collective labour organization based on individual economy (on the basis of private property), not yet the economic units of socialist collective ownership, but they already carried elements of socialism.

Secondly, to support the revolutionary war and guarantee supplies for the Red Army and the Soviet governments, a new type of finance and banking was formed in all revolutionary bases. Primarily, the revenue of the revolutionary bases was to depend on the gains of war and the confiscated property of landlords and despotic gentry. Later, part of it came from the people, mainly including donations from the masses, income from the public fields worked by the Red Army, from the issue of bonds, and from commercial and land taxes. Expenditure was chiefly on war supplies for the Red Army, and only a small part used as administrative fees for the Soviet government and living expenses for working personnel. In all revolutionary bases the supply system (a system of payment in kind) was practiced among the Red Army officers and men as well as the Soviet government personnel. In addition, in all the revolutionary bases feudal usury was banned and pawnshops confiscated. Meanwhile, industrial and agricultural banks were set up in various places. Developing credit cooperatives by raising funds from collectives was encouraged and supported. Early in 1932, following the establishment of the Bank of the Chinese Soviet Republic, branches came into being in every Soviet area. The state bank and its branches issued banknotes.

Thirdly, after the founding of the revolutionary bases, people worked hard to rehabilitate and develop agricultural and industrial production to support the revolutionary war and improve the living standards of the masses. As the bases were located in the economically backward countryside, mostly in mountain or border areas, agriculture occupied a very important position and played a key role in their entire economy, so much so that the economy of the revolutionary bases could be called "agricultural economy." Therefore, the Communist Party and the Soviet government paid great attention to agriculture. To develop agricultural production, measures were taken such as reclaiming wasteland, collecting manure, building water conservancy projects and planting trees in addition to promoting mutual-aid and cooperative movements. In 1932 and 1933, relatively good harvests were brought in. To suit the needs of the revolutionary war, the Red Army soldiers and Soviet government of every revolutionary base started a number of simple industries from scratch. They included arsenals, printing houses and clothing factories, but the military industry was the dominant one. After the First National Congress of the Chinese Soviet, state industries in the Soviet areas made relatively rapid progress. Apart from the military supplies industry, there were civil industries and industries for export to White area such as textiles, coal, tungsten ore, farm implements and paper-making. By January 1934, state factories in the central Soviet area already numbered 32. This was a socialist economy. With government encouragement, handicraft cooperatives in the Soviet areas developed rapidly. By early 1934, handicraft cooperatives in Xingguo and 16 other counties in the central Soviet area increased to 176 with a membership of 32,700.

Fourthly, to break the enemy's economic blockade, stimulate the economy of the revolutionary bases, guarantee supplies for the Red Army, and improve the peasants' living standards as much as possible, much commercial work had been done in the revolutionary areas. For example, the Jinggang Mountains revolutionary base utilized and transformed the *xuchang* traditional place for exchange of rural commodities, set up public stores and booths, and developed trade with the White areas. To maintain the stability of grain prices to benefit the peasants, the grain regulation bureau was established. In some places grain regulation bureaus were established by raising funds from the masses (thus making grain cooperatives). To lessen merchants' exploitation, revolutionary bases one after another started the consumers' cooperatives, whose main task it was to sell industrial items to peasants and purchase agricultural and sideline products from them at reasonable prices. Consumers' cooperatives were new types of commercial organizations in the revolutionary bases. They were a collective economy with socialist elements. "Outside trade" organizations were set up to cope with the export of agricultural products to White areas and the import of industrial items from those areas. Early in 1933, the Outside Trade Bureau was established under the Central National Economy Department. By the end of that year the Chinese Commercial Joint-stock Company, which handled secret trade with Fuzhou, Xiamen, Guangzhou and other places, was founded.

In short, the gradual progress of the agrarian revolution in the revolutionary bases abolished the feudal ownership of land, shook the economic foundation of imperialism and feudalism, and expanded the individual economy of peasants. After land reform, peasants launched a mutual-aid and cooperative movement and set up mutual-aid labour organizations and consumers' cooperatives; handicraft workers started producers' cooperatives; and the Red Army and the Soviet government initiated state factories, stores, and outside trade organizations. All this indicates that with the founding of workers' and peasants' democratic political power, a new-democratic economy was born in the revolutionary bases.

The documents adopted by the First National Congress of the Chinese Soviet, held on November 7, 1931 in Ruijin, Jiangxi Province, such as the Outline of the Constitution of the Chinese Soviet Republic, the Land Law, the Labour Law and Decisions on Economic Policy, still contained "Left" mistakes. For instance, the Land Law stipulated that landlords should have no land distributed to them, and rich peasants only barren land; the Labour Law was divorced from the actual conditions of the revolutionary bases, mechanically stipulating the eight-hour day working system and over-high standard of living. All of these adversely affected the economy of the revolutionary bases.

In the course of establishing its rule over the whole nation, the Nanjing National Government step by step embarked on the monopolization of the national economy. But the semi-colonial, semi-feudal character of the economy in the Kuomintang areas underwent no real change. Since the outbreak of the world capitalist economic crisis in 1929, imperialist powers had vied to expand their economic influence in China and intensify their economic invasion. First, they dumped their surplus goods into China. After 1929 the volume of China's imports shot up and that of exports went down dramatically. The unfavourable balance of trade in 1928 amounted to 300 million yuan in value. The figure in 1931 was over 810 million and that in 1932 reached 860 million. This was unprecedented in history. Among the imported goods, the increase of agricultural products registered the largest in volume. Secondly, they expanded export of capital to China to tighten their control of her economic lifelines. From 1930 to 1936, the annual increase of investment from various countries (including loans) averaged US$ 130 million. By 1936, foreign capital in China totaled US$ 4.3 billion. Now China's heavy industry was mainly monopolized by foreign capital. By 1936, 95 percent of pig iron output, 83 percent of steel output, 66 percent of mechanized coal mining, and 55 percent of generated energy in China were controlled by foreign capital. In the relatively developed light industry, foreign capital also occupied a dominant position. In the textile industry, 46 percent of the spindles and 56 percent of the looms were owned by foreign capital. Moreover, China's finance was controlled by imperialism. The Hong Kong and Shanghai Banking Corporation of Britain manipulated China's foreign exchange prices, and enjoyed the privilege of issuing exchange certificates, handling foreign debt, taking care of tariffs and salt taxes, etc. From 1927 to 1937, the KMT government openly asked for 14 foreign loans which roughly amounted to US$ 400 million. Of these, one contracted for purchase of cotton and wheat in 1933 amounted to US$ 50 million. The economic expansion of imperialism in China made the country more semi-colonial. The northeast was simply reduced to the status of a colony of Japan, and divorced from China's national economic system.

During the intensification of imperialist economic aggression, the National Government depended on its own political and military power to secure and accumulate a large amount of wealth, which gradually constituted state monopoly capitalism. It had formed the important economic foundation for the KMT reactionary regime. The state capital of KMT regime monopolized national financial undertakings. In November 1928, the KMT government set up the Central Bank of China in Shanghai. Around that time, it brought the Bank of China and the Bank of Communications of China under its control through adding "official shares" to them by force. In 1933, the Farmers Bank of Hubei, Henan, Anhui and Jiangxi was established, in 1935 being renamed the Farmers Bank of China. Apart from these, the National Government had erected the Central Trust of China and the Directorate General and Postal Remittances and Savings Banks to monopolize China's trust and insurance undertakings. By making use of political and economic privileges, the National Government further controlled the "four small banks" (the Bank of Xinhua Trust, the Trading Bank of China, the Siming Bank, and the Industrial Bank of China), "the four banks in the north" (the Jincheng Bank, the Bank of Salt Industry, the Central South Bank, and the Bank of the Mainland) and "the three banks in the south" (the Commercial Savings Bank of Shanghai, the Industrial Bank of Zhejiang and the Xingye Bank of Zhejiang). Thus a monopolistic financial network was formed. The National Government set up the National Resources Commission in 1935. Before the outbreak of the War of Resistance, the newly established government-run factories and mines under the National Resources Commission numbered 11. At that time the state capital of the National Government already controlled most of the railways and highways and the circulation of two thirds of domestic commodities, monopolized the national finances and, through monetary, credit and foreign exchange policies, grasped the national industrial and commercial lifelines.

Owing to the expansion of imperialist economic influence in China, the control and plunder of the national economy by state monopolistic capital, the damage done by the years of wars between the KMT warlords, and the increasingly exorbitant taxes and levies, China's national economy was plunged into a state of depression and stagnation. During this period, the development of the national capital was moving along a tortuous road. After the May 30th Movement in 1925, promoted by the revolution and the boycott of foreign goods, China's national capital achieved a slow growth, and the scope of capitalist production relations was enlarged. Because the national capital was not affected by the world capitalist economic crisis that began in 1929, its slow growth continued until 1930. From 1931 on, with the capitalist countries giving up the gold standard and silver prices rising again, commodity prices going down and the loss of the vast market and resources of the northeast, as well as the dumping and smuggling of goods from Japan and other countries into China, the national capital was confronted with crisis, and fell into decline. The number of registered factories and the amount of capital were dwindling, and the then-existing factories were operating under capacity. More and more enterprises were reorganized or closed down. In 1934 this crisis became aggravated because of the devaluation of U.S. currency and the American practice of purchasing silver. As a result of plunder by feudalism plus the warlord wars, backward production and severe natural calamities, China's rural economy went bankrupt. From 1927 to 1935, China suffered serious natural calamities every year. The flood caused by the Yangtze River in 1931 afflicted a dozen provinces with 50 million victims. The floods of 1935 hit the four provinces of Jiangxi, Anhui, Hubei and Hunan, with over 10 million victims.

The National Government was busy handling internal strife and civil war instead of economic construction. In 1931 it worked out a 10-Year Plan for China's industrialization, and in 1935 it launched a national economic construction movement. But in the end it only built a few railways (such as the line from Hangzhou to Nanchang, the section from Zhuzhou to Shaoguan on the line from Hankou to Guangzhou, the Lingbao section on the Longhai Railway, the Jiangnan Railway, the Huainan Railway and the Sujia Railway) and highways (over 40,000 kilometres in total). It nationalized the China Merchants' Steamship Company, and set up a special administrative bureau to develop inland and coastal navigation. The establishment of the China Aviation Corporation was based on cooperation with the United States, and the Europe-Asia Airline was jointly established with Germany. This meant that there were regular flights between a few important cities in the country. The development of post and telecommunications was mainly for military needs. Water conservancy commissions on the Yellow, Yangtze and Huaihe rivers and the rivers of Guangdong were set up to handle affairs such as dredging the waterways, preventing floods and building dykes. The results of the so-called 10-Year Plan ammounted to very little.

In November 1935 with support from Britain, the National Government carried out currency reform by unifying the issuance of paper money called *Fabi* (legal tender) to gather in silver, and at the same time, getting *Fabi* joined in the sterling bloc. This was called the "*Fabi* policy." In May 1936, the National Government signed a silver agreement with the United States, thus linking *Fabi* with the US dollar. The implementation of the *Fabi* policy, on the one hand, strengthened the monopoly of China's finance by state capital. On the other hand, the unification of China's currency was beneficial to the circulation of commodities and, by devaluing the *Fabi*, the volume of currency circulation was enlarged. This made the prices rise again, which stimulated the development of agriculture, industry and commerce. At this time, capitalist countries in the world gradually overcame their economic crises and began the rehabilitation stage. "Prosperity" existed for the time being. China's large-scale civil war basically stopped. In 1936, favourable weather helped harvests for most provinces except Sichuan, Henan and Guangdong. So, the situation of the national economy turned for the better, and the growth of national capitalism reached its peak. In that year the output value of main grain crops amounted to 5.6 billion yuan (*Fabi*), 1.7 million over the average output value of 1933 to 1935, an increase of nearly 45 percent. The output of main crops also registered a substantial increase over that of 1935. Cotton production increased by 78.4 percent, wheat by 8.3 percent, soya bean by 13.8 percent, and production of other crops like rice, sorghum, sesame, and tobacco all increased more than in previous years. The increase of agricultural production raised the purchasing power of peasants, and therefore promoted the progress of industry and commerce. The gross output value of industrial goods in 1936 amounted to 12.2 billion yuan, an increase of 11 percent over 1935. Cotton yarn increased by 29 percent, cement by 26.2 percent, matches by 18.8 percent, and the supply of electricity by 8.1 percent. The increase continued until the first half of 1937. In 1936, the unfavourable balance of trade was greatly reduced. In that same year, the gross output value of industry and agriculture was 8 percent more than that of 1935. In 1936, capitalist production accounted for 58.6 percent of the gross output value of industry. But this all proved to be short-lived. In

Lin Zexu ordered the burning of opium at Humen in April and May, 1839

The Chinese navy fighting invading British warships during the first Opium War

The European-style buildings in the Garden of Eternal Spring in Yuanmingyuan, later looted and burnt down by the British and French allied forces

Office in charge of China's foreign and diplomatic affairs, established by the Qing government in 1861

A customs building in Shanghai (known as Jianghai Customs)

Catholic church at Xuanwumen, Beijing

People Living in Poverty, showing the miserable life at the end of the Qing Dynasty

Beijing students demonstrating during the May 4th Movement

Sun Yet-sen, the first interim president of the Republic of China

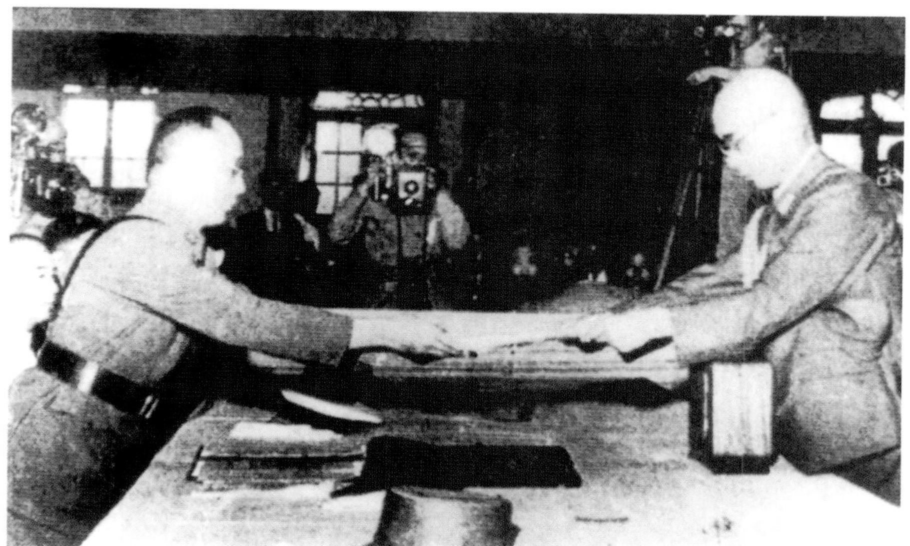

Yasuji Okamura (right), commander-in-chief of the Japanese invasion army, officially surrenders to He Yingqin, commander-in-chief of the Chinese ground force

The Lugouqiao Battle, oil painting depicting the launch of Japan's all-out war against China on July 7, 1937

China's troops ready to resist the invading Japanese army

The sites of the First National Congress of the Chinese Communist Party held in July, 1921.

No. 108, Wangzhi Road, Shanghai

The boat on Nanhu Lake in Jiaxing, Zhejiang Province

Chiang Kai-shek and Mao Zedong drink to each other during the negotiations in Chongqing

Ceremony marking the liberation of Taiwan Province in Taibei on October 25, 1945

Mao Zedong declares the founding of the People's Republic of China in Tiananmen Square on October 1, 1949

July 1937, Japan launched an all-out attack against China. From then on, China was in a state of war. Due to the tremendous damage to the economy by the war, and due to the rottenness of the expanding state monopolistic capital and bureaucrat capital and its destructiveness to the national economy as a whole, the development of China's economy collapsed.

10. Transition from Civil War to the War of Resistance Against Japan

In 1935, the Japanese imperialists created the North China Incident and a series of disturbances, and planned to separate the five northern provinces (Hebei, Shandong, Shanxi, Qahar, and Suiyuan) from China. Their first step for making the five provinces autonomous was to compel the KMT central force to withdraw from Beiping, Tianjin and Hebei so as to weaken the control of the KMT central authorities over the local forces. In May 1935, by creating and making use of pretexts, the Japanese put in an unreasonable claim for the dominance of north China to He Yingqin, the acting director of the Beiping branch of the Military Commission of the National Government. At the same time, they moved their troops from the northeast to threaten the Shanhaiguan Pass, and declared that they would adopt "free actions" if their demand was refused. The National Government once again compromised. In early June it issued a "good-neighbour order." He Yingqin was assigned to hold negotiations with Yoshijiro Umezu, commander of the Japanese forces in north China. After a number of talks, He Yingqin wrote to Umezu, accepting Japanese demands. He's promise included closing the KMT party headquarters in Hebei Province and the cities of Beiping and Tianjin; withdrawing the Northeast Army, the Central Army and the Third Regiment of the Military Police from Hebei; dismissing and replacing the governor of Hebei Province and the mayors of Beiping and Tianjin; banning all anti-Japanese organizations and activities, etc. This letter is usually called the "He-Umezu Agreement." In June that same year, the Japanese invaders found a pretext to force Qin Dechun, head of the Civil

Administration Department of Qahar Province, to sign an agreement with Dohihara, representative of the Japanese troops and special agent chief, known as the "Qin-Dohihara Agreement" (or the "Qahar Agreement"). It included guaranteeing free travel to the Japanese in Qahar Province, withdrawing the KMT organizations and the 29th Corps from Qahar; dismissing the provincial governor; and setting up a demilitarized region in eastern Qahar. From that time, China virtually lost its sovereignty over Hebei and Qahar provinces.

Immediately after the KMT central forces withdrew from north China, the Japanese imperialist actively plotted for the "autonomy" of the five provinces in the north, at the same time intensifying the economic invasion of north China. All these actions constituted an essential menace to the KMT authorities' dominance of the region. In October, the Japanese Cabinet meeting adopted Foreign Minister Hirota's "Three Principles Towards China," namely: (1) China should ban all anti-Japanese campaigns; (2) China should recognize "Manchukuo" and establish economic cooperation between Japan, "Manchukuo" and China; (3) China and Japan should jointly contain the Communist Party. At the same time, the Japanese Cabinet meeting formally adopted "The Bill Promoting the Autonomy of North China." After the meeting, Japan's diplomatic personnel started negotiations with the National Government on "Hirota's Three Principles." Meanwhile, the Japanese Kwantung Army in the northeast and the Japanese forces in north China started to agitate actively for the "autonomy" of north China. On November 6, Dohihara took the "Plan for the High-Level Autonomy of North China" to Tianjin where he intended to force Song Zheyuan to proclaim "autonomy" on November 20. Cooperating with Dohihara's activities, Minami Jiro, commander of the Kwantung Army, ordered his troops to be ready before the 15th to march into north China from outside the Great Wall, and, at the same time, ordered his air force to make preparations to enter and garrison Beiping and Tianjin by the 20th. Now the crisis in north China had reached its peak.

To prevent north China from becoming "autonomous," the National Government adopted a series of countermeasures such as sending Xiong Bing, deputy chief of the Headquarters of the General Staff of the Military Commission, to work on Song Zheyuan while assembling forces and staging large-scale military manoeuvres near Nanjing, and ordering part of these units to move northward to make a feint. After failing to compel Song Zheyuan to proclaim "autonomy" on November 20, the Japanese invaders, by applying continuous pressure, forced him to do so on November 30. Instigated by Japanese imperialists, Yin Rugeng, administrative inspector of the Luanyu Region of Hebei Province, on November 25 proclaimed "autonomy" at Tongxian County and established the "Eastern Hebei Autonomous Committee for Containing the Communist Party" (later changed to "autonomous government"). The Executive Yuan of the government held an urgent meeting and decided to abolish the Beiping branch of the Military Commission. He Yingqin was specially appointed the resident senior official of the Executive Yuan in Beiping; Song Zheyuan was appointed the head of the Hebei-Qahar Pacification Headquarters; and Yin Rugeng was to be dismissed from his post and prosecuted. Although Chiang Kai-shek would allow no "autonomy" of north China, awed by Japan's military force he sent He Yingqin north to confer with Song Zheyuan to find a way out of the crisis. On December 11, the National Government formally decreed the establishment of the Hebei-Qahar Administrative Council headed by Song Zheyuan (1885-1940). The Hebei-Qahar Administrative Council was under the National Government in name, but actually it was relatively independent. Japanese imperialists, traitors and pro-Japanese forces all exerted considerable influence on it and to a great extent brought it under their control. The establishment of the Hebei-Qahar Administrative Council did not relax the tensions between China and Japan. Dissatisfied with the establishment of this political power, the Japanese imperialists continued to support the "Eastern Hebei Autonomous Government for Containing the Communist Party," and attempted to make the Hebei-Qahar Administrative council "join forces" with it as quickly as possible. Now, the National Government would have no other choice but to hand over north

China submissively to Japan.

At this time when the national crisis was further deepening and a new change was taking place in the relations between domestic classes, on August 1, 1935, the Chinese Communist Party's resident delegation to the Communist International published "A Letter of Appeal to All Chinese Compatriots on Resisting Japanese Aggression and Saving the Nation," known as the August 1st Manifesto, in the name of the CPC Central Committee and the Central Government of the Chinese Soviet. The manifesto called on all political parties, compatriots and troops to "stop fighting civil wars so as to concentrate all national resources (human, material, financial and military) for resistance against Japan and for national solvation"; and to organize an all-China united government of national defence and an all-China allied army for resistance against Japan. The manifesto won support from people all over the country. In October, the CPC Central Committee and the Central Red Army arrived in northern Shaanxi, greatly encouraging all the revolutionary people. These two events raised the country's anti-Japanese democratic movement to a new high. On December 9, five to six thousand students from universities and middle schools in Beiping led by the Chinese Communist Party staged a large-scale demonstration. Paraders presented a petition to the representative of the National Government in north China to demand that they "stop the civil war and unite to resist Japan." They shouted slogans such as "Oppose autonomy of north China" and "Down with Japanese imperialism." During the demonstration the students were suppressed by the police and soldiers. The following day the students of Beiping went on a general strike to protest against the reactionary authorities' atrocities and, at the same time, planned a new struggle on a still larger scale. On December 16, when the Hebei-Qahar Administrative Council was to begin functioning, Beiping students numbering over 10,000 broke through the besiegement by police and troops, and held a mass rally and demonstration to voice their opposition to the establishment of the Hebei-Qahar Administrative Council, to any puppet organization in north China, and to the so-called autonomy of north China. The north China authorities once more suppressed the students. The Beiping students' patriotic act brought an immediate response from students across the country and won their support. The December 9th Movement marked the advent of the upsurge of the movement for resistance and democracy. After this movement, progressive youths led by the Chinese Communist Party went to factories, the countryside, and the anti-Japanese front, and embarked on the road of integrating themselves with workers, peasants and soldiers.

The new situation after the North China Incident called upon the Chinese Communist Party to make a scientific analysis of the current situation and formulate a new and correct political line and revolutionary tactics. For this purpose, the CPC Central Committee convened a Political Bureau meeting at Wayaobao in northern Shaanxi from mid to late December 1935. On the 25th, the meeting adopted the "Resolution on the Current Political Situation and the Tasks of the Party." The meeting correctly realized the basic characteristics of the current political situation: Japanese imperialism was paving the way to make China its sole colony instead of remaining a colony under various imperialist powers. The resolution pointed out: "The line and tactics of the Party are to mobilize, unite and organize all revolutionary forces of the nation to oppose today's principal enemies—Japanese imperialism and the arch-traitor Chiang Kai-shek.... Only the broadest anti-Japanese national united front (including the lower and upper strata) can defeat Japanese imperialism and its lackey Chiang Kai-shek." The meeting decided to rename the Soviet Workers' and Peasants' Republic as the Soviet People's Republic and adjust its policies. The resolution also clearly pointed out that at present, "the main danger to the Party is the exclusivism of the "Left", but struggle would also be waged against the Right opportunists. After the meeting, Mao Zedong gave a report on the tactics against Japanese imperialism at a meeting of the Party's activists. The theory and tactics on the establishment of the anti-Japanese national united front as expounded in the resolution and Mao's report made it clear that under the premise of resistance against

Japan, it was possible and necessary to form a united front with the national bourgeoisie and even with a number of landlords and compradors. They especially stated that in the united front the proletariat could and must keep the leadership in hand. In addition to stressing the criticism of the mistakes committed by the "Left" dogmatists on political tactics, they also reminded the whole Party not to forget the bitter experience of 1927 when the revolution suffered great losses due to the proletariat giving up its leadership. This meeting was the starting point for the Communist Party to change its political line and prepared the theoretical and political basis to greet a new upsurge of resistance against Japan.

The North China Incident constituted a grave menace to the KMT's domination in that area. Chiang Kai-shek's policies of compromise and concession had already failed to satisfy the greediness of Japanese imperialists on the one hand, and on the other hand, the rise of the movement for resistance and national salvation would never allow Chiang Kai-shek to continue his policy towards Japan. At that time, tensions between Japan and Britain and the United States were growing. Under these circumstances, with the further splitting up of the Kuomintang and its government and army, the pro-British and pro-American factions were constantly expanding their force and influence, and the pro-Japanese factions being attacked. Early in November 1935, during the Sixth Plenary Session of the Fourth Central Committee of the KMT, Wang Jingwei was seriously wounded in an assassination attempt and went abroad for treatment. The pro-Japanese force suffered a setback. In that same month, the KMT held its Fifth National Congress. In internal affairs, the congress stuck to the anti-Communist policy of "eliminating the remnant Red bandits." In diplomacy, Chiang Kai-shek delivered a speech on foreign relations, saying, "We will never give up peace unless the hope of peace has completely disappeared. We will also never talk of sacrificing ourselves when we have not yet come to the moment of final sacrifice.... With the determination to make the final sacrifice if necessary, we should try our best to struggle for peace and fulfill the goal of laying a foundation for the state and rejuvenating the nation." But he also remarked, "When peace is completely hopeless ... we should take orders from the party and government and steel ourselves for the final sacrifice Chiang's speech showed that the diplomatic relations of the KMT with Japan had begun to change. The congress approved the resolution of the draft constitution, authorized the Fifth Central Executive Committee to amend it and then make it known to the public, and decided to convene a national assembly. Following the Fifth National Congress, the KMT held the First Plenary Session of the Fifth Central Committee, at which Lin Sen was elected president of the National Government and Chiang Kai-shek replaced Wang Jingwei as head of the Executive Yuan. The Executive Yuan was reorganized. Although the faction headed by Chiang Kai-shek still stuck to the principle of "suppressing the Communists" and continued to pursue a policy of compromise with the Japanese aggressors, it was obliged to make some revisions of its original policy.

After the Fifth National Congress, Chiang Kai-shek's policy towards Japan kept changing. He personally took part in the diplomatic negotiations with Japan on Hirota's Three Principles. He declared Hirota's Three Principles could be accepted on the condition that Japan stop instigating the "autonomy" of north China. But no agreement was reached. Chiang was forced to agree to the establishment of the Hebei-Qahar Administrative Council. At that time, an important move by the KMT was that Chiang secretly ordered Chen Lifu to send people to contact the Communist Party through various channels so as to carry out secret negotiations. His intention was to incorporate the Red Army into the KMT forces through talks. This revealed that Chiang was now adopting the policies of both "suppression" and "appeasement" towards the Red Army. This was instrumental in relaxing the sharp antagonistic relations between the KMT and the CPC. Early in 1936, Chiang authorized Foreign Minister Zhang Qun to negotiate with Japan and instructed him to employ stalling tactics. In March, Zhang Qun and Arita, Japanese ambassador to China, held four talks on the adjustment of Sino-Japanese relations. Because the National Government began pursuing an unyielding policy, Japan failed to gain what it wanted through the negotiations.

The Guangdong-Guangxi Incident took place in June. Chen Jitang from Guangdong and Li Zongren and Bai Chongxi from Guangxi declared a shift to the north to resist Japan. At the same time, they jointly dispatched troops into Hunan Province in preparation for fighting Chiang Kai-shek's forces. This move was an open challenge to Chiang in the name of resistance against Japan. The people all over the country demanded resistance against Japan and opposed fighting a civil war. They expected that the Guangdong-Guangxi Incident would be peacefully settled. Chiang Kai-shek bought over Yu Hanmou and others who had been subordinates of Chen Jitang, and then forced Chen out. By September, Chiang reached an agreement with Li Zongren and Bai Chongxi. Therefore, the incident was peacefully settled.

In July, the KMT convened the Second Plenary Session of its Fifth Central Committee. A decision was made to set up the National Defence Council with Chiang Kai-shek as its chairman. At the session Chiang explained the foreign policy approved by the Fifth National Congress, and clearly stated that he would never sign any agreement recognizing puppet regimes. He added, "When we are compelled to sign an agreement to recognize a puppet regime which infringes on China's sovereignty and territorial integrity, that will be the time when we can tolerate no more, and the moment of our final sacrifice will have arrived." In September and October, Zhang Qun held eight talks with Kawagoe, Japanese ambassador to China. The Japanese side asked for a joint containment of the Communist Party in north China while the Chinese side demanded the abolition of the Shanghai and Tanggu truce agreements as well as the puppet regime in eastern Hebei. Chiang Kai-shek instructed Zhang Qun "that complete administrative power in north China must be taken as the lowest limit for adjusting the national relations with Japan today." The negotiations between China and Japan came to a standstill. In November 1936, the puppet troops with Japanese troops' collaboration mounted a massive attack against the province of Suiyuan. The troops under Fu Zuoyi stationed there rose to resist and put the invading forces to flight, and recovered the lost Bailingmiao. Suiyuan's resistance was warmly praised and actively supported by the entire population of the country. The National Government also adopted a relatively positive attitude to this battle of resistance.

Since the December 9th Movement, the domestic situation in China had been rapidly developing towards resistance against Japan. This was a great change. To implement the policies and tactics of the anti-Japanese national united front formulated at Wayaobao, the Chinese Communist Party readjusted its policies in light of its general line and tasks in the new period, and carried out hard and complicated struggles. In February 1936, the Chinese Communist Party organized the Anti-Japanese Vanguard of the Chinese People's Red Army to move eastward across the Yellow River and entered Shanxi Province. Chiang Kai-shek mustered 10 divisions, allegedly 200,000 strong, into Shanxi to cooperate with Yan Xishan's armed forces to obstruct the eastward advance of the Red Army. The marching Red Army withdrew to the west of the Yellow River. On May 5, the Chinese Communist Party published an open telegram appealing to the KMT to "stop fighting, negotiate peace, and resist against Japan in unison." Then the Party Central Committee ordered the Red Army to move west to consolidate and develop the Shaanxi-Gansu revolutionary base, expand the ranks of the Red Army, and strive to unite the forces in the northwest to resist against Japan. To ally with the Hui people for the common struggle against Japanese invaders, the Central Government of the Chinese Soviet issued an appeal to the Hui people on May 25, 1936. It declared, "We would unite with all armed forces of the Hui people and help with their growth ... the two great ethnic groups of Hui and Han should unite closely and overthrow Japanese imperialism and all traitors." After the Guangdong-Guangxi Incident and the Second Plenary Session of the KMT's Fifth Central Committee, the CPC Central Committee decided to abandon the slogan of "opposing Chiang Kai-shek and resisting against Japan," and, on August 25, 1936, wrote to the KMT, formally announcing its readiness to cooperate again with the KMT for salvation of the nation. Afterwards, Mao Zedong and Zhou Enlai respectively wrote to the important figures of the KMT, appealing for them to promote the second cooperation between the two parties. On September 1, the CPC Central Committee issued an inner-Party directive, in which it said, "The chief enemy of the Chinese people today is Japanese imperialism. So it is wrong to equate Japanese imperialism with Chiang Kai-shek, and the slogan of 'Resistance against Japan and opposition to Chiang Kai-shek' is not proper either.... Our general principle is to 'drive Chiang to resist Japan'." In that same month, the CPC Central Committee made a "Resolution on the New Situation in the Resist-Japan-and-Save-the-Nation Movement and the Democratic Republic." It pointed out, "Encouraging the KMT government and its troops to join in the anti-Japanese war is the necessary condition for carrying out a serious, nationwide armed struggle against Japan." Hence the decision to use the name of Democratic Republic to replace that of the Soviet People's Republic.

After the Wayaobao Meeting, the CPC's work in the White area began to change. To bring about a thorough shift of the Party's work in the White area, the North China Sub-bureau of the CPC Central Committee headed by Liu Shaoqi (1898-1969), from Ningxiang, Hunan Province, had done a great deal and contributed much to the establishment of the anti-Japanese national united front.

After the December 9th Movement, the nationwide resist-Japan-and-save-the-nation movement was pushed to a new high. Early in 1936, a flood of students from Beiping, Tianjin, Shanghai and other places went to factories and the countryside to publicize the reasons for resisting Japan. In February, the Vanguard for the Liberation of the Chinese Nation—an organization of revolutionary youths—was set up under the leadership of the CPC. In May, the All-China Students' Union for National Salvation was established in Shanghai. From May 31 to June 1, 1936, an inaugural meeting for the establishment of the Chinese People's Federation for National Salvation was held in Shanghai. The federation published a manifesto and an initial political programme on resistance against Japan and for national salvation. The manifesto stated that the federation was a nationwide united front for national salvation, and its main task at present was to promote the cooperation between various groups of strength in the country for resisting the enemy. In addition, the manifesto suggested that all the parties and factions involved immediately stop armed conflicts and send official representatives for negotiations so as to work out a common programme and set up a unified political power for resistance against the enemy. On July 15, Shen Junru, Tao Xingzhi, Zhang Naiqi and Zou Taofen jointly published a manifesto-like article entitled "The Basic Conditions and Minimum Requirements for Unity Against Foreign Aggression." It expressed the wishes and stand of the Chinese people who demanded an end to internal clashes, unity against Japanese aggressors and struggle for freedom and democracy. This article exerted a tremendous influence. With the expansion of the movement for resistance and the founding of organizations for national salvation in various places, publications on this theme appeared one after another. But any voluntarily organized movement for resistance and democracy out of the KMT's control was considered illegal. On November 23, the KMT government arrested Shen Junru (1875-1963), Zhang Naiqi, Zou Taofen (1895-1944), Li Gongpu, Wang Zaoshi, Sha Qianli and Shi Liang, leaders of the national salvation organizations of various circles, under an accusation of "endangering the Republic of China." This incident, popularly called "Incident of Seven Noble-hearted Personages," aroused the sympathy among people of different circles and a nationwide campaign to rescue them.

As mentioned before, Chiang Kai-shek had sent people to contact the Communist Party, but had never given up his policy of suppression. In October 1936, Chiang went to Xi'an and Luoyang to deploy troops to suppress the Communist Party. He moved 30 divisions under his direct control to stations along the Beiping-Hankou and Longhai railways, preparing to march them to the Shaanxi-Gansu area at any time necessary. He forced Zhang Xueliang's Northeast Army and Yang Hucheng's 17th Route

Army, both stationed in Shaanxi, to continue suppressing the Communist Party. The CPC adopted a policy of trying to win over and unite with Zhang and Yang's troops. In February 1936, Yang Hucheng (1893-1949) reached an agreement with a CPC representative on nonaggression and the exchange of delegates. On April 9, Zhou Enlai went to Fushi, where the Northeast Army was stationed, to hold secret talks with Zhang Xueliang, and reached an agreement of nonaggression between the Red Army and the Northeast Army. In the first half of 1936, the state of hostility between the Red Army and the Northeast and 17th Route armies actually ended. On October 31, Chiang Kai-shek issued orders for a general offensive against the Red Army. The Red Army rose to repulse the enemy attack. On November 21, it wiped out Hu Zongnan's 78th Division at Shanchengbao in Huanxian County, Gansu Province. This last battle put an end to the civil war. In early December, Chiang flew to Xi'an to "supervise the suppression of Communists," making Huaqingchi, Lintong County, his field headquarters. The troops mustered by him now continued their advance to Tongguan, and the clouds of war were gathering over the northwest. Chiang Kai-shek was attempting to force Zhang Xueliang and Yang Hucheng to attack the Red Army, using his Central Army as reinforcement. If Zhang and Yang refused to obey his orders, he would move the Central Army to replace the Northeast and 17th Route armies, to enter and be stationed in Shaanxi and Gansu provinces. This was Chiang's tactic of killing two birds with one stone. Putting national interests above all, Zhang Xueliang again and again advised Chiang to change his policy of civil war and carry out a nationwide resistance against Japan. But all his proposals were rejected. He then held private counsel with Yang Hucheng and decided to have Chiang detained to drive him to resist Japan.

On December 12, Zhang and Yang issued an order to detain Chiang at Huaqingchi. At the same time, Chen Cheng, Wei Lihuang and 10 others were arrested in Xi'an. Following this incident, Zhang and Yang jointly issued an open telegram, declaring that their detaining Chiang was completely out of anti-Japanese and national salvation sentiments, that this was a way to urge Chiang's self-examination, and that his personal safety was guaranteed. They put forward eight propositions such as reorganizing the Nanjing government, stopping all civil wars, releasing all political offenders, lifting the ban on mass patriotic movements, and immediately convening a national salvation meeting.

The sudden outbreak of the Xi'an Incident shocked the whole country and the world. The Nanjing government was thrown into confusion. Out of their own different interests, countries and their domestic forces responded differently. Japanese imperialists attempted to instigate a large-scale civil war in China so as to make use of the chance to expand their aggression. They supported Wang Jingwei, who was then recuperating in Germany, and hoped he would return to China to organize a pro-Japanese government. Britain and the United States were for peaceful settlement of the incident, announcing that they were willing to mediate. The Soviet Union backed China to resist Japan, hoping to settle this incident peacefully, but violently attacked Zhang Xueliang and Yang Hucheng. He Yingqin and company insisted on "sending a punitive expedition" against Zhang and Yang, intending to take advantage of this opportunity to grasp national political power. Initially they got the upper hand, and He Yingqin was chosen as "commander-in-chief of the Punitive Expedition Army." Song Ziwen, Kong Xiangxi and their followers were against punitive expedition. They maintained that Chiang should be rescued through peaceful settlement of the incident. But their intention was to stabilize the positions of the pro-American and pro-British groups in the National Government. Feng Yuxiang, who was then in Nanjing, was also for peaceful settlement to avoid a civil war. The proposition of the Song-Kong group won an advantage in the Nanjing government and finally a decision was made to rescue Chiang. The local Kuomintang warlords were against Zhang and Yang, except Li Zongren and Bai Chongxi from Guangxi and Liu Xiang from Sichuan who expressed support for them, advocating settlement of the Incident through political means. Fu Zuoyi also supported Zhang and Yang. Yan Xishan first stated that he supported Zhang Xueliang, but after the incident took place, he sent a telegram attacking Zhang and Yang, and asked them to hand over Chiang to him so that he could have the situation under his control. Song Zheyuan, Han Fuqu and others pledged their support for the KMT Central Committee, but in fact they were in favour of putting Chiang to death. To the middle classes, the outbreak of the Xi'an Incident was like a bolt out of the blue. Most of them blamed Zhang and Yang and demanded the restoration of Chiang's freedom.

When the news of Chiang's arrest reached northern Shaanxi, Communists, the Red Army and the people of the revolutionary base area were overjoyed, and most of them advocated killing him. But quite a few were worried that killing Chiang would lead to another civil war. After a through discussion of the Incident, the Central Political Bureau, in view of the long-term interests of the nation, quickly negated the idea of killing Chiang and decided on the principle of peaceful settlement. On December 19, the CPC Central Committee clearly pointed out that Chiang should be set free if he agreed to resistance instead of fighting a civil war. At the invitation of Zhang Xueliang and Yang Hucheng, the CPC Central Committee sent a delegation composed of Zhou Enlai, Bo Gu, Ye Jianying and others to Xi'an. There the delegation did a great deal of work and achieved positive results. On December 22, the Nanjing authorities officially sent Song Ziwen and Song Meiling to Xi'an for negotiations. On December 24, an agreement was reached. Chiang Kai-shek was forced to promise to reorganize the KMT and the National Government, release all political offenders, stop suppressing the Communist Party, cooperate with the Red Army to resist Japan, and convene a meeting attended by representatives from various political parties, circles, and armies to discuss and decide the policies of resistance against Japan and national salvation. On the 25th, Chiang was released and the Xi'an Incident was peacefully settled. Zhang Xueliang personally accompanied Chiang's return to Nanjing. But upon their arrival in Nanjing, Zhang was detained. The Xi'an Incident and its peaceful settlement became a turning-point in the current situation. Now the KMT's policy of "internal pacification before resistance to foreign invasion" had failed, and the civil war was basically ended. This provided an essential prerequisite for the second cooperation between the KMT and CPC.

In February 1937, the Third Plenary Session of the Fifth Central Executive Committee of the KMT was held to discuss its policies towards the Communist Party and Japan. To realize the second cooperation between the KMT and CPC, the Communist Party sent the session a telegram, putting forth five demands and four guarantees. The five demands were as follows: (1) Stop all civil war and concentrate all national strength to resist against foreign invasion; (2) guarantee freedom of speech, assembly and association, and release all political offenders; (3) hold a conference attended by representatives from various political parties, factions, circles and armies so as to gather all human resources for national salvation; (4) get everything ready for a war of resistance against Japan as quickly as possible; (5) improve people's livelihood. If the KMT could put these five demands into practice, the CPC would fulfill the four guarantees: (1) Stop the implementation of the policy of overthrowing the National Government by armed uprising on a nationwide scale; (2) rename the Workers' and Peasants' Democratic Government as the Special Regional Government of the Republic of China, rename the Red Army as the National Revolutionary Army and put it directly under the Nanjing Central Government and Military Commission; (3) carry out a thorough-going democratic system of general election in the areas under the Special Regional Government; (4) stop implementing the policy of confiscating landlords' land and resolutely carry out the common programme of the anti-Japanese national united front. At this session, Soong Ching Ling and Feng Yuxiang put forward the "Proposal on the Restoration of Dr. Sun Yat-sen's Three Cardinal Policies." After a fierce debate, the session at last affirmed the principle of cooperating again with the Communist Party. In addition, a resolution on eliminating the "Red Peril" was passed. Its main points included: (1) The establishment and order of a state's army units must be unified, so the Red Army must be completely disbanded; (2) two political powers should not be allowed to exist side by side within a country, so the Soviet government must be liquidated; (3) communist propaganda must be thoroughly stopped; (4) class struggle must be radically ended. Although the resolution still wantonly slandered the Communist Party, it revealed that the KMT's policy towards the Communist Party had finally been changed from "suppression by armed force" to "peaceful unification." This marked a great change in the KMT's policy. However, this was only a change in tactics, for "eliminating the Red peril" remained its cardinal policy. This standpoint and the "peaceful unification" tactic of the KMT decided the relations and form of struggle between the two parties in the coming years.

According to the new developments, the CPC issued a "Letter to All Party Members" on April 15, 1937, putting forth the slogans of "consolidating peace," "striving for democracy" and "conducting a war of resistance." In May the CPC held a conference in Yan'an attended by representatives from the Soviet areas. This conference ratified the political line followed by the Party Central Committee since 1935 and determined the tasks of the Party in the new historical period. Meanwhile, the Party Central Committee convened another meeting in Yan'an participated in by Party representatives from White areas. This meeting summed up experiences and lessons of the Party's work in White areas, criticized the "Leftist" exclusivism and adventurism, and laid down the basic policies and tactics for struggle in the White areas. All these were important preparations made for mobilizing the masses to resist Japan.

After the peaceful settlement of the Xi'an Incident, the historical road for China to take was still tortuous. For example: Chiang Kai-shek had Zhang Xueliang detained in Nanjing; the National Government brought Shen Junru and six other noted patriots to trial, suppressed strikes, repressed and sabotaged the students' patriotic movements, and transferred the Northeast Army from Shaanxi to Henan and Anhui so as to separate them from the Red Army; and Yang Hucheng was forced to quit office and go abroad. Moreover the KMT made use of the people's desire for unity and beat the drum for "corroding the Communists" in an attempt to drive the Communist Party to surrender. In the course of negotiations, the KMT insisted that the Red Army and revolutionary base areas be liquidated. But Chiang Kai-shek was powerless to change the general orientation of uniting all Chinese people to resist Japan. With the negotiations between the KMT and CPC held at higher levels as well as the rising struggle against Japan, a situation of general resistance against Japan by the whole people was in the making.

11. The July 7th Incident and the Start of the Nationwide War of Resistance Against Japan. Three Kinds of Political Power Exist Simultaneously

The all-out war of aggression against China launched by Japan was premeditated. In 1937 when a new economic crisis hit the capitalist world, the Japanese ruling faction found that their domestic political and economic situation was unsteady and that the strength of pro-American and Pro-British forces within the Chinese government was growing, the KMT and the CPC moving towards cooperation, the US and Britain giving aid to Chiang Kai-shek, and the relations between China and the Soviet Union getting close. They were therefore anxious to attack China on a large scale in an attempt to suppress the anti-fascist force at home, establish and extend their colonial rule over mainland China, and strengthen their position in confrontation with the United States, Britain and the Soviet Union.

On the evening of July 7, Japanese troops conducted a military exercise near Lugouqiao (Marco Polo Bridge). On the excuse that a soldier was missing, the Japanese asked for a search of the county town of Wanping. The local Chinese government refused this unreasonable demand. In the process of negotiation, the Japanese troops launched a surprise attack against the town, and then bombarded Lugouqiao. The Chinese garrison rose to fight back. This started the nationwide War of Resistance Against Japan. China now entered a new historical stage.

After the July 7th (or Lugouqiao) Incident, the National Government wavered in its attitude towards the incident and adopted a policy of "neither submission nor aggravation." On the one hand, Chiang Kai-shek sent the Central Army north and ordered Song Zheyuan to resist the enemy on the spot. On the other, he instructed Song to "hold negotiations with Japan on the principle of not losing territory and sovereignty," hoping to see the incident partially settled. On July 17, Chiang delivered a speech at Lushan, reiterating the Chinese government's foreign policy and putting forth four principles for solving the incident: (1) No solution would be allowed to infringe upon China's sovereignty and territorial integrity; (2) the executive organizations in Hebei and Qahar must not be changed illegally; (3) local officials appointed by the Central Government must not be recalled at the casual request of anyone; (4) no restraint would be allowed on the area in which the 29th Corps was stationed. He added, "Whether this matter can.be settled is the final crux.... Once the war starts, every person, young or old, in the north or in the south, must take up the responsibility of resisting the aggressor and defending our homeland." But he also regarded the Lugouqiao Incident as a "local incident" and hoped to "settle it through peaceful diplomatic methods." To preserve his own strength and position, Song Zheyuan strove to reach a compromise with Japan. Although the Japanese government declared its policy was "not to expand the war," actually it was speeding up preparations for expansion of the war. On July 11, the Konoe Fumimaro Cabinet issued a statement on sending troops to north China. On the 19th, the Hebei and Qahar authorities accepted the conditions put forward by the Japanese side and signed them. But the Japanese reinforcements had already arrived in the area of Beiping and Tianjin, and deployed for a battle. Around July 20, the Japanese troops launched attacks in the suburbs of Beiping. In a series of meetings with the ambassadors to China from Britain, the United States, Germany and France, Chiang Kai-shek asked for mediation by their countries. The National Government even indicated that it was ready to accept the settlement decided through negotiation between the Japanese side and the Hebei and Qahar authorities. But all his efforts came to nought. On the 26th, the Japanese troops captured Langfang. They then moved into the city of Beiping and fought with the Chinese garrison at Guanganmen. On that some day, the Japanese army sent Song Zheyuan an ultimatum. Not waiting for the reply from the Chinese side, the Japanese troops launched offensives at daybreak on July 28, and the 29th Corps hurriedly rose in resistance. Tong Linge, vice-commander of the corps, and Zhao Dengyu, a division commander were killed in action. Song Zheyuan was ordered to withdraw his forces from Beiping to Baoding. On the 29th and 30th, Beiping and Tianjin fell in succession.

To put pressure directly on the National Government, the Japanese troops launched offensives against Shanghai on August 13, 1937. The Chinese army fought back. On the 17th, the Japanese Cabinet met and decided to give up the policy of not expanding the war. Shanghai was China's largest financial, industrial and commercial centre. It was also the area where the interests of imperialist powers in China, such as Britain and the United States, were concentrated. On August 14, the National Government issued a statement on the war of self-defence and resistance. It said: "Driven by Japan's unlimited aggression, China now has no other choice but to rise to fight in self-defence and resist this violence." On the 20th, the Military Commission of the National Government divided the northern and southern battlefields into five war zones and worked out the operational policy: "Concentrate part of the National Army in north China to carry out protracted resistance, paying special attention to defending the natural barriers of Shanxi Province; concentrate the main force of the National Army in east China on fighting the enemy in Shanghai and strive to defend the strategically important Shanghai-Wusong area so as to consolidate the capital. In addition, a minimum amount of forces is to be sent to garrison the ports and harbours in south China." The Shanghai-southern Jiangsu-Zhejiang area was designated as the Third War Zone with Feng Yuxiang as commander (later on, Chiang Kai-shek put himself in command of this war zone). On August 15, the Japanese army set up its Shanghai headquarters with Matsui Iwane as commander. From the start of the Shanghai-Wusong Campaign, people from various circles of the whole country actively rendered their support to Shanghai's resistance. The Chinese local armed units marched to the front one after another as well.

On the day after the Luogouqiao Incident, the CPC Central Committee published an open telegram to the nation, calling upon the Chinese people, government and army to unite and build a strong Great Wall of the anti-Japanese national united front. The Red Army was ready to start for the front. To promote cooperation between the KMT and CPC to resist Japan, on July 15, Zhou Enlai, representative of the CPC, delivered to the KMT Central Executive Committee at Lushan the "Declaration of the CPC Central Committee on Making Public the Cooperation Between the KMT and CPC". The declaration put forth basic propositions such as quickly mobilizing national resistance, practising democratic politics and improving people's living standards. It announced that the CPC was willing to strive for the realization of Dr. Sun Yat-sen's Three People's Principles, stop attempting to overthrow the KMT regime and confiscating the land of the landlord class, rename the Soviet political power as the Special Regional Government, and redesignate the Red Army as the National Revolutionary Army. But at that time, Chiang Kai-shek had not yet determined to resist Japan, so the negotiations between the KMT and CPC still achieved no result. After the August 13th Incident, the Military Commission of the National Government announced on August 22 the redesignation of the Red Army as the Eighth Route Army and appointed Zhu De its commander and Peng Dehuai its deputy commander, with the 115th, 120th and 129th divisions under their command. After redesignation, the Red Army immediately marched to the front. Urged repeatedly by the CPC, the KMT at last published the CPC's declaration on cooperation between the KMT and CPC through the Central News Agency on September 22. The following day, Chiang Kai-shek gave a talk, pointing out the necessity of uniting to oppose the enemy, in effect recognizing the legal position of the CPC, though he described the cooperation as the "acceptance" of the CPC by the KMT so as to "enable it to work for the benefit of the nation." The publication of the Communist Party's declaration and Chiang Kai-shek's talk marked the formal beginning of the anti-Japanese national united front based on the cooperation between the

CPC and the KMT.

At the early stage of the war of resistance, the CPC Central Committee repeatedly suggested that the anti-Japanese national united front needed a fixed organization and a common programme for the various political parties and groups. Such an organization could be set up in this way: The KMT would be the national alliance participated in by other parties and groups which could keep their independence, or the national alliance would be jointly organized by various political parties and groups. But these two forms were rejected by the KMT. As the anti-Japanese national united front had no fixed organizational form, consultations could be conducted only when something important happened. The united front did not have a common programme either. As soon as the War of Resistance started, there existed two different guidelines: The CPC determined to fight a war of total resistance while the KMT wanted a war of partial resistance. The difference between these two guidelines and the struggle between them ran throughout the War of Resistance.

To carry out the line of total resistance and formulate the programmes and policies of defeating Japan, the CPC central Political Bureau held an enlarged meeting in Luochuan in northern Shaanxi in August 1937. The meeting adopted the "Resolution on the Current Situation and the Party's Tasks" as well as the "10-point Programme for Resisting Japan and Saving the Nation" drafted by Mao Zedong. The gist of the 10 points were: (1) Calling for the overthrow of Japanese imperialism; (2) general mobilization of all the nationa's military resources; (3) general mobilization of the people of the whole country; (4) reform of the political structure; (5) foreign policies in the resistance against Japan; (6) wartime financial and economic policies; (7) improving people's livelihood; (8) educational policies in the resistance against Japan; (9) liquidating traitors and pro-Japanese elements so as to consolidate the rear; (10) national solidarity for resistance against Japan. These 10 points summarized the basic political propositions of the CPC in the War of Resistance Against Japan, concretely expressed the CPC's guideline on a war of total resistance, and pointed out the road to the final victory in the War of Resistance. The meeting also decided the guiding principles for action at the new stage:

First, place the focal point in the Party's work on war zones and the enemy's rear areas, arouse the masses, carry out an independent guerrilla war and set up anti-Japanese bases behind enemy lines; secondly, take reduction of land rent and interest as the basic policy in solving the peasant problem during the War of Resistance; thirdly, give a free hand to the anti-Japanese mass movement in Kuomintang areas and struggle for people's political and economic rights; fourthly, change the Red Army's strategy, turning regular troops into guerrilla units and mobile warfare into guerrilla warfare.

After the Luochuan Meeting, the Eighth Route Army marched to the front in north China to conduct guerrilla war and establish base areas behind enemy lines. The 10-point Programme stipulated the policy on ethnic minorities: "Mobilize the Mongolians, Huis and other minorities to resist Japan together on the principle of national self-determination and autonomy." Then, the CPC put forth the proposition: National minorities such as Mongolians, Huis, Tibetans, Miaos and Yaos enjoy equal rights with the Han ethnic group; on the principle of joint resistance against Japan, they have the right to administer their own affairs and unite with the Hans to form a unified nation.

Being forced to resist Japan, the National Government still had reservations about fighting the Japanese to the very end. It feared that the people's strength would grow in the War of Resistance and constitute a menace to its rule. At the same time, it felt that it was not strong enough and needed the people's strength to resist Japanese attacks. So, on the one hand, it only relied on the government and its army to fight the War of Resistance, restricted the people's anti-Japanese democratic movement, and refused to reform the existing political and economic systems; on the other, it cherished illusions of intervention by the League of Nations and the signatory states of the Nine-State Pact to check Japan's aggression. However, it had to reduce its pressure on the people and give them freedom to a certain extent in the War of Resistance.

After the start of the anti-Japanese war, the KMT followed a line of partial resistance. The middle-of-the-road group (including the national bourgeoisie, the upper strata of the petty bourgeoisie, the enlightened gentry, and the local groups of strength) were for a war of firm resistance and against compromise and surrender. They demanded the carrying out of the War of Resistance by the entire nation and the realization of democratic politics. They expected the National Government to mobilize the people of the whole country to resist Japan, and supported the arousal of mass movements, thorough reform of the political structure and efforts to promote political democratization. But they put the responsibility of leading the War of Resistance to victory on the National Government and Chiang Kai-shek. The proposition put forward by the middle-of-the-road group played an active and progressive role in the period of resistance against Japanese aggression, although it was different both from the KMT's line of partial resistance and the CPC's line of total resistance.

China's War of Resistance won deep sympathy and active support from people all over the world. The Soviet Union sent China volunteer flyers. Norman Bethune from Canada led a medical team to China, and George Kotnis came with India's Aid-China Medical Group.

Having captured Beiping and Tianjin, the Japanese invading troops in north China separately launched offensives along the Beiping-Suiyuan, Beiping-Hankou and Tianjin-Pukou railway lines. On the Pingsui Railway, the Japanese troops first attacked Nankou, where they met with the Chinese garrison's fierce resistance. On August 13, Nankou fell. On the 27th of that same month, Zhangjiakou fell, too. In the first 10-day period of September, the Japanese troops pushed towards northern Shanxi in an attempt to occupy the province and bring the whole of north China under their control. Li Fuying, commander of the 61st Corps stationed at Datong, the strategically important city in northern Shanxi, led his troops to retreat rather than resist. On September 13, Datong came under Japanese occupation. Then the Japanese army continued its advance towards Suiyuan and captured Baotou on October 16 while directing its attack towards the south. To defend Taiyuan, the National Government concentrated massive forces around Xinkou for a decisive battle. During their march along the Beiping-Suiyuan Railway, the Japanese troops pushed southward along the Beiping-Hankou Railway in late August. Baoding fell on September 24. On October 10, the KMT troops withdrew from Shijiazhuang. After occupying it, the enemy divided its forces into two routes; one continued advancing south along the Beiping-Hankou Railway, and the other marched west along the Zhengtai Railway, in coordination with the Japanese troops in their march on Taiyuan. On October 13, some 60,000 Japnese troops started a fierce attack on Xinkou, where the Chinese defending forces resisted heroically. In 15 days, they wiped out 20,000 enemy troops. Chinese casualties exceeded 100,000. Hao Mengling, commander of the Ninth Corps, was killed in the battle. At this time, the enemy troops marching west captured the Niangziguan Pass on October 26. The KMT troops defending Xinkou suffered great losses through 20 days of bitter fighting. In addition, the war situation in eastern Shanxi was unfavourable. On November 2, they were ordered to evacuate Xinkou and move southward. Originally they planned to reach the position north of Taiyuan and help defend it. But because of enemy pursuit, they failed to do so. Then they crossed the Fenhe River and moved southwest. On the night of November 8, the enemy troops stormed into the city of Taiyuan. After fierce hand-to-hand fighting, the 2,000 remaining garrison troops led by Fu Zuoyi broke through the encirclement and moved to Mt. Xishan, and Taiyuan fell. On the Tianjin-Pukou Railway, the Japanese army intruded into the territory of Shandong Province. To conserve his forces, Han Fuqu avoided combat and abandoned Jinan on December 27 to flee to southwest Shandong. At the end of the year, Japanese troops landed at Qingdao. Now all the main cities and communication lines in north China were under Japan's occupation.

On the battlefields south of the Yangtze River, the Japanese mustered over 200,000 enemy troops, including navy, air and ground forces, to attack Shanghai. The KMT government deployed three lines of defence with more than 700,000 troops. This campaign lasted three months. Supported by the people of Shanghai, the Chinese army fought bravely. The 500 defending troops in Baoshan county town all heroically gave their lives after two days and nights of battling against heavy odds in the streets. The 800 warriors led by Xie Jinyuan were ordered to defend the Sihang Warehouses (Warehouses of the Four Banks) north of the Suzhou River. After four days and nights of bitter fighting, they broke through heavy encirclement and retreated into the public concession in Shanghai. On November 12, the Japanese took Shanghai at a cost of 60,000 casualties. The Chinese troops also suffered heavy casualties.

Having captured Shanghai, the enemy troops immediately marched on to invade Nanjing. On November 20, the KMT government declared they were moving the capital to Chongqing, but actually the government bodies were moved to Wuhan. So Wuhan became the provisional capital. The Japanese troops then advanced along two routes. One column, marching along the Shanghai-Nanjing rail line, took Suzhou and Wuxi in succession and then pressed on towards Nanjing. The other column set out west from the south of Taihu Lake. After seizing Jiaxing and Wujiang, this column divided its forces into two parts, one part starting from Langxi to move north to the south suburb of Nanjing in preparation for joining the offensive against the city. Another part was to attack Wuhu from Xuancheng in an attempt to cut off the Nanjing government's retreat. Chiang Kai-shek hurriedly decided to tenaciously defend Nanjing and established a garrison force composed of 14 divisions—about 100,000 troops, with Tang Shengzhi as commander. In early December Nanjing was already besieged on three sides. On the 8th, battles started near Nanjing. In the evening of December 12, the garrison was defeated. In this campaign the loss of KMT troops numbered 100,000, with countless abandoned weaponry and ammunition. On the 13th Nanjing fell. The Japanese invaders launched a "competition" to kill, rape and loot, which lasted six weeks. Over 300,000 Chinese people and soliders were massacred, and one third of the houses in the city were burned to ruins.

In the earlier period of the War of Resistance, the National Government was relatively active in fighting. At the same time, there were some changes in its domestic policy, such as recognizing the legal position of various political parties and groups, releasing some political offenders, promulgating the "Wartime Military Discipline" and "Regulations Regarding the Punishment of Traitors," revising the "Emergency Acts Regarding the Punishment of Those Endangering the Republic of China," and giving people more freedom. But the KMT only allowed the spread of the anti-Japanese democratic movement to a limited extent. Moreover, it was reluctant to reform the political structure, implement wartime financial and economic policies, and improve people's livelihood. While resisting Japan it also tried to seek compromise and hoped to rely on the League of Nations and Western powers to stop Japanese invasion. However, the League of Nations recognized only the fact of Japanese aggression, and suggested convening a conference of the nine signatory powers of the Nine-State Pact to discuss Japan's violation of the pact, instead of adopting substantial measures to aid China and apply sanctions against Japan. On November 3, the Eighth Conference of the Nine Signatory Powers was held in Brussels, Belgium. But it solved no problems, only raising a proposal that China and Japan cease fire. Meanwhile, the National Government accepted the mediation of Trautmann, the German ambassador to China. Chiang Kai-shek indicated that the conditions put forward by Japan could be regarded as the basis for negotiations. But, due to its occupation of Shanghai, Japan's terms of inveigling Chiang Kai-shek into surrender became more harsh, and also due to Chiang's fear of being opposed by the people of the country, Trautmann's mediation failed. After taking Nanjing, the Japanese government declared on January 16, 1938 (the first declaration by Knoe Fumimaro): "From now on the imperial government will not take the National Government as its opponent. It expects the founding and developing of a new political power in China that will cooperate genuinely with the empire."

As the Japanese imperialists would never stop fighting until the collapse of the National Government, the KMT was obliged to reiterate the policy of conducting a protracted war of resistance. In internal affairs it adopted a pose of being relatively enlightened and progressive. In March 1938, the KMT held a provisional national congress in Wuchang. The congress passed a declaration and the "Programme for the War of Resistance and National Reconstruction." The declaration stated that, "we should exert every effort in the struggle for national survival and independence, and, at the same time, accomplish political and economic construction on the basis of the Three People's Principles." On the one hand, the declaration voiced the determination of fighting the War of Resistance to the very end, and on the other, it hoped for Japan to change its policy so as to work with China to seek "a just peace." The Programme for the War of Resistance and National Reconstruction was the concrete expression of the KMT's political line. It laid down the KMT's policies on military, political, economic and diplomatic affairs. It wished to carry on the War of Resistance and national reconstruction at the same time. Chiang Kai-shek's explanation of the Three People's Principles should be taken as the "top standard" for the War of Resistance and national reconstruction, and that all the resistance forces should be under the leadership of the Kuomintang and Chiang Kai-shek. Apart from these requirements, the programme provided that political training should be strengthened in the army, guerrilla war be widely conducted in the areas behind enemy lines, organizations be set up for the people to participated in government and political affairs, political organs at all levels be improved, etc. These provisions were of positive significance. The documents adopted by the congress were of a dual nature. The KMT could make use of them to decide everything related to the War of Resistance and defend the rule of the big landlords and big bourgeoisie. But people could also take advantage of them to mobilize all forces for resistance against Japan and struggle against the KMT's erroneous policies.

The congress chose Chiang Kai-shek as the director-general of the KMT. It also resolved to set up an Investigation and Statistics Bureau under the Central Executive Committee to extend the secret service, and establish the Three People's Principles Youth League as an instrument to vie with the Communist Party for winning over young people. In July 1938, the Youth League was formed in Wuchang with Chiang Kai-shek as its head and Chen Cheng as its secretary. The congress decided that the National Government should convene the People's Political Council. In April 1938, the National Government promulgated the "Organizational Regulations of the People's Political Council." The Council was a mere consultative body and its resolutions had no binding force for the National Government. It had a membership of 200. All members were first chosen by the Central Executive Committee of the KMT and then announced by the National Government. Most of the councillors were KMT members. The establishment of the council was beneficial to the War of Resistance and promotion of democracy because it offered a place for various political parties and groups as well as people from various circles to voice their views on state affairs. In July 1938, the First Session of the People's Political Council opened in Wuhan.

After capturing Nanjing, the Japanese troops decided to take Xuzhou and open up the Tianjin-Pukou Railway so as to connect the battlefields in the north and south. To defend Xuzhou and pin down the main force of the enemy on the Tianjin-Pukou rail line, the National Government deployed 450,000 troops around Xuzhou. In March 1938, some 80,000 Japanese troops launched an offensive against Taierzhuang. The KMT troops under Li Zongren in the Fifth War Zone carried on a tenacious resistance for more than 10 days, attracted the enemy main force near Taierzhuang, and then encircled them with over 100,000 troops. In this campaign the Chinese troops wiped out 20,000 enemy troops and seized a large amount of weapons and equipment. This was a great victory in the War of Resistance in the frontal battlefields. Despite their defeat at Taierzhuang, the Japanese invaders continued to act according to their original plan and stepped up their deployment of military force to attack Xuzhou. From mid-April on, the enemy mustered 300,000 troops equipped with heavy weapons and besieged Xuzhou from six directions. In mid-May, the Lianyungang-Lanzhou (Longhai) Railway was cut off. To preserve effective strength, the National Government ordered the defenders to abandon Xuzhou and move to the Henan-Anhui border. On the 19th, Xuzhou fell.

After their occupation of Xuzhou, the Japanese mustered troops from the battlefields in the north and south to advance west along the Longhai Railway. On June 5, they took Kaifeng, and prepared to capture Zhengzhou to link up the Beiping-Hankou, Tianjin-Pukou and Lianyungang-Lanzhou railways so as to create a favourable situation for attacking Wuhan. To check the advance of the enemy troops, the National Government ordered the bombardment of the section of the Yellow River dyke at Huayuankou north of Zhengzhou, inundating over 3,000 square kilometres of land in Henan, Anhui and Jiangsu provinces, causing hundreds of thousands of people to drown.

The floods of the Yellow River temporarily stopped the Japanese troops' march west along the Longhai Railway, but they quickly changed their offensive direction. They moved their main force southward to coordinate with their naval vessels going up stream on the Yangtze River to attack Wuhan. Their offensive started early in June. They took Anqing on the 12th, captured Madang in late June, seized Hukou in early July, and occupied Jiujiang on July 26. In early August the enemy mobilized 12 divisions, 350,000 strong, 500 aircraft and 120 warships to attack Wuhan from five directions. The National Government built strong fortifications on the periphery of Wuhan, and concentrated 129 divisions and other armed forces totalling 1.1 million, 40 warships, and more than 100 aircraft there. The Chinese troops fought against the Japanese invaders on the vast battlefields from the northern and southern slopes of the Dabie Mountains to the banks of the Yangtze River. On October 25, the Chinese troops gave up Wuhan. The campaign to defend Wuhan lasted over four months, including hundreds of big and small battles, inflicting 200,000 casualties on the Japanese. At the same time, the enemy troops in south China landed at Daya Bay of Guangdong Province on October 12. On October 21, Guangzhou fell.

During the 15 months from the July 7th Incident to the fall of Wuhan and Guangzhou, the KMT troops had fought heroically on the frontal battlefields and many of them gave their lives for their country. But still, vast expanses of China's territory guickly fell into enemy hands, including areas in the provinces of Hebei, Shanxi, Qahar, Suiyuan, Shandong and Henan in the north, and the Nanjing-Shanghai-Hangzhou region and Wuhan region in central China as well as the Guangzhou area in the south. This was the result of the enemy's strength and China's weakness, of the KMT leading group cherishing illusions of depending on big powers to check Japan's aggression and their use of temporary resistance to achieve the short-lived respite of compromise with Japan, and of the KMT line of partial resistance and the strategic policy of passive defence, as well as many troops becoming corrupt and a number of commanders being incompetent in directing operations or having ulterior motives.

During the War of Resistance, there were the gradually expanding Communist-led battlefields behind enemy lines in liberated areas, in addition to battlefields at the front with KMT troops as the main force. After being redesignated as the Eighth Route Army and the New Fourth Army, the Red Army cooperated with the KMT troops to fight against the enemy. This was the main form of cooperation between the CPC and the KMT at that time. From the start of the War of Resistance, the Eighth Route Army brought about a strategic shift from regular to guerrilla forces and from mobile to guerrilla warfare to meet the military and political needs. This was an important shift related with the fundamental interests of the people. From the end of August to the end of October 1937, the three divisions of the Eighth Route Army and the general headquarters had left northern Shaanxi and crossed the Yellow River to reach the battle front in Shanxi. At that time, the enemy troops were waging vigorous offensives against Shanxi's strategically important sites defended by the KMT forces. To crush the arrogance of the Japanese invaders and coordinate with the KMT troops in military operations, the Eighth Route Army fought many battles. On September 25, a unit of the 115th Division ambushed the 21st Brigade of the Japanese Fifth Division (the Itagaki Division) at Pingxingguan Pass. A full day of fierce fighting wiped out over 1,000 enemy troops. This was the first great victory won by the Chinese armed forces since the start of the nationwide War of Resistance. To support the KMT army in the Xinkou Campaign for the defence of Taiyuan, the 120th Division repeatedly cut off the communication lines in the enemy's rear, ambushed the enemy's motor transport corps and annihilated its reinforcements. On the night of October 19, the 769th Regiment of the 129th Division sent a battalion to attack the enemy's airport in Daixian County, destroying 24 aircraft. On November 8, the KMT troops abandoned Taiyuan and retreated towards southern and southwestern Shanxi. Mao Zedong pointed out: "In north China, the regular war with the KMT as the main force has ended and the guerrilla war with the Communist Party as the main force has entered the major arena." After the evacuation of the KMT army from north China, it was necessary to set up base areas for conducting widespread guerrilla war. Following the strategic plan of the CPC Centrla Committee and Mao Zedong, the Eighth Route Army mobilized the masses, independently expanded the guerrilla war, and established many anti-Japanese democratic base areas.

After the Pingxingguan Campaign, the 115th Division sent its main force south, leaving 3,000 men under Political Commissar Nie Rongzhen in the Wutai mountain area. In November, the Shanxi-Qahar-Hebei Military Area was set up with Fuping and Wutai as its centre. After the besiegement by 20,000 Japanese troops was overcome, a conference was held in Fuping in January 1938, attended by the representatives from army units, government departments and the people of various circles, and the Provisional Administrative Committee of the Shanxi-Qahar-Hebei Border Region came into being. This was the first anti-Japanese democratic political power established behind enemy lines. From April to July 1938, the armed forces of the Border Region launched two attacks on the Beiping-Hankou, Beiping-Suiyuan and Zhending-Taiyuan railways. In September, the enemy mustered 50,000 troops to besiege and attack the central district of the region. A month of hard counterattack caused the enemy to suffer 5,000 casualties. Afterwards, a succession of anti-Japanese base areas were established in western Beiping, central and eastern Hebei. In central Hebei, a Hui people's detachment was formed.

After the fall of Taiyuan, the CPC Central Committee instructed the 120th Division to conduct guerrilla war in the vast mountain area and countryside in northwestern Shanxi. The division opened up the northwestern Shanxi base and the Mt. Daqing base separately. Later on, these two bases were combined as the Shanxi-Suiyuan anti-Japanese base area. In March 1938, the 120th Division destroyed the siege by 10,000 Japanese and puppet troops, and wiped out 1,500 of them.

The 129th Division moved to southeastern Shanxi after Taiyuan fell and opened up an anti-Japanese base area with its centre in the Taihang Mountains. An April 1938, the Shanxi-Hebei-Henan Military Area was set up. In that same month when 30,000 enemy troops attacked southeastern Shanxi, the Chinese troops there wiped out 4,000 of them. In the spring of 1938, the 129th Division marched to southern Hebei and established an anti-Japanese base there. In May, part of the 129th Division and 115th Division entered the border between Hebei and Shandong, where they opened up a base area for resistance against Japan.

In May 1938, the CPC Central Committee sent a number of cadres to Shandong to help set up a guerrilla base area with its centre in Yimeng Mountains. A Shandong Column then was organized as part of the Eighth Route Army.

In October 1937, the Red Army guerrilla detachments in the eight southern provinces were redesignated as the New Fourth Army. In January 1938, the headquarters of the army was established in Nanchang, Jiangxi Province, with Ye Ting as commander and Xiang Ying (1898-1941) as deputy commander. The New Fourth Army had four detachments under its command. In 1938 and 1939, the army set up the southern Jiangsu base area centred around Maoshan Mountain, the southern Anhui base area and the base along the Tianjin-Pukou Railway.

To sum up, the Eighth and New Fourth armies under CPC leadership as well as other people's anti-Japanese armed forces widely launched guerrilla war behind enemy lines, established anti-Japanese democratic bases and gradually opened up battlefields in the enemy's rear area. From September 1937 to October 1938, the Eighth Route Army had fought 1,500 battles, and inflicted over 50,000 casualties on the enemy. In number it grew to 156,000, and the New Fourth Army to 25,000. The population of the anti-Japanese base areas behind enemy lines reacheα 50 million. This showed the tremendous power of people's war; it was also a great victory for the Communist Party's line of total resistance and its strategic policy of independently carrying out guerrilla war in the enemy's rear.

At the same time, the Shaanxi-Gansu-Ningxia Border Region became further consolidated. In September 1937, the regional government was officially set up with 23 counties under its jurisdiction. In November, with the completion of general elections, democratic political power at various levels in the region came into being. After the founding of anti-Japanese democratic political power in the Shaanxi-Gansu-Ningxia Border Region, a series of democratic reforms were under taken as well as struggles against bandits, traitors and special agents, reactionary landlords and despotic gentry. In January 1939, with the establishment of the regional assembly, an administrative programme during the War of Resistance in the region was adopted.

Construction in the political, economic, military and cultural fields now grew vigorously in the region, earning it fame as the model anti-Japanese democratic base. In the course of the anti-Japanese war, the CPC Central Committee had been guiding the people of China politically to resist the Japanese invaders in Yan'an, capital of the Shaanxi-Gansu-Ningxia Border Region.

To direct the people of the whole country to resist Japan and seize the final victory, Mao Zedong wrote two important military treatises in May 1938—"Problems of Strategy in Guerrilla War Against Japan" and "On Protracted War." In the latter, the author made a brilliant exposition on the objective conditions which would lead China to win through waging a protracted war. Proceeding from realities, he analyzed the strong and weak points of China and Japan, and refuted the theory of national subjugation and that of quick victory. He pointed out that the war would undergo the three stages of strategic defensive, strategic stalemate and strategic counterattack. He added that conducting protracted war was the general principle of strategy in the War of Resistance. To carry it out required the employment of the following tactics: the use of initiative, flexibility and planning in conducting offensives within the defensive, battles of quick decision within the protracted war, and exterior-line operations within the interior-line operations. He emphatically expounded the idea of people's war, saying, "The army and the people are the foundation of victory." In these two articles, he elucidated the important strategic position of guerrilla war in the whole process of the War of Resistance, criticized the mistake of looking down upon guerrilla war, and pointed out the way to develop guerrilla war into regular war so as to make the victory of the War of Resistance a victory for the people.

Different guidelines existed during the War of Resistance. As each class and political party had goals and standpoints of its own, the question of leadership was a salient and practical one. This question of leadership was spelled out by Mao Zedong at the Luochuan Meeting. "In the united front, is the proletariat to lead the bourgeoisie, or the bourgeoisie to lead the proletariat? Is the Kuomintang to attract the Communist Party, or the Communist Party to attract the Kuomintang?" On November 12, 1937, Mao made the report "The Situation and Tasks in the Anti-Japanese War After the Fall of Shanghai and Taiyuan" in Yan'an at a meeting of Party activists. In the report he analyzed the differences in principle between the CPC's line of total resistance and the KMT's line of partial resistance, and pointed out that it was essential to follow the line of total resistance and put into effect the 10-point Programme for Resisting Japan and Saving the Nation. In addition, he stressed that capitulationism must be combatted both inside the Party and throughout the country. By the end of November 1937, Wang Ming returned to Yan'an from the Soviet Union. He developed the Rightist tendency existing only among a number of people inside the Party to become a kind of representative opinion, and put forward such mistaken slogans as "Everything through the united front" and "Everything must be submitted to the united front." He went so far as to issue incorrect declarations in the name of the Party Central Committee without its approval. He adhered to his Rightist stand in the work he was in charge of. To summarize the experience since the War of Resistance, formulate the Party's basic policies in the stalemate period of the anti-Japanese war and unify the guiding ideology of the Party, the Enlarged Sixth Plenary Session of the CPC Sixth Central Committee was held in Yan'an from September 29 to November 6, 1938. Mao Zedong made a political report "On the New Stage" and a summarization of the session. Many people gave speeches on the experience of the anti-Japanese war over the past 15 months, and Wang Ming's Rightist capitulationism was criticized. The session passed the "Political Resolutions of the Enlarged Sixth Plenary Session of the CPC Sixth Central Committee" and approved the line of the Political Bureau headed by Mao Zedong. The session called on all Party members to take up the great historic responsibility of playing the leading role in the War of Resistance, reiterated the policy of organizing unrestricted and independent popular armed struggle and concentrating the Party's main work in the war zones and the base areas behind enemy lines. It stressed the necessity for the whole Party to study Marxism-Leninism, especially the Marxist standpoints and methods in observing and solving problems, apply the general principles of Marxism-Leninism in China's concrete circumstances, and oppose dogmatism. This session basically overcame Wang Ming's

Right capitulationist mistakes, made the whole Party take concerted action, worked out an overall strategic plan for the CPC to hold the leading position in the anti-Japanese war and promoted work in various fields.

From the outbreak of the Lugouqiao Incident to the fall of Wuhan and Guangzhou, vast areas in north, central and south China came under Japanese occupation. Most of the main formations of the KMT army retreated to the southwest and northwest. The Eighth Route and New Fourth armies had already penetrated into the enemy's rear in north and central China to conduct guerrilla war and set up bases. Now there were three kinds of areas in China in an interlocking "jigsaw" pattern, namely, the Kuomintang area, the liberated area and the enemy-occupied area. In the Kuomintang area, the Kuomintang was the party in power exercising one-party dictatorship. In other words, political power belonged to big landlords and big bourgeoisie. In the liberated area, political power belonged to the national united front under the leadership of the Communist Party, organized to conduct the anti-Japanese war and uphold democracy. It was the political power of new democracy. In the enemy-occupied area, the Japanese imperialists gathered traitors to establish a puppet regime to exercise colonial rule. This political and military pattern did not come to an end until the day of victory over Japan.

After their occupation of Beiping and Tianjin, the Japanese invaders immediately organized an association to maintain public order and planned the founding of a unified puppet regime in north China. On December 14, 1937, the puppet provisional government of the Republic of China headed by Wang Kemin came into being composed of legislative, administrative and judicial committees separately led by Tang Erhe, Wang Kemin and Dong Kang. The puppet provisional government adopted a five-coloured "national flag" and continued to designate the years of its rule according to those of the Republic of China. The puppet authorities renamed Beiping as Beijing and took it as their "capital." With the appearance of the puppet provisional government, the puppet government in eastern Hebei disappeared. Under the jurisdiction of the puppet provisional government were the administrative offices of Hebei, Shandong, Shanxi and Henan as well as the two municipal governments of Beijing and Tianjin.

In September 1937, the Japanese set up the puppet Southern Qahar Autonomous Government with Zhangjiakou as its centre and including 10 counties south of Qahar. In October, the puppet Northern Shanxi Autonomous Government was established in the area of the 13 counties north of Shanxi with Datong as its centre. In that same month, the puppet Mongolian Coalition Autonomous Government was founded in Guisui with Demchukdonggrub as the president of the Government Administration Council. In November, the three puppet political powers were organized into the puppet Mongolia and Xinjiang United Committee. In September 1939, the United Committee was reorganized as the puppet Mongolian United Autonomous Government with Demchukdonggrub as its chairman, and Li Shouxing, Xia Gong, and Yu Pinqing vice-chairmen.

After capturing Shanghai, the Japanese organized the puppet Shanghai Municipal Government. In January 1938, they set up the puppet Nanjing Autonomous Committee and Hangzhou Public Order Maintenance Association. On March 28 the so-called Reform Government of the Republic of China came into being, headed by Liang Hongzhi. Under the puppet government were the executive, legislative and judicial councils and a secretary office. In addition, the provincial governments of Jiangsu, Zhejiang and Anhui as well as the two special municipal governments of Nanjing and Shanghai were under its jurisdiction.

All of these puppet political powers were set up under Japanese control. Everything was manipulated by Japanese officials and advisors. The Japanese invaders also set up various kinds of "mass organizations" in the areas under their occupation to cooperate with the puppet regime to exercise colonial rule. In December 1937, the Japanese invaders established the "Xin Min Hui" (New People's Association) with Wang Kemin as its president and Miao Bin as the head of the Central Guidance Department. In Shanghai and Hankou, the Japanese imperialists respectively formed "Da Min Hui" (Great People's Association) and the "Zheng Yi Hui" (Justice Association).

12. Changes in the Situation of the Anti-Japanese War from the Stage of Stalemate

Although Japan carried out strategic offensives on a large scale and captured vast areas of Chinese territory during the period from the outbreak of the Lugouqiao Incident to the fall of Wuhan and Guangzhou, they failed to make China give in. Its policy of fighting a quick war to force a decision went bankrupt. Protracted war brought increasing difficulties to Japan. In the course of time from the Beiping-Tianjin Campaign to the decisive battle at Wuhan, Japan had thrown in 24 divisions in north, central and south China, accounting for over two thirds of the total divisions of its ground forces. By the end of 1938, Japanese casualties amounted to 447,000. Due to the protractedness of the war and the extension of the battle line, Japan already found its armed force insufficient, and its military expenditure growing. In addition, anti-war feeling was becoming strong among the Japanese people. In contrast, although China suffered heavy losses in the war, her people were more resolute to fight to the very end. The Eighth Route and New Fourth armies' guerrilla war in the enemy's rear and the many anti-Japanese base areas there had brought into existence large battlefields behind enemy lines. The National Government now still commanded a great number of troops to resist the enemy. Internationally, the expansion of the war of invasion in China had deepened tensions between Japan and the United States and Britain. Thus came the stage of strategic stalemate in the Sino-Japanese War.

In view of the protracted war with China, its increasing difficulties at home and its diplomatically isolated position, the Japanese government was obliged to re-examine its policies towards China. Adhering to the general principle of conquering China, it made a number of revisions in tactics. In November 1938, the Japanese government and the supreme headquarters of the Japanese army formulated a new policy of "readjusting Japan-China relations." This meant strengthening its political offensive instead of expanding the war to force the National Government to give in. Originally the Japanese imperialists had put military offensive first and politically luring China into surrender second. Now they decided to place military attack and political lures on a par. To cope with the protracted war, they planned to further guarantee public order and self-reliance of the areas under their occupation. To reinforce the army on the battlefields behind their lines, they resolved to transfer part of their troops in south and central China to north China. This was an important change in Japan' tactics towards China.

In order to lure the KMT into surrender, the Japanese government issued a declaration (the second declaration by Konoe Fumimaro) in November 1938, which stated that Japan would not decline to negotiate with the National Government so long as it would abandon its current policy and reshuffle the National Government. In December, the Japanese government issued another declaration (the third declaration by Konoe Fumimaro), putting forth the three principles of good neighbourliness, joint containing of communism, and economic cooperation as the general policy of "readjusting relations and building the New Order of East Asia by Japan, Manchukuo and China." The declaration stressed that Japan would "cooperate" with the National Government, and even by willing to consider giving up its extraterritoriality and returning its concession if China would recognize "Manchukuo," sign an agreement of jointly containing communism, recognize Japan's privileges of economy and of stationing its troops in Inner Mongolia and north China, and recognize that Japanese enjoyed freedom to reside and do business in China's interior. Japan's policy change greatly affected China' War of Resistance. Apart from the open capitulation of the Wang Jingwei group, the Chiang Kai-shek clique also began to waver. Furthermore, its reactionary nature became more obvious, and the relations between the KMT and CPC took a turn for the worse. The anti-Japanese war now became more complicated.

At that time, Wang Jingwei was deputy director-general of the Kuomintang, chairman of the Central Political Committee, vice-chairman of the Supreme Conference of National Defence, and president of the People's Political Council. This group included Zhou Fuhai, a member of the KMT Central Executive Committee and director of propaganda, and Chen Gongbo, a member of the KMT Central Executive Committee and minister of industry. On December 18, 1938, Wang Jingwei secretly left Chongqing for Kunming by air. The following day he and Zhou Fuhai fled to Hanoi. On the 29th, Wang Jingwei responded to Fumimaro's third declaration by telegram, announcing that he would like to "negotiate for peace" with Japan on the basis of the three principles set by Fumimaro. Wang's going over to the enemy enraged public opinion. The KMT Central Executive Committee issued a declaration in January 1939, expelling Wang Jingwei from the Kuomintang and dismissing him from all his posts. In May, Wang went to Shanghai to plan setting up a bogus KMT Central Executive Committee and a bogus National Government. In June, the National Government issued an order to arrest him.

Immediately after the Japanese imperialists changed their China policy, the Fifth Plenary Session of the Kuomintang's Fifth Central Executive Committee was held in January 1939. The session focused on the questions pertinent to the anti-Japanese war and national construction at the new stage. On the anti-Japanese war, the session considered that the third declaration by Fumimaro was "a message aimed at inducing China to surrender" instead of one setting conditions for peace negotiations, and that it was a ploy by the enemy to make a quick peace. The session expressed the determination of "carrying the protracted War of Resistance through to the end." But Chiang Kai-shek openly stated that what he meant by "to the end" in the slogan was merely "to restore the status quo before the Lugouqiao Incident." This was the condition set forth by Chiang Kai-shek for peace negotiations when Trautmann was mediating between Japan and the Kuomintang. On national construction, the session concentrated on three matters: Strengthening unity, conducting active struggle, and stepping up construction. But the key points were to "improve party work" and "rejuvenate the Kuomintang," in order to consolidate Chiang Kai-shek's position, and strengthen the force in "active struggle against the Communist Party." To strengthen unified command over the party, government and military affairs the Supreme Committee of National Defence was established after the session to function in the capacity of the Political Council of the Central Executive Committee, with Chiang

Kai-shek as its chairman. The session decided the principle of "containing, restricting and eroding communism," and the establishment of the Committee for Containing Communism. Afterwards, the KMT secretly issued a series of anti-Communist documents such as "Measures for Dealing with the Communist Problem," "Measures for Guarding Against Communist Activities in the Japanese-Occupied Area," and "Measues for Restricting the Activities of Alien Parties." The contents of these documents were: Denying the Existence of the Shaanxi-Gansu-Ningxia Border Region and the anti-Japanese democratic bases; restricting the growth of the Eighth Route Army, the New Fourth Army and the anti-Japanese guerrilla detachments; prohibiting the Communist Party from organizing mass movements; disbanding Communist-led anti-Japanese groups and revolutionary organizations; forbidding communists to serve in the Kuomintang's military and political organs and, especially, strictly preventing Communists from infiltrating the KMT and setting up secret organizations. But all of these measures were carried out in the name of resistance against Japan, or under the pretext of "unifying the administrative system ... unifying military orders and government decrees ... following the programmes of resisting Japan and building the country ... [and] ... putting into practice the Three People's Principles." After the session, the KMT became passive in the War of Resistance while increasing its reactionary anti-Communist activities. However, because the main issue in China at that time was the struggle between China and Japan, the Kuomintang was neither willing to break publicly with the Communist Party nor daring to restore such slogans as "wiping out Communists." On the one hand, it continued to work with the Communist Party in the War of Resistance, and on the other, it did everything it could to guard against and restrict Communists. This dual nature was characteristic of the KMT hard liners during the anti-Japanese war.

Japan continued its effort to lure the KMT into surrender. It changed the original policy of abandoning Chiang Kai-shek to that of recognizing his position. In March 1939, the new Japanese prime minister, Hiranuma, issued an official statement, saying, "If General Chiang Kai-shek and the government under his leadership could reconsider their anti-Japanese attitude and work together with Japan to seek the establishment of the New Order of East Asia, Japan would be prepared to negotiate an end to hostilities." Proceeding from their own interests, the United States and Britain both advised the KMT and Chiang to surrender. In view of the intense situation in Europe, Britain was powerless to take action in the Far East. To maintain its interests in China and Southeast Asia, it hoped that China could reach a compromise with Japan. The U.S., too, was reluctant to be involved in the war between China and Japan. It indicated readiness to take part in negotiations that would be favourable to US interests. In December 1938, British ambassador Carl left Shanghai for Chongqing to meet with Chiang Kai-shek and others. Afterwards, he said that if China and Japan intended to develop closer ties, Britain was more than willing to act as a mediator. Early in 1939, Britain and the U.S. spread news through the press about a Pacific conference to be held to settle the "clash between China and Japan." In April, Carl went to Chongqing again to persuade the KMT government to seek a compromise with Japan. Around October, the American and British ambassadors went together to Chongqing. Wang Chonghui, foreign minister of the KMT government, expressed the hope of promoting the success of the mediation. Kong Xiangxi said, "The restoration of peace in the Far East is essential for the protection of the United States' interests." One after another Zhang Qun and others now went to Hong Kong to explore ways to achieve "peace."

In these circumstances the tendency towards compromise grew among the KMT ruling clique and clashes with the Communists were increasingly frequent. On June 7, 1939, the CPC Central Committee issued a directive on opposing capitulation, which pointed out, "The greatest danger at present is the possibility of the Kuomintang's capitulation." The directive called on the Communist Party to exert all its efforts in the struggle against capitulationists and anti-Communist elements. It made clear that the basic task of the Party was still to consolidate KMT-CPC cooperation and continue the War of Resistance. On June 10, Mao Zedong gave a report opposing capitulation at a meeting attended by senior cadres in Yan'an. He emphasized that the possibility of Kuomintang capitulation has now become the greatest danger and its anti-communist actions were a preparatory step to capitulation. At the same time, he analyzed the Fifth Plenary Session of the Kuomintang's Fifth Central Executive Committee as containing anti-communist and capitulationist elements, but its main orientation was still unity with the Communist Party to resist Japan. He warned that a prudent attitude should be taken towards Chiang Kai-shek and that it would be reckless to restore the slogans opposing Chiang. He added, "The Communist Party should help Chiang to cross over to the good side. On anti-Communist friction, our policy is unity while not forgetting to struggle, as well as struggle while not forgetting to unite, and unity should be our main focus." In its declaration on July 7, marking the second anniversary of the War of Resistance, the CPC Central Committee put forth the following three slogans: "Carry the War of Resistance through to the end—Oppose halfway compromise!"; "Consolidate unity at home—Oppose splits from within!" and "Strive for progress of the whole country—Oppose retrogression!"

After their occupation of Guangzhou and Wuhan, the Japanese found their military strength was insufficient to further expand the war of aggression. Meanwhile, they estimated that relations between the Kuomintang and the Communist Party would not break up for the time being although their frictions took place very often. Based on this judgement, Japanese imperialists decided to ensure the control of all their occupied areas and not to engage in large-scale battles thereafter. From January 1939 to March 1940, Japanese troops in north China had launched three battles in succession to guarantee public order. Confronted with the enemy's fierce attack, people and soldiers in the liberated areas behind enemy lines rose to fight heroically and dealt the enemy heavy blows. In the third year of the War of Resistance, the Eighth Route Army engaged the Japanese and puppet troops in over 6,900 operations and wiped out 113,000 of them. In 1939 and 1940, the New Fourth Army engaged the Japanese and puppet troops in 2,400 operations, putting 51,000 of them out of action. The largest of these in north China was the Hundred-Regiment Campaign from August to December 1940. It involved the participation of 105 regiments composed of 400,000 troops as well as more than 200,000 peasants in logistic support. They fought 1,824 big and small battles altogether, wiping out 46,300 Japanese and puppet troops. Of these,

20,600 were Japanese soldiers. In the three years from the beginning of the anti-Japanese war to 1940, the Eighth Route and New Fourth armies had recovered 150 county seats and a vast expanse of lost territory.

In the course of the struggle against the enemy, the people's revolutionary forces led by the Communist Party had grown rapidly. By July 1940, the Eighth Route Army, the New Fourth Army and the South China Guerrilla Detachment had increased to nearly 500,000, Communist Party members grown to 800,000, and the population of the base areas to some 100 million. The liberated area in north China had been consolidated, the liberated area in central China developed, and that in south China had been set up, due to the concerted efforts of the revolutionary army and people. The Communist-led forces of resistance had now become the main forces insisting on victory.

To cut of the supply lines in China's rear, control its communication hubs and put pressure on the National Government, the Japanese army launched new offensives in south and central China from the beginning of 1939 to autumn that same year. The Japanese troops landed at Hainan Island, and captured cities like Nanchang, Shantou, Changsha (from which they later withdrew) and Nanning. In May 1940, the enemy started the Xiangyang-Yichang Campaign in an attempt to ensure their hold on Wuhan, and threaten Chongqing. Zhang Zizhong, commander of the 33rd Group Army, was killed while directing a battle. Xiangyang and Yichang fell one after the other. From the spring of 1939 to 1941, the Japanese air force carried out extensive bombing of cities in China's rear, especially Chongqing, causing heavy casualties and great losses.

Because of the Japanese army's large-scale offensives against the base areas behind their lines, the pressure brought to bear on the KMT's frontal battlefields was relatively reduced. Therefore, after the Fifth Plenary Session of its Fifth Central Executive Committee, the Kuomintang was capable of strengthening its rule. First, it conducted the large-scale "General Mobilization of the National Spirit". Under the Supreme Council of National Defence, the Association of General Mobilization of the National Spirit headed by Chiang Kai-shek was established, and, at the same time, the "Programme of the General

Mobilization of the National Spirit" was made public. This movement was launched in the name of reforming the national spirit to enable victory over the enemy, but, in the main, it was actually a call for people's loyalty and filial piety to the state under the dictatorship of big landlords and big bourgeoisie, in order to maintain "the unity of military, political and administrative systems," and reject all kinds of "alien views and confused ideas." Secondly, the KMT greatly tightened the control over political power at the grassroots level. Starting from 1939, it pursued the so-called new county system, bringing under its control all the local political affairs, finance and economy, education, and armed forces as well as mass organizations and training. By the end of 1943, the "new county system" had been put into practise in 21 provinces. Thirdly, it employed the trick of "constitutional government." In September 1939, the Kuomintang suddenly resorted to this fraud in order to block people's democratic demands. At the Fourth Session of the First People's Political Council, a KMT councillor suggested the government convene the National Assembly to draw up a constitution and begin constitutional government. The Sixth Plenary Session of the Kuomintang's Fifth Central Executive Committee held in November decided that the National Assembly was to be opened on November 12, 1940. From then on, the people throughout the country launched a movement for the promotion of a constitutional government. Representative figures of political parties, classes and organizations made speeches or published articles on this topic. Thus the question of constitutional government for a time became the focus of people's attention. Knowing well that the Kuomintang had no intention of putting constitutional government into effect, the Chinese Communist Party still actively took part in the movement because practising constitutional government was the people's desire and demand. Mass organizations promoting constitutional government were set up in Yan'an and the anti-Japanese base areas. Awed by the mighty movement, the Kuomintang declared in September 1940 that due to the problem of communications, there were difficulties in convening the National Assembly, and the opening of it would be postponed till further decision. The movement for constitutional government, which had once been lively, now came to an end.

Since the Fifth Plenary Session of the Kuomintang's Fifth Central Executive Committee, anti-Communist clashes had been growing in severity. From April to November 1939, the Kuomintang diehards engineered massacres in Boshan, Shenxian, Pingjiang and Queshan. From the end of 1939 to the spring of 1940, they launched their first large-scale armed clash in north China since the start of the War of Resistance, namely, the first anti-Communist onslaught. During this period, the Kuomintang diehard troops started offensives against the Eighth Route Army in main three regions. Around the Shaanxi-Gansu-Ningxia Border Region, the Kuomintang erected five blockade lines. In December 1939, troops under Hu Zongnan occupied five county seats of the region. In Shanxi, Yan Xishan created the Western Shanxi Incident in December 1939, ordering his troops to besiege and attack the Second Column of the Dare-to-Die Corps and the Independent Detachment of the Eighth Route Army, both garrisoning western Shanxi. In addition, Yan Xishan's troops cooperated with Chiang Kai-shek's army to attack the First and Third columns of the Dare-to-Die Corps in south-eastern Shanxi, destroyed the anti-Japanese democratic political powers and mass organizations of Qinshui and six other counties, massacred 500 people and arrested more than 1,000. In the spring of 1940, Shi Youshan's troops attacked the Eighth Route Army in the anti-Japanese base area in southern Hebei and Zhu Huaibing's troops marched on the Taihang region where the Eighth Route Army headquarters was located. The anti-Communist onslaught plunged the War of Resistance and the anti-Japanese national united front into a serious crisis. The tactic adopted by the Communist Party was to wage a tit-for-tat struggle against the Kuomintang diehards, namely, hitting back at them while not breaking up the overall situation of unity against Japan. Following this instruction, people and soldiers in the liberated areas rose to counterattack and repulse the offensives by the KMT's diehard army. Then, in January 1940 the Communist Party, taking the initative, proposed a ceasefire for negotiations with the Kuomintang. In March, the CPC Central Committee pointed out: "At present, the struggle against KMT onslaughts in Shanxi and Hebei should be ended without delay. It should not be allowed to expand further." Thus the large-scale armed clash basically subsided.

Beginning with the summer of 1939, a controversy over the question of the Three People's Principles developed in China's political and ideological world. For the Kuomintang, this controversy was a part of its anti-Communist activities. To realize the second Kuomintang-Communist cooperation, the Communist Party announced time and again before and after the outbreak of the anti-Japanese war: "The Three People's Principles initiated by Dr. Sun Yat-sen are what China needs today. Our Party is ready to fight for their complete realization." Taking advantage of this announcement, the Kuomintang conducted a vigorous propaganda campaign to "erode communism." They said the Communist Party should give up communist since it had declared that it supported the Three People's Principles. They insisted that the Kuomintang was the only party needed in China to carry out the Three People's Principles and there was no need for the existence of the Communist Party. A massive compaign advocating "one doctrine," "one party" and "one leader" was launched. The Three People's Principles founded by Sun Yat-sen were actually progressive and revolutionary, and as such failed to meet the need of Chiang Kai-shek's clique and were disagreeable to it. However, this was a banner which Chiang Kai-shek would not abandon. The creation of Chiang Kai-shek's version of "Three People's Principles" became necessary. "The System of the Three People's Principles and the Procedure of Putting It into Practice," published by Chiang Kai-shek in May 1939, was a systematic interpretation of these principles. Chiang Kai-shek cast aside the revolutionary spirit of Sun Yat-sen's Three People's Principles, only culling certain phrases out of them for his own composition. He explained history in terms of the people's livelihood and contrasted it to historical materialism. He said that "sincerity" was the "moving force of revolution." Speaking of the implementation of the Three People's Principles, he said, "We must take the period of military government as the basis and, at the same time, step up the work for the political tutelage period." The main task for the political tutelage period was to "start regional autonomy." "The enemy can be defeated and a new China built immediately, so long as people seriously study the Three People's Principles by following this ideology and pursuing this doctrine according to this 'order of practice'," he added. A number of reactionary scholars and bourgeois Rightists also attacked the Communist Party and Marxism-Leninism by adopting a pose of defending the Three People's Principles. Ye Qing, renegade from the Communist Party, published a series of pamphlets such as *China's Present Stage and Future, On the Questions of China's Politics* and *Discussion with Socialists on China's Revolution* to publicize Chiang-brand fascism and oppose the Communist Party and communist ideology with the "theory of single revolution."

In order to defend Marxism-Leninism, defend the democratic revolutionary programme of the Communist Party and the revolutionary Three People's Principles, promote the cause of China's national liberation and hit back against the Kuomintang's political and ideological offensives, the Chinese Communists published many articles setting out their basic views on the Three People's Principles, on communism, and on China's revolution. Their main points exhorted: (1) uphold the genuine Three People's Principles, oppose the fake Three People's Principles and adhere to the New Three People's Principles; (2) correctly understand the relationship between communism and the Three People's Principles; and (3) stick to the theory of revolution by stages, and refute the "theory of single revolution." The controversy over the Three People's Principles was an important struggle in the field of politics and ideology. It spurred the Communist theory of new democratic revolution on to its growth and maturity.

In the course of leading the Chinese peoples to carry out new-democratic revolution, the Communist Party had criticized and repudiated both the "Left" and Right errors, summarized all correct experiences, and evolved its theory of China's new-democratic revolution. In October 1939, the CPC Central Committee published *The Communist*, a journal for guiding the building of the Party, with a special introduction written by Mao Zedong. In this article Mao summed up the historical experience of the Communist Party over the past 18 years and drew the very important conclusion: "United front, armed struggle, and the building of the Party are the three magic weapons for the Communist Party to defeat the enemy in China's revolution. They are the three major magic weapons." In December 1939, Mao Zedong finished writing *The Chinese Revolution and the Chinese Communist*

Party. In January 1940, he published the work *On New Democracy*. In it he discussed the nature of the modern Chinese society, the historical characteristics of the Chinese revolution and its law of development. He pointed out: In the course of its history, the Chinese revolution must go through two stages: first, the democratic revolution, and second, the socialist revolution. This is decided by the nature of the Chinese society. China's democratic revolution underwent a change before and after the May 4th Movement. Before, it was the old-democratic revolution, and after, the new-democratic revolution. The new-democratic revolution must be a revolution led by the proletariat, and it is different from the old-democratic revolution led by the bourgeoisie. The new-democratic revolution must be an anti-imperialist, anti-feudal revolution conducted by the broad masses of the people, and it is different from the socialist revolution of the proletariat. This revolution is a revolution against imperialism and feudalism conducted jointly by the working class, peasantry, petty bourgeoisie and national bourgeoisie. Mao Zedong also put forth the political, economic and cultural programmes of new democracy. He said, "Combine the politics, the economy and the culture of new democracy, and you have the new democratic republic ... the new China we want to create." *On New Democracy* is a Marxist-Leninist theoretical work. Its publication marked the maturity of the theory of China's new-democratic revolution.

In March and December 1940, Mao Zedong completed the two important documents: "Current Problems of Tactics in the Anti-Japanese United Front" and "On Policy." He pointed out: "... in no circumstances will the Party change its united front policy for the entire period of the War of Resistance Against Japan.... In the united front, we can never repeat either the 'Left'-opportunist error of all struggle and no alliance or the Right-opportunist error of all alliance and no struggle. Today our anti-Japanese national united front policy is neither all alliance and no strugle nor all struggle and no alliance, but combines alliance and struggle." Mao Zedong divided the various classes, strata and factions in the national united front into three different political groups: the progressive, the intermediate, and the diehard. He formulated the basic policy of developing the progressive forces, winning over the middle forces and isolating the diehards. The tactical thinking of the Chinese Communist Party is an important component part of the Marxist theory of social revolution.

In September 1940, when the CPC was leading the army and people in the liberated areas to resist Japan, develop the national united front and consolidate the liberated areas, Japan signed a treaty of military alliance with Germany and Italy. To carry out the policy of southward advance, Japan was anxious to end the war with China. So it stepped up its attempts to induce the National Government to capitulate while launching offensives against the liberated areas. In November, the Japanese Imperial Council approved "The Programme for Dealing with the Chinese Incident," and decided that "apart from continuing military operations, every means including political and war tactics should be employed to make the Chongqing regime give in quickly and promote cooperation between Nanjing and Chongqing." After Japan concluded the treaty of military alliance with Germany and Italy, Britain and the U.S. resolved to ally themselves with China for the sake of strengthening their own positions in the Far East and the Pacific region and resisting the Japanese invasion of Southeast Asia and the southern Pacific. They therefore provided the National Government with more aid. Because Germany, Japan and Italy also wanted to drag Chiang Kai-shek into their camp, the position of Chiang's clique was becoming more important. Chiang Kai-shek decided to make use of this opportunity to start another large-scale armed clash to strike at the Communist Party and take China's destiny completely in his own hands.

Beginning with the spring of 1940, the Kuomintang army quickened its pace to create clashes in Central China, and worked out its scheme to attack the New Fourth Army. In July, the Kuomintang put forward "Briefings from the Central Executive Committee" which ordered the CPC to liquidate the Shaanxi-Gansu-Ningxia Border Region, restrict the development of the Eighth Route and New Fourth armies, and fix their operational zones. All these unreasonable demands were refused by the CPC Central Committee. Instructed by Chiang Kai-shek, He Yingqin and Bai Chongxi jointly sent a telegram to the Eighth Route and New Fourth armies on October 19, 1940, ordering them to move completely to north of the Yellow River within a month. On December 8, He and Bai once again telegraphed the Eighth Route and New Fourth armies to withdraw fully to the north of the Yellow River before the end of January 1941. On October 9, Chiang Kai-shek personally issued an order to the New Fourth Army, urging it to move north on schedule. The following day, he secretly instructed Gu Zhutong to make proper arrangements according to the original plan, saying, "They should be wiped out without delay if they still disobey the order to move north on time (before the end of December this year)." Gu Zhutong concentrated seven divisions composed of some 80,000 troops in southern Anhui, getting ready to surround and annihilate the New Fourth Army. In view of this situation, the CPC Central Committee instructed the New Fourth Army headquarters to move as quickly as possible to the north of the Yangtze River. On the night of January 4, 1941, officers and men of the New Fourth Army headquarters and the 9,000 troops in southern Anhui set out from Yunling Mountain of Jingxian County. Arriving in the Maolin area on the fifth, they were besieged and attacked by the Kuomintang armed forces. After fighting a last-ditch battle for seven days and nights, most of them gave their lives due to the great disparity in number and lack of ammunition and food supplies. Ye Ting, the army commander, was detained and Xiang Ying, his deputy, killed. Chiang Kai-shek proclaimed the New Fourth Army a "rebel army," and ordered its designation rescinded and Ye Ting to be tried by military court. This was the Southern Anhui Incident, usually called the Second Anti-Communist Onslaught, which shocked the country and the whole world.

In the wake of the incident, the CPC Central Committee led the whole Party, the whole army and the people of the whole country to struggle resolutely against the anti-Communist diehards. On January 20, the Revolutionary Military Commission of the CPC Central Committee issued the order to re-establish the headquarters of the New Fourth Army, appoint Chen Yi its acting commander and Liu Shaoqi political commissar. Chiang Kai-shek's anti-Communist activities were also censured by international public opinion. He was obliged to say that "the New Fourth Army incident is purely to strengthen military discipline. Naturally it involves no other questions." Later on, he asserted at the People's Political Council that the Southern Anhui Incident was "not related to the politics of political parties and groups" and that he could "guarantee" there would be no military action to suppress Communists in future. The new large-scale armed clash created by the Kuomintang was thus over.

Early in the period of the anti-Japanese war, those political parties and groups which represented the intermediate forces had placed great hopes on Chiang Kai-shek. But soon afterwards their hopes were dashed. To explore and study the policies concerning state affairs, members of small parties and groups of the People's Political Council formed on their initiative the Tongyi Jianguo Tongzhi Hui (Comradely Association of Unity for Building the Nation) in October 1939. Among them were Liang Shuming of the rural construction group, Zhang Junmai (1887-1969) of the State Socialist Party, Huang Yanpei (1878-1965) of the Society of the Chinese Vocational Education, Zuo Shunsheng (1893-1969) and Li Huang of the Chinese Youth Party, Shen Junru and Zou Taofen of the National Salvation Association, Zhang Bojun (1895-1969) of the third party and the non-affiliated Zhang Lan (1872-1955). Before and after the Southern Anhui Incident, the Kuomintang diehards not only put political pressure on and launched military offensives against the Communist Party, but also carried out a high-handed policy towards various democratic parties and democrats. In order to strengthen their unity and cooperation, mediate the clashes between the Kuomintang and the Communist Party, and seek existence and development of their own, these small parties and groups decided to reorganize the Tongyi Jiankuo Tongzhi Hui into the League of Chinese Democratic Political Groups. In March 1941, the League held a secret inaugural meeting in Chongqing and adopted its political programme and general regulations. At the same time, it elected its leading body—the Central Executive Committee, composed of 13 members. Huang Yanpei, Zuo Shunsheng, Zhang Junmai, Liang Shuming and Zhang Bojun were elected standing committee members. Huang Yanpei was the chairman of the Central Standing Committee, Zuo Shunsheng the general secretary, Zhang Bojun the head of the Organization Department, and Luo Longji the head of the Propaganda Department. Soon afterwards, Huang Yanpei resigned his position as chairman of the Central Standing Committee, and this post was assumed by Zhang Lan. In October, the league proclaimed its founding, published a manifesto on its establishment and a statement on its programme in the current situation. The manifesto and programme both represented the interests and political stand of the national bourgeoisie, enlightened landlords and upper petty bourgeoisie. The founding of the league was a great event marking the growth of the political strength of the middle class.

After turning traitor to the country. Wang Jingwei went to Japan in May 1939. There he was guaranteed the backing of the Japanese government in establishing a puppet central government. In August, the "Sixth Congress" of Wang's "Kuomintang" held in Shanghai formulated the so-called Political Programme of the Chinese Kuomintang and called for "peaceful building of the country." In December, the "Japan-Wang Agreement" (also known as the "Programme for Adusting the New Relations Between Japan and China") was concluded. In March 1940, Wang Jingwei convened a political conference of the bogus KMT Central Executive Committee in Nanjing and decided to name the puppet regime "National Government" with Wang as its acting president and the head of the Executive Yuan. On March 30, the puppet "National Government" was founded in Nanjing. In November, the Japanese Imperial Council decided to recognize the puppet government. Then, they concluded the "Treaty on the Basic Relations Between Japan and the Republic of China" and affiliated secret agreements. Meanwhile, Japan, Wang Jingwei and "Manchukuo" jointly signed a "Japan-Manchukuo-China Common Manifesto." The so-called Treaty on Basic Relations turned the secret agreement between Japan and Wang Jingwei into a formal treaty whose contents far exceeded those of the traitorous "Twenty-one Demands."

In the areas under their occupation, the Japanese imperialists carried out inhuman rule and unbridled plunder. In the Northeast, after the Lugouqiao Incident, they set up the Manchuria Heavy Industry Development Stock Company to monopolize the business of iron and steel, light metals, automobiles, aircraft and coal and frantically plundered grain and other farm produce as well as various resources in the northeast. One million peasant households were relocated, and vast areas of land were seized. In the occupied areas south of the Great Wall, Japan established the Central Reserve Bank in Nanjing in January 1941. Military control was exercised over mining and other industries in north China, while "commission business" was adopted in central China. Later on, the plunder was practiced in the name of Sino-Japanese cooperation. In 1938, the North China Development Company and the Central China Development Company were set up with many branches to conduct such businesses as coal, iron, salt, power, communications, and telecommunications. Actually the administration of these enterprises was all in Japanese hands and most of their profits went into Japanese pockets. In the countryside, the Japanese invaders through appropriated land, collected taxes, purchased farm produce at low prices, and directly looted grain, farm animals, and other property. They listed grain as one of the military supplies under their strict control, and bought it by force. For the common Chinese people, they put a rationing system into effect. Many young men were press-ganged into forced labour. People in the enemy-occupied areas were longing for victory over Japan and liberation for themselves as early as possible.

13. The Outbreak of the Pacific War. The Kuomintang Area and the Liberated Area in the Mid-Period of the Anti-Japanese War

After 1940 tensions between Japan and the U.S. were increasingly sharpened because of the Japanese imperialists, southward advance policy. But both sides sought to avoid a direct war. Starting from March 1941, Japan opened negotiations with the U.S. on such issues as maintenance of the status quo in the Pacific, the China question, and the attitude towards the European war.

On June 22 when the Japan-U.S. negotiations were still going on, the German-USSR war broke out. Initially, Germany won one victory after another, bringing about a tremendous change in the world situation. The Japanese imperialists determined to take advantage of this opportunity to intensify their southward expansion. On September 6, the Imperial Council made a resolution that Japan would declare war against the U.S., Britain and the Netherlands, if its demands were not satisfied in the negotiations by early October. Japan's demands included that the U.S. and Britain should neither obstruct the empire's handling of the China incident nor take any action in the Far East to threaten the national defence of the empire. By mid-October, the Japan-U.S. Negotiations had still made no progress. Prime Minister Konoe Fumimaro advocated continuing the negotiations while Tojo Hideki, the minister of the army, argued against the U.S. Forced by the army's strong opposition, Konoe Fumimaro resigned from office and Tojo Hideki took up the responsibility to form a new cabinet. He was very keen on preparations for a war against the U.S. In late November, the U.S. Secretary of State sent Japan a memorandum, demanding that Japan withdraw its troops from China and Viet Nam, and that both Japan and the U.S. should not support any other power in political, military and economic fields except the Chinese National Government. Japan refused this demand. On December 1, the Japanese Imperial Council decided to declare war against the U.S., Britain and the Netherlands.

On December 7, Japan's navy launched a surprise attack on Pearl Harbour, the main U.S. naval base in the Pacific, and destroyed nearly all the warships of the American Pacific Fleet lying at anchor there. After this, Japanese troops attacked Singapore, Britain's important strategic territory in Southeast Asia. The flames of war quickly spread over the vast area ranging from Hawaii in the east to the Malay Peninsula in the west. Germany and Italy declared war against the U.S. on December 11. On that same day, Germany, Italy and Japan signed an agreement for concerted action, pledging to fight the U.S. and Britain to the end. By April 1942, Japan had occupied American dependencies such as the Philippines, Guam and Wake islands, British dependencies such as Hong Kong, Singapore, Malaya, and Burma, the Dutch dependency of the East Indies, and the French dependency of Indo-China. Furthermore, Japan was directing its spearhead of attack towards India and Australia.

The outbreak of the Pacific War and the major victories won by the Japanese army in the early days of the war tremendously affected the global situation, especially Southeast Asia and the Southwest Pacific as well as China's War of Resistance.

As early as the initial stage of the War of Resistance, the Chinese Communist Party had foreseen the possibility of forming a Pacific anti-Japanese front. The CPC Central Committee made a declaration on the Pacific war on the day following its outbreak, and also issued the "Directive on the Pacific Anti-Japanese United Front." The declaration analyzed the international situation after the war broke out, saying that "all the nations in the world have at last clearly been divided into the fascist front which is conducting the war of aggression and the anti-fascist front which is waging the war of liberation." The declaration further pointed out: "The important task for the Chinese government and people is to establish a military alliance with Britain, the U.S. and other anti-Japanese friendly countries, and to cooperate in the war effort. At the same time, it is essential to set up a united front of all the anti-Japanese nations in the Pacific and persist in the war of resistance until complete triumph is achieved." The CPC Central Committee's directive stressed that the united front should be composed of the governments, political parties and groups and people of all the anti-Japanese nations, and that the united front of China with Britain and the U.S. was of special importance. "In order to increase the strength of Britain and the U.S. for resistance against Japan, and to improve the situation of China in the War of Resistance, the Chinese Communist Party should give earnest, all-out cooperation to the British and Americans on every occasion," it added.

The outbreak of the Pacific war enlarged the global anti-fascist front. Many European, Asian and American countries proclaimed war against Japan. In December 1941, President F. D. Roosevelt suggested Chaing Kai-shek set up the China War Zone (including China, Viet Nam and Northern Thailand) with Chiang as the supreme commander. The U.S. government sent General Joseph Warren Stilwell to China to be the chief of staff of the war zone. The U.S. volunteer wing of the Chinese Air Force directed by General Claire Lee Chennault had downed and damaged many Japanese planes since the outbreak of the Pacific war. On January 1, 1942, the U.S., Britain, the Soviet Union,

China, Australia, Belgium, Canada and 19 other countries signed the "Common Manifesto of the United Nations" in Washington, declaring that the governments of the signatory states guaranteed the use of all their military and economic resources for fighting against the fascist allies and their followers, and that they would not sign any separate truce agreement or peace treaty with the enemy countries. Soon afterwards, another 21 nations joined in, including the Philippines, Abyssinia, Iraq and Brazil. In February, China and the U.S. reached an agreement for a loan of US$ 500 million. In May, the Soviet Union and Britain signed a treaty of alliance. In June, China and the U.S. as well as the Soviet Union and the U.S. separately signed mutual-assistance agreements. Thus the International Anti-Fascist United Front was now formally established. China's War of Resistance was therefore combined with the anti-Japanese war of the other countries' governments and people. Meanwhile, the destiny of the National Government became more closely connected with the United States.

At the beginning of the Pacific war, the National Government estimated that Japan could not be a match for the U.S., and so declared war against it on December 9, announcing the abolishment of all the treaties, agreements and contracts involving Sino-Japanese relations. However, Britain and the U.S. suffered disastrous defeats at the initial stage of the war. This disappointed Chiang Kai-shek and made him hesitate to sign the Common Manifesto issued by the 26 countries. In order to appease Japan, he dismissed Guo Taiqi, who was foreign minister when China declared war against Japan. As Japan continued to try to induce him to capitulation, Chiang Kai-shek spread word that he was going to conclude a unilateral peace treaty with Japan. In January 1942, an important Kuomintang official was instructed by Chiang to speak to a U.S. reporter: "China has suffered heavy losses in the war against Japan. She will make peace with Japan unilaterally if she continues to receive no aid." The Japanese newspaper *Asahi Shimbun* reported: "Since a series of victories won by our country in the Great East Asia War, Chongqing has gradually stepped into the crisis of collapse. At present, it has almost completely lost its fighting capacity. The call for peace with Japan has now become the dominant position." But, because the final victory of the Pacific war was hanging in the balance and the Communist-led resistance forces and the people of the whole country were firmly opposed to capitulation, the Chiang Kai-shek clique was obliged to adopt a wait-and-see attitude. It continued the War of Resistance, while keeping channels open to contact the Japanese invaders. At the same time, it made use of this opportunity to ask for aid from the United States.

After the outbreak of the Pacific war, Japan's focus of fighting shifted from China to Southeast Asia and the southwest Pacific. To coordinate with the battling in the south, pin down the Chinese troops in central China, and take advantage of its victories in the Pacific war to compel the Chiang Kai-shek clique to surrender, Japan ordered its 11th Corps to launch the third offensive against Changsha. Late in December 1941, the Japanese troops forced their way across the Miluo River. Early in January 1942, the enemy started a fierce attack on the city. The Kuomintang troops of the Ninth War Zone carried out a tenacious blocking action. In the small hours of January 4, the Chinese troops accomplished the besiegement of the enemy. Finding themselves in an unfavourable situation, the enemy troops withdrew, and in this process were attacked sporadically. On the 15th, they retreated to the Yueyang area. This brought an end to the Third Changsha Campaign.

On April 18, 1942, after bombing Tokyo and other cities in Japan, the U.S. bombers that had taken off from an aircraft carrier now landed at an airport in the Zhejiang-Jiangxi area. In order to avoid the bombing of their metropolitan territory, Japanese authorities instructed their 13th Corps stationed in Shanghai and the 11th Corps in Wuhan to organize the Zhejiang-Jiangxi Campaign to attack the Chinese troops of the Third War Zone from the east and west so as to open up the Hangzhou-Nanchang Railway. The 13th Corps occupied Jinhua on April 28, Quzhou on June 7, and Yushan on June 12 and joined forces at Hengfeng on July 1 with a part of the 11th Corps that had fought their way there from Nanchang, thus bringing the entire rail line under their control. Two months laters, however, due to insufficient military strength, they had to withdraw to the places where they had been stationed, leaving only Jinhua and its surrounding areas still under their occupation. In May and November 1943, Japanese invaders launched two separate offensives on Yichang, Shashi and the area southwest of Shishou. In addition to slowing down the advance of the Japanese army by their blocking actions, the Chinese troops rose to counterattack and made the enemy suffer heavy casualties.

On February 6, 1942, the Japanese army captured Rangoon, the capital of Burma, and then directed its spearhead of attack northward. When Rangoon was in imminent danger, the National Government, at Britain's request, had organized the 5th, 6th and 66th corps into the Chinese Expeditionary Army, which marched to Burma. From mid-March to April, the Expeditionary Army battled against the Japanese troops in Tonggu, Yenangyaung and Lashio. In Yenangyaung, they rescued 7,000 British troops from a siege. But, because the British army had no determination to defend Burma and was not cooperative, the Expeditionary Army retreated northward between April and May. Passing through the Yeren and Gaoligong mountain areas, the main force of the army suffered considerable losses. Dai Anlan, commander of one division, was killed in battle. Then part of the troops retreated to the east of the Nu River while the Japanese troops moved to the west of the river. Another group of the Expeditionary Army entered India and concentrated at Ramgarh in August. There the General Headquarters for the Chinese army stationed in India was set up, with Stilwell as the commander-in-chief. This army and those dispatched later from China into India were reorganized as the New First and New Sixth armies, receiving training and equipment from the U.S.

After the Southern Anhui Incident, the Kuomintang rule became more reactionary. Democratic and progressive forces in the Kuomintang areas were suppressed more savagely. In February 1941, the branches of the Life Bookstore in Chengdu, Kunming, Guilin and Guiyang were ordered closed or forced to stop doing business. Now only the Chongqing branch remained open. Zou Taofen, general manager of the Life Bookstore and noted writer and political activist, was compelled to secretly leave Chongqing for Hong Kong. In March 1942, the Kuomintang government promulgated the "Total Mobilization Law" which included such stipulations as: "Blocking factories, going on strike, holding a slowdown, and other acts hampering production are strictly forbidden.... The government can place restrictions on or stop the establishment of a newspaper office or a news agency, can restrict, order to cancel, add or change the contents of a news report or other printed matter when it deems necessary.... The government can put restrictions on people's speech, on the press, on writings, correspondence, assembly and association." These measures, in fact, had already been put into practice. Their stipulation by law showed the Kuomintang government was bent on depriving people of their civil rights. Early in May, the KMT Central Executive Committee ordered all provinces and cities not to commemorate the May 4th Movement. This was an example of the Total Mobilization Law in action. Chiang Kai-shek himself made use of every chance to strengthen his autocratic rule. When Lin Sen was at his post as the president of the National Government, the post had been one without real power. Lin Sen died in August, 1943. In September, the KMT Central Executive Committee revised "The Organizational Law of the National Government," stipulating that "the president of the National Government is also the generalissimo of the ground, naval and air forces and can hold any other post concurrently." At the same time, the KMT Central Executive Committee recommended Chiang Kai-shek to be president of the National Government, being concurrently head of the Executive Yuan and the Military Commission. In 1943, the Kuomintang invited Mellors, a U.S. secret service expert, to be the deputy head of the newly established "Sino-U.S. Special Technique Cooperative Institute," with Dai Li as its head. This was a setup specialized in training secret agents for the Kuomintang.

The mid-period of the anti-Japanese war was the turning-point for the economy in the Kuomintang area from development to decline. This was also the crucial period of economic changes taking place under the Kuomintang regime. By 1941, factories which had moved inland totalled more than 600, with equipment and materials weighing about 120,000 tons. This greatly promoted the economy in the rear area. At that time, there were several reasons for economic growth. Firstly, factories moved from the coastal war zone to the southwest increased the production capacity of that area which had been backward in industry. Secondly, China's economy was of a semi-colonial type, affected and controlled by foreign capital, but foreign capital had

had little influence in the southwest. In addition, the world war had kept such capital from making an impact on China. This situation was favourable for the growth of Chinese capital. Thirdly, at the earlier stage of the war against Japan, prices in the Kuomintang areas had remained relatively stable, and the financial difficulties the National Government faced were not too great to overcome. Fourthly, the growth of population led to increased consumption, and the War of Resistance meant that the country needed more materials. All this gave a stimulus to industrial and agricultural production. But soon afterwards, development was replaced by decline. In the pre-war year of 1936, there were 300 factories (270 privately owned) in the rear areas. In 1937, 63 factories (60 privately owned) were set up. In 1938, 209 factories were started (182 privately owned). In 1939, factories set up numbered 419 (346 privately owned). In 1940, they were 571; in 1941, 866; in 1942, 1,138 (1,077 privately owned); in 1943, 1,049 (977 privately owned); and in 1944, 549 (533 privately owned). From these figures, one can see that factories established in 1942 were the greatest in number. But counting the sum of capital in terms of conversion of currency value into that of 1936, capital in 1939 was actually the largest in amount, and that in 1938 came next. After 1939, the actual capital was decreasing progressively year by year, except in 1943, when capital was higher than in 1942. For example, of the 871 factories in Chongqing, then the leading industrial centre, more than 270 closed down or lowered production in 1943. All these were indications of the declining industry in Kuomintang areas.

In addition to the decline of national capital and the entire national economy, was the rapid expansion of state monopoly capital and the consolidating of its monopolistic position. During the period of the anti-Japanese war, the National Government and high-ranking officials took advantage of the war-time situation to make their fortunes. This resulted in the rapid expansion of state monopoly capital and bureaucrat capital. State monopoly capital plundered the people of their wealth through the following methods: (1) issuance of bonds, (2) increase of taxes, (3) inflation, (4) controlling foreign exchange and buying and selling gold, (5) monopolizing the sale of particular commodities, (6) practising state monopoly for purchase and marketing certain products. Before the War of Resistance, State monopoly capital had already begun monopolizing the national economy. Now, during the war period, its monopoly was greatly strengthened. In the financial area, early in the period of the anti-Japanese war, a joint general office of the Central Bank of China, the Bank of China, the Bank of Communications of China, and the Farmers Bank of China was set up as the Kuomintang's concentrated financial institution. Chiang Kai-shek was president of its board of directors. In July 1942, the National Government decided that the Central Bank of China should be responsible for the issuance of the national currency. During the War of Resistance, state monopoly capital openly monopolized commerce. The establishment of the Monopoly Enterprises Management Bureau, Trading Committee, and Materials Bureau, as well as the practising of the policies of state monopoly for purchase and marketing, were the important measures for state monopoly capital to realize its monopoly of commerce. High-ranking officials represented by Kong Xiangxi and Song Ziwen operated many commercial companies in private names. With political privileges and financial power, these companies occupied a monopolistic position in the market. In September 1937, the National Government set up the Industry and Mining Adjustment Committee as a monopolistic organ in this field. Apart from quite a few provincial official-operated industrial enterprises, government-run industrial and mining undertakings were mainly under the two systems—the Resources Commission and the Engineering Administration. Privately owned industries, headed by those run by the Kong and Song families, were also monopolies in the market.

In the early period of the War of Resistance, the agricultural situation in the Kuomintang areas was not bad. As the war dragged on, the National Government's financial expenditures were greatly increased. Due to inflation plus the growing need for farm produce, the National Government stepped up its exploitation of peasants. From 1940 on, grain purchase by the state was put into practice and land tax started from the latter half of 1941. In 1943, another measure was adopted: The National Government "borrowed grain" from the peasants by force. Peasants were given only grain loan tickets instead of ready money. This kind of grain loan was free of interest. It was stipulated that each grain loan would be paid back evenly in five years beginning with the fifth year, or could be used as payment for land tax of a new term. According to the statistics in 1942, the amount of farm produce plundered from the peasants through these three measures accounted for up to more than half of what they had harvested. For example, it was 59 percent in Sichuan, 52 percent in Hunan, and 49 percent in Yunnan. Besides grain, other products purchased and sold by the state included cotton, silk, tea, bristles, tung oil, etc. All of these purchases were nominally borne by landlords. But, in fact, the landlords passed them onto the shoulders of their tenants. Land rental rates rose quickly. For instance, the average land rental rate for 27 tenant-peasant households in a county of Sichuan Province was 53 percent in 1941, 73 percent in 1943, and 79 percent in 1944. Heavy exploitation of the peasants made the rural economy in the rear area decline.

State monopoly capital and bureaucrat capital in the Kuomintang area also cruelly exploited the working people, which not only prejudiced the interests of the national bourgeoisie, but also hindered the development of the productive forces and the progress of society. Exploitation and damage by state monopoly capital and bureaucrat capital constantly sharpened the contradictions between various classes. This was one of the root causes for the advance of China's revolution, and also one important reason for the development of the democratic movement during the later stage of the anti-Japanese war. Although the economy of the National Government totally collapsed a few years later, its sharp decline had begun in the mid-period of the war.

With the progress of the anti-Japanese war, the Eighth Route and New Fourth armies rapidly expanded, as did the liberated areas. After the Hundred-Regiment Campaign, the Japanese paid greater attention to the battlefields behind their lines in north China. Chinese areas under Japanese occupation were the bases for launching offensives in the Pacific. To ensure the stability of the bases behind their lines, Japanese troops intensified their attack on the liberated areas. In July 1941, the Japanese army in north China worked out a "Three-Year Plan for Public Order, Discipline Strengthening, and Construction," dividing north China into three types of regions, namely, the "public order region, quasi-public order region and non-public order region." In the "public order region," the Japanese concentrated on "checking on residents", tightening their rule over the Chinese people by extensive puppet organizations, strengthening the *Bao-Jia* system, and issuing the "good person identity card." In the "quasi-public order region," they engaged mainly in building blockhouses and digging blockade ditches to prevent the Eighth Route Army from taking action, and the liberated areas from expanding. In the "non-public order region," Japanese troops in the main adopted "mopping-up" operations, practising the "kill all, burn all and loot all" policy in an attempt to destroy China's resistance forces. From the spring of 1941 to the autumn of 1942, the Japanese launched "Strengthening Public Order Movements" in north China five times in succession; people in the enemy-occupied areas were terribly persecuted, plundered and massacred. But still they failed to reach their goal—guaranteeing their occupation of north China. During 1941 and 1942, Japanese invaders conducted many large-scale "mopping-up" operations against various anti-Japanese base areas. For example: In 1941, operations by 40,000 troops against north Hebei; by 70,000 troops against Beiyue and Pingxi; by 50,000 troops against the Yimeng area of Shandong Province; by more than 30,000 troops against the Taiyue area; and by over 10,000 troops against the Hebei-Shandong-Henan region. In 1942, there was one "mopping-up" operation by 10,000 troops against northwestern Shanxi; one by 25,000 troops against the Taihang area; one by 50,000 troops against central Hebei; and one by more than 10,000 troops against south Hebei. Apart from these, there were many other large-scale operations, each by over 10,000 troops. Small operations were numerous.

The frequent "mopping-up" operations launched by Japanese imperialists, the clashes created and blockade conducted by the KMT diehard army plus the serious natural calamities that north China suffered in 1942 brought grave difficulties to the anti-Japanese base areas behind enemy lines. Most of the bases on the plains such as central Hebei, southern Hebei, the Hebei-Shandong-Henan region and eastern Hebei became guerrilla zones or enemy-occupied areas. The total area of the anti-Japanese bases greatly dwindled, and the population there dropped from 100 million to 50 million; the Eighth Route Army was reduced from 400,000 to 300,000.

At the same time, Japan and the puppet Wang Jingwei government in south China started the "Movement of Checking on Residents" and "mopping-up" operations against the New Fourth Army. During July-August 1941, operations were launched by 10,000 Japanese troops and 15,000 puppet troops against the liberated area in northern Jiangsu. In November 1942, 30,000 Japanese troops and 30,000 puppet troops once again unleashed "mopping-up" operations there. As a result, the total area of the anti-Japanese bases north and south of the Yangtze River diminished greatly.

In light of this situation, the Communist Party adopted a policy of extensive mobilization of the masses for guerrilla war. All the bases emphasized the development of local guerrilla forces and militias, thus creating localized main formations and mass-based armed forces in addition to expanding the militia. In each military area a military organ was set up, joining regular troops, local guerrilla forces and the militia as a body of three in one. In 1941, the local guerrillas and militia under the county level nearly doubled in number. In mass-based guerrilla war, the army and the people behind enemy lines created various methods of fighting the enemy. In the liberated areas, groups of regular troops cooperating with the militia fought against enemy's "mopping-up" operations day and night. They employed landmines, tunnel warfare and "sparrow" warfare to inflict casualties on the enemy at every turn. Meanwhile, they strengthened defence works, evacuated noncombatants, and hid provisions and livestock. Most of the main formations moved to the areas in the enemy's rear to shatter the "mopping-up" operations. In the guerrilla zones, a policy of "squeezing the enemy out" was put into practice to counter their "nibbling" operations. The joint combat by the main formations, local guerrilla forces and militia often dealt the invaders fierce blows before they could get a firm foothold. If the enemy intruded into the hinterland and set up strongholds there, the combined forces would besiege them until they withdrew, or concentrate troops to capture their fortified points. In the areas behind enemy lines, armed forces were dispatched to arouse the masses to overthrow the puppet organizations and attack the enemy from the front and rear. In the enemy-occupied areas, the tactic was to organize numerous armed work teams to launch offensives behind the enemy lines. An armed work team was a small but highly trained combat unit handling Party, government, military and civilian affairs. Its constant task was to arouse and organize the masses, unfold political offensives against the enemy, carry out such struggles as striking blows at the enemy's military police, secret agents and traitors, destroy puppet political powers, attack the enemy's strongholds and set ambushes.

In 1941 and 1942, the army and people in the liberated areas fought heroically. In the fifth year of the war, the Eighth Route and New Fourth armies conducted over 14,600 operations, killing, wounding and capturing 130,000 Japanese and puppet troops. In the sixth year, they fought more than 27,500 battles, killing, wounding and capturing some 200,000 Japanese and puppet troops. During 1941 and 1942, the anti-Japanese base areas were terribly damaged, but they still stood firm. By 1943, after overcoming many difficulties, they had been restored and even expanded to a certain extent. In addition to an expansion in area, the population increased to some 80 million, the army to 470,000, and the members of the Communist Party to 900,000. All these had paved the way for conducting partial offensives against the enemy.

During those hardest days, the Chinese Communist Party not only led the army and people to fight against the enemy, but also devoted major efforts to consolidating the Party itself and strengthening the construction of the liberated areas. In February 1942, Mao Zedong made a report on rectification of the Party's style of work in the Central Party School. In June, the CPC Central Committee issued a circular on rectification study, and the rectification movement was begun. The basic task of this movement was to criticize and rectify subjectivism, sectarianism, and stereotyped Party writing as well as to cultivate and develop the working styles of combining theory with practice, maintaining close links with the masses and carrying out self-criticism, especially concentrating on the criticism and correction of subjectivism, combination of theory and practice, investigation and study, and cultivation of a practical and realistic style of work. The movement was aimed at achieving a high degree of political and ideological unity; the principle was "to learn from past mistakes in order to avoid future ones, thus to cure the sickness to save the patient," and "incorrect thinking should be criticized on the one hand, and the unity between comrades should be achieved on the other." This corrected the erroneous practice of ruthless struggle and merciless blows during the period when the "Left" line was in a dominant position. The rectification movement brought in very good results. From 1942 to 1944, the Central Political Bureau and the senior Party cadres held discussions on the history of the Party and made a summarization of it. Ideas of the Party cadres were unified on the correct line in this way. In April 1945, the Seventh Plenary Session of the CPC Sixth Central Committee adopted a resolution on a number of questions in the Party's history.

In order to overcome difficulties, increase the strength of the liberated areas, and pave the way for completely defeating Japanese invaders, people of the liberated areas worked to build of political power and the economy, and develop culture and education. In the building of political power, the "three-thirds system" was put into effect. In March 1940, the Party Central Committee issued the directive "On the Question of Political Power in the Anti-Japanese Base Areas" which pointed out, "It is the political power of all those who support both resistance and democracy; it is the joint democratic dictatorship of several revolutionary classes over the traitors and reactionaries." The composition in the organs of political power should be one-third for Communists, one-third for non-Party Left progressives, and one-third for the intermediate sections who were neither Left nor Right. "The united front policy on suffrage should be that every Chinese who reaches the age of 18 and is in favour of resistance and democracy should enjoy the right to elect and to be elected regardless of class origin, ethnic group, sex, political belief, Party affiliation and educational level...." In 1941, suffrage in governments at various levels in the Shaanxi-Gansu-Ningxia Border Region was practised according to the "three-thirds system." Local political councils and governments of the liberated areas in north and central China were also elected this way. The anti-Japanese democratic governments in various areas carried out the measures of "better troops and simpler administration."

In the most difficult years, a policy of reducing land rent and interest was implemented in the liberated areas along with the unfolding of a large-scale production movement and the strengthening of economic construction. This promoted the development of the new-democratic economy. Before the end of 1941, reduction of rent and interest was put into effect only in a few places. It was not widespread until January 1942, when the Party Central Committee approved the decision on the land policy for the anti-Japanese base areas. In 1943, it was in full flood. The large-scale production movement started after 1941. In the Shaanxi-Gansu-Ningxia Border Region, the movement was first initiated in a number of army units, and then pursued by all army units, Party and government organizations, and schools. Soon afterwards, it was popularized among workers and peasants. The production movements carried out in the Shanxi-Qahar-Hebei, Shanxi-Hebei-Shandong-Henan, Shanxi-Suiyuan, and central China base areas quickened the pace of economic construction. Developing agriculture was taken as the main task, while the promotion of industry and handicrafts was never neglected. From 1940 to 1942, the people in the Shaanxi-Gansu-Ningxia Border Region reclaimed 1.8 million *mu* (1 *mu* = 1/15 hectare) of wasteland and brought in an increase of 470,000 *dan* (1 *dan* = 50 kilogrammes) of grain. Publicly owned factories increased to 62 with nearly 4,000 workers and staff members, turning out 100,000 bolts of handwoven cloth a year. Other industries like iron-smelting, oil refining, machine repair, and the manufacture of weaponry and ammunition all made progress. The growth of production helped the base areas overcome many economic difficulties and provided material conditions for advancing the revolutionary cause.

The Chinese Communist Party and the governments in the liberated areas attached great importance to the development of cultural and educational undertakings. In March 1940, the Party Central Committee issued a directive on developing national education in the anti-Japanese democratic areas. It pointed out, "To develop national education in these areas is an important link at present for further mobilizing the people to take part in and keep up the War of Resistance as well as to train revolutionary intellectuals and cadres." Education in the liberated areas was new-democratic education, namely, "it is education on national democratic revolution and on science with the theory and method of Marxism-Leninism as its starting point." The directive stated that it was essential to restore and re-establish primary schools in as many areas as possible, and to set up normal schools in several key areas and public middle schools in a number of counties and districts. In 1940, there were 1,300 primary schools in the Shaanxi-Gansu-Ningxia Border Region with 43,000 pupils. In the Shanxi-Qahar-Hebei Border Region, primary schools numbered 7,600 with over 469,000 pupils. The Chinese People's Anti-Japanese Military and Political College, the Northern Shaanxi Public School and the Lu Xun Art Academy in the Shaanxi-Gansu-Ningxia Border Region turned out a great number of trained personnel. In the media field, newspapers and journals published in Yan'sn, the seat of the CPC Central Committee, were the *Liberation Daily, Liberation, Military and Political Magazine of the Eighth Route Army, Chinese Workers, Chinese Youth, Chinese Culture,* etc. Newspapers published in other base areas included *Shanxi-Qahar-Hebei Daily, Xinhua Daily* (North China edition), *Dazhong Bao* (*Newspaper for the Masses*), *Jianghuai Daily*, and *Tingjin Bao* (*Press Forward*). In addition, there were a considerable number of Marxist-Leninist works and Mao Zedong's writings published in the liberated areas. Cultural and educational work in the countryside also made obvious progress. From the achievements in the building of political power, economy, culture and education in the liberated areas, one could see the embryonic form of the new China that was born a few years later.

14. The Political Struggle in the Later Stage of the Anti-Japanese War and the Final Victory of the War

The year 1943 witnessed a significant turn in the world anti-fascist war. At the same time, great changes also took place in the war and the political situation in China, one of the major anti-fascist countries in the world.

The battle of Stalingrad, starting from July 1942, finally ended on February 2, 1943. In this battle the Soviet army wiped out a total of

1.5 million enemy troops, of which 300,000 were German troops and the rest troops from its vassal countries. Germany lost 3,500 tanks and self-propelled guns, and 3,000 airplanes. This battle was not only the turning point of the Soviet-German war, it was also a turning point of World War II. From that time on, the German forces turned from strategic offensive to strategic defensive, while the Soviet forces turned from strategic defensive to strategic counter-offensive. On the North African battle front, the German-Italian forces' surrender in May 1943 to the forces of the Allies marked the end of the war there. The Anglo-American forces' landing at Sicily in Italy in July led to the downfall of the Mussolini government. On September 3, the Italian government signed a truce agreement with the United States and Britain. The victory of the Soviet Union, the United States and Britain in the war against Germany and Italy brought fresh developments to the national liberation movements in the German-occupied countries such as France, Belgium, Holland, Yugoslavia, Poland, Czechoslovakia, Norway, Denmark, Greece and Albania. The people's resistance movements in the countries of the fascist bloc—Germany, Italy, Romania, Bulgaria, and Hungary—were also growing. In 1943, the forces of the Soviet Union, the United States and Britain gained the upper hand on all battlefields. The German fascists suffered defeats one after another. All this brought about a fundamental change in the war.

The year 1943 also saw fundamental and significant changes on the Asian, Australian and Pacific battlefields. Within six months after launching the Pacific war, Japanese imperialists seized a vast area including Burma, Malaya, the Philippines, Indonesia, New Guinea and the Solomon Islands. These, plus the occupied Chinese territory, totalled over 32 million square miles in area, or one sixth of the total area of the earth. Thus the "Greater East Asia Co-Prosperity Sphere," sought by Japanese imperialism, was achieved. But the arrival of its zenith also marked the starting point of its decline.

In May 1942, Japan concentrated large forces for an attack on Midway Island, only to suffer a disastrous defeat. The sea battle around the island was the turning point in the Pacific war. From that point, the Japanese troops lost their ability to stage a strategic offensive; whereas the United States had turned from the defensive to the offensive. In the first half of August the U.S. troops landed on Guadalcanal Island, which marked the beginning of a frontal counter-offensive by the armed forces of the Allies in the Pacific. Japan sent reinforcements for a counter-attack to recover the island. The U.S. forces, also reinforced, put up a stubborn fight. In early February 1943 the Japanese troops, suffering heavy losses, were forced to withdraw from the island, lock, stock and barrel. The U.S. forces began a counter-offensive in the southwestern Pacific in June 1943, and in the mid-Pacific in November. In the face of this offensive, the Japanese forces suffered one defeat after another, which changed completely the complexion of the Pacific war.

In the first stage of the Pacific war, Japanese imperialists, on the crest of victory, pursued an attack policy to force Chiang Kai-shek and the Kuomintang to surrender. In February 1942, they worked out a battle plan to attack Xi'an, Changsha and Changde. In August they schemed to advance on Sichuan to wipe out the KMT forces, take important areas in that province and "speed up the Chongqing regime's surrender or collapse." At this point, as Japan was losing more and more battles in the Pacific, it decided to shift the focus of operations to the southern part of the ocean, laying aside the plan to attack Sichuan. The Tojo cabinet decided to adopt a "new policy towards China," so as to move the troops from the theatre of China as reinforcements to cope with the United States. A meeting of high officials convened in December by the emperor resolved that the Wang Jingwei puppet government's entry into the war was "a favourable turn in the status quo between Japan and China ... Japan will focus its attention on the strengthening of the political force of the National Government [referring to Wang Jingwei's puppet government] ... strip Chongqing of its pretext of resisting Japan ... [and] together with the new-born China march forward towards the completion of the war." With a view to strengthening the "political force" of Wang Jingwei's puppet regime and reducing the Chinese people's hostility towards the regime, the meeting also decided to return Japanese concessions and abolish its extraterritoriality. The economic measures in the new policy towards China were mainly "aimed at obtaining necessary war materials." The new policy also stipulated that "no peace work aimed at Chongqing shall be conducted," and that new provisions should be formulated if the situation changed.

Inducing the National Government to surrender was a set policy of the Japanese government. In late May 1943, after a spell of suspension of surrender-inducing activities, it once again brought up the question of urging the Wang Jingwei puppet government to "do political work on Chongqing." The "Plan of Political Work on Chongqing" was worked out at a joint meeting held in September by the Japanese headquarters and government. The "peace" terms put forward in the plan were: "Disarm the U.S. and British forces in China and make them withdraw from that country ... sever the communications with the United States and Britain... [and] give substantial aid to the Greater East Asian War waged by the empire." All this would be done by Wang Jingwei, but under the "direction" of Japan. However, the war situation in Europe had undergone a great change unfavourable to Japan. In the Pacific war it had suffered military setbacks; moreover, it would not give up the rights and interests it had seized in China. Under these circumstances, "achieving an all-round peace" with the KMT was out of the question.

Thanks to the rise of China's international standing after the outbreak of the Pacific war, and to the attempt of the United States and Britain to make use of Chinese forces to resist Japan, China and the United States reached an agreement in October 1942 to abolish the latter's extraterritoriality and other related rights in China. On January 11, 1943, the "Sino-American Treaty on the Abolishing of American Extraterritoriality in China and the Handling of Related Questions," and the exchanged notes were concluded. On the same day China concluded a treaty of the same nature with Britain. The treaties stipulated that the United States and Britain were to give up their extraterritoriality in China, the rights and interests they had enjoyed in public and other concessions and all relevant rights and interests, and the rights laid down in the Protocol of 1901. American and British nationals within the Chinese territory were put under the jurisdiction of the government of the Republic of China. These were some of the first equal treaties signed by China with foreign countries in her modern and contemporary history. The signing of the treaties indicated a great elevation in China's international status. Grand meeting were held in both KMT-controlled and liberated areas to celebrate the abolishment of unequal treaties. In November Franklin D. Roosevelt, Winston Churchill and Chiang Kai-shek held the Cairo conference. After its conclusion the Cairo declaration was issued, announcing that territories such as Manchuria, Taiwan and Penghu Islands which Japan had seized from China, were to be returned to China. The three big allied powers were to carry on a protracted war for Japan's unconditional surrender. China had emerged in the international arena as one of the world's big powers.

In 1943, Germany in the west retreated one step after another, while Japan in the east suffered constant defeats. The whole situation was on the threshold of a great change. Faced with this situation, the diehards in the KMT felt both joy and fear. Joy, because they imagined that with the war in Europe over, the United States and Britain would be left free to fight Japan on their behalf and that they would win victory in the War of Resistance without any effort. Fear, because with the downfall of all three fascist powers—Germany, Japan and Italy, the rise of people's democratic forces would pound at their own comprador-feudal fascist rule, and even bring them total destruction. Therefore, for the purpose of maintaining and even expanding their fascist rule, they felt it necessary to launch another large-scale anti-Communist action. The publication in March of *China's Destiny* in the name of Chiang Kai-shek signified the start of this action.

China's Destiny was a reactionary, distorted discussion on a series of questions such as the Chinese nation, Chinese history, especially modern and contemporary history, the so-called fundamental problems concerning national revolution and reconstruction, and "the artery of national revolution and reconstruction in China and the juncture deciding her destiny." The book explained the stand, viewpoint, philosophy, and domestic and external policies of Chiang Kai-shek's fascist clique. The spearhead of its attack was mainly directed at the Chinese Communist Party and the communist ideological system, as well as bourgeois democracy. Theoretically it spoke for the comprador-feudal fascist rule, while preparing public opinion for another onslaught against the Communists. Here in this book, Chiang Kai-shek announced his determination to oppose communism and the people. He said facts had proved that only "the line of national revolution" pursued by himself was the "most thoroughgoing and correct." "In the past China's destiny hinged on diplomacy," he alleged. "From now on it lies entirely in domestic affairs." The Communist Party and Communist-led army "set up a local separatist regime ... sabotaging the War of Resistance Against Japan ... [and] hindering unification," so they were "counter-revolutionary ... bringing calamity to the country and people." He clamoured that the Communist Party should "abandon its decision to set up a separatist regime by force of arms" and "do away with feudal warlord ideas." "If it is not willing to thoroughly change its feudal warlord style ... [and] does not have the determination to give up its practice of setting up separatist regimes by force," he declared, "then magnanimity, no matter how great it may be, will never produce any fruitful result, and as such we cannot think out any other reasonable method." China's destiny would be decided "within the next two years," he said.

The publication of *China's Destiny* was followed by a large-scale propaganda campaign against communism and democracy through the media. On June 18, Hu Zongnan called a military meeting at which dispositions were made to attack the Shaanxi-Gansu-Ningxia Border Region. About 500,000 troops were massed around the border region for a large-scale invasion.

In *China's Destiny* Chiang Kai-shek expounded in a systematic way the Chinese-style fascist ideological system and hinted his determination to launch an anti-Communist civil war. This provided the people of the whole country with an opportunity to criticize Chiang Kai-shek by name. The publication of *China's Destiny* and the criticism of the Chiang Kai-shek clique's ideology constituted a high tide in the struggle on the political and ideological front during the anti-Japanese war. It was also a high tide in the struggle between new democracy and Chinese-style fascism in China's contemporary history.

In the political struggle against the anti-Communist onslaught, the Communists published large numbers of editorials and articles in newspapers and periodicals criticizing Chiang Kai-shek and his

China's Destiny. Zhou Enlai made a report entitled "On China's Fascism—a New Autocracy." The editorials, articles, and report elaborated the theory, stand, task and policy of the Communist Party and criticized the reactionary thinking and policy of Chiang Kai-shek and the Kuomintang in various respects. The criticism carried out by the Chinese Communist Party could be boiled down to the following points:

(1) It pointed out that "the current central task of Chinese ideological circles is to thoroughly crush and eliminate fascism ideologically";

(2) It exposed Chiang Kai-shek's "Chinese-style fascism" as a "hybrid" of the dross of Chinese feudal thinking and exotic fascism;

(3) It criticized the fascist "philosophy of devotion" or "philosophy of constancy" as ultra-idealistic obscurantism;

(4) It brought to light the existing fascist programme and tactics; and

(5) It refuted the slander spread by the Kuomintang that the Communist Party was a "traitor party," "traitor army," "new-type feudalism" and "warlord in disguised form"; and made clear the tremendous role the Chinese Communist Party, the Communist-led army and liberated areas had played in the anti-Japanese war.

The anti-Communist action launched by the Kuomintang evoked strong opposition not only from the army and people of the liberated areas, but also from the progressive and middle-of-the-road forces in the Kuomintang-controlled rgions. International public opinion also denounced the Kuomintang for its attempt to split domestic unity and start a civil war. At the same time, the liberated areas were prepared to repulse the Kuomintang army's attacks.

As the conflict between China and Japan remained dominant and the Kuomintang's reactionary moves met with opposition at home and abroad, it had to slow down the anti-Communist onslaught. In his speech at the Eleventh Plenary Session of the Fifth Central Executive Committee of the Kuomintang held in September 1943, Chiang Kai-shek declared that "the Communist problem is a purely political one and should be solved politically." In view of the fact that the Kuomintang had ceased the anti-Communist campaign, the Communist Party, in order to uphold unity and the War of Resistance, expressed its willingness to resume negotiations at any time. Soon afterwards the two parties came back to the conference table as suggested.

The great change in the world situation in 1943 was a great encouragement to the democrats and democratic parties of China. Many political figures across the world described World War II as a war between democracy and fascism. That year the Soviet Union, the United States and Britain shifted to the offensive, Italy's Mussolini government was overthrown and the two fascist powers, Germany and Japan, were doomed to downfall. It was believed that the decline of fascism would be coupled with the rise of democracy. Democratic trends of thought were therefore once again on the upsurge around the world.

These developments had an impact on China, too. In September 1943, Zhang Lan, Chairman of the China Democratic League, published a booklet entitled *China Needs a Genuine Democratic Government.* "Over the past year," he said, "the Allied Powers which have safeguarded the freedom of mankind and promoted democracy have been winning victories, their forces are gathering momentum, and justice is being upheld. The various nations throughout the world have a fresh understanding of democracy and attach greater importance to it. They all regard this world war as a war between democracy and autocracy in the full sense, namely, a war of freedom, equality and independence vs. enslavement, oppression and aggression ... it is generally believed that the collapse of Mussolini will, in terms of importance, exert great influence on the world, not just on the war in Europe. From now on autocracy will gradually crumble and democracy will become the only principle in the political formation of more and more countries in the world."

Another important democrat, Zhang Shenfu, said, "Referring to China, democracy has nearly become the panacea of today. With the general trend of the international and internal situation, objectively speaking, China's democratic future is a foregone conclusion, and this allows no doubt." Because of the influence of the international situation and the darkening political situation in the Kuomintang-controlled areas, because national capital was falling into dire straits, and because the negotiations between the Kuomintang and the Communist

Party were resumed, the movement for democracy in the Kuomintang-controlled areas was on the upsurge after 1943.

In January 1944, the movement for a democratic constitutional government sprang into life. In early January, Huang Yanpei, Zhang Junmai, Zuo Shunsheng, Shen Junru and Zhang Bojun called a forum on constitutional government. Such meetings were held many times in the first half of the year. At the same time, Huang Yanpei and Zhang Zhirang founded *Constitutional Government*, a monthly magazine aimed at studying the problems of constitution and constitutional government, "assisting the government in publicity about instituting constitutional government." *Constitutional Government* invited industrialists, educators and bankers of Chongqing to hold forums and discuss China's constitutional government and the democratic institutions required before its establishment.

In February Zhang Lan, Shao Congen and Li Huang inaugurated the "Chengdu Association for the Promotion of Democratic Constitutional Government" to "actively advocate democracy, practise democracy, promote constitutional government and study the drafting of a constitution." In March the CPC Central Committee issued the "Directive Concerning Constitutional Government," in which it pointed out that the Kuomintang's preparations for constitutional government were intended to dupe the people and stabilize its autocratic rule. In the same month, Zhou Enlai delivered a speech entitled "On the Problem of Constitutional Government and Unity," pointing out that "the constitutional government needed by China should be a new-democratic constitutional government." In May the China Democratic League issued a statement "Our Views on the Current Situation and Our Demands," holding that "China must become a hundred percent democratic country," and that the Kuomintang should abandon its 10-year-old "privileged position." In the same month, the Southwest China Industrial Association, the Union of Factories Removed to Sichuan and the China National Association for Industry held forums on constitutional government, demanding the Kuomintnag retract its policy of economic controls.

In institutions of higher learning in Chongqing, Chengdu and Kunming, groups and meetings were organized to study or discuss constitutional government. The Third Session of the Third People's Political Council took place in September in Chongqing. The Chinese Communist Party, in light of the situation of the time, put forward a formal proposal that the Kuomintnag put an end to its one-party dictatorship and that "the national government call the representatives of all political parties, anti-Japanese armed forces, local governments and popular organizations together to hold a state conference and organize a coalition government composed of the anti-Japanese parties." On October 10, the China Democratic League issued "Our Political Views on the Final Stage of the War of Resistance," calling for an immediate end to the one-part dictatorship and the establishment of a coalition government and democratic rule. Thus China's democratic movement entered upon a new phase.

In April 1944, Japanese imperialism launched the Henan-Hunan-Guangxi campaign in order to support the forces that had intruded into the Southeast Asian countries, relieve its native territory of the threat posed by a China-based American air force, and put up a last-ditch struggle in China's mainland. This campaign, adopted a conservative stratgy. During the eight months of fighting, Japanese troops seized a large part of Henan, Hunan and Guangxi provinces and 146 medium and small cities including Luoyang, Changsha, Guilin, Zhengzhou and Liuzhou, "forcing China's north-south trunk railways open for through traffic." The Kuomintang lost 500,000 to 600,000 men and more than 200,000 square kilometres of territory, placing a population of 60 million under the iron heel of Japanese invaders. The debacle of the Kuomintnag troops was a sharp demonstration of its extreme political and military corruption, and caused a great deal of anger and resistance to the Kuomintang in the areas it controlled.

In contrast to the debacle on the Kuomintang battlefield, a local counter-offensive was launched in the theatre of the liberated areas. By April 1945, the Eighth Route Army, New Fourth Army and South-China Anti-Japanese Column had already expanded to 910,000 men, and the militia had grown to 2.2 million. The 19 liberated areas covered greater or smaller parts of the provinces of Liaoning, Rehe, Qahar, Suiyuan, Shaanxi, Gansu, Ningxia, Shanxi, Hebei, Henan, Shandong, Jiangsu, Zhejiang, Anhui, Hunan, Hubei, and Guangdong, and had a total area of 950,000 square kilometres and a population of more than 95 million. More importantly, all these liberated areas were located in strategically significant regions of the country. Many major cities such as Beiping, Tianjin, Taiyuan, Shijiazhuang, Jinan, Zhengzhou, Xuzhou, Nanjing, Shanghai and Guangzhou were all encircled by people's forces, while a large number of key ports were under the control of these forces or within the scope of their operations. The Communist-led troops and liberated areas had grown into a pivotal force in an all-out general counter-offensive, and a powerful base for winning the final victory in the War of Resistance. These were also a strong force in resisting the Kuomintang's attempt to monopolize the fruits of victory in the war.

On June 6, 1944, the allied forces of Britain and the United States landed in Normandy in northern France to open up the second front in Europe. The Soviet army's victory in its counter-offensive and the opening of the second front pushed the anti-fascist war in Europe into a decisive stage. In the last state of the world anti-fascist war, the United States, the Soviet Union and Britain, especially the United States and the Soviet Union, who were masters of the world war and political situation, convened in February 1945 the Yalta Conference to strive for the final victory in the war and arrange the world order after the war. Present at the conference were Roosevelt, Stalin and Churchill. It mainly discussed the questions of dealing with Germany and Poland, and the war against Japan. The agreement on Japan signed by the three countries greatly infringed upon China's sovereignty. It stipulated that the Soviet Union was to recover the rights and interests enjoyed by tsarist Russia in China's northeast before 1904, i.e., the Soviet "favourable rights and interests" in Dalian port were to be guaranteed; it was to lease Lüshun port as its naval base; and China and the Soviet Union were to jointly operate the Chinese Eastern, and Southern Manchuria railways. This was recognized later in the Sino-Soviet Treaty of Friendship and Alliance signed soon afterwards by the National Government and the Soviet Union. The Yalta Conference affirmed the world order, including China, worked out by the United States and the Soviet Union. However, as the Chinese Communist Party had led the people in fruitful struggles and partially upset the world order under their control, the situation in China developed in a direction favourable to the Chinese people.

On May 1, 1945, the Soviet army conquered Berlin, capital of Germany. On May 8 and 9, Germany signed the instrument of unconditional surrender, and the anti-fascist war in Europe ended in victory for the Allies. The utter defeat of Japanese imperialism had by then become a foregone conclusion. On April 1, the U.S. troops landed in Okinawa. On April 5, the Soviet Union declared the abolishment of the Japanese-Soviet Neutrality Treaty and swiftly moved its armed force to the Far East. The Japanese government had earlier offered to make peace with the National Government on condition that "the status quo in Manchukuo remain unchanged," while its other interests in China might be given up or negotiated. But it had been refused by Chiang Kai-shek. In short the situation of the time was that with the conclusion of the European war, the War of Resistance in China was bound to end in victory and China was on the eve of a great change.

The political struggle in China became more complicated as a result of U.S. interference. In October 1944, Roosevelt, at the suggestion of Chiang Kai-shek, recalled General Joseph W. Stilwell, who was at odds with Chiang. On April 2, 1945, Patrick Hurley, U.S. ambassador to China, issued a statement in Washington, declaring that the United States would cooperate only with Chiang Kai-shek, not with the Chinese Communist Party, and that the obstacle to China's "unification" lay in the "armed political party," the Chinese Communist Party. At the time, the United States was providing and equipping the Kuomintang forces with large quantities of military aid in an attempt to strengthen the Kuomintang's political and military superiority over the Communist Party and prepare the Kuomintang to seize the fruits of victory in the War of Resistance. This would add to the U.S. strength in its contention with the Soviet Union and expand its influence in China after the war.

Early in 1945, the most important task for the political parties and forces in China was still to defeat Japan, but they had already had their eyes on the future—they set about preparing for a bid to control the political situation after the war. The simultaneous convening of the Seventh National Congress of the Communist Party and the Sixth

National Congress of the Kuomintang in the spring of 1945 suggested that China was at a critical juncture. Would the fruits of victory in the people's War of Resistance go to the people or be seized by the Kuomintang? Would China remain a state of the comprador-feudal dictatorship or become a people's democracy? These were major questions to be answered by the two congresses.

The Kuomintang's Sixth National Congress was held from May 5 to 21. One of the topics for discussion was "putting constitutional government into effect," which was actually tantamount to persisting in one-party dictatorship and refusing to establish a coalition government. In his opening speech, while talking glibly about "instituting constitutional government," Chiang said that "after handing state power back to the people," the Kuomintang's responsibility for "defending the republic" would become "heavier rather than lighter." The congress resolved to convene the National Assembly on November 12, 1945 and adopt a constitution. However, the deputies to the National Assembly were still the deputies produced in 1936 from the election stage-managed by the Kuomintang. And the constitution would be formulated on the basis of the "Draft Constitution of the Republic of China" (the May 5th Draft Constitution) promulgated by the Kuomintang in 1936. Thus, "handing state power back to the people" was in essence handing the dictatorship from the left hand to the right one.

The second important topic for discussion was the decision to "thoroughly carry out the Principle of People's Livelihood." The real purpose of its implementation, in addition to the empty talk about "improving people's livelihood," was to "prevent the appearance of capital monopoly," and "eliminate the cause of class struggle." The former was meant to expand state monopoly capital and contain and swallow up national capital, while the latter was mainly intended to oppose the Communist Party. In order to achieve the above two purposes, the congress passed the "Political Platform and Policies," "Agricultural Policy Programme," "Principles for Implementing the Industrial Construction Programme" and "the Labour Policy Programme." These documents stipulated: "All the land in the cities should be turned over to the public ... it should be immediately declared that all mountains, forests, waters, mineral and other natural resources should be owned by the public.... All enterprises of monopolistic nature and enterprises which individuals cannot afford to run privately should be operated by the state or the public ... [and] ... when privately-owned undertakings fail to fulfil the production quotas, the deficiency should be made up by the government." This was the gist of "equalization of land ownership" and "regulation of capital" advocated by the Kuomintang.

The "Resolution on the Problem of the Chinese Communist Party" passed by the congress declared that "all problems can be settled through consultation provided they do not impede the War of Resistance, nor endanger the country." The line pursued by the Kuomintang's Sixth National Congress was a line which persisted in dictatorship and opposed democracy, expanded state monopoly capital and strangled national capital, and opposed land reform. This line not only ran counter to the will of the entire Chinese people, but to the global trend.

The Chinese Communist Party convened its Seventh National Congress at Yan'an from April 23 to June 11, 1945. The congress heard Mao Zedong's political report "On Coalition Government," Zhu De's military report "The Battle Front of the Liberated Areas," Liu Shaoqi's report "On Revising the Party Constitution" and Zhou Enlai's speech "On the United Front." The congress analysed the international and domestic situation and summed up the experience of the Party in leading the new-democratic revolution, especially the experience in the two-line struggle between the Kuomintang and the Communist party in the War of Resistance. It put forward the general line for the present-revolutionary stage and the Party's general programme as well as its specific programme. It adopted a new Party constitution and elected a new central leading body.

In his report, Mao Zedong pointed out that victory in the world anti-fascist war was imminent. After that, the struggle between the anti-fascist people and fascist remnant forces, democracy and anti-democracy, national liberation and national oppression, would still be raging in the greater part of the world. However, it was the people who would win. The situation in China was in accord with the general situation in the world. Hence, "two roads lie before the Chinese people, the road of light and the road of darkness. Two possible destinies await China, a destiny of light and a destiny of darkness." There were two prospects, but the bright future should be the target to strive for. The present task of the Chinese people was to establish a democratic coalition government, finally defeat the Japanese aggressors and build a new China, a China that was independent, free, democratic, united, prosperous and strong. With a view to accomplishing such a task, the congress formulated the line: "Boldly mobilize the masses and expand the people's forces, and, under our Party's leadership, defeat the Japanese aggressors, liberate the entire Chinese people and build a new democratic China."

The most striking characteristic of the new Party constitution adopted by the congress was the stipulation that "the Chinese Communist Party takes Mao Zedong Thought, which integrates the theory of Marxism-Leninism with the practice of the Chinese revolution, as the guide for all its work." The new Party constitution lay much emphasis on the mass line, pointing out that it was the Party's "basic political line" and "basic organizational line." The congress elected 44 members of the Central Committee, including Mao Zedong, Zhu De, Liu Shaoqi, Ren Bishi and Lin Zuhan. At the First Plenary Session of the Party's Seventh Central Committee convened after the congress, Mao Zedong was elected chairman of the Central Committee, and Mao Zedong, Zhu De, Liu Shaoqi, Zhou Enlai and Ren Bishi members of the Secretariat. The congress was a gathering of unity unprecedented in the Party's history, and provided important guarantees for victory in the War of Resistance, and the final victory in the people's democratic revolution.

From mid-July to early August, 1945, Chairman of the Soviet Council of Ministers J. V. Stalin, U.S. President Harry Truman, and British Prime Minister Winston Churchill (later replaced by the newly-appointed Prime Minister Clement R. Attlee) held a meeting at Potsdam outside Berlin and issued the "Potsdam Declaration," demanding that the Japanese government immediately declare unconditional surrender of all its armed forces. On August 6, the United States dropped an atomic bomb on Hiroshima and on August 8, the Soviet government declared war on Japan. In the small hours of the following day the Soviet army launched an all-out general offensive against Japan's elite Kwantung troops along a 4,000-kilometre battle line. On the same day the United States dropped another atomic bomb on Nagasaki. The Soviet army rapidly wiped out the Kwantung forces and liberated China's four northeast provinces and the province of Qahar.

On August 9, Mao Zedong, Chairman of the CPC Central Committee, issued a statement, pointing out "the time has come to inflict final defeat on the Japanese aggressors and all their lackeys," calling on the anti-Japanese army and people to vigourously expand the liberated areas and reduce the areas under enemy occupation, be on their guard to avert the danger of civil war, and promote the formation of a coalition government. On August 10, Commander-in-Chief Zhu De at the General Headquarters in Yan'an ordered the anti-Japanese forces in the liberated areas to quickly launch a big offensive to recover the lost territories and ordered the Japanese and puppet troops to surrender unconditionally within a stated time. On August 11, Chiang Kai-shek ordered the Kuomintang troops to "step up the war effort and actively push forward." Ironically he "ordered" the people's forces to "stay where they are, pending further orders," and forbade them to "take presumptuous action on their own" against Japanese and puppet forces. In the meantime he demanded the Japanese forces "defend themselves effectively" wherever they were, so as to prevent the people's forces from accepting their surrender. He went so far as to order the Japanese troops to recover the "lost land" from the newly liberated areas, and order the puppet troops to "be responsible for maintaining local order." The people's forces refused to execute Chiang Kai-shek's order. The attempt of the Kuomintang army to seize the fruits of victory in the War of Resistance sharpened domestic tensions.

On August 15 Japan's emperor Hirohito formally announced acceptance of the unconditional surrender stipulated in the Potsdam Declaration. On September 2, a surrender signing ceremony was held on the American warship *Missouri*. On September 9, another ceremony was held in Nanjing in the theatre of China, at which Yasuji Okamura, commander-in-chief of the Japanese invading forces in China, signed the instrument of surrender. Thus, the eight-year anti-Japanese war for national liberation ended in victory for the Chinese people.

With the situation viewed as a whole, the victory in the War of Resistance ended the imperialist war of aggression against China. It put an end to the situation in which China was repeatedly defeated by imperialists over the past 100 years. It was a victory for all Chinese except traitors, collaborators and the pro-Japanese group. Because of this victory, China made a big stride forward in the course of new-democratic revolution. The War of Resistance, just as Mao Zedong pointed out, was "a wonder in the history of warfare, a heroic undertaking of the Chinese nation and a great earth-shaking cause."

15. Proposals of Political Parties Concerning National Reconstruction. The Political Consultative Conference

After the war, China was confronted with a new political situation. The new major problems of overall importance were peace, democracy, solidarity and unity, or, to put it briefly, problems of "national reconstruction." These were problems of common concern to every Chinese who stood for political democracy, a prosperous and powerful China, and social progress. Each political party made public their own positions on these problems.

The conclusion of the anti-Japanese war marked the beginning of a new phase in Chinese history. In the "Declaration on the Current situation" issued on August 25, 1945, the CPC Central Committee pointed out, "In this new historical period, the important task confronting the whole nation is to consolidate unity in the country, safeguard domestic peace, bring about democracy and improve the people's livelihood, on the basis of peace, democracy and unity, so as to achieve national unification and build a new China, independent, free, prosperous and powerful." In order to lay the groundwork for future peace and construction, the Declaration demanded the National Government immediately take the following measures: recognize the popularly-elected governments and anti-Japanese forces in the liberated areas; bring about peace and avoid civil war; effect an equitable and rational reorganization of the armed forces and start their demobilization; provide relief to refugees and reduce taxes to relieve the people's distress; recognize the legal status of various parties; abolish laws and decrees which impeded people from enjoying the freedoms of assembly, association, speech, and the press; abolish the secret services and release patriotic political prisoners; and convene immediately the conference of representatives of all parties, and people with no party affiliation, to discuss matters of importance after the War of Resistance, formulate a democratic administrative programme so as to terminate the Kuomintang's political tutelage, set up a democratic coalition government representing the unanimous will of the nation, and make preparations for the convocation of the National Assembly produced from free and unrestricted elections. The Chinese Communist Party stated that it was "ready to make efforts to reach an agreement with the Kuomintang and democratic parties of China for a quick solution to urgent problems and long-term unity to thoroughly apply Dr. Sun Yat-sen's Three People's Principles."

On August 15, 1945, the China Democratic League issued an "Emergency Appeal Amidst the Cheers for the Victory of the War of Resistance," in which the slogan of "democracy and unification; peace and national reconstruction" was brought up. In October the League convened a provisional national congress in Chongqing to pass a programme, political report, declaration and constitution. The first three documents embodied the League's basic political theory and demands. The political report stated the belief that the post-war period was "an extremely rare opportunity for building China into a democratic country," and that the task of the League was to "seize such an opportunity to build China into a totally democratic country." It maintained that since the Anglo-American and Soviet systems each had their merits and demerits, "the economic democracy of the Soviet Union should be adopted to enrich the Anglo-American political democracy" so as to "create a Chinese-style democracy." This was the basic idea of the China Democratic League about democratic politics.

The programme of the League proposed that "land nationalization be accomplished step by step," and that "the state affirm people's private property and establish the property of the state and the public." The declaration put forward the League's demands and policies concerning the Political Consultative Conference, democratic coalition government, National Assembly, freedom for the people, the army, economy, foreign affairs and other important matters. The declaration said, "At present a democratic coalition government enjoying nationwide support is the country's only road to peace, unification and solidarity, and is also the only road to national reconstruction with concerted efforts of the entire nation."

On December 16, 1945, Hu Juewen, Zhang Naiqi, Shi Fuliang and Li Zhuchen called a meeting at Chongqing at which the Democratic National Construction Association was founded; and a declaration and political programme adopted. The aim of the association was to "promote democratic government with joint efforts and develop various undertakings beneficial to national construction by means of mutual help." In its declaration, it made clear its position in all fields. Internationally, it stood for a policy of balance between the United States and the Soviet Union. In domestic politics, it advocated peace and unification, that all political parties exercise forbearance, that the armed forces be nationalized through democratization of politics, and that legislative assemblies at various levels produced by direct general elections exercise different levels of political power. Economically, it demanded a plan for democratic economic construction and full freedom for enterprises within the guidelines of that plan, that at the present stage the state cultivate capital with all its might rather than get rid of it in the name of "regulation of capital," and that the land problem be solved by reasonable means. Socially, it demanded that the government work out an equitable and rational distribution system and lay a foundation for the cooperation between labour and capital, that "free organization of trade unions and peasant associations be encouraged," and that "they should not be controlled or manipulated by any political or social force not connected with the workers or peasants." The declaration expressed its "willingness to establish a model of peaceful struggle in China by dint of concerted efforts of the honest common people, free from deviation or partiality."

Hong Men Zhi Gong Dang issued a declaration abroad as well. The Association of Comrades in the Three People's Principles, the China Association for Promoting Democracy, the Jiu San Society, and the Kuomintang Association for Promoting Democracy were set up in succession and issued their political proposals. Their common desire was to maintain a peaceful environment and establish a democratic government in China.

These parties and their members were making untiring efforts in order to establish a long-sought-after bourgeois democratic state when the golden opportunity came. They entered into an alliance with the Communist Party on the basis of opposing the Kuomintang's fascist dictatorship and demanding the realization of democratic government. They played an important role in pushing the convocation of the Political Consultative Conference and upholding its line, as well as in the movement to oppose civil war, demand peace, oppose dictatorship and demand democracy.

An important aspect deciding China's political situation was the Kuomintang. Its consistent policy was to exercise dictatorial rule and expand state monopoly capital. After victory in the War of Resistance, the National Government took over a large amount of enemy and puppet property. By the end of August 1946, the factories and mines taken over by the Ministry of Economy totalled 2,849, most of which resumed operations under the direct control of the Ministry. The National Government's four banks and two bureaus took over the enemy and puppet banks—the Bank of Strokin, the Bank of Sumitomo, the Bank of Korea and the Central Reserve Bank. As a result, the bureaucrat capital of the Four Big Families drastically expanded to 20 billion U.S. dollars. The basic purpose of the Kuomintang's policy was to defend this state monopoly capital and the political system built on it. Under the conditions of the time, however, it had to use the slogans of "peace and national reconstruction" and "practise democratic politics" as a camouflage. This found expression in a book entitled *The New China of the Post-war Period* compiled by the Ministry of Education of the National Government, which said, "Democratic constitutionalism is the predetermined goal of the national revolution which externally conforms to the trend of the world and internally meets the demand of the people. This must not and cannot be delayed, since this is the mainstream of the politics of the New China after the war." But these slogans were nothing but a means to allay people's demand for democracy and adhere to the reactionary rule. Chiang Kai-shek, while stressing that "democratic constitutionalism must not be further delayed," put forward all kinds of "preconditions" to black the realization of democratic politics. In his "Message to the Military and Civilian Compatriots Throughout the Country" issued on New Year's Day of 1946, he said, "Except that revolutionary responsibility cannot be abandoned, the country's unity cannot be damaged, the basic law cannot be changed, and the foundation of the government cannot be shaken, anything can be tolerated or negotiated." In other words, the Chiang Kai-shek clique brooked no change in the essence of the state of the comprador-feudal fascist dictatorship. This was the basic stand of the Kuomintang on the China problem after the war.

China's politics after the war were inseparable from U.S. imperialist policy towards China. The United States intended to use the National Government as a tool to control China, while the Chiang regime wanted to use American aid as its backing. On this basis the two sides colluded with each other more closely. Restricted by the international situation, the domestic situation of the United States and the development of the domestic problems in China, the U.S. policy of aiding Chiang and opposing the Communists went through a process of evolution. After the war, the United States had to make a choice from the following three possibilities in formulating its China policy:

First, extricating itself from all involvement. This was unacceptable to U.S. imperialism, as it could not give up its policy of aggression against China;

Second, large-scale armed intervention so as to assist the Kuomintang in its attempt to annihilate the Communist Party. Due to the powerful forces of the Chinese people, the opposition of its own people and the people of the world, and the limitations of its national strength, the United States chose not to take such a tremendous risk as to send troops for a large-scale armed intervention when the world war was just over and people wanted peace;

Third, encourage the Kuomintang and Communist Party to negotiate and reach a compromise, while assisting the Kuomintang to establish its power as extensively as possible.

The United States chose the third option, through which it attempted a makeshift measure so as to bring the Communists into the orbit of bourgeois democratic politics, and put them in a position similar to that of the Communists in Western Europe, that is, to form a pro-American, reorganized coalition government headed by Chiang Kai-shek and composed of representatives of the Kuomintang, the Communist Party and democratic parties. The United States reckoned there was such a possibility. However, as this measure was detrimental to the Chinese people, it was continuously exposed and resisted by the Communist Party. Meanwhile, it met with the opposition of the fascist forces within the Kuomintang since it did not altogether cater to the needs of the Kuomintang one-party dictatorship and Chiang Kai-shek's personal autocratic rule. Consequently, the wishful calculations of the U.S. were out of the question. In addition, it was also impossible to form, with the intervention of the United States, another government representing its interests if the Chiang Kai-shek regime was excluded. Under these circumstances, U.S. policy towards China gradually embarked on the road to supporting Chiang Kai-shek in his move to fight a civil war against the Communist Party. In his statement concerning the China policy issued in December 1945, U.S. President Harry Truman, while expressing his support for the proposal for convening a conference of representatives of all major political parties in China to precipitate the unity of China, deemed the existence of the Communist-led armies as not in line with China's political unity. In the same month, George C. Marshall came to China as the president's special representative to carry out U.S. policy towards China. As a "mediator," he participated in the negotiations between the Kuomintang and the Communist Party and supported the National Government in launching a civil war. He left China in January 1947. His activities during his year in China reflected the process of evolution of the U.S. policy towards China.

The Soviet Union was also a major international factor affecting China's internal affairs. According to the Yalta Agreement signed by the United States, Britain and the Soviet Union in February 1945, the Soviet Union would recover all the rights and interests enjoyed by tsarist Russia in northeast China before the outbreak of the Russo-Japanese war. In the meantime, the three countries also reached an agreement on unanimous support for the National Government headed by Chiang Kai-shek. On August 14, 1945, the National Government and the Soviet government concluded the "Sino-Soviet Treaty of Friendship and Alliance" and some other agreements, in which the Kuomintang accepted the Soviet demands for the rights and interests in China in exchange for the Soviet support. The Soviet leaders made it clear time and again to the United States and the Kuomintang that the Soviet Union, like the United States, would support Chiang Kai-shek in his attempt to unify China and back his National Government.

These international and domestic conditions ushered in a short period of sharp, intricate and complex struggles in Chinese history. During this period, the heart of the China problem was the Political Consultative Conference, and the key to the domestic political development at the time was the negotiations between the Kuomintang and the Communist Party at Chongqing.

On August 28, 1945, at the cabled invitation of Chiang Kai-shek, Mao Zedong, accompanied by Patrick Hurley and Zhang Zhizhong, flew to Chongqing with Zhou Enlai and Wang Ruofei for negotiations. Mao and Chiang held talks about the great issues of peace and national reconstruction. Representatives of the Chinese Communist Party Zhou Enlai and Wang Ruofei negotiated with representatives of the National Government Wang Shijie, Zhang Qun, Zhang Zhizhong and Shao Lizi for 40 days, and on October 10 signed the "Summary of Conversations Between the Government and Representatives of the Chinese Communist Party," also known as the "October 10th Agreement." The chief result of the negotiations was the Kuomintang's acceptance of the basic policy of peace and national reconstruction. The Kuomintang and the Communist Party, the Summary said, "must make joint efforts" to achieve "long-term cooperation on the basis of peace, democracy, solidarity and unity" and "resolutely avoid civil war, build a new China, independent, free, prosperous and powerful, and thoroughly bring the Three People's Principles into effect." With this as a prerequisite, the Communist Party would accept the leading position of Chiang Kai-shek. Both sides regarded "democratization of political life, nationalization of troops, and equality and legality of political parties as absolutely essential for achieving peace and national reconstruction." The Kuomintang should terminate political tutelage, institute constitutionalism and convene the Political Consultative Conference to discuss the formula for peace and national reconstruction, and the convocation of the National Assembly.

The problems of nationalization of troops and political power in the liberated areas were the point at issue during the negotiation. Still insisting on "unifying the military command and government administration," the Kuomintang refused to recognize the legal status of the people's army and political power in the liberated areas. On the problem of troops, the Communist Party proposed reducing the anti-Japanese forces under its command to 24 divisions or to a minimum of 20 divisions, and withdrawing its troops currently distributed in the south to the liberated areas north of the Longhai Railway and to those in northern Jiangsu and northern Anhui. To this, the Kuomintang did not give a definite answer. On political power in the liberated areas, the formulas proposed by the Communist Party were all refused by the Kuomintang. As for the problems on which no agreement had been reached, both sides agreed that these would be discussed later or submitted to the Political Consultative Conference for solution. The signing of the "October 10th Agreement" was the prerequisite for the convocation of the conference.

During the negotiations between the Kuomintang and Communist Party, civil war was being fought fiercely in some areas. In September and October 1945, the Kuomintang troops launched attacks on the people's forces along the Beiping-Suiyuan and Beiping-Hankou railways, and around the Shangdang area in Shanxi Province. The people's forces counter-attacked and won the battle. Beginning in November, a popular movement against the civil war broke out in Kuomintang-controlled areas. In order to suppress the movement the National Government manufactured the "December 1st Massacre." To a certain extent, the victory of the people's forces in the counter-attack and the popular movement against the civil war temporarily contained the Kuomintang's policy in this connection. In December the foreign ministers of the Soviet Union, the United States and Britain met in Moscow and reaffirmed their China policy. These factors made possible the convocation of the Political Consultative Conference.

The Political Consultative Conference was held at Chongqing

from January 10 to 31, 1946. Attending the conference were 38 representatives from five quarters: eight from the Kuomintang including Sun Ke (Sun Fo), Wu Tiecheng and Chen Bulei; seven from the Communist Party including Zhou Enlai, Dong Biwu and Wang Ruofei; five from the Youth Party including Zeng Qi and Chen Qitian; nine from the China Democratic League including Zhang Lan, Luo Longji, Zhang Bojun and Shen Junru; and nine public personages including Guo Moruo, Wang Yunwu, and Fu Sinian. Chiang Kai-shek convened the conference and was its natural chairman. In practice the five sides attending the conference represented three political forces. The process of the meeting was a process of sharp, complicated trial of strength among the three political forces, three positions concerning state power and three roads for China to take. During the struggle, the Communist Party and the middle forces joined hands to oppose the Kuomintang's fascist dictatorship. Heated debates were centred around five problems—government reorganization, an administrative programme, the army, the National Assembly and the draft constitution.

On the government reorganization, the Kuomintang proposed "expanding the organization of the government," and refused to reorganize it. The Kuomintang's specific proposals were that the number of National Government Councillors be increased; the appointment of National Government Councillors be approved by the Kuomintnag Central Executive Committee upon the nomination of the chairman; members of the Kuomintang make up "a specified majority" of the National Government Councillors; the National Government Council have no power of appointments to government posts; and the chairman of the National Government be vested with emergency powers. The Communist Party took the position that it accepted the position of Chiang Kai-shek and the Kuomintang as head party, but that the government must be reorganized; that the reorganized government must have a common programme; that the National Government Council should have the power of appointing persons for office; that the number of Kuomintang members in the government should not exceed the limit of one-third; that the choice of National Government Councillors should not be approved by the Kuomintang Central Executive Committee; and that governing by personal decree should be avoided.

The representatives of the China Democratic League put forward three major points on government reorganization: there must be a common programme; the decision-making bodies must be truly capable of making decisions; and the executive organs must be truly capable of applying the decisions.

After debate and consultation the "Organic Law of the National Government" was passed. It provided that the National Government Council was the supreme government organ in charge of state affairs, with powers to discuss and decide legislative principles, administrative policies and major military and administrative measures, financial plans and the budget as well as appoint and remove ministers of the state and appoint members of the Legislative Yuan; that half of the 40 National Government Councillors should be Kuomintang members; and that it required more than two-thirds of the councillors to pass an important motion. This in the main negated the Kuomintang proposals and embodied the demands of the Communist Party as well as democrates and democratic parties.

The problem of the army was the main point of contention at the conference. The Kuomintang adhered to the set principle of "unifying the military command and government administration," maintaining that the "nationalization of troops" must be carried out. The Youth Party stressed that "the nationalization of troops is the precondition for democratization of political life," going along with the Kuomintang. The Democratic League proposed that "all the troops throughout the country should be immediately dissociated from political parties and put under the control of the state." The Communist Party rejected the idea that "only by nationalizing the troops first can the democratization of political life be realized." It held that these two must be carried out simultaneously, and that the purpose of nationalizing troops was to make them troops of the people. Through debates an agreement was reached, though with difficulty. Principled provisions were adopted, such as "the armed forces belong to the state ... military power shall be separated from political parties ... military authority shall be separated from civil authority ... [and] the army shall be placed under the control of the government." However, no practical problems were solved.

The Kuomintang insisted that the delegates elected to the National Assembly in 1936 remain in office and that "a rational number of delegates be added," nearly half nominated by the Kuomintang. This proposal met with strong opposition from the representatives of the Communist Party, Democratic League and non-party progressives. The agreement finally reached provicded that the number of delegates to the National Assembly should be 2,050, including an additional 150 from Taiwan and the northeast, and 700 from various parties and from among public figures. The provision that "the adoption of a constitution shall require the approval of three quarters of the delegates present" basically foiled the Kuomintang's attempt to control the National Assembly.

The Kuomintang insisted that the May 5th Draft Constitution formulated in 1936 remain valid. This, again, met with strong opposition from most representatives, who called for principled revision of the constitution. The Communist Party set forth four principles for working out a constitution: The constitution should protect, not restrict, the rights of the people; the powers of a provincial government in relation to those of the central government should be defined according to the principle of a fair distribution of power; the province should be a unit of local self-government, the provincial governor should be elected by the people, and the province should have a provincial constitution; and the constitution should explicitly lay down democratic policies in military, cultural, educational and economic fields.

After debate, decisions were made regarding the principles for revising the "May 5th Constitution." These were that "the Legislative Yuan is the highest legislative body of the state [whose] functions and powers are equivalent to those of the parliament of a democratic country ... the Executive Yuan is the highest executive organ of the state, responsible and accountable to the Legislative Yuan ... the province shall be the highest unit of local self-government ... [and] the provincial governor shall be elected by the people." These laid down a political system of parliament, cabinet and provincial self-government, denying the one-party dictatorship of the Kuomintang.

The "Programme for Peace and National Reconstruction" on the basis of the "Draft Programme for Peace and National Reconstruction" put forward by the Communist Party was formally adopted as the "administrative yardstick" before a constitutional government was established.

The Political Consultative Conference was a special episode in Chinese political history. The common struggle of the Communist Party, democrats and democratic parties and efforts of the democratic elements in the Kuomintang resulted in the adoption by the conference of some agreements that were favourable to peace, democracy and the people. The conference decided to put into effect a political system of parliament, cabinet and provincial self-government—a negation of the Kuomintang's one-party dictatorship and Chiang Kai-shek's personal autocratic rule. Thanks to these achievements and the solution of problems through consultation, the conference had a great bearing on the political life in China.

The Political Consultative Conference was held against the will of the Kuomintang ruling clique. The implementation of the agreements would mean the denial of the Kuomintang fascist dictatorship. It was natural, therefore, that the conference and its agreements would meet with strong opposition from the deep-rooted reactionary force within the Kuomintnag. During and after the conference, Kuomintang secret agents and hooligans repeatedly disrupted public lectures held at Cangbaitang Hall, beating and wounding speakers Guo Moruo and Zhang Dongsun, both delegates to the Political Consultative Conference. The military police of the National Government unlawfully searched the residence of another delegate Huang Yanpei. Kuomintang secret agents and hooligans engineered the "Bloody Incident of Jiaochangkuo," attacking and wounding more than 60 people including Li Gongpu, Guo Moruo, Zhang Naiqi, Shi Fuliang and Ma Yinchu. Beginning February 22, 1946, the Kuomintang stage-managed a series of anti-Soviet, anti-Communist demonstrations in Chongqing and some other major cities. These atrocities and demonstrations were aimed at sabotaging the ongoing Political Consultative Conference and the political atmosphere of peace and democracy that appeared after the close of the conference.

From March 1 to 17 in Chongqing the Kuomintang called the Second Plenary Session of its Sixth Central Executive Committee, at which fascist elements frenziedly opposed the agreements of the Political Consultative Conference, especially the agreement on the draft constitution. Chiang Kai-shek declared that since some points contained in the principles for revising the draft constitution "contravene the spirit of the five-power constitution ... efforts must be made to remedy the situation." The meeting passed a "Resolution on the PCC Report," setting forth five principles for revising the draft constitution:

(1) The constitution should be formulated on the basis of the Programme of National Reconstruction;

(2) The National Assembly should be a visible organization and exercise its functions and powers through convocation of meetings;

(3) The Legislative Yuan should not be vested with the power of approval and no-confidence over the Executive Yuan;

(4) The Control Yuan should not be vested with the power of approval; and

(5) It was unnecessary for a province to draft its own constitution.

This session also decided that the Central Political Council of the Kuomintang "direct" the work of the National Government; and that the National Government Councillors chosen by various parties from their members should be appointed by the Standing Committee of the Kuomintang Central Executive Committee. These points continued the Kuomintang one-party dictatorship, and utterly repudiated the principles of democratic constitutionalism decided upon at the Political Consultative Conference. These actions by the KMT made it impossible to solve the problem of national reconstruction by peaceful democratic means and a civil war became inevitable.

16. The Outbreak of All-out Civil War. Radical Turn in Military and Political Situation in China

In the first half of 1946, the Kuomintang, while trampling on the PCC agreements, stepped up its preparations for an all-out civil war. It moved 210 brigades, or some 1.3 million men, to the civil war fronts, and seized 40 county towns in the liberated areas. In the northeast it pursued a policy of "taking over by military force." In defiance of the agreement reached by the Kuomintang and the Communist Party, Du Yuming's forces marched west from Jinzhou to attack Rehe, and reached Chifeng and Chengde. The strategic intention of the action was to cut off the link between the two liberated areas: north and northeast China. With U.S. support, the Kuomintang transported five corps, including the New First and New Sixth corps, from Shanghai, Guangzhou and Viet Nam to the northeast to fight the civil war. In May the Chiang troops invaded and occupied Siping, Changchun and Yongji, and advanced north to the southern bank of the Songhua River. Before the outbreak of an all-out civil war, a situation was already created with small-scale fighting south of the Great Wall and large-scale fighting north of it.

On June 26, 1946, more than 300,000 Kuomintang troops launched a massive attack on the Central Plains Liberated Area. This marked the beginning of a nationwide civil war, and also the beginning of a strategic offensive on the liberated areas by the Kuomintang force. On August 10, George Marshall and Leighton Stuart issued a joint statement, declaring that their "mediation" had been a failure. Immediately after the attack against the Central Plains Liberated Area, the Kuomintang employed 58 brigades totalling 460,000 men under Xue Yue and Wu Qiwei of the Pacification Headquarters in Xuzhou to attack the Jiangsu, Anhui and Shandong liberated areas; 28 brigades totalling 240,000 men under Liu Zhi of the Zhengzhou Pacification Headquarters and under the Xuzhou Pacification Headquarters to attack the Hebei-Shandong-Henan Liberated Area; 18 brigades totalling 160,000 men under Sun Lianzhong, governor of Hebei Province, and Fu Zuoyi to attack the Shanxi-Qahar-Hebei Liberated Areas; 20 brigades totalling 90,000 men under Yan Xishan, a portion of the troops under Fu Zuoyi and another portion under Hu Zongnan to attack the Shanxi-Suiyuan Liberated Area; 19 brigades totalling 150,000 men under Hu Zongnan to attack the Shaanxi-Gansu-Ningxia Border Region; and nine brigades totalling more than 70,000 men to attack the guerrilla areas in Guangdong and the Qiongya Liberated Area in Hainan Island.

In early August, seven Kuomintang airplanes bombed Yan'an. In

October, Du Yuming's 16 brigades, with 160,000 men, launched a fresh attack against the Northeast Liberated Area. From July to October, Chiang Kai-shek employed 193 brigades, or some 1.6 million men, to mount an all-out offensive against the liberated areas; they constituted 80 percent of his total regular troops (248 brigades, or 2 million men). On October 11, the Kuomintang troops seized Zhangjiakou, reaching the peak of the offensive, and bringing the total number of occupied cities in the liberated areas to 153. Chen Cheng, Chief of General Staff of the Kuomintang's Ministry of Defence, bragged at a news conference at Beiping that the fighting with the Communist-led forces "can be settled within three or at most five months."

In order to resume or establish reactionary rule in the occupied liberated areas, the Kuomintang officially set up, in October, the Government Administration Committee for the Pacification Regions, with Song Ziwen (T. V. Soong) and Bai Chongxi as director and vice-director. The committee divided these liberated areas and areas in the vicinity into 15 pacification regions and formulated the "Administrative Programme for the Pacification Regions" and "Procedures for Handling Land Problems." Wherever the Chiang troops went, they were followed by the Kuomintang hacks, secret agents, fugitive landlords and their "home-coming legions." In the occupied areas, the Kuomintang set up its party organizations, and instituted the *Bao-Jia* system (by which families were grouped in units which were held jointly responsible for any "unlawful" act), seized the land distributed to the peasants and slaughtered the revolutionary masses. Chiang Kai-shek attempted to consolidate the occupied areas by coordinating administration with military operations.

The Chinese Communist Party had long been prepared for the outbreak of an all-out civil war. When the negotiations between the Kuomintang and the Communist Party and the Political Consultative Conference were in progress, large-scale movements for the reduction of rent and interest and the development of production were initiated to consolidate the liberated areas. A movement to train troops was developed, and artillery and engineer corps were established and expanded. In the "Directive on Question of Account-Settling, Rent-Reduction and Land" issued on May 4, 1946, the Party Central Committee decided to change the land policy in the period of the War of Resistance, that is, to change from the reduction of rent and interest to confiscation of the land of the landlords for distribution among the peasants. This change marked the deep-going development of the democratic revolution.

After Japan's surrender, the Communist Party set the strategic policy of "expanding in the north and defending in the south," and sent large number of cadres and troops to the northeast. In the struggle to clean out bandits, liquidate the remaining enemy and puppet forces, settle accounts with traitors, reduce rent and interest, carry out land reform and support the war for self-defence, vast base areas were gradually built in the northeast, with the people's powers set up on the basis of the united front. The building of the Northeast Liberated Area played a tremendous role in the liberation of the whole country in 1949.

At the time when the Chiang Kai-shek clique unleashed the all-out civil war, it had a total armed force of 4,300,000, with regular troops numbering some 2,000,000, controlled areas with a population of over 300 million, had taken over the military equipment from one million Japanese troops that had surrendered, and had obtained a large amount of military and economic aid from the United States. The People's Liberation Army had just over 1,200,000, of which the regular forces numbered 610,000. They were backwardly equipped and short of weapons; and the liberated areas had a population of just over 100 million. To counter the strategic offensive of the superior enemy forces, the Military Commission of the CPC Central Committee defined a correct operational principle—the principle of concentrating a superior force to wipe out the enemy forces one by one. The concentration of the forces for mobile warfare should be primary, and the dispersal of the forces for guerrilla warfare should be supplementary. The principle was aimed chiefly at annihilating the enemy's effective strength, not at holding or seizing a place. It was permissible to abandon certain cities or places to lure the enemy troops in deep. The next step was to concentrate a superior force and select one of the enemy's weak or isolated parts to destroy its forces one by one in mobile warfare.

After the Chiang troops started an offensive on the Central Plains Liberated Area, the Liberation Army there commanded by Li Xiannian and Zheng Weisan broke through the enemy's encirclement for a strategic shift. In July and August, the East China People's Liberation Army under Chen Yi, Su Yu and Tan Zhenlin wiped out over 50,000 enemy troops in the Central-Jiangsu Campaign, and eight enemy brigades in the Subei area and southern Shandong. In February 1947, the army evacuated Linyi on its own initiative and marched northward. In the Laiwu area it annihilated 50,000 enemy troops at one fell swoop. The Shanxi-Hebei-Shandong-Henan Liberation Army under Liu Bocheng and Deng Xiaoping attacked the Longhai Railway. In the ensuing Dingtao, Juancheng, Huaxian, Jujintai and southwestern Shanxi campaigns, they wiped out 70,000 enemy troops. The Shanxi-Qahar-Hebei Liberation Army under Nie Rongzhen and Xiao Ke engaged the enemy advancing from the east and west to invade Zhangjiakou in September and October. After wiping out 20,000 enemy troops, they withdrew from the city to strike at the enemy in the Baoding sector. The Shanxi-Suiyuan Liberation Army under He Long and Li Jingquan, with the coordination of the Shanxi-Qahar-Hebei Liberation Army, wiped out 8,000 enemy troops in northern Shanxi. The Northeast Liberation Army under Lin Biao (1907-1971) and Luo Ronghuan (1902-1963) annihilated the enemy's whole 25th Division in the Xinkailing region in south Liaoning. Between February 1946 and April 1947 they crossed the Songhua River to attack enemy positions to the south on three occasions, and held the Linjiang region by repulsing four enemy attacks. In these battles they wiped out 50,000 enemy troops and brought the enemy's offensive in the northeast to an end.

During eight months of fighting, the People's Liberation Army abandoned 105 towns and several areas, but wiped out 65 enemy brigades, or 710,000 men. The Chiang Kai-shek troops' occupation of many towns and places in liberated areas resulted in the annihilation of his men in large numbers, an extended battle line, the dispersion of forces, and a great reduction of reserve striking units. Consequently, beginning from March 1947, he had to change the policy of an all-out offensive into one of concentrating attacks on key points in the Shandong and Shaanxi-Gansu-Ningxia liberated areas.

In April 1947, Chiang's troops began their offensive against the Shandong Liberated Area. He moved 60 brigades, or some 450,000 men, to advance northward from the Linyi-Tai'an line. From late April to mid-May the East China Liberation Army first wiped out the enemy's Reorganized 72nd Division at Tai'an, and then the Reorganized 74th Division, one of the enemy's main forces, at one swoop in the Menglianggu sector. The enemy lost altogether 56,000 troops in the two battles. The Menglianggu battle was a decisive one in smashing the enemy's concentrated attacks on key points in the Shandong Liberated Area. Soon afterwards, Chiang concentrated 32 brigades, or 240,000 men, to attack the Yimeng Mountain region. The Liberation Army, while employing part of its forces for head-on resistance, sent its main force to attack the enemy's rear area, which compelled part of the Chiang troops to retreat westward from central Shandong. In March 1947, the Kuomintang massed 25 brigades, or more than 200,000 men, to attack the Shaanxi-Gansu-Ningxia Liberated Area in an attempt to capture Yan'an and smash the leading centre of the Communist Party. The Party Central Committee withdrew from Yan'an on March 19, but continued to remain in northern Shaanxi to direct the War of Liberation throughout the country and in the northwest. The Northwest Liberation Army under Peng Dehuai, which had less than 30,000 men, flexibly seized every opportunity for wiping out the enemy in accordance with the principle of "luring the enemy in deep." Within five months, they annihilated more than 30,000 enemy troops in the battles of Qinghuabian, Yangmahe, Panlong and Shajiadian and frustrated Chiang's troops' attacks against key sectors. In the meantime, the Liberation Army in other theatres launched partial counter-offensives.

In a year of fighting, the Chinese People's Liberation Army wiped out 1,120,000 enemy troops, and beat back their all-out offensive and attacks against key sectors. The total stregnth of Chiang's army was reduced from 4,300,000 to 3,700,000, with only around 40 reserve brigades. The People's Liberation Army lost 358,000 men. Its total number, however, grew from 1,200,000 to 1,950,000, its equipment was much improved and its fighting capacity much strengthened. This brought about a radical change in the war. From then on, the

Liberation Army shifted from strategic defensive to strategic offensive, while the Kuomintang army was forced to switch from strategic offensive to strategic defensive.

The unleashing of a large-scale civil war by the National Government deepened its dependence on the United States. And the latter also needed to sell its commodities in China. Actuated by their common requirements, the foreign minister of the National Government and the U.S. ambassador to China concluded "The Sino-U.S. Treaty of Friendship, Commerce and Navigation" in November 1946 in Nanjing. The unequal and aggressive content and nature of the treaty was covered with phrases of "friendship" and took the form of "equality" and "mutual benefit." It was a treaty by which the United States enslaved China and the National Government sold out China's sovereignty and interests. It provided that U.S. nationals should enjoy in "the whole extent of … the territories" of China the rights to reside, travel, carry on commercial, manufacturing, processing, scientific, educational, religious and "philanthropic" activities, explore and exploit mineral resources, and hold, construct and lease land and building; that U.S. "legal persons and organizations" in China should be accorded the same treatment as Chinese; that in respect of taxation, sale, distribution and use in China, U.S. commodities should be accorded treatment no less favourable than that accorded to the commodities of any third country or to Chinese commodities; that "no prohibition or restriction shall be imposed" by China on the importation from the United States of any article grown, produced or manufactured in the U.S., or on the exportation to the United States of any Chinese article. It also provided that U.S. vessels should have the freedom of sailing in any of the open ports, places or waters in China. After the conclusion of the treaty, Chiang Kai-shek's ambassador to the United States openly stated that "the entire territory of China is open to U.S. merchants." This treaty, just as the public opinion of the time put it, was a "new unequal treaty of national betrayal and unilateral benefit which is absolutely unfavourable to China." The Sino-U.S. Treaty of Commerce met with opposition from the entire Chinese people.

After the Kuomintang tore up the PCC agreements and launched the all-out civil war, with a view to decking its reactionary rule out in legal and democratic finery and currying favour with the United States for more aid, it quickened its pace to "frame a constitution." On July 3, 1946, the Supreme Defence Committee of the National Government decided to convene the National Assembly on November 12 that year. On October 12, the day after Chiang's troops seized Zhangjiakou, the date for convocation was officially announced. With the exception of a small number of representatives of the Youth Party and the Democratic Socialist Party and certain "public figures," all the participants were Kuomintang members. The Assembly was set the task of formulating a constitution, and so it was also known as "Constitution-formulation National Assembly." It came to a close after adopting the "Constitution of the Republic of China." On New Year's Day of 1947, the National Government promulgated the constitution and announced that it would go into effect on December 25. The constitution copied some phrases about freedom and democracy from bourgeois constitutions, but in essence, it could be traced to the same origin as the "Provisional Constitution of the Political Tutelage Period." Its basic feature was that it affirmed in the form of fundamental law the state system of Chiang Kai-shek's dictatorial rule.

The holding of the National Assembly and the formulating of the Constitution were in direct contravention of the PCC agreements and the procedures for the establishment of democratic rule as provided in them. Therefore, the Communist Party deemed the Assembly illegal and refused to participate. On November 19, the CPC delegation headed by Zhou Enlai left Nanjing and Shanghai for Yan'an. Representatives of the Democratic League, and non-party democrats and democratic elements within the Kuomintang also refused to participate. To uphold its correct stand, the Democratic League decided to expel the Democratic Socialist Party, which had attended the National Assembly, from the league.

Immediately after the convening of the National Assembly, the Kuomintang began to "reorganize the government." At a joint meeting of the Supreme Defence Committee and the Standing Committee of the Kuomintnag Central Executive Committee held in April 1947, Chiang Kai-shek appointed the National Government Councillors and the presidents of the five Yuans. He himself took up the post of chairman of the National Government, and Sun Ke the vice-chairman's post. Zhang Qun was president of the Executive Yuan; Sun Ke, president of the Legislative Yuan; Ju Zheng, president of the Judicial Yuan; Yu Youren, president of the Control Yuan; and Dai Chuanxian, president of the Examination Yuan. Of the 29 National Government Councillors, 17 were Kuomintang members, four Youth Party members, four Democratic Socialist Party members, and four "public personages." On April 23 the reorganized "National Government" was officially formed. The Kuomintang described it as a "multi-party government" conforming to democratic principles, and that "the Kuomintang has fulfilled its promise of handing state power back to the people." This government, with only several members of other parties and a few pro-Chiang "public figures" participating, was in practice a dictatorial government controlled by one person, Chiang Kai-shek, and one party, the Kuomintang. Like its predecessor, this government was anti-popular in nature.

After the outbreak of the all-out civil war, a large-scale people's democratic movement erupted in the Kuomintang-controlled areas and was subjected to suppression. In mid-July 1946, the Kuomintang secret agents assassinated within one week responsible members of the Democratic League Li Gongpu (1902-1946) and Wen Yiduo, (1899-1946), who were deeply interested in the democratic movement against civil war and dictatorship. The murder case shocked the country and the world. In December 1946, a female student of Beijing University was raped by U.S. soldiers in Beiping, which triggered off a nationwide movement in protest against their outrageous acts. In May 1947, another nationwide student movement was unfolding under the slogan of "food, peace, freedom" or "against hunger, against civil war, against persecution." On May 20, when students from Nanjing, Shanghai and Hangzhou petitioned at Nanjing, they were beaten by the Kuomintang soliders, policemen and secret agents and many were arrested or wounded.

The poverty-stricken people in many cities, who were suffering from hunger because of soaring grain prices, rose to seize rice in the spring of 1947. On February 28, 1947, the people of Taiwan Province launched a large-scale uprising against the Kuomintang's fascist rule, and were brutally suppressed. From the time when the Kuomintang began to violate the PCC agreements up to the latter half of 1947, a people's democratic movement, developed in the Kuomintang-controlled areas. Students were the driving force behind the movement, and people from all walks of life took part. This, apart from the armed struggle, formed the second battle front in the struggle of the Chinese people against Chiang Kai-shek. In coordination with the victorious operations of the People's Liberation Army, the movement dealt heavy blows to the Kuomintang reactionary regime. As a result, the Kuomintang government was besieged by the whole people—an important indication that a radical change would take place in China very soon.

The unleashing of an all-out civil war indicate Chiang Kai-shek's determination to remain reactionary to the end. He thoroughly cut off the ties between the Kuomintnag and the Communist Party which had been maintained for a decade. In February 1947, the Kuomintang forced the representatives and personnel of the Communist Party stationed in Nanjing, Shanghai and Chongqing for negotiations to leave within a limited time. In March they all returned to Yan'an. At the Third Plenary Session of the Sixth Central Executive Committee of the Kuomintang, Chiang Kai-shek said that a "political settlement" had become "hopeless," proclaiming the Kuomintang's break with the Communist Party. On June 25, the Supreme Court's Procuratorial Office ordered Mao Zedong to be put on the wanted list. Thus the Kuomintang reactionaries totally severed its relations with the Communist Party and disrupted domestic unity, and went a step further on the road to self-destruction.

Owing to the Kuomintang's series of actions—launching an all-out civil war, tearing up the PCC agreements, convening the illegal National Assembly and closing the door to peace negotiations, the hope of establishing a bourgeois republic cherished by democratic parties was getting slimmer and slimmer, a hope which had been high while the PCC was in progress. Those taking the middle road were pushed step by step down a blind alley. They were compelled to rise in struggle as a result of the pressure imposed by the Kuomintang: Because of their miscalculation of the situation and the rejection of people's democracy by those advocating old-style democracy, certain political parties and individuals assiduously spread the middle-of-the-road line and other bourgeois ideas to swell their ranks and put the line into practice. Their basic position was to achieve reconciliation between the Kuomintang and the Communist Party, and maintain close relations with both the United States and the Soviet Union. The China Democratic League repeatedly indicated that as a third party, it would "continue to do its utmost to mediate the armed strife between parties."

The most active advocate of the middle-of-the-road political line was Shi Fuliang (1898-1970), one of the leaders of the Democratic National Construction Association. He defined this political line as establishing a democratic government of the Anglo-American type and developing national capitalism. Politically, he opposed one-party or one-class dictatorship of any type. Supporters of this line, he said, stood for peaceful and reformist action, rather than violent, revolutionary action. It seemed to him that "the present political situation is that the Kuomintang cannot eradicate the Communist Party by military force, nor can the Communist Party overthrow the Kuomintang by military force; moreover, the international situation does not allow the existence of a totally Right Kuomintang regime, nor a totally Left Communist government. Under these objective conditions, the only possible correct road is to resume the middle-of-the-road line of the PCC." For this reason, he argued, it was necessary to form a "powerful middle-of-the-road group ... occupying a decisive position" between Kuomintang and the Communist Party.

Just when this group was going around spreading its ideas, the Kuomintang government had decided to thoroughly suppress it, first making an example of the China Democratic League. In May 1947 the Kuomintang Central News Agency published a fake document, "The Line and Programme of the Chinese Communist Party for Underground Struggle," and a statement by a certain political observer. This statement claimed that "in fact, the China Democratic League and its incarnations—the Democratic National Construction Association, the Association for Promoting Democracy, the Association of Comrades in Three People's Principles—have been taken over by the Chinese

Communist Party, and act in compliance with its wishes." This signified that the democratic parties were about to come under attack. In October the National Government's Ministry of Internal Affairs declared the Democratic League an "illegal organization." The League now was forced to issue a proclamation in the name of its Chairman, Zhang Lan, declaring that all its members would cease their political activities and the headquarters of the China Democratic League would be dissolved. Other democratic parties that had not been compelled to declare their disbandment, also lost freedom of public activities. The forced disbandment of the China Democratic League indicated that the National Government which had flaunted the banner of constitutional government, would not allow the existence of freedom and democracy, even of the bourgeois type. The disbandment of the China Democratic League announced the total defeat of the "third-big-party movement" and the complete bankruptcy of the middle road.

One year after the civil war began, a great change took place in the relative strength between Chiang Kai-shek's troops and the People's Liberation Army. The military posture became highly unfavourable to Chiang's troops. As a result of concentrated offensives, his main forces were massed at the eastern and western flanks, leaving the centre and rear weakly defended. This provided objective conditions for the People's Liberation Army to apply the strategy of breaking through the centre and advancing to the enemy's rear. The People's Liberation Army seized the opportunity and went over to strategic offensive. Selecting the Central Plains region as the point to effect a breakthrough, it directed its spearhead against the Dabie mountain area—the most sensitive area in the Kuomintang's strategy, but with weak forces. In order to start a strategic offensive, the CPC Central Committee drew up a plan of "coordination among three armies" and "pinning down the enemy at both flanks."

Coordination among three armies meant that main force of the Shanxi-Hebei-Shandong-Henan Liberation Army led by Liu Bocheng and Deng Xiaoping would effect a breakthrough in the centre and push towards the Dabie Mountains; the main force of the East China Liberation Army led by Chen Yi and Su Yu would sweep into the Jiangsu-Shandong-Henan-Anhui region as a force at the left rear; and the Taiyue Army led by Chen Geng and Xie Fuzhi, as a force at the right rear, would thrust into western Henan from southern Shanxi. The three armies, deployed in a triangular battle formation between the Yangtze, Hanshui and Yellow rivers, would fight in coordination.

Pinning down the enemy at both flanks meant that Northwest Liberation Army would attack Yulin in northern Shaanxi to lure Hu Zhongnan's troops into going north; the Shandong Liberation Army would start an offensive in eastern Shandong to keep luring Chiang's troops in Shandong towards the sea to facilitate the actions of the three armies.

On June 30, 1947, the strategic offensive began, as the main force of the Shanxi-Hebei-Shandong-Henan Field Army crossed the Yellow River from the Zhangqiuzhen-Linpuji sector and advanced to southwestern Shandong. Early in August, after the southwestern Shandong battle, the field army marched south along three routes, traversed the Yellow River flood plain, crossed the Shahe, Ruhe and Huaihe rivers and entered the Dabie Mountains in late August, without meeting with any forceful resistance throughout its march. By the end of October, after two months of fighting, it had established 33 county-level state powers, and got a firm foothold. On August 22, the Taiyue force of the Shanxi-Hebei-Shandong-Henan Field Army crossed the Yellow River from the Pinglu-Yuxian sector and thrust into western Henan. Soon afterwards it liberated Shanxian, Lingbao, Wenxiang and Lushi to threaten Xi'an. By the end of November, it had built the Henan-Shaanxi-Hubei base area.

In September the exterior-line corps of the East China Field Army swept into southwestern Shandong and crossed the Longhai Railway to advance southward into Henan, Anhui and Jiangsu. By the end of October, it had liberated the vast area west of Hongze Lake, east of the Beiping-Hankou Railway and north of the Huaihe River. At the end of December, the three armies joined forces at the Suiping-Xiping sector in southern Henan, linking up three new liberated areas—Hubei-Henan-Anhui, Henan-Anhui-Jiangsu and western Henan—into one contiguous territory. Meanwhile, the armies also switched from each fighting in its own way to fighting in direct coordination. While battling against the Kuomintang troops in the Central

Plains, the People's Liberation Army in other theatres of war also went over to fighting on exterior lines or counter-offensive on interior lines. The offensives in all these theatres constituted a general, countrywide strategic offensive in the People's War of Liberation.

After six months' fighting, the People's Liberation Army had annihilated 750,000 enemy troops. At the end of 1947, the war was no longer being fought chiefly in the liberated areas but in the Kuomintang-controlled areas. Chiang Kai-shek's army, which had lost practically all its reserve forces, was completely on the defensive. This sent the Kuomintang reactionaries down the road to destruction, as the revolution of the Chinese people was approaching final victory. China now came to a turning point in its history. On October 10, 1947, the Chinese Communist Party issued the "Manifesto of the Chinese People's Liberation Army," raising the general slogan "Overthrow Chiang Kai-shek and liberate all China!" This was an important strategic decision during the Chinese People's War of Liberation.

The manifesto promulgated the basic policies of the Liberation Army, which were also the basic policies of the Chinese Communist Party. These policies included: Overthrowing the dictatorial Chiang Kai-shek government and establishing a democratic coalition government; confiscating bureaucrat-capital, developing the industry and commerce of the national bourgeoisie and improving the livelihood of workers and employees; abolishing the system of feudal exploitation and putting into effect the system of land to the tillers; recognizing the right to equality and autonomy of the ethnic minorities; and abrogating all treasonable treaties and concluding treaties of trade and friendship with foreign countries on the basis of equality and reciprocity. Since the people's revolution was in full flood, the manifesto pointed out for the entire Chinese people the overall goal of overthrowing the reactionary Kuomintang government and building a new China.

Because of the victories in the war and because the war had been carried into Kuomintang-controlled areas, the Communist Party seized the opportunity to consolidate and build the liberated areas and develop production there. In July-September 1947, the Communist Party called the National Land Conference and drew up the "Outline Land Law of China." After its promulgation, the land reform movement in the liberated areas developed more extensively. By the end of 1948, land reform in the old and semi-old liberated areas was basically completed. About 100 million peasants in the areas with a population of 150 million had received land. The reform of the land system raised their enthusiasm for revolution and production, providing an important guarantee of sources of troops, war services and the supply of food and materials needed by the army and people.

In the second half of December 1947, at a turning point in the revolutionary war, the CPC Central Committee called a meeting to discuss the current situation and revolutionary tasks. It adopted the report "The Present Situation and Our Tasks" made by Mao Zedong, and affirmed the economic and political programmes, policies and principles for overthrowing the reactionary Chiang Kai-shek clique and founding a new China. This report expounded the Communist Party's economic programme as "confiscate the land of the feudal class and turn it over to the peasants; confiscate the monopoly capital headed by Chiang Kai-shek, Song Ziwen, Kong Xiangxi and Chen Lifu, and turn it over to the new-democratic state; and protect the industry and commerce of the national bourgeoisie." The principle guiding the national economy was to be identical with the general objective of developing production, promoting economic prosperity, giving consideration to both public and private interests, and benefiting both labour and capital. In the political field, the report reaffirmed the fundamental programme for a democratic coalition government composed of workers, peasants, soldiers, intellectuals and businessmen, all oppressed classes, all people's organizations, democratic parties, ethnic minorities, overseas Chinese and other patriots.

The meeting discussed in detail erroneous tendencies current in the Party and specific policies in the land reform and other mass movements. Soon afterwards certain documents were promulgated to correct the mistakes. The guiding thoughts can be summarized as the following points:

(1) It was extremely important to correctly carry out policies and tactics in the revolution. "Policy and tactics are the life of the Party";

(2) Specific policies could not be separated from the Party's general line for the new-democratic revolution, and it was necessary to

hold fast to the Party's general line;

(3) It was necessary to adhere to the correct criterion for class differentiation, i.e., all different relations between the exploiter and the exploited; and

(4) Proper conditions and correct policies were required for a proletarian party to realize its leadership over its allies.

The promulgation of these correct documents practically put right the "Left" errors. As a result, the people's democratic united front was consolidated and expanded, the Kuomintang reactionaries and other enemies were isolated and the social productive forces protected and developed. These were all indispensable conditions for a total victory in the People's War of Liberation.

When the army commanded by Liu Bocheng and Deng Xiaoping began to cross the Yellow River, the National Government, with a view to overcoming the crisis, adopted at a state conference held in July 1947 a bill submitted by Chiang Kai-shek, "Strictly Enforce a Countrywide General Mobilization to Suppress the Rebellion of the Communist Bandits, Remove the Obstacles to Democracy, Establish a Constitutional Government as Scheduled, and Carry Out the Principle of Peace and National Reconstruction," and issued the "Order for General Mobilization." In the Meantime, Chiang Kai-shek delivered the speech "Suppress the Rebellion and Build the Country." After that the National Government promulgated the "Programme for Mobilization to Suppress the Rebellion and Establish a Constitutional Government." The consultative councils of various provinces and cities and the so-called people's organizations sent open telegrams to express their support. The Kuomintang called meetings in many places to enforce the "general mobilization for suppressing the rebellion." In so doing, one of Chiang Kai-shek's purposes was to alert his counter-revolutionary ranks to the serious danger of "destruction," and urged them to put up a struggle with all their strength. Another purpose was to more savagely extort manpower, material and financial resources in the Kuomintang-controlled areas for the war, and more brutally suppress the people's democratic movements.

On the order for general mobilization to "suppress the rebellion," the Kuomintang carried out the so-called total war. From the winter of

1947 to the first half of 1948, the Kuomintang convened numerous the "bandit-suppressing" and "pacification" meetings to study the problems concerning the "total war in the pacification regions," draw up the "General Plan for a Total War," the "Programme for a Total War in the Pacification Regions," and the "Directive for a Total War in the Pacification Regions." The principle of the "total war" was that "the troops should carry out military, political and economic suppression at the same time; by 'draining the pond to get all the fish,' they should cut off the bandit forces' sources for existence and growth; move or purchase the manpower and materials in the battlefields to achieve as great a degree of centralized control as possible. In this way, wherever they go, the bandits will have nothing to rely on for existence. Both the 'hook' and the 'net' should be used, luring the enemy into a concentrated interception by the troops in the pacification regions, local forces and people's armed forces, who will clean up in separate zones. The national troops can be organized into certain striking corps to encircle and suppress by converging columns, or pursue and suppress with light packs in order to catch the main force of the bandits and wipe them out." This method, however, did not prove successful for the Kuomintang.

The National Government made new appointments for military commands. Minister of Defence Bai Chongxi, with his headquarters at Jiujiang, took overall charge of military affairs in central China, and directed government administration of Hubei, Henan, Anhui, Jiangxi and Hunan. In December 1947, the Baoding and Zhangjiakou pacification headquarters were dissolved and the "North China Bandit Suppression Headquarters" was set up, with Fu Zuoyi as the commander-in-chief. In May 1948, the Kuomintang Generalissimo's Headquarters in Beiping was officially dissolved. In August 1947, the Kuomintang's Peace Preservation Headquarters in the northeast was dissolved, the Generalissimo's Headquarters there assumed the responsibility for political and military affairs, and Chen Cheng was appointed its director. In January 1948 Wei Lihuang was appointed deputy director and concurrently the commander-in-chief of the Northeast "Bandit Suppression" Headquarters. But all this failed to save the Kuomintang troops from their continuous defeats.

In the summer of 1947, though battlefield superiority was still on the Kuomintang side, unfavourable and even critical situations already appeared in the military, political, and economic fields. In his telegram sent to Chiang Kai-shek in June, Hu Zongnan said, "At present our forces are almost all in an inferior position. The crisis is deeper than that in the War of Resistance." The Kuomintang sought American aid to overcome its crisis. Sun Ke, vice-chairman of the National Government, made a statement on two occasions in June expressing the hope of obtaining American "assistance and encouragement" in munitions, loans and political support, of which the munitions were the most important. However, the Americans were well aware of the corruption of the Kuomintang, and so they were skeptical about the effectiveness of the assistance. The U.S. government sent a mission headed by General Albert C. Wedemeyer to China to make investigations so as to determine the specific way of implementing its China policy. Wedemeyer stayed in China for about a month between July and August and toured Shenyang, Beiping, Tianjin, Qingdao, Nanjing, Shanghai, Hankou, Guangzhou and Taiwan. He spoke to a state conference of the National Government and issued a statement before leaving China. In a written report he submitted to President Truman after his return, he said that insensitivity and laziness were a common sight in China, and that the submissive defeatism of many Chinese was discouraging. In order to regain and maintain the confidence of the people, he noted, the central government must immediately carry out thorough and far-reaching political and economic reforms. He pointed out that China's recovery required a leadership with rallying power and a China under the regime of the Communist Party would be detrimental to the interests of the United States. For this reason, he said, it was necessary to aid the National Government. However, he continued, without giving consideration to the fact that there is in China an unpopular government which oppresses the people, any kind of assistance will get nowhere. Therefore, the American aid plan must be carried out under the supervision of American advisors.

At the suggestion of Wedemeyer, the U.S. government pursued a policy of rendering limited aid to the National Government under the supervision of American advisors. This demonstrated that as the tide of the Chinese revolution was surging and the National Government's defeat was inescapable, the U.S. policy towards Chiang Kai-shek had fallen into dire straits. In October 1947, the United States decided to give the National Government aid valued at 27 million dollars; in December the U.S. Congress approved "temporary aid" of 18 million dollars. In June 1948 it decided to grant an additional 400 million dollars. The total value of U.S. aid given to the National Government in the form of loans, materials and services after Japanese surrender was 4.34 billion dollars.

From March 29 to May 1, 1948, the Kuomintang convened in Nanjing the "National Assembly" to elect a president and vice-presidents so as to "hand state power back to the people" and establish a constitutional government. On this election, the United States had predicted that "One cannot expect it to produce a government more representative than the present one." At the time it was impossible to elect anyone other than Chiang Kai-shek as president. Therefore, the United States supported Li Zongren, whose prestige was "getting higher and higher," in his campaign for the vice-presidency, ready to replace Chiang at an opportune moment. After he politely declined and his supporters "appealed to him to accept" the nomination, Chiang Kai-shek was elected president. As for the nominees for vice-president, Chiang Kai-shek was in favour of Sun Ke and against Li Zongren. After a fierce struggle between the two, Li emerged the victor. In May, Sun Ke and Chen Lifu were elected president and vice-president of the Legislative Yuan respectively. The president and vice-president of the Republic assumed office and Weng Wenhao was appointed president of the Executive Yuan. Thus the government, allegedly produced according to the constitution, was formed. The "National Assembly" adopted a "Provisional Clause for the Period of Mobilization for Suppressing the Rebellion," which vested Chiang Kai-shek with the power to take emergency measures. Chiang and the reactionary elements within the Kuomintnag continued to wield power of the National Government.

The National Government's "suppression of the rebellion" failed to hold back the people's revolutionary struggles in the Kuomintang areas. In October 1947, the National Government arrested Yu Zisan, chairman of the Student Self-government Union of Zhejiang University, and executed him. The students of the university rose in protest with the support of President Zhu Kezhen and other professors. The murder created an upsurge against persecution in all Kuomintang areas. Early in 1948, when workers at the Shanghai Shenxi Textile Mill No. 9 went on strike demanding that docked wages be paid retroactively, they were brutally suppressed by reactionary police and troops. Again, when students of Tongji University in Shanghai staged a strike in protest against the expelling of progressive students by the school authorities at the instigation of the Kuomintang, troops and policemen were called in to put down the strike. Between May and June a massive patriotic movement broke out in protest against the U.S. fostering of a resurgence of Japanese aggressive forces. In addition to college students and faculty, large numbers of people of various circles also participated. The United States declared that the Chinese who had "benefited" from American relief had no right to oppose American policies. In response, about 100 people including professors Zhu Ziqing, Jin Yuelin, Zhang Xiruo and Wu Han issued a statement rejecting American "relief materials" and refusing to buy the U.S. relief flour at the government price. The mighty movement against the United States' fostering of the revival of Japanese militarism further isolated U.S. imperialism and the Kuomintang reactionaries. From that time, because of the constant victories in the War of Liberation, the people in the Kuomintang areas shifted from large-scale struggle against Chiang Kai-shek to active coordination with the Liberation Army in the liberation of large cities.

The suppression of the China Democratic League and other democratic parties by the National Government promoted a fresh integration of democratic forces, which in turn further consolidated and enlarged the people's democratic united front. In the winter of 1947, Li Jishen, Cai Tingkai and others of the Kuomintang Association for Promoting Democracy, Tan Pingshan and Cheng Mingshu of the Association of Comrades in Three People's Principles and Wang Kunlun of the Democratic Revolutionary League, together with the democratic groups and democrats within the Kuomintang, called a joint meeting of the Kuomintang's democratic groups to form the China

Revolutionary Committee of the Kuomintang. On January 1, 1948, the Committee issued a manifesto, a programme for action, and a message to the comrades to officially proclaim the founding of the party. The manifesto dwelt on the Committee's two great tasks—opposition to imperialism and opposition to feudalism, and three great policies—"alliance with Russia, toleration towards the Communist Party and assistance to the peasants and workers." "In the present stage of Chinese national democratic revolution," it explained, "if the Kuomintang of China adheres to the two great tasks and three great policies it will still remain in its leading position in the revolution." It advocated land to the tillers, called for the overthrow of Chiang Kai-shek's dictatorial regime, urged the formation of a coalition government, and opposed U.S. interference in China's internal affairs.

After the China Democratic League was banned, Shen Junru, Zhang Bojun and Zhou Xinmin secretly went to Hong Kong. Together with some of the members of the League's Central Committee there, they called its third plenary session in January 1948, at which an emergency statement, a manifesto and a political report were adopted. The session negated the previous statement concerning the "disbandment of the headquarters" and the "cessation of the League members' activities." It made public the League's new policy: totally smash the reactionary dictatorial government in Nanjing and bring about a democratic, peaceful, independent and united new China. The session criticized the ideas of "neutrality" and "middle-of-the-road," calling for "close cooperation" with the Chinese Communist Party. Most members of other democratic parties also persisted in the patriotic struggle against Chiang Kai-shek in the Kuomintang areas and Hong Kong. The founding of the Revolutionary Committee of the Kuomintang and the convocation of the Third Plenary Session of the China Democratic League's Central Committee signified that the bourgeois democratic movement in China and developed to a new stage.

As the Chinese revolution developed in the first half of 1948, the conditions were ready for the establishment of a nationwide democratic government. In the May Day slogans the CPC Central Committee called on "all democratic parties, people's organizations, and public figures to quickly convene the Political Consultative Conference to discuss and carry out the convocation of a people's congress and the formation of a democratic coalition government." This position won an immediate warm response from the people all over the country. On May 5, in response to the call, leading members of the democratic parties and well-known figures such as Shen Junru, Zhang Bojun, Li Jishen, He Xiangning, Ma Xulun, Chen Qiyou, Peng Zemin, Li Zhangda, Cai Tingkai, Tan Pingshan and Guo Moruo sent open telegrams to compatriots both at home and abroad, appealing to them for concerted efforts in this connection. From that time, the democrats and democratic parties, centered in Hong Kong initiated a movement for the convocation of a new Political Consultative Conference. Beginning in August, a stream of democrats and leaders of the democratic parties left Hong Kong and major cities in the south for the liberated areas in northeast and north China, and together with the Communists, began the preparatory work for the new Political Consultative Conference.

17. The Downfall of the Nanjing Regime and the Founding of the People's Republic of China

After two years of fighting, a radical change took place in the war. The Chinese People's Liberation Army grew to 2,800,000 men, of which regular forces numbered 1,490,000. Their military and political qualities, tactics and fighting skill were greatly improved. The army boasted fairly powerful artillery and engineer corps and mastered the tactics for taking strong fortifications. It had organized five powerful field armies—Northwest, North China, Central Plains, East China and Northeast. In two years, Chiang's troops had lost 2,600,000 men, and their total military strength was reduced to 3,650,000, of which 1,980,000 were regular forces. Chiang Kai-shek's army, though it still had considerable strength, had been strategically split by the Liberation Army into six isolated military groups—northeast China, north China, Xuzhou, central China, northwest China and Shanxi. The relative strength and military posture suggested the possibility of a strategically decisive engagement between the Liberation Army and that of Chiang Kai-shek. Reviewing the situation as a whole, the CPC Central Committee and Mao Zedong made a correct assessment, and resolved to wage a strategic decisive battle.

As the war situation was changing in favour of the revolution, the Chiang Kai-shek clique started to seek a military way out. At the beginning of 1948, within his army, discussions were held about the withdrawal from the northeast, but the problem remained unsolved. Early in August at a military meeting in Nanjing, the National Government decided to "defend key points." As for the northeast, it resolved "not to abandon Shenyang in principle, but that preparations be made to pull out." With the Chiang clique unable to make up its mind, the Liaoxi-Shenyang Campaign had got off to a good start.

Between September 16 and 24, 1948, the East China Field Army launched the Jinan Battle. It took the enemy's heavily fortified city of Jinan, completely wiped out 110,000 garrison troops and captured Wang Yaowu, commander of the Kuomintang Second Pacification Zone and concurrently governor of Shandong Province. This was the prelude to capturing the enemy's heavily guarded large cities and surrounding and annihilating his main force on a large scale.

Between September 12 and November 2, 1948, the Northeast Field Army commanded by Lin Biao and Luo Ronghuan launched the Liaoxi-Shenyang Campaign with 700,000 men. On September 12, it made a surprise attack on the Jinzhou-Shanhaiguan section of the Beiping-Liaoning Railway to cut off the railroad and encircle Jinzhou. On October 15, it liberated the city, wiped out more than 100,000 enemy troops and captured Fan Hanjie, deputy commander-in-chief of the Kuomintang Northeast "Bandit Suppression" Headquarters. The links between Chiang Kai-shek's troops in the northeast and those in north China were cut off. Immediately afterwards, part of the enemy forces at Changchun revolted and the rest surrendered. After the liberation of Jinzhou and Changchun, Chiang Kai-shek decided to order his troops in Jinxi and Huludao and Liao Yaoxiang's army in Zhangwu to advance on Jinzhou from opposite directions in an attempt to recapture the city. On October 26, the Liberation Army succeeded in surrounding Liao's troops on the move in Heishan-Dahushan sector and the sector to the east. Two days later it completely wiped out the enemy's 100,000 men there and captured Army Commander Liao Yaoxiang. The Liberation Army followed up this victory with the liberation of Shenyang and Yingkou on November 2, wiping out over 149,000 enemy troops. In the campaign, which lasted 52 days, a total of more than 470,000 enemy troops were annihilated. The whole of the northeast was thus liberated.

The East China Field Army under Chen Yi, Su Yu and Tan Zhenlin, the Central Plains Field Army under Liu Bocheng and Deng Xiaoping, and armed forces from military areas, totalling 600,000 strong, fought the Huai-Hai Campaign from November 6, 1948 to January 10, 1949. On November 6, the East China Field Army launched an attack on Huang Botao's army, which had fallen back from the East China Sea on the area west of the Grand Canal. The enemy fled west, with the Liberation Army in hot pursuit. On November 8, He Jifeng and Zhang Kexia, deputy commanders of the Kuomintang's Third Pacification Zone, revolted with their men, and left the arena. On the 11th the Liberation Army surrounded Huang Botao's army at the Nianzhuang sector east of Xuzhou. By the 22nd, 100,000 enemy troops were wiped out and the commander Huang Botao was killed in action.

After the the Huai-Hai Campaign broke out, Chiang Kai-shek summoned the army under Huang Wei to reinforce Xuzhou. While marching to the Shuangduizi sector southwest of Suxian, it was encircled by the Central Plains Field Army. By December 15, the army was completely annihilated, and Huang Wei, its commander, was captured.

While Huang Wei's army was being surrounded, Chiang Kai-shek ordered Du Yuming, deputy commander of the Kuomintang's "Bandit Suppression" Headquarters at Xuzhou, to give up the city to reinforce Huang's army with the three armies under Qiu Qingquan, Li Mi and Sun Yuanliang, and then flee south together. On December 4, the Liberation Army surrounded all three enemy armies at the area northeast of Yongcheng. Sun Yuanliang's troops attempted to break through, but were completely wiped out. On January 6, 1949, the East China Field Army launched a fierce attack on Du Yuming's forces and completely annihilated the two armies under Qiu Qingquan and Li Mi on the 10th. Qiu was killed and Du captured. The campaign lasted 65 days, and a total of 555,000 enemy troops were put out of action. As a result, the regions of east China and the Central Plains north of the Yangtze River were in the main liberated. Nanjing, centre of the Kuomintang regime, became subject to direct threat by the People's Liberation Army, creating the conditions for the army to advance to the area south of the Yangtze River.

From November 29, 1948 to January 31, 1949, the Northeast Field Army, totalling 800,000 men, and two armies under Yang Dezhi and Yang Chengwu in north China jointly fought the Beiping-Tianjin Campaign. The Liberation Army began its attack on Zhangjiakou on November 29, and launched a powerful offensive on December 5. By the 20th the enemy troops had been encircled and separated at five points—Zhangjiakou, Xinbao'an, Beiping, Tianjin and Tanggu, which were isolated from each other. On December 22, the enemy troops at Xinbao'an were completely wiped out. On the 24th, 54,000 enemy troops, which had intended to flee Zhangjiakou, were put out of action. On January 14, 1949, the Liberation Army started a general offensive against Tianjin's enemy troops, which refused to accept peace terms. On the 15th the city was liberated, the garrison of more than 130,000 was completely wiped out, and Chen Changjie, its commander, was captured. On the 16th the enemy troops at Tanggu fled by sea. The following day, the district was liberated. After the fall of Zhangjiakou and Tianjin, the Kuomintang troops at Beiping under Fu Zuoyi were deprived of any possible way out. Therefore, they had to accept the peace terms put forward by the Beiping-Tianjin Front Headquarters of the People's Liberation Army. Beginning from the 22nd, they moved out of the city waiting for reorganization. On the 31st, the Liberation Army entered Beiping to take it over. On February 3, the Liberation Army held a grand ceremony for marching into the city. The peaceful liberation of China's famous ancient cultural capital brought the Beiping-Tianjin Campaign to a close. In this campaign, a total of 520,000 enemy troops were put out of action or reorganized.

In the three great campaigns—Liaoxi-Shenyang, Huai-Hai and Beiping-Tianjin, which lasted four months and 19 days altogether, a total of over 1,540,000 enemy troops were wiped out. The whole of northeast and north China, except such isolated points as Taiyuan and Datong, were all liberated.

While the Kuomintang militarily suffered fatal blows and found itself politically at a dead end, the finance and economy in the areas under its control also sank into total collapse. Since the later stage of the War of Resistance, the economy there had deteriorated. After the all-out civil war began, the Kuomintang's treasury was overburdened with the huge military expenditure. In 1948 the financial deficit reached 900,000 billion yuan. In June of that year, the revenue merely accounted for 5 percent of the expenditure. The only way out was to issue bank notes in large amounts. By August 1948, the total amount of Fabi (legal tender) issued by the Kuomintang government had reached 663,690 billion yuan, 470,000 times that issued in June 1937. The exchange rate between Fabi and US dollars was 178,000:1 in January, and 11,088,000:1 in August. The Fabi's purchasing power dropped drastically, while commodity prices skyrocketed. The price of rice in Shanghai, for example, was 1,500,000 yuan per picul in January, and 65 million yuan per picul in August. The value of Fabi dropped to such an extent that it could not balance the paper and printing cost incurred for producing this legal tender. The vicious inflation, the flood of American goods, the annexation by bureaucrat capital and heavy taxation forced the industrial and commercial enterprises owned by the national bourgeoisie to cease production or close down. In 1948, the 3,000 large factories in Shanghai were running at only 20 percent capacity. Even normal industrial production and business operations could not be maintained. With a view to preventing its finance and economy from collapse, the National Government promulgated on August 19, 1948 an emergency order and four remedies:

(1) The gold certificate, of which the total amount issued by the National Government was 2,000 million yuan, was adopted as the standard money. Fabi were to be exchange for gold certificates at the ratio of 3,000,000 yuan:1 yuan within a limited period;

(2) All the gold, silver and foreign currencies owned by the people were to be converted within a limited period. These valuables would be confiscated if the holder failed to convert or deposit them within the time limit.

(3) People were required to register any foreign exchange deposited in a foreign country within a limited period. Those who failed

to do so would be punished.

(4) Commodities and services in all places in the country were to be sold for the prices current on August 19, 1948 and converted into gold certificates. This was to be enforced under the strict supervision of the local office in charge. All practices of paying out salaries according to the cost of living index were to be abolished. Workers were forbidden to stage strikes or slowdowns.

These were the so-called monetary reform and price control policy.

The National Government set up management areas in Shanghai, Guangzhou and Tianjin, and appointed Jiang Jingguo, Song Ziwen (T.V. Soong) and Zhang Lisheng economic control inspector or deputy inspector of the three cities respectively. It sent large numbers of special agents and policemen to set up special criminal courts, resorting to arrest and execution by shooting, to compel people to submit. With the extreme shortage of goods and materials, the "government price level" created by robbing industrialists and businessmen could no longer be maintained. Panic purchasing started in early October and spread rapidly to all the large cities in the Kuomintang areas. In November, the National Government had to repeal the "controlled prices" and rescind the gold certificate's limited issue amount of 2,000 million yuan. The gold certificate was devalued at lightning speed as it was printed and issued in large amounts. On April 15, 1949, its value dropped 40 percent within one day. This meant the certificate had practically become waste paper. Still more appalling was the frenzied soaring of comomdity prices. Taking the general price index for August 1948 as the standard, it rose 25-fold in November, 35-fold in December, and 128-fold in January 1949. The National Government's attempt to overcome the economic crisis with gold certificates had totally failed. The complete collapse in the economy accelerated the downfall of the National Government. The only gain was its transportation to Taiwan of the large quantities of gold, silver and foreign currencies it had plundered.

In the second half of 1948, the situation was so unfavourable to the Chiang Kai-shek government in Nanjing that its fate of utter defeat was sealed. Now the United States' plan to compel Chiang Kai-shek to resign, and support Li Zongren as the initiator of peace negotiations, was out into the open. Under pressure from the United States and the Guangxi clique, Chiang issued a statement on New Year's Day of 1949 expressing his desire for "peace negotiations" and "retirement." He alleged that he was willing "to discuss concrete measures to stop the war and restore peace with the Communist Party," on condition that the constituted authority, the constitution and the armed forces must be preserved; and that he would "retire" if peace was achieved. This peace proposal was sternly rejected by the Communist Party. On January 21, Chiang Kai-shek, under the pretext that he could no more attend to business, went to Xikou in Fenghua, asking Vice-President Li Zongren to act for him.

Li Zongren, after taking up the post as acting president, invited Li Jishen and others to promote the peace movement together, and accepted the peace terms set by the Communist Party as the basis for negotiations. However, Chiang Kai-shek continued to control the government, and command the army and special agent system in the capacity of director-general of the Kuomintang. The Propaganda Department under the Kuomintang Central Executive Committee issued instructions against peace negotiations. After Sun Ke offered his resignation as president of the Executive Yuan on March 8, Li Zongren appointed He Yingqin to be his successor. On the 24th of the same month, a peace negotiation delegation of the Nanjing government was formed, consisting of Zhang Zhizhong (1890-1969), Shao Lizi, Huang Shaohong, Zhang Shizhao, Li Zheng and Liu Pei (a later participant). The delegation's minimum demands in the negotiations were: "on-the-spot ceasefire," the formation of the Political Consultative Conference and coalition government composed of equal numbers of the Kuomintang and Communist Party members, and the realization of "ruling the country by both parties with the Yangtze River as the boundary" and "honourable peace." During the negotiations the Communists adopted a tolerant attitude to win Li Zongren over but did not agree to his terms for peace. On March 26, the Communist Party sent Zhou Enlai, Lin Boqu, Lin Biao, Ye Jianying, Li Weihan and Nie Rongzhen (a later participant) as delegates to the peace negotiations which would begin on April 1. After repeated discussions, the "Agreement on Internal Peace" (final amended version) was reached. According to this agreement, war criminals, officers and men in the Kuomintnag army and the government personnel would be accorded lenient treatment. Meanwhile, other problems would also be properly solved. The delegates of the Communist Party declared that the deadline for signing the agreement was April 20. As Li Zongren and He Yingqin refused to sign, the People's Liberation Army began to cross the Yangtze River in the small hours of April 21.

In order to solve a series of important problems facing it, the Seventh CPC Central Committee held its Second Plenary Session in Xibaipo Village, Pingshan County, Hebei Province, from March 5 to 13, 1949, on the eve of the countrywide victory of the Chinese people's revolution. Mao Zedong, Liu Shaoqi, Zhou Enlai, Zhu De and Ren Bishi were present. Mao Zedong made a report. The session discussed a number of major problems such as the strategic plan for the final destruction of the Kuomintang regime and the nationwide victory, the shift of the focus of work of the Party, the basic political and economic policies to be adopted, and strengthening the Party ideologically after the victory of the revolution. Previously the centre of gravity of the Party's work was in the village, the session pointed out. The period of "from the city to the village" and of the city leading the village had now begun. The focus of the Party's work must be in the cities. It was necessary to learn how to administer and build the cities. Of course, attention had to be given to both city and village, the session concluded.

In his report, Mao Zedong pointed out the basic problems to be solved in Chinese society after the countrywide victory and the general tasks of developing from new-democracy to socialism. Considering the forms the class struggle would take in future, and the change in the position of the Communist Party, the session gave timely warning to the whole Party against the growth of arrogance, and the airs of self-styled heroes, and the attack of the "sugar-coated bullets" of the bourgeoisie. A salient aspect of the content of the meeting was to analyse China's economic structure and define economic policies and principles. Before this, the Chinese Communist Party had proceeded with wide-ranging economic work. After conscientious studies on economic problems, Zhang Wentian, standing committee member of the Northeast Sub-bureau of the CPC Central Committee, wrote in September 1948 the "Outline of the Economic Structure and the Guidelines in Economic Construction in the Northeast." This document, to which the Party Central Committee attached great importance, became the foundation for the analysis of China's economic structure and the formulation of basic economic policies.

In his report, Mao Zedong pointed out that the wide gap between industry, agriculture and handicrafts in proportion to China's entire national economy, or the extreme backwardness in industrial production, was the basic point of departure for all questions in China, and that "this gives rise to a series of problems regarding our Party's strategy, tactics and policy." The sectors of China's economy, the report continued, would include the state-owned economy, cooperative economy, private capitalism, individual economy and state-capitalist economy. These sectors of the economy, which were different in character, and their interrelations would "constitute the new-democratic economic structure." As for private capitalism, on the one hand, it should be allowed to exist and expand. On the other, it should be subject to restrictions. "Restriction versus opposition to restriction will be the main form of class struggle in the new-democratic state." These were the guiding ideas for the Common Programme adopted by the Political Consultative Conference convened soon afterwards. After the session, the CPC Central Committee moved from Xibaipo to Beiping and stepped up the preparatory work for the founding of a new China.

As the War of Liberation was going on, the revolutionary struggles waged by the people in Inner Mongolia and Xinjiang registered fresh progress and became an integral part of the whole revolutionary movement in China. The Chinese Communist Party considered the launching of a movement for self-government in Inner Mongolia to be the key link of the people's revolutionary struggle there. On November 25, 1945, the Western Mongolian People's Congress was held in Zhangjiakou, at which it was decided to establish the Federation of Inner Mongolian Self-Government Movements. On January 16, 1946, the Eastern Mongolia People's Autonomous Government came into being. Led and encouraged by the Chinese Communist Party, the Federation and the Eastern Mongolia Autonomous Government jointly held a Conference at Chengde on April 3, 1946, to unify the self-government movements in Inner Mongolia. The meeting decided that the Federation would be the open leading body for the time being and elected Ulanhu as Chairman of the Executive Committee of the Federation of Self-Government Movements, a landmark in the unification of the people's revolutionary forces in Inner Mongolia. On April 24, 1947, the Inner Mongolia People's Representatives Conference was held in Ulanhot. At the conference the "Administrative Programme of the Inner Mongolian Autonomous Government" was adopted and a Provisional Consultative Council elected. On May 1, after the Inner Mongolia Autonomous Government was elected by the Consultative Council, the Inner Mongolia Autonomous Region was officially established, and big strides were made in the economic, cultural and educational fields. Militarily, the region made great contributions to the people's War of Liberation.

The revolution in Ili, Ashan and Tacheng in Xinjiang started in 1944. By the end of 1945, the revolutionary armed forces had put the three areas under their control. They wiped out two divisions of the Kuomintang army and pinned down a considerable number of the enemy troops. The National Government was forced to negotiate with the representatives of the three areas. In 1946 an agreement was made and a coalition government established in Dihua (modern Urumqi), with Zhang Zhizhong as chairman and Ahemaitijiang and Burhan as vice-chairmen. In February 1947, the coalition government broke up and the representatives of the three areas were recalled to Ili. Since July, the revolution in these areas had been reduced to a very difficult position. But the people there continued their armed struggle until Xinjiang was peacefully liberated in September 1949.

On April 21, the day after Li Zongren rejected the "Agreement on Internal Peace," Mao Zedong, chairman of the Chinese People's Revolutionary Military Commission and Zhu De, commander-in-chief of the Chinese People's Liberation Army, issued the "Order to the Army for the Countrywide Advance." It ordered the PLA to "advance bravely and resolutely, thoroughly, wholly and completely annihilate all the Kuomintang reactionaries within China's borders who dare to resist ... liberate the people of the whole country ... [and] safeguard the independence and integrity of China's territory and sovereignty." The PLA began to cross the Yangtze River and embarked upon large-scale operations for a countrywide advance.

After the Huai-Hai Campaign was concluded, the Kuomintang forces on the northern bank of the Yangtze River to the east of Jiujiang, except those holding a few strong points, all withdrew to the south of the river. Nanjing, the capital of the Kuomintang government, was thus exposed to the PLA. Taking advantage of the peace negotiations, the Kuomintnag military authorities set about organizing a line of defence along the Yangtze River. Chiang Kai-shek mustered 115 divisions of his remnant land forces, or 750,000 men, the No. 2 Fleet of his navy, and more than 280 airplanes to defend along the river from Yichang to Shanghai, a total of 1,800 kilometres. The eastern and western sections of the river were commanded separately by Tang Enbo and Bai Chongxi, with Jiujiang marking the bounding between them.

A million PLA troops had already been concentrated in the first half of April on the northern bank of the Yangtze River. After the order to advance was issued on April 21, the army forced their way across the river on a front extending more than 500 kilometres from Hukou in the west to Jiangyin in the east. The Seventh and Ninth armies of the Third Field Army marching along the central route first broke through the enemy's defence line between Anqing and Wuhu, and captured Fanchang and Tongling. The Third, Fourth and Fifth armies of the Second Field Army advancing along the western route broke through the enemy's Guichi-Hukou line on the afternoon of the 21st and seized Dongliu and Pengze. At the same time, the Eighth and 10th armies of the Third Field Army along the eastern route broke through the Zhejiang-Jiangyin line to capture both places. Under the leadership of the Communist Party's underground organization, the officers and men guarding the fortifications of Jiangyin renounced their allegiance to the Kuomintang and blockaded the water route in the Yangtze River.

After the successful crossing of the river by the main forces of the Liberation Army, the Kuomintang's high-ranking officials in Nanjing fled. On April 23, the Liberation Army marched into Nanjing and planted a red flag on top of Chiang Kai-shek's presidential palace. The liberation of Nanjing proclaimed the downfall of the Kuomintang regime.

The Nanjing government had broken up before its collapse. On February 5, the Executive Yuan declared of its own accord that it was "moving the government to Guangzhou" (soon it was moved back). In March, He Yingqin was appointed president of the Executive Yuan to replace Sun Ke. On the morning of April 23, the presidential palace and the Executive Yuan moved to Guangzhou and Acting President Li Zongren fled to Guilin. On June 12, Yan Xishan served as president of the Executive Yuan and Zhu Jiahua as vice-president. On July 16, Chiang Kai-shek organized the Kuomintang's Extraordinary Committee at Guangzhou as the highest decision-making organ of the Kuomintang's remnant forces. Chiang was its chairman, and the members included Yan Xishan, He Yingqin, Zhang Qun, Sun Ke and Chen Lifu. This arrangement was designed to move Chiang Kai-shek from a wire puller to a commander on the stage. This was soon followed by the setting up of a branch committee at Taibei headed by Chen Cheng. After the liberation of Guangzhou, the Kuomintang government fled to Chongqing, and then to Taiwan.

Following the liberation of Nanjing, the main forces of the PLA thrust south along several routes to pursue the enemy. On May 3, they lbierated Hangzhou and put the Zhejiang-Jiangxi Railway under their control. In mid-May, the Liberation Army crossed the Yangtze River from the Tuanfeng-Wuxue sector and liberated Hankou, Hanyang, and Wuchang, three important cities in central China. On the 22nd, Nanchang was liberated. After the liberation of Nanjing, more than 200,000 Kuomintang troops under Tang Enbo entrenched themselves in the Wusong-Shanghai area. On May 12, the PLA launched the Wusong-Shanghai campaign and on the 27th liberated Shanghai, China's largest city and most important economic centre, wiping out more than 150,000 enemy troops. The remnant forces under Tang Enbo fled Shanghai by sea.

The Yangtze Crossing Campaign, fought from April 21 to May 27, ended in the wiping out of more than 400,000 enemy troops.

Meantime, while the North China Liberation Army captured Taiyuan, Datong, Anyang, Xinxiang and other enemy strongholds, the First Field Army liberated Xi'an. The PLA then continued their advance towards the northwest, southwest and south to liberate the whole country.

In east China, the Zhejiang area was liberated between May and July 1949 with the exception of Dinghai. Fuzhou was liberated on August 17, and Xiamen on October 17. Thus the whole of east China was liberated. After that, the PLA fought battles to capture the offshore islands. In the northwest, Lanzhou was liberated on August 26, Xining on September 5, and Yinchuan on September 23. In the latter half of the same month, Tao Zhiyue, garrison commander of Xinjiang Province, and Burhan, the governor, renounced their allegiance to the Kuomintang. On October 20, the PLA forces under Wang Zhen marched into Dihua (now Urumqi), and Xinjiang was peacefully liberated. On September 19, Dong Qiwu, deputy director of the Kuomintang Bureau of Military and Administrative Affairs in the Northwest and governor of Suiyuan Province, renounced his allegiance and the province was peacefully liberated.

After the PLA's Yangtze Crossing Campaign most of the Kuomintang remnant forces were concentrated in south and southwest China. Bai Chongxi's military group was entrenched in Hunan and Guangxi, Yu Hanmou's group entrenched in Guangdong, and Hu Zongnan's group and the local forces of Sichuan, Yunnan and Guizhou entrenched in the southwest. Totalling over 1,000,000 men, these groups organized the Hunan-Guangdong joint defence and the southwestern defence line to put up stubborn resistance. If this failed, they would withdraw to Yunnan, Guizhou and southern Guangxi. If they still could not gain a foothold within the country, they would flee abroad. To the Bai Chongxi group and the enemy in the southwest, the PLA adopted a policy of going all out to outflank, encircle and then swing back to eradicate the enemy as much as possible within the boundary of China. In July 1949 the Liberation Army mounted a powerful attack on Bai's group, which fled south from the Changsha sector. On August 4, Cheng Qian, governor of Hunan Province, and Chen Mingren, commander of the First Army, renounced their allegiance to the Kuomintang, and Changsha was peacefully liberated. In the Hengyang-Baoqing battle fought between September and October, the bulk of Bai's army was wiped out. On October 14, Guangzhou was liberated. On October 26, the forces under Yu Hanmou were annihilated in the Yangjiang sector when they attempted to flee to the Leizhou Peninsula. On November 22, Guilin was liberated. On December 4, Nanning was liberated, and two armies of the forces under Bai were encircled and annihilated on the border between Guangdong and Guangxi. All the forces of the Guangxi clique were wiped out except some 10,000 men who fled to Viet Nam.

The People's Liberation Army started the battle to encircle and annihilate the enemy in the southwest in early November. It liberated Guiyang on November 15, and Chongqing on the 30th. Then it pushed on to Chengdu. In coordination with the peoples' forces marching south from Shaanxi, it forced Hu Zongnan's troops and the remnant enemy troops in Sichuan, totalling several hundred thousand men, to dig themselves in at the Chengdu sector. Awed by the might of the victorious Liberation Army, Lu Han, governor of Yunnan Province, Liu Wenhui, governor of Xikang Province, and Deng Xihou and Pan Wenhua, deputy directors of the Bureau of Military and Administrative Affairs in the Southwest, renounced their allegiance to the Kuomintnag on December 9, and the two provinces of Yunnan and Xikang were peacefully liberated. Chengdu was liberated on December 27. The forces under Hu Zongnan and other remnant enemy troops which had retreated to and assembled in the Chengdu sector were completely wiped out. Thus, China's entire mainland except Tibet was liberated. From July 1946 to September 1949, the People's Liberation Army wiped out a total of 6,250,000 enemy troops. While mopping up the enemy remnants, it crushed the Kuomintang local political powers at different levels and established people's democratic governments, preparing for the founding of a new China.

While the PLA mopped up the enemy remnants and smashed the Kuomintang reactionary political powers at various levels, preparatory work for the establishment of the central people's government, symbol of the new China, was being speeded up. The Preparatory Committee of the New Political Consultative Conference held its inaugural session at Beiping from June 15 to 19, 1949. The task of this committee was to complete all necessary preparations for swiftly convening the New Political Consultative Conference and forming a democratic coalition government. Present at the session were 134 members representing 23 organizations and groups, including the Chinese Communist Party, the democratic parties, the people's organizations, democrats from all walks of life, the ethnic minorities of the country and overseas Chinese. It adopted the "Organic Rules of the Preparatory Committee of the New Political Consultative Conference" and the "Provisions Regarding the Organizations and Groups Participating in the New Political Consultative Conference and the Size of Their Delegations" and elected a standing committee with Mao Zedong as director and Zhou Enlai, Li Jishen, Shen Junru, Guo Moruo and Chen Shutong as deputy directors. Six groups under the standing committee were responsible for various aspects of the preparatory work.

A new China would be born. What was its nature and character? What were the position, role and interrelations of the classes in this country? What were the political and economic systems? And what were its basic political and economic policies? The Chinese Communist Party had expounded on these issues long before, but under the new historical conditions, it was necessary to elaborate them further. On June 30, 1949, Mao Zedong published an article entitled "On the People's Democratic Dictatorship," explaining the theory and basic policies of a new-democratic state, or a people's democratic dictatorship. It provided the guiding ideology and theoretic basis for discussions on major problems relating to the new state and the institution of a state system.

In his article, Mao Zedong first brought up the question of the long-range perspective of the people's democratic dictatorship and the extinction of the state, and made clear the basic viewpoints of the Communists about classes, state power, and political parties. He declared to the whole country that the Chinese Communist Party, unlike the exploiting classes which worked for the interests of a few, was selfless in its aim to lead the Chinese people in establishing a people's democratic government. Then Mao Zedong went on to explain how the Chinese people found in Marxism-Leninism the ideology to guide the revolution, how the old-democratic revolution had failed and the new-democratic revolution had triumphed, and elucidated the historical inevitability of establishing a people's republic in China. He also discussed democracy and dictatorship, the central issue of the theory of the state. This republic would enforce its dictatorship over the landlord class, bureaucrat-bourgeoisie, and the Kuomintang reactionaries. Democracy would be practised within the ranks of the people—the working class, the peasantry, the urban petty bourgeoisie and the national bourgeoisie. The working class was the leading class. The people's democratic dictatorship was based on the alliance of the workers and peasants. The national bourgeoisie at the present stage was of great importance. The state would eventually be abolished, but at present it must be strengthened. Without the existence of the state, it would be impossible for China to develop from an agricultural into an industrial country and from a new-democratic into a socialist and Communist society. These were the basic problems discussed in "On the People's Democratic Dictatorship."

What was the economic system of the new state? This would decide the nature of the state and hence was a major concern to people in all walks of life, and also the problem the session of the Political Consultative Conference discussed most. Some Communists, according to the decision of the Second Plenary Session of the Seventh CPC Central Committee, further explained this question. In June, Liu Shaoqi talked at an inner Party meeting about the guidelines for the economic construction of New China. The economy of New China, or the new democratic economy, he said, mainly consisted of the state-owned economy, the cooperative economy, the state-capitalist economy, private capitalism, small commodity economy and semi-natural economy. These five economic sectors should all be encouraged, but the development of the state-owned economy should take first place. Cooperatives should be extensively established and closely combined with the state-owned economy. Assistance should be given to independent small producers, and their individual economy be led step by step towards cooperation. The state-capitalist economy should be organized. Private capitalist economy should be allowed to expand insofar as it was beneficial to the national economy and the people's livelihood. However, the economy that was monopolistic in character should be gradually nationalized and operated by the state, or operated in the form of state-capitalism and under the supervision of the state. As far as possible, socialist elements should be gradually increased in the national economy, and the planning of the national economy should be strengthened so as to steadily and safely achieve the transition to socialism. This transition was to go through a long, intense and arduous struggle. On September 22, Zhou Enlai explained at a meeting of the Political Consultative Conference the basic spirit of the new-democratic economic policy.

The collapse of the Nanjing government and the preparations for the founding of New China indicated the complete bankruptcy of the U.S. policy towards China. This fact shocked the U.S. government and provoked an argument within the ruling party over its China policy. Douglas MacArthur and others attacked the China policy formulated by President Truman and Secretary of State Acheson. In order the defend themselves, Truman and others published on August 5, 1949 the U.S. White Paper, "United States Relations with China." The White Paper, divided into eight chapters, dealt with Sino-U.S. relations in the period from 1844, when the United States forced China to sign the "Treaty of Wanghea," to 1949, when the whole country was basically liberated. It went into particular detail about how, during the War of Resistance and the War of Liberation, the United States interfered with the internal affairs of China and met with defeat. Thus, in its objective effect, the White Paper became a confession of the United States to its crimes of aggression against China, and useful material with which the Chinese people exposed the aggression.

On August 12, 1949, the Xinhua News Agency published an article "A Confession of Helplessness," starting the criticism of the White Paper. It was followed by five commentaries written by Mao Zedong for the Xinhua News Agency. Under the sponsorship of this news agency, all democratic parties, people's organizations, the press, universities and schools, and public figures from all walks of life held extensive discussions and issued many declarations, statements and comments. The discussions covered Sino-U.S. relations, China's foreign relations, the mutual relation between the Chinese revolution and the revolutionary forces of the world, the relationship between the Kuomintang reactionaries and the Chinese people, the proper attitude to be adopted by the democratic parties, people's organizations and public figures in the struggle against imperialism, the proper attitude to be adopted by liberals or democratic individuals towards the country's internal and external relations as a whole, and how the Chinese people should deal with new imperialist intrigues, etc. These wide-ranging discussions on so many important problems were unprecedented in China's modern history. The publication of the white paper and the criticism of it proclaimed the conclusion of imperialist aggression against China over the past 100 years—one of the major indications of the victory in the new-democratic revolution. It was a big clearing-out of devotion to and worship of America, and was a further criticism of the bourgeois-republic road. This criticism swept away many ideological obstacles to the founding of a state of the people's democratic dictatorship.

On September 21, 1949, the first plenary session of the Chinese People's Political Consultative Conference opened in Beiping. The conference was composed of 662 delegates representing all political parties—the Chinese Communist Party, the China Revolutionary Committee of the Kuomintang, the China Democratic League, the Democratic National Construction Association, the China Association for Promoting Democracy, the Chinese Peasants' and Workers' Democratic Party, the Chinese People's Association for National Salvation, the Association of Comrades in Three People's Principles, the China Kuomintang Association for Promoting Democracy, the China Zhi Gong Dang, the Jiu San Society, and the Taiwan Democratic Self-Government League; the non-Party patriotic democrats, the various regions and ethnic groups of the country, the People's Liberation Army, the people's organizations, the patriotic overseas Chinese and the religious circles. There were also representatives by special invitation. This was an unprecedented, impressive gathering. In his opening address, Mao Zedong, chairman of the CPC Central Committee, said, "Ours is a conference embodying the great unity of the people of the whole country.... Our work will go down in the history of mankind, demonstrating that the Chinese people, comprising one quarter of humanity, have stood up … from now on our nation will belong to the community of the peace-loving and freedom-loving nations of the world, and work courageously and industriously to foster its own civilization and well-being, and at the same time to promote world peace and freedom."

Through full discussion and consultations, the session adopted the "Common Programme of the Chinese People's Political Consultative Conference" on September 29. On the 30th, it elected the First National Committee of the CPPCC, with Mao Zedong as chairman, and the Central People's Government Council with Mao Zedong as chairman of the Central People's Government, Zhu De, Liu Shaoqi, Soong Ching Ling, Li Jishen, Zhang Lan, and Gao Gang as vice-chairmen, and composed of 63 members, including Zhou Enlai, Chen Yi, Dong Biwu, He Long, Lin Boqu, Ye Jianying, Chen Yun, Deng Xiaoping, Tan Kah-kee, Ma Yinchu, Ma Xulun, Guo Moruo, Shen Junru, Shen Yanbing, Huang Yanpei, Zhang Zhizhong and Fu Zuoyi. The delegates unanimously passed a declaration, a message of greetings to the People's Liberation Army, the measures to erect a monument to the heroes of the people and the epitaph on it. The session chose Beiping as the capital of the People's Republic of China, and renamed the city Beijing. It adopted the Christian era as the chronological system of the People's Republic of China, *March of the Volunteers* as the national anthem until a formal one was composed, and a flag with five stars on a field of red as the national flag. On the afternoon of that day, the delegates went to Tiananmen Square for the ceremony of laying the foundation stone of the Monument to the People's Heroes.

The Common Programme defined the character of the People's Republic of China and the fundamental principles governing the structure of the state, its military system, and its economic, cultural, educational and foreign policies. The programme was an important document with the nature of a provisional constitution. It stipulated that "the People's Republic of China is a new-democratic, or a people's democratic, state, a people's democratic dictatorship led by the working class and based on the alliance of workers and peasants, uniting all democratic classes and ethnic groups of the country"; that "state power belongs to the people. The organs through which the people exercise power are the people's congresses and people's governments at all levels"; and that "the guideline for economic construction is to develop production and promote economic prosperity by giving consideration to both public and private interests, benefiting both labour and capital, stressing mutual assistance between city and country and exchange between China and other countries." All sectors of the economy should be readjusted so that, under the leadership of the state sector, they would function satisfactorily with a due division of labour to promote the development of the whole economy. Culture and education was new-democratic, namely, national, scientific and of mass character. All the ethnic groups would be equal. Regional national autonomy would be exercised. The tenet in foreign affairs was to safeguard the country's independence, freedom, sovereignty and territorial integrity, uphold international lasting peace and friendly cooperation between peoples of various countries, and oppose imperialist policies of aggression and war.

The session decided that the People's Political Consultative Conference was the organizational form of the national people's democratic united front. It exercised the functions and powers of the National People's Congress until the convocation of the congress. After the convocation of the congress, the CPPCC would continue to exist for a long time as a consultative organ of all the democratic parties and peoples organizations.

At 2 p.m. on October 1, the Central People's Government Council took office in Beijing. It appointed Zhou Enlai premier of the Government Administration Council of the Central People's Government, Mao Zedong chairman of the Revolutionary Military Commission, Zhu De commander-in-chief of the Chinese People's Liberation Army, Shen Junru president of the Supreme People's Court, and Luo Ronghuan chief procurator of the Supreme Procuratorial Office. At 3 p.m. 300,000 people of Beijing assembled at Tiananmen Square to participate in the inauguration ceremony at which the establishment of the People's Republic of China was proclaimed.

The founding of the People's Republic of China marked the victory of the new-democratic revolution in China. Several thousand years of feual oppression, 100 years of imperialist aggression and 22 years of Kuomintang rule were buried by the Chinese people. The semi-colonial, semi-feudal age was over and Chinese history entered a new era.

The founding of the People's Republic of China marked the end of a long-term struggle between three political lines, or three destinies of the state—a comprador-feudal dictatorship, a bourgeois republic and a people's republic. From that time, the people became the masters of the country, the working class became the leading class, and the socialist state-owned economy became the leading sector of the national economy. This not only provided China with essential conditions to become a prosperous, powerful and modernized country, but it also opened up a road to socialism.

The victory of the revolution in China dealt a severe blow to the world colonial system, hence greatly weakening the strength of imperialism and promoting the growth of the national liberation movement around the world.

The victory of the Chinese people's revolution added a glorious chapter to the history of mankind.

18. Philosophy, Historiography, Natural Science and Literature

From 1919 to 1949 was a period in Chinese history of victory in the new-democratic revolution, and featured prominently the change of China from old to new. This was an epoch in which the people's will and enthusiasm for revolution were high and they forged ahead courageously. It was also an epoch of initiations. Almost everything in this period had a transitional character. In the sphere of learning and culture, in many respects the significance lay in the beginning of studies rather than actual achievements; towards foreign things, attention was focused on introducing and copying rather than careful digestion and assimilation; towards Chinese traditions, stress was on contempt and discarding rather than reasonable development and utilization. The refining and distillation of theories lagged far behind what the masses had achieved in their revolutionary practice. In scientific research no brilliant results from a comprehensive study of things both Chinese and western, ancient and modern, were registered at the time. On the whole, however, the achievements in learning and culture were worthy of this great epoch. In this changeable, abrupt, transitional period in history, immaturity in many respects was inevitable. In some areas, however, not a few achievements were among the best either viewed from the world spectrum or the history of the development of Chinese learning. Of course, the development in each specific cultural field was not uniform, and hence the attainments could not be equal either.

Just as the Chinese grow up in the land of China, their culture grows in the soil of previous society and culture shaped over a long period of time. The development in modern culture, positive or negative, cannot be divorced from the country's tradition. In this period, therefore, while fine heritage was inherited and carried forward, dregs also came to the surface. Of the foreign things introduced to China by the Chinese, some were good, and some were bad. The bad ones, like the good ones, also had their influence on the country.

Since it is impossible to touch on culture in all its aspects, accounts of only a few are given below.

Philosophy

Western philosophy began to spread to China towards the end of the Qing Dynasty. Marxist philosophy was introduced to this country during the Marxist publicity campaign started after the May 4th Movement. Basic rudimentary ideas of historical materialism were spread through early Communist's works. *My Conception of Marxism* by Li Dazhao and *Marxist Theory* and *Reply to Shizhi* by Chen Duxiu played an important role in publicizing Marxism and criticizing non-Marxist ideas. In the meantime, schools of philosophical thought in the West such as pragmatism, Machism, the philosophy of Immanuel Kant, and the philosophy of Georg W. F. Hegel were also introduced to China. Between 1924 and 1926, Qu Qiubai published *Modern Sociology, An Introduction to Social Philosophy, An Introduction to Social Science,* and *An Introduction to the Materialist World Outlook,* making a systematic exposition of historical and dialectical materialism. Qu made indelible contributions in introducing Marxist philosophy and promoting its development in China.

In the 1930s, large quantities of original works on Marxism and works on Marxist philosophy from other countries were translated into Chinese, such as *On Feuerbach, Anti-Dühring, Dialectics of Nature, Materialism and Empirio-Criticism* and *On the Development of the Monastical Outlook on History.* For a while dialectical materialism and materialist dialectics became popular across the country, which aroused worry and opposition among bourgeois scholars and idealists. As a result, polemics on the new philosophy and materialist dialectics continued for several years from 1931 in philosophical circles. Zhang Dongsun published articles—such as "I Also Comment on Dialectical Materialism," "General Review of Materialist Dialectics" and "Is the Logic on Motion Possible?"—and books entitled *Theory of Knowledge, Moral Philosophy* and *Value Philosophy.* He also edited the book *Polemics on Materialist Dialectics.* Through these writings he propagated his own philosophy in opposition to Marxism. Zhang's "Framework Doctrine" maintained that the objective world "is merely an empty framework"; that "there is physics but no matter," and "there is physiology but no life"; that "everything is a framework but without substance," but the "framework" could not be separated from "our knowledge." In theory of knowledge, Zhang held that knowledge consisted of four essential factors—proper arrangement of the external world, innate pattern, standards set by name and reason, and experience conception. He called this the pluralistic theory of knowledge. He denied the three laws of dialectics, describing dialectics as an "outdated curio" and Marxist dialectics as "hopelessly erroneous."

Ye Qing, who styled himself defender of the new materialism and dialectics, rose to criticize Zhang Dongsun's philosophy and wrote *Whither Philosophy, Critique of Zhang Dongsun's Philosophy* and other books. Ye stood for "abolishing philosophy." "In an age when science dominates exclusively the intellectual world," he argued, "philosophy has lost its ground"; therefore, "any attempt to establish any philosophical system is reactionary." Thus he negated completely the Marxist philosophy.

Ai Siqi and others published a series of articles to rebuff Zhang Dongsun's attack, expose Ye Qing's true colours as a false Marxist, and propagate Marxist philosophy. The struggle in the realm of philosophical thought promoted the growth of Marxist philosophy in China. Beginning from November 1934, Ai Siqi published in succession in *Study and Life*, a magazine published in Shanghai, "Talks on Philosophy." He explained in popular, vivid language the basic principles of dialectical materialism and basic laws of materialist dialectics. The fourth edition of his *Talks on Philosophy* offprint published in 1936 was renamed *Popular Philosophy*. Up to 1948, a total of 32 editions were printed. The book played an important part in popularizing Marxist philosophy.

Li Da printed *Outline Sociology* and published its revised and enlarged edition in May 1937; it was a systematic exposition of Marxist philosophy. Li Da, on the basis of studies by Soviet scholars, correctly explained that "the law of the unity of opposites is the basic law and kernel of dialectics," and this law was "a basic law governing the knowledge of all things." He set forth the idea of antagonistic and non-antagonistic contradictions. Regarding the Marxist-Leninist theory of knowledge, he discussed the dynamic theory of reflection and the "movement in cycles" in relation to knowledge, stressing that practice was of decisive importance to knowledge. *Outline Sociology* occupied a very important position in the history of development of Marxist philosophy in China.

In the later half of the 1930s, Mao Zedong researched philosophy. The outstanding characteristic of his studies was the close combination of the tenets of Marxist philosophy with China's revolutionary practice, using the former to guide the latter, and using the experience of the latter to explain and enrich the content of the former. In *On Practice* and *On Contradiction* written in 1937, he made scientific explanations of the theory of contradiction, the kernel of Marxist theory of knowing and doing, or the theory of knowledge, and dialectics. In *On Practice*, he stressed the dependence of knowledge on practice, pointing out that "practice should be first and fundamental in the dialectical materialist theory of knowledge." He expounded and proved the whole process of cognition, pointing out, "Practice, knowledge, again practice, and again knowledge. This form repeats itself in endless cycles, and with each cycle the content of practice and knowledge rises to a higher level. Such is the whole of the dialectical-materialist theory of knowledge, and such is the dialectical-materialist theory of the unity of knowing and doing."

In the 1930s and 40s, the Chiang Kai-shek clique, in order to tighten its reactionary rule, energetically peddled the "philosophy of constancy of action" (also called the philosophy of devotion) and vitalism. Chiang Kai-shek set forth a philosophy which distorted Sun Yat-sen's theory of knowing and doing, and drew on fascist philosophical standpoints. He said, "Through the ages, only by 'action' can everything be created in the universe.... The philosophy of 'action' is the sole philosophy of life.... The starting point in constancy of action lies in 'devotion' ... [and] devotion is the moving force of action." This philosophy was the fascist doctrine of action.

It was Chen Lifu who strongly advocated vitalism. Quoting the term "shengyuan" (origin of life) used by Sun Yat-sen, he wrote *On Vitalism* and *Principles of Life*. He opposed both "idealistic monism" and "materialistic monism," but stood for "vitalistic monism." He held that the noumenon of the universe was "shengyuan." "Shengyuan," which "has admirable wisdom and great ability," was the "all powerful, highly intelligent arbiter who creates life without cessation in the universe." This was "what the Westerners call 'God,' and what we call the 'creator'." This idea was utterly idealistic.

In addition to the above, those who had their own philosophical systems and views included Feng Youlan, Jin Yuelin, Xiong Shili and He Lin. Their philosophical ideas and systems took shape mainly in the 1940s. Among Feng Youlan's representative works were *Xin Li Xue* or *New Neo-Confucianism, Xin Shi Lun* or *China's Road to Freedom, Xin Yuan Ren* or *New Treatise on the Nature of Man, Xin Yuan Dao* or *The Spirit of Chinese Philosophy, Xin Zhi Yan* or *New Treatise on the Methodology of Metaphysics,* and *Xin Shi Xun* or *New Social Admonitions*—all about new Neo-Confucianism.

The new Neo-Confucianism principally inherited and developed the Neo-Confucianism formulated by Cheng Yi, Cheng Hao and Zhu Xi. Meanwhile it incorporated some elements from Buddhism, Taoism and Western philosophy. Feng invented a "rationalistic world ... prior to the practical world," where "all reasons are ready." The "matter" of the actual world, he believed, was nothing but the "realization of reason." This was objective idealism. On the question of life, Feng divided it into four "realms," of which the loftiest was the "realm of heaven and earth." In this realm, "all things on earth are prepared for myself." In this context, "self" became the "arbiter of the universe." Here Feng switched from objective idealism to subjective idealism.

Jin Yuelin's representative works were *On Dao* and *On Knowledge*. In *On Dao*, he formulated the conception of *dao, shi* and *neng*. According to him, "*shi* is similar to reason and shape," "*neng* is similar to vital energy and quality," and *dao* is the combination of *neng* and *shi*. "There is no *shi* without *neng*, and no *neng* without *shi*. ... It makes no difference as to which one should come first." He believed that *neng* could not be felt or described. Jin's philosophical system tended to materialism.

Xiong Shili's representative work was *New Theory of Knowledge*. He maintained that the noumenon meant function and phenomenon. The three were the same thing. He opposed taking the noumenon, which was above the world of phenomena, as the basis of phenomenon. He insisted that "the mind of man" was the noumenon. Xiong's philosophy was subjectively idealistic. Hard to understand, it carried little weight at the time.

Representatives of He Lin's works were *Chinese Philosophy of the Contemporary Era* and *Brief Explanations of Modern Idealism*. His philosophy was the product of integrating Lu Jiuyuan-Wang Shouren school with Neo-Hegelianism of the West. He Lin believed that "the mind is the noumenon of matter and matter is the use of the mind. The mind is the essence of matter, and matter is the manifestation of the mind." On the relations between knowing and doing, he advocated the unity of the two. He held that knowing and doing "take place at the same time ... with neither being the first"; that knowledge was the essence and conduct was the phenomenon; knowledge was primary and conduct was secondary. At the same time, however, he asserted that the materialist conception of history only studied the "outward phenomenon" with the "method of outside observation."

Only the "method of inside observation" of the idealist conception of history "gives attention to the essence." He Lin's philosophy was also idealistic.

Chen Jiakang, Du Guoxiang and Hu Sheng wrote articles pointing out Feng Youlan and He Lin's mistakes in their philosophical views.

Historiography

After the May 4th Movement, Chinese historiography stepped into a new stage. With the spread of Marxism, China's Marist historical science began to make its appearance. Li Dazhao, who was the first to disseminate Marxism in China, was also the pioneer and founder of Marxist history science. He published a series of articles on history, and opened courses such as "materialist conception of history" and "history of thoughts on historiography" in universities in Beijing, starting to bring Marxism to history studies in China. His *Important Points on History* (published in May 1924) was the first introduction to the science of history written from a Marxist viewpoint in China.

In the 1930s, polemics on the nature of Chinese society and the history of social development were conducted among people in China's theoretical and historical circles in a bid to probe into the nature of Chinese revolution and its perspective. These touched on questions such as: was China at that time a capitalist, or a semi-colonial, semi-feudal society?, had a slave society ever existed in Chinese history?, was China after the Qin and Han dynasties a feudal or a commercial capitalist society, or a society of some other sort?, why had China failed to enter an industrial capitalist age?, and the question of the Asian mode of production. Participants in the polemics were Marxist theoretical workers and historians, Chinese Trotskyites, people of the "New Life" school and scholars in other fields. Through the debates, rudimentary principles of materialist conceptions of history were extensively propagated, a variety of historical problems were discussed and historical science was promoted in China. Marxist historical and theoretical workers refuted all sorts of erroneous views which mispresented Marxism and which did not give a true picture of how matters stood in Chinese history. They expounded and proved that the Chinese society over the past hundred years was a semi-colonial, semi-feudal society, and initially sorted out the historical sequence of Chinese social development—from primitive society through slave society, feudal society to semi-colonial, semi-feudal society.

Guo Moruo's *Essays on Ancient Society of China* published in 1930 was the first work in China to apply Marxist theories to explain historical events in the country. The later works of Guo Moruo (1892-1978) on oracle-bone and bronze inscriptions included *Studies of Oracle-Bone Script, Studies of Inscriptions on Bronzes of the Yin and Zhou Dynasties, Notes on Bronze Inscriptions, Compilations of Oracle-Bone Inscriptions*, and *The System of the Inscriptions on Chinese Bronzes of the Zhou Dynasty, Illustrated and Annotated.* These works provided a basis of philological and documentary studies for the research on the social history of the Yin and Zhou periods.

Lü Zhenyu, another Marxist historian, wrote between 1934 and 1937 *Studies of the Chinese Society During the Pre-Historical Period, Chinese Society in the Yin and Zhou Periods* and *History of Chinese Political Thought.* Mao Zedong directed the writing of the textbook *The Chinese Revolution and the Chinese Communist Party* in the winter of 1939. It scientifically discussed China's feudal society in ancient times, the semi-colonial, semi-feudal society in modern times, the revolutionary movements over the past 100 years and all fundamental problems of the Chinese revolution.

Marxist historical science further developed in the 1940s. The outstanding achievements in this field were the completion of a number of works on general history. These included *A Concise History of China* by Lü Zhenyu; *A Brief History of China* and *A Modern History of China* (Volume I) by Fan Wenlan; and *An Outline History of China* (Vols. I and II) by Jian Bozan. In addition, progress was also made in the research on social history, history of thought and history of other fields. Works on these subjects included *A Course in History of Chinese Society* by Deng Chumin; *On History of Ancient Chinese Society; A History of Thought of Ancient China, A History of Thought of Modern China* and *A General History of Thought of China* (Vol. I) by Hou Wailu; *Studies of the Schools of Thought in the Pre-Qin Period* and

Essentials of the Schools of Thought in the Pre-Qin Period by Du Guoxiang; *The Bronze Age* and *Ten Critiques* by Guo Moruo; and *Imperialism and Chinese Politics* by Hu Sheng.

As Marxist historical science took shape and developed, and a number of historians made many contributions in the fields of their studies. Liang Qichao, founder of the Chinese bourgeois theory of history, wrote *On History of China* and *New Historical Science* as early as the beginning of the 20th century. In the 1920s, he wrote some more works including *An Introduction to the Qing Dynasty Learning, History of Political Thought in the Pre-Qin Period, The Method of Studying Chinese History* and *History of Chinese Scholarship During the Past Three Centuries.* Liang Qichao made wide-ranging studies which touched on historical theories and some important aspects in Chinese history. He also drew up a tentative plan for writing a general history of China and a history of Chinese culture.

Gu Jiegang, known for being sceptical about things ancient, set out the idea that the "history" of ancient China was invented layer after layer. Having studied ancient history for a long time, he put out *Investigations on Ancient History* in seven volumes, a collection of articles published at the time. His work, aimed at ascertaining authenticity, helped to clean up some preposterous legends and push forward the study of ancient Chinese history. However, it basically remained in the stage of sorting out related documents, and went a little too far in his doubts about certain specific problems in ancient history. Wang Guowei (1877-1927), Chen Yinke and Chen Yuan also contributed to history and the textual research on historical documentation. Wang initiated the study of oracle bones. He was the first to apply the oracle-bone inscriptions to the studies of history and institutions and systems of the Shang Dynasty (c. 16th-11th centuries B.C.). A man of great erudition, he made achievements in ancient script and vessels, epitaphs of the Han and Wei dynasties, literature relating to the Dunhuang Grottoes, and in the history of the Shang and Zhou dynasties, the history of the Han and Tang periods, the history and geography of the northwest and the history of Mongolia. Among his important works were: *A Study of the Inscriptions from the Yin Ruins Preserved in the Hall of Bliss and Longevity, Studies on Great Kings and Dukes of Early Periods as Seen in Oracle-Bone Inscriptions of the Yin Dynasty,* and its sequel, *Discourses on Systems of thé Yin and Zhou Dynasties, Investigations of Guifang, Kunyi and Xianyun Ethnic Groups, Investigations on the Tartars,* and *History of Drama of the Song and Yuan Dynasties.*

Chen Yinke devoted himself to studies on the history of ethnic groups on the border regions, history of the Wei, Jin and Southern and Northern Dynasties, and the history of the Sui and Tang periods, blazing a new trail by proving historical events through the study of poetry and essays. His *Sketch on the Origin of the Systems of the Sui and Tang Dynasties* and *Discourse on the Political History of the Tang Dynasty* had great impact on the study of the history of the Sui and Tang dynasties.

Chen Yuan contributed much to the history of Chinese religions and the study of historical literature, with emphasis on historical origin and examples. His *Investigations on the People in the Western Regions Assimilated by the Hans, Outline History of the Introduction of Islam into China, An Introduction of Historical Records of Buddhism in China,* and *Doubtful Chronicles About Sakyamuni* were important works on the history of ancient religions, relations between ethnic groups and relations between China and other countries. He made contributions to subjects relating to the science of historical literature, such as bibliography, chronology, study of historical taboos and textual criticism. His main works included the *List of the First Day of Each Lunar Month and Intercalary Years in the Twenty Histories, The Calendar of the History of Islam in China and Western Countries, Examples of Historical Taboos* and *Examples of Textual Criticism.*

Natural Science

In the early years of the Republic of China, institutions and organizations engaged in the study of natural science appeared in China, such as the Institute of Geological Survey under the Ministry of Agriculture and Commerce, and the Chinese Society of Science. The Chinese Society of Science was set up in 1915 in the United States by Zhao Yuanren, Bing Zhi, Yang Quan, Ren Hongjun and other Chinese students studying there. It moved to China in 1918 and settled in Shanghai 10 years later. Most of its members were people known for achievements made in scientific research, engineering and technology at home or abroad. Quite a few were founders of various branches of China's modern science. The activities of the society ranged from publishing and circulating *Science* and *Science Pictorial*, establishing the Mingfu Library, a museum and a biological research institute, to sponsoring lectures and exhibitions on science, and holding academic seminars. With a membership of 3,776 in 1949, the society played an important role in the development of scientific undertakings. The Biological Research Institute of the China Society of Science, under the direction of Bing Zhi and Hu Xiansu, was contributive to the development of zoology and botany. It featured prominently in the academic circles of the world.

In May 1927 the Central Executive Committee of the Kuomintang decided to set up the Academia Sinica, which was officially established in June the following years, with Cai Yuanpei as president. It was the state's highest academic organ of the time. By early 1930, it had nine research institutes—institutes of physics, chemistry, engineering, geology, astronomy, meteorology, history, linguistics, psychology and social science—and a museum of natural history. The institutes had altogether 91 full-time, part-time, honorary and specially invited research fellows, and 64 assistants, initially forming a contingent for scientific research made up of specialists and scholars in many branches of natural and social sciences. By 1949, the number of research institutes had increased to 12. The Beiping Research Institute came into being in September 1929. Universities across the country also set up quite a number of research institutes, which, up to 1947, totalled 157, mainly engaged in science and engineering. In addition to *Science*, a periodical of general interest, major academic periodicals on natural science were *Records of the Chinese Society of Geology, Book Series Published by the Biological Research Institute of the China Society of Science, Physiology in China, Chinese Journal on Physics, Journal on Meteorology* and *Records of the Chinese Society of Chemistry*.

In a semi-colonial, semi-feudal country like China, the low standard of knowledge, shortage of trained personnel and administration expenses, plus the constant political upheaval, all placed great restrictions on research on natural science. However, thanks to the industrious efforts of scientists and technological workers, a great many successes were registered in research and invention in natural science. This enabled China to switch from simply introducing scientific achievements from other countries to boasting of its own fruits in scientific research, some of which were up to the world's advanced level. Meanwhile, personnel was trained and experience accumulated.

Major achievements in natural scientific research and inventions in engineering and technology can be listed as following:

Mathematics: Chen Jiangong, Su Buqing and Hua Luogeng made important contributions in the research on the Fourier series, differential geometry and analytic theory of numbers respectively.

Geology: The Institute of Geological Survey, under the successive leadership of Ding Wenjiang, Weng Wenhao and Li Siguang, conducted field surveys and theoretical research in laboratories, advancing geological science in China. Li Siguang, in his article "Several Special Structure Types in East Asia," set forth principles and methods in geomechanics. He did research on the glacier geology of China's mountain regions and advanced his own views. Huang Jiqing came up with the idea that the earth's crust structure in China could be divided into units in accordance with the relations between platform, geosyncline, and orogenic movement.

Physics: Wu Youxun, Qian Sanqiang and Qian Xuesen made achievements in the research on the Compton effect, the atomic nucleus of uranium and the theory of thin-air dynamics respectively.

Geophysics: Zhu Kezhen, in his "The Motion of Air-Currents in China," found the law governing China's climatic changes in four seasons according to large quantities of observation data. Tu Changwang's "The Relation Between Atmospheric Motion and the World's Atmospheric Temperature" provided a foundation for the research on long-term weather forecasting in China.

Anthropology and Palaeontology: Pei Wenzhong discovered at Zhoukoudian the first skull-cap of Peking Man and a large quantity of palaeontological fossils. The great event caused a sensation throughout the world and played an important role in anthropological research.

Astronomy: The Academia Sinica's Research Institute of Astronomy established an observatory on Purple Mountain in Nanjing to start observations by Chinese astronomers themselves. When a total solar eclipse occurred on September 21, 1941, China sent an observation team to the northwest where it recorded data which had been hard to secure before.

Archaeology: Between 1928 and 1929, the Research Institute of History and Linguistics began digging at the site of the Yin ruins at Xiaotun Village near Anyang, Henan Province. This was the first large-scale underground excavation Chinese archaeologists conducted with modern scientific methods. It yielded an abundance of bronze vessels and oracle bones. The excavation was among the great events in the archaeological history of China and the world.

Industrial Chemistry: Hou Debang invented a new soda-manufacturing method, an internationally-renowned contribution to industrial chemistry.

Bridge Engineering: The Qiantang River Bridge was built under the direction of Mao Yisheng.

Literature

One of the important aspects of the new cultural movement was the literary revolution. In January 1917, the *New Youth* magazine carried Hu Shi's "Some Suggestions for the Reform of Literature" — marking the rise of the new literary movement from the stage of deliberations by a few. This was immediately followed by the pulication of "On Literary Revolution" by Chen Duxiu, "raising high the banner of the 'literary revolutionary army'." This was an official manifesto of the literary revolution. Before and after the May 4th Movement of 1919, discussions about the revolution became more extensive and deep-going; human literature, literature for the common people, realistic literature and literature for life's sake were advocated, and more complete and systematic theories of the new literature were put forward. After the May 4th Movement, writing in the vernacular became the main vehicle for literary expression. The literary revolution vigorously expedited the movement for the liberation of the mind, and thus played an effective supporting role in the anti-imperialist patriotic struggle of the May 4th Movement. It was a truly great revolution in the history of the development of Chinese literature. It laid the foundation for contemporary literature and opened a new chapter in the history of literature.

After the May 4th Movement, pure literary groups and societies sprang up like mushrooms, giving rise to different literary schools. According to statistics, more than 100 such societies and about the same number of literary periodicals appeared from 1921 to 1925, and these could be found in almost all large and medium-sized cities. The most influential and successful of these organizations were the Literary Research Society and the Creation Society. The Literary Research Society was founded at Beijing in January 1921 under the sponsorship of Zheng Zhenduo, Shen Yanbing and Ye Shaojun. It stood for literature for life's sake, belonging to the realistic school.

The Creation Society was established in July 1921 in Tokyo by Chinese students in Japan, such as Guo Moruo, Yu Dafu, Tian Han and Cheng Fangwu. It believed in art for art's sake, belonging to the romantic school.

The literary revolutionary movement which arose during the May 4th Movement was moving step by step towards "revolutionary literature." This manifested itself in the following respects:

First, the guidance of Communist ideology in culture over the new literature movement was further strengthened. The Chinese Communist Party took *New Youth,* reorganized in June 1923, as a compass through which to guide all ideological fields with Marxism. The "New Manifesto" of *New Youth* declared that it would inherit and carry forward the militant tradition of the May 4th new cultural movement, an indication of the Communist Party's conscious direction over the new literature.

Secondly, the elements of proletarian thinking in literature and art were on the increase in literary theoretical proposals. After 1923, Deng Zhongxia, Yun Daiying, Xiao Chunü and other Communists published articles initially popularizing Marxist ideas on literature. In 1925 Shen Yanbing published an article entitled "On the Proletarian

Art," tentatively explaining the proletarian literature and art in nature, subject matter, content and form. One year later Guo Moruo published "Revolution and Literature," pointing out the literature needed by the time was "literature that sympathizes with proletarian socialism and realism."

This period witnessed unprecedented achievements in creative writing. These included short stories by Lu Xun (1881-1936), such as *A Madman's Diary, The New-Year Sacrifice* and *The True Story of Ah Q* and Guo Moruo's *Goodesses*, a collection of new poetry. In *The True Story of Ah Q*, Lu Xun created a typical image of backward peasants exploited by feudal forces. Ah Q habitually uses the self-respecting, self-consoling, self-abasing and self-deceiving "method of spiritual victory" to relieve his sufferings and satisfy his mentality of resistance and retaliation. However, this can only bring him greater humiliation. Once the revolution comes, Ah Q, burning with spontaneous revolutionary zeal, also wants to make revolution. But the countery-revolutionary forces will not allow him to do so and sentence him to death.

The True Story of Ah Q reflects profoundly China's social physiognomy around the 1911 Revolution and class relations in the countryside. It also reflects the impact of the torrential revolution and the reason for its failure, delineates the deep-rooted revolutionary force latent in China's countryside, and lays bare the bad points in Chinese national character, and the tremendous negative effect they have on the advance of Chinese history. *The True Story of Ah Q* is world famous for its deep social content and high artistic value.

Guo Moruo's *Goddesses* is imbued with tremendous momentum for social reforms, rebelling spirit against the dark society and patriotic feelings. *Goddesses* reached the peak of new poetry both in ideological content and artistic quality. It initiated a new style in poetry.

The poems by Wen Yiduo and Bing Xin's short philosophical poems were also well-known during this period.

After the failure of the First Revolutionary Civil War against the Northern Warlord rule in 1927, a group of men of letters directly engaged in revolutionary work quit their posts and flocked to the cultural front. At the same time, a group of new revolutionaries joined them. This promoted the development of literature. In January 1928, the Creation Society and the Sun Society initiated the revolutionary literary movement. The members of the two organizations strove to create a militant literature which would serve the purpose of accomplishing the historical mission of the proletariat under the guidance of "proletarian class consciousness." Thus the history of the development of Chinese literature entered a new phase. However, "Left" mistakes were made in the movement, i.e., the spearhead of criticism was for a time directed at Lu Xun, Mao Dun (pen name of Shen Yanbing) and some others. This gave rise to a controversy about revolutionary literature. This controversy, which lasted until the first half of 1929, was conducted within the revolutionary literary ranks. The result was that the level of understanding of both sides was enhanced and their unity strengthened through mutual criticism.

In order to wage a common struggle against the Kuomintang's cultural campaign of "encirclement and suppression" and spur the development of revolutionary literature, the Chinese League of Left-Wing Writers was established in Shanghai in March 1930 under the leadership of the Communist Party, with Shen Duanxian, Feng Naichao, Qian Xingcun, Lu Xun and Tian Han as its standing committee members. Led by the League, the Left-wing writers launched a stubborn struggle against the Kuomintang's cultural campaign of "encirclement and suppression" and criticized fascist ideas about "nationalistic literature and art" and bourgeois and petty-bourgeois ideas on art and literature. The proletarian art and literature was forging ahead steadily during the struggle, an important manifestation of the cultural revolution developing in depth during the Second Revolutionary Civil War period.

The Left-wing writers conscientiously put their creative activities at the service of the Chinese revolutionary struggle and declared the literature to be part of the entire proletarian revolutionary cause. To this end, they produced many indelible works. Revolutionary realism was the greatest and most important school in China's literary world. In the final analysis, however, literature is the reflection of social life. As aspects of people's life are manifold, it can be reflected from different literary angles. Meanwhile, the varied life in society can be partially reflected in different artistic ways. The rich and varied literary and artistic works of different schools and styles reflecting different aspects of life are what people need to cater to their literary and artistic taste. Apart from the proletarian revolutionary literature, of the writers of other literary schools with different styles, quite a few wrote widely appreciated works. Though not directly dealing with revolutionary themes, some of these works delineated people's social life, thoughts and feelings more extensively and more deeply, and may be handed down from generation to generation. Some produced tremendous effects at their time.

Great achievements were made in literary creation in this period. In the last 10 years of his life Lu Xun wrote a large amount of prose, mainly in the form of short satirical essays known as *zawen*. His works of this type covered a broad range of topics, which centred around the exposure and criticism of political and social reality and touched on a series of political and ideological struggles. They were political commentaries of a literary nature with a trenchant, pungent and humourous style. They achieved the unity of great ideological content and high artistic quality. In addition to Lu Xun, Qu Qiubai also wrote many satirical essays.

Achievements in fiction were also outstanding. The novel *Midnight* and the short story *The Shop of the Lin Family* by Mao Dun (1896-1981) were famous masterpieces. *Midnight* shook the literary world of China after its publication in January 1933. It vividly and realistically depicted China's social reality and class contradictions in the 1930s, and successfully created typical representative figures of the comprador bourgeoisie and national bourgeoisie. Through concrete and vivid artistic portraits, the author explained why semi-colonial, semi-feudal China could not step into a developed capitalist society. This novel was a major achievement in revolutionary realist literature.

Ba Jin's best-known novel was *Family*. With Chinese society around the May 4th Movement as its background, it described the collapse of a big feudal family, laid bare the darkness and decadence of feudal society and praised the awakening of young intellectuals and their anti-feudal struggle. The novel had great impact on young people.

Camel Xiangzi, also known as *Rickshaw-Boy*, was a fine, realistic work by Lao She. Through the tragedy of a rickshaw puller named Xiangzi in Beiping, the novel portrayed the miserable life of the urban poor. The justified pursuit of the upright, honest and kind-hearted ordinary labourer Xiangzi for a decent life finally vanished like soap bubbles in the dark, evil old society, and he himself also became degenerate. The tragic life of Xiangzi was a devastating indictment of the old society. Major novelists of this period also included Ye Shaojun, Shen Congwen, Zhang Tianyi, Ding Ling and Xiao Jun.

Cao Yu is a well-known playwright who came to the fore in this period. His plays *Thunderstorm* and *Sunrise* enjoy popularity in the history of literature. *Thunderstorm*, a tragedy delineating the family life of an extremely feudal capitalist, reveals this family's evil history and reality, reflecting the corruption of upper class society in China. This play, with strong artistic appeal, reached the peak in dramatic literature of this period. Other notable playwrights of this period included Tian Han and Hong Shen.

Major poets of the period were Xu Zhimo and Zang Kejia. Xu's poems, though some had serious defects in ideological content, were noted for their high level of artistry. His poems, admired for vivid images, succint language, colourful ornate phrases and sonorous, harmonious tones, contributed to the development of new poetry. Zang Kejia's poems, solidly based on life, were filled with sincere thoughts and feelings. In terse verses, the poet described the peasants' industry, perseverance, sufferings and adversities, and expressed the longing for the light and the hatred for the darkness of society. His major works included *The Brand* and others.

After the War of Resistance Against Japan broke out in July 1937, large numbers of cultural workers plunged into the mighty struggle against the enemy and directly served the resistance by making propaganda in various forms of literature and art. In March 1938, the National Chinese Writers' Anti-Aggression Association was established in Wuhan, calling on writers to "use our pens to mobilize the masses to defend the motherland, smash the enemy and win victory." In April of the same year, the Third Section of the Political Department under the National Government's Military Commission was set up, with Guo Moruo as its head. The section carried out literary and art propaganda work. In order to bring the literary and art movement into the orbit of its partial resistance line, the Kuomintang advocated the literature and art on the Three People's Principles, namely, works were required to take the Chiang Kai-shek clique's Three People's Principles as their "central theme." Meanwhile, there were also some other erroneous ideas on literature, such as the theory of opposition to "stereotyped writing on the War of Resistance," theory of "opposing writers doing political work," and the fascist concept on literature and art. These ideas were criticized by progressive writers. Running counter to the global situation and not conforming to China's reality, they had little influence. Discussions were conducted around 1940 in the literary and art circles about the question of national form—a continuation of the question of the popular-style literature and art in the first half of the 1930s. The discussions advanced the development of literature.

The gunfire of resistance sparked off the writers' patriotic actions and their creative enthusiasm. For a period of time literary and art works in different forms emerged in large numbers which roused people to rise up in resistance and exposed negative phenomena hampering them from doing so, bringing about the flourishing of literary creation. Nevertheless, after the fall of Wuhan, especially after the Southern Anhui Incident, as the Kuomintang stepped up its cultural tyranny, the resistance literary and art propaganda movement, once extremely active, was reduced. Under these circumstances, many writers switched their main energy to literary creation, with the result that a multitude of finer literary works were produced.

Among the historical plays intended to serve the present, the best was *Qu Yuan*. In it, Guo Moruo created a typical figure—the patriotic, open and aboveboard, and strong-willed Qu Yuan who gave his life for justice. The performance of the play achieved tremendous political as well as artistic effect. Xia Yan's *The Fascist Bacillus* was a popular short story written in the early stage of the War of Resistance. In a satirical tone the author lashed out at the bureaucrats of the Kuomintang and the darkness and corruption under its regime. The story was quite a hit at the time. Successfully-written novels included Mao Dun's *Decay*. Best-known works of new poetry included Ai Qing's *Dayanhe, Facing the Sun* and *The Torch*, and Tian Jian's *To the Fighters.*

In May 1942, the Yan'an Forum on Literature and Art was convened, at which Mao Zedong delivered his famous *Talks at the Yan'an Forum on Literature and Art.* In it he explained a series of fundamental questions relating to revolutionary literature, such as: literature and art must adhere to the orientation of serving the workers, peasants and soldiers; writers must go deep among the masses and familiarize themselves with social life; and the petty-bourgeois literary and art workers must reform their own world outlook. After the forums, the literary and art world took on a brand-new appearance. With its influence spreading to the whole country, Chinese literature developed to a new phase. New changes took place in all aspects of many writers' works—ranging from content, thoughts and feelings, and characterization to language, artistic style and technique of expression. From then until the founding of the People's Republic of China, outstanding works appeared one after another. Zhao Shuli's novels *The Marriage of Young Blacky, Rhymes of Li Youcai* and *Changes in Li Village* reflected profoundly the transformation of old villages in China into new ones, creating images of peasants of a new type. His works, characterized by marked Chinese flavour and style, were well received by the masses, and made important contributions to national and mass literary style. Sun Li's *Lotus Lake* was a short story with a unique style. Ding Ling's *The Sun Shines over the Sanggan River* and Zhou Libo's *The Hurricane* were two best-know novels dealing with struggles in the land reform movement.

A new art form—new opera—came into being in the librated areas. The most famous new opera was *The White-Haired Girl.* It was created by adding elements from traditional Chinese drama and Western opera to a foundation of a new *yangge* opera, and reached a higher plane both in ideological content and artistic quality.

Li Ji's long narrative poem *Wang Gui and Li Xiangxiang* was the most important achievement in new poetry. Using the folksong form and the traditional literary devices of metaphor and allusion, the poem expressed new revolutionary content and achieved the harmonious unity of ideological content and artistic quality. *The Waters of the Zhang River* by Ruan Zhangjiang was another well-composed long poem.

The founding of the People's Republic of China on October 1, 1949 marked the end of the semi-feudal, semi-colonial age in Chinese history and the beginning of its advance to the socialist epoch. With the political and economic developments, philosophy, history science, natural science and literature entered a new era.

INDEX

图书在版编目（CIP）数据

中国通史纲要：英文／白寿彝主编；《中国通史纲要》英译组译.
—北京：外文出版社，2008（学术中国）
ISBN 978-7-119-05296-0

I. 中⋯ II. ①白⋯②中⋯ III. 中国－通史－英文 IV. K20

中国版本图书馆CIP数据核字（2008）第051711号

责任编辑：吴灿飞
装帧设计：姚 波
印刷监制：韩少乙

中国通史纲要（修订本）

白寿彝 主编

出版发行：
外文出版社（中国北京百万庄大街24号）
邮政编码 100037
http://www.flp.com.cn
制 版：北京维诺传媒文化有限公司
印 制：北京外文印刷厂
开 本：787mm×1092mm 1/16（精装） **印 张**：51
2008年第1版第1次印刷
（英）
ISBN 978-7-119-05296-0
11-E-1611S（国图号）
定 价：116.00元